ENGLISH RECUSANT LITERATURE
1558–1640

Selected and Edited by
D. M. ROGERS

Volume 269

RICHARD SMITH
The Prudentiall Ballance
of Religion
1609

RICHARD SMITH

The Prudentiall Ballance
of Religion
1609

The Scolar Press

1975

ISBN 0 85967 269 7

Published and printed in Great Britain by
The Scolar Press Limited, 59-61 East Parade,
Ilkley, Yorkshire and
39 Great Russell Street,
London WC1

NOTE

Reproduced (original size) from a copy in the library of St. Edmund's College, Ware, by permission of the President. In this copy pages 225, 373 and 374 are damaged, and in this facsimile these pages are reproduced from a copy in Cambridge University Library, by permission of the Syndics. For the second part of this work, see Allison and Rogers 774.

References: Allison and Rogers 777; STC 22813.

—

THE PRVDENTIALL

BALLANCE OF

RELIGION,

Wherin the Catholike and Proteſtant religion are
weighed together with the weights of
Prudence, and right Reaſon.

THE FIRST PART,

*In which the foreſaide Religions are weighed together with
the wsights of Prudence and right Reaſon accordinge to
their firſt founders in our Englishe Nation, S. Auſtin and
Mar. Luther . And the Catholike religion euidently deduced through all our Kings and Archbishopps of Canterburie from S. Auſtin to our time, and the valour and
vertue of our Kings, and the great learninge and Sanctitie
of our Archbishopps, together with diuers Saints and
miracles which in their times proued the Catholike faith;
ſo ſett downe as it may ſeeme alſo an abridgment of our
Eccleſiaſticall Hiſtories.*

With a Table of the Bookes and Chapters con-
teyned in this Volume.

PSALM. 118.
The wicked haue told me fables, but not as thy Law.

Printed vvith Licence. 1609.

EPISTLE

TO THE MOST

Noble and renovvned
ENGLISH NATION

my most deere Countrimen.

1. **R**IGHT Honorable, right worshipfull, and dearelie beloued Countrymen giue me leaue to ioyne you all in one Epistle, whom I contayne in one brest of loue, and include in one lincke of entire affection. Becaufe the end for which I write vnto you concerneth you all alike and equallie, to witt, the true Religion and worshipp of God, and saluation of your owne foules. A matter vs of the greateft weight and worthieft of Search, so in these our miferable dayes of moft controuerfie and perplexed difficultie. Wherin to helpe you the better to difcerne true gold from shyninge braffe, true religion from falfe and counterfeit. I haue framed for you *a Prudentiall Balance of Religion.* by which euery one of you, may by the weightes and rules of right reafon,

and

and true prudence weighe the Roman
Catholique and the Proteſtant religion
together, and diſtincklie perceaue whither of them is more likelie to come from
God and to lead you to him.

VVhy this
courſe of
compa-
ringe reli-
gions is
taken.

2. And this courſe of comparinge theſe
two religions together I haue taken
before any other, becauſe as the Philoſopher teacheth and experience confir-
meth. *Contraria iuxta ſe poſita magis eluceſcunt:
Contraries put together do more apppeare.* As
beautie in preſence of deformitie ſeemeth more gratious and deformitie more
vglie; Truth before lies appeareth more
loue lye, and lies more odious; vertue before vice more amiable, and vice more
deteſtable. Euery thinge as it were ſtriuin-
ge to ſhew it ſelfe more when it is ſet as
it were to wraſtle with the contrarie. And

VVhy the
compa-
ringe of
religions
accordin-
ge to rules
of vviſdo-
me is cho-
ſen before
others.

I haue made choyſe of comparinge theſe
religions accordinge to the rules of true
prudence and right reaſon, rather then
otherwiſe, as the moſt generall, moſt
eaſie, moſt euident, and moſt effectuall
for all ſortes of people. for albeit Catholiques & Proteſtants agree that to be the
true religion of God which is moſt agreable to his word, yet ſith they neyther
agree which is his word, (Proteſtants
reiectinge much of that which Catholiques reuerence for Gods heauenly word)

nor

nor which is they fenfe therof, they can
not be brought to agree about one
balance of Gods word wherby they may
weigh their religions together. Befides
that not onely Catholicks teach but alfo
Proteftants confeffe, that *the weaker forte of*
Chriftians can not iudge which is the true expofi-
tion of Scriptures . And therfor to weighe
religions to them by the balance of
Scripture, were to weigh one vnknowne
thing by an other . But the weights of
Prudence and right reafon are both
commun and euident to all,& therfor the
weighinge of religions by them muft
needs be moft generall , moft eafie , and
moft effectual with all fortes of people.
And if anie refufe to haue their religion
tried by thefe kinds of weights, they confeffe therby that they fear their religion
to be contrarie to wifdome and reafon,
which is as much as to be fabulous and
foolifh . For what can be oppofit to
wifdome and reafon but follie and fables?
3. Nether let anie think that that religion
which is moft agreable to Prudence and
the light of reafon, is not alfo moft agreable to Scripture . Becaufe reafon and
Scripture are both God his word and
Gods truth,the one naturall , written by
his owne hand in our foules by creation ;
the other fupernatural , written in paper

Thus
Tertulliã
lib. de
præfcrips.
reafon the
Cath.reli-
gion to be
preferred
befor anie
herefie.

D. Reinolds
Confer.
pag. 149.

VVhat re-
ligion is
againft
vvifdom
and rea-
fon is
follie.

á 3   with

The agreablenes of Religion and reason.

with the hands of his holie Scribes by
reuelation . And therfor though these
two words be of different degree they
can not be contrarie, but rather as twinnes
of one and the selffame parent haue great
sympathie and connexion together . For
as God doth not by his grace destroie the
naturall inclination of our will to good
but perfecteth it: So by his word and faith
he extinguisheth not but increaseth the
naturall insight which our vnderstanding
hath of truthe. yea such is the force of our
vnderstanding to pearce into Gods truth
as that by it the Philosophers (as the
Apostle witnesseth Rom. 1.) came to

S. Paul.

know *the inuisible proprieties of God and his
euerlasting power & diuinitie.* And sith we see
that men by the light of reason know so
much of othermoral vertues as without
all other teaching theyperceaue in manie
things what is honest, what dishonest,
what iust, what vniust, what is vertue,
what vice , why should we doubt that
God hath giuen to vs equal knowledge of
matters of religion and worship of him
self. Which vertue as it is the cheefest of
all morall vertues , so the knowledge
therof is most necessaire of them all vnto
vs. Yea S. Austin accounted so much of

S.Austin.

Reason as *lib. de vtil. credendi cap.* 12. he
said that *Recta ratio est ipsa virtus.* because it
is the

is the naturall square and rule which God euen in creation giueth to euery one to know what he ought to do . And Caluin saith that *Semen religionis est in mente humana.* And Iewel *art. 6 .diuis. 12. that naturall reason holden within her bondes is not the enemye, but the daughter of Gods truth . And therfor he must be very vnreasonable that will without cause be angrye with reason.* And Doctor Reinolds in his conference *pag.* 207. saith, *Reason is a notable helpe of mans weaknes.* This rather for of naturall reason and prudence giuen vnto vs by God, common and euident to all authorized by verdit of the Apostle, confirmed by reason and approued by consent both of Catholiques and Prote-stantes is that wherwith I intend to direct you in the choyce of Religion, and the Balance wherwith I purpose to to weigh before your eyes the two more famous religions which are in our Lande. 4. Not because I thinke that onelie natu-rall light of reason is able without all supernaturall illustration from God to discerne in all points which is the true religion. But because it is able to disco-uer which is false Religion, and amongst many religions it can iudge, which is most likelie to be the true for albeit God hath not made his faith and religion euidentlie true, because then as S. Gregorie saith our

marginal notes:
Caluin.
Iuel.]
Doct Rei-nolds.
S. Greg. hom. 26. in Euang:

faith

faith fhould haue no meritt. Nay.as Saint
Thomas,and the faid S. Gregorie fhew,it
fhould be no faith , becaufe faith , as the
Apoftle defineth,it is. *Argumentum non
apparentium,of thinges not feene.* Yet hath he
made his faith and Religion euidently
credible,and worthie to be beleeued, or
as the Pfalmift fpeaketh , *Credibilia nimis.*
for if both God and mans law iudge the
teftimonye of two or three fuch eye
witneffes,as no iuft exception can be taken againft them, to be euidentlie credible and worthie of belife euen in matters
of life and death, much more will they
iudge the teftimonie not of two ,but of
twelue eye witneffes,which (as they fay)
haue heard,haue feene,haue fullie percea-
ned with ther eyes,and haue bene behol-
ders,their handes haue handled , and fin-
gers haue touched , and againft whofe
fidelitie no iuft exception can be made;
yea whofe vertuous and vpright cariage
in all other matters the world admired,
and befides haue ther faying and teftimonie contefted by fuch wonderous facts
as no mans witt can deuife how they
fhould be done by any power of nature or
arte , but be true miracles wrought onelie
by the diuine power of God who is aboue nature,much more(I fay)will the law
of God and of man too,(if it proceede accordinge

Margin notes:

S. Thomas.
2.2. q. 1.
art. 5.

Hebr.11.

Pfal.92.

Gods re-
ligion
euident
ly credi-
ble.

Deuter. 17.

Math. 18.

1. Ioan. 1.
2. Pet. 1.
Ioan. 20.

Eye vvit-
neffes,and
they many
holie.
fortold
by pro-
phetie
paft and
confirmed
by prefent
miracles.

cordinge to it selfe) iudge the teftimonie
of so many, and so fubftantiall witneffes,
contefted both by diuine propheties
afore hand (as is euident by the old law,
which that they feyued not nor Deuifed
themfelues, is manifeft to the woild by
the atteftation by their enemies the Iewes) and by many wonderfull factes prefent, and thofe facts fo authentically recorded and regeftred, as it can not be
doubted, but they were done , vnleffe
againft all fenfe and reafon we will denie
all recordes of time paft ; and fo wonderous, and fo far aboue the courfe and
order of nature and arte , as no man can
iuftlie thinke, but they be true miracles
and conteftations from God himfelfe.
And this is that kind of authoritie wherof S. Auftin fpeaketh when he faith, that *Lib. de*
if God haue any care of mankind he hath *vtil. cred.*
vndoubtedlie appointed in earth fome *cap. 16.*
kind of authoritie, vpon which we re-
lyinge, may as it were by fome fteppes
mount vp to God. And no maruell ; for
fith we haue no meanes to be certayne
of a thinge, but by euidencie of the truth
or by fufficient authority, and that we
cannot haue euidencie of the true way to
heauen, becaufe it is as fupernaturall as
the end it felfe, and therfor as well out of
the reach of our vnderftanding , as other

ā 5   fupernatu-

fupernaturall thinges are, vnleffe god had prouided fome certayne authoritye, wherby we might be affured of that way, we could neuer be certayne therof but euer either erringe or doubtful. But god hauing left fuch fufficient authoritye as he hath to fhew vs the way to heauen, hath made it therby euidentlie credible, and worthie to be beleued, and far more certayne to vs, then, is they way to a traueller in a ftrainge countrie by the teftimonie of thofe that dwell in the countrie. 5. And on the other fide as he hath endewed our will with a naturall tafte and relifhe of vertue, wherby of nature we abhorre all vice and loue vertue. So alfo hath he infufed into our vnderftandinges a proportionable and correfpondent light and naturall infight of truth, which fheweth vnto the will, which is indeed vice, which vertue. This light cheiflye cōfifteth in certaine generall principles of vertue which God hath giuen to our vnderftandinge as it were rules and fquares to direct it felfe in particular actions, by meanes of which it is affured that what is agreable to them is true and vertuous, and what difagreable falfe and naught, and what feemeth to be moft futable to them, moft likelie to be true and good. Of thefe kind of principles for choyce of

                                    religion

religion one is that principle which S.
Paule mentioneth *Hebr. cap.* 11. That god
is rewarder of them that serue him . And
that which the Psalmist mentioneth that Psalm. 18.
Lex Domini est immaculata ; condemninge
no vertue, nor admittinge anie vice, but
contrarywise most exhortinge to vertue.
and deterringe from vice ; That onelie
Gods religion can be confirmed with
true miracles . That his Religion hath
preachers lawfully sent by him, and the
like. And what religion we see clearlie to
be contrarie to these principles, we may
be sure cometh not from God. And contrarie wise amongst all religions, what
we see most agreable to them, that we
may thinke most likelie to be Gods Religion. As what religion we finde amongst
all to be most immaculate from vice, and
most vrginge to vertue, whose Preachers
we see to shew best warrant for their cō-
mission from God to preach it, and to
bringe best proofes of Gods miracles to
testifie it, that we may be full assured is
most likelie to be Gods religion. For if
all reason iudge him to be the most likelie
to be the true Embassadour frō a Prince,
who bringeth the best assurance and letters of Commission from that Prince,
and consequently that which he deliue-
teth to be the Prince his message, rather
than

than any other! what reaſon, what wiſdome, what ſenſe can ther be to <u>tinke</u>, but that is moſt likely to be Gods meſſage & meaning which being in it ſelfe voyd of vice, is deliuered by thoſe, who ſhew better proofes of ther ſendinge and teſtimonies of ther doctrine then any others? And heervpon it comes to paſſe that whenſoeuer Gods true religion came in queſtion with hereſie before men addicted to neyther, but guided onely by the rules of reaſon and naturall inſight of religion giuen to them by God, it was allwayes iudged more likely to be Gods truth then hereſie. When in the tyme of the old law the Samaritanes contended with the Iewes for the truth of religion before the King of Egypt, the King hauinge heard the reaſons and proofes on both parties, gaue

Ioſeph.18.
Antiq.

ſentence for the Iewes. And in the tyme of the new law, when Manes the here-

Hieron in
Archlao
Epiphan.
hær.66.
Cyril. Ca-
techeſ. 6.

ticke contended with Archilaus a Catholicke Biſhop before Heathen Philoſophers, iudgment was pronounced againſt the Hereticke. Yea generally all ſects, as Iewes, Turkes, Heretickes in iudgment

See infra
l.2.c.13.

preferre the Catholicke Chriſtian religion before all other religions beſides ther owne. Which is a great argument, that it alone is indeed the true religion of God. For as when diuers Citties of

Greece

Greece contended whether of them Plutarch.
deſerued greateſt praiſe for a victorie
which they obtained againſt the Perſians,
the iudges before whome the cauſe was
brought demaunded of euery one of them
whom they thought to haue deſerued
beſt after them ſelues, and all anſweringe
that the Lacedemonians; the wiſe Iudges
gaue ſentence that indeed the Lacedemonians had deſerued beſt of all, for they
ſeinge euery cittye to preferre the Lacedemonians before others, they perceaued
therby, that if their affection had bene as
indifferent betwene them ſelues and the
Lacedemonians, as it was betwene the
Lacedemonians and others, their iudgment would haue preferred the Lacedemonians before them ſelues, as well as it
preferred them before others. And in like
ſort all ſectaries who preferre the chriſtian
Catholique faith before all others but
ther owne, would alſo preferre it before
ther owne, if ther iudgment were guided
with as much in differencie to ther owne
religion, as it is to others, and not ouer-
weighed with cuſtome of likinge ther
owne and affection to ther preconceited
opinions.

6. Wherfore ſeinge that on the one ſide
Gods true religion is thus euidently
credible, and on the other ſide our vnder-
ſtandinge

standinge when it is not miseled with passion or affection, but guided by the principles of religion engrafted in our soule by God and directed by the light of reason is of such force that euen by Creatures it can come to the knowledg of God as it is said *Rom.* 1. that my deare Countrynen may with more facilitie and perspicuitie find out this so important matter as vpon which dependeth their eternall saluation, I haue framed this *Prudentiall Balance* in which by the weightes of prudence and light of Reason they may weighe and compare the Romane Catholique, and Protestant religion, and see whether of them is more like to come from God, and direct men to their euer-lastinge happines. And in the first parte therof (which heere I offer to them) I compare these two religions accordinge to their first founders in our English nation: And in the second God willinge, I will compare them accordinge to their claimes to the word of God, their transla-tions or Copies of that word, accordinge to their manner of expoundinge it and other such generall groundes of Religion: In the third I will compare them accor-dinge to their Doctrines : And in the fourth and last parte accordinge to the effectes which eyther of them hath
wrought

(margin note:) Force of vnder-standing.

wrought, especiallie in our Englifh Nation.

7. In this firft parte I proue that the Romane Catholique, and Proteftant Religions in our Englifh Nation, came firft and originallie from S. Auguftine, and Martyn Luther. And therfor I compare thefe two religions together in thefe two firft founders of them in our Nation: and lay the qualities and conditions of them fitt for Preachers, in the two firft bookes, as it were ech of them in his feuerall Scale. And in the third I compare them together according to the qualities difcribed, that therby the Reader with indifferent iudgment may weigh them, and confider, whether is the more likelie to come from god and to bringe his religion, whether, from the Deuill and to preach his deceites. The qualities wherin I compare them are thefe fiue. *Learninge, vertue, motiues to preach, lawfull vocation or miſſion, and right orders to preach the word of God and adminifter his facramentes.* And the pointes wherin I compare the Doctrins which they brought, are thefe fewe *Approbation of Chriftendome, allowance of aduerfaries, Diuyne atteftation by Miracles, and continuance.* And I fhew euidently by many irrefragable proofes (wherof euer one is the confeffion of Proteftantes) that S.

Auftin

Se l.1. c.2. l.2.cap.1. vvhat is fevved of luther many by alfo Proved of Calvvin or anie other fect maifter of our time.

In vvhat S. Auftin and luther are compared.

vvherin their doctrins are compared.

Auſtin was very learned, Luther ignorant; S. Auſtin vertuous, Luther vicious; S. Auſtin moued to preach by heauenly motiues, Luther by humaine & naughtie; Saint Auſtin lawfully ſent to preach his doctrin, Luther not ſent at all to preach his; S. Auſtin rightly ordered to adminiſter his ſacraments, Luther not ordered at all to adminiſter his; Saint Auſtins doctrin to haue bene the vniuerſall doctrin of Chriſtendome in his time, Luthers doctrin to haue bene contrarie to the vniuerſall beleife of Chriſtians in his time; Saint Auſtines doctrin to haue bene confeſſed by his aduerſaries then, & ours now, to haue bene ſufficient to ſaluation, Luthers doctrin neuer acknowledged of vs to be able to aſſure any; And finally Saint Auſtines doctrin to haue bene confirmed by true, euident and confeſſed miracles, Luthers to haue wanted all color of ſuch confirmation.

8   All theſe pointes (I ſay) I haue prooued by euident and irrefragable proofes and teſtimonies, yea euen by the confeſſion of Proteſtants. Which, what man of iudgment and carefull of his ſaluation conſidereth, will (I hope) make choyce rather to follow Saint Auſtin and his doctrine, than Luther and his. For what wiſedome or reaſon , yea what ſenſe ſhould

ſhould ther be to thinke that God and
his truth were with ignorance , vice,
naughtie intention , want of miſſion and
orders , want of conſent of Chriſtianitie,
of confeſſion of aduerſaries, and of miracles ; And the Deuils lyes ſhold be with
learning , vertue, holie motiues , lawfull
miſſion , right order , conſent of chriſtianitie, confeſſion of aduerſaries,and diuine
miracles . If any ſay that though Luthers
Doctrin want the fore ſaid titles of commendation and credibilitye, yet it hath
the ghoſpell which is to be preferred before them all : I deſire ſuch to conſider
with themſelues , how vnlikely it is, that Note
the ghoſpell ſhould ſtand with ignorance
againſt learninge , wirh vice againſt vertue, with wordlie againſt holie motiues,
with runninge of his owne head againſt
lawiull ſendinge, with no orders againſt
right orders , with auerſion of Chriſtendome againſt conſent of the ſame , with
deteſtation of aduerſaries againſt ther allowance,and finally with want of all miracles, againſt certaine and confeſſed heauenlie miracles ; and I hope they will be
eaſely perſuaded that ʼowſoeuer ſome
make ſhew therof,yet the ghoſpell cannot
indeed, and in the right ſenſe ſtand with
Luther againſt Saint Auſtin. Or if I cannot perſwade ſuch men thus much , yet

ē   let me

let me entreat them to suspend their
iudgment concerninge the Ghospells
being on either side, till they see the second part of this Ballance, wherin God-
willinge I shall weigh Saint Austins and
Luthers religiō according to their claimes
to the ghospell, and the right sense therof,
and by Gods afsistance euidently shew,
that Saint Austins religion hath as much
aduantage ouer Luthers, touching the
true pollefsion of the ghospell, and right
sense therof, as it hath concerning the
forefaid titles.

All our
ancient
Clergie,
Catholik.

9   I haue also in this parte shewed that
the Romane religion of Saint Austin hath
continued euer fince vnto our time in all
our Bishopps, Prelats, Pastors, Deuines,
and Cleargie (except Wiclife and his
small crue)by the example of their heades
the Archbishopes of Canterburye, whom
I shew to haue bene in number sixtie
nyne , and in religion perfect Romane
Catholiques. The like I shewe of the
Queenes, ladies, Princes, Dukes, Earles,
Nobles,gentile and commons,and generally of all the lay tie by the example of
their heades the kinges and princes of this
land,who fucefsiuely(befides Seauentie
more , who raygned in some parte of
England, whiles this land was deuided
into many kingdomes) haue bene in
                                         number

Likvvife
all our
laitie.

number fixtie three, and in religion as
perfect Roman Catholickes as may be.
In fo much that it is confeffed by Proteftants that they knew not fo much of
Proteftancie, as that which they tearme
the head, fountayne and foule therof.
Amongft whom you fhall fee the ancient
and renowned kinge Inas of the Saxons,
profeffinge S. Peters fupremacie all moft
nyne hundred yeares agoe, and that by
letters engrauen in ftone; buildinge a
Seminarie in Rome for his fubiectes ther,
and makinge his kingdome tributarie to
S. Peter. And of the Normans blood you
fhall fee the moft victorious Prince
Edward the third profeffinge by publicke
letters, that it is herefie to denie the Popes fnpremacie, or (as the kinge fpeaketh)
that the Popes iudgment, *omni humanæ
præfidet ceeaturæ.* Amongft them you fhall
fee the auncient and worthie kinge
Ethelred, fo deuout to maffe, as he would
rather aduenture the loffe of his armie, of
his kingdome & life, than he would miffe
the hearinge of a whole Maffe: And yet
by his deuotion miraculofly puttinge
his enemies to flight. You fhall fee that
wife Prince Henry the third to heare
many Maffes euery day, to kiffe Preifts
handes at Maffe time, and preferre the
feinge (as he faid) of his Sauiour ther,

Side notes:

See infra
lib.1.6.21.

lib.1.6.23.

Hentic. 2.
led P.
Alexãdets
horffe.
Hen.5.
fued to
haue his
Countrie
accounted
a nation
that
ovveth
deuotion
to the
Church
of Rome.
lib.1.cap.
25. 26.

lib.1.c.26.

lib.1.c.23.

cap.26.

ē 2   before

before the hearinge of the beſt preacher ſpeaking of him. finallie to omitt many other euident teſtimonies heerafter rehearſed not onelie of their aſſured Romayne Religion, but alſo of ther zeale and feruour therin, fourteene of them euen in the two hundred yeares after the conuerſion of our Nation ſurrendred ther ſcepters, Crownes, and kingdomes, and became either Monkes at home, or trauelled in pilgrimage to Rome.

cap. 23.

And as many Queenes.

10. And were all theſe Archbiſhopps and their clargie, were all theſe kings and ther people blind? And hath time (to imitate Saint Auſtins wordes in the like caſe) ſo changed all things vpſide downe, that light is accounted darknes and darknes light, that (to omitt very many others confeſſed of Proteſtants to be profound diuines as you ſhall ſee herafter) *S. Auſtin, S. Theodor, Lanfrancke and S. Anſelme* who were the very lights of the land and of Chriſtendome alſo in ther time for learninge and vertue were blind, and *Cranmer. Parkar. Grindall and VVhitgift* (men of meane learninge and as litle vertue) did ſee? what in Gods name ſhould make any thinke ſo. for number we haue all moſt ſeauentie for fower, for continuance all moſt a thouſand yeares for fiftye; for learninge we haue profound knowledge euen

Lib. 2. cont Iulian. cap. 10.

euen by Proteſtantes confeſſion againſt meane skill; for vertue we haue famous and confeſſed ſanctitie againſt ordinarie, if not vicious life . If therfore either number, or time, or learninge helpe any thinge to finde out Gods truth, our Catholique Archbiſhopes are far more like to ſee and eſpie it than the Proteſtant Prelates: or if vertuous life moue God to reueale his truth, ſurelie the Catholique Archbiſhops are more like to know it than the Proteſtants. And in the like ſort touching Princes, for two which Proteſtants can produce, we can bring aboue one hundred and twentie: for their child of Nyne yeares old, and ther woman we can produce aboue an hundred, mature, graue, and wiſe men; who haue they in valour comparable to our Kinge *Egbert*, firſt authour of our Engliſh mon archie? to Kinge *Alfred the great* vanquiſher of the daines, and deliuerer of his Countrie; to our Kinge *VVilliam Conqueror* of England? to our *Edward the firſt*, *Edward the third*, *Henrie the fift*; and many moe moſt valiant and victorious Princes? whom in magnanimitie haue they aunſwerable to our Kinge *Ethelſtan*, to our Kinge *Edgar*, King *Canute*, Kinge *Richard Ceur de lyon*, and diuers others? who in largenes of Dominion to our Kinge *Canute*, our

e 3   Kinge

Kinge *Henery the fecond* King *Richard the firſt* and others? who in learning to our Kinge *Ethelwolf*, Kinge *Alfred the great,* Kinge *Henrie ſirnamed beuclarke* & others? who in wiſdome to Kinge *Inas* Kinge *Alfred*, Kinge *VVilliam* conquerour, Kinge *Henry the firſt*, ſecond, fourth, and Seauenth? whom finallie haue they to compare for vertue and fanctitie with Kinge *Ethelbert*. Kinge *Edmund*, the two *Edwards*. *Henrie the ſixt* and very many more?

11. And ſhall we thinke that one child and a woman in ſo ſhort time ſhould eſpie that diuine truth which ſo many Princes in a thonſand yeares could not finde? That the infancie of a child and weaknes of a woman ſhould diſcouer that which the rare learninge, wiſedome, and iudgement of ſo many graue Princes could not attayne vnto? That the fruitles life of a child, and the ordinarie, (if not farre worſe) life of a woman ſhould deſerue of God to haue that reuealed vnto them, which the rare vertue and holynes of ſo many excellent Princes who preferred his ſeruice before their kingdomes, could not obtayne? what were this but in matter of religion and euerlaſtinge ſaluation to giue that iudgment and make that choyce which

in no

in no other matter we would do ? for
who is ther if it lay in daunger of leasing
liuinges libertie or life would not
make choice to follow rather seauentie
then fower, an hundred rather than two,
men than children and women , and
men of famous and confessed learninge
wisedome and vertue than others of
meane learninge and ordinarie (if not
naughtie)liues? And will we when it is
daunger of losse of soule and saluation
make the contrarie choyce? what defence or excuse can we make of this pro-
ceedinge either before God or man? will
we say it is prudence in monye matters
and temporall affaires to follow many
rather then few, men then children and
women , learned wise and vertuous, before others lesse qualified , and not to
trust to much to our owne iudgments;
And can we thinke it prudence to obserue the contrarie course in matters of
religion and eternall saluation ? doth the
matter so alter the case ? Is prudence
become contrarie to it selfe? or is Gods
religion so against all reason wisdome
and iudgment? Can we not become
christians , but we must leaue to be
reasoable men, admitt Christes faith, but
we must banishe all reason discreation
and wisedome? No surelye.

12. I would

12. I would to God proteſtantes would conſider with what confidence and ſecuritye of côſcience we may aunſwere and appeare before god at the latter day for our faith. For if any faith or beleife of Chriſtianitye be laudable or excuſable before God, ſurelie our is. Becauſe we haue taken no new faith, but (to omitt all externall profes and keepe within the compaſſe of our nation) we retayne that faith of Chriſt, to which that our nation ſhould be conuerted from ther Paganiſme, was prophetied and foretold by holie men, as both Catholikes and Proteſtants record, that faith, which our forefathers and nation receaued aboue a thouſand yeares agoe and from great learned and holie men, lawfullie ſent, and rightlie ordered to preach it, which all chriſtendome, then and euer ſince held, which the aduerſaries of it then and now confeſſe to haue bene ſufficient to ſaluation; and finallie which was conteſted by God by true and confeſſed miracles. And therfor we may confidentlye ſay to god in the day of iudgment, that if we were deceaued in our faith, vertue, learninge, lawful miſſion, right order conſent of Chriſtedome, confeſſion of aduerſaries, heauenlie miracles, and conſequentlie Gods owne teſtimonie haue deceaued vs

Conuerſion of our Nation to the Cath. faith prophetied of.

Boeth Hiſtor. Stst. lib. 9. pag. 159. Bale Cent. 1. cap. 61.

Canſes of Catholicks confidence for their faith.

ued vs, which is alto gether impoſſible.
And contrariewiſe I would Proteſtants
would thinke with what feare they
muſt come to render account to God, for
forſakinge ſo auncient a faith and the
faith of their forefathers for ſo long time,
which ſo great learninge, ſo much vertue
ſo lawfull miſſion, ſo right orders, ſuch
conſent of chriſtendome, ſuch acknow-
ledgment of aduerſaries ſuch diuine miracles did comend vnto them, for a new
faith neuer hard of by their forefathers,
nor commended vnto them ſelues by
any of the forſaid titles, but rather diſ-
commended by the contrarie; as comminge from an ignorant and vicious
man, neither lawfullie ſent, nor rightlie
ordered, and which was contrary to the
faith of chriſtendome, condemned by
all the cheifeſt aduerſaries, and wholie
deſtitute of all miracles, or diuine te-
ſtimonye. Surelie if want of learninge, of
vertue, of lawfull miſſion, of right orders,
of conſent of Chriſtianytie, of confeſſion
of aduerſaries, of atteſtation from God;
Nay if ignorance, vnlawfull comminge,
naughtie orders, Doctrine condemned
of chriſtendome and of the chiefeſt aduerſaries, be like (as they are moſt like) to
deceaue, then ſurelie our Proteſtants be
deceaued.

13. Open

Canſes of diſtruſt of Proteſtants.

13. Open therfor your eyes for Gods fake, my most deere Countrimen, and be not wilfully deceaued, for wilfull ignorance doth not excufe, but increafe yonr fault before God. And confider that we exhort you not to a new religion, but to a most auncient, and as it is commonly tearmed *the old religion* ; not to a ftrange religion but the religion of our owne Countrie, Prelates, and forefathers for almoft a thoufand yeares together ; Not to an vntryed Religion, but that which hath bene tryed fo many hundred yeares, and by which it is confeffed of our aduerfaries that diuers haue bene faued and are yet faued. Our firft Chriftian forefathers had good reafon to relinquifh the Pagan ftuperftition of their progenitors, and to imbrace the Chriftian Religion, which Saint Auftin and his fellow labourers preached vnto them, becaufe they faw it taught by great learned and vertuous men, to worke great pietie and godlines in them that imbraced it, and to be con-firmed from God by affured miracles, fuch as Britons then and Proteftantes now confeffe to be true miracles. And we their children haue the fame motiues, and befides the experience and approba-tion, of one thoufand yeares continuance to abide and perfeuer in the fame reli-gion,

See this proued *lib.1.cap.4. s.13.23.*

gion . But what caufe alas had you my
deare countrymen Proteftants to forefake
fo auncient , fo godlie a Religion of your See all
forefathers,and embrace this new ? what this proued.*lib.* 2.
excufe or colour of reafon can you make *c.* 6.7.8.
of this your condemninge your Anceftors 12.14.
for blind , and their religion for follie ?
Did you fee their religion confuted by
publicke difputatiõ?No.Did you feeyours
defended by fuch rare learned men , as
neuer were in England before ? No. Did
you fee it preached by fuch vertuous men
as neuer England had before?No.Did you
fee it bringe forth fuch vertuous effects
and holie life as neuer was the like before?
No.Did you fee it publifhed by men that
had better proofe of ther commiſsion and
orders from God than any had heer to
fore ? No. Did you heare it to be more
approued of the reft of Chriftendome
than before?No. Did you know it to be
approued for good of aduerfaries more
than the religion before? No.Finallie did
you fee it confirmed by more certaine
and true miracles than was the auncient
Religion? No.What reaſon then can you
giue either to men now or to God at the
day of Iudgment,of your forfakinge your
forefathers faith fo grauelie,fo aduifedlie
and prudentlie embraced of them , and fo
long time continued,but a vayne pretence
of Gods

of Gods word wronglie vnderftoode, which euery Hereticke can and doth giue, and which when it is oppofite (as it is heere) to true vertue, lawfull miffion, right orders and vndoubted miracles, is (as is fhewed before and fhall more heerafter) but a vayne colour fhew and fhadowe of reafon, much leffe able to defend your doinges either before men now or God at the latter day. I will heere make an eud, onelie requefting you for Gods fake to lay all pafsion afide whiles you reade this booke, but perufe it with as great diligence, and defire of your owne Good as I compofed it, and prefented it vnto you. And God who is the Authour of all truth, graunt that it worke that effect in you which him felfe defireth. farewell my moft deare Countrymen this 6. of Ianuary. 1609.

TO

TO THE READER.

TVVo onelie meanes (*Gentle Reader*) hath allmightie God giuen vs to be aſſured of truth. The one by Science of euident truth which we our ſelues do know . The other by Beleefe of euident authoritie of others , who in like manner do know , and whoſe teſtimonie we haue no iuſt cauſe to miſtruſt . And therfor as he who should reiect euident reaſon , should both be vnreaſonable in fightinge againſt reaſon and iniurious both to God and himſelfe by refuſinge a meane which God hath giuen him to atttayne to truth . So likewiſe he who should reiect euident Authoritie should both do againſt reaſon which biddeth him giue creditt to ſuch authoritie , and be iniurious to God and him ſelfe by caſtinge away ſuch a meane as God gaue him to aſſure him ſelfe of ſuch truth as by himſelfe he could not know , and finallie should be an enemie to humaine ſocietie which cannot ſtand vnles men do creditt one an other in thinges wherin they haue no cauſe to diſtruſt them for what should we know of things paſt before our time, or of thinges done out of our ſight, if we would not beleeue ſuch as were preſent and knew them, and either by word or writing haue reported them to vs . How should we know ſuch to be our parents but by beleeſe ? How should any matter be tryed in Law but by beleeſe of mens wordes or writinges what familiaritie , humayne ſocietie or frendship could ſtand if we admitt not beleeſe ?

VVherfor

Wherfor abbeit it be a fault to beleeue vpon light or small testimonie (which kind of beleeuers the scripture tearmeth light of hart) as it is a fault to assent to any friuolous reason : yet contrariwise it is a greater fault not to giue credit to euident sufficient authoritie, as it is not to yeild to euident reason. For in beleeuinge vpon weake authoritie we do but preiudice our selues, but in not beleeuinge sufficient authoritie we hinder our selues from knowledge of truth, discredit our owne reportes to others, do against reason which as well bindeth vs to yeild to euident authoritie, as to euident reason, discredit our neighbors and cut in sunder the very sinowes of humane frendship and societie.

lib. de vtil. Cred. cap. 16.

Wherfor wel said S. Austin in that though it be miserable to be deceaued by authority, yet most miserable it is not to be moued with authoritie. *And most vnreasonably do some Ministers, say that they are not bound to beleeue the great vertues or miracles of Saints in times past, though neuer so authentically recorded, because they be not in scripture. Indeed if we vrged them to beleue these thinges with diuine and christian faith they might haue some colourable excuse of such speech, because (as they say) all poyntes of christian faith are in scripture. But sith we vrge them onelie to giue humane beleefe to such matters, either they must shew some cause why the authority of such writers is not sufficient to giue humane credite vnto the thinges by them recorded, or they must reiect all humane authoritie.*

How manie things vvhich are not in scripture are yet to be beleued.

ritie, all mens wordes or writinges, and beleeue
nothinge but what either God hath written, or
them selues haue seene. for if Scripture must be
the onelie square of all our beleife both humane
and Dyuine, we must beleue nothing but what
God hath written, no not that such were our
parentes, that ther are Turkes Moores ar any such
thinge as the Scripture mentioneth not. Or if we
admitt (as we must needes) that humane authority by either word or writinge may be sufficient
for vs to beleue thinges with humayne faith, as
vve beleue such to be our parentes, and the like,
vve must not thinke it reason to reiect a thinge,
because it is not in Scripture, but vve must allso Inconue-
shevv some reason, vvhy such authoritie as testi- niences of
fieth it, is not sufficient for a vvise man to giue not bele-
credit vnto: or els we must confesse our selues to uing mens
be vvilfull, to reiect sufficient authoritie vvithout, authoritie
yea against reason; to be in iurious to God and
our selues in reiecting a meane vvhich he hath
bestovved vpon vs, for to knovv truth; Iniurious
to our neighbours in discrediitinge them vvithout
cause; and finallie pernicious to all good freundshipp
and societie vvhich vvithout beleefe of humane
authoritie cannot stand. And to preuent Ministers
that they shall not delude the Reader by sayinge
that the authoritie vvhich I alleadge for vvhat I Onely
say of Saint Austin and Luther is not sufficient. I Protestāts
beseech him to consider that the Authors vvhich I alledged
alleadge for vvhat I say of Luther are onelie Pro for vvhat
testantes, uch as by other Protestantes are greatlie is said of
Luther.
commen-

commended. *for albeit I might iuftlie alleadge the
teftimonies of Catholiques againft Luther as I shew
heerafter lib. 2. cap. 1. yet partelie to avoyd all
cauills , but principallie becaufe Proteftantes
teftifie yuough againft him, I omitt this aduantage.
And the vvitneffes vvhich I produce for vvhat I
vvrite of S. Auftin, are partelie the faid Proteftants, partely Catholikes, but fuch Catholiques as
fome of them are great Saintes, fome great Clarkes,
fome lyued vvhen tha thinges vvere done vvhich
they vvritt, fome vvere domefticall, fome forrayne,
and all vvere before this controuerfie betvvene
Proteftants and Catholikes arofe , and all are
greathe efteemed of Proteftants as shall appeare
in the Catalogue enfuinge, and finallie all are contefted and approued in their teftimonies of diuers
Proteftants as shall appeare heerafter. VVhich kind
of teftimonie I hope no indifferent man guided
vvith reafon vvill account vnfufficient. And for
other obftinat perfons* who (as S. Hierome faith)
are wount fhutting their eyes to denie
what they will not beleue, I wrot not this
vvorke for as S. Auftin aduifeth vs vve should
rather pray for thefe kind of men than reafon
vvhith them. But novv let vs come to the Catalogue of the Catholike vvriters, and after of the
Proteftantes.*

For
vvhat
Readers
this boo-
ke is
vvritten.

A CA-

A CATALOGVE
Of the cheife Catholike vvriters

*Vpon whose testimonies the Authour relieth for
what he writeth of Saint Austin.*

A

ALCVIN, liued in the eight age after Christ   **1**
which was the second of the conuersion of
our Nation to the Christian faith. He was scholler
to S. Bede and Maister to the famous Emperor
Charles the great of whom what high esteeme
Protestants make, you may see. Infra. *lib.* 1. *cap.* 12.

B

BEDA, liued within the first hundred yeares after   **2**
the conuersion of our Nation and therfore might
well learne the truth therof. How greatlie he is
accounted of by Protestantes both for vertue and
learninge, you may read. *lib.* 1. *cap.* 12. cit. onelie
because his testimonie is that, vpon which I
principallie relie in what I say of S. Austin. I
would heere add what Godwin in the life of
Tatwin Archbishop of Canterburie saith, that
*His historie is the most auncient that England hath
worthie of credit*, And that Cambden in Britan.
pag. 12. giueth him this testimonie that he is.
*Inter omnes nostros scriptores veritatis amicus
amongst all our writers a frend of truth*. And what
himselfe hath in his Epistle to King Cealwulph
to put (as he saith) *all that heare or read it out of
doubt of the veritie therof*, *that vvhat he writeth
of S. Austin and his fellowes he learned of Albinus
a man*(saith he)*of great learninge, brought vp vnder
S. Theodor Archbishop, and Adrian both men of
great worship and learning*, *which thinges* (saith
he) *the said Albinus knew partely by writinge,
partlye by tradition of Elders, and sent to me by*

i   *Nothel-*

Bale.
Cent. 2
cap 8,cal-
leth this
Nothel-
mus alear-
ned and
graue man

Nothelmus , who after was Archbishop of Can-
terburie.Besides this the said Historie vvas approued by the said King Cealwulph , and by all
writers since,and is the verie fountayne of all our
English Chronicles,whose credit depend vpon it.
And therfor if it be reiected , all our auncient
Chronicles may be contemned as fables , or
vncertayne tales.

C

3

CAPGRAVE, lyued vnder King Henry the
sixt. *He was* (saith Bale Centuria. 8. *cap.1.*) *Doctor
of Diuinitie of Oxford,and Prouinciall of the Austin
fryers,the cheife diuine and Philisopher of his tyme,
of a cleare witt and vtterance, he loued the Scriptures singularly , and commented the greatest part of
the Bible, and was Confessour to Humfrey Duke of
Glocester.*

E

4

EALRID liued vnder King Henry the second.
He was (saith Bale Cent. 2.cap.99 *famous for birth,
for learning , and for innocent life. He in short time
excelled all his fellowes in all ornaments of life , left
no kind of learning vntouched , refused a Bishoprike
the better to excercise vertue , and to preach the
Gospell.He was an other Bernard,mild in disposition,
pious in action, and most modest in Counsell, and was
a godlie man , And in all kind of vvriting most like
to Bernard.* Thus Bale.

5

ETHELWERDVS, *seemeth* (saith Cambden *in
descrip Brit.* 100. *) to haue bene great grand child
to King Adulph , and liued about the yeare . 950.*
His booke was published by Protestants with
Malmesburiensis and others.Sauill who published
him,saith, he is *to be commended for his nobilitie
and antiquitie.*

F.

6

FLORENTIVS, liued vnder King Henry the
first.*He vvas* (saith Bale. Cent.2.c. 66.) *very lear-*
ned

ned both in diuine and humane literature , *and gett great fame by his vvriting. He had*(saith Bale) *a vvit apt for any thinge,and an excellent memorie, let no day paſſe vvherin he did not ſome vvhat for the honour of his Countrie,* and calleth his Chronicle *an excellent comment* , which alſo is printed by Proteſtantes .

G

S. GREGORY, *tho great* was the cheefe Author next after God of the conuerſion of our Engliſh Nation vnto Chriſtianitie , and lyued eight yeares after he had ſent S. Auſtin hither, and had heard of great fruit of his labours. He is one of the famous Doctors of the Church , and greatlie reuerenced of Proteſtantes as you may ſee infra. *lib.1.cap.5.*

GILDAS, ſyrnamed *the vviſe,*a Britan, floriſhed about the yeare. 580. which was eighteene yeares before S. Auſtins comming hither. *He vvas*(ſaith Bale Cent.1.cap. 66. out of Polidor) *a moſt graue Author, hauinge vvell learnt liberall ſciences,gaue himſelfe vvholie to ſtudie the Scriptures and ledd a moſt innocent life.* This mans writinges alſo haue bene publiſhed by Proteſtantes, and I produce his teſtimonie cheiflie to ſhew what was the Religion of the auncient Britons.

GEFFGREY *of Monmonth* lyued vnder King Stephen. *He vvas* (ſaith Bale Cent. 2. cap. 86,) *a Briton and learned both in verſe and prooſe,* and he highlie commendeth his diligence , and ſaith he *excellentlie deſerueth of his Countrie* . Thus he and other Proteſtantes account of this Geffrey, which maketh me to alleadge his authoritie againſt them though Catholickes for the moſt part account him but a fabulous Authour , and his bookes be forbidden by the Councell of Trent , and Cambden Britan. *pag.* 8. calleth his hiſtorie,*Ineptias,* fooleries.

7

8

Ho-

H

10. HO **V E D E N** lyued vnder kinge Iohn , *He vvas* (faith Bale Cent.3.*cap.55*) *of a noble race , and a famous Chronographer.* His hiſtorie was publiſhed by Savill, and dedicated to Queene Elizabeth, wher togither with Huntington he is called *a very good and diligent Authour, and moſt true guide of the times paſt.*

11 HV N T I N G T O N, liued vnder King Stephen. *He vvas* (faith Bale cent. 2. cap. 82. out of Polidor and Leland) *an excellent Hiſtoriographer , and approued Authour , and vvrit* (faith he) *finely and learnedly.* He is acounted of Cambden in Britan. pag. 306. an Authour *priſcæ fidei.* Of Doctor Caius lib. de antiqu t.Cantabr.pag.64.*Summus Hiſtoricus.* And his hiſtory was publ.ſhed by Savill with the foreſaid commendations. Fluyd in deſcript. Monæ calleth him *egregium Hiſtoricum.*

I.

12 INGVL PH V S, lyued in the time of the Conqueſt,& *is much deſired*(faith Sauil who publiſhed him)*of very many , vvho d ſire to knovv our Antiquities.*

M

13 MA L M E S B V R I E N S I S, lyued vnder Kinge Stephen,*He vvas*(faith Sauil who publiſhed him, in his epiſtle to Queene Elizabeth) *amongſt the faithfull recorde s of thinges done the cheefe ,both for truth of Hiſtorie and for Maturitie of iudgment, very learned . and hath compriſed the hiſtorie of Seauen huu red yeares vvith ſuch fidelitie and diligence, that he may ſeeme of all ours to haue bene the onelie Hiſtor ographer.* Camb. in Brit pag. 514. calleth him . *Optimum Hiſtoricum. an excellent Hiſtoriographer.* Bale Cent. 2. cap. 73. fai h playnelie he was *the moſt learned of his age in all kinde o good learning . and of ſingular vvitt , diligence and induſtrie in ſearchinge all Antiquites . and*

compiled

compiled a fine and most excellent Historie. And this man so highlie commended by Protestants is the Authour vpon whom next after S. Bede I relie, and the edition which I cite of his historie and of Huntington, Houeden, and Ingulph, is of Franckford Anno. 1601. infol.

MARIANVS, liued at the time of the Conquest, *He vvas* (saith Bale Cent. 14. cap. 45.) *learned both in diuinitie and Humanitie, and lyued all most thirtie yeares solstarie vvith admiration of all men and contiunallie studied He is accounted an excellent Historiographer a singular Calculator, and a graue diuine, vvhich titles saith he to this day all vvriters de giue him.* Thus Bale. Cambd. in Brit. pag. 321. calleth him an Historiographer. *Antique fidei.*   14.

N.

NEVBRIGENSIS, lyued vnder Kinge Iohn. *He vvas* (saith Bale Cent. 3. cap. 53.) *Doctor of diuinity, scarce let any hovver passe vvithout reading of learned bookes, and vvrote a Historie vvith a cleare stile.*   15.

O.

OSBERNE, liued vnder Kinge William Conqueror. *He vvas* (saith Bale Cent. 2. cap. 54.) *most familiar and invvard vvith Archbishop Lanfrancke, vvas the excellentest Musycion of his time, and had a florishing and eloquent stile.*   16.

OTTERBVRNE, *He vvrote* (saith Bale Cent. 7. cap. 75. out of Leland) *a historie sincerely, though his cheefe studies vvere in Philosophy and Diuinitie.*   17.

P.

PARIS, lyued vnder King Henry the third. *He vvas* (saith Bale Cent. 4. cap. 26.) *from his infancie brought vp in learning, and continuallie at studie. And vvrote a Historie*

  from   18.

*from the conqueſt vnto the thirtie fift yeare of the
ſaid King Henrie vvith moſt great diligence and
fidelitie. And for his ſingular giftes both of bodie
and minde vvas deere to that King, at vvhoſe
commande he vvrot his Actes.* This authour is
much eſteemed by Proteſtants, becauſe ſome
times he inueigheth bitterly againſt ſome acts of
the Pope of his time, and therfor was publiſhed
by them, and greatly commended in the preface
by the pretended Archbiſhop Parker, as it is
thought.

W.

19 VV A L S I N G H A M, lyued vnder King Henry
the Sixt. *He vvas* (ſaith Bale Cent. 7. cap. 88. out of
Leland) *ſtudious & diligent in Hiſtories.* He is much
commended by the Proteſtantes, who publiſhed
him, in a Preface before his hiſtorie, who is
thought to haue bene pret. Archbiſhop Parker.

20 VV E S T M O N A S T E R I E N S I S, lyued vnder
King Edward the firſt. *He did* (ſaith Bale Cent. 6.
cap. 31.) *labour ſingularlie in vvriting, and vvas in
all kind of learninge of his time very learned, and
compoſed a Chronicle vvith notable paynes,* which
Bale tearmed *an excellent and fruitfull vvorke,*
and it hath bene printed by Proteſtants with
great commendations. And in the arraigement
of F. Garnet, he is called by a Proteſtant noble
man *a vvitnes of beſt regard accordinge to the ſtate
of whoſe times.* Thus many, thus auncient (to omitt
the famous Baronius and other later writers alſo
alleadged) & thus eſteemed of Proteſtants themſelues are the Authors whoſe teſtimonies I produce for what I ſay of S. Auſtin and his ſucceſſors,
and of our Kings, and our forefathers religion.
VVhoſe teſtimonie whether Miniſters admitt or
refuſe they are ouerthrowne. For if they admitt
them they are clearlie condemned, and if they
refuſe them, they are contemned. For in matters
of

of Antiquitie to refuse to be tryed by so many, so aunciet, so indifferent writers, and so much commended by them selues, and to say, and that without testimonie of one equall writer to the contrarie, that they were all either deceaued or lyed, what other is it, than vtterlie to condemne them selues and their cause, as not able to abide the onelie triall, which can be made of auncient matters, that is by histories and auncient recordes? will they not credit such histories as them selues iudge worthie of credit? will they not beleeue such writers as them selues account especiall freinds of truth, of singular fidelitie, diligence, and indifferent and most excellent Historiographers? will they not follow them in matters of Antiquitie, whom them selues tearme *the most true guides of the times past?* What other thinge were this than obstinatelie to refuse truth it selfe. But much more will this appeare when they shall be found not onelie to refuse our writers, though neuer so auncient and indifferent and esteemed of them selues, but euen their owne best writers or els be condemned. Let vs see therfor the Protestant writers whom we produce as witnesses in this triall of Religions.

A CATHALOGVE
Of the cheefe Protestát vvriters

On whose testimonies the Authour relieth for what he writeth of S Austin and Luther.

A.

ABBOTS, Doctor and Professour of Diuinitie, & now an earnest writer both against Cardinall Bellarmin, and Doctor Bishop.

BALE

1

BALE, Bishop of Ossorie in Ireland in King Edward the Sixt time, as him selfe writeth Cent. 8. cap. 100. and one of the first English Preachers of Protestantisme in time of King Henrie, for which both vnder him and after vnder Queene Marie he suffered as he saith much. As for his skill in Antiquities, he writeth of himselfe in his Epistle before his foureteenth Centurie that he had *Antiquitatum penetralia*, *& incognitas orbi Historias*, and in the Epistle before the thirteenth Centurie that he *had read the histories and Chronicles allmost of all Antiquities*. And how earnest a Protestant he was, appeareth both by his said sufferinges, and allso by his most spitefull kind of writinge against Catholiques, which is so great, as it seemeth malice did possesse the hart, tongue, and penn of that man, and himselfe is fayne to excuse it in his epistle to the Counte Palatin. Of the Authour of the daungerous positions he is reckoned amongst their learned men who in the beginning of Queene Elizabeths raygne Came out of Germanie and of other Protestants often times cited. The booke which I alledge of this man is his Centuries of the writeers of Britanie, edit. Basileæ. 1559. in fol.

(margin: Reinoldes in his Confer. Abbots de Antichrist)

BILSON, at this present the pretended Bishop of winchester, and well knowne for his writinges both against Catholiques and Puritanes.

C.

4 CAIVS, Doctor of Phisicke and halfe founder of Gonell and Caius Colledge in Cambridge. So well seene in Englishe Antiquities, as by an Oxonian Orator, he is tearmed *the Antiquarie*.

5 CALVIN, is more famous among Protestants than I need note him, and of such account amongst many as Doctor Couel saith his writinges were made *allmost the rule of Controuersies*.

CAMB-

CAMDEN, well knowne for his discription of Britanye, and tearmed of Protestants *an excellent Antiquarie* and greatlie commended of diuers in verses before his booke. The edition of his booke cited by me is Londini Anno.1600. in quarto.

COWPER, pretended Bishop first of Lyncolne and after of Winchester, well knowne for his Dictionarie and his Chronicle.

D

DAVNGEROVS Positioner, So I tearme the vnnamed Authour of a booke called *Daungerous Positions*, by some thought to be the worke of Doctor Bancrofte now pretended Bishop of Canterburie, by others of Doctor Sutcliffe.

F.

FOX, most famous amongst Protestants for his Acts & monuments of their Martyrs, which they haue so credited, as they haue set it in diuers of their Churches to be read of all. To omitt diuers high praises giuen to him, as you may see in the beginning of his booke. Ford vpon the Apocalips calleth him *most holie father*. Doctor Abbots in his booke of Antichrist cap. 8. tearmeth him *a man of most famous memorie; a most graue, and most pious man, and plainlie a diuine man*. Bale Cent. 9. cap. 92. saith he was his Achates.

FVLKE, Doctor of diuinitie and a great writer against Catholiques: whom I. B. alias Bacster in tayle of two legged foxes. cap. 13. thus prayseth *profound fulke, vvhose truth and great trauell the Church of God hath tryed, many a fox hast thou had in chase not able to abide thy bote pursuite*. Doctor Reynolds in his

i 5   preface

6

7

8

9

10

preface before his Six Conclusions calleth him
a stout and faithfull souldier of Christ.

G

11 GODWIN, now Subdeane of Excester, & sonne
to Godwin pret. Bishope of Bathe, as himselfe
saith in his Cathalogue of Bishopes.

H

12 HOLINSHED, notorious for his great Chronicle, and most earnest against Catholikes as you
may see by what he writeth of S. Austin.

13 HVMPHREY, Doctor of Deuinitie and the
Queenes Reader therof in Oxford, whom I. B.
loc.cit.thus comendeth *Humphrey of much reading
in thy time past, vvas then a cheefe hunter of the
Romish fox.* And Bale Cent. *9.* cap. 93. highly
commendeth him.

l

14 IEWILL, so famous and knowne to Protestantes as I need say nothinge.

L

15 LVTHER, the father of Protestancie, and of
what high account he is amongst Protestants you
may see infra *lib.3. cap* 1.

R.

16 REYNOLDS, Doctor of Diuinitie who, saith
I. B.loc. cit. *hath the old fox and his cubbs in the
chase.*

S.

17 STOW, well knowne for his Chronicle and
others his writinges of Antiquitie.

18 SVTCLIFE, Doctor of Diuinitie and Deane of
Excester, and a great writer against Catholikes.

19 SVRVEYER, so I call the vnnamed Authour of
the *Survey of the pretended holie Discipline*, by
some taken to be the worke of the said Doctor
Sutclife, by others the worke of the Lord of
Canterburie.

WHITA-

WHITAKER , Doctor and Professour of Diuinitie, and a great writer against Catholiques, whom I. B. loc. cit. calleth *vvorthie VVhitaker of neuer ãyinge fame* . Doctor Willet in his Tetra-stylon pag. 9. tearmeth him *a vvorthie and learned man*. pag. 10. *à godlie learned man*. Doctor Bucley in his Apologie of religion pag. 84. *An excellent man of blessed memorie* . These and thus esteemed of Protestants are the Protestant writers , vpon whose confession or testimonie I cheefly relie in what I write of S. Austin and Luther . Against whose verdict no Protestant can iustlie take exception either of ignorance , because they are of the cheefest writers they haue , or for partia-litie, for they were all most earnest Protestantes. And therfor no Protestant can iustlie reiect their testimonie as insufficient.

THE

THE BOOKES AND
Chapters conteyned in this
firſt parte of the prudentiall
Ballance of Religion.

Firſt Booke or Scale in which the
qualities of S. Auſtin and of his doctrine
are ſet downe.

The ſecond Booke or Scale wherin the qualities of Luther, and his doctrine are ſet downe.

The

The third Booke in which S.

Auſtin and Luther and their Doctrines
are weighed together, according
to the foreſaid qualities
of them.

THE FIRST
BOOKE OR SCALE,

IN VVHICH

The qualities of S. Auſtin, and
of his Doctrine are ſet
dovvne.

THE FIRST CHAPTER.

*VVhat Religion was in this Land,
before the comminge of
S. Auſtin.*

T HE ancient Inhabitans
of this Iland, were the
Britons, whome wee
now call Welch-men.
Amongſt whome the
faith of Chriſt was firſt
planted by the glorious Apoſtles S. ᵃPeter
S.ᵇ Paul, S.ᶜ Symon, and the Apoſtolick
men S.ᵈ Ioſeph of Arimathia (who buried our Sauiour) and S.ᵉ Ariſtobulus, of
whome S. Paul maketh mention in his

a *Metaph. in
Sur. Iun.
Cambd.
deſcript.
Brit.pa.52.
Baron. an.
58. p. 197.
401.*

A   Epiſtle

b *Theod.l.9 de Grac. Sophron. Natal. A- post. Fortu- nat. Bale cent.1.c.26 Cambd. in Britan.p. 52.* c *Nicep.l.2. c.40. Do- roth.in Sy- nop.* d *D. Caius de antiq. Cātabr. Capgrau. in Ioſ. Bale cent.1.c.22. vbi & citat Fleming. Scrop. Po- lid. Geo. maiorem Cambd.l. cit.* e *Doroth.in Synop.* f *Camb. pa. 30 627. 628.de Ba- ron.* g *D. Bucley B.Reaſ.art. pls. p. 175. of Camb.*

Epiſtle to the Romans. All theſe, Proteſtants grant to haue preached Chriſts
faith in this Iland, except Saint Peter; to
whome ſome of them will not haue this
Land ſo much behoulden. Which queſtion, becauſe it is beſides my purpoſe, I
wil not ſtand to diſcuſſe. Onely I aſſure the indifferent Reader, that S. Peters
preaching to the ancient Britons on the
one ſide is affirmed, both by Latin and
Grecke, by ancient and newe, by foraine
& domeſticall, by Catholick writers (ſuch
as f Proteſtants them ſelues account *moſt
excellent,learned and great Hiſtoriographers*) &
by Proteſtāt Antiquaries, ſuch as g Proteſtant Diuines terme *excellent Antiquaries,
and excellent men*: And on the other ſide denied by no one ancient writer, Greeke or
Latin, foraine or domeſtical, Catholick or
other. And what better proofe will wee
require to beleeue a thing done ſo long
agoe, than the aſſertion of men ſo many,
learned, of ſuch different ages, of ſuch different contries, of ſuch different religion,
who haue not ben gainſaid by any one ancient writer? To argue againſt ſuch varietie & grauitie of teſtimonies without any
anciēt writers teſtimony to the cōtrary, is
indeed rather to cauill (which is no mai-
ſtery to doe againſt ſuch anciēt facts) than
to reaſon, & to ſhew a minde more auerted

ted from S. Peter and his Succeſſors, than desirous of truth or honor of his Contrie.

2. This faith thus planted amongſt the Britons by the Apoſtles and Apoſtolick men, periſhed not after their departure, but remained, as Gildas *c. 7.* writeth *apud quosdam integrè, amongſt ſome entire.* and about the yeare of our Lord 158. was meruaillouſly increaſed, and cõfirmed by meanes of Pope Eleutherius, who ſending hither at the requeſt of Lucius then King of the Britons, his two Legats, S. Fugatius and S. Damian, the King, Queene, and almoſt all the people were baptized, and this Land was the firſt that publickly profeſſed the faith of Chriſt, and iuſtly deſerued the title of *Primogenita Eccleſia.* For teſtimony of this, we can produce not onely ſuch variety, and weight of witneſſes, as for the former, to wit [a] Latin, Engliſh, domeſtical, ſtrangers, Catholick, and Proteſtãts, but euen all our Engliſh hiſtories, and in a maner all foraine writers, which intreate of theſe tymes. And finally, the letters patents of King Arthur alleaged by D. Caius a Proteſtant *lib. 1. de Antiq. Cantab.* where he ſaith, that all *know this to be true,* and Godwin in the life of S. Paulin, addeth, that it *can not be denyed.* Wherby we may ſee the impudẽcy of a Miniſter, who is not aſhamed, without all teſtimony to

A 2 the

[a] Engliſh.
Bedal 1.c.
4. *Malmeſ. in faſt. Ethelvverd l. 1. Huuting liſ. 1 Florent. an.* 184.
VVeſtm. an. 185 *Sander. lib de ſchiſ. 1. eland in Baleo* 23.
VVelch.
Gaiſrid l. 4. c. 19. *Nannius hiſt. Landaffen. King Arthur.*
Foraine.
Damaſus in Pont. Ado. Marian in Chron. Platina in Eleu ther. Geneb. Martin. Polon. Pontiſicus Virum. Polidor. Boethius l. 5. *hiſt. Baron. mart. Rom.* 26. *Maij.*
Proteſtãts
Bale cen. 1. *c.* 22. 18. 29 *Camb. in Brit p* 51. *& 628. Stovv and* 179 *Holinſ. p.* 74. *Caius*

l.1.de ant.
Godvvin in
S. Austin
Bilson of o-
bedience p.
57. Cooper
an.180.
Fox l. 1. p.
51. l.2.p.
106.107.
D. Sutclif.
ansvver to
3. Conners.
d.2.

the contrary, to deny this Conuersion of Britany by the Popes meanes, and to say, that *no authenticall author auoucheth it* : but that *it is a fable, and seemeth to be deuised by some fauourers of the Church of Rome.* Which here in the beginning I note, to aduertise the indifferent Reader, that he giue no beleefe to such impudent fellowes deniall without any sufficient witnesse.

3.   The Christian faith thus receaued, the Britons kept not onely found, and vndefiled from heresies a long tyme, but quiet also from troubles, and persecutions vntil the reign of Diocletian the Emperor, who began in the yeare of our Lord 286. & for ten yeares space raised a more cruel persecution against the Christians, than euer had ben before : which passing into this Iland honored it with the glorie of many holy Martyrs, who constantly stood, and died in the confession of their faith. Of whome cheefly are named Saint Alban, (whose miracles and martyrdom are largly set downe by S. Beda *lib.1.c.7.*) and Iulius, and Aaron. This storme of persecution being ouerblown, Constantin the Great, a Briton borne, receaued the Christian faith, & exalted it in the whole Empire of Rome. In whose tyme arose the Arian heresie, which running through the world, corrupted also this Iland, and

*Gildas de
excid c.7.
Bed, l.1.c.4*

*Gildas c. 7.
Bed.l.1.c.6*

Gildas c.8.

shortly

shortly after *all manner of herefies flowed in,* & was there receaued of the inhabitants, being men (as faith S. Gildas their Countryman) *euer delighted to heare new things, and stedfastly retainning nothing certain.* And for thefe herefies, and other vices were the Britons plagued by God with extreme famin, wonderful peftilence, in fo much as the quick were not fufficient to bury the dead, and with moft cruel, & blooddy warre of the Picts and Scotts, as yow may read in Gildas, and in Beda *lib.1. c.12.* & 14. But for the accomplifhmet of their iniquities, after all this, they admitted the Pelagian herefie, which haftned their defolation, and almoft vtter deftruction brought fone after vpon them by the Saxons, or Englifh. For as S. Beda faith *lib. 1. c.17. a few yeares before the coming of the Saxons into this Land* (which faith he *lib.1. c.15. was in the yeare of our Lord 429.*) *the Pelagian herefies were brought in.* But of this herefie the Land was after rid by the difputation and miracles, firft of S. German and Lupus fent by Pope Celeftinus *anno* 429. & after by the fame S. German and Seuerus *anno* 435. *ex Baronio.*

4. After this tyme in this place the faith long tyme (faith S. Beda *lib.1. c. 2 1.*) *remained found and vndefiled.* But at laft, in all, or moft of the Britons it was corrupted

A 3 by

(marginal notes:)
Herefies enter into England.

Herefie bane of a Country.

See S. Bed. *l.1.c.17. & feq.*

TheBritōs error about Eaſter far differēt from the Quartadecimās See Euſeb. 5. hiſt c. 24. 25. Juſtin ſer. 29 Epiph. har. 50. Theod li. 3. de hæreſ.
by an erroneous opinion about the tyme of keeping Eaſter, which was not (as Beda well quoteth *lib. 3. c. 4.*) the error of the Iewes, or Quartadeciman hereticks. For the Quartadecimans alwayes kept their Eaſter on one ſet day of the moone, to wit on the 15. day after the equinoctial, and regarded no ſet day of the weeke. The Britons contrary wiſe celebrated their Eaſter alwayes on one ſet day in the weeke, to wit on Sonday, as Catholicks doe, and obſerued not any ſet day of the

VVherin the Britōs erred touching Eaſter.
moone, as the Quartadecimans did. The onely differēce betwene them & Catholicks was, that wheras Catholicks according to the appointemēt of the Cōncel of Nice kept their Eaſter on the Sōday from the 15. day of the moone to the 21. the Britons kept it on the Sonday from the 14. of the moone to the 20. and ſo they both included one whole day within the cōpas of celebrating Eaſter, to wit the 14. day of the moone, which neither Iew nor Chriſtian

Exod. 12.
els included, and excluded the 21. day, which the law expreſly commanded. Which proceeded of mere ignorance in them. For as S. Beda ſaith *lib. 3. c. 4. They knew as Chriſtian men doe, that the Reſurrection of our Lord ought alwayes to be celebrated on Sonday, but as ignorant men (in that point) they had not learned, when that Sonday ſhould come.*

Becauſe

Becaufe (as S. Wilfrid in S. Beda *li. 3. c. 25.*
faid) *no cunning Calculator of tymes or Aftro-
nomer had come to them.*

Herby it appeareth how fondly fome
Minifters haue inferred that the Britons,
becaufe of this error in keeping Eafter,
learned their faith of the Afian Churches,
where the Quartadecimans were. Both
becaufe the Britons error was not the
Quartadecimans error, but much different; as alfo becaufe the Britons in Conftantins tyme (when Religion began firft
to florifh) agreed with the Roman vfe of
celebrating Eafter, as teftfieth the faid Cô-
ftantin their Countrey man, who in Eu-
feb. *lib. 3. de vita Conftantini, c. 8.* witneffeth
that the fame keeping of Eafter was obferued *in the Citty of Rome in Italie, Africk,
Egypt, Spaine, France, Britannie, Lybia, and all
Greece, in the Dioceffe of Afia, and Pontus, and finally in Cilicia, Vnâ & confentiente fententiâ,
with one vniforme confent.* Moreouer becaufe
as S. Beda *li. 1. c. 11.* faith, that after the forfaid expulfion of the Pelagian herefie, the
Britons kept the faith, *founde and vndefiled,*
which he neuer would then haue faid,
if then they had held their error of Eafter,
becaufe this error he *vtterly detefted,* as him
felf faith *lib. 3. c. 16.* and *lib. 2. c. 19.* calleth it
Herefie. And finally B. Colman pleading in
England for the Britons obferuation of
A 4 Eafter,

*Magd. cent.
2. c. 2.
Fox p. 95.*
The Britôs
errorcame
not from
Afia.

1.

2.

3.

Eafter, and alleadging therto the antiquitie of his Countrymen, afcendeth no hi-

When the
Britōs er-
ror rose.
gher than Abbot Columba, who came
out of Ireland into Britanie, but *anno* 563.
as Beda faith *lib. 3. c. 4.* which was 33.
yeares before S. Auftins comming hither,
and dyed as Sigebert in Chron. and Bale
write *anno* 598. that is, two yeares after
S. Auftins entrance here. Nether did he
euer auouch that the Britons, or Scotts
had ben taught that coftom of the Afians,
but gathered it themfelues by mifunder-
ftanding S. Anatholius his writings, and
by imagining that S. Iohn Euangelift kept
it fo, wherof nether was true, as S. Wilfrid prooued to his face, in Beda *lib. 3. c. 25.*
The author therfore of this error among
the Britons was no Afian, but their owne
ignorance (through *rude fimplicitie,* as Saint
Wilfrid faith) of true calculation of finding the true tyme of Eafter. And the
tyme when this ignorance tooke effect
(as it apeareth by S. Beda's forfaid words
lib. 1. c. 11.) was not long before S. Auftins
comming. And for Scotland, Beda *lib. 2.
cap. 29.* writeth that by the letters of Pope
Iohn 4. written in the yeare 638. or as
Baron. faith, 639. to the Scotts, *it appeareth plainly, that at that tyme this herefie was but
a litle before rifen in Scotland, and that not all the
Contrie, but certain of them onely were infected
ther-*

5.

Pope Iohn
4. *in Bed. l.
2. c. 9. attri-
buteth it to
ignorance.*
Whence
it arofe.

therwith. Which also appeareth by S. Gregory *lib.9.epist.61.* which he writeth *to Quirinus & cæteris in Hibernia Episcopis Catholicis.* But as for the Britons it seemeth by Saint Beda *lib. 2. cap.2.* that they were generally all infected with this error, when S. Austin entred this land. And as for the rest of this Kingdom where the English dwelt they (as both Welch & English Historiographers agree) *pagana superstitione cæcati &c.* blinded in Heathenish superstition they had extinguished all Christianity *in that parte of the Land where they dwelt.* And as S. Beda writeth *lib.2.c.1.* were all then *Pagans* and had ben euer vntill that tyme *bondslaues of Idols.* This was the lamentable estate of England and Wales before S. Austin came, miserably opprest, partly with heresy, partly with infidelity.

Galfrid monum.li.11. c.12. VVestmon. an. 596. Godwin Catalog. of Bishops, in S.Paulin.

Miserable estate of Britany before S. Austins comming.

CHA-

CHAP. II.

That S. Austin was the first Prea-
cher of the Christian Faith to
our English Nation.

Hat our English Nation came hither
out of Germanie, being sent for of the
Britons to ayde them against the Scotts,
and Picts, all Historiographers agree, but
they disagree somwhat about the tyme.
For some write that it was in the yeare of
Christ 449. but S. Beda *lib.* 1. *c.* 15. saith
that it was in the yeare 449. and later indeede it could not be. Because at S. Germans first comming hither (which was in
the yeare 429. as S. Prosper who then
liued recordeth) the Saxons (as S. Beda
*lib.*1. *c.* 20. affirmeth) waged war with the
Britons. For being Pagans, and ignorant
of God, and seeing the Land fruitfull, and
the Britons feeble, they measured right
by might, and turned their wepons a-
gainst the silly Britōs, whome they partly
killed, partly droue ouer seas or into those
hilly places, which now are called Wales.
And in this parte of the Land, which
they possessed, extinguished (as both En-

glish

Sigeb. Chro.
saith. an.
431. Mal-
mesb. l. 1.
an. 449.
Bal. cent. 2.
c. 43. an.
448. Cābd.
in Brit an.
450.
Vvhē our
English
nation
entred
this land.

Galfrid
Mon l. 17.
c. 12.
Godwin in
vit. Paulin.

glish and Welch writers record)all Christianitie, and continewed in their Paganisme, which they brought with them,
for the space almost of 200. yeares, til (as
S. Beda *lib.* 2. *c.* 1. and others record) S.
Gregory seeing certaine English youths
sould for slaues in Rome, and learning of
them that their nation was Heathen, got
leaue of the Pope (being then him selfe a
Monke) to come to preach to them: but
was recalled at the importunitie of the
Romans: yet him self being after made Pope (and as S. Beda speaketh *high Bishop ouer*
the whole world)did in the yeare 596 send
hither S. Austin, and his cōpany to preach
Chrsts faith ynto them. Which truth,
that S. Austin was the first preacher of
Christian faith vnto our English Nation
here in England, hath bene alwaies hitherto as vndoubted, as it is euident, and
manifest. But now becaufe D. Sutclif in
his Subuersion of the three Conuersions,
*c.*3. hath called it in question, and is desirous rather to giue the glorie to a French
man and woman, to Queene Bertha, and
Bishop Luidhard, who were then in
England, or to captiue Britons, whome
he supposeth to haue liued amongst the
English, than to S. Austin, I will prooue it
by as many proofes as can be desired for
the beleefe of any ancient thing.

S. Gre-

Vpō vvhat
occasion
S. Gregory
sent S. Au
stin hither

S. Austin
the first
preacher
of Christi-
anity vn-
to our na-
tion.

S. Grego-
ry.

2. S. Gregory himself, who sent S. Auſtin, writing *lib. 7. Epiſt. 30.* to Eulogius Patriarch of Alexandria, ſaith thus: *VVhiles the English Nation dwelling in a corner of the worlde, remained til now inſidel in the worship of wood and ſtones, by the help of your praier it ſeemed good to me, God being the Author, to ſend a Monk of my monaſtery to preach to them.* The ſame he teſtifieth *lib. 27. Moral. c. 8.* and in diuers letters *lib. 9. Epi. 52. 56. 59*, and in S. Beda *lib. 1. c. 27. 29. 30. 31. 32.* which for breuitie I omit. And the ſame witneſſe diuers other Popes as *Boniface, Honorius, Vitalian, Sergius, Gregorius* and *Formoſus*, wherof ſome were aliue in S. Auſtins tyme, and others liued not long after, whoſe letters are extant in Malmesb. *lib. 2. Pont. Ang. pag.*

S. Auſtins
compani-
ons.

208. *pag. 209.* Likwiſe *S. Laurence, S. Mellit, S. Iuſtus*, three companions of S. Auſtin, in their publick letters to the Scotts in S. Beda *lib. 2. c. 4.* write, that the Engliſh, to whome they were ſent to preach the word of God, were *Paynim people, and hea-*

English-
men,

then men. In like maner the Engliſh youths before mentioned being asked of S. Gregory, whether they were Chriſtiás or no, anſwered (as teſtifyeth Ethelwerd an ancient Hiſtoriographer of the blood royal of England) *No: nor as yet hath any preached*

The mer-
chants.

this vnto vs. And the merchants added *ex Beda lib. 2. c. 1.* that *they were all Paynims.* And
                                        the

the very Epitaph set vpon Saint Austins   S. Austins
tombe after his death testifieth, that he   epitaph.
conuerted *King Ethelbert and his Realme from
the worſhiping of Idolls to the faith of Chriſt*, in
Beda *lib. 2. c. 3.* Thus yow ſe both priuat
and publick, both foraine and domeſtical
teſtimonies, euen of that tyme when S.
Austin liued, conteſt, that beforehis comming our Engliſh Nation was Heathen.
wherto I wil add a few witneſses in the
ages after, that the reader may be aſſured how vndoubted a truth this hath ben
hertofore.

3. S. Beda who liued within 80. yeares   S. Beda.
after S. Austin saith plainly *lib. 2. c. 1.* that
our Nation *had ben euer to that time the bond-
ſlaue of Idols.* And Alcuin his ſcholler, but
maiſter to Charles the Great in Malmesb.   Alcuin.
lib. 1. Pont. Ang. pag. 199. & *1. Reg. c.* 14. calleth
S. Austin *our Firſt Teacher*, and Canterbury
the *Firſt Seat of faith.* King Kenulph, who   King Ke-
liued within 200. yeares after S. Austin,   nulph.
writing letters to Pope Leo 3. in his own
name, & in the name of the Biſhops, Duks
and all the Nobility of his Realme,
confeſſeth, that from Rome *Nobis Fidei
veritas innotuit*, and that, that Sea imbued
his Nation *rudimentis fidei.* King Withlaf in   K. VVith-
his Charter in Ingulph. *pag.* 858. calleth S.   laf.
Austin *the Apoſtle of our Nation.* Odo Arch-   Odo.
biſhop of Canterbury, writing about
                       800.

800. yeares agoe to his Suffragans, saith
that *from the Sea of Canterbury, Augustini &*
aliorum studiis Religio Christianitatis primùm
cunctis finibus Anglorum innotuit. And in a Synod held in the yeare 747. of all the Bishops of England in presence of the King,
and Nobles, S. Austin is called *Pater noster,*
and in honour of him they were wont
to keepe his day most solemnly. And in
an other Synod held about 500. yeares
since, Lanfranc Archbishop of Canterbury
saith: *Quis nesciat quòd à Cantia manauit Chri-*
sti credulitas in ceteras omnes Angliæ Ecclesias.
Superfluous it were to add to these the
testimonies of such as haue lyued since,
both foraine and domesticall historiographers, who all deliuer this for as certain a
truth as can be. Onely for the confusion
of Sutclif and such as he, I will add the
confession of some Protestants. Fox in
his Acts and Monuments *lib.* 4. *pag.* 172.
The Saxons overcomming the Land deuided them
selues into seuen Kingdoms: And so being Infidells,
and Pagans continued til the time that Gregory,
being Bishop of Rome sent Austin to preach vnto
them. The like he hath *lib.* 2. *pag.* 110. 115. and
in his Protestat: *pag.* 9. Holinshead in descript. of Britany *lib.* 11. *c.* 7. *Austin was sent*
by Gregory to preach to English men the word of
God, who were yet blinde in Pagan superstition.
And an. 596. *Gregory sent Austin into this Ile*
to preach

Tvvo Eng-
lish Sy-
nods.

Protestãts
confesse
S. Austin
to haue
ben our
first prea-
cher.
Fox.

Holins-
head.

to preach the Christian faith vnto the English-Saxons, which Nation as yet had not receaued the gospel. Godwin in the life of S. Auftin: *The Saxons not onely expelled Christian Religion, but the followers of the same into a corner of this I-land. And our Contrie being in a maner all growne ouer with Paganisme, for ther was no publick allowance of Christian Religion any where, but in VValles, It pleased God to giue this occasion of re-plãting the same here again.* And telleth, how Saint Gregory seeing English boies sold at Rome, was mooued to send Preachers. And in the life of S. Paulin: *VVhen the Saxons had gotten possession of this Realme, the Britons that were the ould Inhabitants being driuen into a corner therof; The rest was without any knowledg, or inckling* (Note) *of the Gospel.* And Cambd. *in descript. Brit. pag.* 104. Writeth, that S. Auftin *hauing rooted out the Monsters of Heathenish superstition, ingrafting Christ in English mens mindes with most happie successe conuerted them to the faith.* Who will see more Protestants, may read Bale *cent.* 1.*c.* 73.*cent.* 13.*c.* 1. Whitaker *contr. Dur. pag.* 394. Fulk 1. *Cor.* 4. Cooper *Chron. an.* 599. Stow 596.

4. Now let vs see what Sutclif can say against this so confessed a truth. For sooth that the English had notice of the Christian Religiõ before S. Auftin his cõming, because some Britons liued amongst them,

(marginal notes:) Godvvin. The English vvithout any inckling of the gospel before S. Auftin. Cambden

them, and alſo becauſe King Ethelberts
wife Bertha was a Chriſtian, and had a
Chriſtian Biſhop with her named Luidhard. Are not theſe (think wee) ſounde
reaſons to wraſtle withal againſt ſuch
vniform conſent both of his owne, and
our writers? As if we denyed that the Engliſh had any notice of Chriſtianity before
S. Auſtins cōming, but ſuch it was as the
great Turk hath without any beleeſe,
or liking therof. And as for the Britons
they were ſo far from preaching of their
owne accord, as by no perſuaſion, en-
treaty, or threatful propheſie of Saint
Auſtin they could be brought to do it,
as teſtifieth S. Beda *lib.* 2. *c.* 2. and Galfrid *lib.* 11. *cap.* 12. Beſides that as Bale
writeth *cent.* 1. *c.* 7. & Boeth.*hiſt.Scot..lib.*9.
pag. 171. *Aſpernabantur Angli dogmata Britāno-*
rum. The *Engliſh* (for the hatred of the men)
deſpiſed the Religion of the Britons. And concerning the Engliſh Queene, ſhe was no
Engliſh but a French woman, and before
S. Auſtins comming ſhe had negleɗed to
perſuade her husban as S. Gregory *lib* 9.
Epi. 59. teſtifieth, who rebuketh her therfore. And her Biſhop was not ſent to
preach to the Engliſh, but as Beda ſaith
*lib.*1. *c.* 25. *to aſſiſt her, and help her in her faith.*
Nether doth he make any mention of this
Biſhops preaching to our Nation. And for
other

Britons
refuſed to
preach to
the En-
gliſh.

Q. Berta
negleɗed
to perſu-
ade King
Ethelbert
to the
faith.

Other na-
tions ne-
glectvs,
and onely
Rome
helpeth.

other Nations about vs S. Gregory *lib.* 5.
Epist. 59. writeth that he heard that the
English would willingly be come Christians. *Sed Sacerdotes qui in vicino sunt Pastora-
lem erga eos Curam nō habere: but that the Priests
about them tooke no care of them.* Be it therfor
certaine that the first that preached Christian faith to our English Nation was S.
Austin, whome therfor Pope Honorius
lit. ad Regem Edwin. apud Bedam lib. 2. *c.* 17.
King Withlaf as we heard before, and catholick English writers, and some Protestants also as Cambden *Descript. Britan.*
pag. 515. and 178. Bale *cent.* 13. *c.* 7. *cent.* 14. *c.*
13. call the *Apostle of England*. Nether ought
Sutclif or others to be offended with this
title, because wee call not him absolutly
an Apostle, or Apostle of the whole world
as the 12. were, who were sent in *Vniuer-*
sum mundum, but with this restriction of
England. So S. Paul called Epaphroditus
the Apostle of the Philippians, *Philip.* 2.
and Protestants call Tindal and Latimer
Apostles of England, as yow may
see in Bale *cent.* 8. *c.* 72. 85.
and Fox.

Hovv S.
Austin is
our Apo-
stle.
Malm. l. 1.
Hist. c 2.
Goduvini
vit. Augu-
stin. Holin.
head Chr
an. 602.
Apologie
for oath of
allegiance.
92. 93.
Iouius des-
cript. Bri-
tan.

B   CHA-

CHAP.   III.

That S. Auſtin and his fellowes prea-ching tooke great effect in our Engliſh Nation.

BEcauſe ſome Miniſters albeit they can not deny but S. Auſtin preached the faith of Chriſt here in England, yet will extenuate his benefit as much as they can, & ſay that *onely a few Saxons were behoulding vnto him, and that nether Auſtin nor Gregory de-ſerued any great praiſe for the conuerſion of the Saxons, or Engliſh.* I will breefly touch what great good he and his fellowes here did. Firſt therfor him ſelf, though (through the exceſſiue paines which he tooke) he liued but a ſhort time: yet did he conuert Ethelbert King of Kent, whoſe dominion reached vnto Humber, & *many of his people* as S. Beda witneſſeth *lib.* 1. *c.* 26. and chriſtened at one tyme ten thouſand as Saint Gregory *lib.* 7. *Epi.* 30. Fox A⟨ct⟩s *pag.* 119. Cambden in Britan. *p.* 105. and others do teſtifie. Fox. *p.* 116. addeth, that *he con-uerted innumerable.* And *pag.* 118. *Baptized a great parte.* And Godwin *in vit. Aug.* ſaith, *he conuerted all the ſaid Kings people.* Beſides
this

Miniſters vngratful. *Sutc. lf lib. cit.* 6. 3.

Kingdom of Kent conuerted by S. Auſtin.

Epitaph. of S. Auſtin ſaith he conuerted this Kings people.

this he sent S. Mellit to London, where he conuerted Sebret King of Essex. And after *he bad gained* (saith Malmesb. 2. *part. histor. p. 250*) *Kent to Christ, trauailed throughout all the rest of the English Prouinces, so far as the Kingdom of Ethelbert reached.* Yet Fox *Acts p. 119.* and Cambden *lib. cit.* say, that he passed beyond the dominion of King Ethelbert, and christened many thousands in the riuer Swale. And *this trauail he tooke* (saith Capgraue in his life) *on foote, and for the most parte barefoote; and had great knobbs on his knees with continual kneeling in prayer.* Besides in his tyme he procured the erecting of the Archbishoprick of Canterbury, and the Bishoprick of London, and Rochester, & the foundations of the Monasteries of the Austins in Canterbury, Westminster in London, Ely in Cambridgshier, and Cernel in Dorsetshier. And as S. Beda *lib. 2. c. 4. Laied the foundation of our Church well and strongly.* And not content to labor thus for the couersion of English mé, endeuored also to reduce the Britons to the right faith, and *tooke therin* (saith Godwin) *much paines.* Gathered (as yow may see in Beda *lib. 2. c. 2.*) two meetings of their Diuines, & conuinced their error both by disputation and miracles. Wherby wee may see that all parts of England both South, West, East, North, and Wales

S. Austin trauaileth through almost all England.

Christened ten thousands at once.

Trauaileth barefoote.

Erecteth Archb. Bishopricks and monast. Beda l. 1. c. 26. 33. li. 2. c. 3. Capgr. in vit. Austini. Cambden in Brit. p.178. 438.490. Ealred in vit. Edvvardi.

Laboreth to reduce the Britons.

All partes of Englãd beholden to S. Austin.

to are greatly behoulden to Saint Auſtin.

The laborers of S. Auſtins fellowves. S. Laurence.

2.   After Saint Auſtins death (which was as ſome write about ten yeares after his cōming hither)S. Laurence his fellow laborer, and ſucceſſor, conuerted Edbald ſecōd Chriſtian King of Kent.And taught the Papiſts faith(ſaith Bale *cent.13.c.2.)almoſt in all the dominions of the Engliſh men.*And beſides wrote letters which are extant in Beda *lib. 2.c.4.* to the Scottiſh, and Iriſh people who were entangled in the Britons error.And as Bale writeth *cent.1.c.74.* held a Coūcell with thē for that purpoſe in the Ile of Man. Yea as Capgraue hath in his life,he went to Scotland, and there conuerted Tenan Archbiſhop of Irland

S. Iuſtus. to the true obſeruation of Eaſter. S. Iuſtus alſo another fellow worker,and ſucceſſor of S. Auſtin,conuerted ſo many,as Pope Boniface in Beda *lib. 2. c. 8.* writeth to him thus, *yow may ſhew whole Contries plentifullie multiplied in the faith by yow.* And

S. Mellit. both of him, and S. Mellit his Predeceſſor S.Beda *lib.2.c.7.*giueth this teſtimony,*they ruled,& gouerned the Engliſh Church with great*

S. Paulin. *labor , and diligence.* Finally S. Paulin an other of S. Auſtins fellow laborers, and firſt Archbiſhop of York, conuerted, and baptized Edwin King of the North parte of England, and by conqueſt ouer England,Wales and the Hebrides Iles, *with all the*

the nobility (faith Beda *lib.* 2. *c.* 14.) *of his Contrie and most parte of the common people.* And,
as he addeth *c.* 17. *all his subiects of the Northen
parts.* And such paines herein S. Paulin
tooke, that as S. Beda faith *c.* 14. *cit.* he
stayed in one place 36. dayes togeather
from morning to euening, instructing
and baptizing the people. And by meanes
of King Edwin was also Redwald King
of Est-england and for a while the poten-
test King of England, conuerted and
Christened, and also his sonne Carpwald.
Finally to conclude by Saint Austin and
his fellow laborers were six English
Kings conuerted from Paganisme to
Chrifts faith, to wit, Ethelbert, Sebert,
Edbald, Edwin, Redwald, Carpwald. A-
mongst whome Ethelbert, Edwin, and
Redwald were the most puissant Kings
of their tyme. And of the 7. Kingdoms
which then were, they conuerted foure
viz. the Kingdom of Kent, Kingdom of
Est-Saxons, Est-angles and the Kingdom
of the North, and preached, and founded
Churches in the fifth Kingdom of Mercia
at Lincoln, & in the sixt of Westsaxons at
Cernel in Dorsetshier. Founded the two
Archbishopricks of Canterbury, & York,
and the Bishopricks of London, and Rochester, erected the Cathedral Churches
of Canterbury, Rochester, London, Lin-

S. Austin
& his fel-
lovves
conuerted
fix English
Kings and
foure
Kingdōs.

Beda *lib.* 2.
c. 16.
Cambd. *p.*
178.
Founded
tvvo
Archb.
tvvo Bis-
hop. fiue
Cathedral
Churches,
fix mona-
steries.

Beda sup.
Cambd. p.
490.
Capgrau in
Augustino
Ealred in
Edvuardo.

coln, and York, and the Collegiat Church in Southwel. Began the monasteries of the Austins, and Chrifts Church in Canterbury, of Westminster in London, of Ely in Cábridgshier, of Cernel in Dorsetshier. Wherby it appeareth that not onely a few Saxons (as Sutclif speaketh) but the whole nations of English, Scottish, Welch

English.
Scottish
VVelch, Irish greatly bound
to S. Austin and
his fellovves.

and Irish were infinitly behoulde to Saint Auftin, and his fellowes, for leauing their Contrie, for comming fo far a iorney as is from Rome, for venturing into a barbarous, and vnknown Contry as ours then was, for hazarding their liues among fierfe, and fauage people, for recalling fo many Kings, and Kingdoms from Paganifme to Chriftianitie, for laboring fo much to reduce Hereticks, for erecting fo many Episcopal Sees, and Monasteries, and finally for fpending their liues here among vs. And if any parte of this land tooke no great commoditie by them, it was not to be attributed to them, but to the peoples owne negligence, and obftinacy. Wherfor D. Whitaker as far more

D. VVhitak. more
gratefull
than Sutclif.

gratfull than Sutclif *lib. 5. cont Dur. pag.* 394. speaking of our conuerfion by S. Gregory meanes, faith : *That he did vs a great benefit we will alwaies gratfully remember.* And now hauing shewed that S. Auftin was the firft Preacher of Chrifts faith to our Nation

tion in England, let vs fee what qualities
he had fit for fo high a function to wit
what learning and vertue.

CHAP. IIII.

That Saint Auſtin was a great Clerk and excellent Diuine.

SOme Miniſters are fo ſpitefull againſt
S. Auſtin our Apoſtle, as they feeke all
occaſions they can to diſhonor him. Wher
vpon Bale *cent.* 13. *c.* 1. faith he was *ignorant
in holy ſcriptures*, and the queſtions which
he ſent to S. Gregory and are extant in
S. Beda *lib.* 1. *c.* 27. were *moſt vnſauorie and
voide of all knowledg of the Goſpel, and law of
God*. But no maruell if he, and fuchlike
condemne S. Auſtin as vnlearned, who
dare condemne the glorioufeſt lights of
Chriſtianitie, the greateſt Doctors of
Gods Church of blindnes, and ignorance. But how great a Clerk S. Auſtin was,
though we had no euident teſtimony, we
might our felues gather by many waies.
For as touching his wit, and capacitie of
learning, it may fuffice that he was an
Italian, and Roman, whome in wit we
know to excell. The place where he ſtu-

Argumēts
of S. Au-
ſtins great
learning.

His vvit.

B 4   died

died was Rome, where at that tyme as Ioan. Diacon. *in vit. Gregor. lib. 2. c. 13. Rerum sapientiâ cũ septem artibus floruit.* His Maiſter was S. Gregory him ſelf, one of the foure Doctors of the Church, as witneſſe S. Beda *Epi. ad Ceolwolph Regem,* Ethelwerd *lib. 2. c. 1.* Malmesb. *lib. 1. Pont. p. 195.* Amongſt his ſchole-fellowes one was (as it ſeemeth) that great Doctor of Spaine S. Iſidore. For as Genebr. and Sigebert *in Chron.* do write, he was ſcholer to Saint Gregory. And for S. Auſtins indeuor to attaine to learning, for proofe therof it may ſuffice that he was a Monk of Saint Gregoreis owne Monaſtery, where men were not (doubtles) ſuffered to looſe their tyme, brought vp there vnder regular diſcipline, and at laſt made *Præpoſitus eiuſdem Monaſterij, Superior of the ſame Monaſtery.* All which teſtifieth S. Gregory him ſelf *lib. 7. Epi. 30. 112.* and *lib. 2. c. 13.* and S. Beda, *lib. 1. c. 27.* And finally for his profit in learning, it may ſuffice that it appeareth by the choice made of him among ſo many learned men, as then were in Rome, and made by ſo great a Doctor as S. Gregory was, and ſo careful to chuſe ſufficient men, and made for ſo great a matter as to be *Dux verbi, Firſt Preacher* of Chriſtian ſaith to Infidells, and conuerter of learned hereticks. For if S. Gregory required ſo

great

(marginal notes:)
His place of ſtudie.
His Maiſter.
His ſcoole fellowes.
His endeuour.
His profit.

great skill in euery Pastor of soules as he wrote *lib. Pastor.* that *Gouernment of soules is the arte of arts*; How much would he require in him to whome he committed the care of all the Infidells, and Hereticks in so great a Kingdom as this is? And besides this the care of S. Gregory to send hither a great learned man, may apeare by the like great care which Pope Vitalian had afterward, as is to be seene in Beda *lib. 4. c. 1.* to prouide a great, and famous Deuine for the Archbishoprick of Canterbury euen after all England was conuerted. For neither was Pope Vitalian more ready to furnish England with learned Pastors, thā S. Gregory was, nor was he more able to iudg of their learning, nor had he more choice of learned men. If therfor Pope Vitalian sent hither such learned men as S. Theodor and S. Adrian were, what shall we think of S. Austin and his fellowes sent by S. Gregory?

2. But besides these collections of ours we haue a testimony of S. Austins great learning *Omni exceptione maius.* For S. Gregory his Maister who best knew him, and was best able to iudg, and for his holines and rare humilitie was least likly to lye, or praise his scholler beyond his deserts, writing to King Ethelbert in Beda *lib. 1. c. 32.* and exhorting him to follow S. Austin in all

S. Gregories testimonie of S. Austins great learning.

all points faith. *He was replenished with knowledg of the holy scriptures*. And Ethelwerd,
one of our anciéteſt hiſtoriographers, *lib.
2. c.1.* ſaith he was *diuino eloquio nimu inſtructus, excedingly inſtructed in the ſcriptures*. Iuſtus one of S. Auſtins fellowes, and ſucceſſors, Pope Boniface writing to him
ſaith: *He had brought vp King Edbald with great
learning, and inſtruction of holy ſcriptures*, as is
to be ſeene in Beda *l. 2. c.8.* And doubt we
that S. Auſtin had not done the lyke to
King Ethelbert? And of Honorius, another of S. Auſtins fellowes Beda *lib. 5. c.
20.* ſaith he *was a mā profoundly learned in holy ſcripture.* And why ſhoud we think that
S. Auſtin was inferior to him? Beſides S.
Beda *lib. 1. c. 22.* ſpeaking of the Britiſh
Preachers, whome he accounted moſt
learned men, yet comparing them with
S. Auſtin, and his fellows ſaith, that theſe
were *more worthy Preachers.* And beſides
theſe teſtimonies of S. Auſtins great learning we haue an euident proofe by the
effect therof. For albeit there were among
the Britons many *viri doctiſſimi, moſt learned men.* as Saint Beda ſaith *lib.2. c.2.* Yet
Saint Auſtin feared not twiſe to challeng
them all to publick diſputations, and at
the firſt ouercame them, and at the ſecond
they durſt not (as it ſeemeth) encounter
with him. The like diſputations had after

ter

Ethelwerd.

S. Iuſtus
great learning.

S. Honorius great
learning.

S. Auſtin
confuted
moſt learned Hereſicks.

ter S. Laurence, and other of S. Austins
fellowes in the Ile of Man with Scottish
and Irish Deuines, and wrote also to the
Britons as saint Beda *lib.* 2. *c.* 4. speaketh
worthy letters, and fit for their Degree. Yea the
Protestants them selues when they are
voide of passion confesse saint Austin, and
his fellowes to haue bene great scollers.
For B. Cooper Chron. *an.* 599. saith that
*Austin, Iohn, Mellit, and others were godly, and wel
learned men*. Holinshead *an.* 596. calleth
saint Austin, and his fellowes *learned men*.
And Godwin *in vita Honorij,* saith: *Honorius* (*a fellow* and successor of saint Austin)
*was very learned, and some tymes disciple of Saint
Gregory*. And *in vita Laurentij*, that *S. Laurence*(his immediat successor)*was a wel learned man*. That Deusdedit who was an English man, & scoller to saint Austin, was
very famous for his learning, and other vertues.
And if the scoller were very famous, what
may we think of the Maister? Yea Bale
him selfe *cent.*13. *c.* 2. saith that saint Laurence, successor and fellow of saint Austin
was very skilfull in logick and other Philosophie.
3.   But how think yow doth Bale pro-
ue that saint Austin was ignorant of scripture, or his questions voide of all knowledg of the Gospel? Surely not at all. But
it must suffice that this Aristarchus hath
so iudged. But perhaps it displeased Bale
that

(margin notes)
Protestãts
confesse S.
Austin
and his
fellovves
learning.
Cooper.

Holinshed

Godvvin

Bale

that ſaint Auſtin ſhould in them enquire aboute the ceremonies of Maſſe, and about the offering vpon the Altar, of ſaying Maſſe after pollution in the night, or of receauing the bleſſed Sacrament after a man hath carnally known his wife, which queſtions (no maruell) if they ſeeme vnſauorie to Bale, and voide of all knowledg of his new Goſpel. Indeed the queſtions are not of any profound diuinitie, but of practical matters about the gouernment of the Church and holy ceremonies, and adminiſtration of Sacraments, in which matters the greateſt Deuines vnleſ they haue bene practiſed therin (as S. Auſtin had not bene in his monaſterie) are not alwaies the moſt ſkilful. Beſides that Saint Auſtin propoſed thoſe queſtions to ſaint Gregory not vpon ignorance, but vpon humilitie, and deſire to be directed by him euen in ſmalleſt matters. This ſaint Gregory him ſelf teſtifieth in theſe words in Beda *lib. 2. c. 23. I doubt not but yow haue required Counſell in theſe matters, and I think alſo I haue alredy made yow anſwer herein, Yet that which your ſelfe could ſay, and think herein, I think yow would haue it confirmed with my anſwer.* The like account made the French Miniſters of Caluin as appeareth by the Surueie of the holy diſcipline *c. 3. p. 43.* in theſe words. *As any doubtes did ariſe amongſt them*

VVhy S. Auſtins queſtions vvere vnſauorie to Bale.

S. Auſtin could haue anſvvered his ovvne queſtions.

them concerning Church caufes, though they were
but very fimple , and fuch as any ftudent of meane
capacity and iudgment might very eafely haue fa-
tisfyed , yet no man but M. Caluin for his tyme,
and M. Beza afterward was accounted of fuffi-
ciency er able to diffolue them. Yow heare what
fimple queftions the French Minifters
fent to Caluin and Beza, and yet without
any preiudice of their opinion in learning.
And why fhould not S. Auftin do the like? And furely I here admire the goodne-
nes of God towards our Nation , that he
would Saint Auftin fhould enquire fuch
fmall matters of S. Gregory, and that his
queftions fhould remaine to our dayes.
both to fhew vs by our firft Apoftle what
account we fhould make of the refolution
of the Sea Apoftolick, and (as S. Irenæus
lib. 3. c. 3. wrote aboue 1400. yeares ago)
in all difficulties recur to her, and alfo to affure
vs that S. Auftin, who in fo fmall mat-
ters would do nothing of himfelfe, but by
the direction of S. Gregory, would much
leffe vary from him in matters of faith or
religion; And confequently, that the faith
which he taught our Anceftors , was the
faith of the greateft Doctor that euer fince S. Peter fate in the Church of Rome,
and by the confeffion of Proteftants was
as famous and as learned a man as euer was Bishop
of Rome, yea *omnium Pontificum,* Of all the *Bis-*
hops

VVhat ac-
count S.
Auftin
made of
the refo-
lutions of
the See
Apoftol.

Belt VVo-
ful cry *p. 3.*

bops of *Rome*, the *moſt excellent for life and lear-*
ning. Bale *cent.1.c.*68. Which thing wel cõ-
ſidered, can not but breed great comfort
in them, who had the faith of their Forfathers deliuered to them by S. Auſtin, and
as great diſcomfort in them, who haue
forſaken it. And thus much of S. Auſtins
learning: now let vs ſee his vertue.

CHAP. V.

That Saint Auſtin was a great Saint, and holy man.

By how
manie
kinds of
teſtimo-
nies S-
Auſtins
great ho-
lines is
proued.

I F Miniſters were before vnwilling to
grant that S. Auſtin was our firſt Preacher or a learned man, much more loth
they are to confeſſe that he was a holy
man. And not without cauſe, becauſe
therby they perceaue it will follow, that
his faith was the true faith of Chriſt. For
as S. Paul ſaith Rom. 10. *The iuſt man liueth*
by faith. & Heb. 11. *without faith it is impoſſi-*
ble to pleaſe God. But I will prooue not onely by the teſtimonie of them that ſaw
and knew S. Auſtin, but alſo by the teſtimony of his Maiſter, his own life and
death, by publick and priuat teſtimony
of them that liued with him, by all kind
of

of writers following, by the vertuous life
of the Church which he founded, and finally by the confession of diuers Protestants that S. Austin was a saint and vertuous holy man.

2. As for S. Austins Maister, Ambros. *lib.*
2. de Virginibus. saith: *The first spur to learning is*
the excellecy of the Maister. And no doubt but
the example of an excellent Maister is a
great spur to vertue. And what Maister
ether in that age, or long before, or after
could S. Austin haue had comparable to
S. Gregory, who for his great vertue, and
noble acts is surnamed *the great*: whome
S. Isidor *lib. de viris illustrib. c. 7.* who knew
him saith, *was by compunction ful of the feare of*
God, in humilitie cheefest, and endued with such
light of knowledg, as the like was not then, nor be-
fore. And the 8. Councel of Toledo doubteth not to prefer him in morall doctrine
before all other Doctors. S. Ildefonsus al-
so *lib. de vir. illustrib. c. 2.* writeth that he *ex-*
celled so high in perfection of all vertues, as setting
a side all famous men, antiquitie could not shew the
like. For in holines he surpassed S. Antony, in elo-
quence S. Cyprian, in knowledg S. Austin. S. Gregor. also of Tours, who knew him great-
ly comendeth him *lib. 10. de Gestis Franco-*
rum. c. 1. S. Beda *lib. 1. c. 13.* saith, *He was a*
man of the greatest vertue & learning of his tyme.
And who will see more of this vertuous

Hovv ver-
tuous S.
Austins
Maister
vvas.

S. Isidor.

8. Coun-
cel Tolet.

S. Ilde-
fonsus.

S. Gregor.
Turon.

S. Beda
See S. Da-
masen. orat.
2. de defun-
ctis.

man

man may reade his life in **Ioannes Dia-**
con. in S. Beda *lib.* 2. *c* 1. Here I will content my felf with the iudgment of our famous and ancient King Alfred: who thus
commendeth him. *The true feruant of God*
the Roman Pope Chrifts Vicar Gregory, a man of
confiderat fortitude, without rashnes, indued with
cheefe wit, wifdome and Counfel, an infinit trea-
for, becaufe he wonne the greateft part of man-
kinde to heauen, the beft man of the Romans, moft
abounding in greatnes of courage, and moft free of
Maieftie. This was the iudgment of our
great King touching S. Gregory, and of
the fame minde were all our Catholick
writers, as yow may fee in Florẽt. *an.* 605.
Malmesb. 1. *Reg. c.* 3. Weftmon. *an.* 605.
and others. In fo much as D. Reinolds in
his Confer. *p.* 583. writeth that *our Ance-*
ftors had a reuerend opinion of the Pope long after
S. Gregory for S. Gregories fake. To thefe Catholicks I will ad alfo the verdict of a
few Proteftants. D. Whitaker *cont. Dur.*
p. 397. faith : *He was a learned and holy Bishop*
and *p.* 502. *I confeffe Gregory to haue bene a good*
and holy man. Godwin *in vita Auguft. a good*
man that bleffed and holy Father Gregory. Item
This good man being made Pope tooke efpeciall ca-
re of fending Preachers into this Land. D. Sutclif Subuerf. *c.* 2. Gregory and Eleutherius
were Bishops, and famous men in the Church for
their painful labors, and conftancy in teaching the
truth

King Alfred

King Alfred Prefat. Paftoral.

Ancient English men.

Proteftãts. D. Whitaker.

Godwin.

D. Sutclif.

truth. Bale *cent.* 1. *c.* 68. ſaith he *was the ex-cellent of all the Biſhops of Rome for learning and life. That againſt his will and ſtriuing to the con-trary, and at laſt compelled, he ſucceded Pope Pe-lagius . That he was a learned, and good man, founded hoſpitals, inuited pilgrims to his table, ſent things neceſſary to the Monks of Hieruſalem, and maintained three thouſand Virgins .* And *c.* 7 He *reduced the Goths from Arianiſme to the Church, profeſſed himſelfe by writing the Seruant of Gods ſeruants, that therby he might appeare moſt far from all ambition, and deſire of command.* Bell in his Wofull Cry p. 62. ſaith: *Gregory was a holy Biſhop indeed.* And in his Suruey p. 156. He *was vertuous and learned.* pag. 480. *A man of ſufficient credit.* Willet in his Syn-opſis, *A modeſt and humble Biſhop.* D. Hum-frey, Ieſuitiſmi part. 2. pag. 624. *Gregory ſurna-med Great, and indeed great, a great man, and indued with many vertues of deuine grace.* Thus Proteſtants account of ſaint Auſtins Mai-ſter.

2.   As for S. Auſtin himſelf, Godwin *in Aug.* ſaith: He *was a man of exceeding tall ſta-ture, well fauoured, and of a very amiable counte-nance.* And as for his great holines it appea-reth many wayes. For firſt, being very yonge, he forſooke all the pleaſures and commodities of the world, and became a Monk, entering into S. Gregories mona-ſtery, which no doubt was a Nurſerie of

C   vertue,

Bel.

D. Hum-frey.
Luth, *Gal.* 4 I tink Greg. vvas ſaued. *c.* 5. the vvorld hath in ad miration the holi-nes of Gregory.

S. Auſtins vertuous deeds.
1.

vertue. Where, (as Greg. faith *ex Beda lib.*
1 *c.*27.) *he was brought vp from his youth in regular difcipline , and according to his rule imitated the forme , and rule vfed in the Primitiue
Church of the Fathers, among whome all things
were common.* where he fo exceeded in vertue as he was made Superior ouer the
Monaftery. *ex Greg. lib. 7. epiſt.* 112. Secondly, at Saint Gregories commandement
he left his owne Contry, where he ferued
God in quietnes, and came to preach the
Gofpell both fo far of as our Contry is
from Rome, & to fuch barbarous people,
as our Nation then was. Thirdly, after
he entred into England, he liued fo ver-
tuoufly, that albeit he prooued, no douor,
his doctrine by great learning, and confirmed it (as fhalbe fhewed hereafter) by
many and great miracles, yet as faint Beda
affirmeth *lib.* 1. *c.*26. our Contry was conuerted more by the holines of him, and
his fellowes liues , than by any other

See Hun-
ting. *lib.* 3. meanes. *After they were now entred* (faith Beda *lib. cit.*) *into their lodging they began to exercife the Apoſtolick order of liuing of the primitiue

S. Auſtins
and his
fellovves
Apoſto
lick life.* Church , feruing God in continuall prayer , watching, and faſting, and preaching the word of life
to as many as they could, defpiſing the commodities
of the world as things none of their owne , taking
of them onely whome they inſtruƈted fo much as
might ferue their necefſities, liuing them felues*
                                           according

according to that they taught other, and being redy to suffer both troubles and death it self in defense of the truth they taught. VVherby many did beleeue and were baptized, marueling much at the simplicitie of their innocent liuing , and at the sweetnes of their heauenly doctryn. Infrà. The King him self being much delighted with the puritie of their life, and the example of their godly conuersation, as also with their sweete promises , which to be true they prooued with many miracles did beleeue, and was baptized. VVhat paines he tooke first in persuading our Nation the Christian faith, which was then addicted to Idolatrie , after in instructing them, who were so rude and ignorant in all faith, and lastly in baptizing, and administring the sacraments hauing some times to Christen ten thousand at a tyme, none can expresse. Capgraue in his life saith, he went trough England on foote preaching, and most commonly barefoote , and had *callum in genibus* by frequency of prayers. Much paines also he tooke vvith the VVelch men in two Councels, & besides disputation wrought miracles in their sight. He had the gift of miracles *ex Greg. apud Bedam lib. 1. c. 31.* And of Prophecie , *Beda lib. 2. c. 2.* This briefly was the admirable and Apostolick holines of life of Saint Austin and his fellowes, which no doubt he cocluded with a happie death. For his Epitaph recorded by

S. Austins paines and frequent praier. Had the gift of miracles and of Prophecie.

C 2   S. Be-

S. Beda *lib. 2. c. 3.* witneſſeth *after he had conuerted King Ethelbert and his people to the faith of Chriſt, fulfilling in peace the dayes of his office, died the 26. of May.*

4.   Thirdly, for the witneſſe of thoſe, that liued with S. Auſtin. Firſt is S. Gregory himſelf, who beſt knew him, and was beſt able to iudg of his vertue. He writing to King Ethelbert *in Beda lib. 1. c. 32.* ſaith, that S. Auſtin had *bene brought vp in the rule of Religion, and was by the grace of God of much vertue.* And *lib. 9. epiſt. 58.* writing to S. Auſtin him ſelf, ſaith: *I haue much hope, that by the grace of God thy Creator, and our Redemer, Lord and God, Chriſt Ieſus, thy ſinnes are alredy forgiuen thee, and that thou art therfore chooſen, that by thee other mens ſinnes may be pardoned. Nether ſhalt thou haue ſorow of any ſinne hereafter, who endeuoureſt by conuerſion of many, to make ioye in heauen.* And ſurely who conſidereth what great perfection Saint Gregory *lib. 4. epiſt. 24.* requireth in a Paſtor, to wit, that he be *Pure in thought, notable in work, diſcret in ſilence, profitable in ſpeeche, neare to all in compaſsion, aboue all in contemplation, fellow by humility to all that do well, ſtout through zeale of Iuſtice againſt the vices of the offending,* will nothing doubt but Saint Auſtin, whome he choſe to ſo high a function, was an excellent perfect man. And *lib. 5. epiſt. 52.* he ſaith : *Auſtins zeale and inde-*

indeuor is well known to vs. and repeateth it
*epiſt.*53.58.59. Likwiſe of the Popes, ſoone
after ſucceeding to S. Gregory, he is high- *Diuers o-*
ly commended : Of Pope Boniface 4. in *ther Popes*
Malmsbury *lib.* 1. *Pont.* p. 208. he is called
the holy Doctor: Of Pope Honorius *ibidem p.*
209. *Auſtin of holy remembrance.* Of Gregory
3. *ibidem p.* 210. *Auſtin of bleſſed memorie:* Of
Leo 3. *ibid.* p. 211. *Bleſſed Auguſtin.* Beſides by
them who liued with him, and ſaw his
happy end, he is called in his Epitaph, *Authors*
Bleſſed Auſtin. Stow *Chron.* p. 67. or as God- *of his epi-*
win hath, *Saint Auſtin.* *h. tap*

5. Fourthly, touching the teſtimony of *Vvitneſſes*
thoſe that liued after Saint Auſtins tyme, *of S. Auſt.*
the firſt is Saint Beda, whoſe teſtimony *after his*
of his holy life is already ſet downe, to *tyme.*
which I add, that *lib.* 2. *c.* 3. he calleth him *S. Beda.*
the deerly beloued man of God, holy Father Auſtin.
and *lib.* 4. *c.* 27. *The bleſſed Father Auſtin.* In a
Councell of all the Biſhops of England *A Coun-*
held *anno* 747. in preſence of King Ethel- *cell in*
bald and all his Nobility, it was apoin- *England.*
ted, That *the day of our Father Saint Auſtin be*
kept holy, as writeth Malmesbury 1. *lib. Pont.*
p. 197. and Fox *lib.* 2. p. 128. After that, King *K. Ke-*
Kenulph and all his Biſhops, Dukes, and *nulph and*
Nobility writing to Pope Leo 3. ſay thus: *his Biſ-*
Auſtin of bleſſed memory moſt gloriouſly gouerned *Nobles.*
the Churches of England. ex Malmesb. 1. *Reg.*
p*ag.* 31. In the letters of S. Odo Archbiſhop *S. Odo.*

of Cantey̆bury in Malmeſbury 1. *Pont. pag.*
201. he is called *Auſtin of bleſſed memory*. Of
Ethelwerd *lib.* 2. *c.* 1. *& 5.* he is called *Holy
Auſtin ſeruant of Chriſt, and innumerable miracles wrought by him.* Malmesbury 1. *Pont.
pag.* 196. ſaith thus : *How great the merits of
Auſtin are before God, the great miracles do ſhew,
which after ſo many ages he worketh, not ſuffering
Kent, yea all England to become ſlow in honoring
of him.* Of Huntington *lib.* 3. *pag.* 321. he is
called *the ſeruant of God, man of God, to haue
imitated the Apoſtolicall life of the Primitiue
Church, to haue led a moſt clean life.* Of Houeden 1. *part. Annal.* he is called *the glorious
Doctor of the whole Kingdom, the notable Founder of Chriſtian Faith and Religion.* And in like
ſorte is he commended for a great ſaint, of
Weſtmon. *Chron. an.* 596. Marianus *ibidem.*
And finally of all writers domeſticall and
foraine, who writt of him before our
times.

6.   Fifthly, touching the proofe of Saint
Auſtins holines by the holy life of the
Church which he here founded, that is
euident to all them that reade our Eccleſiaſticall Hiſtories. And ſo manifeſt as
Fox *lib.* 2. *pag.* 114. citeth and approueth
theſe words out of ancient Chronicles: *In
the Primitiue Church of England Religion ſhined
moſt purely, ſo that Kings, Princes, Dukes, Conſuls,
Barons & rulers of the Church incenſed with a de-*
                                                ſire

Ethel-
werd.

Malmesb.

Hunting-
ton.

Houeden.

VVeſtm.
Marian &
others.
Odo *chron.*
583 cal-
leth them
*timentes
Deum.*

The ho-
lines of
our church
founded
by S. Au-
ſtin.

fire of heauen entred into Monkerie, volontary exile and solitarie life, forsooke the world and followed Christ. And the same hath Huntington *lib. 5. in Prolog.* and Houeden *1. part. Annal. pag. 412.* And the same Fox *p. 123.* saith : *I do reade and also do credit that the Clergy of that tyme (S. Austins tyme) of England applyed nothing that was worldly, but gaue themselues to preaching, and teaching the word of our Saviour, and followed the life that they preached by giuing good example.* Cambden *in descript. Britan. pag. 345.* saith : *that tyme was most fruitfull of Saints.* And *pag. 628.* he braggeth that no Kingdom hath so many canonized Martyrs and Confessors as England hath, and that it, which before tymes was called a *fertill Prouince of Tyrants*, may now be called *a fertill Contrie of Saints.* And who will see more of the great holines of our Clergy may reade Beda *lib. 3. c. 26.* Othlon *in vita S. Bonifacij.* Marcellin. *in vita S. Suiberti.* Serrarius *de Mogunt. lib. 3.*

7. Lastly, for the confession of Protestants, Fox in his Acts *pag. 105.* saith of Saint Austin and his fellowes thus : *At length when the King had well considered the honest conuersation of their life, and mooued with their miracles, wrought through Gods hands by them, he heard them more gladly and lastly by their holsom exhortations and example of godly life, he was by them conuerted and christened in the yeare*

Confessed by Protestants.
Fox.

See more in Fox p. 132. 133.
Cambden

Of some England was called religiosa Anglia of others Paradisus Dei. See Baron. to. 9. Serra. do reb. Mogunt. lib. 3. nota 55.

Protestāts confesse S. Austins holines. Fox.

C 4   596.

596. And the same he repeateth againe *pag.*
116. Bilson *lib.* Of Obedience, *pag.* 57. saith:
Austin and his fellowes came with religion to God,
and submission to Princes. Bishop Cooper *anno*
599. calleth Austin and his fellowes, *godly*
and learned men. And *anno* 630. calleth Paulinus (one of the company) *a holy Bishop:*
Stow Chron. *pag.* 65. saith, that *S. Austin and*
his fellowes liued in the feare of God. Godwin
in vita August. saith: *He was a Monke of great*
vertue; and calleth him, *Saint Austin.* And
in vita Paulini, saith: *Paulin* (his companion)
was called away to receaue the glorious reward
of his blessed labors. And Holinshed in the
Historie of England: *Austin and his company*
arriued at Canterbury, where he made his abode
by the Kings permission, exercised the life of Apo-
stles in fasting, watching, and prayers, preaching,
the word of God to as many as they could, despi-
sing all worldly pleasures, as not appertaining to
them, receauing onely of them whome they taught,
things seeming necessary to the sustenance of their
life, and liuing in all points according to the do-
ctrine, which they set forth. Ite: *King Ethelbert*
was persuaded by the good example of S. Austin &
his company, and by miracles shewed, to be bapti-
zed. Hereto I might add what diuers Protestants haue written of the great holines
of some of S. Austins company, who succeeded him in the Archbishoprik of Canterbury: But for that we shall haue more
conue-

Bilson.
Cooper.
Stow.
Godwin.
Holinshed

conuenient place hereafter. Now let vs
fee what the malice, and hatred of fome
Minifters againft Saint Auftins doctrine,
hath caufed them to obiect againft his
perfon.

CHAP. VI.

*Certain flanders impofed vpon Saint
Auftin, difprooued.*

Icero, in his Oration for Rofcius,
faith: that as fier falling into water
is ftraight put out: fo a flander put vpon
an innocent man, is quickly extinguifhed.
Which (I doubt not) will prooue true
in the calumniations obiected againft S.
Auftin. The firft wherof is cruelty (fay
they) in exhorting Ethelfrid a Heathen
King of the North, againft the Britifh
Monkes, of whome he flew at once aboue
200. But this is an impudent flander, deuifed firft (for any thing that I can finde)
by Bale, who *centur. 1. capit. 70.* fearfully
broached it, and therfor referreth it to reports, faying: *Vt ferunt, as fome reporte.* But
afterward *Cent. 13. cap. 1.* he confidently a-
uoucheth it. After him tooke vp that
flander Iuell *Defenf. Apolog. part. 5.* Abbots

*Bale flan-
dereth S.
Auftin v-
pon re-
ports.*

botsin his Anſwer to Do. Biſhop, *p.* 198.
Sutclif Subuerſ.*c.* 3. *&* 7. and others.

That S.
Auſtin
vvas no
cauſe of
the death
of the Bri-
tiſh Mōks.

1.

This falſe ſlander is many wayes refu-
ted. Firſt, becauſe it is auouched without
all teſtimonies of antiquity. Bale (as I ſay)
hauing no one to name before, referreth
him ſelfe to vncertain reports, if he be
not both Author, and reporter too. Abbots citeth Iuell, Sutclif, alleageth Thomas Grey, & a nameles Chronicle which
he calleth ould, as if they ſhould haue ſaid,

2.

ask my fellow if I be a theefe. Secondly,
becauſe the Britons albeit enemyes to
Saint Auſtin, blamed not him, but others,
for this ſlaughter, as is euident in Galfrid
lib.4.cap.4. Thirdly, becauſe the ſlanderers

3.

of Saint Auſtin diſagree in their tale more
than the accuſers of Suſanna, and therfor
if Daniel might be iudge, theſe would be
condemned as well as they were. For
ſome ſay S. Auſtin excited King Ethelfrid to this murder, others ſay, not Saint
Auſtin but K. Ethelbert his ſcoller: Some
ſay, that Ethelfrid made this ſlaughter:
others, that K. Ethelbert, as Grey cited
by Sutclif. So they agree nether in the
Author nor Actor of this matter. Fourth-

4.

ly becauſe as Beda teſtifieth *lib.2.c.2.* Saint
Auſtin was long before that ſlaughter,
taken out of this life to the Kingdom of heauen,
and no way cauſed it but rather forwar-
ned

ned the Britons therof by prophecie. *But it came to passe* (saith Beda) *by the secret working of Gods iudgement vpon that vnfaithfull and naughty people* . And the same testifie our best Historiographers both Catholicks and Protestants. Namely Malmesbury *lib.* 3. *Reg. pag.* 325 Hunting. *lib.* 3. Florent. *an.* 603. Westmon. *an.* 603. Sigebert *an.* 602. 615. Stow *Chron. pag.* 66. Godwin in the life of Saint Austin. Fox *Acts pagina* 119. where he writeth that *Saint Austin forspoke the destruction, and by report of others was dead before it hapned.*

2. To this Sutclif *cap.* 7. *cit.* answereth, that those words of Saint Beda touching Saint Austins death before the slaughter, are added by some forger. First, because after this war Saint Austin ordained Iustus and Mellitus Bishops, as Beda (saith he) reporteth . Secondly, because they are not in the Saxon Translation of Beda made by King Alfred. Thirdly, because the Chronicle of Peterbrough and Flores Histor. testifye, that Saint Austin dyed three yeares after this execution. But this surmise of forgerie in Saint Beda his Latin History is altogeather incredible, both because all Latin copies (in which language Saint Beda wrote) haue the sayd words, and impossible it is that ether one forger should corrupt all the copies in

Christen-

Sutclif feigneth corruption in S. Beda.

Confuted.

I.

Chriftendome, or that in all Chriftedome
men would agoe to corrupt Beda in that
place, and in no other. And alfo becaufe
till Sutclif no man fufpected any fuch forgerie. Finally, becaufe, as it fhall appeare
anon by true Chronologie of tyme, Saint
Auftin was indeed dead befor the flaughter. And no little prefumption therof it is,
that the Britons, who layd the blame
therof on King Ethelbert Saint Auftins
fcoller, would foner haue layd the blame
therof on Saint Auftin himfelfe *who threat-
fully* (faith Saint Beda) *prophecied it*, if he
had bene aliue, as King Ethelbert was,
when it chauced. But little will he maruell to hear Sutclife to fufpect Saint Beda
as corrupted, who confidereth how many
and how vndoubted bookes of Fathers
in his Challeng he had reiected as either
forged or corrupted, as Saint Athanaf. *de
vita Antonÿ*, Saint Hierom *de vita Pauli &
Hilarionis*, S. Gregories Dialogues, Saint
Ambrofe *de Viduis*, & many others. Which
kinde of fhift, at it is moft vfuall with Sutclif, fo in the eye of any wife man it is moft
defperat. As for his proofes, the firft is a
manifeft vntruth. For Saint Beda reporteth not that S. Auftin ordained Bifhops
after the faid flaughter of the Britifh
Monkes, but onely talketh of the flaughter before he fpeaketh of the ordination.
                                                    The

2.

3.

Vfuall
vvith Sut-
clif to fay
Authors
are forged

Sutc. be-
lieth S.
Beda.

The cauſe wherof was, becauſe hauing
tould of Saint Auſtins prophecie of the
Britons deſtruction, which prophecie
was before he ordained Biſhops, to ſhew
that it was a true prophecie addeth, that
after it hapened as S. Auſtin had fortould,
and how long after, he ſoone after declareth, to wit, long after S. Auſtins death.
Sutclifs ſecond proofe I greatly ſuſpect to
be a forgerie of his owne. But how ſo euer
that be, ther is nether reaſō that he ſhould
vrge, nor that we ſhould beleeue one
tranſlation before all originalls. For who
would not think that, that trāſlation were
defectiue in that place, rather than that all
Originalls had more than they ſhould. As
for the Chronicle of Peterbrough and
Flores Hiſtor. wee might take iuſt exception againſt them, as hauing paſt
through the corrupt fingering of diuers
Proteſtants, but who are they to oppoſe
againſt ſo many cited before to the contrary, eſpecially ſeeing that Flores Hiſtor.
cleareth Saint Auſtin from this ſlaughter,
and attribueth it to Prophecie. And beſides his Chronologie (as Godwin in the
Biſhops of York *pag.* 442. a Proteſtant
confeſſeth) *is very vncertain,* & in this point
is very falſe. For as Sigebert *in Chron.* and
Bale him ſelf *Cent.* 1.*cap.* 74. reporteth out
of Maſſeus the ſlaughter was done *an.* 615.

At

*Originals
to be be-
leeued be-
fore trāſ-
lations &
many be-
fore one.*

*VVhē the
British
Monks
vvere
ſlaine.*

At what tyme as all writers agree S. Lawrence was Archbishop, and Saint Austin

VVhen s.
Austin
died.

dead, ether *an.* 614. as Malmesbury saith
in Hist. and *in Fastis*; or *an.* 605. as Sigebert
saith *in Chron.* or 608. as Bale hath *cent.*13.
cap. 1. or *an.* 604. as Baron. gathereth out
of Beda, and Florent. *in Chron.* and Stow
pag. 62. affirmeth. How then could Saint
Austin cause this slaughter, which was so
long after his death, and much les goe in
the army to the slaughter as Sutclif citeth
out of an ould Chronicle, if he do not lye
himselfe.

3.   For this Bilson in his Booke of Obedience *pag.* 114. saith, that the King Ethelbert King of Kent (whome Saint Austin
conuerted) mooued King Ethelfrid to
commit this massacre, and citeth therto
Galfrid of Munmouth *lib.* 8. *cap.* 4.
and so indirectly deriueth the faulte to
Saint Austin his teacher. But first, if this

That K.
Ethelbert
caused
not the
British
Mōkes to
be slaine.

slaughter were done (as we haue seene
out of Bale) in the yeare 615. certain it is,
that Saint Austin liued not till that tyme,
but dyed before, as is alredy shewed, and
therfore he could not be the author of this
fact. Secondly, in defence of King Ethel-

2.

bert I oppose against Bilson what Fox

Fox defē-
deth King
Ethelbert.

saith *p.*119. *that it seemeth rather suspicious than*
true, that Ethelbert being a Christian King, ether
could so much preuaile with a Pagan Idolater or
                                                    eh

el, *would attempt so far as to commit such a cruell*
deede. And in truth who so considereth   **3.**
the disposition of that Pagan King in Be-
da *lib. 1. cap. 33.* where he is compared *to a*
rauening wolfe, will easely see, that he
needed no stirrer vp to make war against
the Britōs. And therfor Fox *loco cit.* rightly ascribeth it to the *fierse furie of Ethelfrid*,
which was so great as he is sirnamed *Fe-*
rus. Besides that K. Ethelbert was more   **4.**
potent than King Ethelfrid, for he had all
the South part of England at command,
as testifyeth Saint Beda *lib. 1. cap. 25.* and
Ethelfrid onely the North. And therfor if
he would haue reuenged Saint Austin by
war, and bloodshed, he would rather haue
done it him selfe, than stirred an other
Heathen King against them. But this   **5.**
good King was so far from causing the
Britons to be murdered, because they
would not receaue S. Austins doctrine,
as that, (as writeth Saint Beda *lib. 1. c. 26.*)
he would not force his owne subiects to receaue it.
As for Galfrid ther is no such thing in the
place cited by Bilson, which argueth that
he cited it out of Iuell without seeing the
booke. But indeed *lib. 11. c. 13.* Galfrid saith
that Ethelbert excited Ethelfrid to goe
to Bangor and destroy Abbot Dimoth &
other Monkes, who had resisted S. Austin.
But Galfrid is a very fabulous Author, the
first

firſt broacher of Merlins Prophecies, and
of other incredible fables, and liued many
hundred yeares after Saint Beda, who teſtifyeth *lib. 2. cap. 2.* that King Ethelfrid
came not of purpoſe to kill the Monkes,
(but to get Cheſter, as he, *loco cit.* and Malmesbury *lib. 1. Reg. c. 3.* do inſinuat) and
being to ioyne battell with the Britons,
eſpying the Monkes at prayer, and vnder-
ſtanding that they came to pray againſt
him, ſet firſt vpon them, and ſlew them.

4.   The ſecond fault, which Miniſters
impute to S. Auſtin, is pryde, becauſe he
ſat ſtil in his chaire when the Britiſh Biſhops, and Deuins came to confer with
him. True it is, that S. Auſtin did ſo, but
that it proceeded not of pryde appeareth,
becauſe nether S. Beda nor any Engliſh
1. or foraine writer vnto our times beſides
the Britons (who were hereticks then,
& conſequétly moſt proude themſelues)
imputed it to pryde. Secondly, becauſe
2. Saint Auſtin and his fellowes, as them
ſelues write in Beda *lib. 2. cap. 4. Honored
the Britōs with great reuerēce while they thought
they were Catholicks.* Therfor Saint Auſtins
not riſing to them proceeded not of pride,
3. but of ſome other iuſt cauſe. Thirdly, becauſe the Britiſh Prieſts were ſuch then,
as they deſerued no honor, yea much diſhonor, and therfore it could be no pride
in

in S. Auſtin to giue them none. For beſides that they were hereticks, S. Beda *lib.*
2. cap. 2. calleth them *vnfaithfull , naughty and*
deteſtable people. And Gildas their owne
Contry man ſaith, that they were *wolues,*
enemies of truth , and friends to lyes ; enemyes of
God, and not Prieſts ; merchants of miſcheef , and
not Biſhops, Impugners of Chriſt , and not his Mi-
niſters, more worthy to be drawn to priſon, or to
the cage, than to Prieſthood. And much more
of the like ſorte. And Fox addeth out of
an ould Chronicle Acts *lib. 2. pag.* 114.
that *all things whether they pleaſed or diſpleaſed*
God , they regarded alike , and not onely ſeculer
men did this, but their Biſhops & teachers with-
out diſtinction. Which being ſo I appeale to
the iudgement of any indifferent man,
whether theſe men deſerued any honor
at S. Auſtins hands, eſpecially he being
lawfully apointed their Archbiſhop and
Superior by Saint Gregory. And whether
it were not great humility in him to ſeeke
conference with this kind of people now
the ſecond tyme after he had once before
confuted them both by diſputation and
euident miracle , which made them to
confeſſe that he taught the truth . The
cauſe therefor why he aroſe not to them,
was ether becauſe he followed the aduiſe
of his Maiſter Saint Gregory , who albeit
he were one of the humbleſt men , that

Vvhat
kind of
men they
vvere to
vvhome
S. Auſtin
did not ri-
ſe.

Great hu-
militie in
S. Auſtin
to confer
vvith tho-
ſe to vvho
me he did
not riſe.

Vvhy S.
Auſtin a-
roſe not
to the Bri-
tons.

        D   euer

euer was , yet *lib.* 4. *Epiſt.* 36. giueth this counſell to Biſhops : *Let vs kepe humility in minde and yet maintain the dignity of our order in honor.* Or els perceauing the Britons to

2   be obſtinat , which well appeared when for ſo ſmall occaſion they would forſake the doctrine, which themſelues had ſeene confirmed by miracle, and confeſſed to be truth he followed the aduiſe of Saint

Proteſt. Iohn *Epiſt.* 2. *If any come to you and bring not this doctrine , receaue him not into your houſe, nor ſay to him, God ſpeede.* But whether S. Auſtin would not ariſe to the Britons for theſe or other iuſt cauſes to him known, Protestants can no way condemn his fact,

Fox *Attn:* who commend a far les excuſable fact of edit: 1596. Cranmer, Latimer , and Ridley. For p. 1599. Cooper *Chron. an.* 1555. ſayth, that *becauſe the Biſhops of Lincoln, Gloſter, & Briſtow declared themſelues to be in the Popes Commiſſion , nether Ridley, nor Latimer would ſhew any reuerence to them, nor put of their capps.* The ſame he writeth of Cranmer *pag.* 373. And if this behauiour be commended in proteſtant Prelats , towards their ſuperiors and Iudges, why ſhould the like be condemned in S. Auſtin towards his inferiors?

5.   The third fault is that which the ſoldierly-Miniſter Sutclif obiecteth to him *c.* 3. *cit.* to wit , *extreme Cowardice not beſeeming an Apoſtolick man.* Becauſe being ſent

with

with his company to England they determined with common consent that it was
better to return than go forward. This
wee confesse was a fraylty. Yet first, such
a one it was as a far greater fel not only to an Apostolick man , but euen the
Prince of the Apostles S. Peter, when, for a
womās word he denyed his maister, & to
all the Apostles when they forsooke him.
Secondly such a feare it was as might *ca-*
dere in constantem virū. For our Nation was
then (as they sayd truly) *Barbarous fierse, and*
Infidel , and who daylie made war vpon
Christians , and whose Ancestors saith
Beda *l. 2. 6. 15. had slayne Priests at the Altar,*
and murdered Bishops with their flocks without
respect of dignity . And, as our stories record,
had made such hauock of Christians , as
they made great hills , yet extant, of their
bodies, and were therfor as S. Gildas termeth them, *Deo & hominibus inuisi.* Let Sutclif goe now to preach to such Pagans , or
to the Indian Caniballs, and then he may
be the better suffered to obiect feare to
Saint Austin. Besides , that Godwin also
in his life cleareth Saint Austin of this
feare. For that he saith not all, but *in a ma-*
ner all were afraid to prosecut the iorney, and they
as it were compelled Saint Austin to go back to
craue licence to return. Wherby we see that
Saint Austin was little or nothing faulty
in

S. Austins feare for a tyme, ex- cused.

1 *See inf. l. 2. c. 11. Hovv the Protesti Apostles alture their faith.*

2

Godvvin excuseth S. Austin.

D 2

in this point. Thirdly, I say, that such a
feare it was as Saint Auftin and his company manfully ouercame, and ftoutly performed the iorney, and abode here, *being
ready* (faith Saint Beda *lib.1.cap.26.*) *to fuffer
both troubles, and death it felf in defence of the
truth they taught.* Which is courage well be-
feeming Apoftolick men.

6.   The fourth flander or rather many
flanders is that, wherwith Iuell chargeth
him *Art.1. diu. 21.* where he writeth thus:
He was by iudgement of them that faw him ne-
*ther of Apoftolick fpirit, nor any way worthy to
be called a Saint, but an hypocrit, and fuperftitious,
cruell, and bloody man.* and citeth Galfrid
lib.8.cap.4. But this is moft flanderous.
For nether is ther any word in that place
of Galfrid of Saint Auftin, or the Briton
Bifhops, nether *lib.11.cap.12.* where he talketh of this matter, doth he fay that the
Britons charged Saint Auftin with any
crime, but that they refufed either to be
fubiect to him, or to preach to the Englifh.
Becaufe fayd they (as he reporteth) *they
had an Archbifhop of their owne, and the Englifh
continewed taking their Contry from them.* And
this was all the caufe which Galfrid faith
they gaue. But as for thefe other crimes of
hypocrit, fuperftitious, cruell, and bloody, as Iuell
faith, they that faw him and knew him,
iudged him, that no Briton though then
                                                    his

his enemyes, but the vngratfull Englisfh
hereticks Iuell hath imposed vpon him,
And if Cham were iustly accused of his
Father for reuealing his carnall Fathers
fhame, what deserueth he who falsly im-
poseth vpon his & vpon all Englifh mens
spirituall Father, *for* (to vse Saint Paules
words) *in Christ Iesus he begat vs through the*
Gospell, fhamefull crimes neuer imputed to
him by his enemies. And this dealing of
Iuell with Saint Austin bringeth me in
mynde of his damnable writing against
the Catholick faith. For a little before his
death he charged his Chaplin named Iohn
Garbrand, that as sone as he was dead, Iuel wre-
Garbrand should publifhe to the world, te against
that what he had written, he had done conscien-
againft his owne knowledg & conscience ce.
onely to complie with the State, and to
vphould that religion which it had set vp.
And albeit Garbrand did not for feare pu-
blifh this so openly as he was charged, yet
did he auouch it to diuers in Oxford. Author of this is a Proteftant of good account, whome I could name, yet liuing at
Lewis in Suffex, who tould it to two Catholick Gentlemen of whome I learnt it.
And the more credible this is, becaufe I
could name a Minifter, a Doctor, and of Learned
great account among the Minifters, who immugne
confeffed to a freind of his, of whome I truth.
heard

heard it, that he taught againſt the truth
and his owne knowledg. And the ſame
he doubted not to affirme of the reſt of his
brethren that are learned. And thus hauing ſhewed that Saint Auſtin had great
learning and vertue , requiſit for a firſt
preacher of Chriſts faith vnto Infidells:
let vs ſee what authority he had to preach
and how he was ſent to do it.

CHAP.   VII.

That S. Auſtin was mooued with holy motiues to come to preach to our Nation.

ALthough what can be ſaid of this
matter, will be clear inough, partly
by what hath bene already ſaid , partly by
what ſhall hereafter:yet becauſe it helpeth
much to the perfect iudgmēt of religions,
to know what mooued the firſt Authors
& Founders of thē in any Cōtry to preach
& publiſh them,for therby they may iudg
of their ſincerity or fraudulent meaning,
and whether they ſeeke the glory of God,
and ſaluation of the Cōtry,or their owne
good: Therfore I will declare now what
motiues Saint Auſtin had to teach vs his
reli-

religion, and afterwârd, in the Second
Booke, what motiues likewife Luther
had to teach vs his. Firft therfore, Saint
Auftin could not be mooued by that proper motiue or fpur of all Archereticks or
Sect-maifters to *abducere difcipulos* (as the
Apoftle faith of them) *poft fe*: that is to be
the head and founder of a Sect, becaufe
(as fhalbe fhewed anon) his religion was
the vfuall and common religion of all
Chriftendome in his tyme. Secondly, he
could no be mooued in hope of honor, for
in Rome he was head of his monaftery,
& in England among a fierce, ftrange &
barbarous Nation, he could expect none.
Wherfore albeit (beyond all humaine ex-
pectatiõ)he was made Archbifhop, yet hauing no hope therof, that can not be iuftly
thought to haue moued him to vnder-
take that voyage. Thirdly, profit could not
moue him to this enterprife. For what
profit could he expect here, or what profit did he expect, who (as Saint Beda *lib.*1.
cap. 26. faith of him and his fellowes) *defpi-*
fed the commodities of this world as things none
of their owne, taking of them whome they inftru-
cted, onely fo muc h as might ferue their neceffities.
And being made Archbifhop did accor-
ding as Saint Gregory appointed him in
Beda *lib,*1.*cap.*27. liue according to his religious rule, not a part from his Clergie,

D 4   but

but *followed that tr*ã*de and forme of liuing
which was vfed in the primitiue Church among
the Fathers* , *among whome there was none that
faid that to be his owne* , *which he poſſeſſed* , *but
all things were comon*.

2 And as for worldly pleaſur what ſhould
moue Saint Auſtin (think we) to leaue his
native Contry, and to feeke pleaſure in a
ſtrange Contry, where he knoweth nether place, perſon nor language? What
pleaſure ſhould moue an Italian to chãge
Italy for England, Rome for Canterbury,
eſpecially when our Contry (as then it
was) was ſauage and barbarous? What
pleaſure can we imagin can moue a Chriſtian to goe to preach Chriſts faith among
barbarous infidells? Or what pleaſure did
Saint Auſtin feeke here who with his
fellowes liued here fo Angel like, that as
Saint Beda writteth *lib.*1. *cap.* 26. our Nation *maruailed much at their ſimplicity, of their
innocent liuing* , *and our King was then much
delighted with the puritie of their life and the
example of their godly conuerſation.* And being
Archbiſhop, yet left not his religious
life, and as is before ſhewed, tooke exceeding paines in teaching, and baptizing our Nation, and wonderfully labored to conuert the Britons alfo . Who
(as is before faid) went ſtill on foote, and
for the moſt part barefoote, and had his
                                                    knees

knees hard like the knees of a camell by continuall prayer. Wherfore no human motiue, but the diuine motiues of obe- dience to his Maister and lawfull Bifhop the great Saint and glorious Doctor of Gods Church Saint Gregory, who fent him and commanded him to come hither to preach. And of Charitie, to faue our Nations foules, by bringing them out of heathenifh infidelitie to the faith of Chrift. And glorie of God were the in- citements, motiues and caufes of Saint Auftins comming hither, and preaching that religion which he did. And this is manifeft both by the teftimonies of Ca- tholick Writers and confeffions of Pro- teftants which we cited before touching Saint Auftins holines, and fhall alleadge in this next Chapter where we fhall prooue that this great Clerck and holy man Saint Auftin moued by thefe faintly motiues to preach to our Nation, was alfo lawfully fent therto with fuf- ficient authoritie and commiffion.

Motiues of S. Auftins preaching

Obediéce.

Charitie

Gods glo- rie.

CHAP.

CHAPT. VIII.

That Saint Auſtin was lawfully
ſent hither to preach, prooued by di-
uers authorities and confeſſion
of Proteſtants.

TWO things ther are requiſed to euery lawfull Paſtor, to wit, both right
Orders, and lawfull Commiſsion to adminiſter the Sacraments and Word of
God. And albeit by order of doctrine,
wee ſhould ſpeake firſt of Saint Auſtins
orders, yet becauſe his Commiſsion being
cleared, his orders will eaſely appeare to
be good, I will ſpeake firſt of his Comiſ-
ſion where with he was ſent to preach.
And that he was ſent of Saint Gregory,
wee need not prooue. For as Sutclif ſaith
in his Subuerſion *cap. 3. It is not denied, that*
Gregory ſent Auſtin. The onely difficulty can
be whether he were lawfully ſent, and by
ſufficient authoritie or no. But that he
was lawfully ſent to preach I will prooue
firſt by ſacred teſtimony from Heauen;
Secondly, by authority of Catholicks;
Thirdly, by confeſsion of Proteſtants;
Fourthly, by examples; and laſtly by reaſon.

Howv ma-
nie vvayes
S. Auſtins
miſsion is
prooued.

son. The testimony from Heauen is of
Saint Peter, who appearing in a vision to
Saint Laurence successor of Saint Austin,
when he vpon the reuolt of our Contrie
to Paganisme intended to abandon the
Land, *scourged him* (saith Saint Beda *lib. 2.
cap. 6.*) *with sharp stripes a great while in the
close night, and asked why he would forsake the
flock which he him self had committed vnto him.*
Behould Saint Peter from Heauen testifieth that he had cōmitted English men
to the teaching of Saint Laurence, one of
Saint Austins fellow labourers, & whome
Saint Austin him self appointed & consecrated for his successor. And *when Saint
Laurence awaked* (saith Godwin) *he found it
more than a dreame, for all his body was gore blood.
VVherfore going immediatly to the King Edbald,
he shewed him his woundes, and together related
to him the occasion of them, which strook such a
terror into the King, as by and by he renounced his
Idolls, and caused him self to be baptized.* Now
that this apparition to S. Laurence was
no dreame or illusion appeareth many
wayes. First, by the reall wounds, which
both Saint Laurence felt, and the King
sawe. Secondly, by the authority of Saint
Laurēce, who being so holy a man would
neuer auouch an idle dreame, or illusion
for a certain vision. Thirdly, by the beleefe giuen therto by King Edbald and
his

By S. Pe-
ters testi-
monie
from hea-
uen.

The appa-
rition of
S. Peter to
be true.
1

2

3

his people, who doubtles examined it throughly, before they would vpon the credit therof forsake their Idolls

4. Fourthly by the heauenly effect, which it wrought, which was the recalling of our Contry from Paganisme to Christianity, to which ende the Diuell would neuer cooperat any way. **5.** Fifthly, by the authority of S. Beda and our best Chroniclers Malmesbury *lib.* 1. *Reg & lib.* 2. *Pont.* Huntington *lib.* 3. Marianus *an.* 617. Westmon. *anno* 616. *ibidem.* Florent and others, who haue credited and recorded it as a true vision. **6.** Lastly, by the confession of diuers Protestants, as Godwin in the life of Saint Laurence, and Holinshed in the life of King Edbald. And surly who well considereth it, can not but account it a singuler fauor of God, and honor to our Contrie, that first in the Britons tyme it should receaue the faith of Christ by the preaching of S. Peter, by whose mouth as he saith *Acts* 15. *From ancient tyme God hath made choice that Gentils should heare the VVord of God and beleeue.* And afterward in our English Ancestors tyme should recouer the same faith againe by the meanes of Saint Gregory one of the glorioufest successors of Saint Peter that euer was, and mooued therto by him from Heauen. Which amongst other things declareth

that

(marginal notes)

6.
Protestãts confesses. Peters apparition.

S. Peters care of this Coū trie.

that to be true which the same Saint Peter said to Saint Brithwald, *Regnum Anglo-rum, regnum Dei est. The Kingdom of England, is the Kingdom of God.*

2. As for the authoritie of Catholicks, the first place is due to Saint Gregory, who writing to Eulogius Patriarch of Alexandria *lib. 7. epist. 30.* saith : *VVhiles the English Nation abiding in a corner of the world, remained hitherto in infidelity in the worship of wood and stones, by the help of your prayers it seemed good to me, God being the Author to send a Monke of my Monastery thither to preach.* Loe he ascribeth the sending of S. Austin to God as Author, and to holy mens prayers as helpes therunto. And againe writing to Saint Austins company in Beda *lib. 1. c. 23.* saith: *Let nether the trauaill of the iorney, nor talk of euill tongues dismay yow. But with all force and feruor make vp that, which yow haue by the motion of God begun.* And *lib. 5. epist. 52.* saith, he sent Austin, *auxiliante Domino; By Gods help.* and 54. *disponente Domino; by Gods disposition.* Superfluous it were to cite the rest of the Popes, who followed Saint Gregory, and cooperated all they could to our conuersion, as Boniface 4. and 5. Honorius, Vitalian, and the rest who vndoubedly taught Saint Austin to haue bene lawfully sent. Onely I will add the names of those Princes & Bishops whome
Saint

Ealred in vit S. Edvvardi. Sur. tom. 8.

S. Austins mission proued by authoritie of Catholicks.
S. Gregorie.

Diuers anciant Popes.

Saint Gregory testifieth to haue holpen,
and encoraged Saint Auſtin in his Godly
enterpriſe. Firſt, he ſaith *lib. 7. epiſt. 30.*
that by his licence *Saint Auſtin was made*
Biſhop of the Biſhops of Germanie, and with their
comforts brought to the Engliſh Nation. And *epi.*
114. he ſendeth a Pall to Siagrius Biſhop
of Auſt, & maketh his See next to the See
Metropolitan, becauſe *in the buſines of Saint*
Auſtins miſſion (ſaith he) *we know thou ſhewedſt*
thy ſelfe ſo carefull, deuout and helper in all
things as thou ſhoulde ſt. lib. 9. epiſt. 53. writing to Theodorick King of France. *VVhat*
great fauours your Excellency ſhewed to our moſt
reuerent brother, and fellow Biſhop Auſtin in his
iorney to England certain Monkes comming from
him haue tould vs. And 55. to Clotarius another French King writeth thus : *Some*
who went with our moſt reuerend brother, and
fellow Biſhop Auſtin vnto the Engliſh Nation re-
turning to vs haue tould vs with what charitie
your Excellency refreſhed the ſaid brother of ours
in your preſence, and with how great help you
furthered him in his voyage. And 56. writing
to Brunechild the Queene of France, he
hath theſe words : *VVith what fauor and help*
your Excellency ſuccoured our moſt reuerend bro-
ther and fellow Biſhop Auſtin going to the Engliſh
Nation, nether did fame before ſuppreſſe in ſilence,
and afterward ſome Monkes comming from him
to vs haue particulerly related. Yow ſee the
miſſion

Biſhops
of Ger-
manie or
France.

Kings of
France.

Queene
of France.

mission of Saint Austin was not onely allowed as lawfull, but also holped and furthered by the Christian Bishops and Princes of that tyme.

3. After Saint Austins tyme Beda *lib. 1,* S. Beda *cap.* 22. speaking of Saint Austin, and his fellow Preachers, saith : *the goodnes of God prouided them for our English people,* And *c.* 23. saith, that *Gregory being mooued by inspiration of God therunto, sent the seruant of God Saint Austin.* After him Ethelwerd *lib.* 2. *cap.* 1. Ethel-vverd *Gregory sent Saint Austin, confirmat eum. diuino admonitu.* Florent Chron. *ann.* 596. saith: *Gregory mooued by Gods instinct, sent Austin and others to preach the VVord of God to the English Nation.* Of Protestants, Stow *pag.* 65. saith: Protestãts confesse S. Austin to haue bene sent of God. *Gregory was mooued of godly instinction to send Austin to preach to the Angles.* Godwin *in vita August. Yt pleased God, &c.* Apologie for the oath of allegeance : *Albeit Gregory sent Aust.n and others as he said with deuine reuelation into England vnto King Ethelbert, yet &c.* Luther Kings Ma-iestie in his oratio· to the parle. 19. No-uemb.1605. *lib. cont. Anabapt. Fatemur in Papatu esse rerum prædicandi officium.* VVe confesse, that in the Popedom is the true office of preaching. The law- D Couel defence of Hooker. p. 77. Bu·y Treatises, of Pacificat. p. 109. Some in Peury. Hooker fulnes also of Saint Austins sending must needs all such Protestants confesse as do deriue the authoritie of preaching in Lu- ther, and their first Preachers from the Church of Rome, of whome wee shall speake in the second booke. And also all

　　　　　　　　　　　such

3. *booke*
of Ecclef. of
*Polic p.*158
D. *Baron.*
his 4 fer-
*mons p.*448.
*Feild lib.*3.
of Church.p.
183.
Fox
Iuel
*Caluin.*4.
Iuftit c. 17.
paragr. 49.
VVhitak:
cont. Dur.
p. 397. *Bel*
Suruey pag.
257.

fuch as do graunt , that the Church of
Rome is a true Church of Chrift , or that
Papifts may be faued, which commeth to
one, becaufe none can be faued out of the
true Church. For if the Church of Rome
be yet a true Church , and can fend preachers lawfully, it can not be denyed, but
it had the fame goodnes , and power to
fend in Saint Gregory his tyme. And this
alfo are they likly to grant who will needs
haue S. Gregory and likwife the Church
of Rome in his tyme to haue bene Proteftant, or at leaft Saint Gregory was a true
and vertuous Bifhop . Finally they alfo
muft needes grant that Saint Auftin was
lawfully fent who fay (as D. Feild doth
lib. 3. *Of the Church* , *cap.* 6. 8. and others
doe) that before Luthers diuifion their
Church was all one, &the fame Church
with ours. For fuerly that Church alowed
of Saint Auftins mifsion. And therfor if
fhe had authoritie to approoue Saint Auftins mifsion, he was lawfully fent.

S. Auftins
mifsion
proued by
examples.
Rome
1000 years
agoe vfed
to fend
preachers
into all
the vvorld.
4.   Fourthly, I prooue that Saint Auftin
was lawfully fent of Saint Gregory by
examples. For as Saint Laurence , Saint
Mellit, and Saint Iuftus fellowes and fucceffors of Saint Auftin write in their letters to the Bifhops and Abbots of Scotland in Beda *lib.* 2. *cap.* 4. *The accuftomable*
manner of the Sea Apoftolick was to fend into all
places

places of the world to preach the word of God.
And this cuſtom of the Church of Rome,
ſending preachers to all places of the
world may be prooued by induction euer
ſince Saint Peters tyme. For Saint Clement 3. Pope after Saint Peter, ſent Saint
Dennis into France, as teſtifie Hilduinus
in Areopagit. and the French Chronicles.
Whervpon the French Biſhops writing
to Pope Leo *anno* 400. acknowledg the
See of Rome *fontem & originem religionis ſuæ.*
Pope Eleutherius about the yeare 170,
ſent hither Fugatius and Damian, as is
before ſhewed. And Pope Victor his ſucceſſor about the yeare 203. ſent others into Scotland, as witneſſe Boethius *libr.* 6.
Hiſt. Scot. Genebr. in Victor. Baron. and others.
About the yeare 255. Pope Stephen conſecrated Saint Mellonus a Briton, Biſhop
of Roane, and ſent him thither to preach,
as teſtifie the Author of his life, and Bale
cent. 1. cap. 31. In the yeare 432. (ſaith Bale
cent. 1. cap. 43.) died Saint Ninian, who
being a Briton (as he ſaith there after Beda *lib. 3. cap. 4.*) comming from Rome
preached to the South Picts, and conuerted them to Chriſtianitie. About the year
429. Pope Celeſtin ſent hither Saint German and Lupus to confute and expell the
Pelagians, as teſtifieth Proſper *in Chronic.*
Bale *cent. 1. cap. 45.* Baron. *an.* 429. And the

E   ſame

Marginal notes:
S. Clemēt
S. Eleutherius.
S. Victor.
S. Stephen
S. Celeſtin

same Pope about the yeare 434. confecrated Palladius Bishop for Scotland, and sent him thither, as testifie Prosper *Chron.* Beda *lib.*1. *cap.*13. Baron.*an.*429. Hunting. *lib.*1.and others.And about the same tyme also he sent S. Patrick to Irland, as testifie Marianus *in Chron.*Cambd.*in Hibernia.*Bale *cent.*1.*cap.*49.where he saith that Saint Patrick preached *sinceram Christi religionem.* And thus yow see how before S. Gregory, Popes sent preachers hither to all the ancient inhabitants of these two Ilands, and that they receaued his Legats, which Legats also for the most part were Britons.Which declareth plainly what opinion those ancient Nations had of the Popes authoritie to send preachers hither.

Ancient Britons Scotts Picts and Irish receaued preachers frō Rome.

5.   In like forte after S. Gregories tyme, the Pope sent preachers both hither, and into other Contries. For about the yeare 635. Pope Honorius sent hither Saint Birin,who conuerted the West Contrie, as Beda saith *lib.*3. *cap.*7. Godwin *in vita Birini.*Bale *cent.*13. *cap.*4. And *cap.*5. he addeth that he sent also Saint Felix, who conuerted the East-Angles. In the yeare 668. Pope Vitalian sent hither S. Theodore and Saint Adrian,as writeth S. Beda *lib.*4. *cap.*1. Godwin *in Theodor.* Bale *cent.* 13.*cap.*6.and others. About the yeare 690. Pope Sergius 1. sent S. Willebrord and other

P.Honorius.

P.Vitalian

P. Sergius.

other Englifh Mōks to preach to the Fri-
fons and Saxons, as teftifieth Marcellin
in Sur. tom. 2. Beda *lib.* 5.*cap.*11.12. Bale *cent.*
1. *pag.* 78. *cit.* About the yeare 719. Pope
Gregory 2. fent Saint Boniface an Englifh P.Grego-
man, called the Apoftle of Germany, thi- ry. 2.
ther to preach,as teftifie Bale *cent.*1.*pag.*79.
and all German writers.About the yeare
870. Pope Adrian 2. fent Saint Cyrill and P.Adriā 2.
Methodius to preach to the Morauians
and Slauonians, Baron *Martyrol.* 9. *Martij.*
Sigebert. *in Chron.* About the yeare 970.
Pope Iohn 14. *inuited* (faith Bale *cent.*2.*cap.* P.Iohn 14.
30.) *the Kingdom of Polonie to Papifme ,and fent
thither Cardinall Giles.* About the yeare 989.
Pope Iohn 15. fent S. Adilbert to preach P.Iohn 15.
to the Hungarians & Bohemians.About
the yeare 1000. Saint Boniface was fent
by the Pope to the Ruffians. About the
yeare 1145. Pope Eugen 3. fent Adrian
an Englifh man, and afterward Pope,into P.Eugen.
Norway , as Bale faith *cent.* 2. *pag.* 178.
About the yeare 1252. Pope Innocent 4. P.Inno-
fent the Francifcans and Dominicans vn- cent. 4.
to the King of Tartarie,whome they conuerted , and chriftened , as writeth Bale
*cent.*4. *cap.* 17. About the yeare 1494. Pope
Alexander 6. fent Bucill and 11. Monkes P.Alexan-
more into the Weft-Indies then newly der 6.
difcouered by the Spaniards. And at the
fame tyme were Francifcans fent by the

Pope into the East-Indies, and since that Dominicans, Iesuits, and other religious men haue bene sent into diuers barbarous Prouinces of both Indies, Africk, and Brasile. And in almost all these missions haue those which were sent by the Pope, conuerted those Nations, to whome they where sent, *God cooperating with them, and confirming their words with miracles following,* & are therfor termed the Apostles of those Contries. And if this so long continuance of the Popes sending Preachers into all parts of the world, and Gods meruailous and miraculous concurse with them, by the conuersion of the Nations, to which they were sent, be not ynough to prooue that S. Gregory had sufficient authoritie to send Saint Austin hither, I know not what authoritie can be sufficient.

CHAP,

CHAP. IX.

That Saint Auſtin was lawfully ſent hither to preach, prooued by reaſon.

BY reaſon I will 'prooue it. Firſt, out of that which Proteſtants haue granted. For, *It is well knowne* (ſaith B. Bilſon *de Obedien. part. 1. pag. 60.) that the Pope was not onely Patriarch of the VVeſt parts, but of the foure Patriarches which were the cheefe Biſhops in Chriſtendom in order, and accompted the firſt.* And *pag.* 318. *Patriarch of the VVeſt we grant he was.* The ſame in other termes confeſſeth Iuell *art.* 9. *diuiſ.* 26. where he ſaith: *The Pope had in his prouince one great parte of Chriſtendome.* And Reynolds *Confer. pag.* 541. where he calleth his dioceſe *a Princely dioceſe*, and inſinuateth it to contayne all the Weſt Church. For the Eaſt he diuideth among the three other Patriarchs, Likewiſe the graunt that he vſurped not his Patriarchat. *But* (ſaith Bilſon, *pag.* 60. *cit.*) *it was giuen him by conſent of men.* and *pag.* 319. *it came by cuſtom, as the Councell of Nice witneſſeth.* D. Doue of Recuſancy p. 80. *VVhat authoritie the Pope hath had ouer the Latin*

E 3 *Church,*

Church, hath bene giuen him by human conſtitu-
tions, and generall conſent of Princes and States.
Caluin *lib.4. Inſtitut. cap. 7. §.1 Decreto Nice-
næ Synodi primus inter Patriarchas locus tribui-
tur Romano Epiſcopo.* Finally, they grant that

Popes Pa-
triarchat
ancient. the Popes Patriarchat ouer the Weſt is
not new, but begun euen in the tyme of
the primitiue Church. For Feild *lib. 3. of
the Church, cap. 1.* ſaith : *In the tyme of the Nicen Councell, and before, as appeareth by the Acts
of the Councell, there was three principall Biſhops
or Patriarchs of the Chriſtian world, namely the
Biſhop of Rome, of Alexandria, of Antioch.* Thus
breefly yow ſee the Popes Patriarchat
ouer the Weſt granted to be moſt ancient, and lawfull. Hence I argue thus.
A Patriarch hath authority to ſend preachers to all partes of his Patriarchie : *Ergo*
the Pope had authority to ſend preachers
to England, which is a parte of the Weſt.
England
euer vnder
the Popes
Patriar-
chat. The Antecedent none can deny. The Cō-
ſequent notwithſtanding Bilſon *lib.cit.pag.*
320. doth ſtrangly deny. But no maruell
if ſtrange and vnheard of ſhifts be found
to maintaine falſe doctrine. For ſaith he:
*Pope Innocent 1. epiſt. 91.inter epiſt.Aug.confeſ-
ſeth he had no authoritie to call one poore Briton
out of this Realme. And the Britons would yeeld
no ſubiection to Auſtin the Romiſh Legat.* Therfor England was not within the compas
of the Popes Patriarchat.

2. But

2. But the first of thefe proofes is a manifeſt vntruth, and the ſecond a meere folly. For vntrue is it, that Saint Innocent confeſſed he had not authoritie to call one out of Britany. For the Briton of whome he ſpake was Pelagius the heretick, who at that tyme was not in Britany, but in Paleſtine, as teſtifyeth Saint Auſtin *epiſt.* 32. writen the ſame yeare, which was *an.* 416. Nether had Pelagius bene in Britany long tyme before that. For as Baron ſheweth *an.* 405. out of Saint Chryſoſtom and Iſiodor Peluſiot. He was brought vp in the Eaſt, and after that liued, as Saint Auſtin ſaith *epiſt.* 95. *longe tyme in Rome,* where being diſcouered, he fled, as Baron telleth *an.* 412. into Sicilie, and thence into Paleſtine, where (being by his hypocriſy and fraud abſolued from hereſie, and finding fauor at the Biſhop of Hieruſalem, but contrariwiſe condemned by Pope Innocent and Zozimus) he ſtayed, and for any thing I finde ther dyed. For if him ſelf had brought his hereſy into Britany, Beda *lib.* 1. *cap.* 17. Would neuer haue aſcribed the bringing of it to one Agricola long after. And therfor I doubt of that which Bale *cent* 1. *cap.* 38. citeth out of Walden. that Pelagius was *à ſuis Britannis pulſus in exilium ob hereſim,* vnles by driuing into baniſhment he ment keeping

E 4 out

out of the Contrey, as perhaps Pelagius was. Besides Innocent saith not, that he had not authoritie to call Pelagius where soeuer he were, yea he insinuateth the cōtrary; but that Pelagius if he were obstinat would not come at his call, and that others, that dwelt nerer to him myght do it more conueniently, than he who dwelt so far of as Rome is from Palestine. His words are these, *Qui Pelagius si confidit, &c. VVhich Pelagius if he trust and knowe that he deserueth not to be condemned of vs, because he reiectets that which he taught, he should not be sent for of vs, but he himselfe should make haste that he may be absolued. For if he think yet as he did, when will he present himselfe to our iudgement vpon any letters whatsoeuer, knowing that he shalbe condemned? And if he were to be sent for, that might be better done of them who are nerer, than so far of as we are. But there shall want no care of him if he will be cured.*

3.   Bilsons proofe out of the Britons deniall of subiection hath no more color or reason, than a few rebells deniall of subiection hath to prooue a Prince to haue no authoritie ouer a parte of his Kingdome. For their Catholick Ancestors did euer acknowledg themselues vnder the Pope his iurisdiction, as appeareth both by that which hath bene said before as also because the Archbishops of the Britons

Cathol. Britons euer tooke the Pope to be their superior.

tons not long before Saint Auſtins comming were the Popes Legats, as writeth
Galfrid a man of good account among
Proteſtants *lib.9. cap.12. Dubritius* (ſaith he)
Primat of Britannie, and Legat of the See Apoſto-
lick was famous with ſuch great pietie. And had
Palls from Rome, as is euident in the life
of Saint Sampſon. Nether did the heretick Britons refuſe to be ſubiect to Saint
Auſtin, becauſe they thought Saint Gregorie to haue no authoritie to apoint an
Archbiſhop ouer them, (for vndoubtedly they would haue alleadged this as a
reaſon of their refuſal if they had ſo
thought it) but onely becauſe, as Saint
Beda reporteth *lib 2. c. 2.* they ſayd with
them ſelues. *If he would not ſo much as ariſe to*
vs, If wee ſhould ſubiect our ſelues to him he
would deſpiſe vs. If he had riſen to them they
were determined to ſubiect them ſelues
to him, as Beda there ſaith, which they
neuer would haue done if they had doubted his authority inſufficient.

VVhy the Britons refuſed to be vnder S. Auſtin.

Secondly I prooue it by reaſon grounded in ſcripture. The authority which
Chriſt left in his Church to preach to all
Nations he gaue to euery Apoſtle, as appeareth by his words *Matth.28. Docete om-*
nes gentes, Teach all Nations. And Proteſtants
who teach, euery Apoſtle to haue bene
head of the reſt of the Church beſids them
ſelues,

Secōd rea-ſon in proofe of S. Auſtins miſſion.

felues, do not deny: Therfore this authority muſt remaine in ſome ſucceſſor of
one or other of thoſe Apoſtles, and muſt
not be onely in the whole Church, becauſe it muſt deſcend to ſome ſuch as
Chriſt gaue it vnto. Beſides if authority
to ſend to all Nations were not in ſome
one Biſhop or other, but in the whole
Church onely, when ſoeuer there were
Preachers to be ſent to Infidells, ther
ought to be a generall Councell called,
which were both abſurd, and was neuer
practiſed in Gods Church. But authority
to preach or ſend preachers to England
was more likly to be in Saint Gregory,
than any other Biſhop. For touching the
Patriarchs or Biſhops of the Eaſt, it is a
thing vnheard of, that any of them ſhould
haue iuriſdiction ouer England. And as
for the Biſhops of France, certain it is they
neuer had any authority ouer England.
And the ſame I may ſay of Scotland, Ireland, Flanders, Spaine, and all other Contries. The doubt onely may be of Britons,
becauſe they once had authority ouer the
Contry, which the Engliſh poſſeſſed. But
that could yeald them no ſpirituall authority ouer the Engliſh in Saint Auſtins
tyme, becauſe nether was the Engliſh
euer ſubiect to the Britons, nor was ther
in Saint Auſtins tyme any Britiſh Biſhop
aliue

Marginal notes:

Authoritie to ſend preachers to all nations muſt remaine in ſome one Biſhop.

No Biſhop could ſend preachers to Englãd but the Pope.

aliue who had had any diocefe within England: Therfore they could at that tyme clayme no more authority to fend Preachers into England, than the Bifhops of Wales can now. Wherfore if this authority was then in any Bifhop (as needes it muft be) it was in the Bifhop of Rome, who euer fince the primitiue tyme of the Church hath vfed to fend preachers hither as is before fhewed. And if any require the Princes approbation for the lawfullnes of a Preachers miffion, this alfo S. Auftin had as is euident by S. Beda *l.1. c.25.* Befides Proteftants confeffe the Pope to haue bene alwaies the cheefe Patriarch & Bifhop of Chriftédom. Saith D. Whitaker *lib.6.cont.Dur.p.464. I will not deny that the Bishop of Rome was Primat of all Bishops.* And *p.148. Rome the Seat of the first Patriarch. The See of Rome,* faith Caluin *l.4. c.7. §.26. was in tymes past the cheefe of all* Iuell *art.4.diu.16. Of the Patriarches the Pope had the first place both in Councell, and out of Councell.* And *26. Of the Patriarchs the Bishop of Rome was euer the first.* And *32. Victor fayth that Rome is the cheefe or head ouer all others, which of our parte for that tyme is not denyed.* Bifhop Bilfon *pag.60.* faith *it is well knowne that the Pope was the cheefe of the Patriarchs.* D. Reinolds *Confer.pag. 568. Among all the Apostolick Churches, the Roman for honor, and credit had the chiefty*

And

Proteftâts confeffe the Pope to haue bene the cheef B. of Chriftendom. D. vvhitak

Caluin.

Iuell.

Bilfon.

Reinolds

And 554. *Chryſoſtome* and *Baſile gaue the Pope a ſupreheminence of authority. pag. 368. Cyprian giueth a ſpeciall title of honor and preheminence to the Church of Rome. The Fathers apply the name of the Rock to the Biſhop of Rome.* Finally *Fox in his Acts pag* 18. ſaith, *that in Lyrinenſis, Paſcaſin, Iuſtinian, Athanaſius, Hierome, Ambroſe, Auſtin, Theodoret, and Chryſoſt. S. Peter with his ſucceſſors is called Head of the Church, Cheeſe of Biſhops, Prince of the Apoſtles.* And the like confeſſe all other Proteſtants. Therfor if authority of ſending preachers remaine in any Biſhop, it is moſt lykly to remaine in the Pope.

Third reaſon for proofe of S. Auſtins miſſion. 4. Thirdly, I argue thus. Who hath authority to gouern the whole Church of God, hath authority to ſend Preachers to all Nations: But Saint *Gregory* had authority to gouern the whole Church: *Ergo* he had authority to ſend Preachers *&c.* The *Maior* needeth no proofe. The *Minor* I prooue thus. Saint *Peter* had authority to gouern the whole Church, euen as it includeth the reſt of the Apoſtles; But Saint *Gregory* ſucceeded (though not immediatly) Saint *Peter* in that authority: *Ergo*, That Saint *Peter* had authority ouer the whole Church beſides the Apoſtles, the Proteſtants do graunt. For they teach that Chriſt made euery one of them Head and Gouernor of all

Proteſtant graunt euery Apoſtle to haue bene Head of the reſt of the church

the

the Church befides them felues. D. Whitaker *lib. 5. pag. 365. cont. Dur.* Quis Petrum, &c. *Vho confeſſeth not that Peter was the foundation of the Church, ſeeing that it is common to all the Apoſtles?* And *lib.9.pag.745.* Super Petrum, &c. *Vpon Peter is the Church founded, but not vpon him onely,* Et Petro totius, &c. *And to Peter is the care of the whole Church committed, but not to him onely,* Quia hoc commune, &c. *Becauſe this was common with the reſt of the Apoſtles, as the Scripture, and Fathers moſt clearly teſtifie.* Behould how he confeſſeth that both Scripture and Fathers teſtifie, and that moſt clearly, that the care of the whole Church was committed to Peter. D. Reynolds *Confer. pag. 32. As the name of foundation is giuen to the Apoſtles,* Apoc. 21. *ſo the twelue foundations do prooue them twelue heads.* Ibid. *All the Apoſtles were heads.* Item *pag. 26. Chriſt promiſed to build his Church not vpon Peters doctrine onely, but vpon his perſon in ſome ſorte.* And *pag. 28. Chriſts words to Peter import this ſenſe: Vpon thee I will build my Church.* And Bilſon *lib. of Obedience, pag. 87.* granteth, that the Rock on which the Church is promiſed to be built *Matth.* 16. was Peters perſon, and that the Church was built vpon him, but not vpon him onely, but the reſt of the Apoſtles too. And if paſſion did not blynd their eyes, they would ſee that the Scripture and Fathers

do

Declarat. of diſcipl. print at Geneua 1549. Chriſt cōmēded to Peter all his flock.

The ſame ſaith Fulk *Annotat. Mat.16. Ioan.1.*

do as plainly teftifie that Saint Peter was Head of the whole Church, euen as it includeth the reft of the Apoftles, as they teftifie that euery Apoftle was Head of the reft of the Church befide themfelues. For the places of Scripture out of which they do or can prooue that euery Apoftle was head of all other Chriftians (as yow may fee in Whitaker *loco cit. pag.* 147. and Reynolds *loco cit.*) is *Matth.*28. where euery Apoftle is bidden *to teach all Nations.* and *Ephef.* 2. where Chriftians are faid to be *founded vpon the Apoftles.* And *Apoc.* 21. where the twelue Apoftles are called *the foundations of the Church,* by which places they do prooue (and well) thàt euery Apoftle was made Head ouer euery Chriftian, and the whole Church befide themfelues; becaufe there is no exception made of any man, whome they are not to feede, nor of any Chriftian in the Church, which they founded. And therfore in the commifsion giuen by Chrift to euery Apoftle in the word *Nations,* are included all other befide them felues. And in the fpeech of the Apocalyps vnder the word *Church,* are vnderftood all other Chriftians whatfoeuer. And cófequently euery Apoftle is by the plain verdict of Scripture Preacher to all Nations, and Founder of euery Chriftian befide them felues. In which authority be-

S. Peter as plainly o-uer the A-poftles as ouer the reft of Chriftiãs because their Apostleship did consist, and therin all the Apostles were equall to S. Peter (for euery one of them was as well sent to all Natiōs with authority to found Churches euery where, as he was) some Fathers say, that other Apostles had *parem potestatē* with S. Peter, as Anaclet *dist.21.c. Cū in nouo.* Cypr. *de vnit.Eccl.* Chryſ.*in 1.Gal.* & that the Church is equaly foūded on all the Apostles, because ouer the rest of the Church besides, the Apostles euery one of them had equall authority with Peter: & the Church, (not including the Apostles) was equaly foūded on euery one of them.

Hovv ſome Fathers ſay that others vvere equal in the Apoſtleship vvith S. Peter.

5. But by the same maner, and in the same euidency that Protestants do prooue that euery Apostle was Head ouer all the Church besides them ſelues, do we prooue that Saint Peter was head ouer all the Church euen as it includeth the rest of the Apostles. For as in their cōmiſsion, *Teach all Nations*, and the other ſpeech of them *Foundations of the Church*, all are included beſide them ſelues, because none are excepted, as they are by reaſõ of that relatiue oppoſition which is there found betwene *Teachers,* & *Taught, Founders, and Founded*; & therfor euery one of the Apoſtles being in this ſpeech called *a teacher* & *foundatiõ* none of them in the same ſpeech can be ment to be taught, or founded him ſelf. So in

Proued by Scripture that S. Peters commiſsion includeth the reſt of the Apoſtles.

like

like fort in S. Peters Commifsion *Ioan* 21.
Feede my sheepe, Luc. 22. *Confirme thy bre-*
thren. and in Chrifts words of him *Mat.* 16.
Thou art Peter, and vpon this Rock will I build my
Church. No one Apoftle or other befides
himfelf, who alone is fpoken to, and is in
them apointed *Feeder* and *Confirmer* and
Foundation, is any more excepted than any
other Chriftian is excepted in the Commifsion of the Apoftles in generall. And
therfore are they as well and as clearly included in his Comifsion vnder the name
Sheepe, Brethren, Church, as other Chriftians
are included in theirs vnder the name of
Nations and *Church.* And therfor Saint Bernard faid *de Confider. Nihil excipitur, vbi nihil*
distinguitur. There being no diftinction in
thefe words of Chrift, *my Church, my Sheepe,*
thy Brethren, made from the reft of the
Apoftles, they are not excepted, but included in them. Wherfore if Proteftants will
here admit their commō rule of expounding one place of Scripture by an other,
they muft confeffe that Scripture as clearly maketh S. Peter Head of the Apoftles,
as it maketh them Head of all other
Chriftians. Secondly I prooue by confeffion of Proteftāts, that Chrift in his words
My Church, My Sheepe, Thy Brethren, fpoken
to Saint Peter, included the reft of the A-
poftles. For D. Reynolds *Conferenc. p.* 385.
  faith

Secondly
prooued
by confef-
fion of
Proteftāts.

faith, that Christ by, *My Church*, *Mat.* 16. *meant generally the Catholick Church*, *all the chosen*. But the Apostles *were chosen*, yea the chefest of them. And *p.* 386. *It is the Church of Gods elect, and chosen, which Christ doth call in this place (Math 16.) my Church*, where he addeth, that *this is cleare and out of all controuersie.* And *p.* 368. *Christ said of his whole Church that the gates of hell. &c.* Therfore the whole Church was founded on Peter. The same he repeateth *Conclus.* 1. *p.* 615. and *Conclus.* 2. *p.* 625. and generally all Protestāts graunt the same. For out of this place they proue that the Elect can not fall from God, because Christ here sayd that Hell gates should not preuaile against his Church, That is (say they) against his Elect. In like sort the said Reinolds *Conf. p.* 386. saith, that these words, *My Sheepe, Iohn* 10 (where it is sayd *my sheepe heare my voice*) included all the Elect. Therfore *Ioan.* 21. the very same words include all the Elect (beside Peter, who is excepted because he is apointed to feede them) vnles we will, not vpon any different occasion ministred by scripture, but vpon our own preconceited opinion expound the same word, now one way, now an other. Finally the sayd Reinolds *Conf. pag.* 103. confesseth that by, *Thy Bethren Luc.* 22. Christ ment *all the faithfull.* Then surely he included all the Apostles.

F 6. Thyr-

6. Thirdly , I proue that S. Péter was
head of the whole Church by the authoritie of holy Fathers, whome becaufe
Whitaker côfeffeth(as yow heard before)
to teach moft clearly , that the Church is
founded vpon Peter , I wil omit their
words and remit thofe that lift read'them
to Bellarm. *l.* 1. *de Pont. c.* 10. Onely I will
fhew that they teach that the Church
(as it includeth the reft of the Apoftles)is
founded vpon Peter onely. Cyprian. *epift.
ad Iulian. Ecclefia quæ vna eft fuper vnum. The
Church which is one is founded vpon one, who by the
commaundemēt of our Lord receaued the key therof.* In which words we fee , that as the
Church is fayd to be one onely, fo it is faid
to be founded vpon one onely. And *lib.* 1.
epift. 8. *Ecclefia vna & Cathedra vna.* &c. *One
Church and one Chaire was by our Lords word
founded vpon Peter.* And Saint Hierom. *in* 2.
Ifaiæ. after he had faid that the Apoftles
were, *Montes, mountains,* addeth : *Super vnum
montinm Chriftus fundat Ecclefiam , & loquens ad
eum: Tu es Petrus.* &c. *Vpon one of the Montains
Chrift foundeth his Church, and fpeaking to him
thou art Peter.* &c. S. Leo *ferm.* 2. *de Anniuerf.*
faith, Saint Peter was *plus ceteris ordinatus.*
&c. *ordained more than the reft, whiles he is called a Rock, a Foundation, and apointed porter of
the kingdome of heauen.* And for this caufe
the Fathers when they fpeak of Peter in
respect

respect of the reſt of the Apoſtles, they
manifeſtly prefer him in authority before
them, *ceteris prælatus diſcipulis* . *Preferred before the reſt of the diſciples* ſaith S. Baſil. *ho-
mil.de Iudicio Eccleſ.* And this is ſo euident as
D. Reinolds *Confer. pag.* 179. confeſſeth
that the Fathers call Peter the *mouth* , *the
Top, the higheſt, the Preſident, the head of the Apoſtles,* and *.pag.* 562. The *Prince, the Top, the Cheefeſt of the Apoſtolick company, the Teacher of the
whole world, and a Father of the houſhould.* And
graunteth alſo that ſome of theſe Titles
touch gouernment , *and ſignifie a preheminence
in gouernment* . Wherypon he is inforced
pag. 180. to acknowledg that Saint Peter
was ſuperiour among the Apoſtles , as a
Preſident of a Parliament in France, or as
a Conſull among the Romans. But who
wel conſidereth, ſhall eaſely perceaue that
this is but an authoritie deuiſed of purpoſe to delude the words of the Fathers,
who ſpeaking of Saint Peters authoritie
ouer the Apoſtles , vſe the very words
which we do, to declare his ſupremacy.
And cherfor if they be vnderſtood by their
own words, and not as Reinolds pleaſeth
to expound them , they vſing the ſame
words as we do, muſt be vnderſtood as we
are. But becauſe this queſtion is ſome
what beſide my preſent purpoſe, I will
vrge it no farther. Onely I would know

*Reinolds
deuiſeth
an autho-
ritie in S.
Peter to
auoid his
ſuprema-
cie.*

　　　　　F 2　　　of

of Reinolds how Peter did come by his Confulfhip ouer the Apoftles , which he graunteth to him. Did the Apoftles giue it him? But where readeth he that ? Did Chrift beftow it on him? But where ? if not *Math.* 16. and *Iohn.* 21. In which places if Chrift gaue him any authoritie ouer the Apoftles he gaue him as full power ouer them as ouer other Chriftians. For ther is no limitation of his power towards fome more than towards others, but they are as well to be foûded on him as others are, & he was to feede them, as wel as others. Nether doth this his authoritie ouer the reft of the Church, and the Apoftles too, preiudice the fupreme authority of Chrift ouer all, any more than the lyke authority which the Proteftâts graunt euery Apoftle had ouer the reft of the Church. Secôdly, I would know of Reinolds why he doth not graunt this Confulfhip ouer the whole Church to the Pope, or at leaft to fome one Bifhop or other , but wil make euery Prince head of the Church in his Kingdome.

That S. Peters autho rity remaineth in fome Bifhop of the Church. 7. Now that this authority of Saint Peter remaineth ftill in the Church, and def-cended from him to fome Bifhop, I proue, becaufe all the ends for which ether Chrift declared, or the Fathers affirme, that Chrift inftituted this authoritie, to

remaine

remaine as well after his death, as before.
The first was, that the gates of hell should **1**
not preuaile against the Church. *Math.* 16.
Secondly, that what is loosed in earth, **2**
may be loosed in heauen. *ibi.* Thirdly, that **3**
Peter might cōfirme his Brethren *Luc.* 22.
Fourthly , that he might feede Chrísts **4**
sheepe. *Io.* 21. Fiftly , that one being made **5**
head, occasion of Schisme might be taken
away. Hierom. *lib.* 1. *cont. Iouinianum.* Sixt- **6.**
ly , that the origine of the vnitie of the Church
might appeare. Cyprian. de *simpl.* Pralat. because, as he saith , *lib.* 1. *epist.* 3. Priestly vnity
rose from Peters chaire. And *epist. ad Fulcian.*
Our Lord began the origine of vnitie from Peter. This cause alleadgeth also *Leo. epi.* 84.
and *Anast.* and *Optat. l.* 2. contra Parmen. But
all these ends remaine after Saint Peters
death. Therfore the authoritie also remaineth. Besides S. Austin saith *l. de Pastor. c.* 1.
Christiani sumus propter nos, Prapositi non nisi
propter vos. Therfore Saint Peter being
made Cheefe of Gods Church , for the
good of it , left his authoritie in the
Church. Whervpon S. Austin *tract.* 50.
in Ioannem, saith, that when Peter receaued the keyes, Ecclesiam sanctam significauit,
he represented the holy Church , because he receaued them , as her Gouernour vnder
Christ, and for her good. And therfore
as long as she remaineth, the authority
F 3   which

which Saint Peter receaued for her good

Aarons
authoritie
remained
in his Suc-
ceſſors.
Therfore
Peters.

muſt remaine. Secondly, I proue it, becauſe God in the ould law inſtituted one high Prieſt, who vnder him in ſpirituall matters ſhould be head of the Sinagogue, as in plaine termes confeſſe Caluin *lib.* 4. *Inſtit. c.* 6. §. 2. Whitaker *cont. Dur. p.* 151. Reinolds *Conferen. pag.* 204. 205. And his authoritie deſcended to his ſucceſſors, ſo long as the Synagogue continued. Wherfore wel ſaid the Archbiſhop of Canterbury, Suruey *cap.* 8. *VVe muſt not dreame that when the Apoſtles* (S. Peter) *died the authoritie which was giuen to them, ceaſed, no more than we, may that the authority of Aaron, and his naturall ſonnes expired, and ended with them.* But the gouernment of the Synagogue was but a figure of the gouernment of the Church. For as Saint Paul ſaith: *Omnia in figura contingebant illis.* Therfore, &c. Who will ſee more of this matter may read Stapleton. *contr.* 3. *q.* 2.

8. Onely this remaineth, that wee proue that the Biſhop of Rome (& conſequently Saint Gregory) was ſucceſſor to Saint Peter in this authority. Which I proue,

1 Firſt, becauſe no other Biſhop euer claimed it. For albeit the Patriarch of Conſtantinople in Saint Gregoryes tyme claimed to be vniuerſall Patriarch, that is (as Saint Gregory vnderſtood him) to be the onely proper, and formall Biſhop, as ſhall

be

be more declared hereafter , yet ne acknowledged him felf vnder the Pope, as
Saint Gregory him felf withall witneffeth in thefe wordes, *lib . 7. epiſt. 63. De
Conſtant. ſede quis dubitet eam Sedi Apoſtolicæ eſſe ſubiectam* , &c. *VVho doubted but the See of
Conſtāt. is ſubiect to the See Apoſtolick* (of Rome)
*which both the moſt religious Lord the Emperor,
and our (* Eufebius *) religious brother , Bishop of
the ſame Citty do dayly profeſſe.* Where, by the
way I note, that *Eufebius* is not the name
of the Patriarch of Conſtantinople, at that
tyme, but a ſirname giuen vnto him for his
great externall acts of religion , who alfo
was for his abſtinence named *Ieiunator,*
that is, *Faſter.* Secondly, becaufe the Bifhops of Rome haue alwayes challenged,
and often practifed the fame authority.
The Church of Rome faith (Fox *Act. lib. 1. pag. 1.*)
in all theſe ages aboue ſpecified (from the A-
poſtles) *that challanged to it ſelfe the title and
ringleading of the whole Vniuerſall Church on
earth, by whoſe direction all other Churches haue
bene gouerned.* And *pag.* 18. *VVhat ſo euer was
done in other places , commonly the maner was to
write to the Roman Bishop for his approbation.
The teſtimony of the Roman Bishop was ſome-
tymes wont to be deſired in thoſe dayes (* of Pope
Iulius) *for admitting Bishops in other Churches,
wherof we haue examples* in Socrates lib. 4.
c. 37. *VVhen Bishops of any other Prouinces were*

F 4

2

at any diffention, *they appealled to the Bifhop of* **Rome.** Doct. Reinolds *Confer.pag.457.* **Popes** *of the fecond* 300. *yeares after Chrift claimed fome foueraignty ouer Bifhops. pag.* 383. *Zozimus,* Boniface, Celeftin *did vfurp(*faith he*) ouer the Churches of* Africk, *whiles* Auftin *was aliue. pag.* 544. *They would haue Bifhops, and elders appealle to* Rome. And .*pag.*550. *Popes* (namly Innocent,Leo,Gelaf. Vigil.Greg.) *taught that the Fathers by the fentence of God decreed that whatfoeuer was done in Prouinces far of, fhould not be concluded before it came to the notice of the See of* Rome. *And this they fay all Churches tooke their beginning from the Roman, that all Bifhops had their honor from* Peter. *And yet him felfe faith pag.* 545. *that Pope* Innocent *was learned and Catholick.* And *pag.* 540. *That S.* Auftin *alleadgeth his authority againft hereticks. And that in thofe times Popes were learned , and Catholicks. pag.*552. 554. 555. *and fued vnto by S.*Bafil, *S.*Chrifoftom, *and S.* Auguftin, *and the* African *Bifhops, fought vnto them for their aduife and counfell , for their authoritie and credit.* Of fuch acount were thofe Popes that claymed the fupremacie euen amongft the cheefe Doctors of the Church. Doct. Whitak.*lib.* 7. *cont.Dur. pag.*480.*faith,that Pope* Victor *practifed authoritie ouer externe Churches,*who was not long after S. Peter, and by the iudgment of Proteftants *a godly martyr.*

martyr. Wicklif *in Fox pag.* 445. confeſſeth
the Biſhop of Rome to be Chriſts Vicar on
earth. And Luther for ſome yeares after
he began Proteſtancy confeſſed the ſame,
as yow may ſee *lib. de Captiu. Babyl. in initio,*
and *in Fox pag.* 774. *Edit.* 1596.

9. Thirdly, I prooue it, becauſe the Pope
is ſucceſſor to Saint Peter in his Biſhoprick, therfore he is more like to haue his
authority than any other. That the ancient Fathers ſay, that Saint Peter was
Biſhop of Rome, Proteſtants nether do
nor can deny. And therfore I will for breuity omitt their teſtimonies, and content
my ſelf with theſe mens confeſſions. *The
learned and ancient Fathers* (ſaith Bilſon *lib.
of Obedience pag.* 143.) *call the Biſhops of Rome
Peters ſucceſſors. pag.* 380. *Saint Peter founder
of Saint Leo his Church. The Fathers ſay* (writeth Reinolds *pag.* 218. 219). *Peter was Biſhop of Rome,* and he nameth Hierom, Euſeb. Irenæus. Biſhop Cooper in Chron.
Linus firſt Biſhop of Rome after Peter. But ſaith
Reinol. they meant improperly. And why
ſo? Becauſe (ſaith he) Peter being Apoſtle
could not be Biſhop of one Cyttie. Secōdly, becauſe Irenæus *lib.* 3. *c.* 3. nameth Linus firſt Biſhop of Rome, and Euſebius in
Chron. calleth Euodius firſt Biſhop of Antioch, which could not be if Peter had bene a proper Biſhop. But againſt theſe ca-

Third rea
ſon that
the Pope
ſucceeded
Peter in
his autho
rity.

VVhē the
Fathers
call Peter
Biſhop
of Rome
they
meane
properly.

F 5 uils

uils I oppofe the propriety of the word *Bifhop*, which no Father or ancient writer hath fignified that he vfed improperly when he called S. Peter Bifhop: And all words (efpecially in hiftories) are to be taken properly, when the Authors declare not the contrary, els we fhould neuer be fure how we fhould vnderftãd the writer.

2   Secõdly, they fay, that S. Peter was firft B. of Rome. *Negare non potes* (faith. Optatus *l.* 2. writing againft hereticks) *Thou canft not deny that thou knoweft , that to Peter firft was an Epifcopal Chaire fet in Rome, in which firft fate Peter, to whome facceded Linus.* Loe how certain was it thẽ that the very hereticks could not deny, but they knew it to be fo. Wherfor I ask when the Fathers fayd Peter was firft Bifhop, how they vfed the word *Bifhop* ? If improperly, then they meant fo of Linus. If properly, thẽ we ha-ue our purpofe. Thirdly, in reckoning of

3   the Catalogue of the Bifhops of Rome , they alwaies name Peter firft. Iren *l.3.c.* 3. Eufeb. *Chron.* Epiph. *hær.* 27. Hier. *in Clemente*, Optatus *l.* 2. Aug. *ep.*165. But what fhould he do in the Catalogue of proper Bifhops, if he were none him felf? Befides they reckon him firft Bifhop of Rome as they reckon Mark firft B. of Alexandria,

4   but Mark was a proper Bifhop. Fourthly, they call the See of Rome the feat or
chaire

shaire of Peter, S. Cyprian *lib.1. Epist 3. lib. 4. epist. 2.* S. Hierom *in Pet. ep. ad Damasum* Aug. *lib. 2.* cont. Petil, *cap. 51.* Sozom. *lib. 1. c. 14.* Prosper *lib. De ingratis* Bernard *epist. 237.* And in like sort they call it *sedes Apostolica* as Caluin confesseth, and is euident *ex Concil. Calcedon. Act. 16.* And Rein. *Confer. pag. 369. The Fathers in speaking of the Church of Rome mention often the Chair, and seat of Peter. Hierom honoreth the Bishop of that See with the name of Peters Chaire.* Fiftly, they call the Bishop of Rome successor to S. Peter. S. Hier. *ep. ad Damas.* Concil. Ephes. *1. Tom. 2.* S. Eulog. *apud Greg. lib. 6. ep. 37.* And that they meane of a proper successor, appeareth by that they attribute that peculierly to the Pope. Sixtly, & lastly they say that Peter sate in the Bishops Chaire of Rome as they saye his successors did. *Cathedra* (saith S. Austin *lib. 2. cont. Petil.*) *quid tibi fecit Romana in qua Petrus sedit, & in qua nunc Anastasius sedet? VVhat hath the Chair of Rome done to thee in which Peter sate, and in which now sitteth Anastasius?* Therfore either Peter was a proper Bishop, or Anastasius was none. To conclude, Reinolds him self though vnawares confesseth it *pag. 376.* where he sayth that *Damasus succeded Peter as in Chair, so in doctrine.*

5

6

Reinolds sayth P. Damas. succeded Peter in his chaire

10. As for the first of Reinolds cauils. It s no more against Peters Apostleship to be
Bishop

Bishop of one Citty, than it was to take a particuler care of the Iewes, as he did, nor more than it is for the Bishop of Win-fter to be Parson of Eastmean. And for the second, Irenæus doth not call Linus first Bishop of Rome, but onely faith that Peter, and Paul gaue him the Bishoprick to gouern the Church, to wit vnder Pe-ter, and in his abfence. Euseb. indeed cal-leth Euodius first Bishop of Antioch, but that he meaneth of pure Bishops which were not also Apostles. For before he had fayd *Petrus Ecclesiam Antiochenam fundauit, ibique Cathedram adeptus, sedit.* And Rein. *loco cit.* confeffeth, and both he, and all graunt *that Linus was Peters successor.* And as for Ruffin, his words proue no more, but that Peter instituted Linus to help him, especially in his abfence, as Valerius did institute S. Aug. in his life tyme, who after his death succeeded him, and so did Linus to Peter . Thus haue I prooued that S. Gregorie was successor to S. Peter in his Episcopall See, and that he succeded him also in faith I neede not proue, because protestants, although they find some fault with Greg. doctrine, yet they confesse (as is shewed before) that he taught as much as is needfull to saluation, and con-fequently he wanted no thing to true fuccefsion to S. Peter.

11. Four-

11. Fourthly I proue that the Pope was most likely , to succede Saint Peter , by that which the Fathers attribute to him. Saint Hierom *epist. ad Damasum de nomine hypostasis. Ego nullum primum , nisi Christum sequens beatitudini tuæ, id est , Cathedra Petri communione consocior, super illam Petram ædificatam Ecclesiam scio . Quicunque extra hane domum agnum comederit prophanus est.* I following none formost but Christ , communicate with thy Holines,that is with the Chaire of Peter. Vpon that Rock do I know the Church was built , who soeuer shall eate the lambe out of this house is prophane. Norehow he saith,that he followeth first Christ, and next the Pope, and that the reason, which he giueth herof after, was not why he followed Christ first, for that were needles to proue amongst Christians ; And if he would haue giuen any,it would haue bene,because Christ is God ; But the reason which he giueth, was why he followed the Pope next to Christ , to wit, because he knew him to be the Rock, on which the Church was built . Wherby it is euident,that by the Rock,he meant not Christ,as Bilson *lib. de Obed. pag.* 87. and others would , but Pope Damasus as Reinolds cofesseth p. 370. 376. But yet he meant not(saith Reinolds) the succession of the Popes, because Hierom writeth that Pope Liberius had before

sub-

subscribed to Arianisme. But if Hieroms words be well pôdered he will be found to haue said, both that Pope Damasus was the Rock, and that his succession to Saint Peter in his Chaire of Rome, was the cause why he was the Rock. For if a subiect writing to the King should say: *Nullum primum nisi Deum sequens maiestati tuæ, id est, Throno Conquestoris (in temporalibus) consocior. Super illam petram ædificatum Angliæ Regnum scio. Quicumque extra hanc domum aliquid egerit, rebellis est.* He should confesse that both the King were head of the Realme, and with all tell how he came by that authority, to wit, by succession to the conqueror. So Saint Hierome in the forsaid words both sayd that Pope Damasus person, which he meant by *Beatitudini tuæ,* was the Rock on which in his tyme, the Church was built: and sayd with all that his person had that authoriry by his succesion to Saint Peter in his Roman Chaire, and therfore added these words, *id est, Cathedra Petri,* as a further explication of the former. And consequently he meant that the Church is built vpon all Popes that lawfully succeed in the Chaire of Peter.

D. Feild. Which is so euident as Doct. Feild *lib. 1. de Ecclesia, cap. 4.* confesseth plainly that Saint Hierome *loc cit.* said, *that Peters Chaire is the Rock the Church is builded vpon.* As for Reinolds

nolds reasons, were it truth that S. Hierome wrote (as Reinolds saith) of Liberius, which yet diuers deny, and Reinolds
must deny, if he will speak agreably to
him self. For *pag.* 576. he saith, that *the*
words of Austin (*ep. cont. Donat.* and Hierome
ep. cit.) *do import a sincerity of faith in the Roman*
Bishops to their tyme, which would not be
true, if Liberius had fallen. But admit I
say it were true, that Liberius had denyed
his faith, that maketh no more against his
Rock ship, than the like fault in S. Peter
did against his. For as S. Peter though he
denyed his faith, yet taught not infidelitie
as he was Apostle, and Pastor of the
Church, so nether Liberius though he
committed a personall crime, yet taught
he no heresie, as successor to S. Peter, in
which sorte onely he is the Rock of the
Church.

12. Secondly, S. Austin *ep. contra Donat.* saith:
Numerate Sacerdotes vel ab ipsa Petri Sede. Ipsa
est enim Petra quam non vincunt superbæ infero-
rum portæ: Number the Priests euen from the very
Seat of Peter; It is the Rock which the proud gates
of hell do not ouercom. Behould how the very
succession of Popes from Peter, is called
the Rock of the Church, as the Chair of
Peter was before called of S. Hierome.
To this Bilson *pag.* 88. First saith that the
text is corrupted, and that it should be *ipse*
and

S. Austin

Successiō of Popes by S. Austin the Rock of the Church

and referred to Peters perſon. But this is
a mere ſurmiſe refelled in all the copies
in Europe. Secondly he ſaith, that though
it be *ipſa*, and grammatically agree with
the ſubſtantiue *Petra*, which followeth,
yet it may be meant of Peters perſon. But
if Saint Auſtin had meant that Peter alone
had bene the Rock, and that his ſucceſſors
partaked nothing with him in that , he
would neuer haue byd vs number his ſucceſſors too, and then tell vs that that was
the Rock. Wherfore Reynolds *Confer.pag.*
384. confeſſeth that Saint Auſtin applyed
this text *the gates of hell*, &c. *to the Church of
Rome*. And Bilſon himſelf as doubting of
either of the former anſwers ſaith thirdly,
that Saint Auſtin ſaid not that Peters Seat
is the Rock of the Church , but that hell
gates preuaile not againſt it. But to our
purpoſe all is one, that in Saint Auſtins
iudgment Peters Seat (that is Peters ſucceſſors in Seat) are either the Rock of the

Theodo- church, or ſo ſurely founded theron, as the
ret. gates of hell ſhall not preuaile againſt the.
13.   Thirdly, Theodoret an ancient and
Grecian Doctor writing to Renatus, ſaith
of the Roman See: *Tenet enim ſancta Sedes
gubernacula regendarum cuncti orbis Eccleſiarum.
That holy ſeat hath the gouernment of all the
Churches of the world* . Which words are
ſo plaine, as Iuell *Art.* 4. *Diu.*21. findeth no
                                          better

better anſwer than (iudging others by his owne humor) to ſay, *That man naturally aduanceth his power at whoſe hands he ſeeketh help.* As if Theodoret were ſuch a man as would giue an Antichriſtian title (for ſo Proteſtants acount the gouernment of the Churches in the world) or S. Leo accept it for flatery. Finally the great Councel of Galcedon *ep. ad Leonem,* calleth Pope Leo their *head,* and ſay that to him. *Vinea cuſtodia a Domino commiſſa eſt. The cuſtodie of the Vinyard* (that is the Church) *was committed by our Lorde.* And thus I hope I haue ſufficiently proued both by reuelation from heauen, by the authoritie of the Church then aliue, and ſince, by the examples of Popes euer ſince S. Peters tyme bv confeſſion of Proteſtants, and finally by reaſon taken out of ſcripture, that S. Greg.

Concil. Calcedon,

had lawful authoritie to ſend S. Auſtin. Now let vs come to S. Auſtins orders.

G   **CHAP.**

CHAP. X.

*That S. Auſtin was rightly ordered
to adminiſter the Sacraments,
and preach the word
of God.*

1. THat S. Auguſtin was created Prieſt
at Rome is euident by his ſaying
Maſſe, preaching, and Chriſtening as ſoone
as he came to Canterburie , as is before
rehearſed out of Beda *lib. 1. cap. 26.* And
after he had conuerted King Ethelbert *he
came* (ſaith Beda *cap. 27.*) *to Arles, where of
Etherius Archbiſhop of that Citty he was conſecrated Archbiſhop of the Nation of Engliſhmen,
according as S. Greg. the Pope had commanded.
And the King* (ſaith the ſame S. Beda *cap. 26.*)
*gaue him place for his See in the Citty of Canter-
burie.* Here by the way I note, that wheras
S. Greg. *lib. 7. epiſt. 30.* ſaith, that S. Auſtin
was created Biſhop *a Germaniarū Epiſcopis,*
he doth not gain-ſay S. Beda, who ſaith
he was created by the Biſhop of Arles,
becauſe France was of the writers of that
tyme called Germanie , as appeareth by
Venantius Fortunatus *in Carmine de Nuptijs
Sigeberti & Brunechilda ,* which might be,
partly

partly becauſe the French at that tyme
and long after gouerned a great part of
Germany, partly alſo becauſe the Francks
who then ruled in France were Germans
come out of Germanie. But to our purpoſe. That S. Auſtin was rightly created
Prieſt appeareth, by that he was made by
the authoritie of S. Gregory, or his predeceſſors, whome proteſtants account to
haue bene true Biſhops of Rome. And
Doct. Reinolds *Confer.* *pag.* 362. acknowledgeth the Pope to haue yet Biſhoply
power ouer his owne Dioceſſe. S. Auſtin
therfore being a Roman, and made by the
Biſhoply authoritie of the Pope, was
rightly made Prieſt. And in lyke ſort it
may be proued that he was rightly conſecrated a Biſhop. For he was made by the
authoritie of the Pope with the conſent
of the King of England. Secondly I proue
that S. Auſtin was lawfully conſecrated
Biſhop by the conſent of the Chriſtian
world. For S. Greg. commanded him to
be made Biſhop, the French Biſhops made
him, the Engliſh Chriſtians receaued him,
and the Eaſt Church, to whome S. Greg.
wrote of the matter, neuer diſliked him,
and all the Chriſtian world hitherto hath
approued him. Nether did the Britons
(though enemyes) take any exceptions
againſt his orders. Thirdly becauſe all

Side notes:
That S. Anſtin vvas rightly ordered.

1

2

3

prote-

proteſtants call S. Auſtin a Biſhop, and number him firſt in the Catalogue of the Archbiſhops of Canterburie. And if their Biſhops and Miniſters will haue any orders at all, they muſt confeſſe that S. Auſtins orders were good, and ſufficient. For as Doct. Feild ſaith, *lib. 3. of the Church cap.* 39. *In England they which had bene Biſhops in the former corrupt ſtate of the Church* (ſo he termeth Catholick tymes) *did ordaine Biſhops and Miniſters.* And Sutclif. anſwer to exceptions *pag.* 88. ſaith. *Couerdal and Scory* (who were Biſhops in King Edwards tyme) *layd hands vpon Biſhop Parker.* Bel in his Funerall profeſſeth openly that he hath not departed from the ſubſtance of his Popiſh orders, but onely from the ceremonies therof. Beſides, euident it is, that what Biſhop or Prieſt ſo euer had bene made in King Henries tyme, was neuer conſecrate a new in King Edwards dayes. Who had bene made in Queene Maries dayes was acounted to haue ſufficient orders in Queene Eliſabeths Reigne. And yet what Prieſt apoſtateth from his faith is, without more orders, thought to haue orders ynough fore miniſtring the Sacraments and word of God, or proteſtants haue no order at all. And thus hauing ſhewed that S. Auſtin was the firſt Preacher of Chriſtian fayth to our

Engliſh

English Nation, and that he had both sufficient learning and vertue to difcharge
fuch a function, and withall lawfull commiſsion and right orders to adminiſter
the Sacraments, and preach the word of
God; now let vs fee what kind of faith
and religion it was, which he preached;
and firſt what kind in generall, and afterward what it was in particuler.

CHAP. XI.

*That the Faith which Saint Auſtin
preached to our English Anceſtors,
was the vniuerſall Faith of
Chriſtendome at that
tyme.*

1. THis I proue firſt by the teſtimony
of thoſe that liued in that tyme, a-
mong whome the cheefeſt and principal
is S. Gregory him selfe, who hauing bene long tyme the Popes Legat in Conſtantinople, and after being Pope and receauing letters from all partes of Chriſtendome, could not be ignorant what
was the vniuerſal faith of Eaſt, Weſt, and
of all Chriſtendome at that time. He I ſay

S. Auſtins
vniuerſal
religion
proued by
S. Greg.

writing

writing to S. Auſtin. *lib.* 9. *Epiſt.* 58. hath

theſe words. *Quis ſufficiat*, &c. *VVho can tel what ioy aroſe in the harts of all the faithfull that the Engliſh nation by the working of Almighty God his grace, and the labor of thy brotherhood, hauing caſt away the darknes of errors, is endued with the light of the holy faith, that with ſincere deuotion it trampleth the Idolls to which before vvith mad feare it bowed vnto, that with a pure hart it is ſubiect to Almightie God.* Behould S. Greg. witneſſeth that all faithfull of that time acknowledged and reioyced that Auſtin brought the faith to our Engliſh Nation, and that they by his meanes ſerued God with moſt ſincere deuotion and pure harts. But yet more plainly auoucheth he this truth, *Moral.* 27. *cap.* 6. Where glorying in God of the conuerſion of England

he writeth thus. *Behould now the faith hath entred the harts almoſt of all Nations. Behould God hath ioyned the bounds of the Eaſt and weſt in one faith. Behould the tonge of Britanie which knew nothing but to roare rudely, of late hath begun in Gods praiſes to ſound out the hebrew Alleluia.*

O moſt comfortable ſpeach to all thoſe that follow S. Gregory and S. Auſtins doctrine, to heare auouched by irrefragable teſtimonie that it was the faith of the Church of God from the Eaſt to the weſt aboue a thouſand yeares agoe. For as Tertullian ſaith. Admit that God had neglected

glected his Church , and permitted it to run into errors, is it lykly that so many and so great Churches would conspire wholy in error ? No surely.

2. The next is S. Austin him self who in Beda *lib.* 2. *cap.* 2. saith thus vnto the Britons . *Although in many other points yow do contrary to our custome , or rather contrary to the custome of the vniuersall Church of Christ .* Behould how he testifyeth his custome to be the custome of the vniuersall Church of Christ in his tyme. And *lib.* 1. *cap.* 27. in his questions proposed to S. Greg. he asketh, *VVhere there is but one faith , whie be there so many sundry customs of Churches, and one custome of Masses obserued at Rome , another in France ?* Here he manefestly testifyeth that there was but one faith and one masse in substance euery where , and the difference onely in ceremonies. The same also may be proued by the communion which S. Gregory (whose faith was vndoubtedly the same with S. Austin) had with all Christendom . For *lib.* 6. *epist.* 4. & 5. he communicateth with Cyriacus the Patriarch of Constantinople *lib.* 4. *epist.* 34. 36. *lib.* 7. *epist.* 30. he communicated with the Patriarch of Alexandria , and gloried to him of the conuersion of England. *lib* 1. *epist.* 25. *lib.* 4. *epist.* 37. *lib.* 6. *epist.* 24. *lib.* 7. *epist.* 3. 47. he communicated with the

S. Austins. Doctrine proued to be vniuersal by his owne testimonie

S. Greg. communicated vvith all partes of Christendom.

Patriarch of Antioch ; vnder which three
Patriarchs was almoſt all the Eaſtern
Church . And touching the Weſtern
Church *lib.* 1. *epiſt.* 4. *lib.* 4. *epiſt.* 46. He
communicated with Leander Primat of
Spaine. *lib.* 4. *epiſt.* 51. He communicated
with Vigilius primate of France. *lib.* 9.
epiſt. 61. he communicated with all the
Catholick Biſhops of Ireland.*lib.2.epiſt.*28.
he communicated with all the Biſhops of
Italy. *lib.* 1. *epiſt.* 60. 61. he communicated
with Ianuarius of Sardinia. *lib.*1. *epiſt.* 68.
he communicated with all the Biſhops in
Sicilie. *lib.* 1. *epiſt.* 76. with Leo Biſhop of
Corſica *lib.*1. *epiſt.*75. with all the Biſhops
of Numidia.*lib.*2.*epiſt.*15.*lib.*3.*epiſt.*16. with
all the Biſhops of Dalmatia.*lib.*10.*epiſt.* 37.
He communicated with all the Biſhop of
Vizach , and *epiſt.*30 . With the Biſhop of
Iſtria. And *lib.*7. *epiſt.* 30. with the Biſhops
of Germanie , and conſequentlie with all
Catholick Churches in the Eaſt and weſt.
  3.Of thoſe that liued after S.Auſtins tyme.
Firſt is S. Wilfrid Archbiſhop of York,
who was borne ſoone after S. Auſtins
death . For as S. Beda ſaith. *lib.* 5. *cap.* 20.
He went vp to Rome in the tyme of Ho‐
norius Archbiſhop of Canterburie who
was one of S. Auſtins fellowes , and he
was as S.Beda ther writeth *a worthie Prelat
and notable Biſhop* . This man therfore in
Beda.

Beda. *lib. 3. cap. 25.* difputing with the Scotts for the Roman obferuation of Eafter and fhauen Crownes, faith thus, *The Eafter which we obferue we haue feene to haue bene in lyke maner obferued in Rome, in all Italie and France.* This maner we know to be *obferued in Africk, in Eegipt, in Afia, in Grece, and throughout all Nations and tongues of the world where the Church of Chrift taketh place, befides thefe few Scotts, and the Picts, and Britons, with whome thefe men do fondly contend againft the whole world.* Behould how S. Wilfrid auoucheth his Religion euen in that point wherein the Scotts then diffented from vs, to be the Religion of all the Chriftian world. Nether did the Scotts, or could they deny it. The next is S. Ceolfrid S.Ceolfrid Abbot, and Maifter to S. Beda, who liued in the fame tyme, who writing to Naitan King of the Picts in Beda. *lib. 5. cap. 22.* and fpeaking of his tyme faith : *The whole Catholick Church agreeth in one faith, in one hope, and one charitie towards God.* The third is S. Beda him felf who, *lib. 2. cap. 2.* faith, S. Beda. *The Britons preferred their own Traditions before all other Churches, which throughout the whole world agreed with Auftin in Chrift.* What I pray can be fayd or imagined againft thefe fo manifould or irrefragable teftimonies. Were S. Gregory, S. Auftin, S. Wilfrid, S. Ceolfrid, S. Beda ignorant what was

the

the vniuersall faith of Christendome at
that tyme? or were they so impudent as
they would write, yea auouch to their
aduersaries face a knowne vntruth? No
surely. And this truth Protestants also
partly openly confesse, partly tacitly grant
and acknowledg. For Napier vpon the
Reuelation of S. Iohn, saith. *Betwene the
yeare of Christ* 300. *and* 316. *the Antichristian
and Papisticall Religion reigning vniuersally
without debatable contradiction* 1260. *yeares.*
And Brocard also vpon the Reuelation
pag. 110. writeth that *the Church (*of Protestants) *was troden downe and oppressed by the
Papacy euen from Siluesters tyme vnto these times.*
Bale cent. 1. *pag.* 69. saith. *From this tyme (*of
Boniface 3. who succeeded S. Greg. with
in a yeare or two) *the puritie of heauenly
doctrine vanished in the Church. pag.* 65. *After
Greg. tyme puritie of doctrine perished*, And 73.
From Phocas who liued in S. Greg. tyme *who
(*saith he) *begot the Papacy till the renewing of
the Gospel (*by Luther) *the doctrine of Christ was
all the while among Idiots in holes.* Now if the
heauenly doctrine of protestants perished
straight after S. Greg. tyme, and euer since
hath bene onely in Idiots, and lurking
holes, how could it be the vniuersall faith
of all Christendome in his tyme? Could
the vniuersall faith of Christendome
perish in one or two yeares? Would
all

See more
infr. *lib.* 2.
cap. 3.

all learned men, and open Churches forfake it in fo fhort time, and onely Idiots
and holes keepe it ? See more of this
matter *lib. 2. cap. 1. infra.*

CHAP. XII.

That the doctrine vvhich Auſtin taught vvas the true vvay to faluation.

Proued by the open confeßion of his Aduerſaries, and other things affirmed by them.

1. THe firſt aduerſaries which S. Auſtin
had to his doctrine were the Britons before mentioned. Of whone S. Beda
l. 2. cap. 2. writeth that S. Auſtin hauing
cured a blind man whome they could not,
The people praiſed S. Auſtin as a true preacher of
all truth and veritie ; And the Britons confeſſed
indeed that they vnderſtood that to be the true way
of righteouſnes, which Auſtin had preached, and
ſhewed to them. The fame writeth Huntington *lib. 3.* Stow Chron. *pag.* 66. and others.
And albeit his preaching to them, then
tooke not that effect, which he intended,
                                                    yet

Britons
approue
S. Auſtins
doctrine.

yet if Fox fay true *lib. 2. pag. 123.* that *in
Ina his time began the right obseruing of Eafter
day to be kept of the Picts and of the Britons,*with
in fhort tyme the whole Nation not onely
approued, but alfo admitted S. Auftins
doctrine. Yea if it be true that Godwin
writeth in vit. Theod. *That to him all the
British Bishops, and generally all Britany yeelded
obedience, and vnder him conformed them felues
in all things to the rites and difciplin of the Church
of Rome,*they performed this longe before,
about 60. yeares after S. Auftin.

Proteſtãts account S. Auſtins doctrin fufficient to faluation.

2. The next open Aduerfaries of Saint
Auftins doctrine in England haue bene
the Proteftants; Of whome, diuers haue
in their writings openly acknowledged
as much as the Britons did. For Iuel in

Iuel.

his famous challeng, offered to recant if
any of the holy Fathers who liued in the
firft 600. yeares after Chrift were found
contrarie to him in his Articles. In which
compaffe of yeares both S. Greg. and S.
Auftin liued . And cryed out faying, *O
Gregorie, O Auftin &c . If we be deceaued yow*

Fulk.

haue deceaued vs . Fulk in 1. Cor. 15. *Seeing
Gregorie and Auftin,* (faith he) *taught the truth
in all points neceffarie to faluation , our Contrie
hath not beleeued in vaine, nor all our fore Fathers*

Fox.

are dead in their finnes. Fox in his Acts *pag.*111.
120.122. Calleth the faith planted here by
Auftin and his fellow-laborers *the Chriſtian
faith*

faith. p. 115. 116. *the faith and doctrine of Christ.*
pag. 121. *Christs Religion,* and that Church, *the*
Church of Christ. And *pag.* 112. *The perfect faith*
of Christ. Bishop Cooper Chron. Anno. 636. Cooper.
calleth it, *the right beleefe* . Stow Chron. Stow.
pag. 9. calleth it *the Christian faith.* And *pag.*
72. *pure and incorupted Christianitie.* Cambden Cambden
in descript. Britan. *pag.* 519. *The true Religion*
of Christ. Apologie for the oath of allea- Godwin.
geance , *The faith of Christ* . Godwin in
Paulin. *The Gospel* ; And in Mellit. *The faith*
of Christ . Holinshed in Brit . *The Christian* Holins
faith . *The faith of Christ* . *The word of God.* head.
Bilson of Obed. part. 1. *pag.* 57. calleth it Bilson.
Religion to God. Sutclif Subuers. *cap.* 3. ter- Sutclif.
meth it *Faith, Religion, Christian Religion ,* and
saith the people *were conuerted to Christ,*
Finally Fox *lib.* 2. *pag.* 124. after he had Fox.
tould in particuler how euery one of those
seauen Kingdoms which then were in
England, was conuerted, cohcludeth thus;
And thus by processe of tyme we haue discoursed
from tyme to tyme, how and by what meanes the
Idolatrous people were induced to the true fayth of
Christ . And who considereth with him
selfe, that not onely our Catholick English
Ancestors imbraced the doctrine of S.
Austin, but also the erroneous Britons, and
Protestants account it the *true way of*
righteousnes, the Gospel, the Faith of Christ . *The*
perfect faith of Christ, the right beleefe , the true
Religion

Religion of Chrift, pure and incorrupt Chriftianitie, and finally *true faith of Chrift* , neede feeke no more , but what S. Auftins faith was, and follow it. To thofe that grant that S. Auftins faith was the true way to faluaiion, I might adde alfo the Proteftants, who affirme the fame of the prefent Romã faith, whofe teftimonies yow may fee in the Apologie of Proteftants Tract. 1. Sec. 6. Onely I will content my felfe with his Maiefties wordes to the parlament 9. of Nouember An. 1605. put forth in print thus: *VVee do iuftly confeffe that many Papifts efpecially our Forfathers laying their onely truft vpon Chrift and his meritts* (as they them felues teache in Bellarm.) *may be and often tymes are faued , deteftinge in that point and thinking the crueltie of Puritans worthy of fyer that will admit no faluation to any Papift.*

3. Befids this open confefsion of diuers Proteftants for the truth of S. Auftins Religion, it may be alfo conuinced out of diuers other things which them felues teach. For it being fuppofed out of Gods word heb. 11 that without the right faith it is impofsible to pleafe God: and withall confeffed of diuers Proteftants that S. Auftin and his fellowes were holy men, it neceffarily followeth that his faith was the true faith of God. Of S. Auftins holines, & the Englifh people in general fome thing

thing hath bene sayd before . Of others
Fox *lib .2. pag. 123.* saith *Cutbert Iaruman,* S. Cutbert
Cedda and *VVilfrid I iudge* (saith he) *to be of a*
holy conuersation. pag. 125. Aldelm a worthie and S. Aldelm,
learned Bishop, of notable praise for his learning
and vertue. Ibid. he calleth S. Iohn of Be- s. Iohn
uerly and S. Egwin *Saints. pag.* 127. Tou- Beuerly.
ching the integrite and holines of Bedas S. Beda.
life. *It is not to be doubted, with great comfort of*
his spirit he departed this life. pag. 128. He
intituleth S. Boniface a Martyr of God. S. Boni-
And yet *pag .129. calleth him a great setter vp* face.
and vphoulder of Popery. pag. 112. calleth S. Edmōd.
king Edmond three tymes *Saint.* Item *pag.*
121. *King Oswald a Saint* (saith he) *had great* S. Osvvald
vertues, and by prayer ouercame his enemies.
Cooper Chron. an. 636. calleth Birin
Saint an. 643. *O swald a holy king.* 869. *holy*
king Edmond. Stow Chron. pag. 78. *Cedda a*
holy man. Iaruman a Bishop of great vertue. Ibid
King Sebbi, *very deuout and godly. pag.* 81.
Kinesburg and Kineswith for holy conuersation
excelling. pag. 99. Cutbert *Saint. Bale cent.* 1.
cap. 76. saith of S. Aidan , that *he was a*
man of most innocent life and ful of the spirit of
God , and yet was Oswald his scholler a
manifest Papist, praying before crosses
and for the dead, euen when him selfe was
redy to dye. ex Bed. *lib. 3. cap. 2. &* 12. The
same Bale cent 1. *cap.* 83. saith, that Aldelm
went happilie to Christ , and yet withal confesseth

feſſeth that he wrote *for ſhauen crownes after*
the Roman maner, feaſts of Saints, ſingle lyfe, and
ſuch things, and was long tyme familiar with P.

S.Ceolfrid *Sergius.*cent 1. *cap.* 93. He calleth Ceolfrid,
S.VVille- Beda, Willebrora, Boniface and the like
brord. *moſt holy monkes*, And addeth cent. 2. *cap.* 1.
that Beda *had a moſt happie end* ; And yet
the ſame man ſaith of Boniface *pag.* 79.
that *he brought the Germans to Papiſme*: and
pag. 103 . *VVas the next to the Pope the greate*
Antichriſt, and ſigned a hundred thouſand men in
Bauaria with the Popes mark . And cent. 2.
cap. 5. writeth that Willebrord *preached*
Papiſtrie. Of S. Beda he ſaith cent. 2. *cap.* 1.
That *he can not be excuſed from all ſuperſtitious*
doctrine . And in the ſame place ſaith that
Ceolfrid *vſed the new ordinations of the Roman*
*ſuperſtition.*And that he was a plaine Papiſt
appeareth by his epiſtle in Beda *lib.* 5.
cap. 22. where he teacheth *one ſacrifice of the*
bodie of Chriſt, rounde ſhauing of Monks, Calleth
Peter *head and Primat of the Apoſtles* . Whervpon Fox *lib.* 2. *pag.* 126. termeth him *a*
*ſhaueling,*condemneth him for calling *Peter*
a Mediator , and termeth it *a Monkish epiſtle,*
And in lyke ſort Bale ſpeaketh of diuers
S.Hilda. others. For cent 1. *cap.* 94. he ſaith:S.Hilda
Abbeſſe *was a moſt holy woman* , Ibid. *Iohn of*
Beuerly a man very learned and pious, accounted
it moſt ſweet to preach Chriſts Goſpel out of the
Pulpit , and ended his life in great conſtancie of
Exan-

gelical spirit. And *cent.2. cap. 1.* Calleth him
a most holy prelat. Cambden also Descrip:
Britan.*pag.*518. Calleth S. Werburg *Saint.*   S. VVer-
pag. 526. *S. Milburg a most holy virgin.* p. 612.   burg.
King Oswald *Saint* and *pag.* 150. *Lhat that*   S.Botulph
*age was most fruitful of Saints. pag.*473. Botulph
most holy. And *pag.* 472. *Guthlac lead his life in
great holines* . This by the confession of
Protestants was the fruit of S. Austins
religion . And if it be true, (as most true it
is which our Sauiour said) that we can
not gather grapes of thornes nor figges of
brambles : And if it be true that vertue
springeth not out of the Diuels seede, nor
Saints out of his Religion; Sure it is also,
that S. Austins Religion came not from
the Diuel but from God. Can any man of
sense thinke that so great sanctitie can
stand with ignorance of the true way to
saluation ? With ignorance of the true
worship of God ? That men become
Saints and attain to heauen by Religion
of Diuels? Are Diuels so bountiful to men,
as they will teach them the waye to
heauen? Or haue they such skil as they can
inuent new wayes to heauen besides the
way that Christ taught? And this for the
vertue of S. Austins followers ; Now let
vs see what account Protestants make of
the learning of some of them.

4. That we may be assured that it was
                              H   not

That our Ancestors follovved not S. Austin vpon ignorance

S. Aldelm.

not ignorance which made our Ancestors imbrace S. Austins doctrine, S. Aldelm, Bale saith *cent.* 1. *cap.* 83. *Did so studie both Deuine, and Human learning, that he far passed all the Deuines of his tyme, most learned in Greeke, and Latin, in Verse, and Prose, and cleare in wit and speeche.* Fox Acts 125. saith, *he was a learned Bishop of worthy praise for his learning.* Cambd. *Descript. Brit.* 210. saith, *he was surely worthie that his memorie should remain for euer. For he was the first Englishman that wrote in Latin, and first that taught Englishmen to make Latin Verses.* Godwin *in Vit. Aldelm. He became Very learned, in Poetrie excellent, and writ much in Greek and Latin, Prose and Verse, but his cheefe studie was Deuinitie, in the which no man of his tyme was comparable vnto him.* And yet to assure vs also of his Religion *lib.cit.* affirmeth, that *he wrote at the commandement of Monks for shauing and anointing of Priests, for feasts of Saints, and single life, and other,* (saith he) *new rites, and that he had great familiaritie with Pope Sergius.* And *cent.* 14. *cap.* 26. saith, that Maidulph maister of S. Aldelm was *sullied with Papistical blemish,* and was *a most eager defender of the Roman constitutions.* And yet the same Maidulph, (saith Cambden Brit: *pag.* 210,) *was of great learning and singuler pietie.* Of S. Beda Bale *cent.* 2. *cap.* 1. giueth this testimonie. *He was so practised in Prophane writers that he scarce had*

had his match in that age, he learnt Phisick, and Metaphisick out of the purest fountains. He knew the misteries of the Christian faith so soundly, (note)*that for his exact knowledg both of Greeke and Latin many preferred him before Gregorie the Great. There is scarce any thing worth reading to be found in all Antiquitie which in due places is not read in Beda. If he had liued in the tymes of Austin, Hierom, Chrisostom; I doubt not but he might haue contended for equalitie with them. He put forth many bookes ful of all kind of learning.* Thus Bale of S. Beda: and in like sort Fox Acts. *pag.*127. saith, *he was a man of worthy and memorable memory and famous learning,* The whole Latin Church *at that tyme gaue him the maistry in iudgement, and knowledg of the holy scripture.* Stow Chron. pag. 93. *Beda a famous learned man.* Cooper Chron. *An.* 729. *Beda for his learning and godly life was renowned in all the world.* Bel in his Downfal *Beda for vertue and learning renowned in all the world.* Cambden. Brit. pag. 670. *Bede the singuler glorie of England, by pietie and erudition obtained the name of venerable, wrote manie volumes, most learnedly.* And yet how plaine a Papist S. Beda was shalbe shewed both by his owne doctrine, and by open confession of Protestants *cap.* 17.

5. The third wherof I will speake is Alcuin scholler to S. Beda, but maister to Charles the great. Of whome. Bale cent.2

Alcuin.

H 2   *cap.* 17.

§. 17. *VVriteth thus. He was thought by far the most learned Diuine of his age, yea of all English men from the beginning after Aldelm and Beda, in so much that he was maister to Charles the great, and the first beginner of the Vniuersitie of Paris, skilful in Latin, Greeke, and Hebrew.* Cambd. in Brit: *pag.* 629. Calleth him *the onely glorie of York.* And yet who readeth this Alcuins booke *de Diuinis Officijs* shall clearly see that he, and our Contry then was as perfect Papists as any now are . For there heshal finde all our Ceremonies at Baptisin of exsufflation, exorcising, of salt , Chrisme,

Our An-cestors. vsed all our pre-sent Cath. Ceremo-nies in baptisme.

and the lyke. Our three Masses on christ-masse day, Our Candlels on Candlemasse day, Our Ceremonies in the holy weeke of keeping the Sepulcher, hallowing the font, putting out all the candels but one. Ther he shall see our seauen orders , our attire of Bishops at masse, our Transub-stantiation, our Extreme Vnction , and that acounted a Sacramét, our Confession of all our sinnes , our singing Masse , and praying for the dead. These, to omit in-numerable more, confessed in lyke máner by Protestáts to haue bene great schollers, and profound Diuines , shew that it was not ignorance or want of knowledg which made our Forfathers to follow S. Austins doctrin, nor that the Protestants learned men haue by their learning dif-

couered

couered in it errors, as they call them. For
whome haue they had comparable to
any of thefe in learning, and induſtry
whome of their owne haue they ſo much
commended as they haue done thefe ? Let
any Proteſtant deſirous of truth take
Tindal, Latimer, Ridley (whome they
terme the Apoſtles of England) and conſider whither in learning, or vertue they
be comparable to thefe three. And then
iudge with indifferency on whofe ſide
truth is moſt lykely to ſtand. For all reaſon
teacheth that they are moſt lykely to find
truth, who abounded with moſt learning
to ſearch it, and were indued with moſt
vertue to haue it from God. What reaſonable man then is ther that forſaking the
Doctrine of S. Aldelm , S. Beda , and
Alcuin, whome not onely wee, but very
Proteſtants confeſſe to haue bene moſt
induſtrious to finde truth, moſt ſkilful to
diſcerne it, and moſt vertuous to deſerue
to haue it taught of God , will follow
Tindal, Latimer, Ridley, whofe learning
by the iudgment of Catholiques was very
meane , and their life very vicious; and
by the iudgement of their own men are
but meanly commended either for good
life, or good learning.

*Compa-
riſon of
Proteſt:
learned
men
without*

CHAP. XIII.

That the Doctrine which S. Austin preached he sealed and confirmed by true miracles.

Hovv manie kindes of proofes for S. Austins miracles.

1. THat Saint Austin confirmed his doctrine by miracles, I will proue. First by the testimony of those who liued in his tyme, secondly by the testimony of those that liued soone after, and lastly by

VVitnesses then liuing.
the plain confession of Protestants. Of those that liued in his tyme, first is S. Gre-

S. Gregorie.
gory who writing to Eulogius Patriarch of Alexandria *lib. 7. epist. 30.* saith. *Both he (Austin) and they, vvho vvere sent vvith him shine vvith so great miracles in that* (English) *Nation, that they may seeme to imitat the vertues of the Apostles by the miracles, vvhich they vvorke.* And *lib. 9. epist. 56.* writing to the Queene of France saith. *VVhat and hovv great miracles*

The Q. of France knevv that our nation vvas conuerted by great miracles.
our Redeemer hath vvrought in the conuersion of the forsaid (English) *Nation, yt is alredy knovvn vnto your Excellency.* And can any man thinck that this great Doctor would write to a Queene of France that she knew what miracles were done in England, if they
were

were not manifest, and out of all doubt? And *lib. 9. epist.* 58. writing to S. Austin him selfe he saith. *Reioice that English mens soules are by outvvard miracles dravvne to invvard grace.* Ib. *Diligently discusse thy self, vvho thou arte, and hovv great the grace is in that Nation, for whose conuersion thou hast receaued the gift of miracles.* And *lib.* 27. *Moral.. cap.* 6. *VVheras by good precepts, and heauenly words, yea with manifest miracles too, the grace and knowledg of God is powred into it* (English harts) &c. *By which words* (saith S. Beda *lib.* 2. *cap.* 1.) *this holy Father doth declare that Austin and his company brought the English men to the knowledg of truth, not onely by preaching to them in word but also by shewing them heauenly signes and miracles.*

2. The second testimonie is the publick Epitaph which the English men set vpon S. Austins Tombe after his death in these wordes. *Here resteth the body of S. Austin first Bishop of Dorobernia, that was sent into this Land by S. Gregorie Bishop of the Cittie of Rome, approued of God by the vvorking of miracles, and brought Ethelbert and his people from the vvorshiping of Idolls vnto the Faith of Christ.* The third testimonie of those that liued in S. Austins tyme, are the Britons, who by the miraculous cure of a blind man, wrought by S. Austin in their sight were compelled to confesse (as S. Beda saith, *lib.* 2. *cap.* 2.)

S. Austins Epitaph.

The Britons.

H 4 *that*

that to be the true vvay of righteousnes, vvhich
S. Auſtin preached . And this teſtimony is
much to be regarded, for it is the teſtimonie of many, of enemyes, of eye witneſſes,
and of thoſe *among vvhome* (ſaith S. Beda
lib. 2. cap. 2.) vvere plures viri doctiſſimi. So they
can be no way ſuſpected ether of partia-
litie, being enemies, or of inſufficiencie
being many and preſent, and through
their learning moſt able to iudg . Cambden alſo citeth a peece of a Hiſtorie,
written (as he ſaith) in that time, which
recordeth that S. Auſtin hauing bleſſed
the Riuer Swale, and apointed that of ten
thouſand men (beſides weomen and
children) twoe and twoe ſhould goe in,
and Chriſten eche other, beſides that
none periſhed in ſo deepe a water, this
miracle alſo happened, that all ſicknes and
deformitie was cured by that Chriſtening.
3. After S. Auſtins tyme liued S. Beda who
lib. 1. cap. 26. writeth. *The King being much
delighted vvith the puritie of their life* (S. Auſtin
and his fellowes) *and the example of their
godly conuerſation , as alſo vvith their ſvveet pro-
miſes, vvhich they proued to be true by the vvorking
of miracles, did beleeue and i vas baptized.* And
lib. 2. cap. 2. he reporteth the Prophecie of
S. Auſtin of the deſtruction of the Britons
for their obſtinacie , and the euent
anſwered therto after his death. Which is
ſo ſure

VVhy the teſtimo-
nie of the Britons for S. Auſtins mi-
racles is much to be regarded.

An vnna-
med Au-
thor of S.
Auſtins time.

Great mi-
racles.

VVitneſſes of S. Au-
ſtins mi-
racles af-
ter his tyme.

S. Beda.

ſo ſure a token of diuine reuelation as the
Prophet Eſay. *cap.* 41. ſaith, *Tel vs vvhat things
are to come herafter, and vve ſhall knovv that yovv
are Gods*. The like prophetical knowledg
of things paſt is attributed to S. Paulin,
one of S. Auſtins fellowes, by him *lib.* 2.
cap. 12. and Godwin in vita Paulini, Fox
Acts *pag.* 121, Holinſhed *pag.* 108. and others.
Likwiſe *lib.* 2. *cap.* 6. He recounteth the
miraculous ſcourging of S. Laurence
ſucceſſor to S. Auſtin by S. Peter for in-
tending to abandon our Contrie, vpon
the reuolt rherof to Paganiſme. Which
miracle is conteſted alſo by our cheefeſt
hiſtoriographers Malmsbury *lib.* 1. Reg. and
lib. 2. Pont. Huntington *lib.* 3. Marian. an.
617. Weſtmon. an. 616. Florent. an. 616.
and confeſſed by ſome proteſtants, as
Godwin in vit. Laurentij, and Holinſhed
pag. 158. In like manner *lib.* 2. *cap.* 33. Beda
telleth how Peter a companion of S.
Auſtin being drowned, *Our Lord* (ſaith he)
*made that euery night there appeared a light
from heauen vpon the place vvhere he lay buried.* Ethel-
After S. Beda liued Ethelwerd who *lib.* 2. vverd.
cap. 1. writeth. *That by the prayers of S. Auſtin
Biſhop our Sauiour Ieſus Chriſt ſheweth innumerable miracles to his faithful, at whoſe Tombe vnto
this day no ſmall miracles are wrought.* To theſe Malmesb.
witneſſes we may ad Malmſb. *lib.* 1. Pont. Huntingt.
Hunting *l.* 3. weſtmō. an. 603. and Capgraue Capgraue.
vveſtmon.
H 5   alſo

also, who in the life of S. Auſtin writeth.
That there were none or few in S. Auſtins company
who had not the gift of curing , that they lightned
the darknes of the heathens no leſſe by miracles,
than by preaching . And he addeth that S.
Auſtin *cured all the weak and ſick that were*
brought vnto him, or viſited of him.

Proteſtāts
confeſſe S.   4. Thirdly amongſt proteſtants Fox *lib.* 2.
Auſtins
miracles.   *pag.* 116. writeth that *when the King had wel*
conſidered the honeſt conuerſation of their (Auſtin

Fox.   and his fellowes) *life, and mooued by the mira-*
cles wrought through Gods hand by them, and in
the margent putteth this note , (*Miracles*
vvrought by God for the conuerſion of this land)
he heard than more gladly. pag. 118. he mentioneth S. Gregories letter teſtifying Saint
Auſtins miracles, and *pag.* 119. he ſaith that
Beda, Ceſtrenſis, Huntington, Iornalenſis,
and Fabia teſtifie the forſaid miracle of
Godvvin. the blind man . Godwin in the life of S.
Dauid, *I doubt not but God aſſoarded many mira-*
cles to the firſt infancie of our Church . *Nether*
therfor would I be to peremptory in derogating to
much from ſuch reports as we ſee no reaſon why
they may not be true . And in the life of S.
Auſtin . *Auſtin wrought a miracle by healing a*
blind man for confirmation of his doctrine.
Holinſhed *in Deſcript. Brit*. *King Ethelbert*
was perſuaded by the good example of S. Auſtin
and his company , and for many miracles ſhevved,
to be baptized. And *pag.* 602. *Auſtin to proue his*
                                                                          opinion

opinion good, vvrought a miracle by restoring to sight one of the Saxon Nation that vvas blinde.
And the same miracle acknowledgeth Stow Chron. *pag.* 66. and of forrein Protestants Hemingius *in expofit. psal.* 84. *parte* 1. *cap.* 6.

Stovv.

Hemingius.

5. Concerning the witnesses which I haue produced to testifie that S. Austin wrought these things which wee call miracles, I would haue the Reader to consider, first that some of them were then liuing, as S. Greg. the Britons, and Authors of the Epitaph. Others liued after as the rest. Secondly, some were forrein as S. Greg. others Domestical in England. Thirdly some are publick as the Epitaph, others priuat. Fourtly some were enemyes to S. Austin as the Britons, the others, freinds. Fiftly, some were great Clercks as S. Greg. S. Beda, and some of the Britons, who by their learning could iudg of the miracles; others of lesse account. Sixtly some were great Saints, as S. Greg. and S. Beda were, who would not deliuer an vntruth, or vncertain fables for true and certain miracles; others of meaner qualities. Seuenthly some were eye witnesses, as the Britons (and they enemyes too who would finde what falt they could) and the authors of the Epitaph; others by report. Lastly some are Catholicks, some Protestants.

The qualities of the sayd vvitnesses for S. Austins miracles.

1
2
3
4
5

6

7

8

ſtants. And what greater variety of teſtimonies, or better qualified witneſſes,
would we aſke to beleeue a thing than
theſe be?

6. This great weight and varietie of
witneſſes we haue to beleeue that S.
Auſtin did theſe things which are
accounted miracles, wether they be true
or falſe, which we ſhall ſee anon. And to
the contrary ther is no Author, forrain or
Domeſtical; eye witneſſe or other; freind
or foe; Catholick or Proteſtant, before our
daies: nor any reaſon at all beſides that
which Fulk Anotat. in Io.14. giueth againſt
S. Auſtins miracles, and Fox *lib.* 2. *pag.* 122.
againſt other miracles. vz. *That they are not
in ſcripture : therfor they are not bound to beleeue
them.* As if God were bound to write all
the miracles, which he worketh, or we
not bound to beleeue with human faith
(of which alone we ſpeak in this matter)
that which is auouched by ſo ſufficient
human authoritie, as we can take no iuſt
exception againſt it, either for ſkil to know
the truth, or for will to ſpeake it. If not,
then farwel all human beleefe, which can
require no more than ſo ſufficient human
authoritie, farwel all human authoritie,
which can affoard no greater certaintie;
farwel all human conuerſation, which
can not ſtand without the beleefe of ſuch
autho-

No author before our Daies nor reaſon againſt S. Auſtins miracles.

Se more of this in the preface to the Reader ſup.

vve bound to beleeve vvith humane faith vvhat is deleeuered vvith ſufficient authoritie.

Inconueniences of not beleeving humane authoritie.

authoritie, and let vs beleeue nothing but what God hath written or our felues haue feene. Let vs not beleeue any Records or Hiftories of times paft, no that euer there was fuch a man as S. Auftin. And for times prefent, let vs beleeue no Iurie, nothing done in far Contries, nothing done out of our prefence, no not that fuch were our parents, becaufe none of thefe are written in Gods word, but are deliuered to vs by human authoritie, to which (as they fay) we are not bound to giue credit. Thus yow fee to what inconueniences this kind of fenfles reafon would lead vs, if we fhould follow it in other lyke matters. But befides, it is fond in it felfe, for it is taken from negatiue authoritie : *which kind of argument* (faith Iuel Art. 2. Diu. 13.) *Vnles it be in confideration of fome other circumftance is fo fimple as that a verie child may foone anfwer it.* And iuftly, for negatiue authoritie is no authoritie, and filence no witneffe. Whervpon the law faith. *Qui mutum exhibet nihil exhibet* ; efpecially when the filence is of fuch which had no caufe to fpeake of the matter, as the fcripture had none to fortel S. Auftins miracles. And therfor to argue from fuch negatiue authoritie is to argue from noe authoritie and to feeme to vfe reafon, when indeed ther is none. For who would fuffer a

See S. Auft. *lib. de vtil cred. cap.* 12.

Negatiue authoritie no authoritie.

Male-

Malefactor, against whome many honest men haue deposed, to clear him selfe because diuers standers by say no thing against him? Would their silence, which in any mans iudgment maketh no more for him than against him, be preferred before the depositions of diuers witnesses *omni exceptione maiores*? And so, besids that the scripture was written many hunderd yeares before S. Austin was borne and therfor could not speak of his miracles but by prophecie, the silence therof in his miracles maketh no more against them than for them. For as it affirmeth them not, so nether doth it denie them. And therfor as Fulk argueth; The scripture affirmeth not S. Austins miracles;therfor they were not. An other might with as good reason say. The scripture denieth them not;therfor they were. But leaueth them to the authoritie and credit of those that report them. Which (as hath bene shewed) is as great as can be required to human beleefe: and therfor bindeth vs to giue human

S. Austin. credit vnto them. For as S. Austin said wel *lib. de vtil. cred. cap.* 16. *It is miserable to be deceaued by authoritie, but most miserable not to*

A part of *be moued by it.* Because to be deceaued ether beasts not by probable reason,or sufficient authoritie to be mo- ved vvith is a thing incident to man. But not to be authoritie. moued with conuincent reaion, or such

suffi-

sufficient authoritie, as no iust exception can be taken against it, hauing no reason or authoritie to the contrarie, is the part of a beaste vncapable of reason, or authoritie.

7. For this cause, perhaps some will grant that S. Austin did these things, which are reported of him, but yet will say, that they are not true miracles, but false, such as may be done by nature, arte, or the Diuels helpe. But against these I oppose. First that they say this without the authoritie of any ancient writter at all or any other before our dayes. Secondly they say it without any reason taken from the miracles them selues. For the sudden cure of a blinde person, whome the Britons could not cure, what suspition giueth it of a false miracle? That he was blind the Britons saw, that they could not cure him, them selues experienced. Thirdly I oppose the manes wherby S. Austin cured him, which was as Beda testifieth *lib.* 2. *cap.* 2. *By prayer to the Father of our lord Iesus Christ, beseeching that he would restore light to the blind person that by corporal illumination, and lightning of one man his spiritual grace might kindle many.* Which meane of prayer to God, is quite opposit to the working of false miracles, which is by calling vpon the Diuel. Fourthly I oppose the ende for which most

That S. Austins miracles vvere true miracles.

1
See Alan. Copus Dial. 5. cap. 18.

2

3

4

moſt of S. Auſtins miracles were done, which was to draw Pagans from Infidelitie to Chriſtianitie, and from vice to vertue, as the effect did ſhew. But the Diuel would do no thing(and much leſſe a miracle) to draw men from Infidelitie, and vice to which he enticeth them all he can; or to Chriſtianitie and vertue, from which he driueth them by all meanes that in him lyeth. Therfor S. Auſtins miracles came not from the Diuel. And this trial of miracles by the end of them proteſtants allow as the true touchſtone to try them by. As Fox Acts *pag.* 351. where he crediteth the miracle wrought in the king of Tartaria his child, which when it was born was vgly and deformed, and being Chriſtened became faire and bewtifull. *Becauſe* (ſaith he) *it ſerued to the conuerſion to the Chriſtian faith, to which vſe properly all true miracles do apertain.* And yet that faith to which that King was brought, and for which that miracle was wrought was Papiſtical as Bale granteth *cent.* 4. *pag.* 303.

5   8. Fiftly I oppoſe the admirable, and by Proteſtants confeſſed holines of Saint Auſtin and his fellowes. What affinitie or commerce had ſuch great vertue with the Diuel; From which how far he was, ſo far was he from working thoſe miracles

cles. which Auftin and thofe vertuous men did. Sixtly I oppofe the iudgment of 6 S. Gregorie, Beda, and other learned, and holy men hitherto who accounted them for true miracles. Who if learning, or vertue can defcrie falfe miracles, were as like to defcrie them as any now liuing. yea better, becaufe many of them were prefent, and might confider many circun-ftances, which might help them to finde out the truth, which now we do not know. Seuenthly I oppofe the iudgment 7 of the Britons amongft whome ther were as S. Beda faith, *plures viri doctiſſimi*, and who all were oppofit to S. Auftin, and therfor they wanted nether fkil, nor wil to difcouer the falfitie of his miracles, if any had bene. Laftly I oppofe the confef- 8 fion of the fornamed Proteftants, who hauing duly confidered all circunftances, haue not onely iudged, but confeffed, written, and fubfcribed that S. Auftins miracles were true miracles *wrought* (as Fox fpeaketh) *through the hand of God.*

9. For this, perchance, fome may be perfwaded to confeffe that both S. Auftin wrought thefe wonderous things which are recorded of him, and alfo that they be true miracles, and yet may fay as Fulk doth Annot. in *Marc.* 9. *That Hereticks may work miracles to confirm their erroneous opinions.*

That a miracle can not be vvrought to confirme an vntruth.

I   That

That is direct blasphemie against God.
For a miracle can not be wrought but by
God his diuine power , who vseth it as a
seal to confirm his Doctrin with . Whervpon S. Paul. 1. *cor*. 12. called miracles
signes of his Apostleship, And *marc*.16. they are
called *confirmations from God* , and our
Sauiour Io. 5.*calleth them a greater testimonie
than S. Iohn Baptist*. And biddeth the Iewes
if they will not beleeue him , beleeue his
miraculous works. And S. Austin *lib. de
vtil. cred. cap.* 14.saith , that Christ *by miracles got authoritie , by authoritie deserued credit,
by credit gathered multitudes , by multitude got
antiquitie , by antiquitie strengthned Religion*.
Certain it is therfor , that as God can not
contest, or confirme a lye, so he can not
with hereticks cooperat to a miracle to
confirme their erronious opinion. Wherfor as our Sauiour sayd to the Iewes . If
I cast out Deuils in the finger of God
suerly the Kingdom of God is come
amongst yow . So might S. Austin say,
if I by the finger of God work miracles,
surely the Kingdome of God is come
amongst yow.

10. The last euasion which any Protestant can finde why he should not beleeue
the doctrine of S. Austin confirmed of
him by true miracles , is that which Fulk
also giueth 2. *cor*. 12. To wit : *that we are*

not

not certain whither his miracles were to confirme
any of that corruption which he brought in. To
which I reply, that this is but a gheſſe of
a diſtruſtful mind . For who tould him
that S. Auſtin wrought no miracles for
confirmation of that which he accounteth
corruption. Secondly that God in conuerſion of Infidels vſeth not to work
miracles for confirma.ion of euery Article
of faith, but to authorize the Preacher for
a true meſſenger of God, and the faith
and Religion which he teacheth for his
diuine truth and way of ſaluation . And
this Saint Auſtins miracles did proue
ſufficiently, and it is all wee ſeeke. Thirdly
I ſay that S. Auſtin wrought a miracle to
confirm that which Proteſtants now
account corruption . For the ende for
which he cured the blind man in the
ſight of the Britons, was as S. Beda ſaith
*lib.2.cap.2.*that they ſhould conforme them
ſelues to the holy Roman Church,
namely in adminiſtring of baptiſme . But
the maner of adminiſtring of baptiſme
which S. Auſtin exhorted the Britons
to, was vndoubtedly the ſame which his
maiſter S. Gregor. *lib.de Sacrament.* and our
ancient Contreyman Alcuin *lib. de diuinis*
offic. deſcribe , which Catholicks now
vſe, and Proteſtants reiect , to wit , beſids
baptiſing with water , to exorcize the

1

2

3

child, and to breath in his face , to make the figne of the Croffe in the childs forhead, and breft, to put falt into his mouth, and to touch his noftrels and eares with fpitle , and to anoint him betwene the fhoulders . Surly thefe things confidered, me thinks S. Auftin may fay to vs as Saint Paul did to the Theffalonians . *My Goſpel was not to yow in ſpeech onely , but in veritie and in the holy Ghoſt , and in much plentie.* And that our Anceſtors and we may fay with the great Doctor Richard de S. Victore . *The things which we beleeue were confirmed with ſo many, ſo great, ſo wonderful miracles, that it may ſeeme a kind of madnes any way to doubt of them. I would the Iewes* (Proteftants) *would mark. I would the Pagans* (Puritans) *would conſider, with what ſecuritie of conſcience we may appeare before God touching this parte . May we not with all confidence ſay to God, Lord if it be an error we were deceuied by thee ?* *For the things which we beleue were confirmed amongſt vs with ſo greate ſignes and wonders , and with ſuch , as could not be wrought but by thee. Surely they were deliuered vnto vs by men of great holines, and approued with great and authentical teſtimonies , thy ſelf cooperating and confirming their ſpeeche with ſignes following.*

11. Finally if any men be founde fo Thomas-lyke, and hard of beleefe, that he will not beleeue that S. Auftin wrought

any

any miracle, let them anſwer that which
S. Auſtin ſaith *lib. 22.de ciuit. cap.5.* againſt S. Auſtin,
the Pagans, who would not beleeue the
miracles of the Apoſtles. *If they beleeue not,*
that miracles were wrought by the Apoſtles of
Chriſt (by S. Auſtin and his fellowes) *that*
they might be credited ; thu one miracle alone
ſufficeth,that all the world ſhould beleeue without
miracles . That our Engliſh Anceſtors
ſhould without al miracles forſake their
ancient, and eaſy Religion, and follow
a new , and difficult both for points of
beleeſe, as the myſterie of the Trinitie,
Incarnation ,Euchariſt, and more difficult to practice, as to refrain both act,
and thought.

12. If any aſk why are not miracles now VVhy miracles are
not novv.
done for confirmation of S. Auſtins
doctrine as wel as then , I anſwer with
S. Gregorie homil. 29. in Euangel . *The* S. Auſtin
multitude of the faithful was to be nouriſhed 1
with miracles , that it might increaſe to faith.
Becauſe we water the plants , which we ſet til we
ſee them to haue taken roote , but after that we 2
leaue watering them . And with S. Auſtin S.Greg.
lib. 22.de ciuit.cap. 8. I might ſay that miracles
were neceſſarie before the world (of Britanie)
did beleeue . VVho ſo euer now requireth wonders
to beleeue, he is a great wonder that beleeueth not
when the world beleeueth . Was it ſufficient
for the Iewes to beleeue the doctrine of
I 3　　　　Moyſes,

Moiſes , that their Forſathers ſaw it confirmed of him by many wonders ? And ſhall it not ſuffice vs that our Forſathers teſtifie that they ſaw S. Anſtins doctrine confirmed in lyke ſorte ? Were not our Forſathers to be credited as wel as thoſe Iewes? Or are we more incredulous than their poſteritie ?

vvhat
hath bene
hitherto
proued. And hitherto Gentle Reader we haue ſhewed that Saint Auſtin had all things requiſit to a ſufficient and lawful Preacher of Gods word, to wit great learning, famous vertue, lawful vocation and right orders : we haue alſo ſhewed that the Doctrine which he preached was the vniuerſal faith and religion of all Chriſtendom at that time, is confeſſed by the greateſt Aduerſaries therof to haue bene ſufficient to bring men to heauen and was aproued and conteſted by God by manie miracles to be his diuine and infallible faith; what now remaineth but to ſeek out what S. Auſtins Religion was in particuler, that finding it we may be ſure to haue found a Religion taught vnto our Ançeſtors aboue 1000. years agoe by a great Diuine, by a famous Saint and a lawful Preacher rightly ſent and ordered , which ſo long ſince was the Religion of all Chriſtendom, was approued by God him ſelf by true miracles , and is confeſſed of

the

the aduerſaries to haue bene ſufficient to ſaluation. Than the which I know not what more amy reaſonable man can deſire.

CHAP. XIIII.

That S. Auſtin was a Roman Catholick, proued by his Maiſter S. Gregorie.

1. HOw careful S. Auſtin was to follow the doctrin and Religion of his Maiſter S. Gregorie apeareth by what was ſayde before out of S. Beda. *lib.* 1. *cap.* 27. of the queſtions, which S. Auſtin ſent vnto him ſo far as from England concerning ſmall matters. And therfor his Religion may be euidently gathered by that of S. Greg. But becauſe it would be tedious to proue that Saint Greg. was a Roman Catholick in all ſubſtantial points of Religion, I will for proofe hereof make choice of two eſpecial points: To wit. The Popes Supremacie, and the Sacrifice of maſſe. Becauſe in the firſt of theſe points Do: Reinolds in his Confer: *pag.* 568. affirmeth *the very being, and eſſence of a Papiſt to conſiſt.* And D. Whitaker cont. Dur. *pag.* 503. ſaith.

S. Auſtins Rom. religion proued by S. Gregorie

I 4

faith: *It is the head of popish Religion of which almoſt all the reſt depend.* And *in the maſſe* (faith D.Sutclif in his Anſwer to Exceptions *pag.11) The very ſoule of Poperie doth conſiſt.* And D.Whitak.*loc.cit. pag.*426. affirmeth that, *Nothing is more holy and diuine in our conceipt.* And laſtly I will proue it be the open confeſsion of diuers Proteſtants.

S. Greg. beleued the Popes ſuprema- cie.

2.   As for the firſt pointe of the Supremacie S. Greg *lib.*4. *Epiſt.*32. faith of Saint Peter (who as Bilſon faith *lib.*1. of Obed. *pag.*380. was *Founder of the Roman Church*) *It is manifeſt to all that know the Goſpel, that by our Lords voice the care of the wholle Church was committed to S. Peter Prince of all the Apoſtles.* And *lib.*1. *epiſt.*24. *Peter houlding the Princedome of the Church accounted him ſelf the cheefe in the Church.* And *lib.*11.*epiſt.*44. he calleth the Roman Church *Caput fidei*, *the head of the faith.* His words are theſe: *Admonemus vt Apoſtolicæ ſedis reuerentia nullius præſumptione turbetur . Tunc enim ſtatus membrorum integer manet, ſi caput fideinullapulſeturiniuria.* Likwiſe *lib.* 7. *epiſt.* 49. he faith, *The care enioyned to vs of all Churches doth bind vs. lib.*7. *epiſt.* 6. *VVho doubteth but that ſhee* (Church of Conſtant.) *is ſubiect to the See Apoſtolick.* And *epiſt.* 64. *If any falt be found in Biſhops I know not vvhat Biſhop is not ſubiect to her* (Church of Rome) Which laſt words do ſo plainly auouch S. Greg. opinion of the ſupremacy, as
Doct.

Doct. Reynolds Confer. *pag.* 547. findeth
no better shift than impudently to say
that *either Greg. wrote not so, or he wrote an*
vntruth to cheere vp his subiects. Caluin *lib.* 4.
cap. 7. §. 12. saith that', *There is no word in all*
Greg. writings wherein he more proudly
boasteth of the largenes of his Primacie *than this.*
Furthermore S. Greg. *lib.* 7. *epist.* 69.
VVithout the authoritie and consent of the See
Apostolick *what so euer is done* (in Councells)
hath no force. And contrariwise *lib.* 7. *epist.* 115.
That reuerence is caried of the faithfull towards
the See Apostolick, *that what is apointed by her*
decree shall not after be disturbed. And the
Archbishop of Rauema writing to him
lib. 10. *epist.* 36. saith. *The* See *of* Rome *sendeth*
her lawes to the Vniuersal Church. And him
selfe *lib.* 12. *cap. vlt. The* See *of* Rome *doth looke*
ouer the whole world, and sendeth newe con-
stitutions vnto all. And *lib.* 11. *epist.* 56. writeth
that the cause of a Bishop who had no
Patriarch or Metrapolitan ouer him,
was to be iudged (immediatly) *of the* See
Apostolick, *which* (saith he) *is omnium Eccle-*
siarum caput, head of all Churches. Which
proofe sheweth that he meaneth not head
ship in excellency of gifts as Reinolds
would Confer. *pag.* 548. but in gouernment. In like sort in *psal.* 4. pœnit. he
calleth Rome the head of all Churches
and Lady of Nations, which Title of *the*
I 5   *head*

head of all Churches becaufe Pope Boniface
3. who fucceded S. Greg. within one
yeare or two procured the Emperour
Phocas to declare to appertaine to the
Bifhops of Rome, he is accounted of all
Proteftants generally to be the firft true
Pope and Antichrift of Rome. But if S.
Greg. authoritie were not fo great in the
Church as Minifters are afhamed to ac-
count him an Antichrift, they would as
foone call him Pope and Antichrift, as
they do Pope Boniface, becaufe he
auoucheth the fame Title which
Boniface did.

3. Nether did S. Greg. onely claime this
Supremacie but alfo practized it often
tymes. For. *lib.* 2. *Epift.* 14. He excommu-
nicated the Archbifhop of Salona in
Dalmatia. *lib.* 4. *Epift.* 50. He depofed
Anaftafius Archb. of Corinth in Greece.
And *Epift.* 15. made the Bifhop of Prima
Iuftiniana his Legat, and likwife the
Bifhop of Arles in France. *Epift.* 51. And.
*lib.*5.*Epift.*24. When there arofe a controuerfie betweene a Prieft of Calcedon, and
the Patriarch of Cóftantinople *according to
the Canons* ('faith he) *it fel to the See Apoftolick
and was ended by our iudgement.* And *lib.* 10.
Epift. 30. He maketh a Bifhop fweare that
he will *In all things abide in the Communion of
the Bifhop of Rome.* And in Bed. *lib.* 1. *cap.* 27.

S. Greg.
practizeth
the fupre-
macie.

Taketh

Taketh vpon him to commit all the Bishops and Priests of Britany to S. Austins
charge, and without asking the Prince
his leaue, apointed him to erect two
Archbishoppriks, and 24. Bishopricks.
Finally he tooke vpon him to depose
kings, and princes. For *lib. 11. Epist.* 10. He
saith *Siquis* &c. *If any king Priest Iudge or seculer person knowing this constitution of ours shall
attempt to break it, Let him want al Dignitie of
his povver, and honor.* And *lib. 12. cap. vlt. If any
king Prelat Iudg or seculer person of vvhat Degree
or highnes soeuer* (doe violat the priuiledgee
of S. Medards Monasterie) *Let him be deposed.* And (as Baron: An. 600 writeth out
of the Chronicles of Millan) gaue the
Bishop of that Cittie authoritie to chuse
what king he woulde after the race of
the Lomburdian kings was ended. For
these speeches and acts of Greg. Doct.
Reinolds *Confer. pag.* 549 saith of him and
of all the Popes for 300. yeares before him
that *they auouch more of their See than is true
and right.* But now the question is not
about right, but about S. Greg: opinion
of Supremacie. And *pag,* 545. saith that *S.
Greg. is somewhat large that waye. pag.* 550.
*The primacie which Greg. Leo and others giue to
the See of Rome doth so exceed the truth that* &c.
And *pag.* 17. he saith that Leo the great
(who was Pope 130. yeares before Greg.)
cherished

Protestā opinion of S. Gregorie about the supre-macie.

Reinolds.

cherished the egge of the Popes Supremacie. And
pag. 16. faith, *Leo made Peter a fellow, head, a*
partie, Rock, and half foundation with Chrift.
Which faith he *pag.* 10. Leo did that he
might rife vp with S. Peter. And Doct.

VVhitaker Whitak, *lib.* de confil. *pag.* 37. *Leo was a*
Fulke. *great builder of the See of Antichrift.* Fulkin 2.
Theffal. 2 *Leo and Greg. were great workers*
and futherers of the See of Antichrift, and of the
myftery of iniquity. And ibid. he doubteth
not to fay that *the myfterie of iniquitie did*
vvorke in the See of Rome in Peters tyme, and
did shew it felf in Anicetus, Victor, Cornelius,
Sozimus, Bonifacius, Celeftinus. By which
confeffion of Proteftants a man of mean
eyefight will eafely fee, what S. Greg. and
his Predeceffors thought of the fupremacie. For if they were not of greater authoritie for their learning holines and anti-
quity, they would haue bene as wel
accounted Popes and Antichrifts as their
fucceffors are.

In what 4. If any object that S. Greg. vehemen-
fenfe S. tly impugneth the Title of the *vniuerfal*
Gregorie *Bishop,* which the Patriarch of Conftanti-
impugned
the Title nople in his time vfurped, calling it
of vniuer- proude, facrilegious, and fuch like, which
fal Bishop. he would neuer haue done if he had
thought him felfe to haue bene head of
all the Churches in the world; I anfwer,
that S. Greg. could not doubt, but that the
Title

Title of vniuerfal Bifhop might in fome
fenfe agree to the Pope . Becaufe the
Councel of Calcedon which *lib.1. Epift.24.*
he profeffeth to reueuence *as one of the fower
Ghoſpells*, offered it to his Predeceflors as
him felf teftifie h *lib.4. Epift.32.* Whervnto
he addeth *Epift.* 37. That his adduerfarie
the Patriarch of Conftant. knew wel that
*per Calcedonenſe Con ilium huius Apoſtolica Sedis
Antiſtites Vniuerſales oblato honore vocati ſunt.*
And *lib. 4. epiſt.36.* faith that the Patriarch
of Alexandria knew it alſo to be ſo.
Which he would neuer haue ſaid, vnles
it had bene both certain and euident, ſo as
his Aduerſaries could not deny it.
Wherto *lib.7. epiſt.30.* he addeth, that it
was giuen to his Predeceſſors by Fathers
after the Councel. And in the ſaid
Councel, *VVhich* (as Reinolds faith
Confer. *pag. 563.*) *was a Company of 630.
Biſhops found in Religion and zealous of the glorie
of God,* (although it hath bene falfified by
the Grecians as witneſſeth S. Greg. *lib. 5.
epiſt.* 14.) yet thriſe is Pope Leo called
Vniuerſal Patriarch without the gain ſaying
of any one. Which ſo many and ſo zealous
would neuer haue permitted, if it had
bene altogether vnlawful. And the ſame
Reinolds *confer. pag. 562.* profeſſeth that
the ſaid Councel *named Pope Leo their head.*
And *pag. 561.* That he was *Preſident of the
Councell*

S. Beda
calleth S.
Gregorie
Bishop
ouer the
vvhole
vvorld.

Councel. And of Bed. *lib. 2. cap.1. S. Greg.* is *called high Bishop ouer the whole vvorld*. Besids that, Popes were before that time called Bishops of the Vniuersal Church, as it is to be seene in Pope Leo *epist.* 54. 62. 65. Sixtus 1. *epist.* 2. Victor *epist.* 1. Pontianus and Stephanus *epist.* 2. Which in sense is all one with *Vniuersal Bishop*, if this Title be taken in the proper sense. But S. Greg. condemned it in the Patriarch of Constant. both because it could no waye pertain to him in the proper sense, for that he was not head of all the Church, and also because he claimed it in such a sense, as is vtterly vnlawful both to the Pope, and to any Bishop els, and is in deede sacrilegious. For as S. Gregorie witnesseth *lib. 4. epist.* 34. 36 38. *lib.5. epist.* 60. *lib.6. epist.* 31. 37. and *lib.7. epist.* 29. and 30. He would be called *Vniuersal Bishop* in such sort as *his brethren being despised, he alone might be called Bishop*, or that *he might seeme to haue denyed his brethren to be Bishops*. That is, so as if him self alone were the onely true and proper Bishop, and others but his Deputies or Vicegerents, and not so formal nor true Bishops as he. In which sense that Title is truly sacrilegious; as robbing all other Bishops of their Episcopal Dignitie.

vvhy the
Patriarch
of Constant. vn-
lavvfully
tooke the
title of
vniuer-
sal Bishop.
1

2

S. Gregorie for
Masse.

5. And for the second point of Masse;
S. Greg.

S. Greg. him self saith, *lib. 7. epist. 29.* thus : *VVee do the solemnitie of the Masse euery day in honor of them* (Martyrs). Sutclif in his Answer to the Catholick supplication denieth these words to be in the place cited. Which who will seeke shall take a taste of his impudencie. Doct. Reinolds in his Confer. *pag.* 532. Iuel *art.* 1. *diui.* 31. And *art.* 3. *diuis.* 21. and others saye, that S. Greg. Masse was a Communion, because in the Canon therof are these words, *vvho so euer shal receaue of this participation of the Altar the holy body and blood of thy sonne.* But so they might prooue that our Masse were no true Masse, because the sayd wordes are in the Canon therof. And they proue no more, than that the Church prayeth for all such as shall communicat at masse, and there shall receaue (not bare bread and wine) but the body and blood of Christ. For to say that S. Greg. masse was a Protestantish Communion *of very material bread and wine*, as Iuel speaketh *Art.* 8. *Diui.* 2. were great impudency. First, because in S. Greg. Masse is the Canō of our Masse, in which the substance of our Masse consisteth. And therfor his masse can be no more a Protestant Communion than ours. And besides in the same booke of S. Greg: is the very forme wherwith our Priests are made

That S. Greg: masse vvas no Protestant Communion.

2.

made to fay our Maſſe, v.z : *Take power to*
offer Sacrifice and to ſay Maſſe as wel for the
liuing as for the dead. Secondly Saint Greg.
Maſſe was a true facrifice of the body and
blood of Chriſt, as appeareth by theſe his
words *lib.* 4. Dialog: (which book Bale
*cent.1.cap.*68.confeſſeth to be his) *cap.* 58.
V-Ve muſt ſacrifice the daylie hoſts of his(Chriſts)
fleſh and blood; for this holſome ſacrificie doth ſaue
the ſoule from euerlaſting death, which myſtically
repreſenteth to vs that death of the onely ſonne,
who albeit riſing from death now dyeth not , and
death hath now no more power ouer him , yet he
liuing in him ſelfe immortally and incorruptibly, is
ſacrificed for vs in this myſterie of the holy Obla-
tion. For his body is there receaued, his fleſh is deui-
ded for the ſaluation of his people. His blood is not
powred now into the hands of the Infidells but into
the mouth of the faithful. Loe how he profeſſeth that we daylie facrifice Chriſts
body and blood , and that this daylie
facrifice faueth the foule from eternal
death, and that though Chriſt be not killed
therby, yet is he facrificed ; and his fleſh
and blood diſtributed to the people when
they communicat at Maſſe. which is the
verie doctrin which we teach. Again, in
S. Gregories Maſſe Tranſubſtantiation
was beleeued , as appeareth by theſe
wordes of Doct. Humfrey Ieſuit. *part.* 2.
rat. 5. *pag.* 626. 627. *Gregorie and Auſtin*
brought

Marginal notes:
2

The hoſte facrificed at Maſſe faueth the ſoul according to S. Greg.

Chriſt facrificed at maſſe vvithout dying.

Chriſts blood povvred into the mouths of the faithful.

S. Greg. beleued Tranſubſtätiation.

brought *in Oblation of the holy hoſt, Tranſub-*
ſtantiation &c. How then could his Maſſe
be a Proteſtant Communion? Morouer
in the Maſſe which his ſcholler S. Auſtin
taught our Forfathers, *The myſtery of the*
fleſh and pretious blood (ſaith Beda *lib.* 5.*cap.* 22.)
of the immaculat lamb is offered to God the Father
in hope of redemption ? And S. Greg.*lib.* de
Sacram. ante Canonem calleth the hoſt ^{The hoſte of Maſſe a vital hoſte expelling ſinnes.}
of his maſſe *the holeſome hoſt of the whole*
world, the vital hoſt, which expelleth all ſinnes
and cauſeth warines to auoid them for ener.
Is this likly to be very material bread?
And again *l.* cit. Dial. *cap.* 57. he telleth
vs that while one was captiue amongſt ^{Maſſe louſeth the bonds of a captiue.}
enemies, *his wife got ſacrifice certain dayes*
to be offered for him, who longe tyme after
returning to his wife tould her what dayes his
bonds were looſed, which ſhe knew to be the dayes, ^{Maſſe ſaueth from drowning as manie faithful vvitneſſes teſtifie.}
when ſhe got ſacrifice offered for him. Ibid.
VVhen *a Biſhop* (ſaith S. Greg.) *offered the*
Sacrifice of the holeſome hoſte for the ſoule of
him whome he thought was drowned, he was
ſaued from drowning, as many (ſaith he) *faithful,*
and religious men haue witneſſed to me and doe ^{S. Greg. apointed 30. Maſſes to be ſaid for one dead.}
witneſſe. And *cap.* 55. he telleth of two
deliuered out of the paines of Purgatorie
by his Maſſe. wherof 30. Maſſes were
ſayde for one of them by his owne
apointment. Thirdly S. Greg. Maſſe was   3
ſaid in honor of Martyrs, as is alredy
K   ſhewed

shewed , and offered for the dead as is euident ; and Reinolds *loc. cit.* confesseth, but so is not their communion . Fourthly Bal. *cent. 1. cap.* 68. saith that *Greg. ordered the ceremonies of the Masse and made vp the Canon therof*. And Ibib. telleth what parts he added to the Masse. Again Kemnit. in Examen. *pag.*826.827. confesseth Masse as it is now, to haue bene finished in S. Greg. time . But now it is far different from Protestants communion . And it is euident that nothing since his tyme is added to the Canon, which includeth the substance of the Masse . Finally Fox Acts *pag.* 130. saith that about the yeare 780. Pope Adrian ratified and confirmed the order of S. Greg. Masse, *At what tyme* (saith he) *this vsuall Masse of the Papists began to be vniuersal, and vniforme and generally receaued in all Churches* Loe he confesseth that our vsual Masse came from S. Greg. and telleth the tyme when it began generally to be receaued in all Churches, To wit about 900. yeares agoe.

6. Lastly I will proue S. Greg. to haue bene a Roman Catholick by the open confession of our Aduersaries , Fulk. in Apoc. 6. saith, *Greg. was superstitious in reliques* And 2. Thessal. 2. *Greg. was a great worker and furtherer of the See of Antichrist* , *and of the mystery of iniquitie.* Io. 21. *Gregorie gathered some*

4

5

Protestãts confesse S. Greg. to haue bene a Papist.

Fulk.

some thing for Peters Primacie. Ib. *VVe go not about to clear Gregorie from all vsurpation of Iurisdiction more than to his See appertained.* He thought to highly of his See And Math. 4. *Gregorie alowed of Images* Hebr. 11. *Allowed Images to be in Churches* Acts. 17. *Greg. alowed Images to be lay mens bookes* Math. 16. and 1, Cor. 3. *Gregorie granteth Purgatorie.* Sutclif Subuers. *cap.* 4. *Greg. vsed litanies, allowed Purgatorie, esteemed much reliques of Saintes.* Whitak. cont Dur. *pag.* 480. Greg. *Purgatorium vt certum dogma tradidit.* Fulk 1. Timoth. 4. *Gregorie indeed willeth holy water to be made and to he sprinkled in the Idols Temples, Altars to be built, and reliques to be layd vp. Gregorie indeede did send many superstitious tokens, as a littel Key from of S. Peter for his blessing.* Math. 16. *Greg. fauoreth the supremaey of S. Peter.* Bale Cent. 1. *cap.* 68. *Greg. burdened the Church and Religion of God more then all, with more than Iewish Ceremonies. He ordered the rites of Masse, commanded Masses to be said ouer the Dead bodies of the Apostles, deuised Letanies, and Procession, permitted the Image of the blessed Virgin to be caried about, confirmed Pilgrimage to Images by Indulgences for the peoples deuotion; he was a Maintainer of Pardons, granted Indulgences to those that visit Churches on certain dayes, made four bookes of Dialogues for strengthning Purgatorie. Admitted adoration of the Crosse, and Masses for the dead, Called the*

Sutclif.

VVhitaker.

Bale.

S.Greg.de scribed to haue bene a profest Papist.

S. Greg. granted indulgences.

K 2 *English*

English men to Romish rites by Auſtin the Monk.
And much more there . And *cap.* 70.
Gregorie brought in Ceremonies , Proceßion,
Suffrages, adoration, Maſſes , truſt of mens works.
Item. *After Greg. tyme puritie of doctrine de-*
creaſed & the Inuocation of dead Saints together
with ſale of Maſſes increaſed , and the Myſterie of
the Euchariſt began to be offered for the dead.
Biſhops alſo from the doctrine of faith , fled to truſt
to mens works , and human ſatisfactions , which
(ſaith he) *is manifeſt of Gregorie.* Item. *Greg.*
ſent Auſtin to the Engliſh men that he might bring
in not Chriſt , but the Roman Religion ſtuffed with
the commandements, and traditions of men. And
finally *cap.* 71. he ſaith in plain termes that
Greg. brought Papiſtrie into England. Alſo Doct.

Humfrey. Humfrey *Ieſuitiſmi part.* 2. *rat.* 5. *pag.* 626.
627. *Greg. and Auſtin brought into the Church*
a burden of Ceremonies , The Biſhops Pal to vſe
onely at Maſſe, Purgatorie, Oblation of the holſom
hoſt, prayers for the dead, Reliques , Tranſubſtan-

Tranſub-
ſtātiation. *tiation , new halowing of Churches. Of all which*
what other proceeded but that Indulgences,
Monkerie, Poperie , and the reſt of the Maſſe of

Anſwer
to the
Examinat. *Popiſh ſuperſtition ſhould be builded thervpon.*
And all theſe things did Auſtin a great Monk being
printed at *taught of Gregorie a monk, bring into England.*
Geneua
1566. pag. Who will ſee more of S. Greg. confeſſed
45. Papiſme by Proteſtants may read
Oſiander *cent.* 6. *pag.* 288 . But what we
haue cited out of Engliſh Proteſtants will
ſuffice

suffice I hope to perswade any indifferent man that S. Greg. was a Papist. Who will see more out of S. Greg. himself may read *lib.7.epist.53.*and 109.*lib.9.epist.71. lib.12.cap.vlt.lib.1. epist. 25. 33. lib.8.epist. 22.*

CHAP. XV.

That Saint Austin and his fellowes were Roman Catholicks, proued by their own deedes and Doctrine.

1. **F**Irst Saint Austin was a Benedictin Monk, or (as Doctor Abbots calleth him of the colour of his habit) *a black Monk,* Which kind of Monks Bale *cent.13.cap. 4.* accounteth *one of the hornes of the beast,* so he termeth the Pope; And *cent.1.cap.100.*saith *they filled all with superstition , and Idolatry.* And Fox *lib.3. pag. 153.* condemneth these kinde of Monks *as superstitious , tyed to a prescript forme of dyet, apparrel, and other things, and forbidden to marry.* Secondly he was a *Romish Priest* and *Romish Archbishop* as Doct. Abbots calleth him *pag.* 198. And *Romish Legat* as Bilson termeth him *lib.* de Obed. *pag.* 114. And what masse or seruice of God , a Romish Priest vseth euery one knoweth. K 3 Thirdly

Answ. to D. Bish. pag.197. 1

2

Thirdly, when he and his fellowes came into England, they came as S. Beda *lib. 1. cap. 25.* and all other writers agree *carying before them in place of a banner a Croſſe of ſiluer, and the Image of our Sauiour painted in a table, and ſinging the Letanies* . Which Letanies (ſaith Bale Cent. *1. pag. 62.*)*were ſuperſticious.* Fox *lib. 2. pag. 116.* ſaith they *went in Proceſſion.* Beda *lib. 2. cap. 26 . In Canterburie they reſorted to an ancient Church built in the honor of S. Martin, made while the Romans yet dwelled in England, and began there firſt to ſay ſeruice, ſay Maſſe, pray, preach and Chriſten. cap. 27.* Saint Auſtin was made Archbiſhop by the authoritie of Pope Greg. (or as S. Beda ſpeaketh of,) at the commandement of S. Gregorie. He enquireth of Gregorie how *offerings at the Altar ſhould be diſtributed, what Ceremonies he ſhould vſe at Maſſe, and* the like *cap. 29.* He receaued from Gregorie all ſuch things as were *neceſſarie for the furniture, and miniſtrie of the Church . As holy veſſels, Altar clothes, Ornaments for Churches, apparrel for Preiſts, and Clergie, and a Pal to were onely when he ſayd Maſſe* & authoritie to inſtitute 12. Biſhops vnder him and 12. vnder a Biſhop of York, and ſuperioritie ouer all the Prieſts of Britanie *cap. 30.* S. Auſtin is apointed by Gregorie *not to pul downe the Temples of Idols, but to make holy water, and ſprinkle about the ſame Temples, to build Altars,*

Holie
vvater,

and

and place reliques in them. cap. 33. *Saint Auſtin
builded a Monaſterie in which King Ethelbert
through his aduiſe built a nevv Church in the honor
of S. Peter and Paul lib.* 2. *cap.* 2. Saint Auſtin
exacted of the Britons *to celebrat Eaſter, and
adminiſter baptiſme after the maner of the holy
Roman Church.* And *cap.* 35. Beda ſpeaking
of the Church of the Auſtins in Canterbury ſaith, *This Church hath almoſt in the midſt
of it an Altar dedicated in the honor of S. Greg.
Pope, on the vvich Altar euery Saterday their
memories are ſolemly celebrated by the Prieſt of
that place. cap.* 4. S. Paulin vſed *an Altar of
ſtone.* And *cap.* 20. *a great goulden Croſſe and a
goulden Chalice conſecrated for the miniſtrie of
the Altar.*

2. Beſides Pope Boniface 3. was by the
Emperor Phocas declared to be the true
Oecumenical Patriarch, or head of the
Church as all writers Proteſtants and
Catholicks do agree which was done in
the yeare 605. as ſome ſay, or 606. as
Baron. And this Pope Boniface therby
(as generally all Proteſtants affirme) became the firſt Pope and Archbiſhop of
Rome. Whitak. cont Dur. *pag.* 501. I
affirme (ſaith he) *that in the tyme of Boniface* 3.
*Antichriſt openly placed his Throne in the Church
of Rome.* Fulk Anſwer to a Counter Cath.
pag. 72. *The Popes from Boniface* 3. *were all
blaſphemous Hereticks and Antichriſts.* And in

margin: 4 S. Auſtin aliue vvhen the Pope (as Proteſt: ſay) be-came An-tichriſt.

K 4 1. Ioan.

1. Ioan. 2. Boniface 3. *went manifestly out of the Church and became Antichrist.* Fox *lib.* 2. *pag.* 120. *Rome euer since Boniface* 3. *hath houlden maintained and defended his Supremacie* . The same hath Cooper Chron. An. 611. The like hath Bale *Cent.* 1. *pag.* 69. 70. Downham of Antichrist, and generally all Protestants. But S. Austin was both in this Popes time, for he subscribed to the Charter of king Ethelbert made An. 605. and after. For as Bale saith *Cent.* 13. *cap.* 1. He dyed. 608. or as Malmsb. in fastis saith 613. and yet is he not found but to haue obeyed this Pope Boniface as he did obey Gregorie. Which he would neuer haue done if he had thought it Antichristian for the Pope to

S. Mellits communion vvith a Pope vvhome Protestāts account the second Antichrist

be head of the Church. Yea S. Mellit one of his fellowes and Successors went to Rome about the yeare 610. to *commune* saith Beda *lib.* 2. *cap.* 4. *and counsel with the Apostolick Pope Boniface* 4. the immediat successor of Boniface 3. *for necessarie causes of the English Church*, sat in a Councel with him, subscribed to what was decreed of that Councel, and brought the Precepts to be obserued of the English Church.

Also S. Iustus.

And *cap.* 7. S. Beda writeth, that this S. Mellit and S. Iustus (an other of S. Austins companions and successors) receaued eftsons exhorting Epistles from this Boniface. And *cap.* 8. he saith that Iustus *receaued also*

also authoritie to ordain Bishops from the high Bishop Boniface and a Pal. And *cap.* 17. *and* 18. that S. Paulinus and S. Honorius *receaued* *also their Pals from Pope Honorius.* Which Pa. was giuen by Popes to Metropolitans as a token of agreement in faith. And therfor Pope Pelagius Predeceffor to S. Greg. decreed D. 100. That *what Metropolitan fo euer after three monthes of his Confecration fhall not fend to Rome to declare his faith and receaue his Pal fhall leefe his Dignitie.* This we fee how S. Auftin and his fellowes by their life and deedes profeffed their agreement and faith euen with thofe Popes, whome Proteftants account the firft Antichrifts. But befids this, we haue alfo the teftimonie of the Popes of that tyme, and of S. Auftins own fellowes. For Pope Boniface 5. writing to S. Iuftus aforfaid in Bed.*lib.2.cap.*8. faith thus. *After vve had read the letters of our deere fonne King Edbald we vnderftood vvith vvhat great learning and inftruction of holy fcripture yovv haue brought him to the beleefe of the vndoubted faith.* Loe this Pope aproued the doctrine and faith of S. Iuftus, which he could neuer haue done vnles S. Iuftus had allowed the Supremacie. And S. Laurence, Mellit and Iuftus writing to the Scottifh Bifhops in Beda *lib.* 2. *cap.* 4. profeffe, that it was *the cuftomable maner of the See of Rome euen in their*

And S. Paulin, and S. Honorius.

Popes vvhom Proteft. account Antichrifts aproued S. Auftins doctrine.

K 5 *tyme*

tyme to fend preachers into all places of the world. Which cuftome they could neuer haue accounted lawful, vnles they had thought that See to haue Iurifdiction , and gouernment in the whole world. Yea S.

S. Auftin calleth the Pope Father of all Chriftendom. Auftin in his fpeech to King Ethelbert in Capgraue calleth S. Greg. *totius Chriftiani-tatis Patrem, the Father of all Chriftendom.* And thus much of S. Auftin and his fellowes deedes , and doctrine out of Chatholick writers. Now let vs come to Proteftants.

S. Auftins acts of Papiftrie out of Proteftants. 3. Bilfon and Abbots as is aforfaid call S. Auftin *a Romish Monk, a Romish Prieft, a Romish Legat.* Which names fhew of what Religion they account him.

Abbots. Godwin in vit. Aug. faith , *S. Greg. being made Pope fent*

Godvvin. *Auftin hither , vnto whome he apointed* 40. *other that fhould aide him in this holy work.* Ib. he teftifieth that *S. Greg. fent him a pal , and Church ornaments.* That *he dedicated a Monafterie to S. Peter and Paul , that he claimed authoritie ouer all this Iland Entred the place of*

Fox. *Counfel with his Banner and his Croffe, and with finging Proceffion.* Fox Acts. *pag.* 116. *They went with Proceffion to Canterburie finging Alleluya*

Sutclif. *with the Letanie.* Sutclif Subuerfion , *cap.* 5. *Auftin brought in an Image of Chrift , and a filuer Croffe, and began* (faith he) *to chant Letanies.* Now whither thefe be fignes of Proteftancie or Papiftrie I leaue to euerie one

Holinf-head. to iudge. Alfo Holinfhed defcript. Brit. teftifieth teſtifieth (as before we heard out of Saint Beda) that *S. Auſtin came with a ſiluer Croſſe and Image of our Lord and Sauiour painted in a table, ſinging Litanies.* And that in Canterburie they accuſtomed to *pray, ſay Maſſe, preach and baptize in S. Martins Church.* And that S. Greg. *ſent to Auſtin a Pal* , which (ſaith he) *was the ornament of an Archbiſhop. And that Maſſe and Letanie was at that tyme in France.* Again that *Lawrence with his fellow Biſhops wrote letters to the Britons to conform them in the Vnitie of the Roman faith.* Item Mellitus *ſolemnizing Maſſe diſtributed* &c. Now what Maſſe it was that Romiſh Prieſts, Romiſh Monkes, Romiſh Legats as Bilſon and Abbots call them , ſayde , I leaue to euery one to iudge. And if any body ſhould doubt , Fulk in Hebr. 10. may put him out of doubt . For ther he writeth S. Beda ſayd that, *Engliſh men in his time vnderſtood the holſome ſacrifice* (of Maſſe *) auailed to redemption both of body and ſoule.* Which Fulk calleth ſuperſtitious , and vndoubtedly meaneth the Maſſe . And thus much of S. Auſtins Papiſtry by his owne deedes both out of Chatholick and Proteſtant writers.

Fulk.

That

CHAP. XVI.

That Saint Auſtin was a Roman Catholick, prooved by the con-feſſion of learned Pro-teſtants.

D.Abbots 1.   DOctor Abbots in his late anſwer to Doct. Biſhop *pag.* 197. calleth S. Auſtin a *black Monk. pag.* 20. *The Italian Monk, brought new obſeruations from Rome, and the English receaued the ſame. pag.* 198. *A Romiſh Prieſt, required the British Biſhops to be ſubiect to his Romiſh authoritie. A Romiſh Arch-biſhop brought in nouelties and ſuperſtitions, and did contaminat the faith of Chriſt, Mellitus, Lau-* Iuel. *rentius, Iuſtus, all of Auſtins company and condition* Iuel Art. 3. *Diu.*21. *It is thought of many that Auſtin corrupted the Religion that he found here* D. Fulk. *with much filth of ſuperſtition.* Fulk 1.Cor. 4. *Auſtin did not beget the Nation of the English men to Chriſt by the pure Goſpel, but with the mixture of Traditions. And that Chriſtian Reli-gion which he found in the Britons he labored to corrupt with Romiſh inuentions.* 1. Cor. 15. *Auſtin did not in all points teach the true faith to the Saxons.* 2.Cor.12. *Auſt. brought in corruption.* Syr Francis Haſtings in his Waſtword

once

once or twife faith, that *Auftin brought in the Romifh Religion*. Ofiander Epit. Hift. Ofiander. *cent.6. Auft. thruft Roman rites and cuftoms vpon the English. To vvit Altars, Veftements, Maffes, Chalices,Croffes,Candlefticks, Cenfars, Banners, holy Veffels, holy vvater, and bookes of Roman cuftoms.* See Magdeburgenfes *cent. 6.* Bale B. Bale. *cent.* 1.*pag.* 19. *After Auftins Apoftleship (* faith he) *vnder the English Saxons there fellowed an other kind of Monkes which corrupted all with moft filthy fuperftitions & Idolatries.* And *cent.* 1. *cap.* 70. *Auftin entred not with the Gofpel (* of Luther*) of Chriftian peace, but with the banner of his Apoftleship, with a filuer Croffe, Letanies, Proceffion,Images, painted Pictures,Reliques, and ritual bookes.* And *cap.* 72. *Auft. made Elbald drinck of the cup of the whore,cap.* 73. *King Ethel- bert firft of all English men receaued of Greg.* 1. *Bishop of Rome by Auftin the opinions of the Roman Religiõ with all (* faith he*)the impofture or deceit, and dyed the one and twentith yeare of his receaued Papifme.* And *pag.*73. he calleth our primitiue church *a carnal Synagogue.* And yet further *cent.*8.*cap.* 85. *Auftin(* faith he*)brought in Popish Monkerie, & befides the Popes traditions (* o filthie and blafphemous mouth*)brought no thing but mans dung cent.* 13. *cap.* 1. *Auftin the Roman brought hither Romish rites without found doctrine. The King receaued Romanifme with the anexed Idolatries.He brought in Monkes, Altars, Veftements, Images, Maffes, Chalices, Croffes, Candlefticks,*

Candlesticks Banners , holy (as they call them)
Veſſels , holy water , and bookes of Roman cuſtoms.
Their cheeffeſt ſtudies were about the oblations of
Maſſes. Aud finally Cent.14.*cap.* 31.he faith,
Auſtin diſpoſed all things in England to the forme
of the Sinagogue of Rome, and made English men
honorers of the Pope. Thus plainly is S. Auſtins
Roman Religion confeſſed by Bale who
was both as earneſt a Proteſtant and as
skilful in antiquities as euer Engliſh Proteſtant was. Holinſhead alſo Defcript.
Brit. *cap.* 27. faith *The Inhabitants of Britanie*
receaued the Doctrine of Rome brought in by
Auſtin and his Monks. Ib. *Auſtin indeed converted*
the Saxons from Paganiſme but imbued them
with no leſſe hurtful ſuperſtition than they did
know before . For beſides the name of Chriſt and
external contempt of their priſtinat Idolatrie , he
taught them nothing at all , but rather made an
exchange from groſſe to ſubtil trecherie , from open
to ſecret Idolatrie, and from the name of Pagans to
the bare Title of Chriſtians . So far were theſe
men from thincking S. Auſtin to haue
bene a Proteſtant , or to haue agreed with
them as Fulk would 2. *Cor.* 12. *in the cheeſe*
and moſt eſſential points of faith.

CHAP. XVII.

That S. Auftin was a Roman Ca-
tholick, proued by the Doctrine
and faith of the Engilsh
Church which he
founded.

1. IN this Chapter I will firft fet downe
what Catholicks haue written of the
faith of our Primitiue Church, and after
what Proteftants. Firft therfor our Primitiue Englifh Chriftians fayd Maffe, and
that in honor of Saints. Beda *lib. 4. cap. 14.*
Let them fay Maffes and giue thanks that their
prayer is heard, and alfo for the memorie of King
Ofwald. Likwife they fayd Maffe for the
dead, and confequently beleued it to be
propitiatorie for finnes. Ibid. *cap. 22. Tuna*
a Prieft and Abbot did often times caufe Maffe to
be faide for his (brothers) *foule* Item *lib. 5.*
cap. 13. and *lib. 3. cap.* cit. They erected
Monafteries that dayly praier might be made for
the dead. Secondly they did beleeue that
they offered to God the pretious body
and blood of Chrift as we beleeue we do
at Maffe. Beda *lib. 5. cap. 22. All Chriftian*
Churches

1
Maffe in
honor of
Saints.

Maffe for
the dead.

2
Offered
to god the
pretious
bodie and
blood of
Chrift.

Churches throughout the world *should prepare bread and wine for the mystery of the flesh, and precious blood of the immaculat lambe, and when all lessons, prayers, rites, and ceremonies vsed in the solemn feast of Easter were done, should offer the same to God the Father, in hope of their redemption to come. lib. 4. cap. 28.* S. Cutbert *offered the host of the holsome Sacrifice to God.*

3
Cōfession of sinnes and pennance for them.

Thirdly, they confessed their sinnes to Priestes, and they enioined pennance. *lib. 4. cap. 25. Adaman in his youth had committed a certain greiuous sinne, resorting therfor to a Priest confessed his sinne to him. The Priest when he had heard his sinne, said, a great wound requireth a great cure and medecin, therfor giue thy self to fasting, and prayer as much as thou art able.* And *lib. 4. cap. 27.* He telleth how Saint Cutbert heard mens confessions, and enioined them pennance. And *lib. 5. cap. 14.*

Miracle for confession.

He telleth a dreadful punishment inflicted by God on one, becaufe in time of sicknes he would not confesse his sinnes.

4
Priests could not marry.

Fourthly, their Clergy after holy orders could not marry. S. Greg. in Beda. *lib. 1. cap. 27. If ther by any in the Clergy out of holy orders that can not liue chast, they shall take wiues.* The fame hath S. Beda *l. 5. c. 22.* Fift-

5
Dirige & Masse for the dead.

ly, they fong dirige ouer night, and in the morning fayd Masse for the dead. Beda *lib. 3. cap. 2. The religious men of Hagstalden haue of long time bene accustomed to come*

euery

euery yeare the eue and the day that S. Oswald was slayne to keepe Dirges there for his soule and in the morning solemnly to offer for him the sacrifice of the holy Oblation. Sixtly they vsed holy water and confecrating Churches. Beda *lib. 5. cap. 4. The Bishop (S. Iohn) sent the sick Lady some of the holy water which he had halowed in the Dedication of the Church,* and also candles lighted, Crosses, and holy oyle as we do now as is euident by Malmsb: *lib.* 2. Pont. *pag.* 235. and Ealred in vit. Edwardi.

Seuenthly, they blessed them selues with the figne of the Crosse. Beda *lib.* 4. *cap.* 14. *Cednam blessing him selfe with the signe of the holy Crosse layd down his head on the Boulster, and so falling a little in a slumber ended his life in quiet. And lib.* 5. *cap.* 22. *Euery congregation of faithful men accustometh to beare the signe of the Crosse on their forheads, that by the Diuin power of the same they may be defended from all assalts of the Diuel.* Eightly, their Priests and Monks vsed round shauen crownes. Beda *lib.* 5. *cap.* 22. *It behoueth them which being either made by vow Monkes or by profession of the Clergie to binde them selues more strictly with the bridle of continencie for Christs sake, to bear in their head by clipping, the forme of a crovvne.* Ibid. *All Priests and Religious men had their heads shauen round after the true shape of a crowne.* But as Bale faith Cent. 14. *pag.* 194. *Tonsura est Romanæ Bestiæ character.* Ninthly they

L   erected

6

Holie vvater, candels. Crosses, holie oile &c.

7

Blessing vvith the figne of the Crosse.

8

Priests haue shauen crovvnes.

9

erected many Altars in one Church with
Martyrs reliques, vsed lights and other
ornaments as Catholicks doe Beda *lib. 5.
cap. 21.* Acca imployed his diligence to
gather together out of all places the holy
*Apostles and Martyrs reliques to the end he might
in honor of them build certain Altars aparte by
them selues in little Chappells made for the same
purpose, within the precinct and walls of the same
Church. Morouer he prepared holy vessels lights
and other necessaries to the better adorning of the
Church of God.* And *lib. 3. cap. 6. They worshiped
Reliques.* Tenthly to omit many more
certain Markes of Roman Religion. They
accounted S. Peter Primat and head of
the Apostles Beda *lib. 5. c. 22. I desire with all
my hart to follow the stepps of Blessed S. Peter head
of the Apostles.* Ibid. *They were reduced to the
order of S. Peter Primat and head of the Apostles,
and committed as it were to his Patronage and
protection.* They accounted the Pope *high
Bishop ouer the whole world.* So in plaine termes S. Beda calleth S. Greg. Pope *l. 2. c. 1.*
Accounted the Church of Rome the *Catholick and Apostolick Church. lib. 3. c. 25.* And
*l. 4. cap. 23. Going to Rome, counted a thing of great
vertue aud deuotion.* And *l. 3. c. 25. Held without
all controuersie that these words (vpon this Rock I
will build my Church) were principally spoken vnto
Peter, and that vnto him the keies of the Kingdome
of heauen were giuen.* And the Bishops being
depriued

depriued of their Bishopricks both by the King and by other Bishops appealed to Rome: Beda *lib. 5. cap. 20. VVilfrid the vertuous Bishop of York appealing to the See Apostolick for his cause and by that ful authoritie absolued* &c. Item. *Fiue yeares after he was accused of King Alfrid and many other Bishops and depriued of his Bishoprick wherin vpon repairing again to Rome and obtayning licence to plead his owne defence before his accusers, Pope Iohn and many Bishops sitting in Iugdment, It was by their Definitiue Sentence concluded, that in some parte his accusers had falsly forged surmises, The Pope wrote to the Kings of England requiring them to see him restored.* And thus much out of Catholick writers: now let vs see what Protestants write of the faith of our Primitiue church.

2. Fox in his protestation before his Acts. *After the coming of Austin and his fellowes from Rome Christian faith began to enter and spring among the Saxons after a certain Romish sorte.* Acts. pag. 154. *The causes why solemn Monasteries were first founded in England by Kinges Queenes and Kings daughters and rich Consuls are these, pro remedio anima mea* &c. *For remedy of my soule, for remission of my sinnes, for the safty of my Kingdoms and people which are vnder my gouernment, In honor of the most glorious Virgin.* Whervpon afterward pag. 170. he concludeth that *the doctrine of Iustification by onely faith,* (which pag. 840. he calleth

L 2   *the*

the foundation of *their Church*) *was then*
*vnknown.*Bale Cent. 1.*cap.* 72.saith. *English*
men after Auſtin did dedicat their Churches to
dead Saints. And *cap.* 73. *King Ethelbert*
receaued the Roman Rites and doctrine with all
*the impoſture.*and Cent. 14. *cap.* 54. faith
that the *two Hewalds* (who were the firſt
Engliſh martyrs) *paſi ſunt pro Papiſmo,*
papiſtici Martyres. Papiſtical Martyrs ſuffered for
*Papiſtrie.*Bilſon of Obed *pag.* 321. *The Saxons*
were ſoone entreated to receaue the Bishop of Rome
for their Patriarch. Stow *pag.* 77. citeth this
Charter of King Ethelbert. *King Ethelbert*
by inſpiration of God gaue to Bishop Mellit for
remedie of his ſoule,the Land which is called
Tiilingham for the Monaſtery of S. Paul, which
kind of giuing goods is quite oppoſit to
Proteſtancie, as yow may ſee more
hereafter. And *pag.* 78. faith:King Sebert
to ſhew him ſelfe a Chriſtian built a Church in
honor of S. Peter. Reinolds Confer. *pag.*12.
This imagination of the key and Porter and
opinion of power to ſhut and open committed to
Peter onely (ouer all the Church as it
includeth alſo the Apoſtles) *King Oſwie*
conceaued, and all his Clergie did agree vnto it.
And of S. Beda the principal Doctor of
our Primitiue Church, Oſiander Epit.
Cent.7. *pag.*231. faith thus. *He was wrapped*
in all the Popish errors and articles in which we
diſagree this day from the Pope. Wherby we
may

Marginal notes (left column):

Bale.

Our firſt
Chriſtian
K. a per-
fect Papiſt.

Our firſt
Martyrs
ſuffer for
Papiſtrie.
Bilſon.

Stovv.

Honor of
S. Peter
counted
ſigne of
Chriſtia-
nitie.
Reinolds.

Keys gi-
uen one-
ly to Pe-
ter.

Oſiander.

S. Beda a
perfect
Papiſt.

may see how perfect a Papist S. Auftin was. Fulk in Hebr. 10. *Beda liued in a ſuper-* Fulk *ſtitious time* (yet liued he 80. yeares after S. Auftin) *long after Antichriſt did ſhew him ſelf.* Beda ſayd *that men vnderſtod that the helthful ſacrifice* (of maſſe) *auailed to the redemption of the body and ſoule euerlaſting.* And in 1. Pet. 3. *Beda was caryed away with the errors and corruptions of his tyme .* And thus I hope I haue ſufficiently proued the Roman Catholick faith of our firſt Apoſtle S. Auftin by the faith of his maiſter S. Greg. by his owne deedes and doctrine, by Confeſſion of Proteſtants, and finally by the doctrine of our Primitiue Church which he founded , and how it was that Chriſtian Religion which was firſt founded in our Nation , and our Engliſh Anceſtors imbraced when they forſooke Paganiſme . Now it remaineth to ſhew that the ſame Religion hath continewed alſo conſtantly vnto this late lamentable reuolt to Proteſtancy in all our Nation both in the Clergie and Laitie , which I will declare in all the Archbiſhops of Canterburie who were the cheefe of the one order , and in the Kings who were heads of the other. And by the way I will name in euery Kings time ſome of the notable men who ſucceſſiuely haue confirmed it by their holy life and miracles.

That

CHAP. XVIII.

That all the Archbishops of Canter-
burie from S. Auſtin to our tyme
were Roman Catholicks
proued by generall,
reaſons.

1

No record
that anie
Archb:
vvas Pro-
teſt: befor
this time.

1. FIrſt, becauſe there is no mention
or memorie in any Chronicle of
England , in any writer domeſtical
or forrein , no record or monument of
antiquitie that til Cranmer any of the
Archbiſhops varied from the faith of his
Predeceſſors. Therfor to affirme the contrary, is ether to profeſſe to know things
paſt by reuelation,or to affirm that which
nether him ſelf knoweth , nor any man
euer tould him. Secondly becauſe all the
Archbiſhops vnto S.Odo his tyme(which
was An.958.)had bene Monks as S. Auſtin was, which Odo himſelfe teſtifieth in
Malmesb.*lib.1.* Pontif. *pag.* 200. And Fox
lib. 3.pag. 151. where he ſaith . *This Odo was*
the firſt from the coming of the Saxons til his tyme
which was Archbiſhop of Canterburie being no
Monke,all the other before his tyme were of the
profeſſion

2

All the
Archb. of
Cant.
Monks til
S. Odo.

profeßion of monkes. And therfor he could
not be perſwaded to accept the Arch-
biſhoprick vntil he had profeſſed him _{In a ma-}
ſelfe a Monke. And after that vnto Arch- _{ner all}
biſhop Baldwin *an.* 1184. in a manner all _{til An.}
the Archbiſhops were Monks, as Godwin ^{1184.}
a Proteſtant yet liuing (which ſhall
ſuffice to aduertiſe the Reader of now
becauſe herafter I ſhall often allegd him)
teſtifieth in the life of Archbiſhop Hubert.
And what kind of Monkes theſe were
and what vndoubted Catholicks, hath
bene ſhewed before . Thirdly , they _{Archb:}
were elected by the Monks of Chriſt- _{vvere cho-}
church in Canterburie where were _{Monks.}
Monks(ſaith Malmsburie *lib.*1.*Pont.p.*203)
euer ſince the tyme of S. Laurence
ſucceſſor to S. Auſtin as is euident by the
epiſtle of Pope Boniface to King Ethelbert Ibid. *pag.* 208. and appeareth both by
their liues in Godwin , and by the
iudgment of Pope Innocent 3. in Paris
*pag.*287. Who , when the Biſhops of
England challenged right in the election
of the Archbiſhop, the Pope hearing both
parties gaue ſentence that *Monachi legitimè
probauerunt* &c. *That the Monks had lawfully
proued , that the Prior and Couent of the Church
of Canterbury haue for long times paſt elected
Bishops in their Chapter without the Bishops euen
vnto this time, and haue obtained their election*
K 4   *to be*

to be confirmed of the See Apoftolick. And Fox
Acts pag. 232. writeth that *the practice of the*
Monks was firft to keepe the election in their own
hands as much as they could , and fecondly either to
giue the election to fome Prior or Monke of their
owne houfe,or to fome Abbot or Bishop which fome
tyme had bene of their company. And Ibid. he
addeth that *the Archbishop of Canterburie was*
commonly fet vp by the Pope; *efpecially fince the*
Conqueft. And *pag*.349.*that it hath bene alwaies*
the practice of the Church of Rome euer to haue
the Archbishops of their owne fetting vp, or fuch a
one as they might be fure of on their fide. And
this election of Archbifhops by Monkes
continewed till Cranmers time. For (as
Godwin writeth) Archbifhop Deane
who was the laft but one before him,
was elected by them. And the fame he in-
timateth of Bifhop Warham who was
the very laft befor Cranmer. Now of what
religion they were whome Monkes did
chufe euery one knoweth. Fourthly they
were all confirmed by the Pope: this is
manifeft by Godwin in their liues. And
no maruel, for before S. Auftins tyme
Pope Pelagius Predeceffor to S. Greg.
made a law, *Vt quifquis Metrapolitanus vltra*
tres Menfes confecrationis fua ad fidem fuam
exponendam,& Pallium fufcipiendum ad Apofto-
licam fedem non miferit , commiffa fibi careat
dignitate. Wherypon Reinolds Confer.
458.faith

4
All the
Archb.
confirmed
by the
Pope.

458. ſaith that *Pelagius leſt he ſhould raſhly give conſent to the allowing of any Metropolitan that were not ſound in faith, required them to make profeſſion of their faith and ſo to ſend for the Pal, that is to ſay to ſend for his conſent wherof the Pall was a token.* Yea pag. 543. ſpeaking generally of the Popes of the laſt 200. yeares after Chriſt, ſaith they required the confirmation of the Metropolitans by their conſent. And beſides this profeſſion of faith, it was after decreed by Pope Alexander 3. ſaith Fox *pag.* 229. An. 1179. in the Councel of Lateran, that no Archbiſhop ſhould receaue the Pal vnles he did ſweare this oath *I. N. Biſhop of N. from this houre forward wil be faithful and obedient to bleſſed S. Peter, the holy Apoſtolick Roman Church and my Lord Pope N. and his ſucceſſors Canonically entring. I will neuer by Counſel conſent or deed be in cauſe that they looſe life member or be wrongfully impriſoned. And what ſo euer they ſhall commit to me ether by them ſelues or their meſſengers I will neuer wittingly reueale to their preiudice to any perſon. VVith due reſpect to my vocation I will aide them in the houlding and defence of the Roman Papacie and S. Peters regalities againſt all men. I wil giue honorable entertainment to the Legat of the See Apoſtolick in his going and returne and aſſiſt him in his need. Being called to a Synod I will come vnles I be ſtayed by ſome Canonical let. I will yearly viſit*

The oath of Biſhops to the Pope.

L 5   the

the Court of Rome if it be on this side the Alpes,
or euery second yeare when it is beyond the mounts
vnles I be dispensed withal by the See Apostolick.
I wil nether sel giue nor pawn nor farm out a new
nor any way alien the Lands and liuings belonging
to my Bishoply maintenance without the priuitie
of the Pope of Rome. So God me help. &c. And
the like Oath did S. Boniface the Apostle
of Germanie in his Confecration fweare
to Pope Gregorie in the yeare 723. and
the Pal was deliuered to him with thefe

Speech at
the deli-
uerie of
the Pall. wordes . *To the honor of Almightie God the*
blessed Virgin Mary and the blessed Apostles S.
Peter and S. Paul and my Lord Pope N. and
the holy Church of Rome, as also the holy Church
of N. committed to yow: VVe deliuer a Pal taken
from the body of blessed S. Peter, that is the fulnes
of Pontifical function, to the intent yow vse the
same on certain dayes expressed in the Priuiledges
granted to it by the See Apostolick &c. Now
that our Archbifhops did receaue their
Pal from the Pope is manifeft and confeffed by Godwin almoft in euery one of
their liues, and fhalbe more plainly
fhewed hereafter, and is acknowledged
by Fox *lib.* 3. *pag.* 152. and *lib.* 4. *pag.* 172.
Therfor there can be no more doubt that

5
Our
Archb.
vvere the
Popes
legats. our Archbifhops were perfect Papifts
than the Popes were Popes. Fiftly, our
Archbifhops were euer the Popes Legats
in England . *The Archbishops of Canterbury*
vvere

were (faith Camb. Brit. *pag.* 296.) *Legats of the Bishop of Rome, and as* Vrban 2. *fayd, as it were Popes of an other world* . And Pope Iohn 12. in his letter to S. Dunftan : We fully confirm thy Primacie in which thou oughteft according to the cuftom of thy Predeceffors to be Legat of the See Apoftolick as it is knowne that Auftin and his Succeffors Bifhops were. And can we think that the Pops Legats were not Papifts. Finally diuers of them haue bene canonized by the Pope, and their memories in the Roman Martyrologe. To wit. *S. Auftin , S. Lanrence , S. Mellit , S. Iuftus , S. Honorius , S. Theodor, S. Dunftan , S. Anfelm, S. Thomas , S. Edmund , S. Elpheg* , to whome Godwin addeth *S. Eadfin* , which would neuer haue bene done if they had not bene known Roman Catholicks.

Hovv manie Archb: of Canterb: canonized

That

C H A P. XIX.

That euery one of the Archbishops of Canterburie from S. Auſtin, to the time of the Conqueſt of England were Roman Catholicks, proued in particuler.

S. LAVRENCE II.

1. THe firſt Succeſſor of S. Auſtin and ſecond Archb. of Canterb. was S. Laurence, of whome S. Auſtin him ſelf made choiſe, and conſecrated him whiles he liued, but in what yeare he entred is not certain, but he died in the yeare 619. as may be gathered out of Beda. *He was* The lear- ning and vertue of S. Lau- rence. faith Godwin in his life *a very Godly and wel learned man and tooke great paines not onely with his owne charge but alſo to reduce the Britons Scotts and Irish men to one conſent in matters of religion.* Bale Cent.13.*cap.*2. writeth that he was very skilful in Logick and other Philoſophie. Beda *lib.* 2. *cap.* 3. ſaith *he endeuored to lift vp the building of the English Church*

Church to the perfect highnes, both by often wor-
des of holy exhortation and also by continual
example of deuout and godly workes, and therin
also telieth how he labored to reduce the Britons
and Irish as a true Pastor and Prelat. And thus
much for the worthines of this our holy
Prelat. But as for his Roman Religion
although that be euident by what hath
bene sayd before of S. Austin, yet will I
add what Bale saith of him Cent.13.*cap.*2.
He was sent of Greg. to instruct the English
Saxons in Roman Religion, he taught the, people
the Papistical faith almost in all the Dominion of
the English men.

S. Mellit Archbishop. III.

2.   THe third Archbishop was S.Mellit
who succeded An.619. For as S.
Beda saith *lib.* 2.. *cap.* 7. he dyed An. 624.
after he had bene Archbishop fiue yeares.
Of whome and his successor S. Iustus
Beda *lib.2.cap.7.*writeth. *That they gouerned*   The ver-
the English Church with great labor and diligence,   tues of S.
that he was noble by birth, but much more noble   Mellit.
for the excellency of his minde, often trobled with
sicknes, yet euer free and sounde of minde, did
alwaies feruently burne with the fier of inward
charitie and was wont with his holy prayers and
holy exhortations to driue from him selfe and
                                                     others

Miracles. *others all ghostly tentations* And Ibid. *reciteth how that by prayer he quenched a great fier that burnt Canterburie.* Godwin *in vita eius* faith: *he was a man of noble birth, but of greater minde, exceeding careful of his charge, despising the world and neuer caring but for heauen and* **His Rom.** *heauenly things.* His Roman Religion is **Religion.** manifeſteſt becauſe as Godwin confeſſeth he was an *Abbot of Rome*, ſent hither by Greg. and went after *to Rome to confer with Pope Boniface* ſate in Councel, and was by him *honorably entertained.*

S. Iuſtus Archbishop. I I I I.

3. The fourth Archbiſhop was Saint Iuſtus who inmediatly ſucceeded S. Mellit An. 624. and dyed (as it ſeemeth **The ver-** by Beda *lib. 2. cap.* 18.) An. 633. *He gouerned* **tue and** (ſaith *S. Beda lib. 2. cap. 7.*) *the English Church* **learning** **of Saint** *with great labor and diligence.* And as Pope **Iuſtus.** Boniface teſtifieth (in Beda *lib. 2. cap. 8.*) *of him ſo greatly and earneſtly labored for the Goſpel, as he could shew whole Contries plentifully multiplied by him, and brought vp king Edbald with great learning and inſtruction of holy ſcriptures.* Godwin in his life ſayth *he tra-* **His** *uailed painfully* 12. *yeares.* His Roman **Cathol.** Catholick Religion is manifeſt by his **Religion.** Pall receaued from Pope Boniface, Beda *lib. 2.*

lib.2. cap.8. And by what Bale writeth of
of him Cent.13. *cap. 3.* Where he calleth
him, *Pedagog of the Roman faith,* And addeth
that *he brought king Edbald to the Roman faith.*

S. Honorius Archbishop. V.

4. The fift Archbishop was S. Honorius, who succeded (as appeareth
by Beda *lib.2 cap.18.* and Baron. affirmeth
An. 633) and died as Beda writeth *lib. 3.
cap.20.* An.653. hauing sate 20. yeares. He
was (saith Beda *lib.5. cap. 20.*) one of *S. Greg.
schollers, and profoundly learned in holy scriptures.*
Pope Honorius writing vnto him (in
Malmsb.1.Pont.*pag.208.*) saith, *He gouerned
his flock with much toile, much labor and troble,
euils increasing.* And the same saith Godwin. As for his Roman Religion that is
manifest by his Pal. which Bed.*lib.2.cap.18.*
saith. He receaued with a letter from
Pope Honorius, which also Godwin confesseth. And Bale addeth, that he first
deuided England into Parishes *after the
Papistical maner.* Which thing also testifieth
Camb.in Brit.*pag.*131.and Stow An. 640.
And all these Archb. were Italians, and
fellow Laborers of S. Austin.

*S. Hono-
rius. his
great lear-
ning and
vertue.*

*His
Cathol.
Religion.*

Deusdedit

Deusdedit Archbishop VI.

5. The sixt Archbishop was Deusdedit an English man, who succeeded (saith Beda *lib.3. cap.20*)after a yeare and a halfe, to wit An.655, and gouerned the See 9. yeares foure Monthes. *He was* (saith Godwin) *famous for his learning and other vertues and attended carefully his charge.* Capgraue in his life saith of him: *He was a man worthy of God, famous for his life and learning, watchful in prayer and of most vnspotted puritie.* But his Roman Religion is manifest by what hath bene saide of his Maisters and Predecessors. After him(saith Beda *lib. 3. cap.20.*)Damian was consecrated. But becaufe he faith no more of him , and Godwin reckoneth him not amongst the Archbishops , but amongst the Bishops of Rochefter, I will alfo let him passe.

The learning and vertue of Archb. Deusdedit.

His Rom. Religion.

S. Theodore Archbishop. VII.

6. The next Archbishop chofen(faith S. Beda *lib.3.cap.29. by the Clergie of England*) *was VVighard a Priest of great vertue and worthie to be a Bishop , whome the kings of England sent to Rome to be confecrated :* but he
dying

dying there before his confecration Pope
Vitalian made choice of S. Theodore a
Grecian borne, whome he confecrated
(faith Beda *lib.4.cap.* 1.) An:668. (and not
666. as Bale fableth to make the time
agree with the number of the Beaft in the
Apocalips) and continued Archb. 22. The ad-
yeares three monthes.*He*(faith Beda *lib.* 4. mirable
cap. 2.) *and Adrian his fellovve vvere exceeding* learning
vvel learned both in prophane and holy litterature of Saint
and gathering a company of fchollers vnto them, Theodor.
powred into their bofoms holfome knowledg and Beda.
befides their expounding of fcriptures they inftruc-
ted their fchollers with mufick Aftronomy and
Algorifme, and fo brought them vp in the tongues
as fome of them yet liuing can fpeake Latin and
Greeke as wel as Englifh. Nether vvas there fince
Englifhe men came to Britanie any time more
happie than that. For England had moft valiant &
Chriftian Princes the people vvere vvholly bent to
the ioyful tidings of heauen, and there vvanted no
cunning and expert Maifters to inftruct them in
the fcriptures. Thus S. Beda of Saint Theodore his great learning. Pope Agatho who
than liued fo highly efteemed his wonderful learning that he deferred the calling of the fixt generall Councel for his
coming. In ep: apud Malmsb: *lib.*1. Pont: Malmesb.
pag. 196. and *lib.* 1. Reg. *pag.*11. faith of him
and S. Adrian *that they had learnt throughly all*
good learning and made this Iland a dwelling
M *place*

place of Philosophie. Godwin faith: *He was*
wel seene in all good learning, that England neuer
had so happy dayes nor so many learned men as
vnder him. And a little after. *Amongst a*
great number of others ther were of his breeding
Beda, Iohn of Beuerley, Albinus, and Tobias, all
excellent and very famous men . He founded
(faith he) a schoole or vniuersitie at Greclad. And
as Caius addeth *lib.* 1. *antiq*; Cantab : an
other in Canterburie. Bale *Cent.* 13. *cap.* 6.
giueth this teſtimony of his excellent
learning. *He was accounted inferior to no*
Romish Monke of his time for ether diuine or
human learning, either Latin or Greck tongue. He
brought hither all artes of calculating, Counting,
Verſifying ſinging, arguing. &c. *He taught Latin*
and Greeke. Thus both Catholicks and
Proteſtants admire thisgreat Archbiſhops
learning. S. Beda *lib.* 5. *cap.* 8. thus witneſſeth that he *was worthie of perpetual remem-*
brance for his ſinguler vertues. And addeth this
ofhim and his Preceſſors. *Of whome with*
the reſt of his Predeceſſors equal both in dignitie
and degree , it may be truly verified that their
names ſhall liue in glorie from generation to gene-
ration time out of minde . For the Church of
England for the time he was Archbishop receaued
ſo much comfort and increaſe in ſpiritual matters
as they could neuer before nor after. Florent.
Chron: An:690, calieth him *Archbishop of*
bleſſed memorie. Capgraue in his life faith
In his

(margin notes)
Godwin.
England neuer ſo learned or ſo happie as in Saint Theodors time.
Bale.
Saint Theodor his great vertue. Beda.
Florent.
Capgraue.

In his time England shined with great aboundance of Saints like most bright starres.

S. Theodor his Cathol. faith.

7. But as for his Roman Religion that is so manifest as all Protestants confesse it. Bale Cent. 13. *cap.* 6. faith. *It is manifest that he came with the Character of the great* Bale. *Beast,* (so Bale commonly termeth the Pope) *He gaue the vayle to Votaries in diuers places for seruice of Popish Religion, and finished many things which serued to further the kingdome of Antichrist.* And Cent. 1. *cap.* 80. *In the yeare* 666. *the Papists Masse began to be made Latin.* Item Pope *Vitalian*(who sent Saint Theodor)*made all things to be done in Latin in the Christian Churches, as in howers, in stations, in Masses and Prayers.* And *pag.* 71. *Vitalian sent the Monkes Theodore and Adrian into England, that they might confirme in the popish* Perfect Papistrie *faith those that wauered, and that they might* of Englãd *signe his beleeuers with the Character of Anti-* in S. The- *christ* (So this heretick termeth Christs dor his Vicar.) *He apointed Latin houres, Latin songes,* time. *Masses, Ceremonies, Masses Idolatries and Profession in Churches in Latin, apointed shauings, commanded* annoyntings &c. And Cent. 13. *cap.* 7. *Theodore apointed many things in a Councel for setting vp of Purgatorie.* Fulke Apoc: 13. Fulk. *Composition of the latin seruice by Pope Vitalian to be obserued in all regions subiect to the Romish Tyrany.* Fox. *lib.* 2. *pag.* 124. *Theodore was sent* Fox. 1. *into England by Vitalian the Pope and with*

M 2   *him*

180   *The prudentiall Ballance*

him diuers other Monkes to set vp here in England Latin seruice, Masses, Ceremonies, Letanies,
vvith such other Romish VVare. pag. 125. He

Saint Theodor a confessed Papist and all folloved him. addeth that *Theodore vvas present at the sixt generall Councel vnder Agatho , vvhere marriage vvas forbidden to the Latin Priests.* Who wel remenbreth this, and marketh also that S.

Priests forbidden mariage. Beda *lib. 4. cap.* 2. writeth, that *Theodore visited all the Contry ouer whersoeuer any English people dvvelled, for all men did receaue him gladly and heare him. He did teach the right vvay and path of good liuing.*

All Engl. gladly receaued S. Theodor. *Vnto him all the vvhole Church of the English Nation did consent to subiect themselues.*

Godvvin. Wherto Godwin addeth *that all the Britishe Bishops and generally all Britanie yeelded him obedience, and vnder him conformed themselues in all things vnto the rule*

Note. *and disciplin of the Church of Rome.* Who (I say) marketh this , will neuer doubt but all England was at that time perfect Roman Catholicks. Besids that as S. Beda recordeth *lib. 4. cap.* 18. Pope Agatho sent

English faith approued of the Pope. hither a Nuntio to examine the faith of the English Church. Whervpō Theodore called a Councel and sending a Copie of their faith to Rome, it was receaued most gladly of the Pope. So that S. Theodore and our English Church in his time, were all of one faith with the Pope.

Brithvvald

Brithwald Archbishop. VIII.

8. THe eighth Archb. of Canterburie was Brithwald, who was elected (saith Beda *lib.* 5. *cap.* 9.) An. 692. and consecrated the next yeare by Godwin Archbishop of France. He sate (saith Beda *lib.*5. *cap.* vlt.) 37. yeares 6 months, and dyed An.731. Beda *cap.* 9 cit. saith. *He was a man doubtles wel trauailed in the knowledg of holy scripture, and very skilful in Ecclesiastical and Monastical orders, censures, and discipline.* The same saith Florent. Chron. An. 692. and Marian Ibid. Godwin in his life saith: *He was very wel learned in Diuinity and other wise.* Pope Sergius (who gaue his Pal) testifieth in his epist. in malmsb. *lib.*1. Pont. *pag.* 210. that Brithwald got not his Bishoprick *fastu aut tumore, sed mente subnixa & humili.* Bale Cent. 1. *cap.* 99. saith he was *a fine yong man borne to great matters and got great fame of vertue and learning.* &c, His Roman Religion appeareth both by that Bale Godwin and others say he was an Abbot. And as Bale writeth. *l.* cit. liued an Ermit from his youth. And held a Councel in London An. 712. *in which according to the decree of Pope Constantine he appointed Images of dead*

The learning of Archb: Brith-vvald.

His vertue.

His Roman Religion.

Images honored in Englād An.712.

M 3   *Saints*

Saints to be honored, and Masses to be said before
them. Item. *How much* (saith Bale) *this man*
profited Papistrie Geruasius declareth in his
Catalog. And *cap.* 94. *About the yeare* 714.
vnder Archbishop Brithwald ther was a Synod at

Priests
forbidden
to marie.

London for confirmation of Latin masse, and for
putting away Priests wiues, so he termeth
Concubins. And *cap* 91. That *he held a Synod*
An. 710. *Cuius Synodi vigore introducta sunt*
Imagines in omnes Anglorum Ecclesias. Besides
he was *nexu spiritualli adunatus* to Boniface
that notorious Papist, as Boniface testi-
fieth ep. apud Baron. An. 734. Capgraue in
S. Egwins life hath Pope Constantins
Epist. to this Archbishop, in which the
Pope writeth that Brithwald sent Saint

Two
Engl.
Kings re-
quest the
P. to con-
firme
their
Charters,
900. years
agoe.

Egwin twise to Rome, and that two
English kings requested him to confirme
their Charters of gifts that they had giuen
to S. Egwins Monasterie.

Tacwin Archbishop. IX.

The lear-
ning and
vertue of
Archb.
Tacvvin.

9. THe 9. Archbishop was Tacwin consecrated in the yeare 731. sate three
yeares, Died An 734. *He was a man* (saith
Beda *lib.* 5. *cap. vlt*) *certes notable for his god-*
lines and wisdome, and wel conuersant in holy
scriptures. Pope Greg. 3. in his letter to the
Bishops of England in Malmsb. *lib.* 1.

Pont

Pont. *pag.* 210. faith that he knew him a *religious man and of great vertue* . Florent. An 731. Huntington *lib.* 3. *pag.* 339. accord with S. Beda. Godwin in his life faith , *he was a man very religious & no leſſe learned.* Bale Cent. 2. *cap.* 3. faith , he was *notable for Religion and wiſdome , excellently learned in ſcripture , and ſpent his youth in beſt ſtudies.* His Roman Re-ligion appeareth by that as Bale faith , *He wholy dedicated him ſelf to the Benedictin Rules.* And as Godwin faith , and Pope Gregory *l.cit.* teſtifieth , *trauailed to Rome in perſon and there receaued his Pal* . Which alſo con-teſt Beda *in Epit* . Houeden *parte* 1. and others.

His Rom. religion.

Nothelm Archbishop X.

10. THe tenth Archbiſhop was No-thelm , choſen an. 734. ſate fiue yeares, died an, 739. Bale Cent 2. *cap.* 8. faith . *He was a learned and graue yong man , of tryed honeſtie and knovvne to the vvhole Iland for his memorable deedes.* Beda in the Preface of his Hiſtorie faith he was much holpen by him. His Roman Religion is cleare by his going twiſe to Rome, where he receaued his Pal , as write Godwin in his life, Hunting *lib.* 4. *pag.* 340. Houeden 1. parte Anal. Weſtmon an. 736. Beſides that S.

The lear-ning and vertue of Archb. Nothelm.

His Rom. religion.

M 4   Boniface

Boniface that notorious Papist asked his aduiſe in matters of religion Ex Ep. Bonif. in Baron. an. 734.

Cutbert Archbishop XI.

11. THe 11. Archbiſhops was Cutbert choſen an 742. and died an 758. or (as Bale ſaith) 760. *He vvas* (as Bale Cent. 2. *cap.* 14. hath) *borne of noble race, a man of great renowne for his rare learning and ciuil behauior.* Godwin addeth to his praiſes that he was *a good Paſtor* . His Roman Religion appeareth both by his great familiaritie with Saint Boniface the Apoſtle of Germany, whome Fox *lib.* 2. *pag.* 128. confeſſeth to haue bene a Papiſt, and Bale Cent. 2. *cap.* 13. ſaith *vvas next to the great Antichriſt* , at whoſe aduiſe he called a Councel in England , In which among other things , he apointed that our S. Auſtins day ſhould be kept holy day . And alſo becauſe he had a Pal from the Pope, Ex Weſtmon. ad 740. Beſids he ſent moſt freindly letters and preſents to the forſaid S. Boniface Ex Epiſt. in Baron, an. 740.

The rare learning ad vertue of Archb. Cutbert.

His Rom. religion.

S. Auſtins day made holie day.

Bregwin

Bregwin Archbishop XII.

12. THe 12. was Bregwin, chosen an. *The great*
759. & sate three yeares, *born* (saith *learning*
Godwin) *of noble parentage , chosen in regard* *and vertue*
of his modestie , integritie , and great learning. *Bregwin.*
Westmon. an. 760. saith he was *a wise man*
and learned . His Roman Religion is *His Ca-*
known, both because he was a Monke, as *thol. re-*
Capgraue saith in his life, and because he *ligion.*
made earnest suit to the Pope that the
Archbishops might be buried in Christ-
church in Canterb. and not in the Austins
as before : as Godwin in vit. Lamberti
writeth.

Lambert Archbishop XIII.

13. THe 13. is Lambert , chosen as *Rom. re-*
Malmsberie hath in Fastis an. 762. *ligion of*
Archb.
sate 27. yeares. His Roman Religion is out *Lambert.*
of doubt , by that as Godwin saith in his
life and Malmsb. *lib.*1. Pont. *pag.*198. he had
bene Abbot of the Austins; and as Florent.
saith Chron. an. 764. receaued his Pal of
Pope Paul.

M 5 *Ethelard*

Ethelard Archbishop XIIII.

14. THe 14. Archbiſhop was Ethelard, created an. 793. or as Malmsb. in Faſtis ſaith 791. and that he ſate 13. yeares, but Godwin ſaith he ſate but 8. or 9. yeares. But he is manifeſtly ouerſeene. For he putteth his entrance an. 793. and his death an. 806. which time includeth about 13. yeares. He was ſaith Malmsb. 1. Reg. *cap.* 4. *a ſtout man and worthy of God.* And *lib.* 1. Pont. *pag.* 199. *very induſtrious and gratious with the Peeres of the Realme.* He caried the Letters of King Kenulph *and of the Biſhops of England to Pope Leo for reſtitution of the Dioceſſe of Canterburie and was intertained benigniy.* And P. Leo in his *epiſt.* to King Kenulph calleth him *moſt holy moſt deere and moſt skilful.* VVhich *words* (ſaith Malmsb.) *that high and holy Pope would not haue iterated vnles he knew them to be true* Ibid. *A man after the firſt Doctors to be compared with the cheefeſt Biſhops. And I had almoſt ſaid* (ſaith Malmsb.) *to be preferred before them.* As for his Roman Religion that is manifeſt by his forſaid going and ſending to the Pope. Which alſo Fox *lib.* 2. *pag.* 134. and Godwin confeſſe. And by that as Godwin ſaith in his life he was a Monke and (in B. of Wincheſter) he

was

The vvorthines of Archb. Ethelard.

His Cathol. religion.

was an Abbot , which also testifie _{Our an^d}
Malmsb. 1. Reg. *cap.* 4. Hunting *lib.* 4. _{cient} _{Kings ho-}
Houeden *pag.* 403. In Ingulph he subscri- _{pe to buy}
beth to a Charter in which King Offa _{heauen} _{by god}
professeth . *Per bona opera mercaris præmia* vvorks.
sempiterna.

VVulfred Archbishop XV.

15. THe 15. was Wulfred who succe-
ded (as Godwin saith) an. 807. _{Rom. re-} _{ligion of}
but Malmsb: saith 804. with whome also _{Archb:} _{vvulfred.}
agreeth Florent. Chron. an. 804. he sate
25. yeares . And his Roman Religion is _{See the}
cleare , because (as Godwin writeth)*he* _{Charter}
was made Archbishop at Rome by Leo 3. And _{to vvhich} _{he sub-}
again the 9. yeare after his consecration _{scribed in}
went to Rome . Florent. an. 804. and _{Indulph} _{pag. 855.}
Westmon an. 806. say he had a Pal of
Pope Leo.

Theologild Archbishop. XVI.

16. TTheologild was the 16. Who
(as Godwin saith) succeded an.
832, but Malmsb. in Fastis saith 829 and
dyed the same yeare . Of him little is
written . But as Godwin saith, he was _{Rom. re-} _{ligion of}
Abbot of Canterburie which putteth his _{Archb.} _{Theolo-}
Roman Religion out of question. _{gild.}

Celnoth

Celnoth Archbishop. XVII.

17. THe 17. place occupied Celnoth an. 830. as Malmsb. in Fastis, Or an. 831. as Florent. in Chron. Or an. 832. as Godwin in his life, and sate an. 41. as Malmsb. and Florent agree ; Godwin

Romreli- saith an. 38. His Roman Religion is
gion of manifest by his Pal wich (as Florent an.
Archb.
Celnoth. 831. and Westmon. an. 832. write) he
receaued of Pope Gregorie. And by his
subscription to a Charter in Ingulph,
Wherin King Withlaf offereth a Chalice
King of and Crosse of gould to the Aultare in
England
giueth his Croiland, and *clamidem coccineam ad Casulam*
princely *faciendam his scarlet robe to make a Chisible.*
robe to
make a And *pag.* 862. publickly professed him selfe
Chisible. to be cured of a disease by the merits of
S. Guthlac.

Athelard Archbishop. XVIII.

The vvor- 18. THe 18. Archbishop was Athelard
thines of An. 893. saith Godwin, but
Archb.
Athelard Malmsb. in Fastis an. 871. he sate 18. years
and his 3. and as Malmsb. *lib.* 1. Pont. *pag.* 199. saith of
Prede-
cessors. him and his three Predecessors they did
many worthie things both towards God
and

and the world, but for want of writers
all is obscure. Godwin saith he was a
great diuine, and some times Monk of
Christ-church in Canterbury by which His Rom.
his Roman religion is out of doubt. religion.

Plegmund Archbishop XIX.

19. THe 19. was Plegmund, Entred
(saith Godwin and Malmsb. in
Fast)an.889. sate an.26.as both agree.But
in *lib.* 1. Pont. Malmsb.attributeth to him
33. yeares. *He was* (saith Godwin) *the most* Most ex-
excellent learned man of his time. And as Fox cellent
saith *lib.* 3. *pag.* 170. *Schoolemaister to King* of Archb.
Alfred. Hunting.*lib.*5.*pag.*351.saith,He was Plegmund
chosen of God and all the people. And
Florent. an. 872. addeth that he was
Venerabilis vir sapientia præditus, and an.889. His Ca-
Literis insigniter eruditus. His Roman thol.
religion is out of question, becauſe as saith.
Godwin writeth, *In his youth he was an*
Hermit. And being chosen Archbishop
trauailed to Rome in person,and was ther
consecrated. And was Legat to Pope
Formosus, as he testifyeth *epist.* 2.in these
wordes. *VVe command Plegmund to be our*
Legat in all matters.

A thelin

Althelin Archbishop X X.

20. **A** Thelin fucceded in the 20. place
an. 915. as Godwin hath, and
Malmsb. in Faft. and fate 9. years *who* (faith
Godwin) *had before bene Abbot of Glaftenbury.*
And therfor no queftion can be made of
his Religion.

Rom.
Religion
of Archb.
Athelin.

VVolfhelm Archbishop. X X I.

21. **T**He 21. Archbifhop Wolfhelm
entring an. 924. as Godwin and
Malmsb. in Faft. agree, dyed alfo 934.
Who was (faith Godwin in the Bifhops of
Wells out of Polidor) *famous as wel for*
vertue as learning.

The fa-
mous
learning
andvver-
tue of
Archb.
vvolfhelm

S. Odo Archbishop X X I I.

22. **T**He 22. Archbifhop was S. Odo
an. 934. as Godwin and Malmsb.
in Faft. accord, and fate an. 24. in great
fauour and authoritie ynder diuers Princes. *His parents* (faith Godwin) *were Danes*
of great welth and nobilitie, who difinherited him
for Chriftian religion. *King Edward fenior*
                                              perceauing

perceauing his great excellency of wit set him to
schole where he profited exceedingly. Bale Cent.
2. *cap.* 30. saith, *He was so skilful both in Greeke*
and Latin that sodenly he could vtter either in
prose or any kind of verse what so euer he would.
Godwin faith he preached painfully.
Florent. an. 958. and Westmon Ibid. say:
Odo a man famous for wit, laudable for vertue
and indued with the spirit of Prophecie. In
Malmsb. *lib.* 1. Pont. *pag.* 200. He professeth
that *he would spend all the riches in the world if*
he had them, and him self for his flock. And
Malmsb. there faith that he wrought
miracles. Fox *lib.* 3. *pag.* 151. faith, *A zealous*
care of the Churches of the Lord reigned in him
and other Archbishops then. And thus much of
his learning and vertue. His Roman
religion is out of all doubt. For Godwin
faith being elected he would not be
Archbishop before he was made Monke
as all his Predecessors (sayd he) had bene.
And as Bale faith *l.* cit. *He receaued a Pal*
from Pope Agapit 2. Decreed that mariages of
the Ministers of the Church are to be accounted
Heretical, and exalted Popish monkerie. Thus
Bale. But it spiteth Fox most that Osbern
in vit. Odonis writeth that in his tyme
certain Clercks seduced by wicked error ende-
vored to auouch that the bread and wine which
are set on the Altar after consecration remain
in their former substance and are onely a signe of
                                          the

S. Odo
his rare
learning
both in
greek and
latin.

His great
holines.

His mira-
cles.

His Rom.
religion.

Priests
mariages
forbidden

Some
denied
Transub-
stātiation.

the body and blood of Chrift . And for their
conuerfion. Odo did (as Osbern Malmsb.
and an other Author who as Fox faith
wrote in the time of Alfricus the 4. Arch.
after Odo, write) by his prayers obtaine
of God that the Sacrament fhould appeare
in forme of true flefh and blood , and
againe returne to their priftinat fhape.
This hiftorie Fox *pag.* 1139. diflyketh. Firft
becaufe Osbern faith but *quidam* . But fo
alfo writeth his brother Bale *loc.* cit.
Capgraue in Odone and others. Secondly
that Osbern faith this miracle was done
to conuert the Clerkes , and the other
Author faith it was done to teftify Odo
his holines. As if it could not be done for
both endes. But it fufficeth us, 1. that Odo
and England then beleeued Tranfubftan-
tion, fo odious a thing now to Proteftants,
2. that S. Odo confirmed it by fuch
a miracle as fome Priefts who then began
to deny it , beleeued to be a true miracle
and were conuerted therby . Now
whether they , who were then prefent
and faw it, or Fox who liued aboue 600.
yeares after, were more like to know the
truth of that miracle let euery one iudg.
But here I would wifh the careful Reader
to note , firft that the denial of Tranfubftantiation and the real prefence of Chrift
in the facrament began in England aboue
300. yeare

Marginal notes:

A great miracle to confirme Tranfubftantiation.

Fox denieth a miracle which diuers that faw it confeffe and were conuerted by it.

300. yeares after the land was conuerted to Chriſtianitie, to wit, circa An .950. as Bale ſaith, which ſheweth that the ancient Engliſh Chriſtians beleeued Tranſubſtantiation. Secondly that Tranſubſt. was denied but of a few, and conſequently the general faith of England beleeued it. Thirdly, that this hereſie was ſoone extinct, and the Authors confuted of S. Odo Primat of this Land both by miracle and by writing, which writing (ſaith Bale *l. cit.* he entitled) *Defenſio Euchariſtiæ.* And for this Fox. *lib. 3. cap.*151. ſaith that *Odo might ſeeme to be the worſt that occupied that place.* So he termeth light darknes, and darknes light. But for Tranſubſtantiation yow heard before confeſſed by Doct. Humfrey that Saint Auſtin brought it into England. And before S. Odo, that great Engliſh Deuine Alcuin profeſſeth it clearly in theſe words. *Bread of it ſelfe hath not reaſon, but the Prieſt prayeth that it be made reaſonable of Almightie God by paſſing into the bodie of his ſonne.* Item. *After Conſecration it is one thing and ſeemeth an other. For it ſeemeth bread and wine, but it is in truth Chriſts body and blood. VVherfor God prouiding for our weaknes who vſe not to eat raw fleſh nor duink blood maketh that theſe two gifts do abide in their ancient forme and yet it is in truth Chriſts body and blood.*

Transubſtantiation the ancient faith of England.

Denial of Traſubſt. confuted of S. Odo by miracle and vvriting.

S. Greg. ſent hither the beleef of Tranſubſtant.

S. Odo. Alcuin.

Lib. de diuin offic. o. de miſſa.

Tranſubſtant. plainly profeſſed

N And

s. Beda.
Tom.2.
cap.82.

And S. Beda cited by Walden. *There is
feene the shape of bread where the substance of
bread is not: nether is it any other bread then that
which came from heauen.*

S. Dunstan Archbishop. XXIII.

23. IN the year 959. fucceeded S. Duftan,
and died in the yeare 988. as all

The great
learning
and rare
vertue of
S. Dunftã.

agree. *He was* (faith Godw.) *borne of good
parentage and for the most parte brought vp in the
Abbay of Glaftenburie, where befides other good
learning he was taught to fing, to play vpon
Inftruments, to paint and carue, In all which he
prooued very excellent. For his manifould good
partes made much of the Kings, most gratious vnto
King Edward and King Elbred vnder whome he*

His mira-
cles.

*ruled all things at his pleafure, and for the most
parte admired for a most holy and vertuous man,
and after canonized for a Saint.* The like hath
Bale Cent. 2. *cap.* 38. Malmsb *lib.* 1. Pont:

Surius
Tom.3.
vvriten by
Osborn
in the
tyme of
the Con-
queft.

pag. 202. faith, *He adorned the ftepps of his promotion with vnwearied vertues, Thofe times
were happy which had fuch a Prelat as did nothing
leffe than he fayd.* And much there of his
vertue and miracles. But who readeth his
life in Surius will admire him. But his

His Rom.
Religion.

Roman religion is confeffed of Proteftants. For Godwin faith. *He was a Monke,*

Godvvin.

and bewitched (fo he fpeaketh) *the forfaid
Kings*

Kings with loue of Monkerie, and applied all his Maried
indeuors to the rayfing of Monkes and Monafteries, Priefts
and perfecuted maried Priefts. Fox. Acts. persecuted
lib. 3. *pag.* 136. *faith he was drovvned in all* Fox.
superftition. And *pag.* 158. *An ennemy to Prieftes*
vviues. Bale. Cent. 2. *cap.* 38. *He receaued a* Bale.
Pal of Pope Iohn. 13. *at Rome, of vvhome he obtai-*
ned a Breue by vvhich he might condemn the ma- Priefts
riages (the Concubins in deede) *of the Mini-* compel-
fters of the Church and compel them to keepe the led to
voue of fingle life, and that he did annihilat (faith uovv of
Bale) *the vvord of God* (as Luther vnderftan- fingle life.
deth it) *for the Popes traditions.* And *cap.* 40.
That he had a Vifion at maffe though
Bale call it a dreame. And there is extant
the Ep. of pope Iohn. 12. to S. Dunftan,
wherin he maketh him his *Legat* and
giueth him *a Pal to vfe at Maffe.*

Ethelgar Archbishop. XXIIII.

24. A Fter Saint Dunftan fucceeded
Ethelgar in the year 988, and fat
two yeares. His Rom. religion appeareth Rom, Re-
by that (as Godwin faith) he had before ligion of
bene Abbot of Winchefter which Ethelgar.
Malmsh. *lib.* 1. Pont. *pag.* 203. faith he was
made by Saint Ethelwald who was a
notorious Papift.

Syricius Archbishop. XXV.

Rom. religion of Archb. Syricius.

25. THE 25. Archbishop who succeeded An. 990. as Malmsb: hath in Fast: & sate as he sayth fiue yeares, was Siricius, Whose Roman religion can not be doubted of. For (as Godwin sayth) he was a Monk of Glastenburie, and by Saint Dunstan made Abbot of S. Austins in Canterburie, and by him also preferred to the Bishoprick of Wilton.

Alfricus Archbishop. XXVI.

26. GOdwin and Malmsb. in Fast do put this Alfricus after Syricius, although Malmsburie. 1. Pont. *pag.* 203. put him before Syricius. He entred as is said in fastis An. 995, and died An. 1006. as all agree. Of these three Bishops little is written, because the Danes rage was in Rom. religion of Archb. Africus. their time most furious. But his Roman religion is out of question. For as Godwin testifieth he was brought vp in Glastenburie, disciple(as Bale saith Cent. 2. Alfricus counted a craftie Papist. *cap.* 41.) of S. Ethelwald, and Abbot of Abingdon, and *for his crafte* (saith he) *in promoting Papistrie made Archbishop of Canterbury.*

bury. To this man Fox would gladly attribute a fermon in the Saxon tongue publifhed by Proteftants of the Eucharift. But himfelf is doubtful *pag.* 1040. Edit. 1596, And the Proteftants that publifhed the fermon deny it in their Preface before it. And if he were the Author of that fermon, it would not be a point of Proteftancie as you may fee by what Bale hath fayd.

S. Elpheg Archbishop. XXVII.

27. NExt followed S. Elpheg an. 1006. and fate 7. years. He *vvas* (faith Godwin) *of great parentage and vvonderfull abstinence, neuer eating, drinking, nor sleeping more than necessitie compelled him, spending his time altogether in pietie, studie or other necessaire busines,* So that *vvhat vvith preaching and example of holy life he conuerted many vnto Christ.* And in the Bifh. of Winchefter he addeth that he was *a learned man.* Malmsb. *lib.* 1. Pont. *pag.* 203. faith *His life vvas ful of vertues and miracles, beyng at Rome he manifestly teuld vnto his company the death of Kenulph vvho had succeeded him in VVinchester, was slaine of the Danes rather* (faith Florent. An. 1012.) *than he vvould pil his floock to ransome him vvith* 3000. *pounds. His body* (faith Malmsb.)

His vvōderful vertue of S. Elpheg.

His learning and miracles.

His bodie. incorrupt

N 3   *retaining*

retaining marks of fresh blood remaineth to this

daye vncorrupted. The Roman religion of this bleſſed man is euident, both by his going to Rome after he was choſen Archb. which vndoubtedly was to fetch his Pal; and becauſe (as Godwin ſaith

and Florent : and Veſtmon An. 984). he was Abbot before he was Biſhop , and finally Canonized by the Papiſts.

Liuing Archbishop. XXVIII.

28. Liuing ſucceded an. 1013. and ſate 7. yeares . Of whome little is written , but that he fled the Realme for feare of Danes . But his Roman religion is certain by that which hath bene ſayde of his Predeceſſors.

Agelnoth Archbishop. XXIX.

29. THe 29. is Agelnoth ſirnamed *the good* (ſaith Godwin and Florent. an.1020) *and ſonne to the Earle Agelmar.* He entred an.1020.and ſate 18. yeares. He *was*

ſo deere (ſaith Bale Cent.2. cap. 46.) to *King Canut that he vſed his wit and help cheefly in diſpatching matters.* His Roman religion is manifeſt For as the ſame Bale writeth he

vvent

went to Rome as the manner (faith he) *was that
receiuing his Pal he might sweare Antichrists* (so
he stil termeth the Pope) *faith*. The like
saith Godwin. And of his going to Rome
for his Pal testify Malmsb. *lib. 4.* Pont.
pag. 289. Hunt. *lib. 6.* Florent. *an.* 1021.
Houeden 1022. Fox *lib. 3. pag. 163.* addeth
that *King Canut following much the superstition
of Agelnoth went a Pilgrimage to Rome*. And
Bale *l. cit* addeth. That he perswaded
King Canut to resigne his crowne to the Crucifix,
and calleth him *a Bishop of superstition.*

Eadsin Archbishop XXX.

30. IN the yeare 1038. succeeded Eadsin, The vertue
and died 1050. His Roman religion of Archb.
and vertue appeareth by that (as Godwin Eadsin.
saith) after his death he was made a Saint.
Malmsb. *lib.* Pont. *pag.* 204. and Florent·
an. 1043. write that he anointed King
Edward Confess. who was a notorious
Papist.

Robert Archbishop. XXXI.

31. THe next was Robert who,
succeeded *an.* 1050. and sate two,
or (as Malmsb. in Fastis saith) 3. yeares. His

N 4   Roman

Roman religion is manifeſt by that he was a Monk , brought vp (as Godwin faith) in the Monaſterie of Gemetica in Normandie : had a Pal from Rome as he faith in the life of Stigand . And being accuſed went (faith Malmsb. 1. Pont *pag.*204.) to Rome, from whence he came with letters to clear him, and to recouer his See.

Stigand Archbishop XXXII.

32. THe laſt Archbiſhop before the Conqueſt was Stigand , who an. 1052. vſurped the feate whilſt his Predeceſſor liued, and was depriued an. 1069. *He was* (faith Godwin) *ſtoute and wiſe inough.* His Roman religion is manifeſt, by

that (as Godwin writeth) *he laboured to procure a Pal of the Pope,* but could not becauſe of his vnlawful entrance. And therfore as Ingulph who liued then, writeth. *pag.* 898, Malmsb. *lib.* 1. Pont. *pag.*204. Florent. An. 1058. he procured

The firſt
and laſt
Archb. in
the Sa-
xons time
ſaid Maſſe
and had a
Pall,

one of an Antipope which then was, *and vſed it* (faith Florent. An. 1070,) *in Miſſarum celebratione .* Thus you fee all the Archbiſhops of Canterburie in the Saxons tyme for 466. yeares together were Roman Catholicks . And as S. Auſtin the firſt of them

them had a Pal from the Pope and sayd Masse, so did the very last. Now let vs shew the same of all the Archbishops from the Conquest vnto our time.

CHAP. XX.

That all the Archbishops of Can-terb. from the time of the Conquest vnto our tyme were Roman Catholicks.

1. THe 33. Archbishop of Canterburie and first after the Conquest of England was Lanfranck. He entred an. 1070. being Monke and Prior of Becco *in regard* (saith Godwin) *of his singuler wisdome and great knowledg of all good learning that those times could affoard.* Was first called by Duke William to be Abbot, and after hauing conquered England *for his wisdom and faith-fulnes he made choise of him for Archbishop of Canterburie, as one in all respects most fit and worthie, which being wel known to all men, the Couent of Canterb. at the Kings first nomination readily chose him. The nobilitie and Laitie willingly receaued him with great applause.* Bale

The singuler great learning and vvisdom of Arch: Lanfranck

Godvvin.

Bale.

N 5 Cent.

Cent. 13. cap. 12. faith he was the moft perfect of his tyme in all kind of Logick or fubtilitie of Ariftotle. He corrected and amended according to the right faith all the bookes of the olde and new Teft ament which had bene corrupted by faulte of the writers and alfo the writings of the holy

Fox.

Fathers. Fox lib. 4. pag. 184. From his commendation and worthines I lift not to detract anie

Stovv.

thing. Stow Chron. pag. 148. Lanfranck skilful in fcience prudent in Councel and gouernment of

His holines.

things and for religion and life moft holie. And pag. 171. reporteth that King William Conqueror being redy to die faid that he fuppofed that the praifes of Lanfranck and Anfelme his Succeffor found in the vttermoft corners of the Earth. He was bufie (faith Godwin) in exhorting King Rufus to vertue

Proteftāts forced moft highly to commend their learning and vertue vvho condemned their Doctrin.

and godlines. And as long as Lanfranck lived (faith Stow pag. 179.) Rufus feemed to abhor all kind of vice in fo much as he was counted the mirror of Kings. This high praife for learning and vertue Proteftants giue to this Archbifhop whome to their confufion they confeffe (as yovv fhall heare anon) to haue bene a moft notorious Papift and the greateft enemy of

Archb. Lanfranc firft confuted the deniers of Tranfubftātiation.

Berengarius, whome they account their Patriarch for the denial of the real prefence. If I fhould alleadg the fayings of Catholick writers in his commendation, I fhould neuer make an ende, Onely
therfor

therfor I will cite two who liued in his time, and quote some others . Malmsb. *lib.* 3. Hist. *pag.* 109. saith *he was a man comparable to the Fathers in Religion and learning, on whom in earnest may be verified A third Cato came from heauen. So heauenly sauor had embued his brest and mouth So all the Latin Church did by his learning stir it self vp to the study of the liberal sciences . So by his example or feare Monastical perfection did goe forward in religion.* And much more he hath of Lanfranck 1. Pont. *pag.* 213. & sequ. Ingulph also: Hist. *pag.* 901. saith , *he was the most commended and clear Doctor of all liberal sciences, and most expert in temporal affaires and most holy in life and religion.* The like also hath Marian who liued at that tyme Chron. an. 1070. Florent: and Westmon. Ibid. Huntington *lib.* 7. Neubrigen *lib.* 1. *cap.* 1. Paris. Hist. *pag.* 8. Walsingham in ypodigmate. Capgraue and Trithem in Lanfranco.

2. And no les notorious was the Roman religion of this worthie Archb. than his learning and vertue was famous . Which for breuitie sake I will onely proue by the confession of Protestants . Bale Cent. 13. *cap.* 12. saith plainly. *He did many things for the exaltation of Papistrie . Defineth him to be an Heretick who differeth from the Church of Rome in doctrine of faith.* Which is as much as any Papist now can or wil say. And Cent. 2. *cap.* 62.

Margin notes:
Malmesbur.
Ingulph.
Marian
Florent.
Huntingt.
Rom. religion of Archb. Lanfranc.
Bale.
He an Heretik vvho in faith differeth from the Church of Rome.

cap. 62. *Lanfranck and Anselm set vp the mouldy* (so this wretch blasphemeth) *Idol of the Masse , and condemned the holy marriages of Priestes.* Fox *lib.* 4. *pag.* 173. citeth this beginning of his letter to Pope Alexander . *To the Lorde Pope Alexander high ouerseer of all Christian Religion, Lanfranck due obedience with all subiection.* Pag. 394. he calleth him *a stout Champion of the Pope.* Pag. 1147. *cheefest trobler of Berengarius* . And *pag.* 1148. citeth this profession of Lanfranck, *I beleeue the earthly substances which vpon the Lords table are diuinely sanctified by the ministration of the Priest to be conuerted into the essence of the Lords body , the outward formes onely of the things them selues and qnalities reserued* . Bilson of Obed. *pag.* 681. *Lanfranck and Anselm came in with their Antichristian deuises and inuentions* , and chargeth him to haue first brought Transubstantiation into England. But how false this is appeareth by that no one Author of that time chargeth him with altering any point of the faith of the English , and also by that which before we shewed out of Protest. that S. Greg. sent in Transubstantiation into England, and that S. Odo defended it both by writing and miracles. And who wil more of Lanfrancks earnestnes in Roman religion, may read his Epistle to Pope Alexander 2. and Alexanders to him , and his

booke

Priests mariages condemned.

Fox.

Lanfranck his profession of Transubstant.

Bilson.

Lanfranck altered nothing in our English faith.

booke againſt Berengarius for the real
preſence.

S. Anſelm Archbiſhop. XXXIIII.

3. **T**He 34. Archbiſhop was S. Anſelm
an. 1093. and died an. 1109. *A moſt*
worthie man (ſaith Godwin) *of great learning,*
as his works yet extant teſtifie, and for integritie
of life and conuerſation admirable. Vndoutedly
he was a good and holy man and as worthy the
honor of Saint as any I thinck (ſaith he) *euer*
was canonized by the Pope ſince his tyme. Thus
the Proteſt. them ſelues commend this
bleſſed mā. Of whome who liſt to know
more, may read his life in Surius written
by Edner his Chaplin. Malmsb. who
then liued *lib.* 4. Reg. ſayth *none was more*
obſeruant of iuſtice, none at that time ſo ſoundly
learned, none ſo wholly ſpiritual, the Father of the
Contrie, the mirror of the world. And much
more *lib.* 1. Pont. *pag.* 216. & ſeq. As for his
religion that is manifeſt to be Roman.
For he was a Monk and ſcholler to Lanfranck as Fox ſaith *pag.* 185. had his Pal
from Rome, appealed from the King to
the Pope, and *pag.* 186. he writeth how he
tould King Rufus to his face that *it was*
vn iuſt to command Biſhops not to appeale to Rome.
pag. 195. *He was ſuperſtitious in religion.* Bale

Cent.

(marginal notes:) The admirable learning and holineſs of S. Anſelm.

His Rom religion.

Vniuſt to forbid appeals to Rome.

Cent. 13. *cap.* 16. and others write that he procured that Kings should not inuest Bishops. Cent. 2. *cap.* 50. *He augmented the impudencie of the Popes being their Counsellor in Rome, and their Vicar in England.* Finally they all agree that he forbad Priests marriages, and as Godwin speaketh *persecuted maried Priests extremely.* In so much as Fox *pag.* 191. Bale Cent. 2. *cap.* 59. make him the first that forbad Priests in England to haue wiues, and Cambd. in Britan. saith, *wiues were not forbidden to Priests in England before the yeare* 1102. Which how vntrue it is appeareth by S. Greg. words to S. Austin in Beda *lib.* 1. *cap.* 27. where Saint Greg. apointeth that , *if there be any among the Clergie out of holy orders which can not liue chast they shall take wiues.* wherin he clearly excludeth all in holy orders from wiues. and in Concil. Rom. *If any Priest or Deacon mary a wife be he accursed* . And about 100. yeares after that , Beda *lib.* 5. *cap.* 22. said plainly that *English Priests professed to binde them selues to chastitie* . And Prolog. in Samuel writeth thus, *VVe who haue purposed according to the custom of Ecclesiastical life to abstain from wiues, and to liue single* . And S. Bedas scholler Alcuin *l.* de Virtutibus *cap.* 18. *Chastitie is necessarie to all but cheefly to the Ministers of the Altar of Christ. For he must haue such Ministers as be not corrupted by any contagion*

Priests fordidden to marrie

pag. 163.
Priests forbidden to marrie. from the first infancie of our Church.

S. Gregorie.

S. Beda.

Alcuin.

contagion of the flesh , but rather shine with con-
tinencie of chaſtitie. Bale alſo Cent 1. *cap.* 64. Bale.
writeth thus . *About the yeare* 719. *vnder*
Brithwald Archbiſh. was a Synod held at London brithvvald
for prohibiting of Prieſts wiues, as Nauclerus
(ſaith he) *and others affirme.* And after that
again. S. Odo Archb. as the ſame Bale hath S.Odo.
Cent. 2. *cap.* 30. *Decreed that the mariages of*
the Miniſters of the Church were Heretical. Yea
Cambd. him ſelfe *pag.* 259. writeth that Cābden.
King Ethelwolph about the yeare 855.
had a diſpenſation of the Pope to marry
becauſe he was *ſacris ordinibus initiatus in*
holy orders. But what diſpenſation had that
King needed , if it had bene lawful for
Prieſts thē to marrie. And after this Kings
time , *Dunſtan and his fellows* (ſaith Fox Acts S.Dunſtā.
pag. 156.) *cauſed King Edgar to call a Councel of* Fox.
the Clergie, wher it was enacted and decreed that
the Canons of diuers Cathedral Churches
Collegiats, Parſons, Vicars, Prieſts, and Deacons
with their wiues and children ſhould either giue
ouer that kinde of life, or els giue rome to Monkes.
And Cambden in Brit. *pag.* 211. ſaith this
Councel was held an. 977. how then
could he ſay that Prieſts wiues were
neuer forbidden before, an. 1102. After
that alſo *Lanfranck* (as Fulk Annotat. in Lanfrank.
Math. 8.) *in a Synod at Wincheſter made a*
decree againſt the marriage of Prieſts. And Fox Fulk.
Acts *pag.* 195. citeth an Epiſtle of S. Anſelm
where

where he hath thefe wordes . *Becaufe fo
curfed a marriage* (of Prieſts) *was forbidden in
a Councel of his Father* (he meaneth the
Conqueror) *and of the ſaid Archbishop Lan-
francus lately ,* I command *that all Prieſts that
keepe women ſhalbe depriued of their Churches
and Ecclesiaſtical Benefices .* Wherby it is
euident that Prieſts were not firſt forbidden to marry or haue wiues by Anſelme,
but by manie both Archbiſhops and
Councels, euer ſince the infancie of our
Engliſh Church.

*Wiues
forbidden
to preiſts
in Englād
both by
Archb.
and coun-
cels.*

Rodolph Archbishop. XXXV.

4. THE 35. Archbiſhop was Rodolph,
Entred an. 1114. and died an. 1122.
He behaued (ſaith Godwin) *him ſelf wel in
the place , was very affable and curteouſe , and
willing to pleaſe.* Malmsb. 1. Pont. *pag.* 250.
ſaith, *he was meruaylouſly learned and eloquent*
And *pag.* 252. *very religious .* His Roman
religion is euident, for as Godwin teſti-
fieth he was a Monke and ſcholler to
Lanfranck, receaued a Pal ſolemly from
Rome , and after trauailed in perſon to
Rome.

*The mar-
veilous
learning
and pietie
of Archb:
Rodolph.*

*His Rom.
religion·*

VVilliam

VVilliam corbel *Archbishop* XXXVI.

5. TO him succeeded William Corbel an.1122.and departed 1136. He was (say Marian.and Continuat. Florent.) *vir eximiæ religionis*. His Roman religion is vndoubted, because as Godwin saith, he was a monk and the Popes Legat. Called a Synod wherin many Canons were made againſt the mariage of Prieſts. And finally crowned King Stephen at Maſſe. Continuat.Florent.who then liued saith he went to Rome for his Pal, and had it of Pope Calixtus, and again an other time ; and was honorably receaued of Pope honorius, who made him his Legat in England and Scotland.

Pietie and Rom. Re-ligion of Archb. Corbel.

Theobald Archbishop XXXVII.

6. THe 37. was Theobald chosen an. 1138. and deceased an. 1160. *He was* (saith Godwin) *of so svveete and gentle behauiour, being very vvise vvithal, as he vvas greatly eſteemed of high and lovv, Kings, Nobles and Commons.* His Religion is known, by that as Godwin witneſſeth, he was a

The vvor-thines of Archb. Theobald.

His Rom. religion.

O   Bene-

Benedictin monke, and Abbot, cõsecrated of the Popes Legat, receaued his Pal from Pope Innocent.2. who also indued him and his successors for euer with the Title of *Legatus natus*, which they all kept til the later end of King Henrie 8. Continuat. Florent. addeth that being called of the Pope he went to a Councel held in Rome.

S. Thomas Archbishop. XXXVIII.

7. THe 38. Archbishop and first Englishman after the Conquest was S. Thomas, Elect an. 1161. & martyred an. 1171. *He was* (saith Neubrigen. who

The excellent partes and vertue of S. Thomas Archb.

then liued *lib. 2. c. 16.*) *vir acris ingenij: A man of a sharp wit and competent eloquence comely in fauor and finely handed, comparable to the best in the effectual dispach of any busines, he had so speciall a prerogatiue of honor and loue in the Princes hart that he seemed to be his fellow mate in the Crowne.* And Paris who liued soone after *pag.* 272. saith, *a primis adolescentiæ annis. From his very youth he was adorned* with manifould grace. And *pag.* 167. *Carnem cilicijs attritam cum femoralibus cilicinis edomuit. His flesh worne*

His vvonderful austeritie of life.

with hairecothe, he tamed with britches of the same. Houeden Parte 2. Anal. saith, *Irreprehensibilis vita singulis diebus* &c. *Irreprehensible*

fible he receaued day by day three or fyue difciplines
at the Prieſts hand , his inner garment was of
rugged haircloth of Gotes haire wherwith his
whole bodie was couered from the elbow euen to
the knees he lay vpon the bare ground before his
bed,and neuer ceaſed from prayer vntil for very
wearines he layd downe his head vpon the ſtone he
there placed inſteed of a boulſter. The ſame and
much more is written in his life by four
writers of great credit who then liued.
Fox Acts. pag. 206. ſaith of him thus.
Threatnings and flatterings were to him both one,
great helps of nature were in him , In memorie
excellent good, ful of deuotion . Godwin ſaith
he was *moſt canonically elected and preſently*
after his conſecration became ſo graue ſo auſtere
ſo deuoute in al outvvard shevv as he ſee med quite
an other man . And as Weſtmon an. 1162.
writeth *a Courtiers life he changed into a moſt*
faintly . Thus both Catholicks and Prote-
ſtanıs write of this bleſſed martir . His His Rom. religion.
Roman religion is doubted of no man.
Fox Acts pag. 206. ſaith he was *without all*
true religion , ſuperſticious to the obedience of the
Pope, and *pag.779.* ſaith *Lanfranck Anſelm*
Beket brought the Popes Iudicial authoritie from
Rome into this Land, both ouer Kings and ſubiects,
which euer ſince hath continewed til theſe later
yeares. Bale Cent. 2. *cap.* 100. ſaith he was
Legatus a latere. The Popes Legat.& aſſiduus labor
&c. and *his continual labor was to ſubiect the*

Princes Maieſtie to Antichriſt. What great pennance King Henrie 2. did of his owne accord for being ſome cauſe of this bleſſed mans death, and how God the ſame day rewarded him with a miraculous victorie ouer the Scott, yow may read in the Chronicles. And how great the deuotion of our Forfathers was to this Saint appeareth by the ineſtimable riches which they gaue to his ſhrine, of which

Eraſmus writteth *viliſſima pars* &c. *The baſeſt part was golde, all ſhined, glittered and caſt forth lightening by reaſon of the rare and mightie gemmes and precious ſtones yea the whole Church in euery parte abounded more than with royal riches.* Godwin in vit. Baldwin, *Euery one thought him ſelfe happie that could doe any thing to his honor.* (Of theſe riches King Henry 8. had 24. waine Loades beſides that which others embezeled) And our Anceſtors deuotion towards him appeareth by the hard marble ſtones which are to be ſeene worne round about the place where his ſhrine ſtood with the knees of thoſe that came to pray there. As Proteſtante with admiration do ſhew to thoſe that come thither.

Richard

Richard Archbishop XXXIX.

8. IN the yeare 1173. succeded Richard. and departed this life an. 1183. *A man (*saith Godwin*) very liberal, gentle and paſsing wiſe*. His Roman religion is certain. For as the same Godwin and Fox *pag.* 394. confeſſe, he was a Benedictin Monk and conſecrated of the Pope. Which also teſtifieth Weſtmon. an. 1174. Houeden 1175. saith he held a Councel wherin he decreed *Patrum* (saith he) *regulis inherentes inſiſting in the rules of ancient Fathers that Prieſtes ſhould haue no wiues, and be ſhauen.*

The vvorthines of Archb. Richard.

His Rom. Religion.

Prieſts commanded to put avvay vvomen and to be ſhauen.

Baldwin Archbishop XL.

9. THe 40. Archbiſhop Baldwin ſucceeded an. 1184. and deceaſed an. 1190. *a very comely man* (saith Godwin) *modeſt and ſober, of ſuch abſtinence as fame durſt neuer ſtamp auy ſiniſter report vpon him. Of few wordes ſlovv to anger, and very ſtudious from his child hood.* Fox Acts. *pag.* 230. addeth, that it is ſaide, *that he neuer eat fleſh in his life.* He went with King Richard into the holy land, where saith Godwin *by preaching, counſel, liberal almes, and continual example of a*

The admirable vertue and learning of Archb. Baldvvin.

O 3   most

most vertuous life he did great good, and there dyed. Bale Cent. 3. *cap.* 27. faith he was *eloquent in speech an exact Philosopher and was accounted in those dayes fit for all maner of studie. He was very diligent and careful in the discharge of his Archiepiscopal function behauing himselfe as a worthie Pastor.* **His Rom. religion.** The Roman religion of this holy Prelat is manifest. For as Fox Godwin and Bale L. cit. say he was a Ciftertian Monke and at the commandement of the Pope razed down to the ground a Church which him selfe had built.

Reginald Fiz Iocelin Archb. XLI.

10. THe next was Reginald fiz Iocelin, elected faith Godwin by the Monkes of Canterburie an. 1191. **Rare humilitie of Archb. Reginald.** but he at firſt withſtood what he might, and with teares vnfainedly befought them to make choiſe of ſome other, and dyed within few dayes after. **His Rom. Religion.** Yet his Roman religion is cleare. For as Godwin faith the Pope prefently afforded him his Pal.

Hubert

Hubert VValter Archb. XLII.

11. IN the yeare 1193. succeeded Hubert Walter and dyed an. 1205. *VVho was (saith Paris Hist. pag. 26.) vir profundi pectoris &c. A man of a deepe reache, and a singuler piller in the Realme, of incomparable stabilitie and wisdome.* (The same hath Stow *pag.* 244.) and *pag.* 324. *A magnifical and faithful man, who as long as he liued kept King Iohn from mischeefe and miserie. He was* (saith Godwin) *an excellent and memorable man, a bridle vnto the King, and an obstacle of tyrany, the peace and comfort of the people, And lastly a notable refuge both of high and lowe against all manner of iniurie and oppression, faithful and loyal to his Prince, louing and very careful of his Contrie, in which he caused many excellent lawes to be established. King Richard ceur de Lion had experience of his great wisdom, and other manifould vertues. Nether was ther euer Clergie man ether befor or after him of so great power, neuer any man vsed his authoritie more moderatly.* And as for the religion of this worthie Prelat it is manifest. For as Godwin testifieth he founded a monasterie *for his owne soules health, and for the soules of his Father and mother, as him self speaketh in the foundation, and an other of Cistercian Monkes*. After his election pro-

Great vvorthines of Archb. Hubert.

His Rom. Religion.

O 4   fessed

fessed him selfe a Monke, had a Pal from
the Pope, and was his Legat. Pope
Celestin the third (in Houeden *pag. 763.*)
praiseth him exceedingly, and maketh
him his Legat at the request (as he saith)
of King Richard and all his Suffragans,
and testifieth *that of Huberts deserts, vertue,
wisdome, and learning, the vniuersal Church
reioyceth.* And *pag. 755.* Houeden writeth,
that this Archbishop held a Councel,
wherin he apointed diuers things concerning Masse, and Priests, espetially that
they should not keepe women in their
houses.

Priests
forbidden
to keep
vvomen.

Stephen Langton Archbishop
XLIII.

12.   THe 43. Archbishop was Stephen
            Langton an. 1207. and died an.
1228. *He was* (saith Westmon an. 1207.)
*A man of deepe iudgment, of comely personage,
fine behauior, fit and sufficient (as much as lyeth
in a man) to gouern the whole Church.* Paris *in
his Hist. pag. 297.* addeth *that there was none
greater nor equal to him for maners and learning,
in the Court of Rome.* Godwin saith *he was a
mā, in regard of many excellent gifts both of mind
and bodie very fit for the place, brought vp in the
Vniuersitie of Paris, and greatly esteemed by the
King*

Singuler
learning
and vvor-
thines of
Archb.
Stephen.

*King and all the nobilitie of France, for his
singuler and rare learning, made Chancellor of
Paris, was admirablie learned, and writ many
notable bookes.* He deuided the Bible into Chapters in such sort as we now account them, and
built in a maner all the Archbishops Palace at
Canterburie. The like commendations of
learning yeldeth Bale vnto him Cent. 3.
cap. 87. As for His Roman religion there
can be no doubt. For he was both Cardinal of Rome and made Archbishop by the
Popes absolute authoritie as the said Authors and all Chronicles testifie. He built
also a sumptuous shrine for the bones of
S. Thomas of Cnnterburie, and as Bale
speaketk after his maner, *He largely poured
out dreggs out of the goulden cup of the harlot.*

> who built the Archb. palace in Canterb.

> His Rom. religion.

> Incompa-
> rable lear-
> ning and
> vertue of
> Archb.
> Richard.

Richard Magnus. Archbishop.
XLIIII.

13.   THe 44. Archbishop was Richard
Magnus, elected An. 1223. and
continued about two yeares. *He was* (saith
Paris who then liued Hist. *pag.* 494)
Incomparable for learning and vertue. Fox
Acts. *pag.* 274, saith that *he was of a comely
personage and eloquent tongue.* Godwin
addeth that *he was a man very vvel learned,
vvise graue vvel spoken, and of good report stoute*

O 5   *in*

*in defending the rights and liberties of the Church
and of a personage, tall streight, and well fauored
and that the Pope delighted much with the
eloquence, grauitie, and excellent behauiour of*

His Rom.
Religion.

this Archbishop. The Roman Religion of
this notable Prelat is euident. For as
Godwin saith he was elected by the Pope
him self, and so great in fauor with the
Pope, as both he and Fox *l. cit.* write,
that he obtained of the Pope what so
euer he asked.

S. Edmund Archbishop. XLV.

Famous
learning
and vertue
of Saint
Edmund.

14. THe 45. Archbishop was S. Edmund
elected an. 1234. and deceased an.
1244. *A man* (saith Westmon. an. 1234.)
*mira sanctitatis & mansuetudinis of admirable
sanctitie and meeknes, desiring the peace and honor
both of the King and Realme.* Paris (who then
liued Hist. *pag.* 730. 743.) writeth much of
his miracles, which Westmon an. 1244.

His Mira-
cles.

saith were so many. *Vt viderentur* &c. *that
the Apostles times seemed to be returned again.*
And Bale Cent. 3. *cap.* 96. confesseth that
eum aqua lustrali &c. VVith holy water he
wrought many miracles. *That omnium litera-
rum* &c. He exercised him self *in all maner of
learning and vertue.* Fox Acts. *pag.* 339.
calleth him *a Saint.* Godwin saith *he was*

a man

a man very wel knowne, and indeede famous for his vertue and great learning. The Roman religion of this holy Archbishop is certain. For as Godwin writeth he *was chosen by the procurement of the Pope, and had his Pal from him,* as both he and Fox *pag.* 279. do testifie, and opposed him selfe against the marriage of a noble womā, who vpon the death of her first husband had wowed chastitie; and was after his death canonized for a Saint by Pope Innocent 4. Bale saith he was chosen *Tanquam ad Rom. Pont.. &c. As one more redy at the Popes beck. And that vt Virginitatis assequeretur donum. To attain the gift of Virginitie, he betrathed him selfe with a ring to a woodden Image of the blessed Virgin* wore hearcloth, preached the word of the Crosse for the Pope.

His Rom. Religion.

Mariage after vovv of chastitie forbidden.

Strange deed of S. Edmund to keep his virginitie.

Boniface Archbishop. XLVI:

15. **I**N the yeare 1244. was chosen of the monks at the instance of king Henrie 3. Boniface sonne to the Earle of Sauoie, who deceassed An. 1270. He *was* (saith Godwin) *of a comely person, and performed three notable things whorthie memorie. He payed the debt of two and twentie thousand Marks that he found his See indebted in, He built a goodly Hospitall at Maidston'. And lastly fineshed the stately*

Notable deeds of Archb: Boniface.

Hall

Hall at *Canterburie with the buildings adioyning.*
Of his Roman Religion there can be no
doubt. For as Godw. writeth he was
cōsecrated with the Popes owne handes,
and obtained of the Pope the Bishoprick
of Valentia, and diuers other spiritual
promotions.

Robert Kilwarby Archbishop.
XLVII.

Famous
learning
and sanc-
titie of
Archb.
Robert.

16. THe 47. Archb. was Robert Kil-
warby , elected An. 1272 , and
continued about six yeares . *He was* (saith
Paris, Author of that tyme, Hist:pag.1348.)
Non solum vitæ religiosa sanctitatis· &c, *accoun-*
ted most famous *not onely for the holines of a reli-*
gious life *, but also for knowledg and learning.*
Godwin writeth that he was *a great Clerk,*
and left many monuments of the same in writing
behind him. In both Vniuersities disputed excellent-
His Rom.
Reiigion. *ly, and shewed him self in diuers kinds of excer-*
cises . Of his Roman religion can be no
question. For as Godwin and Bale cent.4
*cap.*46.write, he was made Archb. by the
Pope *ex plenitudine potestatis, by his absolute au-*
thoritie . And besides he was a Franciscan
frier as Godwin rightly saith , and Bale
wrongly maketh him a Dominican , and
Prouincial of their order in England,&
· built

built the Gray Friers houſe in London,
and finallie was Cardinal.

John Peckam Archbiſhop.
XLVIII.

17. **I**N the yeare 1278. ſucceeded Iohn
Peckam, anddeparted this life An.
1292. *A man* (ſaith Weſtmon An. 1278.)
Perfectiſſimus in doctrina moſt Perfect in learning.
Godwin ſaith *of rare learning vſed great
lenitie and gentlenes euery where* , *and of an
exceeding meeke facil and liberal minde* . His
Roman religion is vndoubted . For all
write he was a Franciſcan Frier , and
their Prouincial as his Predeceſſor had
bene, and made Archbiſhop as Weſtmon.
And Godwin.*l*.cit. and Fox Acts *p.* 349.
and Bale Cent. 4. *cap.* 64. affirme by the
*meere authoritie of the Pope.*wheryupon he is
teatmed of Bale *magnus & robuſtus Antichriſti
miles a mightie and ſtout Champion of Antichriſt.*

Margin notes: Rare learning and behauiour of Archb. Iohn. His Rom. Religion.

Robert VVinchilſey Archb. XLIX.

18. **T**He 49. Archbiſhop was Robert
VVinchelſey , elected an. 1294.
& deceaſed an.1313. Walſingham ypodig-
mat.*pag.*100. writeth of him that . *He ruled*
                                        the

Excelent learning vertue and vvifdom of Archb. vvinchelfey.

the English Church notably in his dayes. Godwin *faith that being a childe he was admired for his towardlines, and loued for his modeft, and gentle behauior, gouerned the Vniuerfitie of Paris with great commendation of integritie and wifdom, gaue proofe of excellent knowledg of all good learning by preaching and difputing, and was chofen to be Archbishop with the Kings good liking and applaufe of all men, and coming to Rome the Pope a good and vertuous man* (faith Godwin) *and Cardinals vvere amazed at his rare learning ioyned vvith difcrecion and vvifdom. He vvas a ftout Prelat and a feuere punisher of finne. Such preferments as fel to his difpofition he euer beftovved on men of excellent learning, maintained many poore fchollers at the Vniuerfities, and to all kinde of poore people vvas exceding bountiful. In fo much as therin I thinck he excelled all the Archbishops that euer vvere before or after him. Befides the daylie fragments of his houfe he gaue euerie Friday and Sonday to euery Begger a loafe*

VVere not thefe admirably learned and vertuous men more liklie to knovv the truth than Cranmer and fuch like.

of bread. And there vvere euerie fuch almes daies four or fiue thoufand people. Befides this euerie great feftiual daye he fent 150.*pence to fuch poore people as could not fetch his Almes.* Thus writeth Godwin of this admirable Archbishop, which ioined to that which hath bene recited out of him felfe and others of the rare learning and vertue of many Archbishops, before, and fhalbe of many others hereafter, were ynough to confound any
Prote-

Proteſtant, and condemn their religion. As for his Roman religion it is apparant. For he was choſen by the Monkes, went to Rome, admired of the Pope and Cardinals, and anſwered thus to the Kinge, *Vnder God our vniuerſal lorde vve haue tvvo other lordes, a ſpiritual lord the Pope, and a temporal lord the King, and though vve be to obey both, yet the ſpiritual rather than the temporal.* as Godwin teſtifieth.

VValter Reinolds Archbiſhop L.

19. IN the yeare 1313. ſucceded Walter Reinolds and died an. 1327. *He vvas* (ſaith Godwin) *but meanly learned, but very vviſe and of good gouernment, ſingulerly fauored of King Edward, 2. for his aſſured fidelitie and great wiſdome.* At the inſtance of the king (ſaith Godwin) he was *thruſt into the Sꝛe* by the Pope, receaued his Pal, and procured diuers Bulls from the Pope, which putteth his Rom. religion out of queſtion.

Simon Mepham Archbiſhop LI.

20. THe 51. Archbiſhop was Simon Mepham, cõſecrated An. 1327. and died

His Rom. died An.1333.*He was* (faith Godwin) *verie*
Religion, *wel learned, and Doctor of Diuinitie.*his Roman
relegion is certain. For as Godwin wri-
teth *He was elected by the Monks,* and afforded
confecration by the Pope at Auinion.

Iohn Stratford Archbishop. LII.

21. **T**He 52. Archbifhop was Iohn
Stratford, elect An.1333. and con-
Famous   tinued about 15. yeares. *He was* (writeth
learning
of Archb. Godwin)*famous for his learning, and gouern-*
Stratford. *ment of the Archdeaconrie of Lincoln, a good*
Bishop, and both diligently and faithfully ferued
his king to the laft hower, a verie gentle and mer-
ciful man, and gaue almes thrife euerie daye to 13.
His Rom. *poore people.* His Roman religion is euident.
Religion. For he was (as Godwin faith firft made
Bishop of Winchefter by the Pope, and
after preferred by him alfo to the Archbifhoprick of Canterburie.

Iohn Vfford Archbishop LIII.

Nobilitie
and lear- 22. **I**N the yeare 1348. fucceded Iohn
ning of   Vfford, and died the fame yeare. He
Archb.
Vfford.   was fonne of the Earle of Suffolke, and
Doctor of law. And as for his Roman
His Rom. Religion that is out of doubt, becaufe (as
Religion.
Godwin

Godwin faith , he *was pronounced Arch-bishop by the Pope.*

Thomas Bradwardin Archbishop. LIIII.

23.   THe 54. was Thomas Bradwardin, elected an. 1349. and deceased
the same yeare . He *was* (saith Godwin) *a*   Eccellent
good Mathematician, a great Philosopher , and an   learning
excellent Diuine. But aboue all (saith he) *is to*   and holi-
be commended his sinceritie of life and conuersation.   nes of
He was Confessor to King Edward 3. and in that   Bradvvar-
office he behaued him selfe so as he deserueth   din.
eternal memorie for the same . He was wont to
reprehend the King with great bouldnes for such
thinges as were amisse in him, and in that long
war of France he would be neuer from him , but
admonished him often secreatly , and all his army
in learned and most eloquent sermons publickly,
that they waxed not proud of their manifold
victories: And some there be that haue not doubted
to ascribe that notable conquest rather to the
vertue and holines of that man than to any prowes
and wisdome of others. It is certain he was elected
Archbishop without his seeking, and hardly (saith
he) *should yow finde any Archb. in any age to haue*
obtained his place in better sorte . This high
commendation giueth Godwin vnto this
great and worthie Prelat , and withal as
                    P   great,

great a difcommendation to his Prote-
His Rom. ftant religion . For (as Godwin him felf
Religion. faith) he was confecrated at Auinion by
a Cardinal in the Frier minors Church
which fufficiently ynough teftifieth his
Roman religion in fo much as Bale Cent.
15.*cap.*87.calleth him *Papiftam a Papift.*

Simon Iflip Archbishop. LV.

Learning   24.   IN the yeare 1349.was elect Simon
and good   Iflip, and died an.1366. He *was* (faith
deeds of   Godwin) *Doctor of Law* , *a verie frugal man,*
Archb.   *and built the Colledg of Canterb. in Oxford.*
Iflip.   which is now a part of Chriftchurch.
His Rom. His Roman religion is vndoubted. For as
Reiigion. Godwin writeth the Pope beftowed the
Archbifhoprick vpon him . And in his
Epitaph. *S. Peter is profeffed Princeps Apofto-*
lorum, The *prince of the Apoftles.*

Simon Langhorn Archbishop LVI.

25.   THe 56. Archbifhop was Simon
            Langhorn , elect an. 1366. and
continewed but two yeares . He was
(faith Godwin)firft a Monke,then Prior,
laftly Abbot of Weftminfter . Thence
elected Bifhop of London , then of Ely,
                                    and

and laftly of Canterburie. How Roman a
Catholick he was, appeareth by Godwin,
who writeth that the Pope remoued him
from Ely to Canterburie, fent his Pal, and
laftly made him Cardinal and Legat into
England as appeareth by his Epitaph. In
this Archbifhops time Wicklef began *to*
be angry (faith Godwin) *with the Pope, Arch-*
bishops and Monks, becaufe this Archbishop
difplaced him out of Canterb. Colledg. And the
better to wreak his anger vpon them,
went out of the Church and began his
herefies.

VVilliam VVitlefley Archbishop.
LVII.

26. THe 57. Archbifhop was William
Wittlefley, elected an. 1368. and
died an. 1374. He *was* (faith Godwin) *Doctor*
of Law, and preached in Latin verie learnedly.
He was a Roman Catholick as the fame
Godwin declareth faying that *he was*
aduanced by the Popes onely authoritie.

Simon

Simon Sulburie Archbishop.
LVIII.

Notable
learning
and qua-
lities of
Archb.
Sudburie.

His Rom.
Religion.

27. THe 58. was Simon Suldburie,
elected an. 1375. and died an. 1381.
He was (faith Godwin) *a noble Prelat , verie
wife , learned , eloquent , liberal , merciful , and
preached in Latin very learnedlie.* Stow Chron.
pag. 458. faith *he was an eloquent man , and wife
beyond all wife men of the Realme , and fulfilled
moft worthie martirdom ,* being flaine of the
rebellious commons . His Roman religion is notorious. For (as the faid Godw.
writeth) he was houfhould Chaplin to
Pope Innocent , and one of the Iudges of
his Rota , who beftowed vpon him the
Archbifhoprick, and fent him his Bulls.

VVilliam Courtney Archb. LIX.

Noblenes
and great
learning
of Archb.
Courtney.

His Rom.
Religion.

28. IN the yeare 1381. fucceeded William
Courtney , and deceafed an. 1396.
He was (writeth Godwin) *fonne to hugh
Courtney Earle of Deuonshire , and was a great
Lawyer.* As for his Roman religion ther
can be no doubt . For (as Godwin faith)
the Pope beftowed the Archbifhoprick
vpon him , fent him his Pal, and (as Walfingham

fingham writeth) made him Cardinal.
And Fox Acts *pag.* 505 faith , *He fet King
Richard 2. Vpon the poore Chriftians of VVicklefs
fide,*condemned fome,made diuers abiure
and do pennance.

Thomas Arundel Archbifhop. LX.

29. IN the year 1396. fucceded Thomas Noblenes
Arundel , and died 1413. *He was* and wor-
(faith Godwin)*fonne to Robert Earle of Arun-* Archb.
del and VVarren, was vndoubtedly (faith he)*a* Arundel.
worthy Prelat, wife and very ftout. And Wal-
finghan who them liued, Hift. *pag.* 432.
faith he was *eminentiſsima turris Ecclefia.*&c.
*A moft eminent Tower, and inuincible Champion
of the Church of England.* As for his Roman His Rom.
religion there can be no doubt therof. Religion.
For Godwin writeth that by the Popes
prouifion he was made Archb : of Canterb ; and receaued his Pal. Fox Acts
*pag.*524. citeth his Conftitution wherin
he profeſseth S. Peters fupremacie , and
*pag.*507. faith *He was a great enemy of Englifh*
(Wicklefian)*bookes,and the Authors of them.*
Bale Cent. *7.cap.* 50. faith he imprifoned
the Wiclefifts , and made them abiure
their hærefie.

Henrie Chichley Archbishop. LXI.

The lear-
ning and
vvorthi-
nes of
Archb.
Chichley.
30. THe 61. Archb : was Henrie
Chichley in the yeare 1414. and
departed this wordl. An. 1443. *He was* (as
Godwin writeth) *Doctor of lawe , much em-
ployed in Embassages of the King, wherin he euer
behaued him self wisely , and to the kings good
liking. He alwaies enioyed his Princes fauor , was
wise in gouerning his See , laudably bountiful in
bestowing his goods to the good of the common
vvelth , and lasly , stout and seuere in administration of iustice.* In Hiham Feris he built a
goodly Colledg, and also an hospital, and
in Oxford two Colledges, and called one
His Rom.
religion.
Bernards Colledg an other *Al soules.* As for
his Roman religion there can be no
qneftion of it . For as the said Godwin
writeth the Pope beftowed the Archb.
vpon him, fent him his Pal, and made him
Cardinal, and his Legat in England. And
Bale Cent. *7. cap.* 50. accounteth him a
perfecuter of Wicklefifts. And as is faid in
the Fpitaph of his Tombe was made
Bifhop by the Popes owne hands.

Iohn

Iohn Stafford Archbishop LXII.

19. IN the yeare 1443. fucceeded Iohn
Stafford, and died. 1452. *He vvas* (faith
Godwin in the Bifhops of Bathe) *a man*
very noble, and no les learned, fonne vnto the Earle
of Stafford and Doctor of Lavve. As for his Roman religion that is manifeft, becaufe as
Godwin writeth he was made Archb. *by*
the Popes *abfolute authoritie* , and before
obtained of Pope Martin the Bifhoprick
of Bathe.

Nobilitie and great learning of Archb. Stafford. His Rom. Religion.

Iohn Kemp Archbishop. LXIII.

15. IN the yeare 1452. fucceeded Iohn
Kemp and deceafed An. 1453. He
was faith Godwin *Doctor of Lavve* . And
his Roman religion is certain for as Godwin writeth, The Pope beftowed the
Archb. vpon him, fent him his Pal , and
after made him Cardinal which alfo teftifieth Bale Cent. 11. *cap.* 55.

The learning and religion of Archb. Kemp.

P 4 *Thomas*

Thomas Bourchier Archbishop.
LXIIII.

33. THe 64. Archb: was Thomas
Bourchier elect An. 1454, and
deceased An.1486.He was sonne to Henrie Bourchier Earle of Essex , brought vp
in Oxford,of which Vniuersitie he was
Chancelor.Bale Cent·11. *cap.* 75. saith he
was *a man honorable for his learning,vertue, and
the blood of the Earles of Essex* . His Romane
Religion is manifest by Godwin.

*Nobilitie
and lear-
ning of
Archb.
Bourchier.*

*His Rom.
religion.*

Iohn Morton Archbishop. LXV.

34. THe 65. Archb:was Iohn morton
An, 1487. and dyed An.1500. *He
vvas*(saith Stow Chron.*pag.*789)*of excellent
vvit learning and vertue.* Godwin saith, he
was *Doctor of lavv , had manifould good partes,
great learning in the lavv , vvisdom , discretion,
and other vertues, notable loyaltie ,and faithfulnes
to his Prince.*Bale Cent.11. *cap.*85. *Vir moribus
& c.A famous man in that age for vertue and
learning , seuere , and a louer of iustice A man
that in his time surpassed all the Prelats of England in vvisdome and grauitie* . As for his
Roman religion that is manifest. For he
was

*Eccellent
learning
and vertue
of Archb.
Morton.*

*His Rom.
religion.*

was elected by the Monks, confirmed
redily by the Pope, and made also Cardinal, and procured Saint Anselm to be
canonized.

Henrie Dean Archbishop. LX VI.

35. THe 66. Archb. was Henrie Dean
An. 1501. and died An. 1502. He was (saith Godwin in Bishops of Salsburie) *Doctor of Diuinitie, a wise and indu-strious man* . And of his Roman religion none can make doubt for he was an Abbot, chosen by the Monks, had his Pal from the Pope, and tooke his oath of fidelitie to the Pope set downe before *c.* as yow may see in Godwin.

Atchb. Dean learned and vvise.

His Rom. Religion.

VVilliam VVarham Archbishop LXVI.

36. THe 67. Archbishop. was William
Warham an. 1504. and deceassed an. 1532. He was as Godwin writeth *Doctor of lavv, and greatly commended for his wisdom by King Henrie 7.* That he was a Roman Catholick is manifest . For as Godwin writeth, he said masse, and was chosen by Queene Catherin for one of

The vvis-dom and learning of Archb-vvarham.

His Rom. religion.

her

her Aduocats to defend her mariage
with King Henrie 8. which was con-
tracted by the Popes Difpenfation. And
vndoubtedly when he receaued his Pal
he tooke the forfaid oath of fidelitie to
the Pope.

Thomas Cranmer Archbishop
LX*V*III.

37. *T*He 68. Archb. but firft forfaker of
S. Auftin and his Predeceffors
faith was Thomas Cranmer in the year
1533.and put to death 1556. He was not
chofen for any deferts, but being Chaplin
to Anne Bullen, and known to defire her
preferment and to further King Henries
lufts, was by him firft fent in Embafsie
about the diuorce, as yow may fee in Fox

VVhẽ
Cranmer   *pag.*1689. and after nominated to this dig-
vvas made nitie, to the end that if the Pope refufed to
Archb.   pronounce fentence of diuorce betweene
him and Queene Catherin, Cranmer
might do it. He was fo carnal and fo
His car-   womanifh, as his own mother would
nalitie.   often fay, fhe euer thought women
would be his vndoing. Wherin fhe was
nothing deceaued. For as Godwin con-
feffeth. *He being yet very yong left his felliwfhip*
in Iefus Colledg in Cambridg for loue of a woman
whome

whome he maried. And after, being Archb. in his return from Rome , he brought with him a Duchwoman, *to whome* (faith Fox *pag.* 1037.) *it is suppofed he was married,* whome all King Henries time he carried vp and downe with him in a Trunck, and in King Edwards tyme married her. He was alfo trecherous to his Prince. For abbeit he had receaned fo great fauors of King Henrie 8. and was by him, apointed one of the Executors of his will , yet ftreight after his death he agreed to the breaking of it . And after King Edwards death wrought all he could to the aduancing of Queene Iane, & vtter excluding from the crowne of King Henries lawful daughter and his right Prince Queenc Marie and firft fubfcribed to the difenheriting of Queene Marie, and to that rebellious letter which he and his accomplices fent to Queene Marie, And Fox to his euerlafting confufion hath fet downe in his Acts *pag.* 1299. edit. 1596. and maruel it were if one who thus forfooke God and his Prince, fhould not alfo forfake his Predeceffors faith ? If he who had thus loft, as Saint Paul fpeaketh , a good confcience fhould not alfo make fhip wrack of his faith. For firft he was a Roman Catholick, and fo continewed from his childhood til he was

Arch-

His treacherie to his Prince.

His rebellion.

Fox. pag. 1698.

Cranmer forfoke God and his prince

Hovv long a Rom. Cathol.

Archbiſhop, and a while after. At his firſt
going to the Pope was by him made his
Penitentiarie as Fox hath edit: 1596.
pag. 1690. went to Rome for his Pal and
there tooke the vſual oath of fidelitie to
the Pope. But in the next yeare after, to
wit in the yeare 1534. When king Henrie
by Parliament procured him ſelf to be
tearmed head of the Church he alſo forſooke the Pope in that point yet in all
other agreed with him as the king did,
and both by words and deedes perſecuted
the Proteſtants, as you may ſee in Fox in
Lamberts death and others. And after
King Henries death vnder king Edward
ſonge Maſſe with great maieſtie for the
king of France his ſoule aſſiſted with 8.
Biſhops as writeth Stow Chron.*pag.*1547.
yet after he fel to Lutheraniſm, and ſet out
a Cathechiſme wherin with Luther he
taught the real preſence of Chriſt in the
bleſſed Sacrament; But ſtaying not long
there, from thence turned with the Duke
of Somer. to Zuinglianiſme, and publiſhed
an other Cathechiſme which denyed the
real preſence. After all this vnder Queene
Marie for hope of life recanted all his hereſies, and both by tongue and penne
profeſſed the Roman Catholick faith. But
perceauing that he ſhould die, chooſing
rather to die in account of Proteſtants a
martyr

Song Maſſe ſo-lemnly in King Edvvard 6. time.

Incon-ſtant euen in hereſie.

Sliedan lib.26. An.1555.

In his recanta-tion in fox pag. 1710.He taketh god to vvitnes he recanted of his ovvne martyr, than in iudgment of both them and vs a malefactor, he finally ended his life in Zuinglianifme, being both condemned for Herefie againft God, and for rebellion againft his Prince as Fox confeffeth *pag.* 1698. Edit. 1596. And fo as his faith had bene far different for a time from his Prededeffors fo was his end ignominious and far from the glorie of their happie departures.

minde and for confcience fake, and yet foone after recalled his retantation. Cranmer condemned for rebellion and herefie. Sleidan l. 25. f. 429. The miferable end of the Archb: that firft forfooke S. Auftins faith. The great nobilitie rare learning and vertue of card. Pole.

Reginald Poole Archb. LXIX.

30. THe 69. and laft Catholich Archb. hithertho, was Reginald Poole confecrated an. 1555. and departed this life an. 1558. the fame yeare and day that Queen Marie died. He was fonne to Syr Richard Pool Cofin german to King Henrie 8. and of Margaret Counteffe of Salsburie Daughter of George Duke of Clarence and brother of King Edward 4. *He was a man* (faith Godwin) *of manifold and excellent partes, not onely very learned, which is better known than it neede many wordes, but alfo of fuch modeftie in behauiour and integritie of life and conuerfation, as he was of all men both loued and reuerenced.* And beyond feas he was fo famous, that without all feeking of his he was firft made Cardinal, after

Legat

Legat to the Councel of Trent and twise elected Pope; to which supreme dignitie wanted nothing but his owne consent. He was by the confesion of Ridley in Fox Edit. 1596. *pag.* 1595. *a man worthy of all humilitye reuerence and honor, and indued with manifould graces of learning and vertue*. As for his Roman religion it might seeme needles to proue it if Doctor Bukley and some other Ministers were not ashamed to challeng him for a Protestant whose impudencie I will refel with the testimonie of their owne Authors. For Godwin saith in King Henries time he dealt by letters to his frends to exhort them from all conformitie to reformation and being accused in the Conclaue of fauering protestants and of other matters, *He cleared him self* (saith Godwin) *of all these suspitions absolutely so that the next day they were more resolute to make him Pope than before.* And infra he saith Queene Marie loued him for his learning and nobilitie but aboue all for his religion and finally that he reconciled England to the Pope and receiued from him his Pal. Bale Cent 8. *cap.* 100. saith *he was a Cardinal soldier of Antichrist, not to be commended for any vertue by the seruant of God,* and saith that in an Oration to the Emperor he called the German Protestants *newe Turks, and their Gospel Turcicum pestiferum*

Card. Poole might haue bene Pope.
Ridley highly commended Card. Poole.
His Rom. Religion.

Sleidan lib. 10. in fin.

pestiferûm & adulterinum semen Turkish pesti- *ferous and adulterous seede.* which Crashew was not a shamed in his sermon at Paules Crosse to affirme that Poole said o the written word of God. Farther more Bale termeth this worthie Prelat and great ornament of our Nation *horrible beast a rooter out of the truth of the Gospel a most wicked Traitor to his Contrie,* and prayeth God *to confound him.* So vndoubted it was while Cardinal Poole liued that he was no Protestant but a most earnest Roman Catholick. Which who readeth his booke and See Andreas Dioditius in vit. Polt. considereth his deedes may yet see more fully. But by him may the iudicious reader see with what truth or face our Ministers challeng S. Austin and other holy and antient Archbishops of Canterburie to be of their religion.

Epilog.

39. THus yow see the first and the last of the Catholick Archbishops of Canterburie, namely S. Austin and Cardinal Pole to haue said Masse and had their Palls from Rome, and all of them (except one) euer since the first Christianitie of our Nation vnto our daies, for number thre score and nine for continewance of nine hundred fifty and eight

First and last Cath. Archb. of Canterb. said Masse and haue palls from Rome. The number of our Archb. Their continuance, learning vertue and wisdom.

yeares,

yeares, for learning many of them moſt famous, for wiſdom moſt excellent, and for vertue diuers of them moſt admirable, as you haue heard by the very confeſsion of Proteſtants them ſelues. Thus manie (I ſay) thus excellently qualified Primats and Paſtors of al England, thus long to haue taught the Catholick faith, to haue followed it them ſelues, to haue defended it with their great learning, maintained it by their miracles, authorized it by their notable vertues, and finally to haue liued in it moſt religiouſly, and died moſt happely; What ſhall wee thinck of them? That ſo many, and great Clerks were ſo many hundred yeares ignorant of the truth? That ſo many and ſo great Saints ſo long tyme miſſed of the way to heauen? That all our Anceſtors who ſo many yeares followed them were chriſtened in vaine, beleeued in vaine, and worſhiped and ſerued God in vaine, and finally died in their ſinnes; and are damned and gon to hel? As we muſt needs thinck vnles we graunt the Roman Catholick faith to be the faith of Chriſt and right way to ſaluation. Shall, I ſay ſuch an vnchriſtian, vnnatural, and vnreaſonable thought enter into our harts? And not rather follow the aduiſe of S. Paul ſaying *Memen-tote Præpoſitorum veſtrorum qui vobis locuti ſunt verbum*

Who wil not adventure his ſoule rather with theſe than with Cranmer.

No waie to heauen but by Chriſt and his true faith.

verbum Dei, quorum intuentes exitum conuersationis imitamini fidem, Let vs behould the holy conuersation and happie & vertuous ende of those holy and worthy Prelats and primats of England, assuring our selues that vertue can not follow the Diuel, nor Gods Saints be condemned to Hel. Let vs embrace their faith which was the roote of their vertue, and their cheese guide in their way to heauen, whither they are happily ariued and we shall assuredly follow if we keepe their faith and imitat their vertue. And thus hauing shewed that all our Archbishops of Canterburie, and consequently all our Clergie, Bishops, Archdeacons, Deacons Canons, Pastors, Vicars, Monkes, and Friers were Roman Catholicks euen from the first Christianity of our Nation to our age, Let vs proceed an shew the same of our Christian Kings and Laitie.

Beholding the end of the conuersation of your Prelats follow their faith.

All besides VVicles and his small number.

Q　　　*That*

CHAP. XXI.

*That all our Christian English kings
to king Henrie 8. time were Roman Catholicks proued by
general reasons.*

1
**No record
that anie
of our old
christian
Kings
vvas;Pro-
teſtant.**

1. FIrſt becauſe(as I ſaid of the Archbiſhops)ther is no ſcript, no ſcrole,
no record,no monument, to teſtifie that
our former Chriſtian kings were of any
other religion than king Henrie 8. was
before he began the change. Therfor they
that afiirme the contrarie either know it
by reuelation , or ſpeake without booke.
Beſides it is impoſſible that ther ſhould be
an alteration in religion which is the
moſt markableſt thing in a Common
welth,and that there ſhould be no mention therof ; and altogether incredible
in England , where we ſee the firſt
alteration from Paganiſme to Chriſtianitie, and now lately from Papiſtrie to
Proteſtancie recorded in all Hiſtories.
yea priuat mutations made by kings
in ſome Churches from Prieſts to monks
or contrary wiſe. And can we thinck that
a mutation from Proteſtancie to Papiſtrie
                                              (if any

(ifany such had bene) would haue bene
omitted and forgotten. 2. All the Archbishops of Canterburie were Roman
Catholicks as is before shewed, and yet
none of them trobled by the kings of
former times for his religion. yea most
of them greatly honored by them, and
diuers made Archbishops by their kings
procurment. 3. They suffered the said Archbishops to go to Rome (where diuers
of them were consecrated of the Pope) to
receaue their Pal, to be his legat, and take
their forsaid oath of fidelitie to the Pope,
which if they had bene Protest. and not
perfect Roman Catholick they would
neuer haue permitted. yea some of the
kings procured Pals for their Archb: as
King Edwin for S. Paulin in Beda *lib.* 2.
cap. 17,. King Alfwald for Archbishop
Eanbald, Florent. An. 779. Huntington
lib..3. king Rufus for S. Anselm, Fox
Acts.*pag* 185. 4. Nine of the ancient kings
left their Kingdomes and became monks,
as Fox confesseth Acts. *pag.* 133. whose
names are these, king Kinegilfus, K. Cedwalla, king Ina, king Ethelred, king Sigebert, king Coenred, king Offa, king Edbert, to whome *pag.* 131. he addeth king
Kenred. Now mokes in that time vowed
chastitie as is euident in S. Beda *lib.* 5.
cap. 22. *lib.* 4. *cap.* 25. *lib.* 3. *cap.* 25. And

2
All their
Archb.
were Ca-
tholicks.

3
They suf-
fered
Archb. to
be conse-
crat of the
Pope. &c.

Kings
procure
palls from
the P. for
their
Archb.

4
Manie
ancient
Kings
became
Monks.

Monks
vowved
chastie
pouertie
and obe-
dience.

Pouertie *lib. 1.cap. 25.* And obedience. *lib. 4. cap. 5.* And how Papiſtical this is, and contrary to Proteſtancie euery one knoweth. Beſide as Fox ſaith *pag.* 115. *moſt like they did this for holines ſake, thincking in this kind of life to ſerue or pleaſe God better, or to merit more* which Kinde of act or ende of theirs is plain Papiſtical, and quite oppoſit to Proteſtancie. And therfore Fox ſaith, that *theſe Kings were far deceaued.* To theſe

Manie ancient Queenes and K. Daughters nunnes.

Kings we may adioin 19. Queenes and Kings daughters whome Fox alſo *pag.* 134. confeſſeth to haue left their royall eſtate, and becommen Nunnes. Yea *pag.* 137. he citeth out of an ancient Chronicle, *That in*

Deuotion of English to monkish life.

the Primitiue Church of England Kings, Princes, Dukes, Earles, Barons, and Rulers of Churches incenſed with a deſire of heauen, laboring and ſtriuing among them ſelues to enter into Monkerie into voluntarie exile and ſolitarie life, forſooke all and followed the Lord. The ſame hath Huntington. *lib. 5.* Houed. and others. Is this thinck we a proceding of Proteſtants or rather of earneſt and deuout Roman Catholicks?

5 Our ancient Kings deſire the P. to confirme their Charters.

2. Fiftly. They deſired the Pope to confirme their Charters which they made. This you may ſee of King Ethelbert the firſt Chriſtian King, in Malmsb: *lib. 1. Pont. pag.* 208. Of King Coenred and King Offa in Capgraue in vita Egwin.

Of

Of King Egbert in Florent. Chron.
An. 676. of King wulfer in Ingulf *pag:* 884.
Of an other King Offa in Paris An. 794.
Of King Edgar in Malmsb. *lib.* 2. Reg.
pag. 57. 6. They suffered appeals to Rome **6**
from them selues. This is euident in King Kings
Egbert and King Alfred in Beda *lib.* 5. suffer ap-
cap. 20. 7. They beleeued S. Peter to be Rome.
Prince of the Apostles as is to be seene in
King Offa his Charter in Cambden in **7**
Brit. *pag.* 613. and S. Peter to be *higher in* Kings
degree than S. Paule, as is to be seene in beleeue S.
King Ina his verses there *pag.* 193. and premacie.
Peter onely to haue *had the keies.* to witt
of all the Church, as Reinolds confesseth
Confer. *pag.* 12, And finally the Church of
Rome in their time to be *the Catholick and
Apostolick Church,* as Beda testifieth *lib.* 3.
cap. 29, at what time the Protestants account the Roman Church the whoare of **8**
Babilon, and the Pope Antichrist. 8. Seuen Manie of
of these our English Kings are Canoni- our Kings
zed by the Roman Church in the Marti- by the
rologe, to wit, *Ethelbert, Richard, Oswald,* Pope.
*Sebbi, Edmund, Edward martir, Edward
Confessor,* which would neuer haue bene **9**
done if they had not bene Roman Ca- ancient
tholicks. knovv not
9. Our ancient English Kings could be iustifica-
no Protestants therfore they were Ro- tion by
man Catholicks. For no others challenge faith.

Q 3 them

them for theirs. That they could be no Proteſtants is moſt manifeſt. Firſt becauſe the opinion of iuſtification by onely faith is accounted of Proteſtants the *foundation, head, and cheefeſt point and ſoule of their Doctrin and Church,* It is (ſaith Luther Prefat. in Ionam) *the head of Chriſtian Religion , the ſumme of the ſcriptures.* Prefat: ad Galath: *If the article of Iuſtification* (by onely faith) *be once loſt, then is all true Chriſtian doctrin loſt. And as many as hould not that doctrin are Iewes Turks Papiſts or hereticks.* Item. *By this onely doctrin the Church is built and in this it conſiſteth.* And in *cap.* 1. Galath. *If we neglect the Article of Iuſtification we leeſe all together .* And in *cap.* 2. *It is the principal Article of all Chriſtian doctrin all other Arcicles are comprehended in it.* Fox Acts. *pag.* 840. ſaith *It is the foundation of all Chriſtianitie,* And *pag.* 770. *the onely principal origen of our ſaluatian.* Chark in the Tower diſputation ſaith. *It is the ſoule of the Church.* And the ſame ſay all other Proteſtants. But this foundation, this head, this ſoule of Proteſtancie, our ancient Kings knew not, as Fox plainly confeſſeth in theſe wordes *pag.* 170. *The Doctrin of Iuſtification* (by onely faith) *was then vnknown.* And *pag.* 133. writeth thus of our antienteſt Chriſtian Kings. *They lackt the doctrin and knowledg in Chriſts Goſpel, eſpetially* (ſaith he) *in the Article of free Iuſtification by faith and*

VVhat is the foundation and ſoul of Proteteſtancie Luther.

Fox.

Chark.

Our Kings knevv not the Proteſtant Goſpel.

and therfor (saith he) *they ran the wrong way.*
Loe he granteth that they were ignorant
espetially of that which Protest : esteeme
the especialleft point of Proteftancie.
And Ibid. speaking of our ancient Chriftian Kings hath these wordes : *How great
the blindnes and ignorance of these men was who
wanting no zeale wanted knowledg, seeking their
saluation by their meritorious deedes, which I
write* (saith he) *here to put vs in mind how
much we at this present are bound to God for the
true sinceritie of his truth hidden so long before to
our fforancestors, and opened now to vs. This onely
lamenting to see them haue such works and want
our faith ; and vs to haue right faith and want
their workes.* Could he say more plainly
that our Ancient Princes and Chriftian
Ancestors knew not so much as the foundation of Proteftancy, and wanted their
faith? And with what face then can any
man challeng them for Proteftants. And
heere I challeng Abbots or what minifter
so euer, to fhewe one ancient Englifh
man, Woman, or Child that held this
forfaid foundation, head, and foule of
their religion ; And if they can not (as
indeede they can not) let them confeffe,
that there was neuer ancient Englifh Proteftant, vnles they will make Protest :
without head or or foule.

3. Moreouer to build or indow Religious

[marginal notes:]
A plaine
confeffion
that none
of our
Anceitors
vvere Pro-
teftants.

Vvhat
muft be
fhevved
of mini-
fters that
faie our
Anceitors
vvere Pro-
teftants.

pag.100.

For vvhat end our Kings built and endevved mona-steries.

gious houfes (as Doc. Abbots faith Anfwer to D. Bifhop) *for redemption of their finnes and purchafe of their foules health proceeded of the wāt of the fight of the funne of righteoufnes.* And Fox. *pag.* 133. faith it is contrary to the rule of Chrifts Gofpel. But the fame Fox Ibid. teftifieth *that our fift Chriftian kings built monafteries feeking for merit with God, and remedie of their foules and remedy of their finnes,* and prooueth it by a Charter of King Ethelbald, which he might haue proued by as many Charters of thofe ancient kings as are extant. One of King Ethelbald I will cite out of Ingulph. made to free monks from taxes the third yeare of his Reigne which was 718, fome what more than a hunderd yeares after S. Auftin. *Ego Ethelbald & c, I Ethelbald King of marchland for the loue of the cele-*

Good vvorks done to free the foul from bond of fin.

ftical Contry, and for the redemption of my foule haue prouidently decreed to free it by good worke from all bond of finne. King Ethelbert alfo *Pro anima fua remedio & c, for the good of his foule gaue to Mellit Bishop the land called Tillingham* out of Stow Chron. *pag.* 77. And

Our firft Chriftian K. gaue land to Churches for help. of his foule.

fo of the reft. Again Fox *pag.* 154. *The caufes why folemn Monafteries were firft founded by Kings, Queenes, Kings daughters, and rich Confuls, are thefe, Pro remedio animæ meæ, pro remiſsione peccatorum meorum, pro redemptione peccatorum meorum, & pro falute Regnorum meorum*

meorum quique subiacent regimini populorum in honorem gloriosæ virginis. For the redemption of my soul for the redeeming of my sinnes and for the saftie of my Kingdoms and people subiect to my gouernment to the honor of the glorious Virgin. And therfor by D. Abbots his verdict, and by euident inference our auncient Princes wanted the sunne of Protestants righteousnes. 10. And lastly I proue it by the plain confession of Protest. For Fox Acts. *pag.* 132. saith *our first Christian Kings were deuout to Church men, espetially to the Church of Rome.* Which was, in the opinion of Protestats, when the Pope was known Antichrist, That is, in Boniface. 3. time, and since. Bale *Cent.*1.*cap*,73,saith of king Ethelbert our first Christian king that *He receaued the doctrin of the Roman Religion with all the imposture therof, and died the 21. yeare of his receaued Papistrie,* Could he speake more plainly? And *Cent.*13. *cap.* 5, Felix saith he *conuerted the East parte of England to Papistrie.* And *Ibid cap.* 4. he saith that *Birin vnder colour of the Gospel taught the VVest saxons Papisticam fidem Papistical faith.* The same confesse diuers other Protestants, as hath bene shewed before when we proued that S. Greg. and S. Austin were by the confession of Protestants plain Rom. Catholicks.

10

Our Kings deuout to the P. vvhen he vvas in opinion of Protestants. Antichrist

A Plaine confessiō of Protestants that our nation vvas first conuerted to papistrie.

Q 5   **4. To**

4. To all thefe particuler proofes I ad a general one vz the Englifh names which our ancient Kings and people gaue to their feruice and their Paftors ; alfo their Churches Tombs and Epitaphes and finally all their ancient Monuments do teftifie and proclame their Catholick Roman religion. For their feruice of God they called *Maffe*,Nether can it be fhewed, that euer they called it other wife , and of it haue they tearmed the cheefe feafts of the yeare, as Chriftmaffe, Candlemaffe, Michelmas,Martin maffe. As likwife they haue tearmed Shreuetide of their Shreiuing and confeffing them felues before they began their lent Faft, Palmefonday of the Palmes which they caried on that day,as Catholicks at this day doe ;Ember dayes of the Catholick faft of *Quater tēpora* corruptly pronouncing the laft word. Their cheefe Doers of their feruice they termed Prieftes. That is (as Proteft. confeffe) *Sacrificers,* and therfor their minifters abhor the name. Their cheefe Churches they built in forme of a Croffe. The cheefe Altar therin on high and toward the Eaft, and diuers Altars in little Chappells about ; erected therin a Roodloft with the Roode or Croffe of Chrift vppon it,adorned their Chappells euen the very glaffe windowes with Pictures. In

like

See in Ingulph. hovv antient Knights vvere vvont to goe to confeffion before they vvere knighted.

Name of Maffe.

of Prieft.s.

Reinold conf. pag. 466 467.

Forme of Churches.

like fort they buried their dead with
Croffes as was feene on the tombe of
King Arthur, and their Bifhops with
Chalices as in the Tombe of S. Birin, and
vfually on the Epitaphs defire men to
pray for the foule of the dead. And where
I pray yow was the Proteftant Communion when our firft Chriftian Anceftors
termed their cheefe feruice of God, *Maffe*,
and therof named their principall feafts
in the yeare? where were their Minifters
when they termed their Paftors. *Priefts and
facrificers*. Wher were their Churches
when all the Cathedrall Churches were
built in forme of a Croffe, with one high
Altar, and diuers little Altars in the
Church about; where were they them
felues when our Anceftors euen dead did
by Croffes wher with they were buried,
and the Epitaphs of their Tombes profeffe the Roman Catholick religion.

Certayne

CHAP. XXII.

Certayne obiections of Ministers that our auncient Kings were not Romane Catholiques disproued.

L. **A**Lbeit euery one of iudgment will eafely fee that what can be obiected againft this fo cleare, and by the Aduerfaries confeffed truth , is but cauils which want not againft almoft the euidenft truth that is: yet for fatisfaction of all forts of people , we wil propofe what D. Abbots in his Anfwer to D. Bifhops epiftle *pag.* 199. lately hath collected for proofe that our ancient Kings were Proteftants, or at leaft not perfect Roman Catholicks. Firft he faith that our antient *Kings had the fupremacie in caufes Ecclefiaftical* . This is euidently falfe by what hath bene faid in the 5. 6. and 7. proofe of the former Chapter . To which I add that (as it fhalbe fhewed herafter) King Edward 3. whome Proteftants account to make moft for them, profeffed it to be a fauor of herefie to deny the Popes fupremacie in caufes ecclefiafticall.

2. Abbots

D. Doue of Recufancie vvil haue Bellarm: to be a Proteft: or no perfect Gatholik.

1. obiection.

Ansvver.i

2. Abbots faith that the kings founded Bifhopricks and inuefted them at their pleafur , as did Edward Confeffor the Bifhoprick of Exefter. That in S. Auftins time or long after the King founded Bifhopricks and inuefted Bifhops is apparantly falfe. For it is euident in Beda *lib.1. cap.*29. That S. Greg. at his owne pleafure apointed two Archbifhopricks, & vnder each of them twelue Bifhopricks to be erected in England. And *lib.2.cap.*4. That S. Auftin by his authoritie founded the Archbifhoprick of Canterburie , and the Bifhopricks of London and Rochefter, and that the King then did onely build them Churches , indow the Bifhopricks with lands and *giue them* (faith Beda *lib.* 1. *cap.* 28.) *Poffeffions neceffarie for their maintenance.* And aboue 800. yeares agoe when King Offa would alter the Bifhoprik of Lichfeild in to an Archbifhoprick , he took not vpon him to doe it by his owne authoritie or of the Bifhops of his realm, but procured Pope Adrian to send two legats for that purpofe. Malmsb. *lib.1.* Reg. *cap.*4. And. 700. yeares agoe mhen King Edward Senior erected fiue Bifhopricks in the Weft Contrie, it was done by the expreffe commandement of Pope Formofus. Malmsb. 2. Reg. *cap.* 5. And about 500. yeares agoe, when King William Conqueror

2. obiection.

Anfvver.

Our ancient Kings tooke not vpon them to erect Bifhopriks.

K. Ethelbert.

K. Offa.

K. Edvvard Sen.

K. Vvilliã Conq.

Conqueror would haue fome Englifh
Bifhops depofed , and Bifhopricks tranflated from litle Tounes to greater
Citties,he procured Pope Alexander.2.to
fend a Legat hither to doe it. Malmsb.1.
Pont.But yet we grãt that a while before
the Conqueſt,and ſomwhat after, Kings
tooke vpon them to inueſt Biſhops and
Abbots as appeareth in Ingulp. *pag.* 806.
But this faĉt of theirs done of ſom igno-
rantly as muſt be thought of King Edred
and others before the Conqueſt who
were perfeĉt Catholicks in faith (as ſhall
appeare herafter)and alſo vertuous in life;
of others perhaps preſumptuouſly and
couetouſly againſt the order of the
Church,proueth no more that they were
no Catholicks,than worſe faĉts of theirs
againſt the law of Chriſt proueth them
to haue bene no Chriſtians. For if Princes maye by euery faĉt of theirs be iudged
of what religion they are , they would
fometimes feeme no Chriſtians nor yet
to haue a God.As for S.Edward he might
wel doe what he did, for he was apointed
by the Pope to be his Vicegerent and as
it were Legat as we ſhall ſhewe in his life.

3.obiec-
tion.   2. Thirdly,*they made* (ſaith Abbots) *lawes
for the order and gouernment of the Church , as
is to be ſeene in the lawes of Edward , of Alfred,
of Ethelſtan,and Canutus in Fox Volum.*1.*in fine,*
                                                    and

*and by many laws made since the Conquest against
intrusions of the Pope , as is to be seene in Syr
Edward Cookes reports part 5.* Touching the
lawes of the Chriſtian Kings before the
Conqueſt , I anſwer that they are not
Eccleſiaſticall lawes ſuch as define any
thing as a point of faith , or preſcribe any
thing concerning Religion and worſhip
of God , but are meere commandements
partly for execution of former Eccleſiaſticall lawes, partly for procurement and
conſeruation of externall peace, quietnes,
and order of the Church, which kinde of
lawes Princes may make, as is to be ſeene
in Stapleton Relect. Controu. 2.q.5.Ar.1. See ſta-
Beſides that , Chriſtian Princes apoint pleton.
thus ſome times things in eccleſiaſticall
matters not of authoritie, but vpon zeale,
and not to diſpoſe of faith and religion.
As for the lawes made ſince the Conqueſt
which may ſeeme preiudiciall to the
Popes authoritie, the cheefeſt Authors of
them, were Edward 3. and Richard 2. who
(as ſhall appeare heerafter) plainly profeſſed the Popes Supremacie. And therfor
what lawes they made , were no way to
denie his authoritie , but to reſtrain the
execution therof in ſome caſes : becauſe
as the Apoſtle ſaith *Omnia licent ſed non
omnia expediunt . All things are lawfull but all
things are not expedient* . So they thought
that

that fome execution of his authority in
fome matters would be preiudciall to
their temporall ftate, and therfor thought
it not expedient that in thofe cafes it
fhould be practifed. As for Cookes reports
they haue bene fo anfwered as I thinck
neither him felf nor any for him will
replie. Fourthlie, faith Abbots *Then were*
the fcriptures in foure feuerall languages of fo
many feuerall Nations, befides the Latin tongue
common to them all Beda lib. 1. cap. 1. This is
vntrue, and Beda rather faith the contrarie. His words are thefe. *This Iland at this*
prefent to the number of the 5. bookes of Moifes,
doth ftudie and fet forth the knowledg of one
perfect truth, that is with the language of the
English the Britons the Scotts, the Picts, and the
Latin which by ftudie of the fcripture is made
common to all the reft. In which words he
faith, that the Inhabitants preached and
publifhed Chrifts truth in fiue feueral
languages, but the fcripture they ftudied
onely in Latin, and therby it became
common to all the Inhabitants. And before in the life of Theodor, we fhewed by
the confeffion of diuers Proteftants, that
maffe was in his tyme, (which was before
S. Beda) in Latin onely. But admit that
the fcripture were then in Latin and in
English too, how proueth that, that
English men then were no Catholicks.

Haue

4. obiec-
tion.

Anfwer.

Haue not Englith Catholicks now the scripture in Englith? Fiftlie, faith Abbots, *Then were they in Monafteries commanded to be exercifed in the reading of fcriptures, and euery one was required to learn the Lords prayer and Creede in the English tongue.* This is not worth the anfwering. For what doth the Monks reading fcripture, or the peoples learning the Lords prayer and Creed in Englith make againft Catholick Religion?

5. Obiec-tion.

Ansvver.

3. Sixtly, faith Abbots, *Then was the Com-munio miniftred in both kindes as Paris in Heral-do and Rafo reporteth of fome foldiers.* What Paris faith of foldiers I knowe not. For at this prefent I haue him not at hand. But that Englith men in our Primitiue Church communicated onely with form of bread, appeareth by Beda. *lib. 2. cap. 5.* Wher Pagans fay to S. Mellit, *VVhy doft thou not giue vnto vs of that white bread which thou didft giue to our Father Seba, and doft yet giue to the people in Church?* But if S. Mellit had communicated people in both kinds, it is lykly they would haue demanded both. Befids that Beda expoundeth that place of Luke : (*Cognouernnt eum in fractione panis* (where mention is of one onely kinde) of facramental communion: Therfor he (and confequently our En-glith Church then) alowed communion

6. Obiec-tion.

Ansvver.

R in one

in one kinde. But whether they communicated in both or one kinde, maketh little to proue that they were not Catholicks, becauſe til lay people were forbidden, it was lawful for them to communicate in both kindes.

7. Obiection.

4. Seauenthlie thē (ſaith Abbots) *was Tranſubſtantiation vnknowne, and when it began to be broached or not long after, Elfricus Archbiſhop of Canterburie contradicted it.* How vntruethis

Ansvver.

is of Trāſubſtantiation hath bene ſhewed before in the life of S. Greg: and S. Odo

See befor hovv Bale confeſſeth Archb. Alfric to haue bene a Papiſt, and of Tranſub- ſtant.in.S. Odo Archb.

As for Elfric the Proteſtant Biſhops thēſelues who publiſhed that ſermon confeſſe, that the Author therof was no Archbiſhop of Canterbury. More likly it is to be trũe which Fox Acts. *pag.* 1148. ſaith that it was Elfric ſurnamed Bata, an Heretick, who (as S. Dunſtan appearing to one in a viſion ſaid (as reporteth Osbern) *attempted to diſherit his Church, but I haue ſtopped him* (ſaith S. Dunſtan) *& he could not preuaile.* Albeit indeed that ſermon doth more approoue Tranſubſtantiation than diſprooue it. For in that is ſaide, that *Chriſt turned through inuiſible might the bread to his owne body and wine to his blood.* And that *holy howſel is by might of Gods word truly Chriſts body and his blood:* And that *after their halowing, bread and wine trulye are Chriſts body and blood.* And what other do Catholicks now
ſay, but

fay, but what here is faid? Vz. That bread
and wine are by inuifible power turned
into Chrifts body and blood, and become
after confecration truly (not figuratiuly)
his body and blood. And though the Author of the fermon ad, that the facrament
after confecration *is not bodily but Ghoftly
Chrifts bodie* , yet the word *ghoftly* is not
added to deny the word *(Truly)* which is
abfolutly affirmed , but onely to deny the
word *(Bodily)* that is carnally and after a
Capharnaitical maner which is Catholick doctrin. For though the Eucharift be
truly and really Chrifts body, yet is it not
Chrifts bodie after a carnal maner , but
after a fpirituall & myftical maner. Now
wher he faith (which Bilfon *lib.* of Obed.
pag. 681, and Proteftants vrge) *that holy howfel after bodily vnderftanding, is a corruptible
and mutable creature* , maketh nothing
againft Tranfubftantiation . For his meaning is, that the facrament according to
bodily vnderftanding, that is , according
to the outward forme which with bodily eies we fee and vnderftand, is a corruptible thing , which no Catholick denieth. Again wher he fayeth , *that there is
much betwen the body that Chrift fuffered in, and
the body that is hallowed to howfel* . He
neither faid nor meant that ther is much
betwene Chrifts bodie wherin he fuffred

and

and the bodie of the howſel.(Albeit this
alſo be true, becauſe Chriſts body when
he ſuffered was after the maner of viſible
bodies, palpable, and parte in one parte of
place, and parte in an other: and here it is
inuiſible, and after the maner of ſpirits, all
in euerie part of the ſacramēt: For which
difference and leſſe S. Auſtin *lib.* de ſymbo-
lo *cap.* 10. ſaid much mo e, to wit, that in
the reſurrection ſhalbe no fleſh and blood.
In Reſurrectione non iam caro erit & ſanguis,
becauſe they ſhall be in far different maner) But he ſaid *that ther is much betweene
the body of Chriſt and the body that is* halowed
to houſel, which is moſt true, for thisbody
is the body of bread.

8. Obiec-
tion.
5. Eightlie ſaith Abots *Then the, Biſhops
and Princes of this Land did condemn the ſecond
Nicen Counſel for worſhiping of Images, out of*
Anſvver. *Houeden parte.* 1. *An.* 792. To this I anſwer,
that it is no waye likly that our Engliſh
Biſhops would then cōdemn ſuch honoring of Images as Catholiks vſe, becauſe
they knew that not onely their Chriſtianitie began by S. Auſtin with vſe of Images, but alſo that Archb. Brithwald (as is
before rehearſed out of Bale Cent. 1. *cap.*
99.) held a Councel in London *An.* 712.
*VVherin he commanded vpon the Decree of Con-
ſtantine Pope of Rome that Images ſhould be
worſhiped* . But that which our Engliſh
Clergie

Clergie then disproued was, as Houeden
writeth *Imagines adorari debere*, that is, *ado-
red or worshiped as God.* which Houed: wel
vnderstood when he added. *Quod Ecclesia
Dei execratur, which the Church of God doth detest.* Which (he being a perfect Roman
Catholick as Abbots can not denie) could
neuer say of such honor as Catholicks
giue to Images, but might most truly say
of worshiping them as God. For this the
Church of God did allwaies and doth
accurse. Nether, though some Catholicks
term that worship Latria which is giuen
to the crosse of Christ, did euer any Catholick affirm that any Image or creatur
whatsoeuer, was to be worshiped as God,
as I could easely shew, if it were not besids my purpose. But in that our English
men were mis-informed of the Councel
of Nice, as if it had commanded Images to
be worshiped as God, which it did not, as
(to omit other testimonies) testifieth D.
Feild *lib.*3. of the Church *cap.*20. and 36.   9. Obiec-
tion.
6. Lastly he saith that *then were tithes payd
to married Priests, and so continued to Pope Hilde-*   Malmsb.
lib.2 Reg.
brand (who liued in King William Con-
querors time) *and our most ancient Cathedrall*   cap.7. calleth these
Priests
Churches were places for maried Priests not for
Popish Votaries, as appeareth by the Records of   *irregulares*
the Church of Worceter. That there were   *and vagos.*
maried Priests or rather that Priests kept   *Ansvver.*

woemen as their wiues in Pope Hilde-
brands tyme, and before we deny not.
But that ther were such euer since the
first Christianitie of English men till that
time, or that mariage of Priests was not
alwaies forbidden in England, is most
vntrue, as hath bene sufficient clearly
prooued in the life of S. Anselm, and by
the testimonie of Protestants. Likwise
most vntrue it is, that our most ancient
Cathedrall Churches were places for
married Priestes. For the most ancient of
all is Christchurch in Canterburie, wher
King Ethelbert the first Christian King
of England placed monks (as Pope Boniface in his letter to him in Malmsb. *lib.* 1.
Pont. *pag.* 208. testifieth. And Malmsb.
Ibid. *pag.* 203. addeth this: *It is manifest that
ther haue bene Monks at Christchurch in Canterburie euer since the time of S. Laurence Archbishop who first succeded S. Austin* . As for the
Record of VVorceter if ther be any such
ancient thing, and not forged by some
Minister, it is like to haue bene deuised
by some married Priest, when in King
Edgar and King Edward martyrs tyme
they pleaded for that Church against
Monks, (who were restored to diuers
Cathedrall Churches which had bene
possessed of Preistes euer since the destruction of England by the Danes) by the
                                    iudgment

iudgment of S. Dunftan S. Ofwald King,
Edgar, & two Councels or Parliaments
as yow may read in Osbern (who liued
in the time of the Conqueft) in the life of
S. Dunftan . As for the firft Cathedrall
Church of Worceter, it was, (as Godwin
faith in the Bifhops of Worceter) a monafterie built by S. Egwin . I fay the firft,
For that which is now , was long after
founded by S. Wulftan Bifhop of Worceter, as yow may fee in his life in Godwin. Or if the firft were built of Sexwolf
(as Cambden faith in Brit. *pag.* 512. It is
nothing likly that he would build it for
married Prieftes , feing (as Beda faith
lib. 4. *cap.* 6.) he was a monke him felfe,
and built that Monafterie which now is
called Peterborough . But efpecially becaufe nether then , nor long after there
were any maried Prieftes in England , as
is euident by thefe words of S. Beda *lib.* 5.
cap. 22 written long after the foundation
of Worfter Church . *It behoueth them who
being ether made by vow Monks , or by profeſſion
of the Clergie , do bind them felues more ſtrictly*
(then maried men) *with the bridle of continencie* . Behould how in Bedas time
Monks by vow, and the Clergie by pro-
feſsion, did (as they do now) binde them
felues more ftrictly to chaftitie then
other men did . Which in other words is

R 4   to fay,

to fay, they did not marry. And thus much for the refelling of thefe flender obie&ions, which if they be compared with the former proofes wherwith wee fhewed that our ancient Kings were Roman Cathol. will (I fuppofe) feeme to any of indifferent iudgment to deferue no anfwer.

CHAP. XXIII.

That all the Chriftian Kings of England from their firft Chriftia-nitie to the time of the Monar-chie of Englǎd, were Roman Catholicks, prooued in particuler.

1. VVHen S. Auftin entred there were 7. Englifh Kings in this Land . Wherof foure were conuerted by S. Auftin and his companions. But partly becaufe it were to tedious to difcourfe of all thefe Kingdoms, partly alfo becaufe what is prooued of one of them, will cafelie be beleeued of the reft, I will difcourfe onely of the Kings of the Weft Contrie, who in time fubdued the reft, and

and whose roiall blood yet inioyeth the crown in their rightfull heire both by the English and Scottish line, our Souerain Lord King Iames. If any askt me why God permitted the Western Kings to conquer the rest? I will not take vpon me to haue bene of Gods counsel, yet haue I noted diuers notable things peculier to them, which whither they might moue God to blesse them with such temporall benediction or no, I leaue to the reader to iudg. The first is, that the first Christian King of that Contrie, namely Kinegilsus left his Kingdome and became a Monk as testifieth Fox *Acts.pag.* 110. 134. which we read not of the first Christian Kings of the other Kingdoms. The second is that the kings of this Contrie, first left their Kingdoms and went on Pilgrimage to Rome. This is manifest by S. Beda *lib.* 5. *cap.* 7. in the valiant King Ceadwall. Who in the year 689. before all other kings wēt on Pilgrimage to Rome. The third is, that these kings first of all other our Princes made this land tributaire to Rome for the Peter pence. This all our Chronicles write of King Ina in the yeare 726. These three notable things these Kings performed first, and therfor perhaps their Kingdom continewed longest. But now to come to the Kings in particuler.

His maiestie descended of the VVest Saxon Kings by both the English and the Scottish line.

First Christian K. of vvest saxons became a Monke.

VVest saxon Kings first vvent to Rome.

First made their kingdom tributary to the See Apostol.

R 5   *King*

King Kynegilsus first Christian King of the west Saxons or west Countrie.

2. THe firſt Chriſtian King of the Weſt Saxons was Kinegilſus alias Cynegilſus, who began his reigne An. 611. as ſome write, or as others. 612. two or thre yeares before the death of S. Auſtin our Apoſtle, if he died not before 614. as Malmsb.recordeth; and reigned 31.yeares. He was côuerted to the Chriſtian faith & Chriſtened by S. Birin in the yeare of our Lord 635.& was a valiant Prince, and had proſperous ſucceſſe in his warrs againſt the Britons, and againſt Penda the cruel Pagan King of the Mercians or Middle Engliſh. As for the faith of this ancient and valiant King, that appeareth to be Roman Catholick many wayes. Firſt be-cauſe he was conuerted by S. Birin, who-me both Catholicks and Proteſt. grant to haue bene ſent hither by Pope Honorius, who was the fourth Pope after Boniface 3. which Pope Proteſtants (as is ſhewed before *cap.13*) account the firſt Antichriſt and head of the Papiſt ¡Church, becauſe he procured Phocas the ¦Emperor to de-clare that he was head of the Church, and in like ſort they account of all the Popes

ſince

Kinegilſus 1. Chriſtiâ K. of the VVeſt Saxons.

The va-lour of K. Kinegilſus

K. Kynigil-ſus a Rom Catholick

1

Beda lib. 3 cap. 7.
Godvvin in Birin.
Cooper.
An. 6;6.
Bal. Cent. 13.cap.4.

since that time. And it is not likly that Pope Honorius would send any hither that did not beleeue him to be head of the Church, in which point (as D. Reinolds and D. Whitaker say) *the essence of a Papist doth consist.* Besides this Honorius in his Epistle in Beda *lib.* 2. *cap.* 18. plainly calleth S. Peter *head of the Apostles,* and *cap.* 17 he sendeth two Palls, one to the Archbishop of Canterburie, and another to the Archb. of York; more ouer he was a Canon regular as saith Ciacon in his life, as also was S. Birin whome he sent, which order Bale Cent, 1. *cap.* 82. calleth *one of the hornes of the beast,* and Cent. 1. *cap.* 70. plainly refuseth Honorius as a Papist saying, *He instituted the feast of the Exaltation of the holy Crosse, added the inuocation of the dead Saints to Greg. Letanies, and ordainet that there should be a Procession euery Saboth day. Hence the Procession in Churches seeme to haue had their beginnings.* Secondly the same S. Birin, Apostle (as Camb. calleth him in Brit. *pag.* 338.) of the Westsaxons, was so addicted to masse and things belonging therto, as for the loue of a Corporas which he had left on the shoare when he tooke shipp for England, when he could not perswade the mariners to returne to fetch it, he aduentured his life by walking on the sea to goe for it, as Malmsb. *lib.* 2. Pont. *pag.* 241.

Iornelasensis,

(marginal notes:)
K Kinegilsus connuerted by a Canon regular.

P. Honorius a Papist.

2

s. Birins esteeme of a Corporas.

Miracle touching a Corporas.

Iornelasensis, and so many Authors affirme as (saith Fox *lib. 2. pag. 122. I can not but
maruel*, And if he were not obstinat could
not but beleeue. And Capgrane in his life
saith that his bones were founde in Pope
Honorius 3. and Archb. Stephens time
with a leaden Crosse vpon his brest a little Chalice

3 *and two stoles.* Thirdly this King became a
Monk as Fox testifieth *lib. 2. pag. 110.* and
134. and for what ende hath bene before
declared, which is an euident badg of

4 Papistrie. Fourthly his Godfather in
baptisme was King Oswald as Beda
saith *lib. 3. cap. 7.* which Oswald erected
Crosses and prayed before them, and
being to die him selfe prayed God to haue
mercy on the soules departed, out of Beda

5 *cap. 2. cap. 12.* which are euident tokens of
Papistrie. Fiftly, This truth is euident by
the open confessions of our aduersaries.

For Bale Cent. 13. *cap. 4.* writeth that,
Birini opera &c. *By the industrie of Birin in the
yeare of our Lord* 635. *Dorchester with the Contrie
therabout vnder pretence of the Gospel receaued
the Papisticall faith.* And that *S. Birin was
enrolled amongst the Papisticall Saints.* Thus
the Roman religion of this first Christian

King is both euident, and confessed.

3. In this Kings time, besides S. Austin
and his fellowes, of whose miracles
wrought for the testimonie of the Roman

Catholick faith is before spoken, liued See Bed. *lib.3.cap.7.* the saide S. Birin, whome to omit Catho- Sur. tom. lick authors Cooper Chron. An. 636. 6. Malmsb *lib.*2 Pont. calleth *a holy man.* Cambd. in Brit. *pag.*338. Capgraue faith, *He was admirally famous for the opinion of* in Birin. *sanctitie.* Godwin in his life saith he was *a very zelous and deuout man.* And Fox Acts The holines of the *lib.* 2. *cap.* 122. saith, *that by his godly labors he* conuerter *conuerted the King to the faith of Christ.* And of K. Kinegilsus to amongst others his miracles waiked as is the Cath, faith. said vpon the seas (a thing scarce heard of since S. Peeters time) to fetch his corporas, which is so certain as Fox. L. cit. Fox dare dare not deny, yet saith he(if we will be- not denie S. Birin leeue him on his word)that if this miracle VValking were done, it was not done for the holi- on the sea nes of the man (yet yow see how holy, to fetch a him selfe, and other Protest. confesse him Corporas. to haue bene)or corporas, but for conuersion of the heathen. But it sufficeth that God would work so great a miracle for conuersion of the heathen to the Roman faith. In this Kings time liued also King Oswald, whome Fox Acts *pag.*133.calleth Miracle for con- *a Saint*, and who by vertue of prayer firmation (which he made before a Crosse) with a of praiers made be- far lesse army vanquished his enemies, as for Crosses not onely S. Beda *lib.*3. *cap.* 2. and Catholick writers, but Fox also Acts *lib.* 2. *pag.* 121. Cambd. in Brit. *pag.*720.and others do **grant.** So wel did God then lyke praying
before

before Croſſes . As for diuers other miracles done by S. Oſwalds reliques and by
very chipps of his Croſſe , which S. Beda
lib.3.cap.2. 10.11. & other Engliſh writers

Fox dare not denie Saint Oſwalds miracles. do record , Fox loc. cit. ſaith, *he hath not to affirme what the people of that time affirmed of him,* As if he were amazed , not knowing whether to confeſſe the miracles, and ſo condemne his religion of falſitie ; or deny them,and ſo condemne him ſelf of impu-

Proteſt. confeſſe miracles to haue bene done by reli- ques and the Croſſe dencie ; Eſpecially ſeeing that Iuel Art. 1. diu.19.Bel.Suruey *pag.*353.and D.Whitak. *lib.*10.cont.Dur.*pag.*866.confeſſe that God hath often times wrought miracles by the reliques of Saints,and alſo done ſtrang miracles and driuen away Diuels with the Croſſe,as teſtifie Iuel Art.14. Diu 3. And

Feild. lib.3. of Church cap.10. lib 4. cap.31. Fox him ſelfe Acts *pag.* 85. teſtifieth that Conſtantin the great profeſſed that he did ouercome his enemies *ſalutari Crucis ſigno : by the holſom ſigne of the Croſſe .* In this Kings tyme alſo Sigebert King of the Eaſt Angles left his Kingdom,and became

A King a monk and diuers Kings Daughters Nonnes. a Monke , and S. Edburga daughter to King Ethelbert, S.Eanſwid daughter to King Edbald, and S. Ebba a Lady of the bloud royall left their eſtates, and became Nonnes. Beda *lib.3.cap.*18.Capgraue in vita Eanſwidæ,Cambd.in Brit.*pag.*670.Hun-ting. *lib.* 2.

King

King Senwalch the 2. Christian King.

4. THE second Christian King of the Westsaxons was Senwalch, sonne (as Beda *lib.* 3. *cap.* 7. and others record) of Kinegilius, began his Reigne An. 643. and reigned 31. yeares twice vanquished the Britons, and tooke a great part of land from the Mercians, and as Malmsb. writeth *lib.* 1. Reg. *cap.* 2. *was comparable to the best Princes, the middle and last of his time.* and so religious that (as Florent. An. 843. Fox. Acts. *pag.* 122. Stow *pag.* 96. write) he built the Cathedral Church at Winchester, and gaue all the Contrie within 7. miles about for maintenance of Priests that should serue therin, though Godwin in vita Agilberti say his Father began the worke, and that he did but finish and confirme his Fathers deed and grant, and adde therto thre Manners. But as for the Roman Religion of this religious and vertuous King it is manifest, first by what hath bene sayd of his Father. Secondly because after the decease of S. Birin aforsayd, his Bishops was Agilbert, as Beda *lib.* 3. *cap.* 9, Malmsbus. *lib.* 1. *cap.* 2. Godwin in Agilbert and all agree.

Which

The vaiour and vertue of K. Senwalch.

K. Senwalch a Rom. Catholick

1

2

which Agilbert was so notorious a Papist
as Fox in his Protestation before his Acts
reckoneth him amongst Romish monkes
much drowned (as he saith) *in superstition with
Dunstan, Lanfranc, and such lyke* . And in a
Synod defended the Roman vse of Easter
and round shauing of Priests crownes, as
is to be seene in Beda *lib.3.cap.26.* and Fox
Acts *pag.*123 . Thirdly because after Agilbert his Bishop was Elutherius , who at
this Kings request as Beda *lib. 3. cap. 7.*
Godwin in vita Elutherij write, was côse-
crated by S. Theodor, whome(as is before
shewed)Protestants confesse to haue bene
a notorious Papist . Fourthly because S.
Egelwin or Egwin was brother to this
King, as testifieth Malmsb. *lib. 2. Pont.
pag.*255. Which Egwin Bale Cent.1.*cap* 91.
saith was a Benedictin Monk *ad supersti-
tiones natus, borne for superstitions ,* helped, *vt
statuæ ponerentur in Templis & venerarentur :
for the placing of Images in Churches and worshiping of them,* and was after canonized, and
how great he was with Pope Constantin
appeareth by his life in Capgraue. Fiftly,
because in this Kings tyme came the said
S. Theodor into England , *vnto whome*
(writeth Beda *lib. 4. cap.* 2. and Godwin
in his life) *all the whole Church of the English
Nation did consent and submit them selues:*
Therfor then this King and all his Chriſtian

3

4

5

ſian people were as ſincerly Papiſts as
S. Theodor him ſelf was.

5. In this Kings time among other holy
men liued the bleſſed Biſhops S. Chad
and Tedda, whoſe vertue and miracles
are recorded by S. Beda *lib.* 3. *cap.* 23. and
lib. 4. *cap.* 3. likwiſe ther liued in that time
K. Oſwin who vowing to God to make
his daughter a Nonne if he ouercame his
enemies, got the Victorie though he had
but one Legion againſt thirty ex Beda
lib. 3. *cap.* 24. Hunting. *lib.* 3. Weſtmon An.
855. And if he had not bene preuented by
death ment to go to Rome, and there to
ende his life, as witneſſeth Beda *lib.* 4.
cap. 5. There liued alſo S. Sebbi King of
the Eaſt ſaxons who together with his
ſonne Sighard became a Monke as may
be ſeene in Beda *lib.* 4. *cap.* 1. Malmsb. 1.
Reg. *cap.* 6. Stow Chron *pag.* 79. In like
ſort ther liued Oſwie *a meruailous deuout
and godly man* (ſaith Beda *lib.* 3. *cap.* 14.) and
Sigibert a holy King of Eſſex, of whome
writeth Beda *lib.* 3. *cap.* 22. And at the ſame
time S. Eartongatha daughter of Ercombert King of Kent; S. Edelburg daughter
to Anna King of Eaſt England, and
Sedrido his daughter in law, with diuers
others went into France, and there became Nonnes floriſhing with great vertue
and miracles, as yow may read in S. Beda

S *lib.* 3.

Holie
men in K.
ſeauvalch
his time.

K. Oſvvin
vouing to
make his
daughter a
Nonne
get teth a
miracu-
lous vic-
torie.

K. Sebbi
and his
ſonne bea-
come
Monke.

Diuers
Kings
daughters
holie
Nonnes.

S. Earton-
geth.
S. Edel-
burg
Sedrido.

*lib.*3. *cap.* 8. Likwife Herefwid mother to Adolph King of Eaſt Angles ex Beda *lib.* 4. *cap.* 23. And in England became Nonnes S. Withburg daughter to the faid King Anna ex Florent An. 798. Elfled daughter to King Oſwiex Beda *lib.*3. *cap.*24. and alſo S. Hilda a Lady of the blood roiall ex eodem *lib.* 4. *cap.* 23. and diuers others. Bale Cent.10.*cap.*9.and

Then alſo
liued S.
Bathilda
in Engl.
vvoman
Q. of Frā-
ce and
after non-
ne.Sur.
tom. 7.

Capgraue in Botulpho maketh mētiō of certain fifters of King Athelmond King of Suffex who in this kings tyme An. 650. were Nonnes in Gallia Belgica. And Fox *lib.* 2. *pag.* 133. faith king Ciffa built the Monaſterie of Abington An. 666. Cooper faith, 665. In this tyme alſo as S. Beda writeth *lib.*3. *cap.* 26. *Euen the*

Honor of
our An-
ceitors to
Prieſts
nnd
Monks.

habit of religious men was had in great reuerence. So that where any of the Clergie or religious perſons came he should be ioifully receaued of all men as the feruant of God. If any were met going on iorny they ran vnto him and making low obeiſance deſired gladly his benediction ether by hand or mouth who would euer *haue thought* that the children and poſteritie of theſe Anceſtors would make it treaſon to be a Prieſt, or thinck it a pleaſing thing to God to make them away with cruel deaths.

Queene

Queene Sexburga. III.

6. **T**he next Chriſtian Prince was
Sexburga viſe to King Senwalch.
Who began to reigne An. 672. or; 674.
as others ſay, and held it one yeare. *Non*
Deerat ſaith Malmsb. lib. 1. *Reg. cap.* 2; *The* The va-
woman wanted not ſpirit to diſpach the affaires of Sexburg.
the Realme, ſhe raiſed neu armies, and retained
the ould in obedience, ſhe gouerned her ſubiects
with clemencie, threatned her enemies terribly,
executed all things in that maner that beſides her
ſex nothing made any difference. The Roman Her Rom.
religion of this noble Queene is manifeſt Religion.
by what hath bene ſayde of her husband,
and by the Counceel which S. Theodor
in her time (as Huntington *lib.* 2. *pag.* 318.
ſaith and appeareth by Beda *lib.* 4. *cap.* 5.)
kept at Hereford with all the Biſhops of
England. Stow Chron. *pag.* 96. ſaith ſhe
builded a Nonuery in Shepei, and became
her ſelfe a Nonne and Ableſſe in Ely: But
I think that was an other Sexburga
Queene of kent, of whome we ſhall ſpeake herafter. For Malmsb: ſaith ſhe died
after ſhe had reigned one yeare. In the
reign of this Queene Florent: ſaith in
Chron: befel that famous act of a far more renowned Queene Ethelred of Northumberland, who was twiſe married

S. Ethel-
red tvvise
maried
and yet
a virgin.
Bed.lib.4.
cap. 19.
Camb.in
Briton.
pag.438.
Stovv
chron.
pag 92.
Florent.
An.672.
Huntingt.
lib.2. vve-
stmon.
An 679.
S.Ethel-
reds bo-
die incor-
rupt.
Also S.
Edilburgs.
Miracles
by reli-
ques.

and liued 12.yeares with herlast husband
Egbert a yong man and King of Northumberland,and yet(as both Catholick
and Protestant writers haue deliuered)
could by no meanes be perswaded to
haue carnal companie with ether of
them, and this yeare with her husbands
licence left the wordl , & became a Nonne. Sixteene yeare after her death her body,in testimonie of her incorrupt virginitie. was found incorrupt in S. Bedas
time,as him self testifieth. *lib.4.cap.*19.The
like he reporteth *lib.3.cap.*8. of Saint Edilburgs bodye after 7. yeares burial. And
he addeth that Diuels were cast oute, and
diuers diseases cured by the clothes in
which Edilburgs body had bene wraped.

King Escuin 4.Christian King.

The Va-
lour of K.
Escuin.

7. **TO** Queene Sexburg succeded
King Escuin in the yeare 674. or
675. as others say. *He was*(saith Malmsb.)
Kinegilsus great nephen by his brother,and of nota-
ble experience in the warres.For the Mercians he
ouer thrue with a dreadful slaughter..But as for

His Rom
Religion.

his Roman Religion that can not be
doubted of, For therin ther is no mention made that he varied from his Præ-
decessors,and because his Bishop was the
forsaid Elutherius,and Heddie,of whome
we,

we, wil speake herafter. In this Kings S. Ercen-vvald and his mira-cles. time liued S. Ercenwald Bishop of London whose great vertue and miracles wrought euen by the chipps of his litter (as in the Apostles time by S. Peters shadow aud S. Pauls napkins) are mentioned in S. Beda·*lib.* 4.*cap.*6. Where also *cap.* 7. and seq: he relateth the great miracles done by God in the Nonry of Booking which Ercanwald founded, and wherof his sister Edilburg was Abbesse. In this Florent. An.675. Cambd. Brit.pag. 453.Stovv, pag.81. Kings time also dyed Wolsher king of the middle English who builded Peterborow.and whose wife S, Ermenild and his daughter S. Werburg and his twosisters S. Kinesburg and kineswith became Nonnes. Likwise his brother merowald had by his Queene S. Frmenburg One Q. and 3. King. daughters Nonnes. three holy virgins S. Milburg, S. Mildred, and Milgith and one vertuous sonne Saint Meræsin. This account those great Princes then made of monkish life. Florent. An.675. malmesb. 1.Reg. cap.4.

King Kentwin 5. *Christian Prince.*

8. The 5 Christian Prince was King Kentwin, who began his reigne An.677,as Malmsb. hath in Fastis,or 676. as Florent hath in Chron , and ruled 9. The valour of K Kentvvin. yeares. He was as they saye sonne to the forsaid Kinegilsus,and *nota in bello experientia*

tia maruelous expert in war as Malmsb. hath
*lib.*2. Reg.*cap.* 2. And as Florent addeth
An :704. *He chafed the Eaſt Britons by the dint*

His Rom.
Religion.

of the ſword. His Roman religion is manifeſt. Firſt becauſe(as Fox writeth Acts

1

*lib.*2.*pag.*110.) He died at Rome, and be-

2

cauſe his Biſhop was S. Heddie made
Biſhop , (as Godwin ſaith in his life,)
An 673. and died 750.as Beda hath *lib.* 5.
*cap.*19.and was(ſaith Bale Cent.1.*cap.* 86.)
a Monk , and conſecrat by that famous
Papiſt S.Theodor; which alſo affirmeth
Florent. An. 676. Thirdly becauſe in

3

the fift yeare of this king (as Huntington
ſaith *lib.* 4.) was that Councel in hat-
feild by Saint Theodor in preſence of
Iohn Legat of Pope Agatho ,where the
Engliſhe Biſhops profeſſed their faith in
ſuch ſort, as it was wel liked of Pope

Saints in
K. Kenti-
wins time

Agatho,as may be ſeene in Beda *lib.* 4.
cap. 17. and 18.In this kings time liued the
for ſaid S. Heddi *a verie vertuous and holy man*
ſaith Godwin in his life, And Beda *lib.* 5.
*cap.*19.ſaith *vndoubtedly that he was a iuſt man,*
and teſtifieth that S. Aldelm his familier

Great mi-
racles by
the Duſt
of S. Heddi
his graue.

frend and ſucceſſor, and greatly eſtemed
of Fox Acts *pag.* 125. Cambd. in Brit:
pag. 210,Bal Cent.1. *cap.* 83, was wont to
tel that at the place where he died many
great miracles and cures were done , and
that men of that Prouince had made a
deepe

deepe pit by carrying a way the Duſt therof, which cured many both men and beaſtes. In this kings time An. 679. did S. Wilfrid conuert Suſſex, and wrough diuers miracles as is to be ſeene in Beda *lib.*4. *cap.*13. And Stow confeſſeth Chron: *pag.*7. And yet is he confeſſed to haue bene a Papiſt by Bale Cent.1. *cap.* 88. and Cent. 14. *cap.*21. to haue maintained *Non interpretabilem Papæ authoritatem*, as he termeth it; And then allſo lyued the moſt deuout woman Abbeſſe Hilda of the blood royal, ex Beda *lib.*4.*cap.*23; And in this Kings time alſo An.679. befel that great miracle for the approouing of Maſſe and praying for the dead which S. Beda recounteth *lib.*4.*cap.* 22. of a Prieſt Who thincking his brother had bene ſlaine in a battel but indeede was taken priſoner *did often times* (ſaith Beda) *cauſe Maſſe to be ſaid for his ſoule.* By the ſaying of which Maſſes it came to paſſe that no man could bind him but he was ſtreight looſed again about eight a clock in the morning when Maſſes began to be ſayd. This miracle fel not out vpon an obſcure perſon but in one that ſerued Queene Edelred and in an Earles houſe, and not in Englád onely but in Friſland alſo, whither the man at laſt was ſould. *And many* ſaith Beda *that heard theſe things of this man were ſtirred in*

A great miracles for Confirmation of maſſe.

S 4 *faith*

faith and godly deuotion vnto prayer almes and and charitable deedes and to offer vnto our Lord hofts of the holy oblation and facrifice for the deliuerie and releefe of their freinds that were departed This fame (faith he) *was tould me of them that heard it of the very man on whome it was done And therfor knowing it to be true and certain I doubted no whit to put it into this our Ecclefiaftical Hiftorie.* Which words of this great Doctor and Saint then liuing may fuffice to con-fonnd the incredulitie, of any Minifter. In the fame Kings time alfo

Plagne cealeth by intercef- sion of Saints.

as Beda recordeth *lib.4.cap.4.* was a great mortalitie ftayed by the interceffion of S. Ofwald, and Maffes faid to giue God thancks therfor at the apointment of S. Peter and Paul appearing in a vifion

Tvvo Queens nonns.

Which vifion to be true, appeared by the miraculous effects folowing. In this Kings time alfo liued Sexburg Queene of Kent who hauing left her Princly ftate became a Nonne vnder her fifter Saint Edelred in Ely, and fucceeded her in the Abbeffefhip And Alfo as Beda faith *lib. 4. cap. 26.* Eanfled Queene of Northumberland wife to King Ofwin with her daughter Elfled in the Monafterie of Whitbie.

King

King Cedwalla VI.

9. IN the yeare 686. succeded king Cedwalla who saith Beda *lib.5. cap. 7.* held it two yeares, and leauing it An. 688. (as Beda hath in Epit.) was baptized of the Pope at Rome on Easter euen An. 689; and there died. He was as Beda writeth *lib. 4. cap. 15.* a valiant yong man, Subdued Sussex and the I le of wite. And as Malmsb. addeth *lib. 1. Reg. cap. 2.* often times ouercame the Kentish men. His Roman religion is vndoubted. For as Beda hath *lib.5.cap.7.* being not yet Christened, he left his kingdome and Contrie and went to Rome, *thincking it to be singuler glorie and renowne to him to be regenerat at the Sea Apostolick with the Sacrament of baptisme. And withall hoped that as sone as he was clensed from sinne he should depart this world, Both which* (saith Beda) *by the prouidence of God were fullfilled. For he was baptised by Pope Sergius and named* Peter , *that he might beare his name whose Tombe he came to see , and died while he wore his white aparrell of innocencie was buried honorably in S. Peters Church* where in our tyme his body was found neere to S. Peters Sepulcher. In this kings time dyed S. Cutbert. For as S. Beda saith *lib. 4. cap. 27.* He was consecrat Bishop An. 685.

The valiantnes of K. Cedvvalla.

His. Rom. Religion.

Saint Cutbert, and his religion and miracles.

S 5   and

& hauing bene two yeares Biſhop ſoone after died, and was wont, (as there and ſequ. Beda writeth) to heare mens confeſſions, to offer ſacrifice to God, and whoſe body eleuen yeares after his death was (as S. Beda ſaith who then liued) found whole and ſound, and the Iointes and ſinowes ſoft and pliable and many miracles wrought therby. In this time ſaith Beda *lib. 4. cap. 27. it was the maner of the people of England when any of the Clergie er any Prieſt came to a Village, they would all by and by at his calling come to gether to beare the word and willingly harken to ſuch things as were ſayd, and more willingly follow in works ſuch things as they could heare and vnderſtand.*

Deuotion of Engl: people. (margin)

King Ina. VII.

10. THe 7. Chriſtian king was Ina who began his Reign An. 688. as appeareth by S. Beda in Epit. & Malmsb. in Faſtis, and held his kingdome (as Beda *lib. 5. cap. 7.* and all teſtifie) 37. yeares. He was ſaith Malmsb. *lib. 1. Reg. c. 2. fortitudinis vnicum ſpecimen: The onely mirror of fortitud, the Image of wiſdom, and his lik in religion yow could not finde. How worthie he was in the affaires of God the lawes may witneſſe, which he made for correcting of the peoples maners wherein to this day appeareth a liuely repreſentation of his pietie* Bale Cent. *1. cap. 97.* ſaith, *magni con-*

ſilij

The admirable vertues of K. Ina. Malmsb. (margin)

Bale. (margin)

filij & fortunæ homo a man of profund iugment and great fortune. Fox Acts. pag. 127. *A worthy* Fox. *and valiant King* Cooper An. 687. *Ina of great* Cooper. *power and wisdome and ther with valiant and hardie and in feats of armes very expert .* To which Stow Chron pag. 96. addeth *that he* Stow. *was the patern of strength and manlines, an Image of wisdome, and his like of no man known at that time for religion and framing his life therafter.* These high praises for religion Valor and His Rom. wisdom (three singuler properties of a Religion. Prince) do both Catholicks and Protestants giue to this renowned Prince. Now let vs see what his religion was. First his Bishop was S. Aldelm a notorious Papist, as is shewed before *whose* **1** *commādements* (faith Malmsb. L. cit) *audiebat humiliter ad-implebat hilariter .* He humbly listened vnto, and cheerfully fullfilled, Secondly **2** he built faith Stow loc. cit. and others Glassenburie Abbey , and erected also *a Chappell of gould and siluer* (so termed of Chlaices the ornaments) *with ornamentes and veffels of* Images *gould and siluer, gaue to the Altare 264. pounds* of gould *of gould, a Chalice with a Paten of ten pounds of* and siluer. *gould, a Censor of 8. pounds, a holy water bucket of 20. pound of siluer Images of our Lord and our Ladie and the 12. Apostles of 175. poundes of siluer and 28. pounds of gould, a Pall for the* **3** Altar. &c. Thirdly his wife Queene Ethel- Thre burga liued a Nonne at Berking as Fox Queene nonns.

saith

faith A&ts *pag.* 125. and others . His fifter
Queene Cuthburga of Northumberland
a Nonne at Winborn as Camb. in Brit.
pag. 182. and Likwife an other fifter of his
called Quen-burga as writeth Florent
An. 718. Weftmon and others . Fourthly
him felfe as Fox faith *pag.* 125. *fetting a fide
all the pompe and pride of this wordl affociated
him felf in the fellowship of poore men and tra-
uailled to Rome with great deuotion, wher* (as he
faith *pag.* 110) *he became a Monke* and *pag.* 125.
*granted a peny of euery houfe to be payd to the
Court of Rome.* And *pag.* 136 *founded the
English Scoole or Seminarie there* . Fiftly as
Cambden teftifieth in Brit. *pag.* 193. he
made verfes to be engraué in the forfront
of Gloffenburie in which he plainly confeffeth S. Peters fupremacie (faith he)
that he was in Degree higher than S.
Paul ; had the Keyes of heauen , was the
Porter, and the firm Rock . The verfes
are thefe.

Cælorum portæ lati duo Lumina mundi
 Ore tonat Paulus, fulgurat Arce Petrus.
Inter Apoftolicas radianti luce coronas
 Doctior hic monitis, celfior ille gradu.
Corda per hunc hominum referantur , & aftra
 per illum
Quos docet ifte ftilo, fufcipit ille Polo.
Pandit iter Cælo hic dogmate clauibus alter
 Eft via cui Paulus, ianna fida Petrus.

Behould

Marginal notes:

X Into pilgrim to Rome and granteth the Peter Pence.

Beda. lib.5 cap.7.
malmsb: loc. cit.
Cooper An 725.
Bale Cent. 11. cap. 97.
Sleidan. lib 9.
Stovv pag. 96.
Bal. lib. cit Cambd. in Brit. p. 192.

5

S. peters fupremacie profeffed by letters engfauen in ftone.

Behould Chriftian Reader this ancient and famous King and confequently all England in his time, which is 900. yeares agoe beleeuing, and not beleeuing onely but profeſsing, nor profeſsing but engrauing in ftone for teſtimony to all pofteritie that S. Peter was in degree aboue all the Apoftles, was the peculier Rock of Chriſtians, the proper Porter of heauen, and efpetially had the keyes of the coeleſtiall Kingdome; Which is plain-ly that fupremacie which their Pofteritie Catholicks doe attribut vnto S. Peter and his fucceſsors. And of the royall blood of this vndoubted Catholick and renouned King and fo deuoted to the Church of Rome as firſt of all Chriftian Kings of the wordl, he made his Kingdom and euery houſhould therof tributary therto by payment of yearly penſion by his brother Ingles came King Egbert, who after reduced England to a monarchie as teſtifieth Paris Hiſt. *pag.* 126. and of this King Egbert by liueall fucceſsion defcendeth our prefent Souereign Lord King Iames. *S. Peter in degree aboue all the reſt of the Apoſtles.*

His maieſtic defcendeth of K. Ina. by his brother.

11. In this Kings tyme beſids him felf three other Engliſh Kings left their Kingdoms alfo and became Monks, to wit, Ethelred, and Coenred Kings one after the other of mercia or middle England, *Four Kings leaue their kingdoms and became möks.*

and

and Offa King of Eſſex . The two laſt
went to Rome,and there entred into Re-
ligion.The third remained heere in England,& after was made Abbot of Bardney
neere Lincoln . And beſides the Queens
before mentioned Kineſwitha daughter,
of King Penda and alſo eſpouſe to the
ſaid King Offa became a Nonne hauing
before perſwaded him to giue ouer both
his Kingdom and ſuite to her . And beſides theſe Oſrick King of Northumberland as Godwih in the Biſhops of Gloſter
ſaith , but indeede King of the Victians
as Beda called him *lib.*4. *cap.*23.about the
yeare 700.founded a Nonnery in Gloſter,
in which Kinebnrg Eadburg and Euaall
Queenes of Mercia were ſuccesſiuly
Abbeſſes.The ſame ſaith Cambd.in Brit.
pag. 316. Such rare and admirable loue of
God,and contempt both of pleaſures and
glorie of this world , reigned in our
Kings , Queenes , and Princes of thoſe
dayes,that iuſtly Cambd.in Brit.*pag.*345.
calleth this age *feraciſsimum Sanctorum ſecu-*
*lum:a moſt fruitfull wordl of Saints.*Oh when
will Proteſtants breede ſuch an age . In
this Kings time fell that moſt dredfull
pumiſhment of God vpon that Captain
who in his ſicknes would not confeſſe
his ſinnes leaſt he ſhould ſeeme fearfull.
Which S. Beda recounteth *lib.* 5. *cap.* 14.
where

Three
Queens of
mercia
Abbeſſes
one after
the other.

Proteſtāts
glorie of
the holi-
nes of our
Cath. An-
ceiſtors.

wher he telleth how a little before the mans death Angels appeared and shewed to him a faire booke, but little in quantitie wherin all his good deedes were written, and after there came a huge multitude of Diuels, who in a great black booke shewed him all his ill deedes and sinnes, and one of them strooke him on the head and other on the feete which, strokes crept into his body & when they met he dyed in desperation. In this Kings time also dyed S. Iohn of Beuerley who made S. Beda Priest, whome he recounteth *lib. 5. cap.* 2. that by making the signe of the Crosse vpon the tongue of a Domb man he restored his speeche, and that he helped an Earles wife with holy water, and *cap.* 5. cured an Earles sonne and his Chaplin by his blessing. In this time also liued S. Wilbrord an English man, who An. 697. was consecrat Bishop by Pope Sergius, and sent to preache in Frisland and Germany, which also S. Swibert and many English more did Marcellin. 1. mort Surio tom. 2. Beda *lib.5.cap.*11. In this time also liued S. Boniface the Apostle of Germanie, whome Pope Greg. 2. sent thither to preache An. 719. whose oath of fidelitie and plain Papistrie yow may read in Surius Tom. 3. and Baron An. 723. At that same time also liued that great Eremit

Dreadful punishment of one that differed his confession.

Westmon. An. 921. Godw. in B. of york.

Miracles of S. Ihon of Beuerlay.

See also Surius de rebus mogun-tin.

and

s, Guthlac and S. Antonie of England S. Guthlac.
the S. An- Of whome becauſe Fox *Acts pag.* 125.
toine of
England. ſaith, *that he ſeeth no great cauſe, why he ſhould
be Sainted, Nether beleeue I* (ſaith he) *his miracles.* I will in this Saint giue the reader a
His holi- taſte of Fox his impudencie, and a full
nes. aſſurance (if any can ſuffice) of S. Guthlac
his miracles. Wherby euery indifferent
man may iudg of the like miracles of
Saints. As for his holines Cambd, in Brit.
pag. 472. ſaith thus *Guthlacus ſumma ſanct
titate* &c. *Guthlac heere* (at Crowland) *lead
an heremitical life in exceediug great ſanctitie,
in honor of whome King Ethelbald with wonderfull expence founded a Monaſterie in a Mariſh
and vnſtable grounde, for religion and wealth
very famous.* Behould this Proteſtant
acknowledgeth that S. Guthlac led a
moſt holy life, and was ſo eſteemed, that
His mira- King Ethelbald (who liued at that ſame
cles. time) ſoone after his death, built a goodly
Monaſterie in his honor. And who will
read his life in Surius Tom. 2. ſhall finde
that he was an admirable Saint.

12. But as for the miracles of S. Guthlac
if any humane teſtimony or euidence
can make a thing certain and vndoubted, they are ſo. For Ingulph in his
Hiſt. printed and publiſhed by Proteſt:
(who liued in the time of the Conqueſt) ſetteth doune the Charter of King
xenulph

Kenulph a worthie Prince as all our Chronicles testifie , dated *Anno Christi* 806.in which the King saith that he and his Queene were eye witnesses of many miracles done at is shrine in these words *Kenulphus Dei misericordia Rex* &c. *Kenulph by the grace of God King* &c. *Be it known to all men that our Lord hath magnified his Saint, the most blessed Confessor of Christ S. Guthlac , who corporally resteth in Crowland Monasterie with most famous signes and worthy wonders , yea with fresh and innumerable miracles,as both I and my Queene haue seene with our owne eyes in our Pilgrimage.* And there the king freketh all Pilgrims that come to S. Guthlac *cum signis eius in caputijs aut capellis ,with his images in their hatts or capps.* from all tax and tole. And to this Charter subscribe the said king kenulph , and Cuthred king of kent , Celwal brother to King Kenulph, Wilfrid Archb. of Canterb.two Bishops, and one Abbot,and diuers others. And he setteth doune an other Charter of king Burdred, in which he testifieth that Crowland. *Pro frequentibus miraculis* &c. *In respect of the frequent miracles of the most holy Confessor*(S. Guthlac) *is alwaits a fertil mother amongst the vinyards of Engaddi.*And that *God by apparant myracles of S. Guthlac hath vouch saffed to shew his mercie.* To which Charter subscribe the king An. 851. with

The King and Q. of England faire say were eye-vvitnesses of S. Guthlacs miracles.

English Pilgrims vvith images of Saints in their hats.

Testimonie of K. Burdred for Saint Guthlacs miracles.

T the

the whole confent (as he faith) of the
Parliament then gathered againft the
Danes, Archb. Ceolreth, fix Bifhops , two
Duks, three Earles, and diuers others. And
Ingulph addeth that in the Parliamét the

Manie cured miraculeufly in the Parliament.

Archb. Ceolreth and diuers others, *aswell
Prelats as Nobles were fodenly and miraculoufly
cured of a kinde of palfie,* which at that time
much offended England and ther vpon
omnes ad vifitandum &c . *All prefently bound*

The vvhole parliament voweth pilgrimage.

*them felues in confcience by a moft ftrict vowe to
vifit in a deuout Pilgrimage with all poßible
fpeede the moft facred tombe of the moft bleffed
Saint Guthlac at Crowland.* What now will
Fox fay againft this cloud of witneffes
*omni exceptione maiores?*Will he fay(as Minifters vfe to fay of Priefts and Monks)
that they forged thefe miracles for gaine?
But this were madnes to fayi of fuch
great Kings and Princes ; or will he fay

Fox his confufion.

that they were deceaued? But fome of
them were eye witneffes , and fome of
them were fuch in whome the miracles
were wrought, as the Archbifhop , and
Bifhop of London, who teftifie the fame
in their fubfcription. But by this the indifferent Reader may both perceaue,
what credit he may giue to the miracles
of other Saints and with what impu-
dence (without any teftimony to the
contrary) they are denyed of Fox and
fuch

such like. And therfore I will not make any more Apology hereafter for the miracles which I shall rehearse, but only cite my Authors from, whome I haue them.

King Ethelard. VIII.

13. KIng Ina going to Rome An. 728. as Florent hath Chron. left his Kingdome to Ethelard, who *held it most quietly* (saith Malmsb. *lib.*1. *c.*2.) 14. *yeares.* he was saith Malmsb. *Cosin to King Ina, and a valiant Prince.* His roman religion appeareth, both by that King Ina so notorious a Papist chose him to whome he would commit his kingdome, as appeareth by Beda *lib.*5. *cap.* 7. and also by other things which are by Protestants confessed of the religion of this time. In this kings time died S. Egbert Priest *Anno* 729. *Ex Beda lib.*3. *cap.* 27. *vvho led* (saith he) *his life in great perfection of humility and meeknes, continency, innocencie and righteousnes, and conuerted the Scotts to the right obseruation of Easter.* And S. Beda himselfe, that glorious doctor of our English Church, the flower of Christianity at that time for vertue and learning of whose high praises giuen to him by Protestants, and of his perfect roman Religion I haue said ynough before. Here only I will adde

Valour of K. Ethelard.

His Rom. Religion.

Saints.

T 2   the

the Elogy of Malmsb. *lib. 1. cap . 3. Bedam*
(faith he) *mirari facilius &c, you may fooner
admire then vvorthly praife Beda , vvho liuing
in the fartheft corner of the vvorld vvith the flash
of his doctrine haue a light to all Nations .* Here
*vvit faileth vvords are vvanting, vvhile I cannot
tell vvhat moft to commend , vvhither the multitude of his volums, or the fobriety of his ftile . For
doubtles the diuine vvifdome had vvith no fparing
draught giue him to drinck, that in fo short a fcat-
ling of his life could perfect fo huge voliues. The report of his name vvas fo famous that the cheefeft in
Rome had neede of him for the refoluing of doubtfull queftions .* And much more there of his
holines. Where alfo he addeth that he died
anoiled and hovvfeled. The like hath Florent:
and Weftmon. Anno 734. and Hunting.
lib. 4. Caius de antiq. Canterb. *pag.* 138. proueth that Beda went to Rome, and there
read his bookes *coram Romana Ecclefia : Before the Church of Rome and then gaue them to
other to copie forth, vvhich vvas (faith he) ordinarie in the Ecclefiafticall vvriters of that age
to deliuer their vvorks firft to the Pope of Rome to
be examined.* In this Kings time Anno 737.
(as is in the Epitome of Beda) Ceolwolfe
King of Northumberland (to whome
Beda dedicated his hiftory) left his Kingdome, and became a Monke . And as
Malmsb. 1. Reg. *cap.* 3. florifhed with miracles. And about the fame time Frige-
dida

(margin notes:)
Florent.
VVeftmon.
Anno. 734.
Huntings.
lib. 4.

VVriters
Procure
their
vvorks to
be appro-
ued of the
Pope.

K. Ceol-
vvolph a
Monke.

dida Queene of the weſt-Saxons went ^{Q.Frige-}
to Rome, Hunting.*lib.4.pag.340.*Godwin _{grim.} dida a pil
in the Biſh. of Salsbery, which *at that time*
(ſaith Beda *lib.5.cap.4.* And Hunting: Deuotion
l. cit) *many Engliſh men both of the nobilitie and* of Engliſh
cōmons ſpirituall & tēporal were wont to vſe with Rome. ingoing tō
much emulation. In this Kings time alſo a-
bout the year 730. as Godwin hath in the
Biſhops of Oxford, (though Capgraue
in her life ſay 750.) liued the holy Virgin
S. Frideſwid , who flying to ſaue her s. Fride-
maydenhood from Prince Algarus , he ſwida.
was miraculouſly ſtrooke blind, and ſhe *Cambd.in*
after became Abbeſſe of a nonry built by *Brit.p.328.*
her Father Didā. Theſe dayes were ſo far
from Proteſtancy, and ſo manifeſtly Catholicke , as Bale Cent. 1. *cap.* 93. ſaith
they were *peſſima tempora pubeſcente Antichri-*
ſto: Very bad time when Antichriſt grew to riper
yeares: And Centur. 2. *cap.* 6. writeth of
Cymbertus an Engliſh Biſhop of S.Bedas
time, *After the cuſtome of the reſt in the ſame age*
he taught and cōmended the Roman cuſtoms to be
obſerued in his Churches. And Fulke Annot.*in*
*Hebr.*10.ſaith *Beda liued in a ſuperſtitious time,*
long after Antichriſt did opēly ſhew himſelf. And
1.Petri 3.*Beda was carried away with the er-*
rors and corruptions of his time . Fox Acts *pag.*
126. calleth this time *a Monkiſh age* , And
S. Ceolfrid maiſter to S. Beda a *Shaue*
ling. So plainly do they confeſſe England
this

this time to haue bene Roman Catholicke.

King Cuthred IX.

14. IN the yeare 741. as Florent hath in
Chron. Anno. 740. Malmsb. in
Faſtis ſucceeded king Cuthred, and died
ſaith Hunting. *lib.* 4. and Malmsb. *lib.* cit.
the 15.yeare of his reign.He was Coſin as
Florent.and Malmsb. and others ſay (as
Weſtmon. hath brother) to king Ethelard , and was as Hunting. *lib. cit.* and
Houeden *pag.* 408. *Rex magnus. A puiſſant
King, and mightie Prince, famous for his proſperous
reign and victories.* His Roman religion is
manifeſt, both by that which hath bene
ſaide of the former king , and alſo becauſe in his time, (as Stow ſaith Chron.
pag. 88.) Pope Zacharie wrote a letter
hither wherin he threatned *to excommunicat
them that would not amend their incontinent life.*
Which was read in preſence of the King
and Nobles; no man thinking that the
Pope tooke more vpon him than he
might.In this kings time S. Richard for-
ſoke his Kingdom and Contrie,and went
on Pilgrimage to Rome, and died by the
way at Luca.His two ſonnes S.Willibald
and Winnibald, and his holy daughter S.
Walburg following their Fathers **example**

The va-
lour of K.
Cuthred.

His Rom.
Religion.

The Pope
threatneth
to excom-
municate
ill liuers
in En-
gland.
S Richard
K. a pil-
grim and
his tvvo
ſonnes
and
daughter.

ple, left also their estates and Contrie and _{Surius}
went into Germanie to help. S. Boniface _{tom. 1.} _{Baron.}
their Kinsman in the conuersion of that _{An.750.}
Nation.

King Sigibert. X.

15. IN the yeare 754. as Malmsb. hath in
Fastis succeeded King Sigibert. who
(as Malmsb. saith 1. Reg *cap.* 2.) after a yeare
was deposed by the consent of all, for his
naughtines. In his time An. 754. (saith
Beda in Epit. Sigebert in Chron : and
others) was S. Boniface an English man,
and Apostle of Germany martyred in
Frisland with 53. more of his company.
This blessed Saint and great ornament of ^{Saints and}
^{martyrs.}
our Nation Bale Cent. 1. *cap.* 79. saith *was* ^{See the}
very superstitious , *and brought the Germans to* ^{manie and}
^{highe}
Papistrie. And other where saith was *next to* ^{praises}
Antichrist meaning (after his maner) the ^{of this S.}
^{Boniface}
Pope. Fox Acts *pag.* 128. calleth him *Martyr* ^{both of}
of God. Stow Chron. *pag.* 85. saith , *He was* ^{Catholiks}
martyred for the profession of Christ and his holy ^{and Pro-}
^{testants}
Gospel. Cooper *pag.* 716. The *Germans about* ^{ancient}
this tyme receaued (by Boniface) *the faith of* ^{and new}
^{*in Sacrario*}
Christ. And yet was this Boniface so noto- ^{*derebus mo-*}
rious a Papist, as Fox. *pag.* 129. termeth ^{*guntin lib. 3*}
^{*not. 57. 58.*}
him *a great setter vp and vphoulder of Poperie.* ^{59.}
Bale Cent. 1. *cap.* 79. plainly saith he
brought the Germans *ad Papisticam fidem,*

to the Papiſticall faith. And Cent. 13. *cap.* 3. citeth theſe wordes of Boniface out of his epiſtle to the Pope. *How many ſcollers or diſciples ſo euer God hath giuen me in this my Legacie I ceaſe not to incline to the obedience of* Surius tom. *the See Apoſtolick.* He impoſed (ſaith Bale)

3. Serrarius *ſingle life vpon Prieſts.* By this & much more de rebus Moguntin. in his life in Surius and Baron *Tom.* 9. yow may ſee what religion England then profeſſed, from whence S. Boniface and all his fellow laborers in Germany did come.

King Kinulph. XI.

16. **I**N the yeare 755. (as Malmsb. in Faſtis, Florent in Chron : and others agree) ſucceeded king kinulph , and reigned 29. yeares as Malmsb. hath in Faſtis,

The va- lour of K. died An. 784. ex Florent, Malmsb. in his Kinulph . Hiſtorie ſaith. 31. years, Houed: writeth the ſame , Malmsb. 1. Reg. *cap.* 2. *Clarus morum compoſitione militiaque geſtis . Honorable both for his vertuous behauiour & warlick prowes.* The like hath Hunting. *lib.* 4. and Houed. *pag.* 408. Cooper. Chron. An. 748. ſaith *the vertue of this man ſurpaſſed his fame .* The

His Rom. Religion. Roman religion of this king is euident by his Charter ſet downe by Godwin in the Biſhops of Bath in theſe words . *Ego Ke-*

Kenulphus. I *Kinulph King of the VVest-Saxons will bestow a peece of Land, humbly ascribing it for the loue of God and satisfaction of my sinnes with consent of my Prelats and Nobles, to Gods blessed Apostle and seruant S. Andrew.* Which kind of gifte is contrary to the foundation of Protestancie, as is before shewed oute of Fox, Abbots and others. And Fox Acts *pag.*130. addeth, that about the yeare 780. (which was in this kings tyme) *Pope Adrian ratified and confirmed by reuelation the order of S. Gregories masse. At what time* (saith he) *this vsuall Masse of the Papists began to be vniuersall and vniforme and generally receaued in all Churches.* In this Kings time Egbert or Edbert King of Northumberland leauing his Kingdom became a Monke, *Epitom. Beda An.* 758. Florent. Westmon. *An.* 757. Malmsb. 1. *Reg. cap.* 3. Stow Chron *pag.* 93. Fox Acts. *pag.* 131. In this Kings time *An.* 781. also died Werburga *quondam* (saith Florent.) *sometime Queene to Ceolred King of Merchland.* By which kind of speech he insinuateth that thē she was a Nonne, which is plainly affirmed by Houeden *pag.* 404. And in Germany liued S. Lullus, S. Burcardus, S. Willebald, S. Liobe, and many other English both men and women, disciples of this forsaid S. Boniface, who with vertuous life and miracles planted there the Catholick Roman

Good deeds for satisfactiō of sinnes.

VVhen S. Greg. order of Masse became vniuersall.

K. Eadbert a Monke.

Q. VVerburg a Nonne.

Saints.

man faith, which they carried with them
out of England.

King Bithricus XII.

17. THE 12. Chriſtian King was
Bithricus, who began his reigne
An. 784. and reigned 16. yeares as Malmsb.

The ver- faith 1. *Reg.* 2. and *in Faſtis* , and dyed An.
tues of K. 800. He was faith he *pacis quam belli*
Bithricus. *ſtudioſior* , *more deſirons of peace than of war*
Ethelwerd. *l.* 3. calleth him *Regem pijſſimum.*

His Rom. *A moſt godly Prince.* Cooper An. 778. faith he
Religion. *Knightly ruled the Land* . His Roman religion is moſt notorious . For as Hunting.
lib. 3. Houed *pag.* 404. Weſtmon An. 739.

Popes and others write, in his tyme came Legats
legats ho- into England from Pope Adrian *antiquam*
norably (fay they) *renouantes* &c. *renewing the ancient*
receaued *League and Catholick faith, who were honorably*
of all En- *receaued both of the Prelats and Princes, and held*
gland. *a Councell at Cealtid* ex Houed. *pag.* 410. Be-

K. Offa ſides he maried the daughter of King
and King Offa, who in his time left his Kingdom,
Kenred *become* went to Rome with Kenred King of
monks. Northumberland , and there bound his
Peter Kingdom to pay the Peter pence , and
pence. finally became a Monke as Fox writeth
Hunting. *lib.* 4. *pag.*
342. Houed *lib.* 2. *pag.* 3. and *pag.* 129. and others. Beſides
pag. 409 ·
Bale Cent. of this King Offa Stow writeth *pag.* 89.
2. cap. 15. that

that he caused the reliques of S. Alban to *Malmsb.* 1.
Reg. cap. 4. be taken vp , and put in a Shrine , and adorned with gould and pretious stones, and builded there a Prinely Monasterie, *His Charter* (saith he) *is dated An.* 793. *with the witnesse of him selfe , his sonne Egferd ,* 9. *Kings,* 15. *Bishops,* 10. *Dukes,* &c. By which we may clearly perceaue the Roman faith of all our Nation then. Westmon. also *An.* 794. Telleth how King Offa with the counsell of his Bishops sent to the Pope to haue priuiledges for that Monasterie , and the Pope con-
firmeth
our Kings
Charters. Pope answered that he should grante what he thought conuenient *Et nos* (saith the Pope) *And we by our priuiledg will confirme our originall.* And as Paris hath *An.* 794. He Manie
Princes
became
monks. excepted it from all iurisdiction of Bishop or Archbishop, & subiected it immediatly to the See of Rome . *His diebus* (saith Bale Cent. 2. *cap.* 15. *In these dayes many Princes in England with shauing tooke vpon them the profession of Monks.* In this Kings time *An.* 793. was the Innocent and holy King Ethel- S. Ethel-
bert. K.
Ethelrida
his spouse
an An-
choresse. bert of East-England slaine, Malmsb. in Fastis & 1. Reg. *cap.* 5. Florent. Chron. Stow *pag.* 74. Fox Acts. *pag.* 129. And Ethelrida his espouse daughter of King Offa made her selfe an Ancoresse or recluse *ex* Ingulph. *In this tyme also was fouud the body of S. Withburg daughter of King Anna after* 55. *yeares buriall ,* *ex* Florent An. 798.

S. Fre-
mund K.

An.798.In his tyme alſo liued S.Fremund King and ſonne to king Offa *Vir* (ſaith Cambd.in Brit. *pag.*500. *magni nominis* . *A man of a worthy name, and ſinguler pietie towards God* was canonized for a Saint . And Ristrith *iamdudum Regina tunc Abbattiſſa*

Q Ristrith
Nonne.

obijt.Ristrith ſomtime a Queene then Abbeſſe dyed, Houed. An. 786. And An.799.died Osbald

K. Osbald
Monke.
Saints.

then Abbot,but once king of Northum-berland , Houed. *Ibid.* In this time alſo died S. Lull. Archbiſhop of Mentz whome not onely Malmsb. *lib.* 1. Reg.*cap.*4. but Bale alſo Cent. 13. *cap.* 56. com-mendeth ſaying *he was homo tum eruditi-onis* & c. *A man of approoued learning and ſanstitie , and gaue him ſelfe as an example of vertue to the Gentills that had any inclination to the Chriſtian faith.* And yet was he ſcoller and ſucceſſor to Saint Boniface that famous Papiſt. Ibid. *cap.* 57. Bale calleth Saint Burchard his fellowe, *Virum pium ac religioſum* : *a godly and religious man* . And *cap.* 70. he ſaith that S. Wilhad Archb. of Brome and fellow laborer with them,

English
deſire to
die for the
Church of
Rome.

Martirij deſiderio pro Rom. Eccleſia flagrabat: *Burnt with deſire of Martirdome for the Church of Rome.* In his time alſo liued that great Clerck Alcuin Confeſſor to Charles the Great of whome ynough hath bene ſayd before.

18. Thus thou ſeeſt Chriſtian Reader how

how clearly the Catholick Roman religion hath bene deduced through all those our firſt Chriſtian ĸings for the ſpace of the firſt 200. yeares after our conuerſion from Paganiſme to Chriſtianity. And what notable contempt of the world and holines of life it bred in that time in our ĸings, Queenes, Princes, Clergy, and Commons, in ſo much that ten of thoſe ĸings that then were are now accounted Saints: To wit, *Ethelbert, Edwin, Oſwald, Oſwi, Sebbi, Sigebert*, another *Sigebert, Richard, Ethelbrit, Fremund,* And fourteene of them forſaking their ĸindomes, either became Monks, or went on Pilgrimages to Rome, namely *Kinegilſus, Centwin, Cedwall, Ina, Sebby, Offa, Sigebert, Ethelred, Coenred,* another *Offa, Cealwolph, Eadbert, Kenred, Osbald, to* whome I may adde *Oſwin* preuented by death. And 13. Queenes nonnes to wit *Bathildu, Ethelreda, Sexburg, kineſwith,* (eſpouſe to King Offa) *Eadburg, Ena, Emenild, Edelburg, Ethelburg. Canſled, Cuthburg, VVerburg, Erigedida, Riĉtirth* to whome I may add *Heseſwid* mother to King Adolph. Beſides, many Kings ſonnes as *Sighord, VVillibald, VVinnibald, Mereſin, Adelbert,* and many more whoſe names we know not. And many Princes Martyrs as *Raſſin VVulfhale, Elbert, Egbrigh,* and

The effeĉts of Catholike religiõ in our nation in 200. yeaɼs.

Ten Kings Saints in 200 yaeɼs.

Fourtene Kings Monks or Pilgrims.

VVho vvold not aduenture his ſoule ſooner vvith thes holie Kings, Queens and Princes than vvith one boye and a VVomã.

Prnnces Côfeſſors. See marcellin in vit. Simbert. Princes martyrs.

and one Confeſſor *S. Pumold*, And many Kings and Queenes daughters that became nonnes as *Edelburg·Eartongath Sedrido, VVithburg*; *Mildred*, *Milbith*, *VValburg, Etheldrida.*

Kings daughters

19. Could ſuch admirable contempt of the world ſpring from the Diuels religion? or rather from his who in our baptiſme bindeth vs to renounce the world and pomps therof. Could ſo great vertue and holines of life riſe from the Diuel, the vtter enemy of vertue? or rather from God, from whome (as S. Iames ſaith) commeth all goodnes? Can Proteſtants imagin that God reuealed his truth to them, and hid it from ſo great Saints and ſeruants of his as thoſe were? who ſought it ſo diligently, folowed it ſo earneſtly, and (as S. Iames ſpeaketh) *by their workes haue ſhewed their faith*, and yet notwithſtāding periſhed euerlaſtinglie as (no doubt) muſt needes be both thought, and ſaid if Proteſtants religion be the only truth of Chriſt, and Chriſts truth the only way (as no doubt it is) to ſaluation. And therfore how ſoeuer ſome Miniſters ſay that they will not iudge their Forfathers, they cannot but thinke that theſe holy Princes and their people are damned (which they are a ſhamed to ſay) or that there are diuers wayes to heauen, which

Can grapes ſpring of thorns.

Did God hide his truth from thoſe vertuous princes and reueal it to a boy and a vvoman.

No hope of ſaluation to our Anceitors if the Cath. faith be not the faith of Chriſt.

which is right Atheiſme, or rather Anti-
chriſtianiſme. For if ther be any other
way to heauen than that which Chriſt
taught, we make Chriſt a lyar. But let
them thinck as they liſt, I hope all men
that are carefull of their ſaluation and
withall conſider that as ther is but one
God and one Chriſt, ſo ther is but one
baptiſme and one faith, to wit the Catholick (which who keepeth not intirely
ſhall periſh euerlaſtingly) will both thinck   *Athan. in*
and ſay: *Moriatur anima mea morte iuſtorum,*   *Symbolo.*
& fiant nouißima mea horum ſimilia. *Let my*
ſoule die the death of the iuſt and let my end
belike to theſe men. And now let vs goe from
the Kings of a part of England to the
Monarchs of the whole.

That

CHAP. XXIIII.

That all the Kings of England from the Monarchy to the Conqueſt vvere Roman Catholicks, proued in particuler.

King Egbert XIII.

1.   THe thirtenth Chriſtian King of the weſt-Saxons an d firſt that reduced England to a Monarchy, was King Egbert, who began his reign An. 800. & reigned 37. yeares, died An. 837. He was (ſaith Malmsb. *lib.* 1. Reg. *cap.* 2.) *worthely to be preferred before all Kings,* And *lib.* 2. *cap.* 1. *Regis Inæ abnepos. King Ina his great grandchild by his brother Inegilſe, ſuldued the mindes of his ſubiects by clemencie and meeknes, and left his ſonne great occaſions of commendations.* Houed. hiſt. *pag.* 407. ſaith *he was Vir ſtrenuiſſimus ac Potens*: *moſt ſtout and puiſſant.* And (as all our Engliſh Cronicles teſtifie) in his time ſubdued all the reſt of our Engliſh Kings. Hunting. *l.* 4. *VVallos vicit: ſabdued the VVelchmen.* Florent An. 836. *Danos fugat*: *Put to flight*

The vvorthines of
K. Egbert.
1 Monarch
of Englād.

flight the Danes . The Roman Catholick His Rom.
religiō of this victorious Prince is euidēt. Religion.
Firſt becauſe he ſuffered his ſonne and
heir Ethelwolph to be a Monke and ſub- **1**
deacon , as both Cátholicks and Proteſtáts affirme,& Godwin in the Biſhops of
Wincheſter ſaith *it is certain.* Wherby (ſaith
Bale Cent. 2. *cap* 20.) *He became the Popes
Creature by both profeßions.* Secondly, becauſe
he committed his ſaid ſonne Ethelwolf **2**
to S. Swithin to be taught , as teſtifieth
Florent. *An.* 827. Gotzelin, and Godwin
in vit. Swithini, And as addeth Gotzelin Surius
inter precipuos amicos numerauit . reconed him tom. 4.
in number of his eſpeciall freinds. Now this
Swithin was a Roman Catholick. For,
as Bale *l . cit .* granteth he was a Monke,
and as Malmsb. *lib.2. Pont:* Gotzelin. *l. cit.*
Weſtmon. *An.* 861. and others report
wrought miracles by the ſigne of the
Croſſe, is canoniſed by the Papiſts for a
Saint. Thirdly becauſe K. Kenulf (who in **3**
his time was King of midlengland.& as
Malmsb. ſaith *lib.1 . Reg. Nulli ante ſe Regi.
Nothing inferior , in power and religion to any
King before him, and whoſe praiſes ſhalbe aduanced on high ſo long as there is found any indifferent
iudg in England,* writing with all his Biſh.
and nobilitie to Pope Leo beginneth his
letter thus. *Domino beatißimo: To my moſt holy
Lord and wel beloued, Lord Leo the Roman Biſhop*
                         V   *of the*

of the holy, & Apoſtolick See, Kenulſ by the grace of God King of Merchland with the Biſhops, Dukes, & all Degrees of honor within our Dominiōs with health of moſt ſincere affection in Chriſt . Infra.

The proſ-
peritie of
Rome, the
ioy of
England.

The ſublmity of the See of Rome is our helth, & the proſperitie therof our cōtinuall ioy. Becauſe whence yow haue your Apoſtolicall dignitie thence had we the knowledge of the true faith. VVherfor I thinck it fit that the eare of our obedience be humbly in-clined vnto your holy commādements, & with our whole forces to fulfill u hat ſhalbe thought cōueniēt by your holines to performe . But now I Kenulſ by the grace of God K. humbly beſeech your Excellēcie to receaue me in quiet peace into your holines lap, & whome no meanes of merits do ſupport, let the large aboūdāce of your bleſſing enrich for the gòuer-mēt of his people, that almightie God by your inter-ceſſiō may together with me encorage the Nation againſt the inuaſion of forren foes which your Apo-

Rome
taught
England
the faith:
All K.
Kenulphs
Predeceſ-
ſors had
the popes
bleſsing.

ſtolical authoritie hath imbued with the rudemēts of the Chriſtian faith. This bleſſing haue all the Kings who ſwayed the Mercian ſcepter deſerued to obtaine at your Predeceſſors hands, this ſame do I in humble māner requeſt & deſire to obtain of yow moſt holy Father, firſt by way of adoptiō to receaue me as your child, as I loue yow in the perſō of a Fa-ther, & ſhall embrace yow with the whole force of obedience. Againe he ſaith: Excellentiæ veſtræ: VVe in moſt humble manner beſeech your Excel-lencie, to whome the key of wiſdome is giuen by God. Again: VVith great humility & alſo affectiō

we

we haue writte these to yow most holy Pope, besee-ching in most earnest wise your Clemecie kindly & iustly to answer these things vvhich vve haue bene vrged to propound. VVe send yovv here as a smale token of my louing minde, that is 120. *Mancuzes vvith letters requesting yovv to accept therof in good part & vouchsafe to bestovv your blessing vpon vs.* And the Pope answering him saith that this K. professed to be willing to lose his life for him , & acknowledged (saith the Pope) that *Nostris Apostolicis;* &c. That no Christian presumeth to goe against *our Apostolicall Decrees.* Yea Fox *p.* 132. speaking of this K. & the others before him saith, *They wanted the knowledg & doctrin in Christ, especially in the Article of free iustification in faith.* Which , *p.* 840. he termeth *the foundation of the Church and all Christianitie, and therfor* (saith he) *they ran the vvrong vvay.* And so concludeth that Protestants truth was hidden to our for-ancestors, In which I verily beleeue him.

Our K. and Peers vvrite vvith great hu-militie to the Pope.

King Ethelvvolph XIIII.

2. THe 14. Christian King was Ethel-wolph, sonne to the forsaid King Egbert, who began his reign An. 837 .and reigned 20. yeares and od monethes. He was (saith Malmsb. *lib.* 2. *cap.* 2.) *by nature gentil, and more desirous of peace than of war.* And yet (saith Malmsb: *l. cit* .) *Danos non semel per se & suos Duces contudit:* The Danes

Vertues and va-lour of K. Ethel-vvolph.

V 2 he

he ouercame more than once by him selfe and his Generalls . And besides other victories at Okley in Surey flew so many Danes (saith Floren : and westmon. An. 851. Houed *pag. 413.* and others) *as neuer was heard in one Realme, and at one time nether before nor after.*

His Roman religion is most notorious. First by that which hath bene said in the life of his Father. Secondly because he procured a dispensation of the Pope because he had byn a Monke and subdeacon that he might marry. which Pope Malmsb. 1. *Pont.* saith was Leo 3. Bale Centur.2 *cap,* 20. saith was Gregor. 4. others say Leo 4. Thirdly he first sent his sonne Alfred to Rome to be instructed (saith Westmon. An. 854.) *of the Pope in manners and religion.* And after went himselfe, and staied at Rome a yeare, and ther (as all Catholicke and Protestant Cronicles confesse) bound all England to pay the Peter pence. And as Bale *pag.* 116. speaketh *Prouinciam suam &c. He made his Couutrey tributarie to the Roman Synagog, & so* (sayth he) *was all England made subiect to the Roman Beast.* Besides this he appointed euery yeare 300. Mancuzes, which were (as Caius faith *lib.* 2. de antiq. cantab. *pag.* 287 .) thirty pence a peece to be sent to Rome wherof one hundred should buy oile for light in S. Peters Church, and one

hundred

Margin notes:

His Rom. Religion.

1

2

3
Kings sonne sent to be instructed of the Pope.

Ethelw. lib. 3. cap. 3
Stovv pag. 89 Coper.
An. 852.
Houeden. pag. 415.
Huntingt. lib. 5 Ingulp. pag 862.
VVestmon An 857.
VVhatmã euza is.

hundred for the same vse in S. Pauls , and
one hundred should be giuen saith Florent *Anno.*855. *Vniuersali Papæ Apostolico To
the Vniuersall Apostolicke Pope* . The same
hath Fox *lib.*3.p.136. Fourthly *he gaue* (saith
Fox) *te holy Church and religious men the tenth
of his goods and Lands in VVest-Saxons with liberty and fredom from all seruice and ciuil charge.*
And Fox setteth downe his Charter in
these wordes. *Ego Etheluolphus &c.* I Ethelwolph King of the *VVest-Saxons with the cõsent
of my Prelats & Nobles will grant an hereditarie
portion of my land to be foreuer possessed by God &
the blessed S. Marie and all the Saints of God.*
Behould how the King by the aduise of
his Bishops and Nobles giueth Land to
God and his Saints, and to what purpose
himselfe declareth in these words fol-o-
wing, *For the redemption of our soules , for the
remission of our sinnes.* Which intention , as
yow heard before out of Abbots & Fox ,
is contrary to the Protestants Gospell.
And therfore Fox vpõ these words saith,
*Note the blind ignorance and erroneous teaching
in these dayes,* and addeth that *they were led
with pernicious doctrine to set remission of sinnes
and remedie of soules in this donation , and such
other deedes of their deuotion.* And further the
King saith, as Malmsb. testifieth *lib.* 2. *cap.*
2. *Placuit Episcopis cum &c.* It hath pleased the
Bishops with the Abbots and the seruants of God

The faith
of King
Ethel-
vvolph
and his
Nobles.

Good
deeds for
remission
of sinnes.

VVestmon
An.854.

V 3   to

K. Ethel-
vvolph re-
quireth
Masses for
him aliue
and dead.

to apoint that all *our brethren and sisters in euery Church shall sing on wensday in euery weeke fifty psalmes, and euery Priest two Masses, one for King Ethelwolph, & another for his Dukes consenting to this gift, for their reward & remission of their trespasses. And for the K. liuing let them say Oremus Deus qui iustificas &c. For the Duke also liuing also* Prætéde Domine &c. *But after their death for the K. alone, & for the Dukes deceassed iointly together, & this be so firmly ordained throughout al the daies of Christianitie euen as their libertie is established, so log as faith increaseth in the English Nation. This Charter of Donation was written in the yeare of our Lords Incarn. 844. Indict. 4. the fift day of Nouemb. in the Citie of VVinchester, in the Church of S. Peter before the head Altar. And this they did for the honor of S. Michael the Archangell, & also for the blessed Marie Q. the glorious mother of God & of S. Peter the Prince of the Apostles, and in like mäner of our most holy Father Pope Greg. and of all Saints.* In this Chapter I

K. Ethel-
vvolph co-
manded
not in
spirituall
matters.

note how, not the King but Bish. apoint Priests to pray & say Masses for him, and that S. Peter is called Prince of the Apostles; the other points of Papistry therin are more euidét than that I neede to point to

All En-
gland Pa-
pist in K
Ethel-
vvolhps
time.

them. And yet (as Ingulph saith *p. 862.*) to this chapter subscribed all the Archb. & Bishops of England, K. Bardred, & King Edmund after martyr, and Princes of a part of Englad vnder King Ethelwolph,
Ab-

Abbots, Abbesses, Dukes, Countes, and nobles of the whole Lād, & innumerable multitude of other people. By which we may see the vniuersall faith of our Contry of that time. And in a Charter of King Berthulphus in Ingulph p. 861. The King praiech God *Quatenus pro intercessione Guthlaci&c. That through the intercessiō of S. Guthlack and all the Saints he would forgiue me & all my people our sinnes.* In this Kings time *An.* 850. S. Wolstā nephew to two KK. was vniustly murdered, and afterward honored by God with miracles, Florét. Chronic. Also S. Ieron, an English Priest martyred in Holand, *An.* 849. Bale Cent. 13. *cap.* 75. In this K. time also liued one Offa K. of Eastengland, who leauing his Kingdome, and trauailing to the holy land, in ould Saxonię (from whence our Nation came into England) electẽd S. Edmund for his heire, and sent him into Englād: Capgraue in vit. Edmundi, Florent. An. 855. Homed. *pag.* 415. Stow *pag.* 76.

Pardon of sinnes asked by intercession of Saints.

Saints.

King Ethelbald. XV.

3. THe 15. K. was Ethelbald eld₁st sonne to K. Ethelwolph who began his reign, *An.* 857. and reigned fiue yeares. He was at first dissolut and naught, as yow may see in Malmsb. *lib.* 2. *cap.* 3. But *peracta pœnitentia* (saith Westmon. *Anno.* 859.) *Hauing done pennance all the time he liued after,*

V 4 *he*

he gouerned the Kingdom with peace and iustice.
Wherfore Hunting. *lib.5.pag.*348.calleth
him *optimæ indolis auenem*: *a youth of very great
towardnes,* faith that all England bewailed
his death.

King Ethelbert XVI.

4.   THE 16. king was Ethelbert bro-
    ther to the former, begā his raigne
An.862.as Malmsb. hath in Faftis, and
held the gouerment fiue yeares. *He was*
Valour of faith Ingulph *pag.*863. *Validißimus adolefcens,*
K. Ethel- *A moft valiant yong man and an inuincible trium-*
bert.   *pher ouer the Danes , he ftoutly for fiue yeares
fpace gouerned the Kingdome.* Malmsb. 2. *Reg.
cap.* 3. faith he ruled *ftrenuè dulciterque :
Manfully and fweetly.*Houed *pag.* 405. faith
pacifice & amabiliter, peaceably and gently. In
Saints.   this Kings time died S. Swithin *Anno*
862· Florent.& Weftmon.in Chron. As
His Rom., for the Roman religion of thefe two
Religion. Princes , that appeareth both by what
hath bene faid of their Father, and
what fhalbe faid of their two
brothers.

King

King Ethelred XVII.

5. THe 17. king was Ethelred 3. fonne to king Ethelwolfe, Who began his reign faith Malmsb. *lib. 2. cap. 3. Anno* 867. and reigned 5. yeares, as his brothers did. Of hi n and his brethren Malmsb. faith, *They bouldly and ftoutly entred battel for their Country,* and addeth that this king befides ordinary skirmifhes, fought 9. picht Battels in one yeare againft the Danes, & was oftener Conqueror : And that he flewe one kiug of them, 9. Earlers, and innumerable people. which alfo teftify Ethelwerd *lib. 4. cap. 12.* Hunting *lib. 5.* Cambd. in Brit. faith , He was *Princeps longe optimus.* Couper *Anno* 863. fatih *he was among his fubiects mild gentle,& pleafant,againft his aduerfaries feuere,fierce, and hardie.* Of this Fox *lib. 3. pag.* 141. telleth that being to ioine batell with the Danes , his brother Alfred gaue the onfet *while the King* faith Fox,*was at feruice and meditations ,* and albeit word were brought him that his brother had the worft, yet *would he not* faith Fox *ftir one foote before the feruice was fully coplet*; And addeth that *through the grace of God,and their godly manhood the King coming from his feruice recouered the victory,* & flew-as Ethelwerd(who as himfelf faith defceded

of

Fortitudo, and pierfe of K Ethelred.

nine battells in one yeare.

Miracle in confirmation of Maffe.

Marueilous victorie.

of that K. *lib.* 4. *c.* 2.) ſaith one King, fiue Earles. And *th: t I may ſay ſo* (ſaith Ethelwerd) *almoſt all the chiefeſt youth of the Barbarians, that nether befor nor after was there ſuch a ſlaughter heard of ſince the English entred Britanie.* See yow heere this meruailous and miraculous victorie cōfeſſed by Fox to be obtained *by the grace of God and the deuotion of the King to his ſeruice!* But what ſeruice this was which God would thus approue by ſo miraculous a victorie, and by which England was then defended from deſtruction of Danes, Fox was aſhamed to tell. But our ancient Hiſtoriographers *Florent.* & *VVeſtmon. An.* 871. & Houed. part. 1. *pag.* 416. ſaith plainly *it vvas Maſſe ſaid by a Prieſt.* Which alone ſufficeth both to ſhew that this King was a Roman Catholicke, and that Maſſe is diuine ſeruice. Beſides that, Malmsb. writeth, that this King entred battel, *cruce Dei conſignatus: Signed vvith the croſſe of God.* And (as Fox ſaith, and Godwin in the Biſhops of Exeter) he builded the Abbey of Exeter. In this Kings time An. 870. ex Malmsb. *vvas holy King Edmund* (Cooper ſaith *Anno.* 869.) *ſlaine of the Danes becauſe he vvould not forſake the faith of Chriſt.* The ſame hath Fox *pag.* 140. Florent. Anno 870. Of his great miracles wrought after his death yow may ſee in his life, in Surius *Tom.* 6.

England defended by deuotion to Maſſe.

K. Ethelreds Rom Religion.

Saints.

VVeſtmon. 870.
K. Edmūd.
His brother Edvvald.

His

His brother and heire Edwald (ſaith ^{Duke} Fox *l. cit.* and Capgraue in vit. Edwald.) ^{Fremūd.} became an heremit. *Fremūd alſo* (ſaith Bale Cent. 2. *cap.* 22.) *ſonne of Algarus Duke of the VVeſt-Saxons, a beutifull yong man , and only ſonne, relinquiſhed the gouerment of the common welth , which his parents left him , that he might follow Burchard the Monke,* and was after as Capgr. ſaith in his life, ſlaine of the ſame Danes which ſlew S. Edmund. In this ^{Chaſtitie} time alſo S. Ebbe (ſaith Stow Chron. *p.* ^{of S. Ebbe} 101.) Abbeſſe of Couldingham, cut of her ^{and her} noſe and vpper lippe , and perſwaded all ^{Nonnes.} the ſiſters to do the like, to keepe her virginitie from the Danes, who therupon ^{VVeſtmon.} burnt the Abbey and Nonnes therin. ^{An. 870.}

King Alfred the great. XVIII.

6. THe next K. was Alfred the fourth ſonne of K. Ethelwolfe, who (as Malm. hath *l. 2. c. 4.*) begā his reign *An.* 872. & ruled 28. years & a half. *He alone of all our* ^{The vvor-} *Kings.* (ſaith Fox *l. 3. p. 141.* `took his crown &` ^{thines of} *vnctiō of the Pope.* And that we may ſee how ^{K Alfred} ^{crovvned} God bleſſed him whome his vicar crou-^{of the} ned and anointed , he alone for his admi-^{Pope.} rable deedes both in war & peace , is ſir-named *the Great.* And the praiſe which not onely Catholicks but alſo Prote-ſtants giue vnto him in all kinde of vertues ſurpaſſe in my iudgement the
                                                            praiſe

praiſes of all Chriſtian kings that euer haue bene . But for breuitie ſake, I will content my ſelf with the praiſes giuen to him by Proteſtants, who (yow may be aſſured) knowing him to be ſo manifeſt a Roman Catholick, as ſhall appeare anon, would giue him no more than he deſer-

Cambden ueth. Cambd. in Brit. *pag.* 243. and 331.
calleth him *Clariſſimum & pientiſſimum*
Bale *Regem. A moſt renouned and godly King* . Bale
*Cent.2.cap.*26.ſaith he was *Egregia indobis & forma adoleſcens : A yong man of a notable towardnes and bewtie , born vnto learning and vertue, He called for the beſt learned men to be his Counſellers and inſtruĉters : Eight howers euery day he ſpent in reading , writing , and diſputing. He gouerned all things with an excceeding good wit, and with ſingular prouidencie . He was eſteemed an Architeĉter , and moſt perfeĉt Geometrian, a Gramarian, a Philoſopher, a Rhethorician. an Hiſtorian, Muſitian, and no vulgar Poet. Three Colledges he founded at Oxford , one for Gramarians, an other for Philoſophers , the third for Diuines. Of ſtudyes and the common welth he beſt deſerued.* Cooper An. 872. *Of faire ſtature, and comely perſonage , and no leſſe renowned in martiall pollicie than ciuil gouernment.* Stow Chron. pag. 105. *Victorious Prince, ſtudious prouident for widowes , Orphans and poore people, endued with wiſdome , iuſtice, fortitude, and temperance, a moſt diſcreete ſercher*
                                        of truth

*of truth a most vigilant and deuout Prince in the
seruice of God, and deuided the day and the night
into three equal portions, wherof the one he spent
in studie prayer and such things as belonged to his
minde and soule, the other in eating sleeping and
other excercise of the body, the third in the affaires
of the common VVelth.* Fox *lib.* 3. *pag.* 141. saith **Fox.**
*Amongst all the Saxon Kings hitherto is found
none to be preferred or all most to be compared with
this Alfred, for the great and singuler qualities in
this King worthie of high renown, whither we behould his valiant acts and manifould trauells for
his Contrie, or his godly and excellent vertues
ioyned with a publick and tender care of the weale
publick or whither we respect his notable knowledg of good letters with a feruent desire to set
forth the same throughout all his Realme.* And
p. 143. 145. giueth him high praises for
continence, valour, and learning, conclu-
ding thus. *This valiant vertuous and learned
Prince Christianly gouerned his realme,* And
much more with great admiration of this
King, which yow may read in him, and
in Malmsb. *lib.* 2. *cap.* 4. Hunting. *lib.* 5.
Ethelwerd *lib.* 4. Ingulfe, Florent. *pag.* 309.
VVestmon. Chron. Houed. *p.* 417. and
others.   **Mislear-**
                                                          ning.
7. Onely I will out of them note some
of his vertuos. Of his great learning is **Forti-**
spoken before. For his valour Bale *Cent.* 3. **tude.**
cap. 43. saith, *he fougt* 57. *tymes with the Danes.*
                                            Cambd.

Cambd.in Brit.*pag.*213.*Nobili prælio contudit,*
and *pag.* 444. *Danos contudit ad libitum: He*
repressed the Danes at his pleasur . And as
Malmsb. and others teſtifie made them
become Chriſtians , or forſwere the
Realme . For his gouernment ſaith Caius
de Antiq.Cantab. pag.328. *Chriſtianiſſimas leges*
ſcripſit & promulgauit.He writ and promulgated
moſt Chriſtian lawes, and cauſed ſuch peace as he
made braſlets of gould be hung vp in the high way
which none durſt touch . For his chaſtitie it
was ſuch , that as Cooper *An.* 872. after
many Catholick writters teſtifieth , he
deſired of God ſicknes that he might not
offend againſt chaſtitie . As for his pietie
and deuotion it was ſuch as Florent.
Weſtmon. *An.*871. and others write *Miſſam*
audire quotidie: That he daylie heard maſſe, and
ſayd his houres and Matins, and in the night ſeaſon
vnknovvn to all his ſeruãts he frequẽted Churches to
*heare ſeruice.*Which alone ſufficeth to ſhew
his Catholick Roman religiõ. But beſids
this(Bale & Fox *l.cit.*& Stow *p.* 99.Caius
*l.cit.p.*325.confeſſe)he was crowned & an-
oinred of Pope Leo, & as Bale ſaith termed *his adoptiue child*. & as is beforeſaid inſtructed of him in maners & religiõ. Moreouer as Caius ſaith.*In reparandis , ornandis*
&c. In repairing beutifying &enriching Monaſte-
ries he labored earneſtly,amongſt which he builded
*two of great renoun.*ButFox reckoneth three,
one

Side notes: Wiſdom. Malmsb. lib.2.cap.4. V Veſtmon. Am.892. Chaſtitie. Deuotion The religion of K. Alfred. 1 2 3

one at Shasburie, one at Ethling, the third S. Cutbert
at Winchester. The cause of the building encoura-geth the
his Monasterie at Ethling, was because he K. to recouet England.
being almost quite vanquisht of the Danes,
and lying there hid for a time, S. Cutbert
appeared to him badd him be of good
corage assuring him both of the present
vision and future victorie ouer the Danes Profes of the truth
by a present miracle. This vision was (as is of S. Cut-
said) confirmed then by a present miracle, berts vi-
and by the perfect conquest of the Danes sion to K. Alfred.
after following, beleeued of this notable
prudent King, and testifyed (as Fox p. 142.
cõfesseth) by Malmsb. Polichron. Houed.
Iornalasensis & others, and yet is termed
of him without any reason or testimony,
a dreaming fable, onely (as we may imagin)
because it is sayd to come from S. Cutbert
For soone after p. 149. he crediteth a Vision
of Egwin a Herlot, albeit it haue nothing
so good testimonie, because therin is no
mentiõ of any Saint. Finally this excellét
King in his preface beforethe Pastorall of
Saint Gregory calleth him *Christs Vicar*, &
sent almes to Rome Westmon. *An.* 889. &
also to India, *to performe* (saith Fox p. 142.)
*His vovv to S. Thomas vvhich he made during the
tyme of his distresse against the Danes*. In this
Kings time Burdred King of Merceland
forsaking his Kingdom went to Rome, A King goeth
and *Anno.* 889. his Queene Ethelswitha to Rome.

followed

Holiemen in time of K. Alfred. followed him. In this kings time also liued S. Grimbald , whome king Alfred called out of France to teach in Oxford, and S. Neotus, *Scientia* (faith Bale Cent. *2. cap.* 1. *In knowledg and manners excelling in counsel good, in speeche wise, by whose counsel Alfred founded a schoole at Oxford.*

King Edward the elder. XIX.

8. IN the yeare 901. succeeded King Edward the Elder sonne to king *The worthines of K. Edward sen:* Alfred, and reigned (saith Malmsb. *lib.* 2. *cap.* 3) 23. yeares, others say 24. *He gouerned the land* (saith Fox *lib.* 3. *pag.* 146. *right valiantly, in Princely gouernment , and such like martial prowes he was nothing inferior to his Father, but rather, exceeded him, subdued VVales & Scotlãd, & recouered all out of the Danes hãds.* The same saith Cooper An. 901. Stow *A great victorie.* p. 107. Malmsb. *l. cit.* Florent and Westmon. An. 924, Houed. *p.*122. And Ingulph. and Hunting. *lib.*5. say that in one battel he slew two kinges , and 10. Earles of the Danes. And Ethelwerd *lib.* 4. *cap.* 4. writeth that in all he slew 4. kings of *His Rom. Religion.* them. The Roman religion of this valiant and victorious Prince is euident. First because as king Edgar his grandchild in an oration (which Fox hath *lib.* 3. *pag.* 170.)

testi-

teſtifieth he accounted S. Duſtan his Father, helper and fellow worker in all
things, choſe him as Biſhop and Shepherd
of his ſoule, and keeper of his maners,
obeyed him in all things, and preferred
his counſel before all treaſure. Secondly
becauſe he obeyed the commandement of   2
the Pope, who threatned him excommu-
nication if he procured diuers Biſhopricks
to be erected, ex. Malmsb. *l. cit.* Cambden
in Brit. *p.* 198. Thirdly becauſe two of his
daughters Edfled and Edburga became   3
nōnes & the third Ethelhild vowed virgi- Tvvo
nitie, exMalm. *l. cit.* Houed. *p.* 421. And as daughters
Bale ſaith Cent. 13. *c.* 77. Gregorie a ſonne Edvvard
of his, became an hermit in Swiſeland. Nonnes
Fourthly becauſe he toke awaye his bro- third
thers or his brothers ſonnes wife from vovved
him, becauſe ſhe had bene a Nonne, Hunt. virginitie.
lib. 5. Weſtmon. An. 801. In his time liued   4
the ſaid S. Edburg his daughter, and S.
Friſtan Biſhop of Wincheſter *a man,* ſaith Saints.
Godwin in his life) *highly eſteemed of, for his*
learning, but much more for his great vertue and
holines.

X   *King*

King Athelſtan. XX.

The Wor-
thines of
K. Ethel-
ſtan.
9. IN the yeare 924. ſucceeded king Athelſtan, ſonne to king Edward, and held the Crowne. 16. yeares, ex Malm. *lib. 2. cap. 6. He was* (ſaith Fox *p.* 147. Cooper. An. 925. and Stow *p.* 107.) *a Prince of worthie memorie, valiant, and wiſe in all his acts, and brought this Lād to one Monarchy: For he expelled the Danes, ſubdued the Scotts quieted the VVelch-men.* The like ſaith Bale Cent. 2. cap. 22. and alſo Catholick writers, as yow may

His reli-
gion.
ſee in Malmsb. *l. cit.* Hunt. *lib.* 5. Houed. *pag.* 422. His Roman religion is moſt eui-dēt. For going to the Battel of Brumford

*Ingulpg.
Florent.
An.* 938.
Hunt. lib. 5.
pag. 422.
againſt many kings, and innumerable enemies, *he viſited* (ſaith Ingulph) *S. Iohn of Beuerley by the waye, with great deuotion,* and God ſo bleſſed his deuotiō as in the battel he ſlew (ſaith Malmsb) the king of Scotts,

A wonder
full victo-
rie.
& fiue kings more, 12. Earles, innumerable multitude of his enemies, and got one of the greateſt victories that euer Engliſhe wonne. And in his return gaue great gifts and priuiledges to S. Iohn of Beutrley, and made it a ſanctuary for all Debters and Malifactors, *Ex* Ingulph, and Cambd. in Brit. *pag.* 636. Beſides he was, ſaith Ingulph and Malmsb, greatly delited with
                                   a peece

a peece of the holy Croſſe, and Crowne of Hovv K.
Etbelſtan
eſtemed
reliques. thorns which Hugh king of France ſent vnto him: Made S. Aldhelm his Patron. Cambd. p. 210. *Builded* (ſaith Fox *pag.*149) *the two Monaſteries of Midleton and Michelney for his brothers ſoule.* VVherby (ſaith Fox) *it* VVhy
Kings
builded
monaſte-
ries. *may appeare that the eſpetiall cauſe of building Monaſteries in thoſe dayes was for the releaſing ſinnes bothe of them departed and of them aliue. which cauſe,* ſaith he, *how it ſtãdeth with Chriſts* (Luthers) *Goſpel, let the Chriſtian Reader try with him ſelf.* Thus Fox, which confeſſion of his may ſuffice to ſhew how all that kings tyme all the Realme was Roman Catholick. And how all Chriſtendome All Chri-
ſtendom
of the
ſame
faith vvith
K. Ethel-
ſton. abroad agreed with him in religiõ appeareth by the marriage of his ſiſters to the Emperor, king of Frãce, & other Chriſtiã Princes. In this kings time befel a miracle in Duke Elfred whome the king ſent to Rome to purge him ſelfe of treaſon by his oath before S. Peters ſepulcher. But (ſaith Miracle
by S Peter. the K. in his charter, which Fox *pag.* 148. Malmsb and others haue,) *hauing taken his oath, he fel before the Altar, and was caried by the hands of his ſeruants to the Engliſh ſchole, and the next night after he ended his life.* Then alſo liued Saint Birnſtan Biſhop of VVin- Saints. cheſter *Qui &c.* ſaith Florẽt. *An.* 932. Malm. Polichron: Houed. Iornelacenſis & others more as Fox confeſſeth p. 148. *who dayly*

*ſong maſſe for the quiet reſt of the ſoules de-
parted.*

King Evvmund X X I.

10. THe 21. Chriſtian King was Edmund ſonne to the forſaid Edward, who began (ſaith Malmesb.) An.
Vvorthi- 940. and reigned ſix yeares and a halfe.
nes of K. He *was* (ſaith Cooper *An.* 940. and Stow
Edmund. p. 108.) *a man by nature diſpoſed to noblenes and
inſtice.* Huntin. lib . 5. calleth him *inuictum,
vnconquered,* & ſaith *omnia illi feliciter ſucceſ-
ſiſſe : all things fel out happily to him :* And Fox
lib. 3. pag. 130. writeth that *he achiued noble
victories againſt his enemies, and ſet his ſtudie in
maintaining & redreſſing the ſtate of the Church,*
His Reli- *which ſtoode all then in building of Monaſteries &
gion.* *Churches, and furniſhing them with new poſſeſ-
ſions. and reſtoring the ould,* Infra. *In the time of*
Strait life this *king Edward or ſhort lie after , hardnes , re-*
vſed for ſtraint of life with ſuperſtition were had in vene-
merit ſake ration, & men for merit ſake with God gaue thēſelues to leade a ſtreight life . which alone
would ſuffice to ſhew of what religion
this King was. Beſides, that (as Stow
ſaith p. 108. Florent. *An.* 942. Weſtmon.
An. 940. Houed p. 423.) he was altogether
coūſelled & lead by S. Dunſtan, at whoſe
requeſt he reedifyed Gloſſenburie, and
made

made S. Dunſtan Abbot therof with a
Chapter extant in Malmsb. *lib.* 2. *cap.* 7.
He granteth many priuiledges to Gloſſenburie *for hope of æternall reward and for-*
giuenes of his ſinnes , In this Kings time liued his wife S. Elfegia who (ſaith Ethelwerd *lib.* 4. *cap.* 6.) was canonized after
her death, and miracles wrought at her
tombe.

Saints.

King Edred. XII.

11.　The 22 . Chriſtian King was Edred, third ſonne of King Edward.
He entred An. 946. and held the crowne
nine yeares and a halfe, as Malmsb. hath
lib 2. *cap.* 7. His *magnanimitie* (ſaith he) *did*
not degenerat from his Father and brethren . He
ſubdued the Northumbers and Scotts. He hum-
bled himſelfe to the feete of holie men, deuoted his
life to God and S. Dunſtan by whoſe counſell he
made his court a ſchoole of vertue. Thus Malm.
Cooper An. 946. Stow Chron. *pag.* 108.
ſaith he was *a great maintainer of honeſtie &*
moſt abhorred naughty & vnruly perſons, in ſeats
of armes much commended, wherby he kept in o-
beiſſance the Northumbers and Scotts and exi-
led the Danes. As for his Roman religion
ther can be no doubt. For as Fox writeth
pag. 152. *He was much ruled by the Connſell of S.*

The wor-
thines of
K. Edred
and his
vertue.

His reli-
gion.

X 3

Dun-

Dunstan, in so much as in histories he is reported to haue subiected himself to much pennance inflicted on him by S. Dunstan: Such zelousdeuotion (faith he) *was then in Princes.* And as Florent. *An. 955.* Malmsb.*l. cit.* Houed.*pag.423.* West-mon.*An.955.* write, when he fel fick *Accerfiuit &c. he fent for bleffed Dunstan his confef-for.* Ingulph faith *Aboue all the Kings his Pre-deceffors he had the pureft confcience, and a fpe-tiall deuotion to S. Paul.* And *p.876.* he citeth his Chapter in the which he erected a new the Abbey of Crowland as he faith *In the regard of the redemption of my foule and is fory* that by the deftruction of that monafterie , prayers for the foules of the kings his prodeceffors haue bene intermitted . To which Chapter fub-fcribe two Arcbifhops, 4. Bifhops, many Abbots, and Earles. And Stow *pag.* 198. faith *the King fealed this Charter with feales' of gould.*

King Edwin. XXIII.

12.   IN the yeare 955. (faith Malmsb. *l.2.c.7.*) fucceded Edwin, fonne to king Edmund, & reigned 4. yeares. He was fo bewtifull as Ethelwerd *lib. 4. c. 8.* faith he was commonly called *Pancalus* , but as Malmsb. he abufed his bewty to
lew-

lewdnes, for which and for banishing of
S. Dunstan (writeth Cooper *An.* 955.) he
was odible to his subiects. Fox *pag.* 152.
addeth that he was deposed of the Northumbers and mercians, & Edgar chosen
in his place, yet as it seemeth he amended.
For Hunting. *l.* 5. writteth that he ruled
his kingdeme not without commendation, & Osbern in vit. Dunstani writeth,
that by the praiers of S. Dunstan he was
at his death deliuered from the Diuels.
His Roman religiō appeareth by the pos- Religion
session which, as Malmsb. saith, he gaue of K.
S. Aldelm, whose body, saith he, was Edvuin.
then found, and *in scrinio locatum*, *placed
in a shrine.* In the Register of the Abbey of
Bury she is said, to haue giuen to that Monastery the towne of Becklis, and diuers
other things.

King Edgar. XXIIII.

13. THe 24. K. was Edgar, secōd sonne
to king Edmund, who began his
reigne, (saith Malmsb. *lib.* 2. *cap.* 8.) *Anno*
959. and reigned 16. yeares. The praises The prai-
which both Catholicks and Protestants ses of K.
giue to this king are exceeding. Malmsb. Edgar.
calleth him *honor & delitiæ Ang : The
honor and delight of English men*, and
saith

faith that *inter Anglos &c.amongſt English men
the report is* , that *no King nether of his or any
former age in England* , *is to be compared with
Edgar.*Ingulph an ancient & graue author
p.889.faith he was *flos & decus* &c. *The ſloure
and ornament of all his Anceſtors,and the mirror of
the VVeſtern climat of the world* , *the bewtie
glorie and roſe of Kings.* Florent An. 975. and
Houed.*p.*426. add, that *he was as worthie to
be remembred of Englishmen* , *as Romulus of Ro-
māʒ,Syrus of Perſians,Alexander of Macedonians,
Arſaces of Parthians* , *Charles the great of the
French.* Huntington *lib.*5. p.356.faith *Edgar
the peaceable,a King magnificent* , *a ſecond Salomon, in his dayes the Land was much bettered, he
was moſt deuout to God,he built many Monaſteries.*
And Malmsb. faith that in the yeare 1052.
(which was about a hundred yeares after
his death)his body was found *Nullius labis
conſcium voyde of corruption* , and that it
wrought miracles.The like praiſes do the
Proteſtants afford him . Cooper An. 959.
*A Prince of worthie memorie, for his manifould
vertues gratly renouned* , *ſo excellent in iuſtice and
ſharp correction of vices as wel in his Magiſtrats as
other ſubiects* , *that neuer before his day was vſed
leſſe felonie and extortion* . *Of mind valiant and
hardy* , *& very expert in martiall policie.* The
like faith Stow Chron.*pag.*109. Fox Acts.
lib. 3. pag. 154. faith he *was much giuen to all
vertuous* , *and princely acts,worthy of much com-*

                                                    men-

mendation and famous memory , excellent in *iuſtice , maintained the godly , loued the modeſt,* *was deuout to God, and beloued of his ſubiects* *whome he gouerned in much peace and quietnes,* *ſo God did bleſſe him with aboundance of peace.* *No yeare paſſed in the time of his Reigne in* *which he did not ſome ſingular and neceſſarie* *commoditie for the common welth . A great* *mantainer of religion and learning . He had in* *redines 3600. ſhips (The ſame ſay* Florent. *and* Weſtmon . *Anno 975.* Houed. *pag.* 426. *) of war, and made 8. Kings to row him* in a boate, he ſetting at the ſterne & gui-ding it. The Romā religiō of this renow-ned K, is manifeſt . For Fox *l. cit,* ſaith *He* *was a great Patron of Monkiſh religion , builded,* *(as ſome ſay) as many Monaſteries as there be* *ſondays in the yeare , or as* Edner *reporteth 48.* *pag.156.* Edgar *was ſeduced by* Dunſtan *, who was* *drowned in all ſuperſtition and did ſeuen yeares* *penance at* Dunſtans *apointment.* And *pag.* 161. and 169. reciteth an oration in King Ed-gar which alſo is in Stow *pag.* 111. wherin the King ſpeaketh thus to the Clergy . *It belongeth to me to rule the lay peo-* *ple, It belongeth to me to prouide neceſſarie things* *to the Miniſters of the Church to the flock of* *Monkes.* Behould how he diſtinguiſheth betwene gouerning lay people , and pro-uiding for cletgie . Item he complaineth there that *Prieſts crownes are not broade nor*
their

Fox cal-leth this King a Pœhnix.

The reli-gion of K. Edgar.

Ingulph *pag.* 883.

lay people , and prouiding for clergie.
Item he complaineth there *That Priests*
crownes are not broade nor their rownding con-
uenient, and that they came not deuoutly
to Masse , and saith to the Bishops , *I haue*
Constantins sworde, and yee haue Peters sword
in your hands , let vs ioine right hands , let vs
cuple svvord to svvord that the Leapers may be
cast out of the Temple . Touching which
oration, Fox noteth the religious zeale
and deuotion of Kings , *and the blind* (saith
he) *ignorance and superstition of that time in*
both estates Ecclesiasticall and ciuil in esteeming
Chrifts religion cheefly to confist in giuing to
Churches and maintaining of Monkery, wherin it
appeareth (saith he)*how ignorant that time was*
of the true doctrin of Chrifts faith. And putteth
this note in the margent. *The doctrin of iufti-*
fication vnknowne. Bale *Cent.* 2. *cap.* 34. saith
Edgarus &c. *Edgar earneftly seruing the desires*
of Monkes , And by the inchantments of Dunstan,
Ethelwald, and Ofwald , being made an Image of
the Beast,did fpeake onely as they gaue him breath,
& all things then were ruled at their beck. Ingul.
pag. 883. setteth downe his Charter of
Peterborowh, wherin he calleth S. Peter
Superum Ianitorem . The porter of heauen , and
saith he apointeth there a market *for*
diuers good purpo^es both of temporall and fpiri-
tual profits, *that Gods minifters may be holpen*
more neare at hand,and that the Chriftian people
meeting

Cōstātins
svvord in
the Kings
hand S.
Peters in
the Bif-
hops
hands.

K. Edgars
time
knevv
not the
Proteftāts
Doctrin.

meeting there amidst worldly affaires may demand Gods help, whiles by demanding *S. Peters* Note.
protection and by hearing the misterie of Masse
according to the faith of eche one the faultes of
diuers sinnes may therin be redeemed. And
again : *Hanc regiferam libertatem &c, we*
haue procured this royal libertie according to the
primitiue institution therof, to be strenghned
from the See of the Apostolicke Roman Church,
by the author him selfe of this writing most re-
uerend Ethelwald . And to this Charter
subscribe two Archbishops , three
Bishops, many Abbots, Dukes, and nobles . And Malmsb. *l. cit.* citeth an other
Charter of that king granted to Glassenburie , which he requested to be confirmed by Pope Iohn 12. which Pope confirmed it saying that he tooke the Monasterie *in protectione Romanæ Ecclesiæ & beato-*
rum Apostolorum Petri & Pauli: In protection
of the Roman Church and the blessed Apostles
Saint Peter and Paule . In this kings tyme Saints in
liued Saint Merwin saith Florent. *An.* this King
967. whome he made Abbesse of Rum- his tyme,
sey , and confirmed that Monasterie
(saith Stow *pag.113.*) in the presence of all
the Nobilitie. Also Saint Editha his own
daughter , who from her infancy was
brought vp in a Monasterie , and
would not refuse that lyfe to enioy
the crowne aftet her brother King
Edwards

Edwards death. Alſo S. Elſted a nonne
whoſe life and miracles yow may read in
Gapgraue.

S. *Edward Martyr*   XXV.

14.   In the yeare 975. began S. Edward the Martyr ſaith Malmsb.
lib. 2. *cap* . 9 . .ſonne to King Edgar, and
reigned three yeares, who did (ſaith he)
follow the ſteps of his Eathers religion, and yeelde
both eare & minde to good Councell. Ingulph
pag. 889. ſaith he was a *ſimple and moſt holy*
yong man, following much his Father in maners.
Cooper An.975, and Stow *pag,* 113. ſay he
was in all kinde of honeſt vertues comparable to
his Father Edgar, began his ſouerainty with much
modeſtie and mildnes, & worthely fauored of all.
Fox Acts. *pag.*159 *Authors deſcribe him to be*
a vertuous and noble Prince , much pittiſull &
bountifull to the poore. And Caius de Antiq.
Cantab:*pag.*294.ſaith he *is worthilie tearmed*
a martyr. Cooper *An.* 977 . ſaith after his
death *God ſhewed for him many miracles,*
which alſo teſtify Malmsb. l. cit. Weſtmon. *Anno.* 979. and others. wherby the
Reader make perceaue what account he
may make of Fox, who l.cit.calleth them
tales. His Roman religion is manifeſt
partly by what hath bene ſaid of his Father

The vertues of K, Edvvard martyr,

Miracles.

His reli-gion.

ther, partly becaufe Fox faith l. cit. He **1**
was by Dunftans meanes elected and
confecrated. Which alfo teftify Malmsb. **2**
l. cit. Florent. *Anno* 975. And becaufe as
Fox & the fame Authors teftify he ftoode **3**
with Saint Dunftan againft Priefts
Wiues. In this Kings time liued three Saints.
great Saints S. Dunftan S. Ethelwald &
S. Ofwald, of whome we will fpeake in
the time of the next King when they
died.

King Egelred. XXVI.

15. IN the yeare 979. faith Malmsb. *lib. 2.*
cap. 10. fucceeded King Egelred,
fonne to King Edgar, and reigned 37. Qualities
yeares. Who (as fay Florent An. 978. of K.
Houed. *p.* 427. and Cooper An. 978.) *was* Egelred.
Moribus elegans pulcher vultu & decorus aspectu.
excellently manered of fayer face and gratious
countenance. His Roman religion is mani- His reli-
feft, by what hath bene fayd of his Father. gion.
Secondly becaufe his mother built two **1**
Monafteries one at Amsbury, an other at
Whorwel and became a Nonne Cambd. **2**
in Brit. *pag.* 177. 221. 228. and as Malmsb.
l. cit. faith *Corpus filicio*, & c. She wrapt her-
bodie in haire cloth. In the night layd on
the

the grownd without pillow fhe toke her
fleepe &c.

3 Thirdly becaufe in his time liued thefe
notorious Papifts S. Dunftan, S. Ethel-

4 wald, and S. Ofwald. Fourthly becaufe
he confirmed the Charter of Euifham
Monafterie, *& libertatis priuilegium*, &c. *And
the priniledg of the liberty confirming, figned it*

5 *with the figne of the Croffe*, Cambd. in Brit.
pag. 327. Fiftly becaufe he receaued the
Legat of Pope Iohn 15. and by him

Miracles. made peace with the Duke of Normádie,
Malmsb. *l. cit.* In this time was S. Edward,
King and martyrs body found incorrupt
An. 979. Houed. *pag.* 407. Then alfo liued

Saints. S. Dunftan of whome fome thing hath
bene faydin the Archbifhops, & S. Ethelwald Bifhop of Winchefter, who (faith
Godwin in his life) *was a great Patron of
Monks and no leffe enemy to married Priefles.* And
S. Ofwald Archb. of York whome God-
win confeffeth to haue *bene very learned and
for his integritie and conuerfation much reuerenced. The greateft faulte* (faith he) *I finde in him
was, in that he was very earneft in fetting forth
that doctrin of Diuels that debarreth men* (who
haue promifed to God the contrary) *from
marrying*. In this time alfo was martyred
S. Elpheg Archb. of Canterburie, And S.
Edmund King and martyr miraculoufly
flew Swain King of Denwark (as in the
Ec-

Ecclesiastical histories it is reported of Saint Mercurie Martyr that he slew Iulian the Apostata) This miracle Fox him selfe dare not discredit, but *lib.3. pag.161.* writeth thus of Swain. *He entred the Ter-* Miracle. *ritorie of Saint Edmund, wasted and spoiled the contrie, despised the holie Martyr menacing the place of his sepulcher. VVherfore the men of the Countrie fel to praier and t fasting, so that shorlie after Swain died sodenlie crying and yelling. Some saye (saith he) that he wasstroken with the sword of S.Edmund. In fear wherof Canutus his sonne granted them the fredome of all their liberties and great freedoms, quitted them of all tax and tribut. And after that time it was vsed that Kings of England when they were crowned sent their Crownes for an offering to S. Edmunds shrine, aud redeemed the same againe with condigne price.* And these times were so euidently Papistical, as Fox in his Protestation before his Acts saith thus: *About the year of our Lord 980. sprong forth here in England, (as did in other places more,) a Romish kind of Monkery much drovvned in supestition. Of this svvarme vvas Egbert, Agelbert, Egvvin, Boniface, VVilfrid, Agathon, Iames, Roman, Cedda, Dunstan, Osvvald, Athelm, Lanfrancke, Anselm and such other.* But well it is that this Iames was (as S. Beda saith *lib·2.c.20.*) *a good & godlie man, &* Deacon to

S.

S. Paulin, who was S. Auftines compani on, by whome we may fee the religion of S. Auftin and his fellowes. Agilbert, Agatho, Wilfrid, Roman, Cedda, were holy men much commended by Beda *lib. 3. cap.*25. and liued in S. Auftins time, or very fone after, long before this time. The others Egbert, Boniface, Danftan, Ofwald, Anfelm, were the famoufeft Saints which England hath.

King Edmund Ironfide XXVII.

16.   THe 27. Chriftian King was Edmund Ironfide, fonne vnto King Egelred, who fucceded *An.*1016.and reigned one yeare. *He was* (faith Malmsb. *lib.*2. *cap.*10. *a yong man of notable towardlines of great ftrength both of minde and body, and therfore firnamed Ironfide of the Englifh men.* The like fay Hunting *lib.* 6. Weftmon. *Anno* 1016. Cooper *Anno* 1016.and Fox Acts *Pag.* 162. write that he was of lufty and valiant courage in martiall affairs both hardie and wife, and could indure all paine. His Roman religion is manifeft by that as the Regifter of Bury faith he reedifyed Glaffenburie deftroied (as it feemeth)by the Danes,and by what hath bene faid of his Father.

The valour of K. Edmund Ironfide.

His religion.

King

King Canut. XXVIII.

17. THe 28. king was king Canut , a
Dane who by force of armes and
dint of sword got the kingdome , beginning his reigne *Anno.* 1017. and reigned
20. yeares, *Composed* (saith Malmsb. *lib.* 2.
c.11.) *his life magna ciuilitate & fortitudine.* Of **Vertues of**
whome Hunting : *lib.* 6. Polidor. *L.* and **K. Canut.**
others recount this story, That as he sat
by the sea side his flatterers magnifying **For p. 164.**
him, called him Lord of the land and sea,
whose flattery to discouer he commanded the waues not to come neere him, but
they rising according to their course be-
wet the king, wherat he smiling said to
his coutriers, loe he whom yee call Lord
of Sea and land cannot cõmand a smale
waue. Cooper *An.* 1018. saith he was *a sage
gentle and moderat Prince.* And An. 1027. *for
his vertuous life worthie to liue perpetuallie . He
was of great magnificence,& vsed such iustice &
temperance that in his daies was no Prince of
such renowne, towards God humble and lowlie.*
Bale Cent. 2. *cap.* 45. saith, he was *Iuuenis
&c. a yong. man of excellent vvit and high minde
and notable in Christian modestie.* That great
king who was withall king of Denmark **His reli-**
and Norway was euidentlie a Roman **gion.**
Y   Ca-

1 Catholick . Firſt becauſe after the ſaid
ſpeech of his, touching the Sea, he went
to Wincheſter as Fox *pag.* 163. Bale *l. cit.*

Florent.
Moued.
An.131.

Stow *pag.* 120. Hunting. *l. cit.* and others
write, and taking his crown from his head
ſet it vpon the head of the crucifix. *Quo* &c.
(ſaith Bale) *By which he ſignified that the Kings
of thoſe times were no Kings, but onely the likenes*

2 *of Kings and Images of the Beaſt.* Secondly Fox
pag. 163. writeth *that following much the ſuperſtition of Agelnoth Archb. of Canterburie he went
on Pilgrimage to Rome,* and ther founded an
hoſpitall for Pilgrims, gaue to the Pope
pretious gifts , and burdened the Land
with a tribut called , *Romeſcot .* In his
letters to the Nobles and Biſhops of England in Malmsb. and Ingulph him ſelf
ſaith that he went *oratum* &c. *to pray for the
redemption of my ſinnes,* and ſaith that he had
longe vowed it, and thancketh God that
he had there honored S. Peter and Saint
Paule, and all the holy places of Rome.
Et ideo hoc maxime, &c. And therfor I haue
done this principally becauſe I haue
learned of wiſe men, that Saint Peter the
Apoſtle hath receaued great power of our
Lord of binding and looſing, and that he
is the Porter of heauen , and therfore I
thought it very profitable 'to require
eſpecially his protection with God.

3 Thirdly in his Charter in Malmsburie he
ſaith

saith, he graunteth priuiledges to that Monasterie by the counsel of the Archbishop Agelnoth and also of all the Priests of God, and with the consent of all my Peeres for the loue of the Kingdom of heauen, and pardon of my offences, and the relaxations of the transgressions of my brother King Edmund. Wherby wee see that both him selfe and his Bishops and nobles were Roman Catholicks. Fourthly he built (saith Fox *l. cit.* Cambd. Brit. *pag.* 415.) Saint Bennets in Norfolk, and turned Saint Edmunds Bury into an Abbey of Monks, And Bale *libro cit.* addeth, *It is found that next after God he endeuored to appease Saint Edmund by prayers and offerings.*

4

*King Herold .*XXIX.

18. IN the yeare 1036. succeded King Herold sonne to King Canut by Elfgina an English woman, as witnesseth Ingulph, and reigned 4. yeares and 4. monethes, *ex* Malmsburie *lib.* 2. *cap.* 12. His Roman religion is manifest both by his Father, & by that which Ingulph writeth of him *pag.*895. *He gaue to the Monasterie of Crowland a Cloake of silk set with goulden*

Rom. religion of K. Herold.

Y 2 *buttons*

buttons which he wore at his coronation, and he had done to vs many moe good things if ouer hasty death had not taken him away.

King Hardy Canut. XXX.

19.   THe 30. King was king Hardi-Canut, sonne to king Canut & Emma, who had bene wife to king Egel-reld. Began his reign *An.* 1040. & ruled two years. *He shewed* (saith Malm. *l. 2. c. 12.*) *exceeding great pitty of minde towardes his bro-*

Rom. re-   *ther S. Edmund the Confessor.* His Roman
ligion of   re'igion appeareth both by his Father, &
K. Hardi   because as testifyeth Registrum Burinese
Canute.   *Dedit S. Edmundo libertatem.*

King S. Edward Confessor. XXXI.

Vertues of   20.   IN the yeare 1042. Edward Con-
K. Edvvard   fessor & sonne to the forsaid king
Cöfessor.   Egelred began his reign, and reigned 24. yeares. *He was* (saith Malmsb. *lib.* 2 *cap.* 13.) *deuout vnto God and therfore directed by him, whilst he reigned, all thing at home and a-broad were quiet and calme.* He flew by his Captaines Machetat king of Scotts, and put another in his place , & brought wales into the forme of a Prouince vnder Eng-

England. *Illud celeberime fertur &c. That is most famously reported that he neuer toucht any womans chastitie.* And Florent. *An.* 1066. calleth him *Decus Anglorum, The honor of Englishmen.* But who will see more of his vertues may read his life written by a most ancient and graue Author in Surio *Tom.* 1. This only I will not omit, that to him did God first giue the vertue of curing the kings euil and the crampe, from whome all our Princes since haue receaued it. Fox *lib.* 3. *pag.* 164. and Cooper *An.* 1043. say that *he was a man of gentle and soft spirit, neuer delt with his wife fleshlie, guided the Kingdom with much wisdome and iustice, from vvhome issued as out of a fountain, much godlinesse pitty & liberalitie tovvards the poore, gentlenes and iustice tovvards all men, and in all honest life he gaue a a vertuous example to his people.* And *pag.* 16. calleth him *vertuous and blessed King.* Cooper *pag.* 1065. addeth *That he purged the ould lavves and piked out of them certain vvhich vvere most profitable for the Commons.* To these high praises Stow Chron. 122. adioyneth that God greatly glorifyed him in his life by wonderfull signes, and cured the kings euil. Now let vs see what the religion of this great and holy king was. First he vowed to God, that if he got the crowne he would go, to Rome on Pilgrimage, Westmon. *An.* 1049. Ealred in vita Edwardi.

The like Cambd. in Brit. *p.* 330. Bal. Cent. 2. *cap.* 12. Stovv. *pag.* 122.

Bal. supra.

The religion of K. Edvvard Confes.

1

Se-

2 Secondly, when his people would not suffer him to leaue the Land for fear of the Danes inuafion, he demanded difpenfation, and obtained it of Pope Nicholas. 2. Nichol. *in ep. ad Edwardum*.Ealred|*in vita*: Thirdly, fent two Abbots to a Concell held at Rhemes by Pope Leo,Florent.and Houed.*Anno.*1050.

3

4 Fourtbly he built the Monaftery of Weftminfter:principally *for the loue* (faith Camb. in Brit. *pag.* 376. *of the cheefe Apoftle*,whome he honored with a fpeciall & peculier affection. Fiftly, whiles he was at Maffe, God reuealed vnto him the drowning ofthe K. of Denmarke which intended to inuade England . Houed. *An.* 1066.Ealred *in vit.*Sixtly, Pope Nicol. writing to him , thanketh God that King Edward had loue to S. Peter *and with vs he confented in all the Apoftolicall Decrees*, and therin abfolued him from his vow, & Weftminfter from all Epifcopall iurifdiction, and faith that to him and his fucceffors *we commit the aduoufion , and tuition of all the Churches of England that in any place yow may determine by the Counfell of the Bishops and Abbots what things be iuft and right.* Whervpon Bale *l. cit.* faith:That *fub Nicolao 2. facti funt Anglorum Reges &c. vnder Pope Nicolas 2.the Kings of Englad were made the Popes Vicars.* Seuétly,writing to the Pope.He profeffeth

5

6

7

feſſeth the Popes ſupremacie, In which (as Proteſtáts ſay) the eſſence of a Papiſt cōſiſteth, in theſe plain words, *To the cheefe Father of the vniuerſall Church Nicolas, Edward by the grace of God K. of England due obediēce.* Ealred *in vit.* And in his lawes in Fox *pag.* 166. appointed that a King ſhall ſweare vpon the Euangeliſts and bleſſed reliques of Saints that he will maintain the holy Church with all integrity. And ſo manifeſt it is, that this K. & our Country in his time were Roman Catholicks, as Syr Edward Cook the Kings Attorney in F. Garnets Arainment (which ſince is printed) openlie called , *the time of Edward Confeſſor* . Henrie 1 . Edward 1¼. Richard 2. Henrie 4, and 5. *the verie midnight of Poperie ,* which were in truth the moſt florishing times, that euer England ſaw. For what King haue we in vertue comparable to King Edward Confeſſor? in wiſdome , to King Henrie the firſt? in valour and victories to King Edward the firſt, the Conqueror of Scotland ? and Henrie 4. of England, and Henrie the fift Conqueror of France ?

That times of England moſt florishing vvhich Proteſt: confeſſe to haue bene Papiſticall.

Y 4

King

King Herold. XXXII.

21.   THe 32. and laſt King of the Saxons was King Herold who
tooke the crown *An.*1066. and held it not

Valour of K.Herold. one yeare.He was ſaith Cooper *An.* 1066.
valiant and hardie. Florent. *An.*1066. ſaith he
was left ſucceſſor by Saint Edward and
choſen of all the nobles of England and
crowned of Aldred Archb.of yorke & began to put down vniuſt lawes & to ſet vp
iuſt to become a Patron of Monaſteries,to
honor and reuerence Biſhops Abbots
Monks and Clerkes , to ſhew him ſelfe
pious humble and affable, to hate malefa-
ctors and to labour by ſea and Land
for defence of his Countrie he ouerthrew
the king of Norway in a great battel,but
was ſone after himſelfe ſlayne and England cõquered in a ruefull battel in Suſſex
His Rom. by William Duke of Normandy and after
Religion. king of England. His Roman religion is
manifeſt both by what hath bene ſaid
of king Edward , and becauſe as Cambd.
hath in Brit *pag.*384. *VValtham Monaſterie*
he founded in the honor of the holie Croſſe where he
made his vowes for victorie againſt the Normans .
Weſtmon *An.*1066. ſaith,*orauit ante crucem*
He prayed before the Croſſe. Thus yow ſee
the

the Roman Catholicke religion deduced
not only fom all our Christian kings for
the 200. yeares vnto the Monarchie but
also from the monarchie all the Saxons
time vnto the conquest therof by the
Normans for the space of 266. yeares: in
which time two of the said Kings haue
bene Saints to wit Saint Edward martyr and Saint Edward Confessor. Three
haue gon on Pilgrimage to Rome, namely king Ethelwolph king Alfred the
great and king Canut: To whome we
may ad king Burdred and king Edward Confessor who would haue gon.
Two kings daughters Saints namely S.
Edburga daughter to king Edward and
S. Editha daughter to king Edgar. And if
we will know why God permitted our
Contry to be subdued of strangers. It was
saith Malmsb. *lib.* 3. in Guilielmo.1. *because*
the studies of learning and religion had decayed,
Not a fewe yeares before the Normans coming
the Clergie could scarce stamer out the words
of the Sacraments, he which knew his grāmer was
a wonder and a miracle to the rest, Monks vvere
fine in apparell and had euery kinde of meat indif-
ferent making a mockerie of their rule, The
nobles giuin to glutonie and Venerie did not go
to Church in the morning after the maner of
Christians but in their chambers dalying vvith
their wiues heard onlie the solemnization of

Y 5   mat-

their wiues heard onely the solemnization of Mattins and Masse by a Priest, making much hast therin. Euery one commonly was giuen to tippling continewing in this exercise nights as wel as dayes, wheron vices ensued companions of dronkenes. But I would not haue these sayinges to be vnderstood of all. I knew many of the clergie at that time walked the path of sanctitie in true simplicitie. I knew many Lay men of all sorts and conditions within this same Contrie pleased God. Hunting. also *lib. 6.* writeth that before the Conquest, a man of God tould them that for their sinnes in murder and treason, and becauſe they were giuen to drunkenes and care-leſnes of the seruice of God, ther ſhould come from France a Lord that ſhould depreſſe them for euer, and not onely they but the Scotts alſo ſhould rule ouer them to their deſerued confuſion. S. Edmund alſo prophesied of this coquest of England which though Fox *pag.* 165. call but a dreame yet the euent following ſheweth it was too true a viſion.

CHAP.

CHAP. XXV.

That the Kings of England from the Conquest to King Edward 3. time, were Roman Catholicks proued in particuler.

1. THe 33. King of England was William the Conqueror who entred this Land *An.*1066. and reigned 21.yeares. He got the crowne of this Réalm partly by dint of fword and conqueft, partly by the graunt of King Edward Confeffor, whofe cofin German remoued he was. For as him felfe faith in his Charter, in Cambd. in Brit. *pag.*111. *He got the Kingdome by the help of the graunt of God and of his cofin glorious King Edward, who apointed him his adopted heir to the Kingdom of England.* And Guitmundus *in oratione ad Regem,* faith: He got England *by the gift of God and by the freindship of Edward his Kinfman.* And Ingulph who then alfo liued, faith. *An.*1065.

Edward

VVhat right K. VVill. had to the Crovvne of England.

Edward chose VVilliam and sent Robert Archb. *of Canterb. who should declare it vnto him. And* pag. 911. *In the Kindred and consanguinitie of Edward our famous King , VVilliam framed his conscience to inuade* England. Paris *pag.* 1057. *It is sayd that blessed S.* Edward *gaue the King-dome to VVilliam as a Legacie on his death bed.* The like hath Walsing. ypodigm *pag.* 28. Houed. *pag.* 609. *and others.* Finally Fox Acts *pag.* 165. King Edward *thought to make* Edgar Adeling *his heire, but fearing partly the mutabilitie of English men partly the malice and pride of Herold and others , perceauing therby that he should not so well bring his purpose to passe directed solemne Embassadors to the Duke of Normandie assigning and admitting him to be his lawfull heire next to succeed him after to the Crowne.* And King William trusting to the right of this title offered Herold (as Fox *pag.* 166.167. and others write) to trye their two titles before the Pope , but Herold refusing, William neuerthelesse sent and got his title approued by the Popes iudgment. This King saith Hunting. *lib.* 6. *pag.*

Valour
and ver-
tues of K.
VVilliam
Conq.

370. *was wise, but crafty, rich but couetous, vainglorious but louing his reputation , louing to the seruants of God , hard to this withstanders , the onely author of peace that a little girle loaden with gould might passe through Englād vntouched.* The like hath Malmsb. *lib.* 3. and Cooper An. 1067 ; Bale Cent. 2. *cap.* 56. addeth
that

that he was of great corage and excellent
in the knowledg of warlick affaires.
His Roman religion is manifeſt . Firſt
becauſe as Weſtmon.An.1085. and others
write,*Euery day he vvas preſent at Maſſe heard
mattins Lauds Euenſong vvith the Canonicall
houres , nether vvould he ſuffer euen vpon moſt
vrgent and difficult affaires,him ſelf to be kindred.*
In the meane ſeaſon he ceaſſed not to kneele and
to pray deuoutly . Seconaly becauſe as ſone
as he had gotten the victorie he ſent
Herolds Standerd to the Pope. Stow in
Herold,Cambd.in Brit. Thirdly he built
two Monaſteries one at Battel in Suſſex
Vt orarent: that they might pray ſaith Weſt-
mon.An.1067.Paris 1066. *Pro ibi mortuis for
the dead there.* And an other at Cane in
Normandie . Fourthly he made his
daughter Cecilia a Nonne:Paris An.1075.
Stow. *pag.*177. S. Oſmund was ſo inward
with this King as Bale ſaith Cent .
13. *cap.* 14.*That he could not be abſent ſcarce
any time from King VVilliams preſence .* And
yet as he both there ſaith, and Fox Acts
pag. 184. Godwin in the Biſhop of Salsburie,this Oſmund in the yeare 1076. was
author of the office or maner of ſaying
Maſſe mattins and adminiſtring Sacraments after the vſe of Sarum which (ſaye
they)was afterward in a manner receaued
through all England Wales and Ireland.

Sixtly

His Rom.
religion,

1

Paris.
An.185.

K. VVill.
Conq.
heard
euery
daie Maſſe
mattins
and
Houres,

2

3

4

K. VVill.
daughter
a Nonne.

5

Sixtlie Pope Alexander writing to him *ep.* 10. saith *Among the Princes and rulers of the world we vnderstand the notable forme of your religion*, and writeth to him to persist in the study of most Christian deuotion. And Pope Greg. 7. whome Protest. call Hilddebrand, and hate most of all the Popes *lib.* 1. *ep.* 31. calleth King William, *the most louing and principall sonne of the Roman Church*. And *ep.* 69. saith: That King William reioised in his promotion, and shewed all the affection of a good sonne from his hart. And *l.* 6. *ep.* 30. *VVe loued alwaies King VVilliam peculierlie amongst the rest of that dignity*. And *lib.* 7. *ep.* 26. saith, that his Queene Mathildis offered him *what soeuer we would haue of theirs he might haue it without delay*. And *lib.* 7. *ep.* 5. saith, *That the King of England although that in some things he behaued himselfe not so religiouslie, notwithstanding becaufe he would not consent to enter into league against the Sea Apostolicke with some, that were enemies to the Crosse of Christ, being requested therto but compelled by oath the Priests to leaue wiues, the lay men to pay the tenths which they detayned, is praysworthie sufficientlie and more to be honored than other Kings*. This thus Pope that then liued. Seuenthlie King William although he deposed almost all the old English nobilitie, yet he tooke not vpon him

to

Loue betvvene P. Hildebrand and K. VVilliam.

to depofe anie one Bifhop or Abbot but
procured Pope Alexander to fend down
two Legats to do it . Eightlie, King
William preferred Lanfrank to the Archbifhoprick of Canterburie as all know,
whome the proteftants confeffe to haue
bene a notorious Papift. Ninthlie, he
glorieth in his death bed (as Stow
Chron. *pag*, 171. Baron *An.* 1084. and an
other author then prefent write) that he
had increafed 9. Abbeies of Monks, and
one of Nonnes, and that in his dayes 17.
monafteries of Monks and fix of Nonnes
were builded: *VVith fuch compaffe*, faith he,
*Normandie is fenced and all things which any
noble men in Lands or Rents haue giuen to God
or Saints for their fpirituallhealth, I haue curte-
oufly graúted and confirmed their Charters. Thefe
ftudies I haue followed from my firft yeares. This I
leaue vnto mine heires to be kept in all times. In this
my children follow me continuallie , that here and
for euer before God and men yow may be honored.*
Finallie as Stow p. 174. and the faid Authors report, being to giue vp the ghoft
with great deuotion he lift vp his eyes to **Heauen,**
and holding abroad his hands faid, I commend my
foule vnto our bleffed Ladie Marie Mother of
God, that she by her holie praiers may reconcile
me to her moft dere fonne our Lord Iefus
Chrift . And with thefe wordes (faith
Stow) he prefentlie yelded vp the
ghoft

marginal notes:

K. VVill. Conq. tooke not vpon him to depofe Bifhops or difpofe of Bifhop-ricks.

8

9

VVhat account K. vvill. made of Monafte-ries.

Monafte-ries fence of Coun-tries.

10

K. VVil-liams laft vvords praying to our ladie.

ghoft. And *pag.* 176. he addeth that he was buried at a Maffe, and that the Preacher defired all to pray for the dead Prince. This was the ende of this victorious and vndoubted Catholick King.

Fox his confes: of the Cath. time vnder K. VVilliam Conq. and fince.

2. And fo Catholick thefe times fince the Conqueft haue bene, as Fox Acts *pag.* 167. fpeaking after his maner faith, *Before the Conqueft infection and corruption of religion vvas great, but in the times folovving it did abound in exceßiue meafure*. Which he faid onely becaufe the hiftories of the times folowing are more exant & perfect, and fo afforde more playne and more frequent teftimonie of the Catholick faith than thofe of the former times, though they as yow fee afford fufficient. Bilfon alfo of Obed. *pag.* 321. faith *that the Pope inforced vpon the Normans the headship of the Church*. Wherin he confeffeth that the Normans admitted a cheefe pointe of

Saints in K. VVilliams time.

Papiftrie. In this kings tyme Iyued that holy Queene of Scotland S. Margaret grandchild vnto king Edmund Ironfide, whofe holy life is written by Tungat an Englifh man Bifhop of S. Andrews in Scotland. Who was faith Bale Cent. 2. *cap.* 60. *ocula\ißimus teŝtis Virtutum eius: a moſt certain eye vvitneſſe of her vertues*. And Fox Acts. *pag.* 185. calleth her *vertuous and deuout ladie*. And yet was fhe a manifeft Papift.

For

For being to die she called for Priests,
and made her confession, and was anoiled and howseled, as testisie the said Tur-
got, Houed. An. 1093. Hunting. *lib. 7. pag.*
373. and others. In her life tyme *She was*
a maintaner of pietie , instice, peace, frequent in
prayer, who punished her body with fasting and
watching. and of this holy Queene is his
present Maiestie descended by both the
Royal lines of England and Scotland.
In this Kinges tyme also liued Berengarius a French Deacon, who is the first
that is named to haue denyed the real
presence of Chrifts bodie and blood in
the Eucharist , *as the holy Church teacheth*
saith malmsb. *l. 3.* who liued about that
time. The same denied some ancient hereticks in S. Ignatius time as he testifieth
ep:ad Smyrn. but nameth none. But they
were then so fully put downe, as from
thence to Berengarius (which is almost a
thousand yeares) none is found to haue
denyed Chrifts real presence in the Sacrament, besides such as denyed that he had
any real body at all. Berengarius denied
also marriag to be lawful and the baptifme of Infants, as Durand then Bishop of
Liege writeth in his epistle to Henrie
then King of France *tom. 3. Biblio. Sanctor.*
in fine. and Protestants confesse , namely Oecolampadius *l. 3. p.* 710. Crispin *l.* of

Florent
An. 1093.
Malb. *l. 4.*

Holines
of Q.
Margaret.

Berengar.
vvhod e-
nied the
real pre-
sence de-
nied also
mariage
and bap-
tisme of
Infants.
Massou.
Annal.
franc. *lib. 3.*

Z   the

the Church p. 289. But at laſt this Berengarius recanted all his hereſies and died a
good Catholick, as the ſaid Malm. wit-
neſſeih. Againſt him wrote our great
learned Preiat Lanfranc & many others.

King VVillam Rufus XXXIIII.

3.   THe 34. Chriſtian King of England was William Rufus *Anno*

Vertues of K. Rufus for a time.

1088. and reigned 13. yeares. *He* (ſaith Stow
Chron. *pag*. 179.) *as long as Lanfranc liued ſeemed to abhorre all kinde of vice, ſo that he was
accounted a mirror of Kings.* Cooper *Anno*
1089. writeth that *in martiall policie he was
verie expert, and diligent in all matters he went
about, ſtedfaſt and ſtable in his promiſſe, and meruailous painfull and laborious. But at laſt
vices ouerwhelmed his vertues.* His Roman

His Rom. Religion
1

religion is manifeſt. Firſt becau'e as
Malmsb. hath *lib.* 4. Paris *An.* 1087. He
was brought vp by Lanfranc, and by his
meanes chiefly, made King. Secondlie

2

becauſe Fox writeth *lib.* 4. *pag*. 184. *Lincoln
Minſter in his time had a Romish dedication.* And
as Paris ſaith *pag*. 767. that being done *the
king called two Cardinalls who were preſent, who
had receaued fulnes of power of our Lord the
Pope for the diſpoſition of Bishopricks, and of the
ſame Church. The ordination was ſuch, that the
                                                      Bishop*

Bishop being chosen & the Canons placed in their possession, from thence forth they should in orderlie discipline of life serue God and his blessed mother day and night. Thirdlie becaule (as **3** Stow hath Chron. *pag.* 160.) Rufus gaue to the Monkes of the Charitie the manner of Berdmonsey, and builded them a new house. And in his Charter yet extant he confirmeth his Fathers graunt to the Monasterie of Batel and saith he doth it *for the soule of his said Father, and also of his* A plaine *mother matildis of godlie memorie, and for the* Papistical *soule of his most glorious predecessor King Edward,* of K. *for my owne saluation likewise and my Successors,* Rufus. *and for the quiet rest of those that were slaine there in batel.* VVhich how euident a signe of Papistrie it is hath bene shewed before. Fourthly Rufus being once very sick **4** made his confession to S. Anselm. Malm. 1. Pont: *p.*217.and nominated him Archb. of Canterb. whom the Protestants confesse to haue byn a notorious Papist. Fift- **5** ly Malm. 1. *pont.p.* 220. Florent. *An.* 1095. Fox *lib.*4. *p.*185. and others testify, that *he sent two messengers to Pope Vrban to entreat him to send his Pal for him (Anselm) and with charge & paines prouided it.* And that Gualter the Popes Legat delt so wirh the King, that Vrban (there being an other Antipope) was proclamed lawfull Pope throughout all the realme. VVherfore though this

Z 2   King

king tooke vpon him to forbid Bishops to account any for Pope, or to appeale to the Pope without his licence (wherin he was resisted by Saint Anselm as yow may see in Malmsb.1. Pont. *pag.* 217. 219.) it argueth not that he thought he might do so lawfully any more, than that he might be (as Fox termeth him *pag.* 1092.) *a piller and rauiner rather of Church goods,* or as Godwin in the life of S. Anselme termeth him *the most Sacrilegious Simonest that euer reigned in England.* In so much as Hunting. and Paris say *An.* 1100. when he dyed, he had in his hands one Archbishoprick, two Bishopricks, 12. Abbeies, &, as Stow saith *pag.* 183. said he would haue all the spirituall liuings in the whole Realme. And Malmsb. *lib.* 4. addeth that he encoraged the Iewes to dispute with the Christians, swearing that if they ouercame he would be of their religion. Other horrible Villanies of his, report Hunt. Paris *l.cit.* and others more, which declare that he little cared to break Gods or the Churches lawes, but conuince no more but that he was an ill Christian, and an ill Catholick for life. In this Kings tyme dyed S. Wulstan Bishop of Worceter, whome Godwin calleth *Saint*, and confesseth that men had a great esteeme of *him for his streitnes of life, and opinion of holines,*

Saints in K. Rufus time.

And

And of other Authors of that tyme he is much commended , Marian , Florent. Chron. Malmsb. 1. Pont. And his life is to be seene in Surius Tom. 1. In this Kings time also S. Stephan Harding an Englishman founded the order of Cistertian or white Monks, as Bale Cent. *2. cap.* 63. Fox Acts *pag.* 185. Malmsb. *lib.* 4. Reg. *pag.* 127. and others write. Malmsb. termeth him *The cheefe Author of the whole fact , and especiall ornament of our dayes.* In this kings time died also the forsaid Saint Osmund Bishop of Salsburie, the Author of that manner of saying masse, Breuiarie, and administring Sacraments , which is called the vse of Sarum.

Cistertian order founded by an Englishman.

King Henrie I. XXXV.

4. THe 35. Christian king was Henrie 1. yongest sonne to William Conqueror, and borne in England, began his Reign *An.* 1100. and reigned 35. yeares. *For his knowledg* (saith Fox *lib.* 4. *p.* 191.) *and science in the 7. liberall sciences, he was Sirnamed Beuclerck.* Cooper and Stow *An.* 1101. say he *was a noble & valiant Prince , & mightie of body of comly visage , plesant , & sweete countenance, excellent in wit & eloquence , & had good hap in battel.* The like write Catholicks of him.

Valour and qualities of K. Henrie. 1.

Z 3   As

1 As for his religion it is euident to be Roman Catholicke. Firſt becauſe his Archb. was S. Anſelm, to whoſe piety he aſcribed his conqueſt of Normandie: Ediner in vit.

2 Anſelm. Secondly becauſe he built a Church at Dunſtable, and *by the authority of Eugenius 3. Pope* (ſaith Cambd. in Brit. *p.* 350.) *placed there Canons regulers.* Paris *p*. 98 and VValſing. *p.* 38. name foure Monaſteries

3 which he built. Thirdly becauſe (as Stow ſaith *p* 204.) Atholph Prior of S. Oſwald

4 was his Confeſſor. Fourthly he yeelded vp the Inueſtiture of Biſhops. Fox 194. Malmsb. 5. Reg *p.* 152. Florent. VVeſtmon.

5 *An.* 1107. Houed. 1108. Fiftly ſaith Paris *p.* 96. Houed. An. 113'. Malmsb. *lib.* hiſt. nouel. *lib.* 1. Pope Innocent the ſecond was moſt honorably entertained of him, and by his help was admitted through all

6 France. Sixthe Fox *p.* 192. ſetteth downe this letter of his to Pope Paſcall. [To the venerable Father Paſcall cheefe Biſhop Henry by the grace of God K. health. I greatly reioice with you at your promotion the See of the Roman Church requeſting that the freindſhip which was betwixt my Father & your Predeceſſors may alſo continew betwexne vs firme & ſure.] And at the ſame time ſaith Fox *pag.* 193. he ſent another letter to the ſaid Pope crauing of him his pal for Gerard Archb.

of

of Yorke, the forme wherof here followeth. To his reuerend and beloued Father
Pascall Vniuersall Pope, Henry by the
grace of God king of England] & endeth
thus [I pray our Lord long preserue your
Apostleship.] Ibid. Fox wriceth that this
kings Embasador said to the Pope [that
England of a long continuance had euer
bene a prouince peculier to the Church
of Rome and paid duely vnto the same
yearely tribute] Finally in this kings
time the Cistertian Monsts entred into
England. Fox *Acts p.* 185. Bale Centur. *2. c.*
63. And in his last sicknes as the Archb. of
Roan writeth to Pope Innocent in
Malmsb. hist. Nouel. *l.* 1. *he confessed his sinnes*
was absolued, and receaued the body and blood of
our Lord with great deuotion , & lastly at his
own request was aneyled. And the Kings
Attorney in the arainment of F. Garnet
calleth this Kings time *the very midnight of*
Popery. In this Kings time say Florent. &
Houed. *An.* 1104. was the Shrine of S. Cutbert opened by Raph Abbot, after Archb.
of Canterb. & found incorrupt, in the presence of Prince Alexāder after K. of Scotland, & many more. In his time died S.
Anselm before spokē of, & Thomas Archb.
of York , who when the phisitians tould
him that he must ether vse the company
of a woman or die, he made choise of

Z 4   death

Marginal notes:

K Henrie
1. Profes-
seth the P.
to be vni-
uersal. P.

Cistertian
monks
enter into
England.

Manner
of King
Henries
death.

S. Cut-
berts bo-
die found
incorrupt.

Saints.
See Saint
Anselmes
miracles
in malb. 1.
Pont.
p. 216. 129.

Archb.
Thom.
vvould ra
ther die
than vfe
the com-
panie of a
vvoman.

death . For which Godwin in his life accounteth him a martyr , though a little before he had faid that Saint Ofwald in debarring Priefts from marriage had fet forth the droctrine of Diuels.

King Stephan XXXVI.

Valour of
King
Stephen.

5. THe 36. Chriftian king of England was Stephan , grandchild by a daughter vnto the Conqueror . He was crowned *An.* 1135. and reigned 19. yeares, *He vvas* (faith Malmsb. *lib.*1. Hift. Nouel.) *Diligent and ftout in war, of an immoderat mind, prompt to enterprife any hard thing, & to his enemies inexorable , affable to all men.* Weftmon, *An.*154. *A notable foldier and in courage excelling.* The like hath Hunt. *l.*8. Cooper *Anno* 1136. And Stow p.206 . faith he was *a noble man and paffing hardie, of paffing comlie fauour and perfonage, in all princelie vertues he excelled, as in Martiall policie, affabilitie,gentlenes , and bountifull liberalitie towards all.* His Roman religion is cleare. Firft becaufe his brother Henry Bifhop of Winchefter was in his time Legat to the Pope. Hunting. *l.* 8. Malmsbur. hift. Nouell. Secondly, becaufe Stow faith *pag.* 215. He founded the Abbeis of Coxall in Effex , of Furnis

His Rom.
Religion.

1

2

in

in Lankafhier, of Feuerfham in kent, a
Nonry at Carew , an other at High-
am. Thirdly , becaufe being to giue battel on Candlemas day, he heard Maffe
(faith Hunting, *lib.* 8.) and the candle
which he offered, broke ; and the *Pix
in which the body of Chrift was put fell downe
vpon the Altar*. which were taken for
aboadments of the loffe of the batell.
Fourthly, becaufe in this Kings time
began (faith Fox Acts *pag.* 201.) *appel-
lations from Councells to the Pope by Henrie* Bifhopp of Winchefter brother to
the King. In this Kings time *Anno*
1137. faith Bale Cent. 2. *cap.* 63. began
in England the Monkes called Robertins
of Robert their beginner. But Capgraue in the life of Robert faith thefe
Monks were Ciftertians. In this time
(faith Bale ibidem) entred into England the Moncks called *Præmonftratenfes,*
Anno 1145, And *Anno* 1147. began the
Gilbertin Monks and Nonnes, founded by S. Gilbert Lord of Sempring-
ham. And this time Nicolas Breack-
fpear an Englifh Monke and Cardinall,
afterward Pope, conuerted Norway,
(fayth Bale *l. cit.*) *ad Papifmum, to Papiftrie.* And fo manifeftly were the times
vnder King Stephen Papifticall , as Bale
Cent.2.c. 74. fpeaking of them faith *here we*
                                                    vnder-

*Fox pag.
201. Cambd
pag. 681.
&. 388.*

3

4

Monks
enter into
England.

Cambd.
Brit. p. 475.
Neubrig.
l. 1. *c.* 16.
Capgraue
in Gil-
berto.

vnderstand that there was great want of the pure doctrine of Christ Iesus . And *cap. 73.* faith it *was a most corrupt age .* In this Kings time died alfo Saint William Archbifhop of York & Kinfman to King Stephan a man (faith Godwin in his life) *very noble by birth but much more noble in vertue and good maners , many miracles* (writeth he) *are faid to be vvrought at his Tombe.*

Saints.

Miracles.

King Henrie II. XXXVII.

6. IN the yeare of our Lord 1155. King Henrie fecond, grandchild by the Empreffe Maude to Henri,1. fucceded and reigned 33. yeares. *He was* (faith Fox Acts *pag.* 234. *Eloquent , learned , manly and bould in chiualrie .* The like hath Cooper *Anno.* 1155. and Stow *pag.* 216. Cambd. *pag.* 247. hath much of his praife out of Catholick writers of that time. *Vnder him* (faith Fox Acts *pag.* 224.) *the Dominion of England extended fo far as hath not bene feene before VVhom Hiftories record to haue poffeffed vnder his rule Firft Scotland, to whome VVilliam King of Scots with his Lords temporali and fpirituall did homage both for them and their fucceffors , the feale wherof remaineth in the Kings Trefurie, as alfo Ireland, England , Normandie,*

The vvorthines of King Henric. 2.

Guiens

Guiens, Aquitan vnto the mountains of Pirenei.
He was offered alſo to be King of Ieru-
ſalem by the Patriarch and Maiſter of the
Hoſpitall. Now let vs ſee what was the
religion of this potent King, and of Eng- His Rom.
land when her Dominion was the largeſt Religion.
that euer it was. Firſt Fox Acts *pag.* 234. **1**
telleth how this King *heard Maſſe*. Se- **2**
condly Stow *pag.* 232. telleth how he built
the Nonrie of Font Euerard, the Priorie
of Stoneley, of S. Martin in Douer, and
of Baſing weck. To which Cambd. in
Brit. *pag.* 488. addeth Newſted in Nottingham ſhier, and *pag.* 321. Cicceſter in **3**
Gloſterſhier. Thirdly he brought Car- Carthu-
thuſians into England and built them a Monks
houſe at Withan, Godwin *in vit.* Hugonis come into
Lincoln. Houed. ſaith this was *An.* 1186. England.
Bale Cent. 2. *cap.* 63. ſaith it was 1180.
And after Carthuſians (ſaith he) *came in*
Kinghts of Rhodes and of the Temple. And
Cambd. Brit. *pag.* 728. ſaith the Carmelits
were brought in at this time. Fourthly, **4**
(ſaith Stow *pag.* 216.) he was directed
cheefely by Thomas Becket in all
things. Fiftly, (ſaith the ſame Stow **5**
pag. 218.) He obtained of Pope Adrian
4. both to haue Dominion of the Bal. Cent.
Iriſh people, and alſo to inſtruct them 2 *p.* 180.
in the rudiments of faith. And the Pope
in the letters of the grant calleth him
a Catho-

6

Baron.
tom.12.

a Catholick Prince. Sixtly, he & Lewis King of France going on foote, performing the office of lackeis and houlding the bridel of his horse on the right and left side, conducted Pope Alexāder with great pompe through the Cittie Taciac vnto the riuer of Loir, Robert Monten. Genebre. in Chron. Bale Cent. 2. *c.* 94. Neubrigen *l.* 2. *c.* 14. Thom. Cant. in Ep. ad Henr. 2. Se-

7

nenthly Houed. *p.* 502. setteth doune the letter of Gilbert Bishop of London to the Pope, in which the Bishop writeth that the K. neuer auerted his minde from the Pope, nor euer meant it, but would loue him as a Father, and reuerence the Church of Rome as his mother, and had afsisted the Pope in all his necesfities with all his hart and strength. And *pag.* 550. relateth a letter of Cardinals who writ of the King, how obedient he shewed him selfe to the Church, of which

8

said they *in this our short relation it is not needfull to relate.* Eightly, Fox. *pag.* 227. Cooper An. 1072. and others write, that he agreed with the Pope that he should not hinder appeales to Rome, and that nether the King nor his sonne should departe from Pope Alexander, so long as he should count him or his sonne for Catholicks. Bale Cent. 3. *cap.* 4. saith *He permitted Appeals to the Pope and willingly submitted*
him

him selfe and his Kingdom to the Popes pleasure.
And English men came into greater subiection
of Antichrist than ever at any tyme before.
Ninthly he persecuted certain German
Hereticks, whome Bale Cent. 2. *cap.* 95.
calleth Christians ; and others whome
Bale *cap.* 97. calleth *preachers of Gods word.*
And Houed *pag.* 1573. reporteth that he
and the King of France purposed to goe
in person against the Albigenses, whome
Protestants commenly acount brethrem
of their Church . Finally his death was
thus: *Cùm eger esset* (saith Houed. *pag.* 654.)
VVhen he was sick vnto deathe he caused him self
to be caried into the Church before the Altar and
there he deuoutly receaued the communion of the
body & blood of our Lord confeßing his sinnes, And
being absolued by the Bishop and Clergie he died.
And the times of this King were so manifestly Roman Catholick, as Fox Acts *pag.*
224. saith, *This age was all blinded and corrupted*
with superstition. And yet *pag.* 225. affordeth
it then the name *of a Christian Realme that*
had the word of God. And p. 227. noteth *the*
blind and lamentable superstition and ignorance of
these dayes. Bale Cent. 3. *cap.* 14. cryeth out
that *sub Honorio* 2. *vnder Honorius* 2. *The life of*
man was corrupted vpon earth by Antichristian
Traditions . In this Kings time liued the
holy Eremit S. Gudrig *Vir* (saith Cambd.
Brit. *p.* 668.) *antiqua & Christiana simplicitate*
totus

9

10

See more
of this K.
Rom. re-
lig. in
Baron
tom. 12.

Saints.

totus Deo deuotus, A man of ancient & Chriſtianliē ſimplicitie wholly deuoted to God. Whoſe holines is deſcribed by diuers, Capgraue,

Houed. *Anno.* 1169. VVeſtmon. *Anno.* 1171.
Neubrigen.*lib.* 2. *c.*20. and 28. In his time
alſo liued and died glorious S. Thomas
of Canterb. of whoſe miracles Fox Acts
*pag.*225. ſaith he hath ſeene a booke to the
number of 270. of curing all diſeaſes belonging to man or Woman , amongſt
which he nameth one moſt ſubiect (as
he thought by reaſon of the matter) to
laughter . But who conſidereth , that all
the membres of our body were alike
created of God,& may as wel be reſtored
by him again when they are loſt , and
weigheth the teſtimony which Fox bringeth him ſelf of the miracle, may by this
iudg of the certaintie of the reſt . The
matter was thus. An inhabitāt of Bedford
hauing had by forme of the lawe (which
then was) his eyes pluckt out , and his
ſtones cut away , but vniuſtly , made
prayer to S. Thomas for the reſtoring of
them, which was done. That the man had
bene thus maimed , the Burgeſſes and
Cittizens of Bedford (ſaith Fox) did teſtifie with publick letters. And whither he
was cured or no, was eaſy to know. All
that Fox ſaith againſt this or the reſt of
the miracles is,that there was no neceſsitie
of a

of a miracle in a Christian Realm hauing
the word of God. Forsooth he must, tel
God when there is necessitie, yea tie Gods
hands to do nothing but for necessitie.
Had not the Iewes the word of God
when they had the daylie miracles of
Probatica piscina? Doth not the vertue of
miracles shine in the Church for euer as
the notes of the English Bible imprinted
An.1576. Iohan.14. do teach ? But wel it is
that Saint Thomas his miracles haue so
many and so authenticall testimonies, as
he must needs contemn all humā authoritie who denieth them to haue bene done.

King Richard Cœur de Lion.
XXXVIII.

7. IN the yeare 1189. succeeded K. Richard Coeur de Lion, so sirnamed of
his corage, sonne to King Henrie 2. and
reigned 10. yeares. He was saith Cambd.
de Brit. *pag.* 331. *Animi excelsi & erecti* &c.
Of an high and vpright mind altogether borne
for the Christian common vrelth, Englands
glorie and terror of the Pagans. Cooper *Anno.*
1189, *big of stature, and had a mery counte-*
nance, in vvhich appeared as vvel a pleasant gent-
lenes, as a noble and princely Maiestie, to his
soldiers fauorable, bountifull, desirous of vvar.
Subdued

Valour of
King
Richard
Cœur de
Lion.

Polid.
lib. 14.

Subdued the Kingdom of Ciprus, conquered the Citty of Acon, vanquished the Soldan in the holy Land , whither he went with an army of 30000. foote and 5000. horse. The Roman religion of this famous and magnanimous King is manifest. First because Houed. who then liued *pag.* 656. 657. Paris 205. and others tel the maner of his coronation was thus . The Archb. Bishops Abbots and Priests in Copes with the Crosse before and holy water and incense brought him to the Church. Again he tooke his oath on the Gospel and many reliques of Saints. After coronation began the solemn Masse, and when they came to the offertorie Bishops brought the king to offer, and in like sorte to take the Pax. And after Masse returned again with Procession, Secondly *pag.* 222. Paris telleth how he redeemed the reliques of Ierusalem
„ with 52. thousãd Bisátes. Quatenus (saith
„ he) To the ende that Saints of God whose
„ bones he redeemed in earth might help
„ his soule by their intercessions in heauen.
„ And *pag.* 497. He obtained of the Soldan
„, that a certain Priest at the Kings stipend
„ might euery day celebrate masse of the
„ holy Crosse at our Sauiours Sepulcher
during the time of the truce . Thirdly retiring to England saith Westmon. *Anno.* 1194. he

His Rom. religion.
1

k. Richard crovvned at masse.

2

3

1194. he visited S. Thomas of Canterb. S. Edmund, and S. Albons Shrines, and after went against his Rebells in Nottingham. Fourthly Houed. *pag.* 658. setteth downe a Charter of his where he graunteth Land to S. Cutbert, [For the soule of our Father and Ancestors, and of our Successors, and for our owne and our heires saluation, and for the confirmation and increase of our Kingdome.] Fiftly Houed. *p.* 677. hath a letter of his to Pope Clement 2. which beginneth thus: [To his most reuerend Lord and blessed Father by the grace of God cheefe Bishop of the holy Apostolick See, health and affection of true deuotion in our Lord. The facts of Princes haue better end whe they receaue assistance and fauour from the See Apostolick. [And *pag.* 706. When king Richard went to the holy Land, he left the care of the gouernment of his kingdome vnto the See Apostolick. And *pag.* 753. The same Houed. setteth downe a letter of Pope Celestin in which the Pope saith thus, [The Church of England hath alwaies kept the sincerity of her deuotion and ancient faith with the Roman Church] Finally a little before S. Richards death (saith Fox Acts *pag.* 249.) *Three Abbots of the Cistertian order came vnto him to whome he was confessed, and when he saw them somwhat stay*

4

5

England alwaies deuout to the Church of Rome.

9

A a   *as*

at his abſolution ſaid theſe words , that he did willingly commit his ſoule to the fier of Pur-

Saints.

gatorie there to be tryed til the Iudgment in hope of Gods mercie . In this publick pro-feſsion of Roman Catholick faith gaue this renowned King vp his ſoule to God. In this Kings time died *Anno.* 1189. the forſaid Saint Gilbert , who of his order erected 13. Monaſteries in

Polid.*l.*14.

England. Then alſo liued Saint Hugh of Lincoln, of whome we ſhall ſpeake hereafter.

King Iobn. XXXIX.

8. THe 39. King was King Iohn, brother to King Richard, who began his Reign *Anno.* 1199. and reigned 17. yeares. Of this King ſome igno-rant Proteſtants brag, as if he had bene a Proteſtant. Bale *Cent.* 1. *cap.* 75. be-

polid.*l.*15.

cauſe for a time he diſobeyed the Pope, commendeth him *of valor, liberalitie, & Chriſtian pietie.* But with ſhame inough for he loſt all in manner that his Pre-deceſſors had in France , which was

Qualities of K. Ihon.

neere as much as England it ſelfe , and had almoſt loſt England too . *VVas,* as the Earle of Northampton ſaith of him in the araignment of Garnet ,

im-

impious, as wel sans foy, as sans terre; and that
he was *as likly to haue departed with his soule
as his Crowne, if neceßitie had preßed him.*
Nether was he ill onely to him selfe,
but to his people and Contrie, from
whome being not content by him selfe
to extort what he would, sent for many
thousand Flemings to do the same, to
whome he ment to giue Norfolk and
Suffolk, Paris *pag.* 360.367. And *pag.* 325.
he nameth the Embassador whome King
Iohn sent to the Mahometan King of
Africk to offer the subiection of him self
and his Kingdom to him, and to accept
the law of Mahomet, which Paris learnt
of them, to whome one of the Embassadors tould it. Neuertheleße what Christian religion he had, is euident to haue
bene Roman Catholick. First because he
was chosen King cheefely by meanes
of Archbishop Hubert, Paris *pag.* 264.
who was a notorious Papist. Secondly
because vpon his coronation he tooke
his oath vpon the reliques of Saints,
Paris *pag.* 263. and next day after his coronation went on Pilgrimage to S. Albans,
pag. 264. at Lincoln offered a chalice of
gould. *p.* 273, helped to carry on his shoul-
ders the body of S. Hugh *pa.* 274. Houed.
pag. 812. Thirdly he heard Maße (saith
Stow *pag.* 246.) and fell downe before the

His Rom:
Religion.
1
Stovv.
pag. 244.
2

3

A a 2   *Abbots*

Abbots of Cistterce desiring to be admitted of them
4   *for a brother.* Fourthly he founded a goodly
monastery at Beulieu, & erected a Nonry
at Godstow *topray* (saith Camb. Brit. p. 329)
*for his Fathers soule, for that perswasion had then
possessed the minds of all men.* And in his Charter to Batel Abbey commandeth all his
Iustices to defend the Possessions of that
monastery *sicut* (saith he) *nostra propria : as
our owne.* And Regist. Burriense saith, he
gaue a great Saphir, and a Ruby to S. Ed-
5   munds Shrine . Fiftly when Grecians
came to dispute against his faith he would
not hear them, Bale Cent. 3. *cap.* 37. ex
6   Paris. Sixtly Fox Acts. *pag.* 253. writeth
that King Iohn submitted himselfe to the
Court of Rome, and as Bale saith Cent. 3.
cap. 75. *Acknowledged the Pope to be head of all
Christians.* And though he disobeyed for a
time the Pope, yet that he did not for a
difference in religion , but because the
Pope would make an Archb. of Canterb.
whome the King misliked . And as

For vvhat   Cooper saith *Anno* 1201. *did this not vpõ iudg-*
cause K.   *ment to set vp true religion* (saith he) *but vpon*
Ihon diso-   *couetousnes and of a forward mind.* Finally,
beyed the   vpon his deathbed (saith Fox *Acts pag.* 256.
Pope   *he much repented his former life,* and had (saith
for a
time.   Stow *pag.* 262.) a Confessor at his death,
7   and receaued the Sacrament at the hands
of the Abbot of Crocston, and died with
thesè

these words: *Deo & sancto VVolstano animam me am commendo*: I commend my soul to God and S. VVolstan, Paris *pag.* 389. Of the manner of his death Fox *Acts. pag.* 256. writeth thus: *Some write, that he died of sorrow as Polidor, some of surfeting, as Redinger ; some of a bloodie flux, as Houed. some of a burning ague ; some of a colde sweat, some of eating apples, some of eating peares, some plummes, &c.* yet (saith he) *most writers agree that he was poisoned by the Monke Symon of Swinsted.* But who those were, he writeth not, nor could name one besides a namelesse Author of that Chronicle, which, because Caxton printed it is cald, *Caxtons Chronicle.* And it is as Stow well saith *pag.* 494. *a fabulous booke.* And therfore Bale *Cent.* 3. *cap.* 75. referreth this to report, saing: *Vt ferunt, as men report.* But who will not beleeue rather Paris *pag.* 389. Westmon. *Anno* 1216. and others liuing in that same time, or sone after, who say, he died of surfit & sorrow, then a Chronicle accounted by Protestants themselues *a fabulous booke* or writen by a namelesse Author long after that time. In this Kings time, died that glorious Saint, Saint Hugh Bishop of Lincolne, and Carthusian Monke, whome Godwin, in his life, calleth *Saint.* And saith, *By his integritie of life and conuersation, and the opinion of diuers Miracles wrought by him,* hath

VVestmon
An. 1216.

K. Ihon
dieth in
profession
of the
Cathol.
faith.

Saints.

hath purchafed vnto him felfe the honor and reputation of a Saint. He addeth alfo, that S. Hugh. *Grew very famous far and neere for his extraordinarie abftinence and aufteritie of life.* And that king Iohn and king William, king of Scotts, for great reuerence they bare to his holines, helped to carry his Corps from the gate of the Cittie, vntill it came to the Church dore.

King Henrie the III.

XL.

9. IN the yeare 1216. fucceded, king Henrie 3. fonne to king Iohn, and reigned 56. yeares, dyed *Anno.* 1273. *He was* (faith Cooper *Anno.* 1218.) *of nature gentle, of minde fage, and wife.* And fo pious, as Leolin Prince of Wales, (faith Fox *Acts pag.* 280.) protefted, that he feared more his almes, than his puiffance. And Weftmon. *Anno* 1272. fpeaking of this king, faith. *Of how great innocencie, of how great patience, and of how great deuotion he was in obeying his Sauiour, our Lord knoweth, and they which faithfully adhered to him, and of how great merit he was with God the miracles after his death teftifie.* The Roman religion of this vertuous king is manifeft. Firft, be-

cause

Marginal notes:
VVifdom and pietie of King Henrie. 3.

His Rom. Religion.
1

cauſe, as Fox ſaith in his *Acts pag.* 257. He
was crowned by Swall, the Popes Legat ; and Stow addeth , *pag.* 263. *Being
crowned , the gouernment of the King and his
Kingdome was committed to the Legat , to the
Biſhop of VVincheſter ,* &c. Secondly , becauſe Continuator of Paris, who then
liued , ſaith *pag.* 1349 . and Walſingham in Edward. 1. *pag.* 19. *Euery day he
was accuſtomed to heare three ſonge Maſſes , and
deſirous to heare moe ſerued daylie Prieſts celebrating priuatly , and when the Prieſt did eleuat our
Lords bodie, he vſed to hould the Prieſts arme , and
to kiſſe it .* And when that Lewis king of
France ſaid vnto him , that he ſhould
oftner heare ſermons, he anſwered, I had
rather ſee my freind often than heare an
other ſpeake of him , though neuer ſo
wel. Thirdly, his Confeſſor was a Dominican Frier named Iohn Derlington,
Bale *Cent.* 4. *cap.* 56. and Walſing. *in Edward.*
1. *pag.* 7. His Queene alſo after his death
became a Nonne , Walſing. *pag.* 14.
Fourthly, in this Kings time came into
England diuers orders of Friers , as the
Dominicans , to whome , ſaith Stow *pag.*
268. the King aſſigned a houſe in Oxford;
The Gray Friers , Cooper , *Anno* 1222.
The Croochet Friers , *Anno.* 1244. Bale
Centur. 4. *cap.* 3. The Auſtins Friers',
Anno. 1252. *Centur.* 4. *capit.* 17. to whome

Marginal notes:

2

K.Henrie
3 daily
heard 3.
ſung
Maſſes.

Deuotion
of King
Hen.3.
Bal. Cent.
4 *cap.* 46.

3

A.Quene
a Nonne

4

Diuers
kinds of
Friers
enter into
England.

A a 4 *cap.*

*cap.*46. he addeth the Paulins, the Friers of Armenia, the 'Friers *de pœnitentia*, the Friers *de Viridi Valle* , and the Bonhomes. Which laſt order Rodulphus *l.* 2.|*de Sancto Franciſco*, ſaith, was iuſtituted by Richard Earle of Cornwall, and brother to King Henrie . Fiftly, when the Pope ſent a Legat into England, ſaith Paris *pag.* 589. *the King met the Legat moſt dutifully at the Sea coaſt, and bowing his head to his knees côducted him moſt reſpectiuely to the inermoſt parts of his Kingdome, when he departed brought him with great honor to the Sea.* Stow *Chron. Anno* 1241.

5

Sixtly, becauſe (as is to be ſeene in Fox *Act.*287.& others) He wrote to the Pope thus: *Sanctiſſimo in Chriſto Patri &c.* [To his moſt holy Father & Lord in Chriſt Innocent, by the grace of God cheefe Biſhop health and kiſſes of his bleſſed feete.] And in the letter, [May it pleaſe your Fatherhood, we beſeech yow that our lawes and liberties which yow may righly repute none other but your owne, yow will receaue to your tuitiô to be côſerued whole & ſound.] Vpon which words Fox maketh this note: *The K. in too much ſubiection to the Pope* . And in a letter in Paris *pag.*839 The K. profeſſeth to the Pope that [In all the time of our reign, we haue ſubmitted our ſelues & our kingdom in all & through all things to the wil of your Father hood.] And

6

K. Henrie 3. calleth the P Lord in Chriſt & offereth to kiſſe his feet.

And *pag.* 863. he citeth letters of the Pope in which he professeth. [That amongst the rest of the Kings of the whole world, we embrace in the armes of our finguler loue our moft deere fonne in Chrift the renowned King of Englãd, who as a Prince Catholick and deuout , hath alwaies ftudied to honor the Roman Church his mother with a filiall fubiection and dutifull deuotion , becaufe he would no way depart from her good pleafure, but rather what things he vnderftood to be gratfull and pleafing to her , he hath performed with a ready carefulnes.] And againe. *pag.* 887. alleadgeth other letters of the Pope to the King, wherin he faith :] Towards your perfon , as to a fonne and fpeciall deuout of the Apoftolick Sea, we carying a Fatherly affection of loue do willingly giue audience to your requefts , as far as we may with God and do impart our benign fauor. To thefe letters I will add two other publick letters of the nobilitie and Commons , and of the Clergie at the fame time, taken out of Fox *p.* 288. Paris *pag.* 901. and others . [To the reuerend Father in Chrift Pope Innocent cheefe Bifh. The nobles with the Communalty of the whole Realme of England fending greeting with kiffing of his bleffed feete. Our mother the church of Rome we loue

with

Profeffion of the King.

The popes teftimonie of K Henric. 3.

Profeffion of the nobilitie and Cõmons of Englãd of their fubiection to the Pope.

with all our hartes as our duty is, and couet the increafe of her honor with fo much affection as we may, as to whome always we ought to fly for refuge. *Item.* Ney ther is it to our faid mother vnknowne, how beneficiall and bountifull a giuer the Realme of England hath bene now a long time, for the more amplifying of her exaltation . *Againe* Our king being a Catholick Prince, & wholly giuen to his deuotions and feruice of Chrift, fo as he refpecteth not the health of his owne body, will feare and reuerence the See Apoftolick , and as deuont fonne of the Church of Rome, defireth nothing more, than to aduance the ftate and honor of the fame.) And the faid Fox *pag.* 291. and Paris and Weftmon. *An.* 1247. fet downe an other letter of the Clergy and Communalty of Canterbury thus. (To the moft holy Father in Chrift Lord Innocent by Gods prouifion cheefe Bifhop: The whole Communalty both of the Clergy and laity of the Prouince of Canterbury fendeth deuout kiffing of his bleffed feete . Like as the Church of England, fince it firft receaued the Catholick faith, haue alwayes fhewed it felfe faithfull and deuout in adhering to God & our holy Mother the Church of Rome ftudying with al kind of feruice

to

England euer fince her firft Chtiftia-nitie deuont to the Church of Rome,

to pleafe & ferue the fame, and thincketh
neuer otherwife to do, but rather to continew and increafe as fhe hath begun : So
now the fame Church moft humbly pro-
ftrat befor the feete of your holines, moft
earneftly intreat, &c.) And the fame
perfons writing to the Cardinals, call
them *Bafes fulcientes Ecclefiam Dei, Pillers vn-*
derpropping the Church of God. Moreouer the
faid Paris *pag.* 929. hath the letters of
the Religious men to the fame Pope
in thefe words. (To our moft holy
Father & deere Lord in Chrift Innocent
by the grace of God chæfe Paftor of the
vniuerfall Church, his deuout fonnes the
Abbots and the Priors of this Prouince
of Canterbury and Yorke health and
kiffes of your bleffed feete. The whole
Church is gouerned vnder one Father &
Paftor, alfo the Church of England is a
moft fpeciall member of the Church of
Rome.) And *pag.* 930. The Nobles, Clergy, and Vniuerfall People (wifh as
their dutyi is health reuerently to fuch
a great Bifhop.) And *ibidem* : The
king writeth againe thus. (He knoweth who is ignorant of nothing, that
we alwayes placed our mother the Roman Church in the bowels of our fin-
cere affedion as her, whome we would
loue, and vnto whome in imminét inftáts
of

of necefsitie, as a fonne vnto his mother, whome fhe ought to fofter and norifh from her dugges of milk, we would recur.

Thus the King, Clergie, Religious, Nobles and Commons doe moft plainly and publickly profeffe their Catholick religiõ, and fubiection to the Pope, and his fpirituall fuperioritie ouer them, in fo much as Godwin in the life of Sewal Archb. of York, faith : *Thſ King fubiected, and as it were proſtrated him felfe to the Pope.* And Bale *Cent. 4.cap.23.*noteth that *King Henrie the third did not reigne but bore the Image of the Beaſt.* And *cap.*6. ſpeaking of the time of this King, faith, *The healthful truth was vanished out of thſ Land, men being led into perdition.* And *cap.34. Vnder King Henry 3.ther was great decay of true faith in Chriſt euen vnto our tyme,* in the merits *of condignitie and congruall of the Papiſts, in Indulgences fuffrages of Saints, vowes, maffes, Purgatorie, Images,* &c. And therfor exhorteth all to trie the doctrine which florifhed from the year 1270. to the yeare 1520. So manifeft a thing it is that this King and all his fucceffors and Realme fince him to the later ende of King Henrie 8. were Roman Catholicks. And albeit this King and the common welth in his tyme repined fome what at the Pope, yet that was not for any points of faith or religion, but onely (as yow may fee in Paris the Kings

Chro-

Proteft.
confeffe
K. Henr.
Cath.
religion.

Proteft.
except
againft all
vvritings
from K.
Hen.3.to
Luthers
time.

Chronicler of that time and others) because he bestowed English Benefices
vpõ Strangers. Which he being then driuen out of Rome and from his own liuing
by a wicked Emperor, was forced to doe.
Finally this King died (as Continuat. Paris then liuing writeth *pag.*1343.) Confessing his sinnes, beating his brest, absolued,
houseled aneiled, & honoring the Crosse.
In this Kings time liued the holy Archb.
of Canterb. S. Edmund, whose body long
after his death was found incorrupt,
Westmon. *An.*1247. and others. Also Saint
Richard Bishop of Chichester, *A man* (saith
Westmon. *An.* 1253.) *Of eminent knowledge,
and singuler or rare sanctitie .* Godwin in his
life saith, *All men greatly reuerenced him, not
onely for his great learning, but much more for his
diligence in preaching, his manifould vertues, and
aboue all his integritie of life and conuersation. In
regard of which and many miracles fathered,*
(saith he) *vpon him, he was canonized .* In this
Kings tyme also died that great Clerck
Robert Grostet Bish. of Lincoln, whome
the Protest. would make one of theirs,
onely, because he mislyked the Popes pre-
ferring of strangers to English Benefices.
But that reason is too friuolous . Besides
that Westmon. *An.*1253. testifieth, that the
same yeare he died he wrote thus to the
Pope, *Salutem,* &c. Your wisedom knoweth

VVestmon
An. 1246.

7

Saints.

See Sur-
tom. 2.

eth that I with a filiall affection deuout-
ly and dutifully obey the Apostolicall
commandements.]And our anciēt wri-
ters are so far from accounting him no
Catholicke, as they esteeme him a Saint,
and relat his miracles, as yow may see in
Paris and Westmon. *Anno.* 1250. Only
Paris *pag.* 1174. saith, that he had *good zeale
but perchance not according to true knowledg.*
In this Kings time liued that great schole
Doctor and Englishman *Alexander de
Hales.*

King Edward I. XLI.

10   IN the yeare of our Lord 1274. succeded Edward. 1. sonne to King
Henry 3. and reigned 34. yeares. *He was*
(saith VValsingham in his Ypodigmate
pag. 98.) *In armes strong, victorious warlick, vvho gained all England from the hands
of valiant Symon de Montfort, VVales he got
from Leolin, Aquitan he wrested from the King*
of Fräce, Scotland he often subdued. Camb. Brit.
pag. 700. saith : *He was a Prince far excelling
in whose most valiāt mind God chosed a most vvorthie lodging, that he might match the heigt of
royal maiesty, not only vvith fortitude & vvisedom
but*

bat with bewtie alfo and comlynes of bodie,
whome fortune in the prime flower of his age
trained vp in many warrs and moft difficult times
of the Common welth, whilft that fhe difpo-
fed him for Brittifh Empire . VVhich when he
was eftablifhed in , he *fo gouerned hauing*
ouercome the VVelch men *, and triumphed ouer*
the Scotts , that by good right he is efteemed
another ornament of Brittanie . The like
high praifes giue him Cooper . *Anno.*
1274. Stow *pag.* 304. Bale *Cent.* 4. *cap.* 58.
and others . As for the Roman religion His Rom. Religion. I
of this renowned Prince , it is moft
cleare . Firft, becaufe (as VValfingham
faith , *Hiftor. pag.* 16.) His wife Queene
Eleoner dying , *with continuall prayers he*
did pray vnto our Sauiour Iefus for her , for
euer ordaining and procuring for her the cele-
brations of Maffes in diuers places of his
Kingdom . In euery place and Vilage where
her Corps refted , the King commanded a Croffe
to be erected in memorie of the Queene , that
her foule might be prayed for of thofe that
paffed by. pag. 33. He Tranflated a ftone
to VVeftminfter, which the Kings of
Scottland at the time of their coronation were wont to vfe for a Throne,
commanding that a Chair fhould be
made therof for Priefts to fit in when
they folemnifed Maffe . Befides *pag.* 13.
His daughter Marie was a Nonne. And

in

in ypodingm. p. 88. He commanded that the Crown of gould that was the king of Scots fhould be offered to S. Thomas the Martyr. And *p. 71. He built an Abbey of Cifter-cian Monkes.* And as Fox faith *Acts pag. 339.* Went on Pilgrimage to our Ladie of Walfingham ; to thanck God for his efcape of a great danger . And of fo great account were religious men in his time, as Stow *pag.* 329. reckneth 61. Abbots , and 8. Priors of the Parliament in his tyme.

2   Secondly , becaufe (as Walfingham hath Hift. *pag* 49.) he writeth thus to the Pope, [To the mofl holy Father in Chrift Boni-faceby the diuine prouidence cheefe Bifhop of the holy Roman and Vniuerfall Church , Edward by the grace of God king of England , Lord of Ireland, Duke of Aquitan , health and deuout kiffes of your bleffed feete. *Beneth.* Wee do hum-blie befeech your holines for as much as &c.] And *p.* 55. He & Fox 341. fet downe a letter , wherin the Nobles and all the Barons affembled together in parliament

This was fealled with 100. feales. *y-podigim pag* 89. write thus to the Pope [We reuerently and humbly befeech your holines, that yow would fuffer our Lord king of Eng-land , who among other fheweth him felf Catholick and deuout to the Roman Church, *&c.*] And Weftmon. *Anno.* 1302. putteth the beginning of this letter thus.

[To

[To the most holy Father in Christ *L.* Boniface by the diuine Prouidence cheefe Bishop of the vniuersall Church, his deuout sonnes Iohn Earle of VVarren, Thomas Earle of Lancaster, *&c.* Deuout kisses of your blessed feete.] Behould how both the king and nobles professe to kisse the Popes feete, & call him cheefe Bishop of the Vniuersall Church. In like manner Pope Boniface writing, in VVestmon. *Anno.* 1301. to king Edward saith: *Scimus fili,* &c. VVe know my sonne, and now a long time experiéce the Mistres of things hath taught vs how towards the Roman mother Church which in her bowels of charitie hath caried yow representing a kingly deuotion, your reuerent regard is shewed, your zeale strengthned, and that in all promptitude yow obeying the true constitutions of the seat make your repose. finally, after the kings death his body lying, at VValtham *Destinati sunt,* &c. saith VValsing. *Hist. pag.* 67. *There were apointed of euery great Monasterie neere bordering six Monks, Cannons, or other religious, which should watch about the body and continually solemnize the funerals. And the Cardinall Legat graunted Indulgence of one yeare to them, which did say our Lords prayer and the Angelicall salutation for the Kings soule.* And so manifestly were the times of this king Roman Catholick, as

3

B b the

the Kings Attorney in the arrainment of
Garnet calleth them, *the verie midnight of*
Poperie. And Bale *Cent. 4. cap. 46.* cryeth
out: *Vnder King Edward the goulden face of*
the primitiue Church was obscured, the cheefest
bewtie of the Gospell changed. The house of Israel
was turned into rubbish, the Ministers of the
Churches degenerated into Dreggs and excre-
ments, the Friers bearing rule. In this Kings
time liued that great schoole Doctor and
English man Richard Middleton, Bale
Cent. 4. cap. 77. and dyed that glorious

saints.

Saint, S. Thomas of Hereford, who in
life was admirable for vertue, and after

Miracles.
See Suf.
tom. 5.

death wonderfull for the greatnes and
multitude of his miracles, which were
examined with such straightnes, and approued with so great authoritie, as who
will beleeue any human testimonie,
can not but beleeue them, as
is to be seene in our an-
cient Manuscript
yet extant.

King

King Edward. 2. XLII.

IN the yeare 1307. Edward 2. sonne to Edward 1. succeeded, and reigned 19. years. *He was* (saith Cooper *Ann* 1308. And Stow *pag.* 337. *faire of body but vnstedfast of maners and disposed to lightnes.* His Roman religion is certain, both by what hath bene saide of his Father, and because Caius *de Antiq. Cantab. pag.* 80. and Stow *pag.* 337. say, *He sued to Pope Iohn* 22. *to renew the priuiledges of the Vniuersities, which he did.* Item. *He builded the Friers Church at Langley.* Stow *pag.* 332. Vowed in the battel of Sterling to build a house for the Carmelits in Oxford, which he performed. Stow *pag.* 334. sent for two Cardinals to make peace betwene him and the Scotts, *pag.* 336. Had a tenth of spirituall goods granted him by the Pope, *pag.* 339. Had a Carmelit for his Confessor Bale *Cent.* 4. *cap.* 96. And as he saith *cap.* 82. *In this Kings tyme came in the Friers De pænitentia into England, to whome the King gaue the Synagogue of the Iewes.* Item the Friers of the order of Martyrs the Sarabitæ, the Paulins, and the Trinitaries. Bale *Centur.* 5. *cap.* 13. calleth these times the middle darknes of Roman superstition. In

Qualities of K Edward. 2. Polid. *l.* 18. His Rom. Religion.

Bb 2   this

The Cath⋅ religion hitherto in Englād vvithout antē op-poſition .

this kings time liued that famous ſubtil doctor Iohannes Scotus. And hitherto haue we proued the Catholicke Roman religion through all our Chriſtian Kings, not only cleare and manifeſt, but alſo without any oppoſition or contradiction ſauing of a few who in Saint Odo his time doubted of the reall preſence, but were ſoone conuerted. Hereafter in our Country the Catholicke religion hath found ſome oppoſition, (though ſmall) by reaſon of VVicklife, (who aroſe in the next Kings time) and his ſellowes.

CHAP. XXVI.

That the Kings of England from Edvvard 3. to Henry 8. vvere all Roman Catholick proued in particuler.

King. Edward. 3. XLIII.

1.

THe 43. Chriſtian King of Eng land was Edward 3. ſonne to

VVorthi-nes of K. Edvvard 3.

Edward 2. Began his reigne *Anno.* 1326. & reigned 51. yeares. *He was* (ſaith Walſin-gahm Hiſt. *Anno* 1376.) *amongſt all the Kings*

of

of the world renowned, benign, gentle, and magnifi- Polid. l. 195
cent, coragious of hart. humble , milde and very
deuout to God . This man (ſaith Cooper *Anno*
1327. And Stow *p.* 438.) *Beſids all other gifts*
of nature was indued with paſsing comly bewty &
fauor, of vvit prouidēt, circumſpect & gentil, doing
nothing without great wiſdome & conſideratiō. Of
excellent modeſty & temperance , and aduanced
ſuch perſons to high dignity as did moſt paſse others
in integrity & innocency of life, in feats of Armes
verie expert. Of his liberality & clemencie he
ſhewed very many great examples . Breefly in
all Princely vertue he was ſo excellent, that few
noble men before his time can be compared to him.
The like praiſe to him giue Fox *Acts pag.*
374. Bale Cent. 6. *cap.* 57. & others. He His victo-
wonne the great battell at Creſsie where ries.
he vanquiſhed the King of France with
two other Kings , tooke Calis , and at
the ſame time ouercame the King of
Scotts ,'and tooke him priſoner. And his
ſonne Edward ſirnamed the black Prince with a very ſmall army got the battell of Poitiers Wherin he tooke the
French king, and after that entred into
Spaine ouercame the king and draue
him out of the Contrie. So that this
king by him ſelfe and his company tooke
two kings, ſlewe one, and vanquiſhed
three others .

Of all our Engliſh kings to Henrie

8. Fox of most all challengeth this King, and faith *pag. 428. That aboue all other Kings to Henrie 8. he was the greatest bridler of the Popes vsurped power. During all his time Iohn VVicklef was maintained with fauor and ayde sufficient.* Indeed King Edward 3 . *Anno* 1374. made a lawe to forbid all procurement of English Benefices from the Pope : But the cause therof was, not that the King thought amisse of the Popes Authority , but becaufe he thought that the execution thereof in this point was incommodious, and inconuenient to his Realme. For other wise none of all our Kings haue auouched the Popes fupremacie , (in which Prote-ftants account the effence of a Pa-pift to confift) fo cleare as he. For in his letters to the Pope extant in Wal-fingham *Anno* 1336, and others he wri-teth thus, (Therfore let not the enuious or finifter interpretation of detractors made of your fonne finde place in the bowels of your mercie and fan&itie who will after the ancient cuftome of our predeceffours , perfift in yours and the See Apoftolickes fauour vntou-ched . But if any fuch fugeftion made againft your fonne fhall forttine to come vnto your holines eares , Let not cre-dit be giuen of your holy deuotion by

your

Otterbor-ne in Ed-vvard: 3.

your holines therunto, before your fonne be heard, who trufteth and euer intendeth to fpeak the tiuth, and to iuftifie euery one of his caufes before your holines iudgement, whofe authority is aboue all earthly creatures which to deny is to approue an herefy.) Behould the King confefsing firft that it was hereditarie to him from his Anceiftors to abide firmely in fauour of the See Apoftolicke. Secondly, that he purpofed euer to do foe. Thirdly that it was herefie to denie the Popes iudgement, *præfidere omni humana creatura* : *To beare rule ouer all human Creatures*. Oh when would this famous King haue thought that any of his Pofteritie fhould make that treafon, which him felfe profeffeth all his Ancestors to haue held, and accounteth it herefie to denie. And Pope Benedict in his anfwer of this letter in VValfingham *pag.* 124. faith thus. [Your Progenitors Kings of England, haue excelled in greatnes of faith and deuotion towards God, and the holy Roman Church, as her peculier fofter-children and deuoted fonnes, and haue preferued the fplendor of their progeny from any darkefome cloud. Betwene the ftate of your Kingdome

King Edvard.3, accounteth it herefie to denie the Popes fuprema-cie.

The fame faith Pope Greg. 11. in VValfing.p.104. Kings of England efpeciall children of the Rom. Church.

and

and alfo of the Kingdome of France we
greatly defire to make a happy fucceffe of
peace and concotd. And againft you my
fonne I cannot fhut vp the bowels of my
Fatherly affe&ion.) To which the King
returned this anfwer in Walfingham *pag.*
130. (VVe haue reuerently and humbly
accepted the letters of your Holines.
Alfo with a cheerfull hart we do befeech
your clemency, that if it pleafe you, you
will duely ponder our iuftice and intentio
founded vpon the truth. And that we as
occafion ferued haue fauored the holy

K.Edvv.3: Roman Church in all fulnes of deuotion
Profeffeth found loue and gratious fauor, as you may
to haue
euer fa- conie&ure of a moft deuout fonne. For
uored the God is the witneffe of our cofcience that
Pope. we haue defired to exalt & defend the ho-
nors and liberties of the Church.) And
againe the king *Anno*. 1343 writing to
Pope Clement in VValfing *pag*. 150.

Profeffeth faith thus, (To his moft holy Lord
the P. is Clement by the diuine prouidence cheefe
Bishop of Bifhop of the facred Roman and vniuer-
the vni-
uerfal fall Church, Edward by the fame grace of
Church. God King of France and England and
Lord of Ireland deuout kiffes of your
bleffed feete &c.) And then calleth him,
(*fucceffor of the Prince of the Apoftles*. Infra. VVe and ours do defire and ought
to reuerence your moft facred perfon
and

and the holy Roman Church. And *pag.* 15. Clement anſwereth him thus. My deerly beloued ſonne yow haue knowne how to exhibit your ſincere deuotion to our Lord and to your Mother the holy Roman Church , as of famous memorie your Progenitors the Kings of England haue done whilſt they liued.] And Fox himſelfe *Acts pag.* 383. ſetteth downe a letter of the K.and nobles to Pope Clement *Anno* 1343. thus. [To the moſt holy Father in God Lord Clement by the grace of God of the holy Church of Rome and of the vniuerſall Church cheeſe and high Biſhop his humble and deuout children the Princes Dukes Earles Barons Knights Citizens and Burgeſſes and all the communalty of England aſſembled at the Parliament houlden at VVeſtminſter the 15. day of May deuout kiſſing of his feete with all humble reuerence and humility. Moſt holy Father yow being ſo high and holy a Prelat and head of the holy Church by whome the holy Vniuerſall Church and people of God ought to be as by the Son beames illightened &c.]Be hould the whole Parlament calling the Pope head and Biſhop of the Vniuerſall Church, and offering to kiſſe his feete with all humilitie and reuerence. And

The vvhole Parlament calleth the Pope head of the vniuerſal Church.

And again Fox *pag.* 387. setteth downe an other letter of King Edwards to Pope Clement in this sort. [Most holy Father, we desire your holines, and in as much as lieth in vs, require the same, that yow that supplie the place of the sonne of God on earth, and haue the gouernment of all Christen men *&c.*] What could be more clearly spoken for the spirituall supremacie of the Pope? And this same Roman religion of his is euident by many other waies. For he founded (saith Stow *pag.* 439.) the new Abbey neere to the Tower of London, where he placed white Monks to *the honor of God and our Ladie according to a vow by him made being on the Sea in great perill.* And a Nonrie at Detford. Cambden. addeth *pag.* 333. a Frierie of Carmelits. He instituted also the order of the garter in honor of God and Saint Georg, and among other rules apointed, that when any of the Knights died the Kinge should make a thousand Masses to be saide for his soule, and others many hundreds according to their Degree. He offered (saith Fox *pag.* 396.) *after the blind* (saith he) *superstition of those dayes in the Church of VVestminster the Vestments wherin Saint Peter did celebrat Masse.* His Confessor was *Thomas Bradwardin,* whome

K. Edw. 3. plainly professeth the Popes supremacie.

whome Bale *Centur.* 5. *cap.* 87. accounteth
a Papift. Finally as Walfingham. *An.* 1376.
writeth he dyed thus . *The King when he*
could not fpeake , with verie great reuerence
taking the Croſſe did kiſſe it moſt deuoutly, ſom-
times ſtretching forth his hand in ſigne of crauing
pardon, and other times alſo letting fall from his
eyes plenty of teares, and kiſſing moſt often the
feete of the Crucifix . And after his death
Pope Greg. 11. *lit.* in Walfingham *Anno*
1378. calleth him, *Catholicum Principem &*
Pugilem fidei . A Catholick Prince and Champion
of the faith.

The Ca-
tholik end
of K. Ed-
vvard. 3.

    And ſo euidently was this King and
the Realm in his time Roman Catholick, as Fox *Acts pag.* 377. vpon a letter
of the King to the Nobles of France
maketh this note: *Note the ignorance of the*
time . And *pag.* 396. *The blinde ſuperſtition of*
thoſe daies . And *pag.* 424. *This is out of all*
doubt that at vvhat time all the world was in
moſt vilde and deſperat eſtate, and that the lamen-
table ignorance of Gods truth had ouershadowed
all the earth, VVicklef ſtept forth &c. Behould
here manifeſt that before Wicklef there
was not one Proteſtant in the whole
world . And how ill a Proteſtant he
was ſhall hereafter appeare . And *pag.*
425. *In this ſo horrible darknes of ignorance*
(ſaith Fox) *at what time there ſeemed in a*
manner to be no one ſo little a ſparke of pure
                      doctrin

Proteſt.
confeſſe
K. Edvv 3.
time to
haue bene
Cathol.

All the
vvorld
ignorant
of Pro-
teſtancie.

doctrine left, VViclef sprong vp, through whome the Lord would first raise vp again the world which was drowned in the depth of human traditions. In like sort Bale *Cent.5. cap.85.* faith, *This age was shadovved vvith the darknes of great ignorance, and blinded with more than Diabolicall fooleries.* And *Cent. 6. cap. 1. the midnight of errors and a dim vvorld.* And *cap.8. In these times darknes of great ingnorance possessed the vvorld. cap.23. The common blindnes of the time vvas in aduancing the Idolatrie of the Popish Masse.* As for the discontentment which some time this king had with the Pope, that was not for any matter of religion, but because (as Cooper saith *Anno.* 1343.) The Pope gaue diuers Bishopricks and Benefices in England, which the king thought not expedient for his temporall estate. And as for the fauour which VVicklef found in his time, that proceeded rather from the Duke of Lancaster who gouerned all in the olde age of the King, and for a time vpheld VVicklef, not vpon any liking of his heresie, but to spite therby some of the Bishops whome he hated, as Stow *Anno.* 1376, (wtih whome Fox agreeth p.393.) testifieth in these words, *The Duke of Lancaster labiring as vvel to ouerthrovv the liberties of the Church, as of the Cittie* (of Lōdon)*called vnto him VVicklef,* &c. And when these contentions betwene the Duke and others

were

[marginal notes:]

In a maner no one litle spark of Protestancie.

VViclef first raised forsooth the vvorld

VVhy K. Edvv. 3. some time discontented vvith the Pope.

VVhy the D. of lancaster a vvhile favoored VViclef.

were appeafed. *He commanded* (faith Fox *pag.*400. *Edit.*1596. *VVicklef to fubmit him felf to his Ordinarie.* Which clearly ynough declareth the Roman religion of that Duke, which alfo other wife were euident by the honor wherwith he was receaued by the Cardinals and Bifhops in the Popes Courte , Stow *pag.* 399. And by his Confeffor *Iohn Kinningham* a Carmelit , who (faith Bale *Cent.* 6. *cap.* 4.) firft impugned Wicklef. And *Cent.* 7. *cap.* 26. faith that Gualter Diffe (*than who none in Antichrifti negotijs actuofior, more bufie in the rules of Antichrifts*) Confeffor to the Duke perfwaded him for the loue at leaft of Papiftrie to make war in Spaine , which then fauored an Anti-pope : to which purpofe Pope Vrban fent the Duke a ftandard and made his Confeffor his Legat, and gaue him authoritie to preach the Croffe with many Indulgences for all them that would follow the Duke. At what time (writeth Bale out of Purney a wiclefift the liuing) *Inualuit tunc Antichrifti furor pra cæteris temporibus. Antichrifts furie preuailed more than in other times.* More ouer Polidor *lib.* 19. faith that two Hereticks were burnt in London in this Kings time, whome Bale *Cent.* 5. *cap.* 74. calleth *feruants of Chrift* . In this Kings time liued the vertuous Ladie Mary Counteffe of Saint Paule, a woman (faith

The Cath. religion of the D. of lancafter:

(.faith Stow *pag.*437) of finguler example for life, who builded Pembrooke
hall in Cambridge, and S. Iohn of Brid-
linghton, of whome we will fpeake in
the next kings time. In this Kings
time liued that witty fchoolmâ William
Occham.

King Richard. 2. XLIIII.

IN the yeare 1377. fucceeded King Richard 2. Nephew to Edward 3. by
his fonne Edward the black Prince and
reigned 22. yeares. *He paffed (* faith Cooper *An.* 1377. and Stow *pag.* 439.*) all his
predeceffors in bountie and liberality.* His Roman religion is moft manifeft.   Firft be-

caufe he was crowned at a Maffe wherof Walfingham *Anno* 1377. fetteth downe

the beginning of the Introit, Graduall,
Epiftle, and Offertorie. Had a Franci-
fcan Frier for his Confeffor, Stow *pag.*
458. In the Commotion of Tiler went
to Saint Edwards Shrine, prayed before the high Altar, offered and Confeffed him felfe to an Anchor, Stow *pag.*
459. and gaue to the faid Shrine a
Ruby then efteemed worth a thoufand
Markes *pag.* 593.   Made foure Kings
of

of Ireland knights at Maſſe *pag.* 501. And
made the Earle of Northumberland
ſweare to him vpon the hoſt after Maſſe
*p.*520.But moſt of all iſ his religion certain
by his owne letters to the Pope and by his
lawes and Acts againſt the Wickleſiſts.
Fox Acts *p.* 590. ſetteth downe his letters
to Pope Boniface 9. thus . To the moſt
holy Father in Chriſt and Lord,L.Boni-
face 9. by the grace of God high Pope of
the moſt holy Roman and vniuerſall
Church, his humble and deuout, Richard
by the grace of God king of England and
France,and Lord of Ireland,greeting and
kiſsing of his bleſſed feete. And.*pag.*511.he
citeth an Act of Parlament then made to
declare that Vrban was true and lawful
Pope; And*pa.*556.ſaith, *King Richard procu-*
red letters Apoſtolicall from the Pope for the con-
*firming of certain ſtatuts of his.*And *pag.*431.ci-
teth a letter of Greg. 11. written in this
kings time to the Vniuerſitie of Oxford,
wherin the Pope ſaith , that England
doth not onely floriſh in power and
aboundance of riches,but is much more
glorious and ſhining in purenes of faith,
accuſtomed alwaies to bring forth men
excellently learned in the knowledg of
holy ſcriptures , grauitie of maners, men
notable in deuotion,and defenders of the
Catholick faith.The like commendations
he

he giueth in an other letter to king
Richard. Yea to teftifie the Roman Catholick faith of this time, and to ftop the
mouth of fome Minifters, who are not a
fhamed to fay the Pope giueth leaue to
finne, It pleafed God this prefent yeare
1608. to raife (in a maner) a knight of that
time, and to make him fpeake. For digging
to make a graue in Saint Faiths Church
vnder Paules, they found the Coffin of
Sir. Gerard Bray brook the cords wherof
were frefh and the herbs of good fauor,
and vppon his breft a Pardon granted
vnto him of Pope Boniface of that time,
intire and whole in thefe words. *Boniface*
Bifhop feruant of the feruants of God. To his be-
loued fonne Gerard Braybrook the yonger Knight
and to his beloued daughter in Chrift Elizabeth
his wife, of the Dioceſe of Lincoln, health and
Apoſtolicall bleſſiug. It hath proceeded from the
affection of your denotion wherby yow reuerence
vs and the Roman Church, that we admit to our
fauorable hearing your petitions, thoſe eſpecially
which concerne the halth of your foules. Hence it
is that we inclining to your requeſts, do by the
Tenor of theſe prefents eaſely grant to your deuo-
tion, that the Confeſſor whom ether of yow ſhall
thinck good to chuſe ſhall by authoritie Apoſtolick
giue to yow a plenarie remiſſion of all your finnes of
which yow ſhalbe in hart contrite and confeſſed,
once onely at the point of your death: Yow perfiſting
in the

*in the sincerity of faith, in the vnity of the holy
Roman Church, and in obedience and deuotion to
vs and our Successors the Bishopps of Rome canonically elected. So notwithstanding that the said
Confessor concerning those things, of which satisfaction shalbe imposed vpon ether, He inioine it
to be done by yow, if yow return from perill of
death, or by your Heires, if yow then chance to passe
from this world, that which yow or they are bound
to performe as is aforesaid. And least (which God
for bid) in regard of such fauor, yow be made more
prone to committ sinne, VVe will that if by any
such confidence yow should fortune to transgresse,
that the foresaid Indulgence shall not any thing
profit yow. Therfore let it altogether be vnlawfull for any man to infringe this our graunt and
will, or with rash bouldnes contradict it. If truly
any shall presume to attempt it, lett him know
he shall incurre the indignation of Almighty God
and his most blessed Apostles Saint Peter and Paul.
Giuen at Rome, at S. Peters, the 9. of Iune, in the
second yeare of our Popedome.*

Behould, gentle Reader, this ancient
pardon, and consider by it: First, the high
esteeme that our Catholick Anceistors
made of the Popes pardons, in so much,
that this worshipfull knight would send
to Rome to procure a particuler one for
him selfe and his wife. Againe how vn-
truly Ministers say, that Popes giue pardon and leaue to sinne, seeing this par-

don could not auaile for any finnes committed vpon hope of the pardon. But,
efpetially I would haue thee confider
Gods wonderfull difpofition in the con-
feruing and reuealing of this Pardon at
this time. What thinckeft thou that thi;
Knights graue fhould be neuer opened
till this day ? That the Pardon fhould be
preferued from corruption fo long lying
in the earth ? That that onely Coffin in
which this Pardon was, fhould haue the
cordes fo long time found & the flowers
fo long odoriferous , what thinck we
this Pardon auailed to the foule of this
Knight (for which purpofe it onely was
giuen) when it wrought fuch benefit to
his dead corps.

But now to come to the Kings lawes
and *Acts* againft the Wicklefifts Fox *Acts*
pag. 441. faith , *The King adioined his affent to*
the margin:

Kings
Richards
lavvs a-
gainft
vviclefifts
vvhom
Proteft.
account
their
brethren.

the fetting downe of an Ordinance which was
indeede the very firft lawe which is to be found
made againft religion and the profeffors therof.
bearning the name of an Act made in the parlia-
ment Anno 5. *Richard* 2. *vvherin* (faith Fox)
VVicklefs doctrine is called herefie , and notorious
errors and flanders, to ingender (faith the Act)
difcord and diffention betvveene diuers eftates of
the realme . And order is taken for to areft and
imprifon fuch till they amend . Ibid Fox citeth
the letters patents of the King againft
Wick-

Wicklef and some other there named, or any other noted by any other probable suspition of heresies Again *pag.* 460. King Richard writeth to the Shriefe of Northamton against the VVicklefists thus. [VVe willing therfor to withstand the Defenders and maintainers of such heresies, Do will and command as wel the fornamed as namely the forsaid Iohn VVoodward to be apprehended, straitly charging the same to be imprisoned by their bodies, or otherwise punished as shall seeme good to the Iustices.] And *pag.* 504. he setteth downe the Kings Commission in these words. [VVe by our speciall Letters Patents in the zeale of our faith haue giuen authoritie and licence vnto the forsaid Archbishops, and all and euery of his Suffragans to arest all and euery one of them that will preach or mantain any such Conclusions repugnant vnto the determination of our holy Mother the Church. And in other letters chargeth all not to hinder the Bishops of hereford in suppressing the Lolards. Yea *pag.* 406. *Edit.* 1596. Fox citeth a lawe made *Anno* 2. Richard 2. for burning of VVicklefists *Thus* (saith Fox *pag.* 505.) *King Richard taking parte with the Pope and the Rom.sh Prelats, waxed som what strait and hard to the poore Christians*

Cc 2   *of the*

of the contrary side of VVicklef, and saith that though none were burnt vnder him, yet some were condemned, diuers abiured, and did pennance. And *pag.* 513. saith. *King Richard chose to serue the humor of the Pope.* To this Bale *Cent.* 6. *cap.* 1. addeth, that Wicklef was banisht for some yeares. And *cap.* 77. that *Anno* 1382. Wicklef was condemned by ten Bishops, and fourty four Diuines, and twenty Lawyers. And *cap.* 82. saith, that King Richard at the commandement of Boniface 9. & *Cent.* 7. *cap.* 11. gathered a great Councell *Anno* 1392 against the Wicklefists. And Fox *pag.* 507. and Walsingham *An.* 1395. & others write, that King Richard being in Ireland, left all as sone as he heard increase of Lollards, and calling the cheefe of them vnto him threatned them greatly, if they followed Lollards any more, and making one of them sweare therto, the K. swore to him, that if he broke his oath, he should die a foul death. So earnest was that King against those ⸗ whome Protestants accountnow their brethren. And albeit he consented to the Law made *Anno* 1391. against those that procured or brought any excōmunication of the Pope against any, yet that Law was not made to deny any point of the Popes authority, but because (as Polidor saith *l.* 20.) *many were vexed*
dayly

*dayly for causes which they thought could not be
known at Rome easely,* The King and Lords Tem-
poral and Commons (for the Lords spirituall
reclamed as Fox witnesseth *pag.* 512.)
*thought it expedient that in this point the Pope
should not vse his authoritie .* Besides that
when Pope Boniface 9. sent to haue
these Lawes recalled, *the King* (saith VValsingham in Ypodigmate, *Anno* 1391.) *Vt fi-
lius obediens . As an obedient child , determined to
fulfill the Popes demaundes, but the Knights of
the Parliament would not abrogate the Statute
against Prouisors , because they would not haue
English Benefices at any time giuen to strangers.*
And the times of King Richard were so
manifestly Roman Catholick , as the
Kings Attorney in the araignment of
Garnet calleth the the *midnight of Poperie.*
Bale *Cent.* 6. *cap.* 96. saith, *that Almost all that* Saints.
*were in those darck times did erre through igno-
rance of Gods lawe .* In this kings time dyed
Saint Iohn of Bridlington whose life is
written in Capgraue who (saith Bale
Centur. 6. c. 63. *Cælesti Theologia assiduus
cultor adhasit.* And VVilliam Fleet
an Austin Frier, who was canonized as Bale *Cent.* 6.
c. 41. reporteth out
of Sabellicus.

Henrie

Henrie 4. XLV.

VVorthi-
nes of K.
Henrie 4.

I N the yeare 1399. succeded king Henrie 4. granchild to king Edward 3. by Iohn Duke of Lancaster, and dyed *Anno* 1413. hauing reigned 14. yeares. *He was* (saith Po-lider *lib.* 21. *of a great corage, & after the ende of*

His Rom.
Religion.

ciuill warrs entertained all most gently. The same hath Cooper *Anno* 1399. and Stow Chron. *pag.* 424. His Roman Catholick religion is most notorious . For as Fox *Acts pag.* 523. and others write, he made the Statute *ex officio* . Where is apointed . *That who so euer is conuicted of* (Wicklefs) *heresie be-fore his Ordinarie or Commißioners, that then the Shriefes. Maiers, and Bay lifs of the Cittie, Con-trie, or Towne, shall take the persons after senten-ce is pronounced, & cause them openly to be burned in sight of the people.* And *pag.* 517. Fox setteth down the Kings Decree in parliament, wherin he professeth to be zelous in reli-gion, and reuerent louer of the Catholick faith, And minding to roote out all here-fies out of his Kingdom , And ther com-mandeth one VVilliam 'Santrey a conu-ict heretick to be burnt, which perhaps is he whome Bale *Cent.* 6. *cap.* 75. saith was burnt in Smithfield *An.* 1401. In this tyme was burnt saith Bale *Cent.* 8. *c.* 5. that relaps William Swinderby a smith in London

for

for denying the reall presence, & a Tayler
the same yeare 1410. for the same cause
Fox *pag.* 481. nameth his brother Iohn
Badby burnt then, who (as VValsingham.
ypodig. *pag* 174, who then liued, writeth)
said that the Eucharist is not the body of
Christ, but worse than a toade or a spider,
And perhaps he is that VViclefist of whome that graue Author Thomas VValden
who (was ther present) reporteth *Tom.2.c.*
63. That standing befor the Archbishop &
Bishops in presence of the Duke of yorke
& many nobles, he said that a Spider was
more to be worshipped thā the Eucharist,
and sodainly from the top of the Church
came a great spider & sought to enter into
his mouth, & would scarce be kept out by
any mans helpe. Moreouer Fox *Acts* 518.
saith that this King was the first of all
EnglishKings, *that began the burning of Christs*
(VViclef) *Saints for standing against the Pope.*
That K. Henrie bnrnt VViclefs Saints is
euident, But he was not the first which
burnt such as stood against the Pope, as
appeareth by what hath bene sayd of Edward 3. And finally he concludeth that
this king was bent altogether to vphould
the Popes Prelacie. And therfore in his
Considerations, Considerat. 10. saith, *Pro-*
testants rather dyed than liued in the dayes of
King Henrie 4. And when the Lollards

Miracle for honor of the B. sacrament

K Henrie 4. wholie bent to the Pope.

Cc 4   or

or Wicklefifts requefted him (as faith
Walfingham *An.*1410.) either to alter, or
mitigate the forfaid Statute, he anfwered
them that he would rather inforce it. And
when they propofing to him the fame
bait, as Proteftants did to King Henrie 8.
defired him to take away the Church
liuings , becaufe with them he might
maintain 15.Earles,1550. Knights,6200.
Squirs, and 100. Hofpitals, he detefting
their malice commanded them to filence.

VVhat
baite the
VViclefifts
Propofed
to K.
Henrie. 4.
to ouer-
throvv re-
ligion.
The like
offer ma-
de Prote-
ftants
vvhich
fyr Thom
more
confuted.

The rare
vertues
of K.Hen-
rie.5.

King Henrie 5. XLVI.

IN the. yeare 1413. fucceded K. Henrie
5. fonne to King Henrie 4. and died
An. 1422. hauing reigned 9. yeares. *He was*
(faith Polidor *lib.* 22.) *the onely glorie of that
time, then whome none borne ether for greatnes of
courage or for vertue was more famous or excellent, whofe loue euen yet remaineth amongft men.*
The like commendations giue to him
Walfingham, who then liued *Hiftor. pag.*
465. and *ypodigm. pag.* 178. Cambden Brit.
pag. 442. calleth him *Optimum Principem.*
Stow *pag.* 595. *Victorious and renowned King.*
He wonne the great battel of Agincourt,
and greateft part of France with Paris,
and was apointed by the French King
Regent of France,and heir after his death,
                                The

The Roman religion of this Victorious　His Rom. Religion. and vertuous Prince is notorious . First 1 becaufe (as Fox faith *pag.* 569.) he made a Statut *An.*2. That all and finguler fuch as were of Wiclefs learning, if they would not giue ouer fhould fuffer death in two manner of kinds, That is, They fhould be firft hanged for treafon againft the king (againft whome they rebelled) and then burned for herefie againft God. Secondly, 2 this king(faith Fox *pag.* 675, *in all his life and*　The valiantest *all his dsings was fo feruiceable to the Pope and his*　Prince of *Chaplins, that he was called the Prince of Priefts.*　England These were the Lollards who as Walfing.　called the faith *Hift.pag.*435. were wont to fay. *Now*　Prince of *the Prince of the Priefts is gone, now our enemy is*　Priefts. *departed.* Thirdly he hanged and burnt Syr 3 Iohn Owldcaftel called Lord Cobham, whome though Fox account a principall martyr of his, yet his brother Stow *p.* 581. calleth him *the publick enemy.* And he was fo phantafticall at his death , as he talked of his own rifing to life the third day *pag.* 582. He burnt alfo diuers other Wiclefifts *ex* Bale *Centur.* 7. *cap.* 5. And Fox *pag.*481. telleth that being yet Prince he was at the burning of the forfaid Iohn Badly, and commanded fier to be put to him when he would not recant. Fourthly, he 4 built three Monafteries VValfingham. *Hift.pag.*452.as Beethlem for Carthufians, Sion

Sion for Brigittings, and another for the Cælestins. which two laſt orders came new into England in his time. Fiftly his ghoſtly Father and whom he moſt truſted and in whoſe armes he died (ſaith Bale Centur. 7. *cap.* 84.) was the great Clerk and greteſt aduerſaire of the Wickleſiſts *Thomas VValden* Prouinciall of the white Friers. Sixtly being to giue the battle at Agincourt, the night before (ſaith Walſing Hiſt. *pag.* 438.) He and his ſoldiers ſpent the night in making their côfeſsiôs, and prouiding for their ſoules. And in ypodigm. *pag.* 188. telleth how at harſtew they had a ſolemne proceſsion before the bleſſed Sacrament. Of this religion was that Engliſh King and Engliſh ſoldiers who won, that glorious battell, who conquered France, and made England renouned. Finally This King as Stow faith *Anno* 1416. ſent his Embaſſadors to the Councel of Conſtance, where Wickleft and his doctrine were condemned, and there procured it to be ordained, that *England* (ſaith Stow) *ſhould obtain the name of a nation, and ſaid one of the foure Nations that owe their deuotion to the Church of Rome which vntill that time men of other Nations for enuie had letted.* Behould Chriſtian Reader how the moſt victorious that England euer had, and England

5

6
Confeſsiô of ſinnes befor victorie.

7
England in her moſt triumphant time accounted it great honor to be eſteemed a Nation that owed deuotion to the Church of Rome.

land

land in the most triumphant time that e-
uer she enioyéd, stroue to be accounted a
Nation that owed deuotion to the
Church of Rome, and accounted that
a ptincipall honor. And at that time did
God blesse our Nation with greatest vi-
&ories . with hapiest succesle , with
largest Empire that euer since or before
she obtained . And these times were so
euidently Roman Catholicke , as the
Kings Attorny in the araignment of F.
Garnet calleth them *the verie midnight of
Poperie.* And Fox in Considerat 10. saith
Protestants rather died than liued vnder this King
In this Kings time liued that great Clerk Saint.
Thomas Walden, who (as Bale said Cent
7. *cap.* 84.) conuerted the *Duke of Lituania
with all his people to popisme* and as he reporteth out of Diuers is canonized.

King Henry. 6. XLVII.

THe 47. Christian King was King
Henrie 6. only sonne to King Henry
5. began his reigne *Anno* 1422. and reigned 38. yeares.. *He was* (saith Cambd. in The pietie
Brit. *pag.* 345. *The best and most pious Prince.* Henrie.6.
and *pag.* 257. *A most holy King a patern of
Christian pietie and patience King Henry* 7 . *so
admired his vertues as he dealt with* Pope Iulius

to

to canonize him. Fox *pag.* 716. saith, I doubt
not but King Henrie 6. *was a good and quiet Prince*
Stow *pag.* 595. saith, *he was of nature gentle
and meeke, suffered all iniuries patiently. pag.* 624.
alwaies naturally inclined vnto good pag. 705.
*after his death worshiped by the name of holy King
Henrie, whose red hat of veluer* (saith he) *was
thought to heale the head ach of such as put it on.
In both states he was patient and vertuous, that
he may be a pattern of most perfect vertue. He
was plaine and vpright onely giuen to prayer and
reading of scripture and almes deedes. Of such
integritie of life as the Bishop that had bene his
Confessor ten yeares auouched, that he had not all
that time committed any mortall crime. So conti-*

Polid. *l.* 24.
saith ma-
nie mira-
cles vvere
vvrought
ly his
bodie.

*nent as suspition neuer touched him. Far from
couetousnes, so religiously affected that on principall holy dayes he would wore sackcloth next
his skin. He pardoned one who had thrust him into
the side with a sword, and of his naturall inclination abhorred all vices as wel of body as of minde.*

Thus do Protestants commend this holy

His Rom.
Religion.

king. And his Roman religion is manifest.
For Pope Eugenius sent to him a goulden
rose as to a Catholick Prince, Stow *pag.*
635. And vnder him were diuers Wickle-
sists burnt *An.* 1415. 1430. 1431. 1428. And
Bishop Pecock made publickly to recant
1457. and had his bookes burnt before
his face, *ex* Bale *Centur.* 7. *cap.* 75. Godwin
in Bishops of Chichester, Fox *Acts Edit.*
1596.

1596.*pag.*605. & *sequen.* setteth down the
names of diuers VVicklefifts , wherof
fome were burnt , fome whipped , fome
made abiure their herefie vnder this
king . And *pag.* 644. he fetteth downe
publick letters of the King dated *An.* 18.
Regni where he auoucheth the burning
of one *VVhite* a VVicklefift, & calleth him
Traitor to God.

King Edward 4. XLVIII.

THe 48. Chriftian Prince was Edward
4. of the houfe of York, who began
his reign 1460. and reigned 22. yeares.
He was (faith Stow *pag.* 689) *of noble courage*   Valour of
and great wit. pag. 722. *a goodly perfonage*   K.Ed-
princely to behould, of hart coragious , politick in   vvard.4.
counfell , in aduerfitie nothing abafhed, in profpe-
ritie rather ioifull than proude , in peace iuft and
mercifull , in war fharpe and fierce. His Ro-   His Rom.
man religion is manifeft , For (Bale faith   Religion.
Centur. 8. *cap.*34.) That his Confeffor was
Iohn Stanborn a Carmelit . *Qui totus*
iurauerat in Romani Pontificis authoritatem:
who wholly fwore to the Popes authoritie. And
Fox *Acts Editione* 1596. *pag.* 659. putteth
one Iohn Goofe a VVicklefift burnt vnder him. And Ibid.noteth *that fince the time*
of King Richard 2. *there is no reigne of any King*
to be

*to be aßigned hitherto wherin some good man or other hath not suffered the paines of fier for the religion of Iesus (*Wicklef*) Besides Stow pag. 690. saith that King Edward vvent crowned in VVestmenster in the honor of God and S. Peter, and the next day in paules in the honor of God and S. Paule.* And his daughter Brigit became a Nonue polidor *lib· 24.*

King Edward 5. XLVIIII.

THe 49. Christian Prince was Edward 5. soune to Edward 4. a child of a 11. yeares old , who liued not many dayes after his Father. As for the religion which this child had, it may easely appeare by what hath bene said of the Father.

King Richard .3. L.

IN rhe yeare 1483 , the 50. Christian Prince was Richard 3. brother to Edward 4, who tooke the Crown & held it two yeares. The qualities of this K. are notorious in all Chronicles. And his religiõ is known both by what hath bene said of his brother. Aud as Polidor *l.*25. he began a Colledg in Yorke of an hundreth Priests.

K. Richards religion.

King

King Henrie 7. **L I.**

IN the yeare 1485. succeeded King henry 7. of the house of Lankaster, and reigned 23. yeares. He *was* (faith Stow) *a Prince of meruailous wisdomme , police iustice temperance and grauity .* Fox *Acts, pag.* 729 . faith the same. His Roman Catholicke religion is euident. For Fox setteth downe diuers Wicklefists burnt or otherwise punished vnder him , as *pag.* 731. four. wherof one the K. caused to be brought before him, but when he would not be perswaded , was burnt. Aud *pag.* 774. he reckneth diuers others, & others abiured and burnt in the cheeke. Wherupon Considerat . 10. he faith, *Proteftants rather died than liued ynder King. Henry* 7. And p. 776. faith thus of K. Henrie 7. *othervvise a prudent and temperat Prince permitted the rage of the Popes Clergie so much to haue their wills ouer the poore flock of Chrift as they had .* Ibid. *The perfequution began novv in the Church to be hoat* aud he attributeth the death of the K. to the perfequution (forfooth) of the Gospellers. Moreouer *pag.* 799. He reporteth out of G. Lilly. how Henry 7. *Anno* 1506. fend three folemne Orators to Pope Iulius 2 . to yeald his obedience, *Ex more* (faith Lilly)

to the

VVorthines of K. Henrie. 7.

His Rom. Religion.

to the See of Rome. And Stow *p.* 811. writeth
that Pope Iulius 2. sent a cap of maintenance, and a sword to King Henrie 7. as
to a Defender of the Church. And Fox *pag.*
799. saith that Pope Alexander 6. and
Pius 3. had before done the same. King
Henrie 7. builded also three Monasteries
of Franciscans Pollidor *in vit.* In this kings
time liued Iohn Alcok Bishop of Elie,
A man (saith Godwin in his life) *of admira-*
ble temperance, for his life and behauior vnspotted
and from a child so earnestly giuen to the studie,
not onely of learning , but of all vertue , and god-
linesse , as in those dayes neuer any man bore a
greater opinion and reputation of holines, He liued
all his time most soberly and chastly subduing the
temptations of the flesh by fasting studie and praier
and other such good meanes.

King Henrie 8. LII.

King Henrie 8. sonne to king Henrie 7.
began his Reign *An.* 1509. From the
which time to *An.* 1530. he continewed an
earnest Roman Catholick . For (as Fox
saith *pag.* 789.) From *Anno.* 1509. to 1527.
diuers VVicklefists *were preseted , troubled &*
imprisoned. And *pag.* 836. He setteth downe
a letter of king Henrie *Anno* 13. *To all Maiors*
Sherifes, Bailifs, and Constables *, and other*
                                                       officers

officers to aßist the Bishop of Lincoln, for punishing Heretieks according to the lawes of holy Church. And Bale *Cent.* 8. *cap.*62. faith, that two were burnt *An.*1515. for the matter of the Sacrament. And *cap.*75. that Barnnes was made to recant *Anno* 1525. And likwise Bilney, Garret, and others *An.* 1527. Stow alfo and others write how king Henrie *Anno* 1511. wrote to the French king to defift from molefting Pope Iulius 2. and in the next yeare fent an army of ten thoufand men into France in the Popes defence. And *An.* 1513. VVent himfelf in perfon with a royall army & conquered Torwin and Turney. And not content thus manfully to haue aduentured his perfon to defend the Pope with his fword, did in the yeare 1521. write alfo an excellent booke in his defence againft Luther. The originall wherof I haue feene in the Popes Librarie with the Kings fubfcription therto in thefe bad verfes, if I wel remember.

K. Henrie 8 zeal in defence of the Pope

> *Hunc librum Henricus Leoni decimo mittit*
> *In fignum fidei & pignus amicitiæ.*
> *This booke to Leo tenth King Henrie the eighth doth fend*
> *In teftimonie of his faith, and token of a freind.*

For which booke Pope Leo gaue to him & his fucceffors for euer the glorious title

Dd   of

of *Defender of the faith*. And again in the
yeare 1527. When Pope Clement 7. was
taken prifoner, he gaue monthly 60.thou-
fand angels, for the maintenance of an
army for the Popes deliuerie. And after
this made long time fuit to the fame Pope
that he would by his authoritie pronounce his mariage with Queene Catherin tô
be none, and diuorce them, which he nôt
granting, King Henrie (as yow fhall heare
in the next Booke) renounced the Popes
authoritie, and made him felf head of the
Church, and yet remained in all other
points a Roman Catholick. Whervpon
Bale *Cent.*8. *cap.*80. faith, that *King Henrie*
did admitt the Doctrine of Antichrift euen in the
matters of greateft moment, and did retain the
*contagious dreggs.*By fuch phrafes this wrech
vfeth to vnderftand Papiftrie. And Fox
*pag.*1291. granteth, *that Obits and Maffes ap-*
peare in his will. And as he faith *pag.* 1135.
made it high treafon to deny the reall
prefence, and fellonie to defend mariage
of Priefts, breaking of vowes, or to
condemne Communion in one kinde,
priuat Maffe, or auriculer Côfefsion, without all benefit of abiuration or Clergie.
VVhich Lawes were feuerely executed
by him. And at his death would gladly
haue bene reconciled to the Roman
Church, as Bifhop Gardiner ('with
whome

K.Henrie
8.neuer a
Proteftãt.

Sleidan
Engl:l.13.
fol.174.

Moft feuer
of all
Engl.
Kings a-
gainft He-
retiks.

whome he delt about that matter) protested openly in a sermon at Pauls Crosse.
And so Catholick was the people of
England in his time euen after his reuolt
from the See Apostolick, as when the
Vicar of Croidon a most famous preacher
of that time, tolde them in a sermon at
Pauls, that as they had denyed the supremacie of the Pope, so in time they would
fall to deny other points of the Catholick
faith, euen the reall presence of Christ in
the blessed Sacrament, The people at that
word cryed out. *Neuer Neuer Neuer.* which
yet now we finde too true.

Zeal of our grand fathers touching the real presence.

Queene Marie LIII.

AFter K. Henrie the eight succeeded
in the yeare 1546. King Edward the
sixt his sonne, a child of nine yeares olde,
which childe wanting the vse of perfect reason, and vnfit to gouern him
self, was the first Protestant Prince that
euer was in England, and turned the
Roman religion which his Father had
left, (though maimed in one principall
point) to open Protestancie. Not for
the miracles or rare vertues of the Preachers therof, or their conuincing their
aduersaries in disputation, as King

Ethel-

Ethelbert changed his Paganifme into the Roman religion , as is before fhewed, but becaufe the Lord Protector and his complices thought it moft futable to their humors , and moft fit for their afpiring pretences . But how vnfortunat this exchange was , not onely to the foules of this King and principall Actors therin, but alfo to their liues and bodies , yow may reade in Stow , where yow fhall fee that the very fame yeare 1548. that Proclamation was made for receauing in both Kindes, the Lord Admirall (a cheefe agent in the change of religion) though brother to the Protector , and Vnkle to the King , was beheaded for a Traitor, And the next yeare 1549 VVhen Proclamation was made againft Maffe , fone after alfo was Proclamation made againft the Protector him felfe , the principall author of the change, and he caft into the Tower. And in the yeare 1552. when the newe feruice booke of Common prayer begun in Pauls , the faid Protector was beheaded , And the next yeare the King died , and the Duke of Northumberland (an other principall actor in the change of religion though againft his own confcience , as he openly declared at his death) was beheaded for treafon, and Cranmer and Ridley and other fauorers

The ill end of the kringers in of Proteftancie.

rers of that change were depriued of their
Dignities,and sone after burnt.This was
the rufull end of the first setters vp of
Protestancie . For maintenance wherof
albeit a new Queene was proclaimed,
Nobles sworne,and the strength of England gathered,yet in short time almightie
God ouerthrew it again without any
bloodshed by one vertuous woman Q.
Marie, whc all the time of her life liued
so chastly and religiously,that all her enemies could not to this day fasten the least
suspicion of vice vpon her. And whome
euen Protestants write to haue *Bene of*
nature and disposition verie milde and pittifull.
VVhich argueth that they wel deserued
the seueritie which shee shewed towards
them.And so earnest a Roman Catholick
shee was, as the Protestants write of her,
that there was , *Not these thousand yeares a*
more obedient daughter to the Church of Rome
than she was. VVherby yow may iugde of
the impudencie of Doctor Reinolds who
in his *Confer.pag.* 583 denieth, not onely
all the former Princes , but euen Queene
Marie euer to haue alowed the Popes
absolute spirituall supremacie , (or as he
speaketh) *the Popes Monarchie ,* but onely to
haue granted him such a preheminence,
as the Duke of Venice hath in that state.
But with her in the yeare 1558. ended all

Dd 3 the

Protestan-
cie ouer-
throne
by a vvo-
man vvi-
thout any
bloodshed.
Vertue of
Q. Marie.
Author of
danger.
positions
l.2. cap.14.
Her Rom.
Religion.
In the
arraign-
ment of
F. Garnat.
D Doue
*lib.*of Re-
cusancie
vvil haue
Bellarm.
to be a
Protest.
or at left
no per-
fect
Papist.

the glorie of Catholick Princes of England . Who (except King Henrie 8. for a
few yeares, and King Edward 6.) had
continewed from the yeare 598. till the
forſaid yeare 1558. the ſpace almoſt of a
thouſand yeares . And after roſe a new
kind of Proteſtancie , differing from that
of King Edward the childs time. Not (as
I ſaid before) through any miracles or
ſtrange vertue of the Preachers therof, or
their ouercomming their aduerſaries in
Diſputation, but againſt the will of all
the Biſhops and a great parte of the Nobilitie, by the counſel of meere Lay men,
and the authoritie of a woman, who was
induced to make this change, not for
zeale of religion (which ſhee little regarded) but to aſſure her ſtate the more , becauſe ſhee feared, if ſhe acknowledged the
authoritie of the Church of Rome , her
birth might be called in queſtion . But of
the cauſe, maner, and meanes of erecting
Proteſtancie, we ſhall ſpeake more in the
ſecond booke.

Epilogue.

Hitherto (gentle Reader) thou haſt
heard 53. Princes of England ſucceſ-
ſuly , beleeuing and profeſsing the Rom.
Catho-

Catholick faith, besides 70. and more others, who reigned ouer certain partes of England, whiles it was deuided into diuers Kingdoms, whose names onely I will here set downe. Kings of Kent 13. *Ethelbert, Edbald, Ercombert, Egbert, Lotharius, Edricus, VVithred, Edbert, Edilbert, Alricus, Edilbert-pren, Cuthred, and Baldred.* Kings of the East Saxons 9. *Sebert Sigebert Sigher S. Sebba, Sighard, Senfred, Offa, Selred, Swithed.* Kings of Eastengland 13. to wit *Redwald, Carpwald, S. Sigebert, Egris. Anna, Ethelere, Eibelwald, Adulph, Elwald, Beorna, Ethelred, Saint Ethelbright, S. Edmund,* kings of middle England 17. Namely *Peda, Vulpher, Ethelred, Coenred, Ceolred, Ethelbald, Bernred, Offa, Egfert, Kenulph, Saint Kenelm, Ceolwulph, Bernulph, Ludecan, VVithlof, Bertulph, Burdred.* Kings of the Northpart of England 18. *Edwin, Saint Oswald, Oswin, Oswi, Egfrid, Alfrid, Ostred, Kenred, Ostrie, Ceolwulph, Egbert, Ostwuld, Mollo, Alred, Ethelbert. Alswald, Ostred, Athelred,* and some kings also of the South Saxons. Consider I pray thee now the number of these kings which is aboue 120, far aboue the smallest number of two Protestant Princes. Consider their sex and age, who almost all were men and of mature yeares, VVheras of the Protestant Princes, one was a childe, the other a womau. Consider their wisdome and

valour, in which they were inferior to
no Princes in Chriftendome. Confider
their vertue, which was fo great, as there
are more Kings of Ingland Saints, than of
all Chriftendome befides. Confider the
end for which they firft embraced the
faith, which was nether to enioy their
luft, nor to get any Church goods, nor to
affure their temporall ftate, but to gaine
heauen. Confider the Counfellors, whofe
aduife they followed herein, were not
ignorant and laye men, but vertuous and
learned Diuines. Confider the motiues
which drew them to the Catholick religion, to witt, rare vertue, great learning,
admirable miracles of their firft preachers.
Finally, confider how long they continewed in their faith, to wit almoft a thoufand yeares, and how almoft in euery
Kings time here liued fome notable men,
who with rare vertue and miracles haue
confirmed their faith.

Confider I fay all this, and then iudge
whither the Catholick religion of fo many and fo worthie Kings, or the Proteftant faith of one Child and one woman,
be more likely to be good and to come
from God. Can we thinke that fo many
Princes of mature yeares and iudgment
fhould be blinde, rather then one child &
a woman, that thefe could fee that in fo
few

few yeares which all they could not perceaue in a thousaud ? That these two
should hit vpō Gods truth for temporall
endes, rather thā they for spirituall? That
that should be Christs faith wherto these
two were moued by wordly (if not vi-
tious)motiues, thē that wherto they were
moued by heauenly vertue and miracles?
That that should be Gods truth which began but the last day, rather thā that which
hath continewed heere this thousand
yeares? Finally that a Child and one woman are gone to heauen, & so many vertuous Princes with all their Archbishops
Bishops Prelats Diuins and Clergy, with
all their Queenes, Princes, Nobles Commons and Ancestors for these thousand
yeares, not withstanding all their wisdom,
learning, miracles, vertuous liues, and
good deedes are gon to hell for want of
true faith in Christ? were (as the ancient
Father Tertullian saith to certain Hereticks of his time) so many millions christened in vaine, beleeued in vaine, serued
God in vaine, and are dead in their sinnes. Perhaps some will say that the for-
sayd Princes and our Ancestors beleeued
so much of the Christian faith as is necessary to saluation. But then it euidently
followeth that the Protestant faith is not
the Christian faith. Because (as I haue
　　　　　　　　　　　　　　　the wne

Lib.1.c. 21. fhewne before out of the confefsion of
Proteftants) thofe Princes knew not fo
much of Proteftancy as that which Proteftants account the *foule head and foundation*
of their religion and without which they
fay all is loft, To wit, Iuftificatiõ by onely
faith. Yea they are by Fox & others plainly denyed to haue known the Proteftants
faith, and affirmed to haue held diuers
pointes quite oppofit to Proteftácy. How
then could they be faued by any point of
Proteftancy who knew not fo much as
the foundation therof, and with other
points of their beliefe ouerturned it ?
Wherfore others afhamed to condemne
fo many , fo worthy, and fo vertuous
Chriftians to Hel, and yet not daring to
afford them hope of faluation left they
fhould condemne their owne religion, anfwere, that they will not iudge their forfathers, but leaue them to Gods iudgement. But thefe ether are afhamed to
vtter what they thinke, or haue no firme
faith at all. For if they firmely belieued
their Proteftant faith to be Chrifts faith
they muft needs thinck that all that haue
died without it are damned , for without
true faith it is impofsible to pleafe God,
or (which is a fpice of Atheifme and right
Antichriftianitie) that there are more
waies to heauen than by Chrift and his
faith.

faith , that there are many faiths,
many baptifms , many Chrifts, many
Gods . From which irreligious atheifme God deliuer my deere country.
And thus hauing fufficiently fhewed
how Saint Auftin was our Englifh Nations firft preacher and what qualities
he had fit for fuch a function and what
kind of doctrine his was and how it hath
continued in our countrie euer fince, let
vs now vew Luther and his doctrine &
fee whither they haue the like or rather
quite oppofit qualities & conditions, that
after hauing weighed both , we
may the better iudge wherof to make our
choice.

Finis Primi libri.

THE SECOND

BOOKE OR SCALE,

VVHERIN

The qualities of Luther and of his Doctrine are set dovvne.

THE FIRST CHAPTER.

That Luther was the first Author of the Protestant Religion.

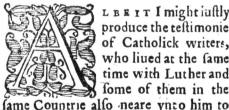

VVhy Catholiks might be alledaged against. Luther.

LBEIT I might iustly produce the testimonie of Catholick writers, who liued at the same time with Luther and some of them in the same Countrie also neare vnto him to proue that he was the first beginner of Protestancie, because they could not be ignorant of so notorious a matter, and being of that fidelitie as they cannot be dispro-

1
2
3

difproued in any other weightie matter, & of that grauity as it can not be thought that they would wittinglie make them felues a fcorne to the world by reporting notorious yntruthes, and finally being Catholicks whofe teftimonie (as we fee in England,) Proteftants vfe to account moft fure, Catholick writers I fay being thus qualified I might iuftly produce their teftimonie efpecially in fo eafie a matter for them to know, and fo eafie to be difproued if it were not true (For what more eafie than to name one liuing man that was Proteftant befor Luther if any had bene) yet partely becaufe I would auoid all cauils, but efpecially becaufe Proteftants themfelues teftifie ynough in this matter, I will abfteine from Catholick witneffes, leauing it to the iudicious Reader to confidet how euident our caufe is, which we will proue onely by the teftimonie of our aduerfaries. And that Luther was the firft Author of Proteftant Religion, I will proue. Firft, by the Proteftants confefsion of the inuifibilitie or no appearance in the world of their Church or religion before Luther. Secondly, by their like Confefsion of the newnes or late rifing of their Church and faith. Thirdly, by their Confefsion alfo of the departure of their firft Maifters and

vvhy their teftimonies are forborne.

Fiue kind of Profes that Luther vvas the beginner of Proteftantifme.

1
2
3

and Teachers from our Church. Fourthly I will proue it by reason. And Fiftly by their plaine affirming and graunting that Luther was indeed the beginner of their religion. To which profes I will adde in the next Chapters a disprofe of such as some Proteſtāts chalenge to haue bene of their religion in Englād in former times.

2.   Thouching the firſt kind of profe that the Proteſtāts Congregatiō was not viſible in the world before Luther, it may suffice that Luther himſelf *lib. de Capt. cap. de bapt.* complayneth that *The Popes tirany* (saith he) *for many ages hath extinguiſhed the faith.* And *lib. de libert.* he crieth out thus. *Alas Chriſtian life is vnkowne in all the world.* Eraſmus a Cōfeſſor with Fox, and a man of good iudgment with Doct. Reinolds writeth that Luther *taught many things which for many ages the Church knew not.* Caluin *Præfat. Inſtitut.* confeſſeth plainly, that his doctrine *diu iucognita sepultaq̃, latuit* ; *Lay long time vnknowne and buried.* Againe: *In the ages paſt ther was no face of a true Church. For some ages all things were drowned in deep darknes.* And *lib. 4. c. 1. §. 11. For some ages the pure preaching of the word vaniſhed.* Doct. Whitaker *cont. Duræum pag.* 274. *we as plainly know* (saith he) *the viſible Church to haue periſhed as thou knoweſt a man to be dead*: Perkins in his *Expoſit: of the Creed p.* 400. *Before the daies*

of

That the Proteſtāts Church was not viſible befor Luther. Luther.

Eraſm. cont. Epiſt. non Sab. Luther. Fox in his Calendar. Reinolds. Cōfer. pag. 151. 155. Caluin. The alteration of religion vvith the beginning of Charles 5. tooke her original. Sleidan. præfat hiſtor. VVhitaker. Perkins.

of *Luther for the space of many hundred yeares an* The pro-
Vniuersal Apostacie ouerspred the whole world. testant
And in his Refor. Catholicke p. 332. *Our* hid for
Church (saith he) *in Luthers time began to* manie
shew it selfe as hauing bene hid by an vniuersall hundred
Apostacy many hundred yeares togeather. Could years to-
one speak more plainly? And expofit.*cit.p,* gether.
370. he saith these *many hundreds:* which
he meaneth were nine hundred yeares.
D. Fulke in natis Apoc. 20. *They* (Prote- Fulke.
stants) *were often driuen into mountaines and*
desert places of the Alpes , Apenin Hercinia silua
and other corners of the world, or els dispersed &
kept close in all regions of Europe. The surueier Surueier.
of the pretended discipline. *c.* 8. *In this latter*
age (saith he) *when after a long darknes, it plea-*
sed God to restore vnto vs the light of the Gospel. c.
4. *Priests of all sortes & likewise the people all of* All priests
thē together from the top to the toe were drowned and peo-
in the pudles of Poperie. And I pray you who ple drow-
was then a Protestant. Poperie
3. But how long was this ignorance, this to toe.
darknes, this drowning of Priests & people
in Poperie . Fox in his *Acts* edit . 1596.
(which edition I cite in this booke) p. 767. Fox.
saith. *From* 400. *yeares heretofore and more the*
religion of Christ was wholie burned into Idola-
trie. And p. 390 . *About the yeare* 1370. *all the*
world (saith he) *was in desperat estate, and igno-*
rāce of Gods truth ouershadowed the whole world
& there seemed in a māner to be no one litle spark
of

of pure doctrine left. Again in his Proteſtatiõ
befor his Acts. *About the yeare* 1215. *&* 1080,
*Chriſtian faith was exſtinguiſhed, then the true
viſible Church began to ſhrink and keep in for
fear.* And further *pag.* 138 *In the time of King
Edgar* (which was *An.* 954.) *and of the ould
Monkes, ſuperſtation began to creep into the Church
for ighorance of free iuſtification by faith .* And
yet further ſpeaking of our Chriſtian
Kings from our firſt Chriſtianitie vnto
the yeare 800. he writeth thus *pag.* 120.

Proteſtan-
tiſme hid-
den to our
Anceitors. *How much are we* (Proteſtants) *bound to God
for the ſinceritie of his truth hidden ſo long to our
Anceſtors and opened now to vs.* Ibid. *They lacked
our faith .* Thus Fox confeſſeth that the
Proteſtants truth was hidden and vnknowne here for one thouſand yeares
al moſt. Nay *p.* 138. he feareth no to write
that. *Shortly after the time of Chriſt and his
Apoſtles the Doctrine of Chriſtian Iuſtification*
(which *pag.* 770. he accounteth, *the onely
principall origin of our ſaluation,* and *pag.* 767.
the foundation of all Chriſtianitie) *began to be
forgotten .* In like manner Bale an other
great Antiquarie *Centur.* 6. *cap.* 69. calleth
the time of King Richard 2. *a darkiſh age.*
And *Centur.* 5. *cap* 85. *The age* (ſaith he) *of K.
Edward* 3. *was couered with darknes of extreme
ignorance.* And in King Henrie 3. time as
he writeth *Centur.* 4. *cap.* 6. *Holeſome truth
periſhed from earth.* And vnder K. Henrie 2.
(an

(as he writeth *Cent.3. c.14.*) *Mannes life was corrupted vpon earth with Antichristian traditions.* So that all this time ther was no roome for Protestants on earth. And yet further *Cent.1.pag.69. From the yeare 607.* (saith he) *puritie of heauenly doctrin vanished in the Church.* And *p.65. After Greg. the first puritie of doctrine* perished. And *Cent.1. c.74. From Phocas* (who liued *An 602.*) *till the renevving* (saith he) *of the Gospel* (by Luther) *the doctrine of Christ was for that space amongst Idiots and in lurking holes.* Doest thou hear Reader in whom and wher this new Gospel was for almost 1000. yeares together ? Napier alſo in his Treatiſe vpon the Reuelat. *pag.145. Euen 1260.years* (saith he) *the Pope and his Clergie hathe poſſeſſed the outward and visible Church of Christians reigning without any debatable contradiction. Gods truth* (saith he p 191.161.156) *most certainly* (note the word) *abiding ſo long latent & invisible.* Behold this Proteſtat cófeſſing that their truth was inuiſible for more than twelue hundred yeares . yea Fulk in his Anſwer to a Counterfeit Cathol. *pag. 35.* will haue the Church *to haue decaied immediatly from the Apoſtles time.* And to conclude with Luthers teſtimonie as I began with it . He Galath 1. *fol. 27.* hath theſe words . *VVhen the light of the Goſpel after ſo great darknes begā first to appear.* And *Galach. 3.fol.154. Of this difference* (taught by me) *between*

Proteſtancie for a thouſand yeares onely in Ideots and in holes.

Napier.

Fulke.

Luthers

Luthers doctrin not knovvne to the antient Fathers.

twene the lavv and the Gospel ther is nothing to be foūd in the books of the Mōkes Canonists Scholemen, no nor in the books of the ancient Fathers. And Galat.5.fol.271. This vvas cōmon in these our daies befor the light & truth of the Gospel was reueled.

4. Thus you see it euidēt by the cōfession of Luther & diuers other Protestāts both domesticall and foraine that their Church, their faith & religiō was inuisible and vnknowne to the world before Luther. And this inuisibilitie of their Church before Luthers time do all Protestāts mantaine, who affirme the calling or sending of Luther Caluin & such like to preach, to haue bene extraordinarie or onely from God, becaufe ether there was no protest. church or ministrie, of which they could be sent ordinarily, or at least none such knowne to them. And hervpō may any mā of iudgmēt gather that indeed their Church & religiō was not at all befor Luther. For if it were not visible how came they to knowledg of it? Or if as Fox saith in his Protest. *it was not reported in Histories* how know they that it was? Can they tell what was in times past without relatiō of those who thē liued, vnles they pretend some such reuelatiō as Moyses had to know the Creatiō of the world? Is it not a meere refictiō or imaginatiō, such as euery new start vp Heretick can auouch? Is it not a witles & witfull assertion.

ſertiõ to affirme that there hath bene euer
ſuch kind of people, & yet not to be able to
name one mã of thẽ, one place wher they
were, one witnes of their being? Doth
Gods word force vs to ſuch poore, miſerable, yea incredible ſhifts? Or rather is it
not wrongly vnderſtood when we are
compelled to inuent ſuch ſhamefull ſhifts,
or els to confeſſe that Gods truth and religion was no wher in the world before
Luther? Surely to vſe euen Iuels words in *Incl.*
the like matter, *Articulo 2. diuiſion. 8. It muſt*
needs be a ſtrãge Church that had nether beginning
nor ending, no defender, no reprouer, no mouth to
vtter or eat to hear it, nor pen to write, nor place to
reſt in. And we may ſay to ſuch as Tertul- *Tertulliã*
lian ſaid to ould Heretiks. *VVho are you?*
whence are you? whẽ came you? VVher lurked you
ſo long? The meetings of witches though
they be brought together by the diuel yet
be often times ſeene. The meetings of Fai- *Prote-*
ries though they be ſpirits ſome times are *ſtants for*
diſcried. And were there Proteſtãts theſe *one thou-*
ſand yea-
thouſand yeares & yet more inuiſible than *res more*
ether witches or Fairies? were ther Cõgre- *inuiſible*
them Fai-
gations of them & yet nether ſeene, heard *ries.*
or imagined of by the world? Surely this
kind of Church hath her being as Proteſt.
haue their Iuſtification, that is merely by
beleef or imaginatiõ, not by reall exiſtẽce.
But as Tertullian ſaid of ould Heretiks ſo

some now VVill beleeue without Scriptures that
they may beleeue against Scripture. For what
more without Scripture ether of God or
man, than that there hath bene a Protestant Church for these thousand yeares
and yet we nether saw any such, nor any
that then liued hath tould vs? And what
more against Scripture than to beleeue
that Christ and his Church kept (especially for so long time) *in penetralibus* in corners and lurking holes, that his Church
and Pastors are not a cittie built vpon a
mountaine, a light set open vpon a cand-
lestick that it may shine to all? Or how
could any of them be saued if they professed it not seing confession is made to saluation. Rom. 10.

*Math 4.
& 24.*

5. And this kind of argument must needs
seeme forcible both to Protestants and
Puritans because they both vse it against
their aduersaries. For hereby the forsaid
Surueyer, *cap.* 5. proueth that the Puritan
disciplin was neuer before Caluin, because in all times afore there is no mention or
record of it. And likwise the Puritans proue that Anabaptisme was not before our
daies as you may see in Colloquio Franca-
tal. whose words because they make
much to our present purpose I will here
rehearse. *If you* (say they to the Anabaptists)
*be the Church of God it vvill follovv that God vvas
vvithout*

*Hovv Pu-
ritans
proue that
there
vvere no
Anabap-
tistsbefore
this age.*

without a people and a Church till the year 1522. *in which Nicolas Storck and a litle after Thomas Muncer laid the first foundation of your doctrine.* And this they proue thus. *For if you read all Histories from the beginning of the vvorld you shall not finde a people which had a Confeßion of faith like to yours. But because say they nether God was from the beginning vvithout a people and Church, nor the euerlasting King Iesus Christ vvithout a Kingdom & your Cōgregation began first An.*1522. *it followeth that you can not be the true Church & people of God.* Thus Puritās against the Anabaptists, & we obiect the same to them.

6. As for the second point of the newnes and late rising of Protestancie Luther *Prefat. Epist. Galat. fol.* 2. saith thus: *In these dayes this healthfull knowledg of Christ is now reuealed and raised vp againe.* And the Apologie of the English Church in plaine termes acknowledgeth the newnes of their doctrin thus: *It was easie for thes men* ('Papists) *fortie yeares agoe to deuise thes and other greater crimes against vs when in midst of that darknes some beame of truth then vnknovvne & vnheard of began first to rise.* Loe he cōfesseth that 40. yeares agoe Protest.doct.was not heard of before but then began first to appear. But let vs hear him further. *VVhen Martin Luther* (saith he) *& Hulderic Zuinglius most excellent men & sent of God to lighten the world began first to preach & the matter was yet new* (note) *& the*

That the Protestāts Church is new and lately risen.
Luther.
Apologie alias luel.

428   *The prudentiall Ballance*

euent vncertaine and ther could be no such heinous
wickednes imagined which for the newnes (Note
again) and strangenes of the matter vvould not
be easily be beleeued of the people against vs. Behold it twise confessed that their doctrin
was new and strange also 40. yeares agoe.
And *pag.*13. he biddeth vs to think of the
beginning and proceedings of their religion. D.
Reinolds also in his Confer. *pag.* 152. writeth thus: *It is more likelie that you* (Papists)
*who by long continuance of time haue had long
occasion to steale avvay truth should corrupt the
Fathers than vve vvho haue not had it.* Loe Reynolds confesseth that Protestants haue not
long continewed. Caluin also 4. *inst. c.* 1.
parag. 2. hath these words. *Albeit a heauie deso
latiõ vvhich vve euery vvhere see, doe cria that ther
is nothing of the Church remaining.* And *c.* 3. *para.*
4. plainly auoucheth that ther were no
Churches *rightly setled*, and therfore they
needed to be sent extraordinarily. Cooper
in his Chronicle *An.* 1535. saith, that *Luther
vvrote that Gods light vvas lately renewed.* And
finally Fox to omit others in his *Acts p.* 788.
cõfesseth most plainly that Luthers doctrin
was new in the year 1524. *For thẽ* (saith he)
*the doctrin of Luther first beginning to spring and
being but in the blade*, *vvas not yet knovvne vvhi-
therto it tẽded, nor to vvhat it vvold grovv.* And in
like sorte *p.* 791. he termeth also Zuinglius
doctrine new. To these I might add that
the

Sleid. præfat
Histor.
saith the
original
of Prote.
stancie
vvas in
the begin-
ning of
Charles. 5.
reigne.
Reinolds.

Caluin.

Cooper.

Fox.

Protestãts
doctrin
but in the
blade. An.
1524.

the Patriarch of Conſtantin. to whome
the Proteſt.ſent their doctrin, condemned
it and calleth, *it altogether nevv doctrine.* And
vpon the newnes of their doct. it cometh
that thes termes are moſt vſuall with Pro-
teſt. *The doctrin of the Goſpel vvas borne a nevv.* Calvin. 4.
The Church reſtored, The Goſpel reſtored. Chriſts inſtit.cap. 7.
doctine renewed, Gods word began to ſhine. The 24.Apol.
renouatiō of the Goſpel.The riſing of the nevv Hie Aug.pag.
ruſalē.The birth of the Goſpel,Secōd birth of Chriſt 56.194.
Religion borne againe. And their *firſt maiſters* VVhisak.
their *firſt Biſhops* their *Apoſtles* or *Euangeliſts,* cont. Dur.
Luther,Latimer, Ridly & the like. Hence 140. Bale
what will follow euery one ſeeth, to wit, Cent. 8.cap.
that the Proteſt.Church or faith is not the 60.68.100.
Church or ſaith of Chriſt, which begun Cent.1. cap.
about 16.hundred years agoe; but a new 74.Feild. of
Church begun not yet one hundred ſince. the Church
Or that Chriſts Church & faith was quite lib.3.cap.
dead & gone, and Luther raiſed it againe 39.Suruey
to life. And what Church then I pray you cap. 8.
was that wherin he was Chriſtened? was
it Pagan? were his Godfathers Heathens?
was he whē he was baptized made a Paynim? whēce came this new Church raiſer?
from what heauen fell he? from what ſea
ſprunge he? from what earth roſe he? That all
7. Touching the third point to be proued the firſt
that the Proteſtants firſt and cheef tea- Proteſtant
chers were once Roman Catholicks and Preachers
went from our Church and religion it is had bene
before
Rom. Ca-
tholiks.

ſo manifeſt as nether is it nor can it be
denyed. For Luther 1.*Gal fol.*37. ſaith thus
of him ſelf:*I was as earneſt for the Popes laws as
euer any was, I honored the Pope of meere cōſciēce.*
And *fol.*38. *I did ſo highly eſteeme the Popes authoritie that to diſſent from him euen in the leaſt
point I thought it a ſin worthie of euerlaſting deathe
and wold my ſelf in defeuce of the Popes authoritie
haue miniſtred fire and ſword.* And *fol.*188.
*VVe that are ould haue bene trained vp in Popiſh
error euen from our youth.* Thus teſtified Luther for him ſelf and his German Prote-

Calvvin. ſtants. Caluin 4.*inſtit.cap.*2 *parag.*4.for him
ſelf and the French Proteſtants ſaith
thus: *VVe haue departed from their (Popiſh)
Church.c.6.para.*1.*VVe haue left the See of Rome
cap.*15.*parag.*17. *VVe confeſſe we were long time
blind and incredulous, vnderſtood not the matters
of baptiſme, now we accuſe our blindnes & hardnes

Iuel. of hart.* The Apologer of England ſpeaking
for him ſelf & the Engliſh Miniſters writeth thus *pag.*188. *VVe haue indeed gone from
the Pope we haue ſhaken of the yoke of the Biſhop

Fox. of Rome.* Finally Fox *Acts. pag.*3. ſpeaking
generally of Proteſtants ſaith : *It is true
that we are remoued from the Church of Rome.*
And D. Reinolds amongſt his Conclu-

Reinolds. ſions maketh this one . *That the reformed
Churches in England Scotland France Germanie and other Kingdoms and Common wealthes
haue ſeuered them ſelues lawfully* (ſaith he)
from

from the Church of Rome. And if this be so notorious and confessed of all the cheefe Maisters & Churches of Protestants that before Luthers reuolt they were all Roman Catholicks, vndoubted it ought to be of al other Protestants of meaner sorte, and consequently there was neuer a Protestant before him.

8. Fourthly I proue by reason that Luther was the first beginner of Protestancy. For as Iuell saith Art. 1. diuis. 7. *Eckius, Pighius, Hosius, and others who liued in Luthers time haue cried out a maine in their books and pulpits where was your religion before Luther began.* The like hath Fox *Acts pag.* 749. and all know to be true. And yet could neither Luther then, nor any since for him name one man woman or child then liuing who had bene a Protestant before Luther. And howsoeuer it may be thought that beforeLuthers preaching Protestants kept secret, yet can it not be thought but when they knew him to preach securely, they wold haue discried themselues and runne to him, if any such had bene. Besides that, there are men yet liuing who can remember that the first Protestants were Catholicks before Luthers new preaching. Fox in his *Acts pag.* 749. proposing the forsaid question to himselfe nameth a few, who rather shew that there were no Protestants in England before

A question neuer answered by Protestats.

1
2
3

fore Luther. For 1. all the persons whom he nameth abiured their faith as him selfe confesseth *pag.* 750. *and died* (as he'writeth) *shortly after for greef or liued with shame.* 2. these abiurers were (as he setteth down) in the yeare 1521. foure yeares after! Luthers new preaching, and we aske for Protestants before his preaching. 3. no one of these abiured persons was accused for holding iustification by only faith which point is the soule head & foundation of Protestancie as hath bene shewed before and shall hereafter : so that without it they could be no Protestants. And if they had held it, it wold haue bene discouered. For as Fox saith *pag.* 650. *The Catholick Prelats made such diligent inquisition and examination as nether was any word so closely spoken of them no articles mentioned, but it was it discouered.* Wherefore indeed those abiurers were but pore reliques of the Lollards of whome we shall speake hereafter.

9. Lastly I proue that Luther was the beginner of Protestancie by the plaine & open confession of diuers Protestants and testimony of Luther himselfe. For, Doct. Couell in his booke of Articles published by authority Art. 19. *pag.* 130. saith thus: *Some Protestāts make Luther & Caluin Authors of the religion among vs.* D. Doue of Recusan-

cie

Fox his Church consisting of abured persons Hovv protested they that abiured.

Fox.

That Luther vvas Author of Protestancie confessed by Protestāts. Covel. Dous.

cie p.32. *Luther* (faith he) *in his time began a* Reformation, And a booke termed the *Harbo-rough* & much efteemed in the beginning of Q. Elizabeth, maketh England to fpeak thus . *I am thy countrie England , who brought forth that bleffed man Iohn VVicklef who begot Hus, who begot Luther,who begot truth.* And in the margent hath this note. *The fecond birth of Chrift.* Fox alfo *Acts* pag. 770, faith *Luther pluckt downe the foundatiō of Papiftrie by opening one veine long hid before,* the *touch ftone of all truth and the onlie principall origen of our faluation, which is our free iuftification by faith onely.* And the Author of the booke called *Prognoftica finis mūdi* or *Antichriftus* writeth thus *The fpirit which telleth things to come vvorketh not but in time of the Gofpell which Luther as it is cōfeffed* (note the word) *tovvards the end of the vvorld did firft bring in.* And p.13. *The feduction of falfe prophets is not manifeft but vnder the Gofpell vvhich before Luther as vve faid neuer vvent fince the primitiue time of the Apoftles.* And Cōrad Schuffelb. *l.2.* Caluin Theol. p.130. doubteth not to call it *impudencie to fay that many learned men before Luther did hold the doctrine of the Gofpell.* Georg. Milius *in explicat . art . 7. Confeff. Aug. If there had bene* (faith he) *right beleuers before Luther there had bene no need of a Luther an reformation.* Benedict Morgenftein *tract. de Euchar . pag.* 145. faith, *it is ridiculous to think that in time before Luther any*

(note)

Right margin notes:

Harbo-rough.

Luther begot truth.

Fox.

Luther opened the veine of all truth.

Progn oft.

Luther firft brought in his Gofpel.

Schuffelb. Impudencie to fay thervvere Gofpelleis befor Luther.

Milius. Morgerftern. Ridiculous to fay any had pure doctrin befor Luther.

(note) *had the purity af doctrine and that Luther should receaue it from them considering it is
manifeft* (note againe) *to the whole Chriftian
world that before Luthers time all Churckes were*

*ouerwhelmed with more than Cymerian darknes
& that Luther was diuinely raifed to difcouer the
same and to reftore the light of true doctrine.* Thus
Proteftāts: but let vs hear alfo Luther him
felfe: *VVe dare glorie* (faith hePrefat. in Corpus doctrinæ lipfiæ 1561.) *that Chrift was
firft published of vs* And de *Captiu.initio.* fpeaking of his impugning indulgences faith:
I alone did then roole this ftone. And 1. *Galat.fol.
26.we by the grace of God haue gottē here at VVit-*

temberg the forme of a Chriftian Church. And 3.
Galat. fol. 109. *many gaue thanks to God that
through the Ghofpell which we firft* (note) *by the
grace of God then preached &c.*fol.142. *we haue
receaued the firft fruits of the fpirit.*4, Galat.fol
205. *Sectaries at the beginning of the reformatiō
of the Gofpell were glad to heare vs and read our*

*bookes.*Ibid. *The truth of the Gofpell, God hath
now againe in thes latter daies reueiled by vs vnto
this vngratefull world.*

:0.   Thus you fee it euident by many
waies that Luther was the firft inftitutor
of Proteftant religion & founder of their
Church, and confequently that their religion and Church, is a deuife and inuention of man. Wherupon what will follow
euery one feeth. And as Luther was the
Au-

Author of Proteſtancy in Germany, ſo
alſo from him it ſpred into England and
other Countries not only by means of his
books, but alſo by his and his ſcholers
Melancthon Pomeran & others particuler letters written to Engliſh men, and
by the example of the German Proteſtāts
which as Stow ſaith King Henry 8. followed in reiecting the Pope, And finally
becauſe Tindal who is termed the Apoſtle *Tindal the Pro-*
of England went as Fox ſaith, *pag.* 983. *teſt. Apo-*
into Germany and *there had conference with* *England*
Luther. Wherupon the ſaid Fox ſaith *pag.* *taught by*
1013. *that from Germany Luthers Goſpell began to* *Luther.*
ſpread his beames here in England. And ſo wee
may iuſtly account Luther the Author or *Proteſtan-*
founder of Proteſtāt religion in our Eng- *cie came*
liſh Nation. And howſoeuer ſome will *out of Germanie*
obſtinatly deny, againſt all the forſaid *into*
profes that Luther was the Author of *Engl.*
their religion, but it was (forſooth) before
Luther, though they know nether where,
nor in whom, norcan produce any witnes:
yet neither doth any, nor can any deny, *K Henrie 8.*
but that this late reuolt of our Engliſh *in Stedan*
Nation from the See of Rome, came ori- *lib. 8. fol.*
ginally from Luther, as the vnion ther of *Proteſtants*
to the ſaid See aboue one thouſand years *came into*
agoe proceded from Saint Auſtin: which *out of*
ſufficeth me to compare the vnion in *Germanie*
faith of our Engliſh Nation with the

See

VVhat is shevved of luther the like may be prooued of Calvin or anie other Sectmaister of our time Besides our ministers say Luther differeth from the in no substantiall point Iuel Apol Feild of Church Reinolds Confer. VViclef no Protestant.

1

VViclef knevv not so much as the foundatiō of Protestancie.

See of Rome with the disunion therof, in their two principall Authors S. Austin and Martin Luther. And thus hauing shewed that there was no Protestant liuing, ether in England or other wher when Luther began , let vs see whether ther had bene any in England in times past.

CHAP. II.

That VVicklefe and his followers were no Protestants.

1. **A**Lbeit Protestants challeng some few others who liued about Wicklefs time, yet becaufe their greatest hope is in him and his followers. in so much that Doctor Fulke answere to a Counterf. Catholick *pag.* 24. faith, that *he weeneth that we will not deny VVicklef to haue bene of their Church* , I will for breuity sake omit the rest, and shew that euen Wicklife and his companie were far from being Protestants. First, becaufe to hold iustification by only faith is as is before shewed *lib.* 1. *cap.* 21.

21. by generall consent of Protestants *the head, the soule, the foundation of their Church and religion*, And as Luther saith *Præfat. Epist. ad Galat: As many as hold not this doctrine are either Iewes, Turkes, Popish, or Hereticks*. But Wicklef and his mates held not iustification by only faith. For as Melancthon cheefest scholler to Luther writeth *Epist. ad Fred. Micon. inter Epist. Zuinglÿ pag. 622. He nether vnderstood nor held the iustice of faith*. Besides nether Wicklef, nor any of his followers were euer accused by any of the Catholick Inquisitors of those times of that point, albeit as Fox saith *pag. 750.* their inquisition was so strait, that *no article could be mentioned amongst them, but it was discouered*. Moreouer many of Wicklefes bookes are yet extant, and neuertheles no Protestant hath yet found this their fundamentall Article of iustification by only faith in any of his bookes'. How then could Wicklefe be a Protestant who knew not so much as the head soul and foundation of Protestancie?

VViclef held not iustification by onely faith.

2. Secondly, Wicklef held diuers things which Protestantes condemne, as that, *if any Bishop or Priest be in deadly sin, he doth neyther order consecrat nor baptize,* which Fox *pag. 400.* sayth can hardly

2
VViclef holdeth diuers things condemned by Protestâts.

Seê more
of his Ar-
ticles in
Concil.
Conftan-
tien.
hardly be defended. And that *fo long as a
man is in deadly fin he is no Bishop or Prelat in the
Church of God. That temporall Lords may according to their ovvne vvill and difcretion take
avvay the temporall goods from the Church men
vvhenfoeuer they do offend.* which articles
Fox *pag. cit.* defendeth no otherwife then
by faying *that preaduenture they vvere not fo
ftrictly ment of him as they were gathered* . Moreouer Fox *pag.* 414. amongft other articles of Wiclete citeth thefe. *To enrich the
Clergie is againft the rule of Chrift There is no
greater Heretick or Antichrift than the Clerke
who teacheth that it is lawfull for Priefts and
Leuits of the lavv of grace to be endued vvith tē-
porall poffefsions.* To which Stow *Anno.*1376.
addeth this other. *That neither King nor any
feculer perfon could giue any thing perpetually
to any perfon of the Church.* Further more as
Fox hath *pag.* 392. he extolled *the perfection
of pouerty of the begging Friers,* and as Stow
faith *l. cit. adioyned himfelfe to them.* And

vvhy
VVıclef
impugned
the Cath.
faith.
the caufe why he inueighed againft the
Church was as there Stow faith *becaufe he
had bene depriued by the Archbishop of Canterb.
of a benefice that he vniuftly as was faid was in-
cumbent vpon.* Laftly Fox *pag.* 410. fetteth
downe a letter which he wrote to Pope
Vrban 6 . *Anno* 1382. (which was about
three yeares before he died) wherin he
confeffeth the Pope to be *Chrifts Vicar on
earth*

earth and addeth thus: *If I haue erred in any of thes points I will submit my selfe to correction euen by death if necessitie so require.* Diuers other points which Protestants detest are collected out of his books by the Author of the Protestants Apologie for the Roman Church *pag.* 106. And more of Wicklefs wicked life and doctrine you may see in walsingham histor.*pag.* 188, 206. 302 ypadig. *pag.* 139 142.

3.   Thirdly diuers Protestants refuse VVicklife for one of theirs and account him an Heretik. As Pantaleon Chronall. *pag.* 119. placing VViclife amongst Hereticks saith thus of him : *VViclife vvith the Lollard preacheth his heresie in England.* And the foresaid Melancthon *epist. cit. I haue looked* (saith he) *into VVicklese, vvho maketh a great adoe about this controuersy* (of the Eucharist) *but I haue found many other errors in him by vvhich vve may iudge of his spirit. Surely he neither vnderstood nor held the iustice of faith. He foolishly confoundeth the Gospell and ciuill affairs, nor perceaueth that the Gospell giueth vs leaue to vse the pollicie of all nations. He laboreth to proue that Priests shold haue no proprietie. He vvill haue no tithes paid but to those that teach. He sophistically and very seditiously cauilleth of ciuill dominion. In like manner he sophistically cauilleth at the common*

F f   *receaued*

receaued opinion of the *Eucharist* . And in
loc. Com. titul. de potest Eccles. he plainly faith that *VVicklefe plaied the made man.*
Doctor Caius alſo *lib. 2. de Antiquit. pag.*
268. obiecteth Wicklife to the oxonians
as a diſgrace to their vniuerſity . And
Stow in his Chronicles deſcribeth Bale
Oldcaſtell and others his followers as
notorious malefacors and rebells to
their Prince . yea Luther himſelfe *explicat. Art.* 30. ſpeaking of Huſſits who
were Wickleſiſts in Bohemia (ſo termed of Hus Wicklefs principall ſcholler) faith. *They do not well who make me
a Huſsit , for he held not with me .* And
in diſput. Anno 40. *tom.* 1. *pag.* 493. Hus
faith he *tought horrible and diueliſh blaſphemie .* So far was Luther from accounting Wicklefs followers for Proteſtants.

4.   Finally the Sheriffes in England
euer ſince Wicklefs time do take on
oath to perſecute Lollards , which was
the vulger name of Wiclefs followers.
Which King Edward 6. Queene Elizabeth and his preſent maieſtie and Miniſters would not ſuffer , nor the Proteſtant
Sheriffs would take ſuch an oath if they
accounted Wicleſiſts Proteſtants . And it
being thus manifeſt that Wicklef and his
companie were no Proteſtants , much
more

Caius.

Stovv.

Lnther.

So D.
Doue of
Recuſan-
cie vvill
haue Bel-
larmiu a
Proteſtant
or no per-
fect Pa-
piſt.

4
The
Sheriffs
ſvveare to
peſecute
VVicle-
ſiſts.

more manifest it is that no other English man before King Henrie 8. his time was Protestant. Which thing Cramner neuer doubted of when (as Bale reporteth *Cent. 8.cap.90.* he offered to defend, *that the religion apointed by King Edward 6. was more pure and agreable to Gods word than what* (said he) *had bene vsed in England this thousand years.* So clear it was in Cramners iudgment that Protestancie had not bene vsed in England for one thousand years before him. But because some Protestants do hope to find some foating of their religion in the ancient Britons before that time, let vs see of what religion they were, that therby it may appear that nether English nor British were euer Protestants before Luthers time.

Cramner.

Protestancie not vsed in Engl for one thousand years befor K Edvv.6.

CHAP. III.

That the ancient Britons were neuer Proteſtants.

VVhy Pro-
teſtants
chaleng
the Bri-
tons.

I

2

1. THe reaſon why Fox, Bale, Fulke & othert calleng the ancient Britons for Proteſtáts, is not becauſe that they can proue that thy held their fundamental point of Iuſtification by faith, or any other ſubſtanciall point of Proteſtancy, but only becauſe for a whil they diſagreed from our S. Auſtin in ſome things, to wit, about the time of keeping Eaſter, and manner of baptizing, and *ſuch rites,* (as S. Auſtin ſpeaketh in Beda *lib. 2. cap. 2.*) *and cerimonies.* And alſo becauſe they thinck, that by reaſon of ſcarſitie of Records, we cannot proue that Britons held theſe points of our faith ,which Proteſtants do deny. Which reaſons will ſerue as wel to proue that the Ancient Britons were Brownifts , or Anabaſtis, as that they were Proteſtants . But God willing we will ſhew by irrefragable teſtimonies of Antiquity , that albeit the ancient Britons were ſome time infected with ſome antient

lib. 1. c. 1.

cient herefy, as hath bene fhewed before, yet they euer held fo many points of Catholicke religiō, as they neuer could be Proteftants, but quite oppofit to them.

2.   And as for the religion of the Britons for the firft 300. yeares after Chrift, which was the time in the perfecution of the primitiue Church, that may be eafily gathered by the religion which they profeffed ftreight after the perfecution was ended, vnder their glorious Contriman the firft Chriftian Emperour Conftantine the great. Both becaufe there is no mention of any alteration made by them in religion all that time, and alfo becaufe Gildas *cap.* 9. and Saint Bəda *lib.* 1. *cap.* 4. and 8. write, that till the time of Arian herefy, or as Bale cent. 1. *cap.*70. Fox in his Proteftat: Fulke *annotat. in* 2. *Cor.* 12. teftify, till the time of S. Auftins comming there was no change of their religion. Let vs fee therefore what religion they profeffed in Conftantins time.

3.   Firft they builded, faith S. Beda *lib.* 1. *cap.*7. *a Temple of a meruailous rich vvorke in the place vvhere S· Alban vvas martired*, and belieued in that place fick perfons to be cured, &many miracles to be wrought. Secōdly they builded, faith he *l.* 1 *c.*8. *Temples of holy Martirs.* And the like did Conftantin himfelfe

Antient Britons Catholiks. Miracles beleued in places of Martyrdoms. Temple of holie Martyrs.

Ff 3

Euseb.lib.3. de vit. cap.47. To this D. Abbots againſt D. Biſhop *p. 173.* anſwereth, That

Obieƈtiō.

Conſtantin by bnilding Churches in the honor of Martyrs ment not to honor their perſons but to celebrat their names. This

Ansvver.

gloſſe deſtroieth the Text. For if the word (*matyrs*) do ſignifie their perſons, he in building Churches in honor of Martyrs, ment therby to honor their perſons . And as to

Obieƈtiō. Ansvver. To honor Martyrs by building Churches is to honor them by a religious aƈt.

buildChurches is no ciuil or prophane aƈt, as is to built Trophes or ſuch monuments, but a religious aƈt, ſo to honor Martyrs by building of Churches is to giue thē religious honor. And if Chriſtians by building of Churches in honor of Saints had ment

1

no more than an honorable memory of their names, whie did they neuer build

2

Churches in honor of Princes, or of any perſons aliue or dead whoſe names they might honorablie remember? beſids that tp celebrat ones name & not to houer his perſon is to implie cōtradiƈtion, For by ce-

3

lebrating a name we intend not to make ſuch a ſonnd or ſuch letters famous, but cheeſly and principally the perſon ſignified therby: And to make a perſon famous is it no honor to him? And if we make him famous, by a religious aƈt, (as Conſtantin made the Martyrs famous by building of Churches) wee

Collins.

giue him a religious honor . Wherfore
                                        Collins

Collins in his sermon at Paules Crosse 1607. dedicated to the Archb. of Canterb. and allowed of him saith *pag.* 52 .that building of Churches to Saints was one cause of Protestants for forsaking our Church.

4. Moreouer Constantin (as Euseb. saith *lib.* 4. *de Constant.* c60. caused himselfe to be buried in the Church of the Apostles *Ita vt post obitum etiam precibus illis quæ eo loci ad honorem Apostolorum futuræ essent dignus haberetur.* Behould Constantin hoping after his death to be holpen by prayers: and those made in honor of the Apostles , which are two especiall points of Papistrie. To this D. Abbots *l. cit pag.* 177. answereth, that Eusebius mistooke Constantins meaning for he desired no prayers to be made for his soule, Because he said *lib.* 4. *cap.* 63, *Now indeed I know that I am a happie man, that God hath accounted me worthy of immortall life. and that I am now made partaker of the light of God. And againe , that he had obtained the true life , & none but himselfe vnderstood of what happines he was partaker*, *and therefore he hastned and would not delay his going to God.* Thus Abbots. To omit that those words *God hath accounted me worthie of eternall life* are not in Eusebius translated by musculus a Protestant , but for them are these *iam me æternam vitam sortitum liquet.* Is it not

I pray

3
Pariers for dead, and in honor of Saints.

See his maiesties allovvance of Constantins religion in all points, in Confer. at Hampton Court, *pag.* 69. Obiecctio.

Ansvver.

I pray the (Reader) ſtrange, that Abbots
born laſt day ſhould know what was
Conſtantins meaning better than Euſeb.
who liued familiarly with him? Nay better than all men than liuing, to whome
Euſeb. ſaith *cap.* 59. that his intent was
factum perſpicuum made manifeſt? Or that
Abbots ſhould gather Conſtantins meaning out of Euſeb. his words better than
Euſeb. that wrote them? Perhaps Con-
ſtatin might, being a very vertuous Prince
eſpecially ſtraight after his baptiſme (as
Euſeb. ſaith theſe words were ſpoken)
ſay, with S. Paule *nihil mihi conſcius ſum,* and
therupon account himſelf happy & wor-
thy of eternall life and *in ſpe* to haue obtained it, yet muſt he needs adde alſo with
S. Paule *nec tamẽ in hoc iuſtificatus ſum,* which
might wel make him deſire prayer for him
both aliue & dead. If Abbots could proue
as he neuer ſhall, that Conſtantin ſaid, as
the Proteſtants do, that he did not pro-
bably think, but certainly know , that his
ſoule not ſoone or late , but immediatly
after it were out of the body, ſhould go to
heauẽ as the ſoules of martirs do, he might
wel ſay that Cõſtatin cared not for praiers
after death. For vpõ certain knowledg of
martyrs happines we pray not for them,
but ſhould do thẽ iniury (as S. Auſtin ſaith)
if we did. For therby we ſhould ſhew that

we

Abbotts
taketh
vpon him
to knovv
the mea-
ning of
Enſeb. his
vvords
letter
then him
ſelf.

we were not fuly affured of their hapines. But with probable knowledg, or hopeful truth, ether of our owne or others felicitie, we may both defire prayers for vs after our death, or pray for others dead. Becaufe though we hope wel, yet we are not fully affured, and till we be affured of a thing, we may pray for it. And this was the cafe of Conftantin and S. Monica, when they defired to be prayed for after their death; And of S. Auftin and S. Ambrofe when they prayed for Monica and Theodofius whome they beleeued (as S. Auftin fpeaketh) to be in heauen, but were not therof certain and fecure.

VVe can not praie for them vvhom vve are affured to bein heauen. But for them vvhom vve onely hope are there. VVhie.

5. Again Conftantin *tranflated* (faith Saint Hierom cont. Vigilant.) *The holy reliques of Andrew Luke and Timothie at which* (faith he) *the Diuels roare, to Conftantinople.* He figned him felfe with the Croffe, and made him felfe be painted with the Croffe on his head, Eufeb. *l. 3. de vit. c. 2. & 3.* He profeffed to haue ouercome his enemyes *by the wholfome figne of the Croffe.* Eufeb, *de vit. lib. 1. cap. 33.* He worfhiped the Croffe, Sozom. *k 1. cap 8.* He *worfhiped the Croffe both becaufe he had had much help by it in battels against his enemies, and by reafon of his heauenly vifion which he favve of it.* But to beleeue we may be holpe by the Croffe (as Conftantin did) is papiftical, as Do. Abbots granteth anfvver to Do.

4 Tranflatiõ of reliques 5 Bleffe vvith the figne of the Croffe 6 Hope of victorie by the Croffe. 7 VVorship of the Croffe. See Confer. at Hamp. Court about the vvorld VVorship. *pag.* 75.

Bifhop

8
Esteemeof Nonnes.

9
Priests
confessed
to haue
pouer to
iudge.
Kings.

10
Profession
of the
Popes supremacie.

11
Priests
and people praie
for Constant dead
His maiestie in
Confer at
HamPt.
Court.
saith he
seeth no
reason
but vvhat
vvas vsed
in Constantins
time
maie still
continevv
pag.69.

Bishop *Epist.pag.*168. His mother also did honor and serue as their mayden , *Virgines. Deo sacratas Dedicated to God.* Ruffin *lib.*1.*c.*8. which Virgines if they were not Cloister Nonnes as Abbots termeth them *pag.*171. they were votaire Nonnes, which Protestants can as ill abide. He professed besides that he had no power to iudg of Priests. *God* (saith Constantin, in Ruffinus *lib.*1.*c.*2.) *hath made yovv Priests , and giuen yow povver to iudg euen of vs : vvherfor vve are rightly iudged of yovv. Yovv are giuen to vs as Gods and it is not conuenient that men should iudg Gods.* Abbots *pag.* 191. saith he spake this of modestie and humilitie. But I ask whither he spake thus as he thought or no? Yf yea? Then he thought Priests to haue power to iudg him, if no ? than he spake against his conscience, and not humbly but falsly. Further more in his Edict he calleth Bishop Siluester *the high Priest and Vniuersall Pope, and the head and top of all Churches in the vvorld* . And finally when he *was* dead, many people (saith Euseb.*l.*4. *de vit c.*71. *together vvith the that vvere dedicated to God, vvith many teares offered prayers to God for the soule of the Emperor* . By which yow may see the Papisticall faith both of that noble Emperor, and of his Priests & people. And to expound their prayers for his soule, of onely wel wishing as Protestants doe to their frends departed , as Abbots expoundeth

deth them p.178. is ridiculous. For if Eusebius had mét that thofe onely wifhed wel,
and not indeed prayed for Conftantins
foule, he could haue fayd fo. Nay he would
haue faid fo. For the lawe of Hiftorie bindeth the writer to proprietie of fpeech.
But, *durum telum neceßitas* , For Proteftants
can not ftand, vnles fcriptures, Fathers,
Hiftoriographers be expounded figurati-
uely. And fo manifeftly was Pope Siluefter
who cathechifed this Emperor, a Roman
Catholick, as Bale *Cent.* 1.*c.* 36. faith. *In thefe*
times (of Conftantin) *Siluefter began to lay the*
foundatiõ of the Popes Monarchie & finding the key
of the Depth he opened the pit, if it be true (which
he nether denieth nor reproueth) *which*
Papifts write of him. And *Ibid.* All the Popes
after Siluefter to *Boniface* 3. he termeth *mit-*
red Bishops preparing by their Cannons & Decrees
the feat for the great Antichrist . And Napier
vpon the reuelatiõ p. 68. calleth the vifible
Church in Conftantins time Antichriftiã,
& Papifticall. This was the Papifticall religion of this worthie Emperor. And vndoubtedly the fame was thẽ the religiõ of
the Britõs, who were his fubiects & Con-
triemẽ, & amõgft whome (as Sozomé faith
l. 1.*c.* 5. he came to knowledg of Chrift. relig.
6. Now for the next 300. yeares vntil S.
Auftins coming, that the Britons were no
Proteftants, may be prooued out of diuers
authors.

Religion of Britons for the second 300. yeares. Gildas.

1

Altars of ftone. Priefts Sacrifices.

2

Vovves of Chaftitie, and of Monkish life. No mariage for monks after their vovv. Sucaring by our ladic and Saints. Beda.

1

Church in honor of Saints. Monks. Anchorets.

2

Holic vvater. Reliques:

authors. Firft Gildas *cap.* 24. teftifieth that the Britons had holy *Altars of ftone*, and *cap.* 26. calleth them *celeftis Sacrificij fedem*. Seats *of the heauenly facrifice*: and reprehendeth Priefts for *facrificing feldom*, & calleth their facrifices *Sacrofancta Chrifti Sacrificia*: *Moft holy facrifices of Chrift*. Which argueth that they then had true facrifices, true Altars, true Priefts. And touching Vowes he condemneth *cap.* 26. Kings for breaking them, condemneth one King for marying a woman who had vowed *Perpetuam Viduitatis caftimoniam*: Perpetuall chaftitie in VVidowbood. And exclameth againft an other King for forfaking Monks life, and calleth his mariage after his vow, *Prafumptiuas nuptias*: Pretended mariage. Finally *cap.* 26. he teftifieth, that the Britons vfed to fweare by God, and by our Lady, and all Saints. All thefe points of Catholick religion Gildas toucheth, and nameth no one point of Proteftancie. As for S. Beda he faith *lib.1.cap.27.* that they had a Church built in honor of S. Martin. *cap.* 11. and *lib.2.cap.* 2. That they had Monks and Anchorets. *l.* 1. *cap.* 17. that S. German (with whome they agreed in religion) *by a fewe fprincles of* (holy) *vvater affvvaged tempefts and droue avvay Diuels. c.* 18. that he caried about his neck a bag of reliques, by which putting it to a blinde womans eye he reftored her fight. *Ibid.*

That

That they went *to S. Albans to giue God praise,*

and thancks by him (S. Alban) *and there tooke of the duft where the holy Martirs blood vvas fhed.* *cap.* 20. Obferued the 40. dayes of Lent deuoutly finging *Aleluia* after Eafter. *Ibid.* God (faith Beda) *gaue S. German and S. Luphus prosperous paſſage home for their ovvne vertues fake, and alſo at the interceſsion of the bleſſed martyr S. Alban.* All theſe proofes affordeth S. Beda that the Britons were Roman Catholicks before Saint Auftins coming, and no one proofe, that they were Proteftants.

Profpe-
rous iue-
ceſſe at-
tributed
in parte
to Saints.

7. Galfrid alſo *lib.9. c. 12.* faith that in this time Saint Dubricius the Archb. of Wales was *Apoftolice fedis Legatus* : that is, the Popes Legat. Malmsb. *lib.1. Reg. c. 1.* And Hunting. *lib. 2.* fay that King Arthur trufting *in an Image of our B. Ladie vvhich he put in his vveapons, he alone put his enemies to flight vvith great ſtaughter.* Stow alſo Chron. *p.* 61. faith that King Arthurs body was found in K. Henrie 2. time with a leaden Croſſe faftned to that fide of the ftone that lay next his body. Caius alſo a Proteft. *lib. de Antiq. Cantab. pag.* 75. citeth letters of Pope Honorius dated *Anno* 624. in which the Pope confirmeth the priuiledges which his Predeceſſors had giuen to the Briton Students, and prohibiteth any Archb. or Bifhop to excommunicat the ftudents. Such authoritie did the Britons acknow-

Galfrid.

Popes
legat.

Malmesb.
Huntingt.

Some ho-
pe of help
by images.

Stovv.
Burial
vvith
Croſſes.

Caius.
Priuiled-
ges procu-
red from
Popes.

ledg

ledg the Popes to haue ouer them. In this time also saith Bale *Cent.14.cap.6. Palladius was sent of Pope Celestin to set order amongst the Scotts after the Roman maner.* And *cap.11. Brigit wrought great wonders with holy water* . And *Cent.1. cap. 53. Aegiptian Monkerie* (so he termeth our Monkerie) *about the yeare* 530. *vnder Abbot Congel tooke great strength and increase.* And that S. Columba and Saint Brendan (who filled France, Germanie, Ierland, with Monkes and which Brendan *Cent.14. cap.78.* he confesseth to haue held Purgatorie) were scollers to this Congel. To which he addeth *Cent.1. cap.* 50. That Gildas a Briton of this time did seeke the solitarie places of the desert, *and vse heirecloth next his skin*; And *cap.*61. That Kentigernus *vsed goatskinnes, and a strait coole.* Which is no fashon of Protestāts. Finally S.Sampson a Briton Bishop going in those times out of Britany into France, his religion was not onely there admitted for Catholick, but him selfalso had there a Bishoprick giuen to him. And his Kinsmā S.Maglorius being a Briton, was ordered by him *to dispense the quickening bodie of our Lord : Did eat barley and beane bread, on VVensday and friday tooke no meate, did afflict his flesh with continuall wearing of hearcloth, did watchfully say the prayers of the night which are termed Mattins, and prostrat before the Altar did* **sing**

sing Letanies, and finally offered sacrifice to God.
Surius *Tom.* 5. VVhat signe is there here
of Protestancie, or rather not of earnest
Papistrie?

Britons
in S. Au-
stins time
differ not
in faith
but about
Easter.
S. Austins
I

8. And as for the faith of the Britons in S.
Austins time, that, (besides some few ceremonies) differed in nothing from S. Austins faith , but onely about the time of
keeping Easter, as may be proued many
wayes. First, by S. Austin him selfe, who in
Beda *lib.* 2. *cap.* 2. speaketh thus to the Britons. *Though in manie other points you doe con-*
trary to our custom (not faith) or rather contrarie
to the custom of the Vniuersall Church . Yet if yee
will agree with vs in three things: That is, to cele-
brat Easter in due time, to accomplish the mistery
of baptisme according to the maner of the holy
Roman and Apostolick Church, and lastly preach to
the English Nation the worde of God, all your other
ceremonies (not heresies) *rites , fashons , and*
customs , though they be contrarie to oures we will
suffer and bear with them. Behould S. Austin
though so earnest a Papist as hath bene
shewed before, yet offering to ioyne with
the Britous, if they would amend onely
three things , wherof the first onely concerned faith , the other two concerned
ceremonies , and charity . Would he,
(thinck we) who was so nice in matters
of religion , as he would not ioine with
the Britons vnles they conformed them
selues.

felues to him in certain ceremonies, haue not much more exacted their conformitie in Maſſe, vſe of Images, and ſuch like points of religion, as it is euident he vſed. if they had differed from him in ſuch matters? Beſides yow ſee, that the other things wherin they differed from him, were but (as he ſpeaketh) *ceremonies, rites, faſhions, and cuſtoms.* Secondly, the Britons them felues in Beda *lib. 2. c. 2.* publickly confeſſed, that that was *the true vvay of righteouſnes vvhich S. Auſtin ſhevved.* And the onely reaſon which they giue there, why they would not ioyne with him, was pride, as they imagined, in him. Thirdly S. Beda though a perfect Papiſt, as hath bene ſhewed before by the confeſsion of Proteſtants, yet findeth no more fault with the Britons than S. Auſtin did.

2

3

The Britons religion by the Irish and Scotts

9. But yet more fully will the Britons religion appeare by the religion of Iriſh and Scots in thoſe dayes. For as, Laurence Mellit, and Iuſtus three follow laborers of Saint Auſtin write in Beda *lib. 2. cap. 4. The Scots did nothing differ from the Britons.* And the Iriſh being couerted by S. Patrick a Britō,

Hunting. lib. 3.

it is moſt lykely they agreed with them in religion, and ſure it is, that they agreed with them in the time of keeping Eaſter. VVhat therfor can be proued of ether of theſe two Nations, may be iuſtly inferred of the

of the Britons. Adamannus therfor an
Irish Abbot in Beda *lib. 5. cap. 22.* professeth
Saint Peter to be head of the Apostles and
looked to haue him as a Patron before
God. And Colman a Scottish Bishop who
altogether agreed with the Britons, and
obstinatly refused to admit the Romã vse
of Easter, yet neuer the les agreed with
the Catholicks *without any cõtradiction* (saith
Beda *lib. 3. cap. 25.*) That these words. *Thou
art Peter & vpon this Rock I will build my Church
were principally spoken to Peter. And that vnto
him the keyes of the Kingdom of heauen were
giuen.* Which brefly is to confesse with
Catholicks, that Peter was head of the
Church. For if these words, *Vpon this Rock
I will build my Church* were principally spoken to him, surely he was principally made the Rock and head of Christs Church.
VVhich Bale *Cent. 14. c. 21.* wel perceaued,
when he writeth that S. VVilfrid (who
then disputed with Colman) founded, *non
interpretabilem* (as he speaketh) *Papæ authoritatem* vpõ these words, *Tu es Petrus* &c. To
whome in this (as yow heard) Colman
agreed without contradiction, and consequently beleeued, *Non interpretabilem Papæ
authoritatem,* as wel as Saint VVilfrid. And
from this vniuersall and former beleefe of
Saint Peters Supremacie, it came that the
Picts when they were reconciled to the

Gg Ro-

1
S. Peter head of the Apostles, and hoped to be patron.

2
Peters supremacie.

Roman vſe of keeping Eaſter and ſhauing Crownes, were all glad that they were reduced to the diſcipline of S. Peter *Prince & head* (as Beda reporteth their words) *of the Apoſtles.* wherby yow may ſee how vndoubted a thing the headſhip of S. Peter was then, euen amõg the Britõs, Scotts, Picts, & Iriſh. In which point the eſſence of a Papiſt (as Proteſt. write) cõſiſteth. Likwiſe S. Furſeus an Iriſh man, coming into Englãd telleth how his ſoule being taken out of his bodie had ſeene the fier of Purgatory, *ex* Beda. And Bale ſaith he preached the Goſpel *not without human Traditions,* ſo Bale termeth Papiſtry. And one Adamã a Scot confeſſed his ſinnes to a Prieſt, & did penance enioined by him, which are ſubſtantiall points of papiſtrie. Saint Oſwald alſo who was (as ſaith S. Beda) inſtructed & chriſtened in Scotlãd, did (as the ſaid S. Beda writeth) erect a croſſe & pray befor it, and being him ſelf, ſaith S. Beda, to be ſlain immediatly, he made his prayer to God to haue mercy vpon the ſoules of the ſoldiers. Thus wee ſee that the Iriſh and Scots, & conſequẽtly the Britons, about S. Auſtins time profeſſed S. Peter to be head & primat of the Apoſtles, beleeued Purgatorie, cõfeſſed their ſinnes to Prieſts, & did the penáce enioined them, erected croſſes & prayed before thẽ, hoped to haue SS. as

Pa-

lib.1.cap.22

Reinolds
Confer.

3
Purgatoire.
Beda.lib.3. cap.19.
Bale Cent. 14.cap.79.

4
Traditions.
Beda.lib.4. cap.25.

5
Confeſſion and penance.
lib.3. cap.3. Ibid.cap.2. Ibid.c.12.

6
Erecting Croſſes praying befor them and for the dead.

Patrons befor God, & praied for the dead.
Which whether they be notes of proteſtācy or Papiſtry rather I remit to the reader.
10. S. Columban alſo an Iriſh Abbot, who
liued both befor & after S. Auſtins coming
& whome S. Auſtins fellow labores ſpoke
with all in Fráce, as thē ſelues report in S.
Beda: This mā (I ſay) was vndoubtedly of *lib. 2. cap. 4.*
the Britons religió, both becauſe he obſer-
ued Eaſter as they did, & alſo becauſe he
was brought vp with the Britō Monks in *Surius*
Bágor vnder their famous Abbot Cōgellus *tom. 6.*
as Bale & Cambd. do affirme; And yet be- *Bale Cent.*
ſides his error about Eaſter, was a perfect *14. cap. 12.*
Papiſt as yow may ſee by his life writtē ſo- *Cambd.*
one after his death by Ionas his diſciple (as *Brit. p. 337.*
Bale ſaith) where amóg many other notes *Cent. 14.*
of Papiſtrie he is reported *cap. 5.* to forbid *cap. 15.*
his Monks to haue any thing proper. *c. 8.* to Monks
bleſſe him ſelf with the ſigne of the Croſſe, haue no
& *c. 23.* by it to reſtore ſight to the blind. thing
And *c. 24.* to viſit S. Martins Tombe. But proper.
much more by the life of S. Gallus cótry- Bleſſing
man & ſcholler to S. Columbā, writtē by vvith
that graue & ancient Author Walfridus ſigne of
Strabo in Surius *to. 5.* where *c. 6.* it is writ- the
ten that S. Columbā dedicated a Church croſſe.
in honor of S. Aurelia with bleſſing holy Church
water & ſprinckling it in the Church, with dedica-
proceſſion & Maſſe ſaid on an Altar. And ted vvith
cap. 10. S. Gallus is reported to haue made holie
                                              vvater,
                                              Proceſ-
                                              ſion,
                                              Maſſe.

a Croſſe

a Crosse and set it vp, and taking from his neck a bag of reliques of our B. Ladie and the holy Martyrs S. Maurice and Desiderius, to haue hanged them on the Crosse, and so prayed before them to Christ that he would in honor of our blessed Ladie and the Martyrs & Confessors make that a fit habitation for him *cap.* 21. he is reported to perswade a Dukes daughter (out of whome he had cast a Diuel by the signe

of the Crosse) to vow virginitie and to refuse the marrying of a King, which she did and prayed to S. Stephen to helpher therin. *c.* 25. he is reported to offer *Sacri-*

ficium Salutare: The wholfome Sacrifice, & to say Masse *pro requie, for the rest* of his Father Columban then dead. And *cap.* 32. When he dyed, the Crosse & candles were caried

before his corps . This , was the religion of Saint Columban & Gallus at the time of S. Austins coming, & consequently of the Britons . And therfor no maruel if S. Austin tooke no exception against any point of their religiõ, but onely about Easter. And so far was S. Columban from Protestaneie, as Bale *Cent.* 14. *cap.* 12. saith, he wrot. *superstitiously* and praised *voluntarie and mens workes.* After Saint Columban and Gallus, liued S. Killian a Scott, whome Bale *Cent.* 14. *cap.* 23. manifestly confesseth to haue bene a Papist, and made Bishop by the

the Pope about the yeare 686. And after him Maidulphus a Scott also about the yeares 690. who (saith he *Cent* 14. *cap.* 26.) *was sullied with Papisticall blemish and Monkish impostures*. And in the same *Cent.* Bale nameth many Scotts who left their Contrie *Prædicare Papismum, to preach Papistrie* . And about the yeare 631. (which was soone after) *the custome of Scotland was* (saith the Author of S. Wirons life) *for the Inhabitants to chuse their Bishop , then to send him to* Rome *to be consecrated by the Pope, as* S. VViro *was*. Of whome it is also written, that King Pepin of France confessed his sinnes to him. Surius Tom. 3. Baron An. 631. Bishops of Scotland consecrated of the P.

11. Thus thou seest gentle Reader , that albeit ther be so great scarcitie of ancient records of British matters, yet on the one side their cōsent with the Rom. religiō in many substantiall points , & such as Beza Parkins , and others confesse to be quite opposit to Protestancie, is euidently proued many waies. And doubtles their like agreemēt in more points would be found, if more ancient monumēts of those times were extant. And on the otherside ther is no one ancient monumēt or scroul which testifieth that they held any one substantiall point of Protestancie, as Iustification by faith onely, Communion of bare bread and Wine, Denied Purgatorie , or prayer for dead, prayer to Saints, & such like. But Beza Præfat Bibl. ad Cond. Perkins Refor. Cathol.

Prote-

Proteſtāts claime them onely, becauſe we for lack of ancient records can not ſhew particulerly that they agreed with vs in all points of faith. As if all were Proteſtants whome we could not ſhew particulerly to haue agreed with vs in all points, or it may not ſuffice any reaſonable man to ſhew particulerly that they agreed with vs in many ſubſtātiall points, & ſhew the ſame generally in all other points beſides one, into which they vpon ignoráce . Becauſe nether S. Auſtin nor others foūd any other falt with the matter of their faith, nor Proteſtants can ſhew any other, in which point alſo Proteſtants diſſent from the Britons as wel as we.

Hovv it is proued by the Britons that the Cathol. faith is the true faith of Chriſt.
Fox.
Bale.

And if vnto this euidency of the Catholick Roman religion of the Britons yow adioine what Fulk, Fox, Bale & generally all Proteſtants write of the certain truth of their religion , it will euidently follow that the Roman faith is the true faith of Chriſt . For Fox in his Proteſtation ſaith, *That religiō remained in the Britons vncorrupt,& the word of Chriſt truly preached till the coming of S. Auſtin* Bale Cent.1. cap.90. *There was alwaies amo · ſt the Britons preaching of truth moſt ſure doctrine,& ſuch worſhip as was by Gods cōmandement giuē of the Apoſtles to the Churches.* And *pag.*73. calleth the Britons Church

Fulk.

of S. Auſtins time *Veram Chriſti Eccleſiam.*

And

And Fulk 2. *Cor.* 12. calleth the Britons of S. Auftins time Catholicks, and faith, *with them Chriftian religion had continewed euer fince the Apoftles times*. And thus hauing shewed that before Luthers time there was nether English nor Britifh Proteftant in all England; Let vs now fee when and how Proteftácie firft began in Germanie, and after in England.

C H A P. IIII.

VVhen, where, wherfore, and how Luther began to preach Proteftancie.

1. LVther hauing bene long time an Auftin Frier and all his life before fo earneft a Romã Catholick as you heard him felf confeffe *fupra:cap.*1. and Fox in his Actsp. 770. and others côteft, began in the yeare 1517. and *on the morrow* (faith Fox *pag.*771.) *after all Saints in the cittie of VVittenberg in Saxonie to oppofe himfelf againft the Catholick faith in the matter of Indulgences by publishing and mainteining certaine Conclufions againft them*. This (as all Proteftant writters agree) was the place, the time, the matter, wherin Luther began firft to publish their doctrine. His Maifters

Sleidan. lib.1. fol.1.

The place, year, and daye vvhen Luther began Proteftancie.

Gg 4   therin

Luthers maisters of protestancie.

Neque abhominibus neque per homines.

VVhen Luther began to preach Protestancie he intēded no reformatiō at all. Fox. Sleidan lib.1.fol. 1. Luther at first impugned pardons onely to boult out truth & vvith submissiō to the Church.

therin were (as he saith 4. *Galat.fol.* 208.) *his gift of knowledg, his owne studie, and his outward and inward tentations*; By which last instructor perhaps he meaneth his black maister, whome (as we shall see herafter) he confesseth him self to haue had.

2. As for the end wherfor Luther began his new doctrin, that could not be any reformation of religion by him then intended. For as Fox confesseth *pag.* 771. *In the beginning of this controuersie Luther nether dreamed nor suspected of any change that might happen in the Ceremonies.* And not in the beginning onely but euen a year after. For Fox *l.cit.* speaking of the year 1516. saith thus. *All this while Luther neuer thought of any alteration to come of any Ceremonie, much les such a reformation of doctrine & Ceremonies as after did follow.* And a Protest. writer of Paralippomena Vspergen: whome Fox much followeth saith *An.* 1518. *Luther shewed him self to come in publick against his will, but could not staie him self.* Yea Luther him self in *loc.Com Clas.4.* confesseth that he fell, *into this faction* (so he termeth it) *by chance and against his wil.* And *L. de Captiu. fol.* 5. *By force* (saith he) *I was drawne into this quarell.* And *epist.ad Leon.* 10. *fol.* 4. Eckius (saith he) *drew me into this vnexpected quarrell, catching me in a small word about the Supremacie which by chance slipt from me.* How then could this man intend

refor-

reformation of religion by his preaching
against the old religion, if, as Fox said,
for a yeare after, be did not so much as
dreame of any reformation, no not in ceremonies? with what conscience think
we did he impugne the old religió whiles
he neither ment nor dreamed to reforme
it? *Luther impugneth a religion and yet meaneth not to améd it.*

3.   In like sorte the end for which Luther began to impugne the Cathol. faith
could not be Gods glorie. For what glory
could he intéd by his new preaching who
ment not to make any alteration at all in
Gods religion. Besides that he often times
offered both by word & writing to giue
ouer his new doctrine if he might not be
bound to recant, or his aduersaries bound
to silence. For as Fox hath *pag.* 772. in
writing to Cardinall Caietan *Anno* 1518. he
promised *to proceed no further in any mention
therof, so that his aduersaries were likewise bound
to keep silence.* And (saith Fox) *if the Bishop of
Rome wold haue bene content with this submission
of Luther he had neuer bene touched any further
of him.* And againe in the yeare 1520. as
Cooper hath in Chron. *he submitted himselfe
to the P. of Rome so that he might not be compelled to recant.* And as Doct. Whitaker *lib. cont.
Dur. pag.* 11. *If at the beginning he could haue
obtained neuer so litle of the Pope he would straight
haue bene quiet.* yet Luther him selfe *epistol.*
ad

Luther sought not Gods glorie begin-ning prote. stancie.

Luther 4 times offered to sup-presse Prote-stantisme. Sleidan. Engl. lib. 1. fol. 6. and in fol. 9.

Luther offered to recant vvhat he had vvritten touching pardons.

2
Sleid.*l.1.
fol.* 10. saith he submitted him self also An. 1519.
Sleid. *lib.1. fol.* 17. See Sleidan *lib.1. fol.1.5.* of Luthers submission to the P. and Church of Rome

3

4

ad Leon. 10. saith, *I promised silence to Caietan and to make an end of my cause, if the same were commanded to my aduersaries. And then* (saith he) *the matter stood in very good termes, but he began to command me recant, and then it fell into much worse estate. VVherfore what after followed came not by the fault of Luther, but of Caietan, who suffered me not to be silent, when I then most desired.* And *ibidem*, after this againe he saith . *I yeelded to your authority and was readie to be silent.* And *fol.* 5. an other time he offered *silence at request of his Friers.* Here Christian Reader I appeall to thy cōscience, whether this man who so often offered to suppresse his new doctrine, so he were not bound to recant it, intended by preaching it any glorie of God? Nay whether by offering to suppresse it, he did not condemne both himselfe and his doctrine? Was his cause good which (he speaketh) was at best when it was to be supprest, and put to pepertuall siléce? and became worse when his silence was not accepted, and what followed therof he wold not haue imputed to himselfe: was it Gods cause which he wold haue buried in silence, if he had not bene bound to recant? was it Gods cause which was at the best when it was to be supprest, became worse wen it was published, and wherupon ensueth such euils as Luther wold

wold not haue imputed to him ? Surely
this sheweth that to be time which D.
Empser an eare witnes auouched that-
he publikly said . *That this matter was* Luthers
nether begun for God, nor shold end for him. prote-
was it not his pride, which could not station
brook the shame of recanting , or his ad- that he
uersaries triúphing ouer him, which made began
him go forward to that which his Cno- not for
science told him was ill begun ? God.

4. VVhat then will you say meat Luther
by his preaching against Indulgences ? The end
Surely no other thing than for a time to for
spite the Dominican Friers, and to hinder vvhich
their credit and gaine which hauing hin- Luther
dred by his new doctrine he ment to haue began
proceeded no further therin, if he had not Prote-
bene boúd to recát what vpó spite against stan-
others he had preached . For wheras the tisme.
Austin Friers had bene wonte to publish
the Indulgences which the Pope sent into
Germany, the Archb. and Prince Elector
of Mentz appointed the Dominicá Friers
to publish those, which were sent in the
yeare 1516. Herupon Luther and diuers of
the Austin Friers were sore offended. And
Luther more impatient than the rest , for
to spite the Dominicans, began first to
preach, and after to publish conclusions
against the valour of indulgences. That
this was the true cause of Luthers
new

new preaching, beside the testimonie of al
Catholick writers, appeareth partly by
what hath bene already said, partly also by
what shall be rehearsed further out of
Protestants. For Cooper in Chron. wri=
thus *An.*1517. *Leo Bishop of Rome according to the
manner of his Predecessours sendeth downe general
pardons and licence of other things into Germany.
By occasion wherof Mar. Luther an Austine Frier
of VVittemberg first began to preach to the people
against Indulgences.* Note how he confes=
seth that P. Leo his sending pardons was
no new thing or peculiar to him, but the
custome of his Predecessors, & yet that Lu=
ther tooke occasiō therof to preach against
them which argueth, that not the pardons
themselues gaue Luther occasion to prea=
ch against them before, but some thing
peculiar to those pardons, to wit, the pu=
blication of them, not by Austin Friers as
the former pardōs were published, but by
the Dominicans.

5. And this cause Fox insinuateth a litle
more plainly *pag.*771. where he saith, *Lu=
ther was moued vpon the sermons of one Tecelius
a Dominican Frier, who caused the Popes indul=
gences to be caried about the coūtrie, to publish cō=
clusions against them.* Loe the Dominicans &
their sermons, or rather their reputation
which they got by publishing the indulgē
ces, and not the indulgences themselues,
        moued

Cooper.
Sleid.lib.
1.fol.1.

Fox.
prote-
stants in
their pu-
blik let=
ters in
Sleidan
lib.8.
pag.110.
saie that
all this

moued Luther to preach againſt indulgēces. And what I pray you ſhould make Luther to impugne indulgences then, more
then before, and to impugne indulgences
before any other point of Catholick faith,
but thatt he Dominicans had then & not
before the publiſhing of them, and they
were made peculiar publiſhers of them, &
of no other point of religiō. And that you
may yet more clearly ſee, that no diſlike of
the indulgēces themſelues moued Luther
to impugne them Fox *l.cit.*confeſſeth that
*Luther in the beginning did not vtterly reiect in-
dulgences; but required a moderatiō in them.* And
the Author of Paralip. Vſpergen. addeth
that *at firſt he did but lihgtly ſtriue againſt them,
only for diſputation ſake:* yea Luther himſelf
in one of his Articles ſet downe by
Fox *pag.* 1167 . ſaith thus . *Indulgences are
in the number of thoſe things which are lawſull.*
And *l. de Captiu. I did not thinke* (ſaith Luther) *indulgences to be vtterly caſt away.* And
Sleidan his ſcholer addeth *hiſtor lib.*13.that
*he ſcarce knew what the name of indulgences
meant when he firſt began to preach againſt them.*
How then could indulgēces be the cauſe
of his reuolt from the Cath. faith ? But as
the wiſe man ſaith that by *the Diuels enuie
death entred into the world:* So may we ſay
that by *Luthers enuie againſt the Dominicās* Pro-
teſtantiſme entred into the world. And as enuie

diſſētiō
in reli-
gion
ſprung
of that
ſome too
much ex
tolled in
dulgen-
ces.

Luther
offered
to re-
cant
vvhat he
had veri
tten tou-
ching
pardons.
Sleid.
*Eng.lib.*1
*fol.*9.
Sleid.*lib.*
1.*fol.* 2.5.
Luther
at firſt
accoun-
ted in-
dulgen-
ces lavv-
full.

of

of other mens good moued Luther to begin this tragedie, so his owne pride (which
wold not permit him to recant what he
had wickedlie taught) made him to proceed, as appeareth by what hath bene said
already. And Luther him self confesseth
in Sleidan *l.* 13. that the Popes excommu-
nication of him made him to defend his
doings and set forth many books; and Fox

VVhat made Luther mantai-ne his doctrin.

*pag.*771. writeth, *that the rage of Frier Tecelius*
who called him Heretik, made him to mantaine
the matter. So that not Gods glorie or the
goodnes of his cause, but euen as him self
& his best freinds excuse him, other mens
supposed iniuries moued Luther to mantaine Protestancie.

The manner of Luthers proce-ding in Prote-statisme. His in-constan-cie.

6. As for the maner how he proceded in
his new doctrine, it was very inconstant,
both in particuler points & in his whole
religion. For in his answer to P. Leo his
Bull in Fox *pag.* 1170. he writeth thus:
I imbrace with the full trust of my spirit thse arti-
cles in the said Bull condemned, and affirme, that
the same ought to be holden of all faithfull Chri-
stians vnder paine of eternall damnation. And
pag. 1174. *I confesse* (saith Luther) *all these*
things condemned here by this Bull for pure, clear,
and Catholick doctrine. And yet Fox noteth
in the Margent *pag.* 1167. thus: *He retracteth*
these Articles, he recalleth these. And 1. *Galat.*
fol. 36. *whether it be* (saith Luther) *Cyprian,*
Austin,

Auſtin, Ambroſe either Peter, Paul, or Ihon, or an Angel from heauen that teacheth otherwiſe, yet *this I know aſſuredly that I teach not the things of man but of God.* And yet him ſelf *lib. de Captiuit.* writeth thus : *I admitted the Papacie to be good by mans law.* And *ibid.* he admitteth three ſacraments for a time as he ſpeaketh. And yet ſoone after caſt away the third ſacrament, and the Papacie vtterly. And *lib. cont. Catharin.* he maketh this recantation. *I confeſſe that in the beginning I thought ill of indulgences, of the Pope, the Church of Rome, Councels, &c.* And yet (as you ſee) he taught his doctrine of indulgences and other things, as pure Catholick, and to be held of all Chriſtians vnder paine of damnation . Wherfore vaine is the excuſe which Feild *lib. 3.* of the Church *cap.* 42. maketh for Luther by the example of Saint Auſtin, who reuoked ſome things which he had taught. For Saint Auſtin reuoked what he had taught as his owne probable opinion, but Luther reuoked many things which him ſelf had taught as points of faith, and to be beleeued vnder paine of damnation, and therfore was inconſtant and wauering in his faith, which Saint Auſtin was not.

Luther reiecteth vvhat he taught vnder paine of damnation,

Feilds excuſe of Luthers inconſtancie reiected.

7. And the like inconſtancie he vſed touching his whole religiõ, doubting for a lõg time

time whether he fhould returne to Catholicke faith or goe on with his Proteftancy. For *Anno.* 1518. which was the fecond

Luthers
fubmif-
fion to
the Pope
after he
had be-
gun pro-
teft.

yeare of his new preaching, he wrote thus
to the Pope as Fox *pag.* 771. Paralip. Vr-
fpergen.and others do witnes:*Moſt holy Father I offer my ſelfe proſtrate at the feet of your
Holines with all that I am & that; I haue,ſaue me
kil me, call me,recall, approue me, reproue me as
you pleaſe. your voice the voice of Chriſt in your
ſpeaking I will acknowledg. If I haue deſerued
death I will be content to die.* And againe made

1

2 a Proteſtation faith Paralip. Vrfpergen.
that *he wold nether ſay nor hold any thing which
the Church of Rome did not.* And after this the

3 fame yeare being cited by Cardinall Caietan to appeare before him at Augufta, *he
came* (faith Fox *pag.* 772.) *yeelding his obedience to the Church of Rome, and by writing exhibited to the Cardinall acknowledged his exceſſe
in ſpeach againſt the Popes dignitie,and premiſed
to make amends for the ſame in the pulpit. And as
touching the matter of pardons* (faith Fox) *he
promiſed to proceed no further in any mention
therof, ſo that his aduerſaries likewiſe were bound
to keep ſilence.* Likewife *An.* 1519. which was
the third yeare of his Proteftácy he wrote
as Sleidan confeffeth,that *in humane things
nothing is more excellent than the Church of Rome
beſide Chriſt only.* And in publick difputation
the fame yeare *confeſſed freely* (as Melancthō
cited

cited by Paralip. Vrſper. writeth) *that the Pope is the vniuerſall Bishop* . And yet againe *An.* 1520. (which was the fourth year of his new doctrine) *he ſubmitted him ſelf* (ſaith Cooper in Chron.) *to the Biſhop of Rome ſo that he might not be compelled to recant his writings* . But finding that all his ſubmiſsions wold not be accepted without he recanted, and that the ſame year his doctrine was condemned as Hereticall, and him ſelf pronounced an Heretick, vnles he recalled it with in 60. daies, and being ſecure by the protection of the Prince Elector, he reſolued to proceed in his wicked courſe, and ſo went on from naught to worſe vntil he died *an.* 1546. But thus you ſee that as long as Luther had any hope to eſcape recantation, he ſtill offered to giue ouer his Proteſtancie, which plainly ſheweth how ill him ſelf liked it, and that onely pride and want of humilitie moued him to maintaine it.

Cooper. An. 1520, Paralip. vſperg. 16. Fox. pag. 1169.

Proteſtāts beholden to Luthers pride for their relis gion.

CHAP. V.

By what means Proteſtantiſme ſpred ſo far.

1. THe ancient writer Tertullian noted, that in his time ſome weak and

lib. de praſcript.

waue-

wauering Chriſtians wondered, that Hereſies ſpred ſo far and preuailed with ſo
many . And perhaps in our dayes ſome
may in like ſorte wonder that Proteſtantiſme is ſo far extended. But let thes *won-*
derers (as Tertulian termeth them) conſider that the· Mahumetans impietie and
the Arian hereſie which denied the
Godhead of Chriſt were far larger. Let
them alſo conſider what Luther ſaieth

Luther.

5. *Galat. fol. 251.* that *their is no doctrine ſo wic-*
ked fooliſh and pernitious, which the world doth
not gladly admit embrace and defend, and more-
ouer reuerently entertaineth cheriſheth and flatte-
reth the profeſſors therof. Let them I ſay conſider this with that which anon I ſhall
add, and they will leaue to maruel of the
ſpreading of Proteſtancie, which (as all
Hereſies vſe to doe) creepeth like a Can-
ker. Beſides that indeed though the name
of Proteſtants and Proteſtant religion be
far ſpred, yet nether could Luther in his
life time far extend his doctrine (For as
him ſelf confeſſeth 4. *Galat fol. 199. 229. he*

Luther
could not
far extend
his doc-
trin.

litle preuailed, And *fol. 253. few* (ſaith he) *are*
by our Miniſterie tranſlated out of the bondage of
the Diuel, And *fol. 154. Euen now whiles we liue*
and employe all our diligence to ſet forthe the
office and vſe of the law and Goſpel ther be very
few euē among thoſe that wilbe counted Chriſtians
and make profeſſion of the Goſpel vvith vs that

vnder-

vnderstand those things rightly. And after his death ther is scarce any prouince cittie or person which entirely holdeth Luthers doctrine. So that as Tertulian said of valentinians that they were in many places but Valentin their founder no wher. So may we say that Lutherans or Protestants are in diuers Countries but Luther in none. Which him self not onely feared but forsaw and fortold *Galat.* 4. *fot* 154. 201. And no maruel, for if Luther were not constant to him selfe how could his scholers be constant to him, if he controlled all the Fathers vpon pretence of greater light why shold his followers forbear him.

2. But to call all that chaos and confused Masse of opposit errors Protestantisme, which this day goeth vnder that name, and sprung first from Luther, and after was increased by others, and to omit the particuler causes of the entrance therof into seuerall Contries, the generall causes of the increase therof were diuers rising partly from some abuses partly from the religious persons and Clergie, partly from the laie people, but especially from Luther and his adherents and their doctrine. For it can not be denied but ther were some abuses in some places of some things belonging to Catholik religió, as namely of

Causes of spreeding Protestasis.

Hh 2   indul-

indulgences . Of which abuſes Luther
tooke his aduantage to bring the holie
things them ſelues into contempt , as appeareth by what hath bene ſaid before.
And this occaſion alſo Caluin & his companions vſed in ſetting vp their religion in
Geneua, as noteth the Surueyer *c.4.* wher
he well obſerueth, that. *when men haue bene
bitten with abuſes , it is an acceptable point to
hear the things them ſelues exclaimed againſt. For
it falleth not (ſaith he) vnder euery ſimple mans
cap to diſtinguish well in that matter.*

Surueyer.

2

3. An other cauſe were the vices of d'uers
religious and Clercks. Amongſt whome
(eſpecially in Germanie) when Luther
began diuers things were out of order.
Whervpon they growing into contempt,
it was eaſie to perſuade the people, that
their religion alſo was contemptuous.
Men commonly affecting or diſaffecting
the things as they do the perſons to whome they belóg . And of this meane principally Luther made benefit for his cauſe as
him ſelf declareth in theſe words 4. *Galat.*
fol. 229. *If the Papacie had the ſame holines & au-
ſteritie of life which it had in the time of the anciēt
Fathers Hierom, Ambroſe, Auſtin, & others, when
the Clergie had not yet ſo euill a name but liued
after the rules & decrees of the Fathers religiouſly
and holily in outward ſhew and vnmaried what
could we doe now againſt the Papacie?* Ib. *If that*
outward

*Luther
confeſſeth
that if
Catholiks
liues had
bene good
he could
haue done
nothing.*

outward shew and apparance of the old Papacie remained at this day, we shold peraduenture do litle against it by our doctrine of faith, seing we do now so litle preuail. This meane vsed also Caluin as witnesseth the forsaid Surueier *c. 4.* wher also he noteth *that it is a plausible matter with the people to hear then depraued that are in authoritie.* In the lay people also Luther found a great greedines, and as the Apostle speaketh *itching ears* to hear nouelties. For as him self noteth *1. Galat. fol.* 14. *The vnscilfull multitude longing to hear news do ioyne themselues to false Apostles.* And in others ther was a desire of libertie, and of power to checke their Pastors. And how many this motiue drew to follow Luther Melanchton his cheefest scholer cited by the Surueyer *c.* 8. telleth in these words. *Many for no other cause I see do loue Luther but for that they thinck they haue cast of their Bishops by means of him, and haue obtained a libertie, which will not be profitable for our Posteritie.* Item. *our fellows* (saith he) *do sight so for their owne Kingdom and not for the Gospel.* And this meane also vsed Caluin and his crew at Geneua as the said Surueyer noteth *L. cit.* saying. *It is a plausible matter with the people, especially to vnderstand of anie libertié which may appertaine to them selues.* And finally in others of the people ther was a vehement thirst for the Church goods, which Luther by

his

Surueyer.

3

Melancthon confesseth that men follovved. Luther onely for libertie.

Surueyer. So the Gracches moued sedition in Rome by their leges Agrarias.

his preaching expoſed to the praye of
Princes and people . This bate vſed the
wiclefiſts in K.Henrie 4.time to cach that
worthie Prince as Stow reporteth,& with
it partely,Proteſtants caught K.Henrie 8.
and vſed it to others . For as the ſaid Surueier writeth.*cap.21. VVhen reformation of religion vvas firſt vrged it vvas thaught ſuch an effectuall motiue as vvould procure attention vz. to
entitle Princes after a ſorte to the Church goods.*
But did theſe reformers mean that Princes
ſhold keep thoſe goods?No.For he addeth.
*The learned men perſwaded them ſelues that if by
anie policie they could ouerthrovv Poperie, it vvold
aftervvard be an eaſie matter to recouer them
againe . Beſides (ſaith he) they did not ſo yeeld
ouer their right in that matter to Princes , but it
was done vvith diuers cautions and prouiſos , by
vertue vvherof they ſuppoſed in time to recouer
all againe into their ovvne hands . But (ſaith he)
they plaied vvilie beguile them ſelues.*

4. On Luther and his partners ſide the
firſt meane of ſpreding their religion was
which him ſelf in theſe words 4.*Galat.*
*fol.21.*noteth in falſe Apoſtles. *They make
great Proteſtations that they ſeek nothing els but
the aduancement of Gods glorie , that they be moued by the ſpirit to teach the infallible truth , and
they promiſe vndoubted ſaluation to thoſe that
receaue their doctrine.* An other meane on
their ſide was their diſſembled ſanctie.
Which

Church,
goods
confeſſed
to be the
effectual
motiue to
Proteſtan-
cie.

Miniſters
moue
Princes to
change
religion
for
Church
goods, but
meane to
get all
them
ſelues.

4
Proteſta-
tion of
falſe prea-
chers.

Which meane Caluin and his companie most vsed as noteth the said Surueyer *cap. 4.* wher he saierh. *It is not vnknovvne to anie of iudgment vvhat the profeßion of anie extraordinarie zeal and as it vvere contempt of the vvorld doth vvork vvith the multitude . VVhen they see men goe simply in the streets, looking dovvnevvard for the most parte , vvringing their necks avvry, shaking their heads as if they were in some present greef, lifting vp the white of their eyes some time at the sight of one vanitie as they walke , vvhen they hear them giue great groanes, crie out against this sin and that sin not in their hearers but in their Superiors, make long prayer, profeße a kind of wilfull pouertie, speaking earnestly against some mens hauing too much and soome men too litle, which beateth into the peoples head a present cogitation of some diuision to be made in time. VVhen I say the multitude doth hear such kind of men they are by and by caried away with a maruelous great conceit and opinion of them, especially when they take vpon them to shew a waie or disciplin vvhich shalbe nothing preiuditiall to the people but rather bring them libertie, and yet shall reforme all things amisse as them selues vvold desire.* Hitherto the Surueyer whose words I haue cited at large because they liuely describe our first Protestant Preachers.

5. But the most effectuall mean which Luther had to spread his religiõ was his licétious

Ministers hypocrisie to seduce the people.

Hh 4

tious and flefhly fweet doctrin, wherwith
on the one fide he tooke from his followers all fear of God both in this world and
the next, and of man too as much as he
could and withal remoued from them the
exercife of all hard and vnpleafing things.
And on the other fide licenfed them to
enioy all the delites and pleafures of this
world:and withall affured them both of
as much iuftice in this life and glorie in
the next, as anie Saint in heauen had or
hathe.For as for the fear of God in this
life he taketh that away by affuring thofe
that haue his iuftifying faith, that all their
finnes are forgiuen and all punifhment
due vnto them remitted . Which fecuritie
Caluin fome what increafed by adding
that who once hath iuftifying faith, can
neuer leefe it which two points, who
foeuer firmely beleeueth I fee not how
or why he can fear God in this life.
For how can he fear God in this life
who is fure that nether he can leefe Gods
fauor nor be punifhed of him for any fin
which he committeth ? And as for fear
of God in the next world , firft Luther tooke quite away Purgatorie, and
though he left Hell, yet not for his followers whome he affured that beleuing as
he tought them they could not be damned what foeuer they did.*So rich* (faith he)

lib.de

Luthers doctrin taketh avvaie the fear of God in this life.

And in the next life too.

lib. de Captiu. cap. de Euchar.) *is a Christian, as he can not leese his saluation with what sinnes soeuer, vnles he will not beleeue for no sinnes can damne him.* And as touching fear of man also he tooke that away as much as he could. *For a Christian* (saith he 2. *Galat. fol.* 66.) *is free from all lawes and subiect to no creature.* And *lib. de Captiu. A Christian is bound to no law but to Gods. No law can be imposed vpon Christians by any right ether of men or Angels, but as much as they will themselues.* Which doctrine D. Whitaker *cont. Dur. pag.* 726. expoundeth thus: *The conscience is bound to no law, but Gods.* And *pag.*731. *The particuler lawes of Magistrats haue no command ouer the conscience.* Which who beleeueth need not fear to break any mās law if he can keep it secret. In like sorte Luther remoued from his followers all difficult and hard things. For he tought them that Gods commandements were impossible to be kept, Confession Satisfaction, Abstinéce, Fasting & austerity of life, he ether condemned, or accounted no more acceptable to God than feasting, and pampering our bodies.

6.　And on the other side, touching pleasures & delites of this world, he licensed Bishops, Priests, Monks, Friers, & Nonnes to break their vowes of chastitie, pouerty, and obedience, and to marie, to

get

Luthers
general.
indulgen-
ce to sin.

to get riches, and to liue at their owne
commād; gaue leaue to the people to read
and vnderstand Scriptures according to
their priuat spirits, to make choise of their
Pastors, and to take all or a good part of
Church liuings. He freed Princes from
all Ecclesiasticall subiection, and graunted to all sortes of people a licence to eate
at what time and what meat they list yea
he gaue a generall and direct indulgence
for to syn. For 2. *Galat. fol.* 66. *A Christian*
(saith he) *hath nothing to do with the law and*
sin. 3. Galat.fol.114.sin in vs is no sin. And *fo.140.*
If sin vex the, think that it is at it is indeed, but
an imagination. ibidem *True diuinity teacheth*
that there is no sin in the world any more fol.138.
Christ saith he *is the only sinner.* And his

Luthers
quiet of
conscien-
ce in
extingnif-
hing re-
morse
of sin.
Luther
Serm.de
nativv.B.
Mariæ.

whole drift in that booke is to extinguish
in his followers all feeling of sin or re-
morse of conscience therof, and this he
termeth quiet of Conscience. And withall
this (as I said) he assureth euery one of his
followers that they are as iust as our blessed ladie, and if they beliue as he teacheth
them as sure of heaune as she is. And do
we maruel to see common people to embrace so secure and pleasing a religion?
Surely we need maruell no more than to
see water run the lower way or stones
rolle downe the hill. But alas poore soules
who like silly fishes are caught with this

pleasing

pleafing bat to their euerlafting death.
For this learning cometh not from aboue
but as S. Iames fpeaketh is earthly fenfuall
and diuelifh what religion of God can
that be which abandoneth al fear of God?
what piety can that be which remoueth
the exercife of hard things as for the
moft parte the acts of vertue are. What
Chriftianity can that be which ioyneth
league with the flefh and the world
which Chriftians renounce in their
baptifme? And thefe motiues I haue noted in the fpreading of Luthers doctrine
But let vs hear the forefayd Suruzyer.

7. *Firft* (faith he *cap.* 8. *Luther and his par-* | Luthers means of fpreading his doc-trin out of the Sur-ueyer.
teners faught to perfuade the Pope and Bifhops to
to their reformation. This is euident by Luthers to P Leo , to the Archb. of Mentz
and others. But finding fmall encourage
ment of them *they vvere driuen* (faith he)
to flie to the ciuil Magiftrats. & the rather to moue
them to their reformation they laboured by all
means they could to make the Popifh Clergie moft
odious vnto them. They inueighed againft their
pride, againft their fuperfluities, againft their cor-
ruptions. They perfwaded the Princes that Bifhops
and Abbots had too much, and told free cities that
notwitftäding their freedome in refpect of the Em-
peror, yet they were fubiect to their Bifhops, and
were not (faith he) *difcontented that fo good an*
occafion was offered them to procure their greater
*   liberty*

1

2
3
4

libertie. *Moreouer Luther and his were content to* *yeeld to much againſt their mind with many vn-* *equall conditions. So at laſt the ciuil Magiſtrats* *began a reformation. The Pope, the Bishops, and the* *cheefeſt of the Clergie impugned it,* *VVherupon* *their liuings which they had in any of thoſe terri-* *tories were feaſed into the hands of the ciuil Magi-* *ſtrates.* Thus you fee euen by the confeſſiō of Proteſtants, that Luther could not per-ſuade his religion to the chiefeſt of the Clergie, but ſpred it by temporizing with Princes and States, with yeelding too much euē againſt his mind, with exciting cities to rebell againſt their Biſhops, and take their liuings from them. VVhich whither it be an Apoſtolike kind of pro-ceeding or no, I durſt make the Surueier himſelfe iudge. Sure I am that he great-ly condemneth the like proceding of Cal-uin *cap.* 2. and feareth that Puritans will in time vſe the like courſe to reforme him and his Company.

CHAP.

CHAP. VI.

VVhen, by whome, wherfore, and how Proteſtancie began firſt in England.

1. IN the firſt booke yow haue heard how all our Chriſtian Kings to K. Henry 8. were Roman Catholickes. Now it commeth to ſhew when, wherfore, & how he altered the Religion of all his Forfathers and Predeceſſors. About the yeare 1527. He fel in loue with M. Anne Bullen daughter to Syr Thomas Bullen, who not condeſcending to his luſt, vnles he made her his wife, he made earneſt ſuit to Pope Clement to be diuorced from Queene Catherin daughter to the King of Spaine with whome he had bene maried 20. yeares, and had had by her diuers children, vpon pretence that ſhe had bene maried before to Prince Arthur his brother. But the Pope taking great deliberation and longe time in the matter, King Henry in the yeare 1531. (not vpon any diſlike of the Popes religion (but *vpon occaſion of delay* (as both Cooper and Stow ſay in their Chronicles, *made by the Pope in*

the

The Proteſt. diuines in German. vvold not auovv. K. Henries deuorce. Sleidan. Engl. lib. 10. fol. 139. Cauſes of K. Henrie 8. reuolt from the Pope out of Cooper and Stovv.

484   *The prudentiall Ballance*

the matter of his diuorcement, & displeasure of
such reports as he heard had bene made of him
to the Court of Rome, & thirdly pricked forward
by some coũsellers to follovv the exãple of Germãs,
cauſed proclamatiõs to be made in the 29.
of Septẽber forbidding all subiects to procure any things from the Court of Rome.
And not content with this, to spite the
Pope more, he compelled the Clergy tha
same year to giue him 130. thouſand poũds
with the Title of the *headship of England*, *ſo*
far forth as the word of God did permit. And in
the year 1533. of his own authority he married Anne Bullẽ, & a good wile after made
Cranmer diuorce him frõ his former wife
thanliuing. For which vnchriſtiã proceeding being excõmunicated by the Pope, he
was more enraged. And therefore in the
year 1534. by Act of Parliamẽt made him
self head of the Church, which title Barnes
a Proteſtãt saith (as Fox recordeth') that
the K. got by his & his fellowes labors.
And Tindal the Apostle; (as Proteſtãts cal
him) of Englãd who thẽ liued, writing *An.*
1532, to Frith of K. Héries intentiõ againſt
the Pope & Clergy saith thus in Fox p.987
I smell a Counsell to be takẽ litle for the Clergies
profit in time to come. But yow muſt vnderſtãd that
it is not of pure hart & for loue of the truth, but to
auẽg himself & to eate the whores fleshe & drink the
marow of her bones. which becauſe it is vrittẽ

                                                    ſom-

(margin notes:)
K. Hen. diuorced from his firſt wife after he had marieda second.

Proteſtãts brag of procuring the title of the head of the Church to K. Hentie.

VVhy K. Henr. reuolted from the P. out of Tindal.

somwhat enigmaticaly. Fox expoundeth in the marget thus, *eating the vvhores fleshe is to spoile the PopesChurch only for the pray & spoile therof.* Thus yow see it euident euē by the confession of Protestants both the yeare when K. Henry 8, began to reuolt frō the Pope. To wit 1530. & his Counsellers therin, to wit, no Bishops nor Diuines but Laymen; who hoped (as they were) to be partakers of the pray. And his motiue ther vnto, not dislike of theP. religiō or like of a better, but malice against his persō, & couetusnes ofthe Church goods. And out of these two foūtains haue sprōg since all the Protestācie of Engl. which whether they were liker to be foūtains of Gods or the Diuels religiō I leaue to euery one to iudg.

2. And as the motiues so his alteratiōwere malice & couetuosnes, so his proceding after was euer cruell couetous & blooddy, quite differēt frō his procedings in theformer time, For wheras before in 22.years of his Regn he had bene gētle & put none of his nobility to death besides the Duke of Bucking ham & Eearle of Suffolk for treason In 16 . yeares after, of six Queenes which he had, he put away two, wherof one diedfor sorow, other twohe beheaded the one for adultery, the other for incest also,a thing vnheard of befor in EnlgishQ. the fift he caused to be opened for to saue

to

K. Henr. forsooke the P. not for loue of truth but for spite and couetousnes. Beginning of Protestancie in Englaud. An. 1530. Counselars, therto laie men. Motiues. spite and Cauetousnes.

Protestancie quite altereth K. Henries procedings.

the child in her belly, and the fixt he ment to haue executed for hereſie. Of Cardi-dals he beheaded one, cōdemned an other, brought the third to death, with greefe and ſorow. Of Lords Abbots he hanged, drawed and quatered ſix, Priors fiue, be-ſids a great number of Prieſts, Monks, and Friers. And of the Nobility he condem-ned one Duke to perpetual priſon, behea-ded a Marqueſſe, beheaded two Earles, one Earles ſonne and heire, and fiue of his Vnckles all in one day, beheaded ſix Lords and one Lords ſonne and heire: & hanged one Lord, beheaded one Counteſſe, at-tainted one Marqueſſe; and of knights, gentlemen, and others, executed great numbers. And for his couetouſnes of Church goods, beſides the 130. thouſand poundes, exacted as before, of the Clergy, the very ſame yeare he ſuppreſſed the Ho-ſpitall of S. Iames nere to Charing Croſſe *Anno* 1532. ſuppreſſed the priory of the Tri-nity in London. *Anno* 1534. ſuppreſſed the houſes of the Obſeruant Friers in Englād and tooke to himſelfe all fruits and tenths of all ſpirituall goods and promotions *An.* 1534. tooke the reliques and cheefeſt Iuells out of Monaſteries, *Anno* 1536. ſup-preſſed all religious houſes to the value of 200. poundes and vnder, and tooke all their lands and grounds. *The number of theſe*

these houses (faith Stow) *were* 276. *the value of their lands then* 32000. *pounds and more by the year. The moueable goods as they were fould at Robin hood penorthes amonted to more tha one hudred thousand pounds. It was a* pitifull thing (faith he) *to heare vvhat a lamentation the poore people in the* Countrey *made for them.* For *there was great hospitality kept among them, and as it was thought more than* 10. *thousand persons Maisters and seruants had loft their liuings by the putting downe of those houses. Anno.* 1538. All Abbeis and religious houses were fuppreffed, and S. Thomas of Canterbury Shrine pulled downe, *which was* (faith Stow) *built of ftone aboue a mans hight. The vpper part of timber which was couered with plates of gould damasked with gould wier, which groud of gould was again couered iewels of gould* 10. *or* 12. *crooaped with gould wier into the faid ground of gould. Many of thefe rings hauing ftones in them brooches Images Angels pretious ftones and great pearles &c, The fpoile of which shrine in gould and pretious ftones* faith he *filled two great* Chefts, *the which fix or eight ftrong men could do no more than carie one of them at once out of the* Church. By which one may gather the ineftimable riches which King Henrie got by all Abbeis and Shrines. Moreouer *Anno* 1540, he fuppreffed the knights of the Rhodes. And finally *An.* 1505. all Chanteries Colledges & hofpitals were giue to the K. And yet not

content

VVhat mifcheef one point of Proteſſancie brought to England.

content. withall theſe Church goods, which were ineſtimable, within two years after, to wit *An.* 1540. impoſed a great tax vpon both Clergy & Layty as neuer was heard of before in England, as yow may read in Stow & other. And withall coined baſe mony in great aboundance

Proteſtancie at firſt entrance vndid English men, ſoules bodies goods, houſes, Churches monuments.

which was after called downe to halfe valowe, Thus yow may ſee how Proteſtancie or rather one pointe therof, to wit, The deniall of the Popes ſupremacie altered this K. from a liberall and clement Prince, to a moſt cruel & couetous mã, & how it entred into our Coũtry, not only with the loſſe of our Contrymens ſoules, but alſo of their goods and liues, & made ſuch hauock of mẽ & weemẽ, of churches, houſes, ancient Monuments, ſtately buildings as if ſome fury had come out of Hel, or ſomme mortall enemy had gon roging vp & down our Contry. Surly who well

Proteſtãts vviſh of Geneua and Beza.

conſidereth this may ſay of Proteſtãcy as Bãcroft in his ſuruey *c.* 3. ſaith of Geneua. *It had bene better for this Iſſad if neuer English mã nor Scotiſh mã had bene acquainted there* And of Luther as he *c.* 8. ſaith of Beza *thoſe Churches that followe Bezas humor may iuſtly wish he had neuer ben born.* And the Dãgerous Poſitioner *l.* 1. *c.* vlt. ſaith he thincketh the Scottiſh Miniſters wrought more miſcheefe in that Country in 30. years thã the P. of Rome ha d done before, in 500.

3. Finally

8. Finally the succes which this King reaped by his alteration was most miserable. For wheras before he was loued of English-men at home, and feared of strangers abroad, after this change made, he was secure of neither. For first Lincolnshyre men rose against him to the number of 20. thousand, & streight after Yorkshier men to the nuber of 40. thousand. And these insurrections being appeased the Yorkshier men twise after attempted an insurrection. And from abroad he was accursed of the Pope, and stoode in continuall feare that some forreigne Prince would inuade his Land. And as Frier Peto then tould him to his face openly in the Pulpit at Greenwich, that if he proceeded in his course it woule befal to him, as it did to Achab. that doogs should lick his blood, & there should not be one left of his issue to pisse against a wall. The first wherof was seene to be fulfilled after his death, when the lead wherin his body was wrapt, whilst in the carriage therof to Winsor, it stood in the ruins of the monastery of Syon broke, and his blood ran out, which the doggs lick vp as a graue writer reporteth out of their mouth that sawe it, and the second we all now see to be accomplished.

Miserable succsse after Probtesancie.

Commotions.

Prophetie of F. Peto.

　　　4. Catho-

4. Catholick religion thus maimed in one point by King Henry, was after his death heere turned into Proteſtancy, Firſt in K. Edwards time and after in Queene Elizabeth reigne. But who conſidereth by what authority by what meanes, & whoſe procurment it was done, may iuſtly think that it was not wrought by God. For Proteſtancie was ſet vp, not by the authority of any man but firſt by the authority of a child of 9. yeares ould ſcarce come to the vſe of reaſon and not fit to gouern himſelf and after by the authority of a woman. The meanes by which it was ſet vp was nether miracle nor extordinarie vertue of the firſt preachers of it or their publick confuting by diſputation their aduerſaries as Catholick religion was ſet vp by S. Auſtin, but meerely the will of the Protector in King Edwards time, and of the Queene in her time, and the terror of lawes. Which meanes are more ſeeming as befitting Turkiſh than Chriſtiã religiõ. And laſtly the procurrers of this change were not Biſhops or Diuins, but ether wholly Laymen ignorant of Scripture & diuinity, againſt the will of all the Biſhops as it was in Queene Elizabeths time, or principally Lay-men againſt the conſent of the beſt learned of the Paſtors as in K. Edwards time. And how little theſe men

cared

A child firſt and after a vvoman authors of Proteſtancie in England.

Meane, onely vvil and teror.

Frocurers laie men.

cared for religion, but euen againſt their
conſcience ſought their owne aduance-
ments, appeareth by the Duke of Northumberland a principall Doer in the alteration in K. Edwards time, who ſtuck
not to tell euen in that time to M. An-
thonie Browne after created Vicount
Mountaigue as I haue often heard of his
honorable and vertuous Lady lately deceaſed, that he knew the Roman religion
to be the truth, but yet (ſaid he) ſince we
haue begon with this new, run God run
Diuel, we wil go forward. And that religion was but a colour of his ambitious
pretences is alſo euident, by what Stow
writeth of him. For firſt he repeateth his
Oration to the Lords wherin he ſaith *that*
Gods cauſe and the preferment of his (new) word
was the originall ground of proclaming Queene
Iane, and after reciteth his words at his
death where he profeſſeth the Rom. Catholick faith, and profeſſed that he did not
for hope of life, but for conſcience, and acknowledged the euils then hapned to
England to haue comen by the new
religion By this iudg of the reſt and now
let vs return to Luther.

D of
Nor-
thumb.
confeſſeth
that a-
gainſt his
conſcien-
ce he ſet
vp the
nevv re-
gion.

Sleidan.
lib 25.
An. 1553.

CHAP. 7.

CHAP. VII.

That Luther was ignorant or meanly learned,

1
Luthers
yong
years.

1. THat Luther was but meanly learned whē he first begā Proteſtátiſme I wil proue many waies. Firſt by his yong years for he was but 34. years ould when he began this new doctrine. At what yeares men haue rather the ground of learning, than are any way excellently learned. Secondly, he ſtudied in no famous

2
Studied
in no
famous
vniuers.
Fox. p. 770.

vniuerſity nor vnder any notableMaiſter. For the chefeſt place wher he ſtudied, was Erphord in Germany, a place of no name, and his Maiſters names are ſo obſcure as they are not knowne, vnles we reckon his black Maiſter wherof we ſhall ſpeack heerafter. I might alſo adde that he was brought vp in a monaſtery becauſe D. Whitak. *cont. Dur. p.* 733. ſaith *what can we expect out of Monaſteries but Monkiſh ſuperſtitions vnlearned?* Thirdly, he had a very great

3
Corporal
impedi-
ment of
ſtudie.

impediment of ſtudie, For *tom.* 2. *pag.* 22. thus he writeth: *I dare not read two whole leaues togeather nor two or three lines of a pſalme, nor looke vpon any thing long; For ſtreight I haue a noiſe in my ears that I am faine to lay dovvne my head to the forme.*

4

2. Fourthly I proue Luthers ignorance by his doctrine. For as Feild *lib.* 4. of the
Church

Church *c.* 24. graunteth, *Luther made que-*
stion of S. Iames epist. & of others. Wittak. *cont.*
Dur. *p.* 12. saith *he vvrote disgracefully of it*, p. 20
doubted of it. & *p.* 22. *called it strawish in respect*
of S. Peters and S. Pauls Epistles. And yet as
the same Feild saith *he had but vveak and*
friuolous reasons to doubt, or as Whitak. *p.* 19.
hath, *had no iust cause of suspition*, or as Fulke
addeth in 2. *Iacob. had no reason.* wherfore
ether Luther had no iudgment or learning to think friuolous yea no reason,
weightie reason or he had lesse grace to
reiect a parte of Gods word for no reason at all. Moreouer Fox *pag.* 1167. setteth
downe these Articles which I think few
wil iudge to proceed from great learning.
To burne Heretiks is against the will of the spirit.
To fight against the Turk is to repugne against God
Soules in purgatory do sin without intermissiõ, &
diuers others which Fox is faine to file
with his expositiõ, D. Couell in defence
of Hooker: *pag.* 42. setteth down this Article of Luther : *Faith vnles it be without euē*
the least good work doth not iustifie. And *p.* 101.
saith *Luther is not afraid to affirme that Sacra-*
ments are effectuall though administred by Sathā
himselfe. Feild also *lib.* 3. of Church *pag.* 127.
granteth that Luther taught. *That when and*
wher noPresbiter cā be foūd to performe the office
a lay mā yea a womā may absolue. which I tink
few learned Protest. wil defend Caluin

4. *Inſtit. cap.* 17. *Parag.*30.ſaith that the Lutherans opinion of the Eucharift *raiſeth vp
Eutiches hereſie.* Luther himſelfe *lib. de Concil. part.* 2.*pag.* 276. *plainly teacheth Diuinita-
tem poſſe pati , that the God head could ſuffer.* And
as Zuinglius reſponſ. ad Confeſ. Luth. *fol.*
458.teſtifieth *clearly & roundly profeſſed that he
wold not acknowledg Chriſt for his Sauiour, if his
humanity onely had ſuffered.* Himſelfe *lib. de
Captiu. cap, de Euchar.* leaueth it free to beliue in the Eucharift ether *tranſubſtantiation
or impanation* and |profeſſeth that he fir-
mely beliueth *panem eſſe Corpus Chriſti , bread
to be Chriſts body.* And *c.* 3. *Galat.* auoucheth
infáts to haue acts of faith & beleef,whils
they are baptized, which S . Auſtin *Ep. ad
Dardan.* counteth moſt ridiculous,

3. Fiftly I proue Luthers ignoráce by the
céſure of diuers Proteſtáts, Fox ſaith p.488
Luther had blemiſhes in doctrine,[1] & went awry.
Sutclif Anſw.to except.p.41. *Luthers opinion
(about the Euchar.)is hereticall by inferéce of
ſuch Cöcluſiös as follovv of it.* To which he addeth *p.* 55. that he is an Heretik who holdeth any point condéned for hereſy, wher-
pö an other may infer that Luther was an
Heretik. Zuing.in his Ep. to ¦Luther *Anno*
1526. ſaith *vve eaſily ſee that thou*(Luther) *art
an vnſcilfull or very ravv diuine* Whitak. cont.
Dur.p. 22.*It maketh not much matter (* ſaith
he *) vvhether Luther ſaid ſo or no.p.*27.*vvhat is
it*

it

Marginal notes:

The God head ſuf-
ſered vvith
Luther.

5.
Proteſtáts
cenſure of
Luther.

Zuinglius
indgeth
Luther to
be igno-
rant.

it to me? I care not what they (Luther and his cheef scholers) *misliked.* And as Fox saith *p. 788. Some Protestants giue clean ouer the reading of Luther, and fall in vtter contempt of his books.*

Some Protest contemne Luthers bocks.

4. Lastly, I proue Luthers ignorance by his owne confession. For as Sleidan reporteth *lib.* 13. he said thus. *VVhen I began to preach against indulgences I scarce knew what the name of them ment.* And in Fox *pag.* 1173. he confesseth that he is not certaine, what is done with a soul which departing without actuall sin yet hath the originall roate of sin, nor whither Fear in a man dying with imperfect charitie let his entrance into heauen or no. In like sorte *in Colloq. Mensal. fol.* 154. he professeth that he knoweth not how discerne, *Legem ab euangelio the law from the Gospel.* And other wher he saith that he knoweth nether Greek nor Hebrew. And *L. de Captiu. cap de* bapt. *Here* (saith he) *I confesse my ignorance.* And *cap.* de Matrim. *vnto this day I am so vncertain about vowes as I know not when they are to be thought to bind.* Ib. *I dare not define whither pluralitie of wiues be lauful.* And *L. cōt. Chatharin.* plainly cōfesseth how ignorant he was in the beginning of his new preaching about Indulgences, the Pope, Church of Rome, Councels & other matters. And 3. *Galat. fol.* 170. *I haue scarsely learnt the first principles* (of the vse of the law) See it *fol.* 12. and 100.

6 Luthers confessiō of his ignorance. *Sleidan Engl. lib.* 16. *fol.* 132. vvhen Luth began first to preach against pardon he knevv not vvhat that matter ment as him self confesseth.

5. And

Think of
this my
deere
Coumtrie-
men.
*Neander
lib.8. expli-
tet.orbis
terra.
Fox p* 416.
Edit. 1563.
*Bul
Apoleg.*

5. And was this the man that controlled
all the Fathers? that condemned al Antiquitie of ignorāce and blindnes? that contemned al the Canonifts & fchole diuines?
was this *the God* (as fome call him) *of diuins*?
was this *the conductor of Ifrael*? was this the
man that *was giuen by God to lighten the vvorld*?
O wilfull blindnes of men, who wil follow fo ignorant and blind a guide! What
muft become of both him and them that
follow him and forfake the ancient Fathers and Catholik Church, but what our
Sauiour faith of the like. If the blind lead
the blind doe they not both fall into the
dich. And if Luther who had (as he faith)
the firft fruits of the fpirit, was thus igno-

Ignorance
of Engl.
Minifters.

rant, what may we think of others who
fucceded him? *Some of our Minifters* (faith
Collins in his fermō at Pauls Croffe 1607.)
are enemies to learning. Godwin in his pre-

Decaie of
learning
in Englād
vvith
Proteftācie

face befor his Catalog of Bifhops writeth
*that the beft vvits daily refufe the vniuerfities or
diuinitie at leaft. And euery age* (of Proteftant)
*bringeth les plentie of learned men among vs than
other, And it is much* (faith he) *to be feared that
our pofteritie vvill truly fay.*

> *Aetas parentum peior auis tulit*
> *Nos rudiores, mox daturos*
> *Progeniem inerudıtiorem.*

The Declaration of difciplin printed at
Geneua *an.* 1580. faith p. 148. *That now in fteed*
of labor

of labor idlenes is comen into the vniuerſities, contention, neglect and almoſt contempt of all religion with diſſolute licence and libertie, wherby they giue them ſelues to all riot and wantones. It greueth me (ſaith that writer) *how far they are from Muſes & learning. Euen the verie temples of religion, the altars the Chapels do waxe prophane vnholie and void of al true religion* . And much more of the like ſorte *ib.* I. B. alias Bacſter in his taile of two legged Foxes *cap.* 11. greatly complaineth of the decay *of learning. pietie and religion; and the contempt and beggarlines of Miniſters.* Wher he ſaith that ſome of them *haue no more knowledg than idols of woad or ſtone*, and termeth them *Syr Ihons lack latin lack learning, lack cõſcience.* O how doth learning decay and ignorance increaſe, when our aduerſaries thus openly confeſſe it. And what wilfull imprudēce is it to think that theſe kind of fellows can ſee more thã our ancient Prelats and diuines. And hauing thus ſeene Luthers ſmall learning. now let vs behold his life and maners.

CHAP. VIII.

That Luther was a naughtie and vicious man.

Three kinds of proof of Luthers vice

1. **M**Y proofes of Luthers vicious and naughtie life I will reduce to three heads

1 heads. The firſt ſhalbe touching his owne
2 deeds. The ſecond touching his doctrine.
3 And the third touching the effects of bothe. As for his life it ſeemeth that for a
while after he entred into S. Auſtins order
he did ſeriouſly giue him ſelf to pietie and
deuotion. For that he writeth of him ſelf

Luthers pietie for the time of his Cath. religion.

while he was a Frier 1.*Galat. fol.*37 *I endeuored my ſelf to keep the Popes laws as much as
was poſſible for me to doe, punishing my poore bodie
with faſting, watching, praying and other exerciſes.
I honored the Pope of mere conſcience & vnfainedly and whatſoeuer I did, I did it of a ſingle hart of
good zeall and for the glorie of God. And fol.* 38.
*I keept chaſtity pouerty and obedience, I was free
from the cares of this preſent life, I was onely giuen
to faſting, watching, praying.* Thus Luther for
a time, and happie had he bene if he had
ſo continewed. But as he entred into religion vpon fear becauſe he with whome
he walked in the feilds was there ſlaine
with a thunderbolt. So fear being an il
keeper of continuance, he afterward fell
from this zeall of his owne good & Gods
glorie, and in ſteed therof *foſtered* (as him

Luther confeſſeth that he hated God

ſelf writeth *fol.* 38.) *cit. cõtinuall miſtruſt doubt-
fulnes and hatred & blaſphemie againſt God.* And
præfat. 1. *operum tom.* 1. *I felt my ſelf* (ſaith he)
*to be before God of a moſt trobled conſcience, I
loued not yea I hated* (ò horor to hear) *God iuſt
and punishing ſinnes, and vvith ſecret if not blaſphemie*

phemie yet vvith great murmuring I repined at Luthers
him. I raged so vvith a feare and perturbed con- fit dispo-
science. Thus Luther of him self before he become
began Proteftantisme . And I pray the an Arche-
Chriftian Reader was this change in Lu- retik.
ther from zeall of Gods glorie to hatred
of God, from God or from the diuel? was
a man in this cafe likelie to haue particuler light from God touching his truth rather than anie in the world befides? Or
rather hauing (as him self confeffeth) loft
a good confcience, was he not like (as S.
Paul fpeaketh) to make fhipwrack alfo of
his faith? was not a man of his difpofition
fit to be made of the Diuel a broacher of
herefies , and an apt inftrument to lead
manie foules to hell ?

2. Of his enuie for which he firft began Hic enuie.
Proteftantifme you haue heard befor, and
likwife of his pride for which he cōtinew- Pride.
ed it . But his pride was otherwife fo
notorious as Proteftants tax him for it.
God (faith Conrad Regius *lib. cont. Heſſum*)
for the ſin of pride wherwith Luther exalted him
ſelf hath taken away his ſpirit from him , and in
ſteed therof hath giuen him a wrathfull lying and
arrogant ſpirit. Oecolampad.*lib. cont. confeſ.*
Lutheri, writeth that , *Luther was puffed vp*
with the ſpirit of pride and arrogancie . And the
Tigurin Minifters in their anfwer for
Zuinglius pronounce that, *Luther is caried*
                                        away

away with too much insolencie. Of his wrath
and anger D. Feild *lib.3.* of the Church *cap.
vlt.* cōfeſſeth that *Luther was of a violent spirit
and caried too much with the violent streame of
his passions, and the Tigurins Gesnerus and others
diſlike his distemperat passions.* Fulk *in cap. 3.
Philip.* giueth this verdict of him. *Luther
purſued contentions more bitterly than was meet.*
The Tigurins *respons ad Luther.* write, that
*he followed too much obstinacie and pride and that
much of the malignant spirit was in him.* Ieſner
in his bibliotheca faith. *He could bear none but
ſuch as agreed with him in all points.* God (ſaith
he) *forbid leſt by his contention and impudencie
he hurt the Church.* Eraſmus a Cōfeſſor with
Fox, and of good iudgment and a plaine
and wel meaning man with D. Reinolds
lib cont. epiſt. non ſobr. Lutheri, giueth this ſentence of him. *Luthers epiſtle breatheth deadlie
hatred, is all full of impotent if not furious reproches
and malitious lies. He malepertly rageth againſt
Kings and Princes when he liſt. Extreme hatred
deſire of command and firebrands of Incitors driue
him out of the waie. He cracketh naught but diuels
Sathans, Hobgoblins, wiches, Magæras & ſuch more
than tragicall speeches. His minde can be ſatiated
with no raling, he is beſid himſelf with hatred, he
hath no ſinceritie, no ſobrietie, no Chriſtian modeſtie. If you take out of his books hyperbols, railing.
ſcoffing, repetition, aſſeuerations, articles of VVic-
leſs & Huſ, perhaps litle will remaine of his owne.*
                                                   Caluin

Caluin in Schuffelburg *lib.* 2. *theol. Caluin.* *fol.* 126. concludeth that . *Luther multis vitijs scatet, hath many faults.* As for Luthers fleſh-lie filthines him ſelf *tom.* 1. *epiſt. Latin. fol.* 334. ſaith that. *I am burnt with the great flame of my vntaimed fleſh. I am feruent in the fleſh ſlothe luſt &c.* And as the world knoweth, contrarie to his promiſe made to God, maried a wi-fe, and her a Nonne.

His lea-cherie. Luther in Sleidan. *lib.* 3. *fol.* 29 my profeſ-ſion is not of life and manners.

3.   But to leaue Luthers carnall vices, and to come to worſe, ſuch as by them we may clearly ſee that Luthers preaching came not from God . Firſt he reiected a good parte of Gods word, as not onely Catho-liks ſay but moſt Proteſtants alſo confeſſe, to wit the Epiſtle to the Hebrues, the ſe-cond of S. Peter, the epiſtle of S. Iames & of S. Iude, the ſecond and third of S. Ihon, and the Apocalips. And this he did vpon friuolous yea vpon no reaſon as is before ſhewed. Now how hatefull a ſin it is to re-ieĉt Gods word euery one ſeeth, and God him ſelf declareth by his curſe *Apoc.* 22. Se-condly, of that part of Gods word which he did admitt he corrupted diuers places namely *Rom.* 3. wher he the Apoſtle ſaith that má is iuſtified by ſaith he added (Alone) And being asked why de did ſo he anſwe-red ſo I comád & ſo I wil, my wil ſhal ſtád for reaſon ſtil *to.* 5. *Germ. fol.* 141. And this heinous vice was ſo notorius in Luther

Reiected a parte of Gods word.

Luther in prologis harum epi-ſtolarum.

Corrup-ted the reſt.

Biblia German.

as

as Zuinglius his Coapoſtle *L. de Sacram.*
Tom. 4. *pag.* 411.412. thus writeth to him.
Thou doeſt corrupt the word of God
thou art feene to be a manifeſt & common
corrupter of the holie ſcriptures . Hew
much are we aſhamed of thee who hitherto eitemed the byond all meaſure and
now proue the to be a falfe man . Fulke
alſo in his Preface to his Annotat ſaith
that Luther in his heat miſliked a true
tranſlacion of the Bible . So far could paſſion tranſport this new Apoſtle. Thirdly,
Went he impugned that which in his conſcien-
againſt his ce he tooke to be truth and ſo committed
conſcience. that heinous ſin againſt the holie Ghoſt,
which our ſauiour faith ſhall be forgiuen
nether in this world nor the next. For as
is before declared he often times offered
to ſuppreſſe his new doctrine if he were
not bound to recant it , wherin he muſt
needs doe againſts his owne conſcience
ether in preaching his new doctrin knowing it to be falſe,or in ſuppreſing it thinking it to be Gods truth . And in *Colloq.*
Luther. *Menfal. fol.* 158. him ſelf confeſſeth thus . *I*
wiſheth *neuer leaut theſe thoughts that I wiſh and deſire*
he had *that I had neuer begun this buſines.* And *in parua*
neuer be- *Confeſſione.I knew* (faith he) *that the eleuation*
gun Pro- *of the Sacrament was idolatrous , yet I kept it in*
teſtancie, *the Church of VVittenberg that I might ſpite the*
*diuel Carloſtadius.*ô what wold not he do or
ſay

say to spite Catholiks, who to spite his
freind and first scholer permitted (as he
thaught) idolatrie against God. And shall
not we wish wo had neuer knowne that
religió, which the Author therof wisheth
he had neuer begun? And albeit both he
and all Protestants account it a thing commanded by God to communicate in both
kinds and forbidden by him to communicate in one onely yet as Iuel *Art.2. diuiſ.6.*
nether doth nor can deny, he wrote. *If per-*
chance the Councell shold appoint (to communicate in both kinds) *we would least of all*
receaue bothe but then first in despite of the Coun-
cell we wold receaue but one or nether and in no
case both kinds. Behold how to spite a
Councell he wold ether not communicate
at all or not so as he thinketh God commanded. And who will see more of this
humor of Luther may read Vbenberg *de*
Cauſis Cathol.fidei &c. cap. 15. But was this
man who thus partly reiected, partly corrupted Gods word, and sinned against the
holy Ghost likelie to be a man chosen by
God to be a new preacher and restorer of
his word, and strangely lightned by the
holy Ghost? No Surely.

4. Yea that we may be assured that it
was the Prince and spirit of darknes who
sent and lightned him, almightie God so
prouided that no aduersarie nor stranger,

but

but him self should vtter, & not vtter onely, but write and print for a warning to all posteritie, that in the dark night he learnt his doctrin of the Prince of darknes. For *lib. de missa angulari tom. 6. Ienen. fol. 28. b.* and

Luthers confession that he learnt his doctrin of the diuel.

edit. Wittenberg. 1577. by Thomas Kelug *tom. 7. fol. 228.* he writeth thus. *Vpon a certain time I sodenly waked about midnight, then Sathan began his disputation with me saying. Harken right learned Doctor Luther. Thou hast said priuat Masse these 15. yeare almost euery day, what if priuat Masses were horrible idolatrie? what if ther were not the bodie and bloud of Christ, but thou worshipedst bread and wine and shewedst them to be worshiped of others. To whome I answered (saith Luther) I am an anointed priest, receaued vnction and consecrtion of a Bishop and did all things by command & obedience of my Superiours. How then should I not haue consecrated seing I pronounced the words of Christ seriously with great earnestnes? Thou hearest this. All this said he (the diuel) is true. But the Turks and Heathens do all in their temples vpon obedience, and do their seruice with deuotiō. The priests of Hieroboam did also all things*

These vvords are left out in the edition of vvittenberge.

with zeall & with deuotion against the priests in Hierusalem. VVhat if their ordination and consecration were false as the Turkish and Samaritans are false Priests, thy worship is false and impious. Here (saith Luther) I began to sweat and my hart to quake and beat within me. The diuel can place and vrge his arguments fitly to oppose & hath

a great

a great and strong voice. And these disputations are not long adoing but streight one answer followeth an other. And I well found then how it falleth out that men are found dead in the morning in their bedds . He can kill the bodie, he can also by reasoning driue the soule into such straites that in a moment it is to forsake the bodie. VVherto he hath almost driuen me full often . Surely in the dispute he caught me, and against my will I wold haue caried such a heap of blasphemies before God, but willingly vvold haue defended my innocencie. VVherfore I marked what cause he had against my priesthood and consecration . Hitherto Luther, whose words whether I haue truly alledged or no may be seene in the editions which I named . And after this Luther setteth downe fiue arguments which he learnt of the diuel against priesthood and Masse. O detestable Maister ! O hatefull scholler! O execrable doctrin! O abhominable schole! And, O heauens be amazed that a Christian wold beleeue the diuel rather than Christs Church, and that Christians shold follow him who professeth to follow the Diuel!

5. Ministers being greatly ashamed at this testimonie of Luther against him self & his doctrin, endeauor to cast manie mists before peoples eyes that they shold not perceaue the horror therof. D. Sutlif *l. de Eccles. pag.* 298. saith it was a dreame. But Luther

Luther confesseth that he vvas caught of the diuel in disputation.

Hov ministers glosse Luthers confession.

Kk 2 saith

faith plainly that it was after he awaked,
and telleth what a voice the diuel vfed, &
how he had like to haue died for fear. Feild
*l.*3.of the Church *c.vlt.*Iuel *Art.*1.*diuif.*2.and
others fay it was but *a fpirituall conflict and
tempting of Luther to defpaire.* But houfoeuer
the diuel ment alfo to draw Luther to de-
fperation,it can not be denied,but that he
ment to perfuade him to detefth his preifthoud and Maffe,as is euident both by the
words cited and by the fiue arguments
which the diuel brought againft the Maffe
with which Luther (as he faith) was
caught , that is perfwaded to reiect his
prieithoud and Maffe which before he
greatly eftemed. It ca not therfore but impudently & againft Luthers owne words
be denied,but that this new doctrin, that
Preifthoud and Maffe are naught,he learnt
of the diuel, houfoeuer the diuel hauing

Forther
confef-
fion of
Luthers
familia-
ritie
vvhith
the diuel.

perfwaded him that,mét with all to driue
him to defpaire. And howbeit our Minifters be afhamed of Luthers learning and
freindfhip with the diuel yet he him felf
braggeth therof.For *10.2.Ieren.fol.*77.*Beleue
me*(faith he)*wel, yea very wel I know the diuel.
He often times walketh with me in the Dorter.
VVhen I am in companie he hurts me not, but vvhen
he catcheth me alone then he teacheth me maners.*
Againe. *The diuel oftener and nearer fleepeth
vvith me than my Kate . I haue tvvo maruelous
diuels*

diuels, vvho among the diuels are great Doctors in diuinitie. And in his letters to the Elector of Saxonie. *The diuel some times so passeth through my braines as I can nether vvrite nor read.* And in Colloq. latin. fol. 32. *I had rather* (saith he) *be killed by the diuel than by the Emperor* . And of the forsaid conference betwene Luther & the diuel Erasmus *cont. epist. non Sobr. Lutheri* writeth thus. *He bringeth in a disputation of the diuel vvith a man, in his book of Masse in corners, & ascribeth such strong argumēts to him* (diuel) *as he saith he could not ansvver them.* And againe. *The diuel did impugne his mynd about Masse vvith strong vveapons.* Thus Erasmus a Confessor and plaine meaning man amongst Protestāts. And the Ministers of Zurich in their Confession *fol.* 25. 26. 127. call Luther *the Minister of Sathan* , and say that he wrote his books *impulsu spiritus* (Satanæ) *cum quo disputationem instituit, quique vt videtur Lutherum disputando superauit, by the motion of that spirit* (Satan) *vvith, vvhome he disputed, and vvho as it seemeth ouercame him in disputation.* This same also testifie Gesnerus, Tossanus Neostadius, Beza, Caluin and others cited by Feuardent. *in lib.* 4. *Iren. cap.* 32. Nether was it peculier to Luther to be thus taught of the Diuel. For to Carolstadius appeared a diuel whiles he was preaching, as Alberus a Protestant witnesseth to which the Ministers of Basil add that

See Feu-ard.in 4. Iren. cap. 32 Vlenberg. Cansa. 21. Apol of Protestants trac. 2. cap. 2 parag. 2. Testimonie of other Prottestants for the same. Erasmus. Fox in Calendar D. Reinol. Conser pag 155. Ministers of zurich.

Gesner and others.

Kk 3   he

he was killed of a diuel. Zuinglius in his
book *de Subſid. Euchar.* profeſſeth that he
learnt his doctrine about the Euchariſt of
a ſpirit which I *know not* (ſaith he) *albus an
alter fuerit, whether it were black or vvhite,* that
is good or bad God or the Diuel. Caluin
epiſt. ad Bucer. confeſſeth he had, *Genium a
familiar ,* to whome he attributeth his
vaine of curſing. And of Knox his conference with the diuel you may ſee Hamilton *Confut. Caluin. pag.* 254. And thus much
touching Luthers deeds.

Luthers
vvicked
doctrin.

6. As for his wicked doctrine ſome thing
hath bene ſaid already, and here we will
add a litle more, referring the cheef to the
third part of this Treatiſe . In behalf of
ſin, he teacheth *l. de Captiu.* thus. *No ſinnes cã
damne a Chriſtian but onely incredulitie.* And a-
gainſt goods works he hath theſe two Articles in Fox *p.* 1167. *In euerie good work the iuſt
man ſinneth. Euerie good vvorke of ours vvhen it is
beſt done is a veniall ſin.* In fauor of carnall luſt
he writeth *ſerm. de Matrim. If the vvife can not
or wil not, let the maide come* again. *As it is not in
my povver that I ſhold be a man: ſo it is not in my
povver that I ſhold be vvithout a vvomã.* I tem. *It is
not in our povver that it ſhold be ether ſtaied or o-
mitted but it is as neceſſarie as that I ſhold be a mã
& more neceſſarie thã to eate drink or ſleepe.* And
*l. de Captiu. l. de Matrim. If a vvomans husbãd be
impotent than* (ſaith he) *I vvold aduiſe that vvith
                                        conſent*

consent of her husband she shold by with an other, Epist. ad
or with her husbands brother, yet with secret ma- Albert d
riage. If her husband wold not consent I wold ad- Mogunt.
uise that mariyng to an other she shold fly into Horri-
some remote & vnknowne place. Ib. I had rather bile est
suffer pluralitie of wiues than diuorce.
si vir in
morte
7. And as for the effects of Luthers new inuenia-
doctrin Erasmus *Epist. ad Vultur.* saith thus. tur sin e
Bring me one whome this Gospel(of Luther)*hath* vxore.
of a glutton made sober, of feirce, mild, of couetous Luthers
liberall, of an ill speaker, wel spoken, of vnchaste vvicked
shamefast. I can shew them many who are made faith
worse than they were. To this Feild *lib. 3.* of
Sleidan
the Church *cap.* 8. findeth no better answer lib. 6 fol. 83
than to say thus, Erasmus *was variable and in-*
constant. But by his leaue otherwise iudged Caluin.
Fox of Erasmus whē he placed him in his
Calendar for a cōfessor, otherwise D. Reinolds whē in his Confer. *p.* 152. he termeth Luther.
Erasmus *a man of excellent iudgment. & p.* 155.
a plaine & wel meaning man. And for his iudg- Men se-
ment of the Lurherās maners Feild cā not uē times
shew that Erasmus was various. But what vvorse
wil he say to Caluin who admonit. *vlt. ad* vvhen
VVestphal. writeth that Lutherans *haue not* they are
one iot of honest shamefastnes, are brutish men, & Prote-
make no account of the iudgment of men or angels? stants
than be-
What wil he say to Luther him self who fore.
5. Galat. *fol.* 252. writeth that his followers
are seuen times worse vnder the name of Christian
libertie than they were vnder the Pope. And

K k 4 *fol.*

fol. 285. Th⅍ (faith he(⅍ *the lot of the* (new)

By Pro-
teſtancie
men
grovv
out of
kind.

Goſpel that when it ⅍ preached men begin to ſpoile to rob, to ſteal and to beguile. To be brief men ſeene ſodenly to grow out of kind and to be transformed into cruel beaſts. And much more he hath of the like ſorte *fol.* 27. 286. 39. 252. And who will ſee more of the wicked effects of Luthers Goſpel may read Schuſſelb. *lib.* 2. Caluin. theolog. Iezler. *de bello Euchariſt,* Feuardent. *in* 2. *Iren. cap.* 9. And alſo Luther poſtil. *ſupra.* dom. 1. *aduentus.* Smidelin. *Cant.* 4. *in* 21. *Luc.* wigand *de malis German.* Bulling. *conc.* Brent. Caluin *de ſcand* and *ſerm.* 10. and 11. *in epiſt. ad Ephes.* Muſcul. *L. de Prophet. & cant.* 4. de planetis. Here I will add a litle of the increaſe of ill life in England ſince Proteſtantiſme entred.

8. King Henrie after he had admitted one point of Proteſtancie, to wit, the denial of the Popes ſupremacie, and permitted the Bible to be read in Engliſh, in his oration to the Parlament in Fox *pag.* 1124. telleth the effects therof in theſe words

Effects
of Pro-
teſtancie
in K.
Henrie
8. daies.

I am very ſorie to hear and know how vnreuerently that iewel the word of God is rymed, ſung, and iangled in euerie alehouſſe and tauerne, contrarie to the true meaning and doctrin of the ſame. And yet I am as much ſorie that the Readers of the ſame follow it in doing ſo faintly and coldly. For of this I am ſure that charitie was neuer ſo faint amongſt you, and vertuous and godly liuin *uing was neuer les vſed , nor God him ſelfe amongſt Chriſtians was neuer les reuerenced honored and ſerued.* Thus King Henry of the effects of Proteſtancy in his time. And as for the effects therof in King Edward 6. time the Proteſtant who publiſhed Cranners booke againſt traditions telleth vs what they were, thus. *VVe were talkers only and not walkers, lip Goſpellers from mouth outward and no further , vve vvere euen ſuch as the Prophet ſpeaketh of ſaying. That people honoreth me vvith their lipps but are far from me with their hart, we could ſpeak of Gods word and talk gloriouſly therof , but in our harts vve vvere ful of pride, malice,enuie, courteouſnes, backbiting , rioting, harlot,hounting no whit bettered at all than vve vvere before vnder the Popes Kingdome. Nothing was amended in vs but only our tonges no nor they nether if I ſhall ſpeak rightly and as the truth was in deed. For vve vſed detraction of our neighbour, filthy talke, with many proud braggs of holines : we read not the ſcriptures nor heard them for any amendment of our ovvne vvicked liues,but only to mak a ſhew and brag therof, to check and to taunt others yea and to eſpie ſmall motes in other mens eyes , but nothing deſirous to ſee the greate beames in our owne. This I ſay to talk and not to vvalk, to ſay and not to doe , vvas not only among the vnlearned ſorte of men, but alſo amõg the graue Cleerks and preachers of Gods word.* And much more their of there like ſtuffe .*

9. And

God neuer les reuerenced than after Proteſantiſme entred. Frnits of Proteſtancie in K. Edvvard time.

Men no vvhit bettered vnder proteſtãtiſme.

For vvhat end Proteſtants read ſcriptures.

VVhat Proteſt. preachers vvere.

9. And touching the effects of Prote-stancy in Queen Elizabeths time Fox him self *Confid.* 3. telleth vs the in these words, *God graunt* (saith he) *vve may do better for vvorse I think vve cannot do if vve English men in these reformed daies walk with monſtrous pride pranking vp our ſelues more like plaiers on a ſtage than Gods chrildren in his Church.* And *Confide-rat.* 4. *who* (saith he)*followeth that he knoweth.* *To rip vp all our deformities in particuler I meane not here, nether need I, the ſame being ſo euident to all mens eyes, that who can not ſe our excesſiue outrage in pompeous apparell, our carnal deſires and vnchaſt demeaners without fear of God, our careles ſecurity vvithout conſcience, as though their were no iudgmēt to come, our ſtudie vpon this vvorld as if there were no other heauen.* And much more of the like tune. And in his latin Ep. he complaineth that *euery blaſt of tentation carieth Proteſtants headlȩng into pride, auarice, pleaſure, filthines, reuȩng and what wickednes not.* And as for the preſent Proteſtants Collins in his ſermō at Paules croſſe 1607. ſaith, his *eyes guſh out vvith vvater to ſee there is no religion amongſt men for the moſt parte, but that which is tainted with a ſpice of faction.* The *declarat.* of diſcipline *pag.* 148. ſaith their *very temples chappels and alters vvax prophan and void of all true religion.* the Surueyer *cap.* 21. ſaith that *men are kept from confesſion to no conference* vvith

Marginal notes:
Fruits of Proteſtancie vnder Q. Elizab.

Proteſt. can not do vvorſe if they vvould.

Proteſtants careles ſecuritie.

VVhat preſent Prote-ſtants are.

Proteſtants churches void of all true religion.

vvith their *paſtor , from long praier to two or three words and farewell, from ſuperſtition to very great ſecurity and prophanation.* And *cap.* vlt. he citeth the words of a principall Miniſters in Scotland touching the encreaſe of vice there , wherof he giueth the cauſe in theſe wordes. *The more knowledge* (of the new Goſpell) *increaſeth, conſcience decaieth.* If any be deſirous to ſee in particuler what kind of men our Miniſters be he may read the danger. Poſitions *lib.* 2.*cap.*11. & ſeq. and *lib.* 4.*cap.* 4. the Surueyer *cap.*3.8.18.I. B. his taile *cap.* 11. and others. For my owne parte I loath to moue this dunghil any further. But O what difference is there betwene S. Auguſtin and his follows, and our miniſters , and betweene our foreſaid vertuous Anceſtors and the preſent Proteſtants. And thus hauing ſhewed how vnfit Luther was both for learning and life to be a Preacher, and eſpecially a firſt Preacher immediatly ſent of God to Preach his heauenly truth, let vs ſee what motiues he had to preach, and afterward what Commiſſion.

Increaſe of Proteſtant knovvledg is the diſaſe of conſcience.

Quo modo obſcuratum eſt aurum mutatus eſt Color optimus. Th. an. 4.

CHAP.

CHAP. IX.

That Luther was moued by humane and naughtie motiues to preach Protestantisme.

WHat can be said of this matter is clear by what hath bene declared in the former Chapter, notwithstanding because we will obserue the like of Chapters in discoursing of Luther which we vsed of S. Austin let vs heere see what motiues Luther had of beginning and continuing his Protestants doctrine. The first motiue of beginning his doctrine was as is shewed before, enuie and emulation against the Dominicans for hauing the publishing of the indulgences which was wont to be giuē to the Austin Friers. And his motiue of continewing and proceding in his new Doctrine was his pride which wold not permit him to recant what himselfe thought so ill of as he offered to suppresse and burie in perpetuall silence. Besid these principall motiues others he had which set him forward in his new doctrine. For being before a Frier

lib.2.cap.4.

vnder

vnder obedience and bound to pouerty &
chastity, by his new doctrine he shaked of
subiection, & got licence to gather riches,
to mary, to enioie the contentments of the
world. To these motiues were added vain
glorie the nurse of all Archeretiks, to haue
followers termed after him Lutherans, the
applause of vulgar and licentious people,
and such like.

CHAP. X.

That Luther was neuer sent or called to preach Protestantisme.

1.　FOr the better vnderstanding of
that which shalbe said in this
Chapter we must note, first that it is not
denied that Luther was once lawfully
sent to preach to wit to preach Papistrie.
For Being made Doctor and Preacher of
Diuinity by Catholicks he was by them
sent to preach their faith and doctrine.
But it is denied that euer he was sent to
preach Protestancie, Secondly we must
note that there are two kinds of sending
to preach, the one extraordinary by God
alone as the Prophets and Apostles were
　　　　　　　　　　　　　　　sent

ſent. The other ordinarie by man alſo, but yet ſuch as God hath giuen authority vnto to ſend others. So were Timothy Titus & all Paſtors in Gods Church ſince the Apoſtles. How Luther was ſent Proteſtants can not agree. For ſome will haue him to haue bene ſent extraordinarily by man alſo, and of theſe ſome will haue him to haue bene ſent by this man, others by that, which variance alone if Daniel might be iudge wold deſcrie the vntruth of their tale. But God willing I will ſhew that Luther was ſent no way to teach Proteſtancie.

2.   Amongſt thoſe who affirme that Luther was ſent ordinarily by man, ſome ſay that he was ſent by his Magiſtrat and Prince the Elector of Saxonie. But this can not be. Firſt becauſe Frederick then Elector at the firſt *nether encouraged* ſaith Fox *pag.771. nor ſupported Luther but often repreſented heauines and ſorrow*, for his procedings. Secondly becauſe the Elector was a Romā Catholick when Luther begā & a whil after. How then cold he firſt ſend Luther to preach that doctrine which before Luther he nether beleued nor knew of? Thirdly becauſe power to preach is ſupernaturall and mere ſpirituall, becauſe it pertaineth to care of ſoules and their direction to a ſuperna-

turall

turall end But the power of Magiſtrates 3
is naturall & ciuil and pertaineth to direction of men to their natural end as common to Heathen as to Chriſtian Princes.
And who will ſay that Heathen can ſend
men to preach and giue them care of 4
ſoules . Againe who can giue power
to preach and adminiſter the Sacraments may alſo himſelfe preach and adminiſter Sacramenrs, for none can giue
what he hath not himſelfe. But woe men
may be Princes who yet can not preach.
Therfor Magiſtrats, can giue no power to
preach. And this diuers learned Proteſt. do 5
grant. For Bilſon *l.* of obed. approued by
pnblik authority p. 296. plainly ſaith that
their Biſhops haue not their authority frō the Prince Bilſon.
and that *the Prince giueth then not Commiſsion*
to preach, but only liberty and permiſsion . And
303. *The charge* (ſaith he) *which the Preachers*
and Biſhops of England haue ouer their flock pro-
cedeth not from the Prince. And *p.* 322. *Princes*
haue no right to call or confirme preachers. which
he repeateth *p.* 323. And Fulke *in* 1. *Cor.* 14. Fulk.
The authority (ſaith he) *of ciuil Magiſtrates doth*
giue Biſhops nothing that is peculier to Eccleſiaſti-
cal Miniſters. Finally howſoeuer ſoueraigne
Princes cold ſend men to preach, yet ſubiects as that Prince Elector was to the
Emperor, cold not againſt their ſouerai-
gnes will ſend any. And therefore Luther
nether

nether was nor cold be sent first, to preach
of Duke Frederik.

Luther not sent by anie Protestant Church.

3.   For this cause, other say that Luther
was set by his Church. So Fulk *in Ioan* 10.
But this is easily disproued by what hath
bene shewed before *cap.* 1. by the Protestants confession of the nullity, or at least
inuisibility of their Church befor Luthers
preaching. For howsoeuer he might be
confirmed of a Church which himselfe
founded, yet cold he not be first sent to
preach of a Church which before he preached was not at all, or at least was not visible. Wherfore I demand whē the people
sent Luther to preach Protestancy? whiles
they were Rom. Catholick? But that can
not be for no man will send one to preach
opposit doctrine to his. Or after that Lu-
therby his preaching had made them Protestants? But then had he preached before
he could be sent of them and they could
not be his first senders.

Ther must be a Protestant preacher befor ther be a Protest. Church and no Church can send her first preacher.

4.   Others finding no Protestant people
or persō who could send Luther to preach
Protestancy before he preached it are
faine to flie to their vtter enemies, to wit
the Roman Church, and say that she first
sent Luther. So D. VVhitak *cont. Dur. pag.*
820. Sutclif Answere to *Except. pag.* 88. Feild
l. 3. of the Church *c.* 6. & 39. Fulk *in Rome*
10. and English Protestants commonly,
though

thought some of them be ashamed to affirme it in plaine termes. Their only rea
son is, because no other can be found to
send Luther. But if they meane of sending
to preach Protestancie, it is most false and
incredible. False, because both P. Leo 10,
and Emper. Charles 5. then spirituall &
temporall heads of the Rom. Catholicks
forbad Luther to preach Protestancy, and
the one condemned him as an heretik for
so doing, the other outlaueth him. And
incredible it is that the Rome Church
shold send a man to preach a religion so
opposit to hers as Protestacy is, this were
for her to set one to cut her own threate.
And if they meane of sending to preach
Papistrie that auaileth them nothing. For
I hope they wil not say that authority or
Commission to preach one religió is authority to preach the contrary, or that the
Roman Church when she gaue Luther
authority to preach Papistry ment to giue
him authority to preach Protestancy any
more than Protest. Bishops when they
giue their Minister authority to preach
Protestancy meane to giue the authority
to preach Brownisme or Anabaptisme.
Besids that the purer sort as our Ministers
teach that *Popish Priests haue no calling* as you
may see in Penry against some *pag.* 31. And
in truth al Protestats shold teach so if they

L l   wold

VVhat
Church
can fend
men to
pteach
Gods
vvoteis
Gods
Church.

would fpeak côfequétly to their own do-
ctrine.For if fhe haue authority & power
to fend men to preach the word of God
then is fhe the Church of God for fure it is
that God gaue this authority to no other
côpany but to his own Church only) And
Proteft.in going out of this Church & impugning her, wét out of Gods Church &
impugne her.Moreouer if the Ro.Church
gaue Luther his authority to preach fhe alfo could take it away, For as willet faith
wel Synopfis *p.2 03. authority of preaching in*
Minifters may be reftrained or fufpéded by Church
gouerners. & we fee the practife herof towards the filéced Minifters.By what authority then preached Luther after he was
fordidden by the Rom,Church.Finally if
Luther had his authority to preach frô the

VVhat
confufion
vvill fall
vpon Pró-
teft:if they
faie their
firft¦ prea-
chers vve-
refent by
the Rom.
Church.

Rom.Church(which in the opiniô ofPro-
teftâts is the whoare ofBabilô the Church
of Antich.the Sinagog of Sathâ) Luther &
his Minifters muft needs be miniôs of the
Babiloniâ whore officers of Antich.Mini-
fters of Sathan, & in their preaching execute the function, which he whore, Antichrift, &Sathan beftowed vpon them.

5. Herupô others vtterly defpairing to find
out any côpany or perfon to whome they
might hanfomly attribute the fendind of
Luther fly to extraordinary fending by
God alone faying that Luther & their firft
                              preacher

preachers were fent only of God & thervpon call the Apoftles or Euangelifts. So
Cal. 4. *inftit. c.* 3. §. 4. the finod at Rochel *An.*
1607. *art.* 32. & others yea the Declaratio of
difciplin printed at Geneua 1580. *pag.* 139.
faith plainly *that in our dayes there was no place
of ordinary calling & therfore the Lord extraordinarily ftirred vp (as it were) certain new Apoftles to
lighte the world again with the light of the Gofpel.*
This is a very miferable & impudent fhift,
For firft it is auoched without al proof or
teftimony befid their owne words. And
therfor maybe as lightly reiected of vs as it
is affirmed of them. 2ly, becaufe al Archeretiks claime this kind of fending & Prote-
ftats bring no efpecial proof why we fhold
beleue Luther in this point more tha other
Archeretiks yea *Erafm. Ep. ad frat. infer Germ.*
writeth that *Mahomet may better chaleg the fpirit tha Luther.* Thirdly becaufe Luther himfelf difclaimeth this kind of fending him.
For 1. *Gal. fo.* 11. he faith. *God calleth two maner
of waies, by means & without means. He calleth vs
to the Miniftry of his word this day not immediatly
by himfelf but by man.* And addeth that *ordinary vocatio hath endured fro the Apoftles to our time
& fhall to the end of the world.* The fame hath
vogel his fcholer *in Thefaur: Biblico c. de vocat.
Miniftror.* & others. And who fhold know
how Luther was fent better than himfelf.
Befids D. Feild *l.* 3. of the Church *c.* 48. as

Luther
not fent
extraor-
dinarily.
1

2

3

diſclaming extraordinary calling ſaith, *we
ſaie our calling and our Miniſtrie is not extraordinary.* And D, Fulke *in* 10. Ioan. Luther (ſaith
he) *had lawfull calling both of God & the Church*
And the 23. Article of the Proteſtāts faith
is this : *Theſe we ought to iudge lawfully called
and ſent which be called and choſen to the work by
men who haue publick authority giuen to them in
the Cōgregation to cal and ſend Miniſters.* Therfore according to our Proteſtāts faith Luther cannot be iudged to haue bene lawfully ſent vnles he had bene ſent by men
& this of publik authority in the Church.
yea Caluin him ſelfe after he had brought
diuers proofes out of Scripture that to
lawful calling is neceſſary the ſending by
men, ſaith thus 4. *inſtit. cap.* 3. *Parag.* 15. *we
haue therefore out of Gods word that that is lawfull calling of Miniſters when they which are
thought fit are made vvith conſent and approbatiō
of the people.* And *Muſcul. loc. Com. pag.* 394.
ſaith *Extraordinary calling is not now in vſe.* D.
Serauiu in booke of degrees of Miniſters termeth extraordinary calling *an
vnknowne cooſt.* See D. Couell in his defence
of Hooker, *pag.* 86.

4   6.   Fourtly ether theſe were Proteſtant
Paſtors befor Luther or no? If there were
what need Luther extraordinary calling
who might be ſent of theſe former Paſtors ? If there were none ? how could
                                   theɪ

ther be a Protestant Church *which* (as Caluin saith *loc. cit.*) *can neuer vvant Pastors and
Doctors.* and as Feild saith *lib.* 2. of *Church
cap.* 6. *The Ministery is an enssentiall note of the
Church.* Yea as Whitaker saith *cont. Dur. p.*
274. *the soul of the Church.* If any say, that
there were Protest. Pastors before Luther
but they were inuisible, and therfore he
was not sent of them. I reply that Feild
l. cit. c. 10. saith that *the Ministrie is alwaies vifible to the vvorld.* and the same saith Caluin
4. *inftit. cap.* 2. *Parag.* 2. *& 11. & c.* 1. *Parag.* 11.
And in truth it implieth côtradictiô that
ther shold haue bene Pastors preaching
the word & adminiftring the sacramêts,
and yet inuifible, especially to such faithfull men (forfooth) as Luther was. In like
sort I demâd whither there were Churchs
rightly setled before Luther or nô. If no
then Luther was the setler of the Proteftant Church. If yea, then was not he
sent extraordinarily. For as Caluin teacheth 4. *Inftit. c.* 3. *Parag.* 3. that *calling hath
no place in Churches rightly setled.* or as Fulke
saith *in* 10. *Rom. it is not neceffary but where
ether ther is no Church, or the Church is no member of Chrift.* If then Luther were extraor-
dinarly sent ether, there was no proteftât
Church before him, or it was no member
of Chrift. Fiftly, Caluin 4. *inftit. c.* 2. *parag.* 14
saith, that *no wife man vvill denie that it is alto-*

5

L l 3   *gether*

ther requifit to lawful vocatiō that Bishops be apointed of mē, seing ther are so many testimonies of scrip
ture to his end. And thē sheweth that though
god had extraordinarily called S. Paul, yet
he kept (saith Cal. disciplinã Ecclesiastica vo-
cationis the disciplin of Ecclesiasticall vocation, in
apointing the Church to segregate him &
Barnabas, & laie hāds vpō thē, to the end that
the Churches disciplin in apointing Ministers by men
might be cōserued. If therfore God had called
Luther or Calu. as extraordinarily as euer
he called S. Paul. & more I hope of their
modesty they wil not chalēg) yet to con-
serue Ecclesiast. disciplin he wold haue bidden thē go to some Church , to be segrega-
ted by her, & haue hāds laid vpō thē. vnles
these new Apostles wil chaleng more priuiledg & exemption from all Churches
approbatiō of their calling thā S. Paul had
7. Sixtly extraordinary & miraculous missiō frō God requireth his axtraordinary &
miraculous attestatiō therof. But Luther
had no such attestatiō. Therfor he had no
such missiō. The first proposition I proue
many waies. First by the exāple of Gods
procedings hertofore. For whē he extraor
dinarily sent Moises to deliuer the Israe-
lits he cōtested his sending by wonderous
miracles, & whē he sēt Apostls he cōfirmed
their missiō by prodiges & miracles, yea
Christ himself though sent most extraordinarily

Luther vvil haue a more extraordi-narie cal-ling than S. Paul.

6

7

narily of his Father yet saith *If I had not done*
(miraculous)*works in them which no other hath
done they shold haue no sin.* And shal we sin it not
beleuing Luther who maketh no one mi-
racle? or wil he desire to be beleued without miracles more than Christ did? 2¹ʸ· I
proue it by the authority of Tertulliã who   z
l. de præscrit. biddeth certain Heretiks who
pleaded extraordinary sending to *proferre
virtutes to shew their miracles.* 3¹ʸ· I proue it by   3
reason. For euery Prince when he sendeth
any extraordinary Embassador giueth him
particuler letter of credéce. And the particuler letters of extraordinary Embassadors
from God are his miracles. 4¹ʸ· I proue it   4
by the incõueniences that otherwise wold
follow·. For otherwise a false Prophet
might make his missiõ as credible to vs as
a true Prophet. At least one that preached
true doctrine but indeed was not sent of
God to preach might intrude himself in
to that office with as much probability as
another that was truly sent. Lastly, I proue   5
that miracles are requisit to extraordinary   *Caluin.4.*
missiõ by the Confessiõ of Protestãts. For   *parag.13.*
Calu. saith *Becaufe the Ministrie of the Apostles*
was extraordinarie, that it might be made nota-   Calvin.
ble with some more markable note it was to be
called and apointed by our Lords own mouth. And   Luther
if some externall note needed to the cal-
ling of the Apostles, I hope it needed more

Luther.

to the calling of Luther, Luther *also lo.* *Com. claf.4. cap.20.* faith, *God fent not any but ether called by man or declared by miracles, no not his fonne.* And *to.5. Germ. fol.* 491. he afketh a Preacher *whence comeft thou vvho fent the? vvhere are the miracles that vvitnes thy fen-*

Faino legem quam ipfa taleris.

fending from God? And *to.2.fol.*455. *If he fay that he vvas fent of God and his fpirit as the Apoftles, let him proue this by fignes & miracles, or fuffer him not to preach for vvhenfoeuer God vvill change the ordinarie courfe there he alvvaies vvorketh miracles.* And 1. *Galat. fol.*40. *It vvas neceffary for S. Paul to haue the outvvard teftimony of his calling.* And fhall not we think it neceffary for Luther? *If any* (faith the Declarat. of difcipline printed at Geneua 1580.) *pleafe themfelues in this gadding abrode throughout the Churches, and vvill contend that they may do fo, let them fhevv vs the fignes of their Apoftlefhip as S. Paul did to the Corinthians, let the proue that they are endued vvith thofe Apoftolicall gifts of tonges, healing, doing of miracles. let the proue that they are immediatly called therunto of God.* Finally I proue that Luther was not extraordinarily fent of God, becaufe he was not extraordinarily affifted by him from teaching falfe doctrine. For as our Englifh Proteft. côfeffe he tought falfe doctrin in many points. But they can produce no other affuredly fent extraordinarily of God who taught falfe doctrin. And in my

iudgement

iudgment Englith Proteftants much condemne their owne doctrine in defending
that Luther was fent extraordinarily from
God. For feing he hath condemned much
of their doctrine for herefie, they muft
therby confefſe that their doctrine hath
bene cŏdemned of a man efpecially lightned of God, and extraordinarily fent of
him to teach his truth. Wherfore I wold
they took better aduife and followed the
counfell of the forfaid Declarator in thefe
words *pag.* 30. *Let enquirie be made into euerie
ones calling, let them ſhew how they were chofen
and ordeined as the letters and feall of their calling.
Let them rehearfe their genealogies and the race
of their defcent. Let them bring their rodds and fet
them before the Arke of God. And who can not
ſhew the marks and tokens of their election and
Creation, they that can not fetch their pedigree
from Aaron, and whofe rodds remaine dead before
the Arke, let them be by the moft iuft authoritie of
Gods word difplaced.* Thus he, whofe aduiſe
if it be followed, I doubt not but Luther
wilbe difplaced as a falfe Prophet.

English
Proteſtãts
condemne
them
ſelues in
defending
Luthers
calling.

Good
aduiſe of
a Prote-
ſtant from
Geneua.

8. The forfaid fixt agument touching miracles much trobleth Proteftants, and
therfor they anfwer it diuerfly. Some by
granting that miracles are neceffarie for
the atteftation of extraordinarie miffion,
and faie as Feild doth *lib.* 3. of the Church
c. 48. and Fox p. 789. that Luther wrought
mira-

miracles. But these we shall disproofe of
purpose herafter. Wherfor others despai-
ring to make anie probable pretéce of miracles, denie that they are necessarie to
assecure vs of extraordnarie mifsió. Because Isaies, Daniel, Zacharias, wrought none,
& becaule S. Paul proued his mifsió rather
by the efficacie of his doctrine than by miracles. And Caluin *l. de scandal.* faith that
howfoeuer miracles were necessarie to the
extraordinarie vocation of others yet not
of thé, becaufe they teach no new doctrin
but the fame which befor hath bene confirmed with miracles, and becaufe their
doctrin is euidét &needeth no miracles to
proue it. But thefe their reafons are manifeftly falfe. For Isaias miraculoufly cured
K. Ezechias prolonging his life 15.years,&
caufed the shadow of his diall to returne
back 10.lines. Daniel miraculoufly tould
both what the K had dreamed, & what
his dreame fignified *Dan.* 2. *&* 4. which is
one of the greateft tokens of Gods afsiftan
ce that is. And in like forte Zacharias *6.1. &*
4.fortold diuers things which foone after
were fulfilled. S. Paul and Barnabas proue
their doctrin by miracles *Act* 15. wher they
tell what great fignes & miracles God had
wrought by them among Gentils in teftimonie therof. And 2. *Cor.* 11. S. Paul proueth
his Apoftleship becaufe faith he the fignes
of my

of my Apostleship were wrought vpon you in miracles prodiges and powers.

9. That which Calu. saith, besid that euery Sectmaister saith it & with as much color as he, is euidently falfe. For as for the newnes of his doctrine it partly appeareth by what hath bene said *sup. c.* 1, & shall euidétly be shewed in the 2. parte of this Treatise. And how anciét & euidét soeuer his & Luthers doctrine wete and therfor that it needed no miracles; yet if their mission to preach their doctrin be extraordinarie, it cã not be denied but their mission is both new & vneuidét, & they needed miracles at least to approue their mission vnto vs. For God hauing no wher auouched by word that he wold send Luther to preach, if he auouch not by deeds nether , what certaintie haue we ether from God or mã (besides Luthers owne word) that Luther came from God nether let anie mã answer that Luther proueth his doctrine by the word. For now the question is not about his doctrine, but about his authoritie to preach, which a mã maie wãt, & yet teach true doct. Wherfor absurd is that which Bilson affirmeth *l.* of obedience *p.* 300. *As long as we teach the faith of the Apostles we haue their authoritie.* For so euerie right beleuer hold haue Apostlick authoritie to preach: hold be Apostles or doctors contrarie to S.

Though Luthers doctrin vvere good yet he needed miracles to proue his extraordinarie calling.

Protestãts beleue that Luther vvas extraordinarily sent vvithout all profe, testimonie or reason. All right beleuers haue not authoritie to preach.

I

to S. Paul 1. *Cor.* 12. all ſhold be Paſtors and
none ſheep, all laie men yea woemen and
children might adminiſter the word and
ſacraments, None could be prohibited or
ſuſpended from preaching. Finally this
3 licence of preaching graunted to all that
haue true faith is graunted beſides Gods
word or warrant. Wherfore Bilſon vpon
better aduiſe perhaps in his booke of
4 gouernment of the Church *cap.* 9. writeth
that *they haue no parte of Apoſtolik Commiſsion,
that haue no ſhew of Apoſtolik ſucceſsion.* And
*that Paſtors do receaue by ſucceſsion power and
charge of the vvord and Sacraments from and in
the firſt Apoſtles.* And I wold he wold ſhew
to whom Luther ſucceeded in his new
doctrine, or els confeſſe that he had no
part in Apoſtolik Commiſsion. Certain
therfore it is that though euerie right beleuer may confeſſe his faith and alſo teach it
priuatly when neceſsitie requireth, yet
none but Paſtors who are lawfully ſent
can preach it of authoritie, take care of
ſoules, and adminiſter the Sacraments.
And how I pray you ſhold we be aſſured
that Luther was ſent of God to do this,
rather than anie other right beleuer? This
Tell me
this o Mi- I wold gladly know, and euerie one ſhold
niſters. know before he commit his ſoul to his
guiding whome he knoweth not to haue
anie charge or commiſsion to direct him.
10. But

10. But diuers learned Proteſtants finding no colorable anſwer to make to this demand, do plainly confeſſe (as Sadeel a Miniſter of Geneua teſtifieth in a book written againſt ſuch) that their miniſters ore *legitima vocatione deſtituti, deſtitute of lavvfull calling.* Others though not ſo plainly do graunt the ſame in ſaying that ſuch as ate ſit may reach the word without ſending. Which Caluin inſinuateth in *cap.* 13. Actorwher he ſaieth that we need no teſtimonie from heauen that God ſendeth ſome. *Becauſe* (ſaith he) *vvhome God hath indued vvith ſufficient gift ſeing they are framed and faſhioned by his hand we receaue them giuen to vs of him no otherwiſe than as the prouerb is from hand to hand.* And to this ſame end tended Bilſons complaint *l. of obed. pag.* 300. that *the wicked* (ſaith he) *alwaies asked the godly for their authoritie as the Ievvs asked S. Ihon Baptiſt and Chriſt.* And 1b. *So long as we teach* (ſaith he) *the ſame doctrin vvhich the Apoſtles did vve haue the ſame povver vvhich they had.* And *pag.* 301. *He that defendeth truth is armed vvith authoritie ſufficient though all the vvorld vvere againſt him.* And that a man may preach without commiſſion he bringeth a ſimilitude that when a cittie is on ſire or entred by enemies euerie one may crie Alarme though he be no officer, and *pag.* 310. and 311. he produceth the example of Frumentius and Ædeſius who taught infidels

(marginal notes)
Proteſtäts confeſſe that their Miniſters vvant laufull ſending and authoritie

Vvhom Calvin allovveth to preach vnſent.

Bilſon.

infidels the Christian faith hauing no sending to that purpofe.

11. Here thou feeſt Gentle Reader that
confeſſed by learned Proteſtants which I
intended in this chapter, to wit, that Luther & his firſt partners were not ſent to
preach ether of God or man, but ſeing
(forſooth) the Church al on fire with idolatrie, & entred by enemies and thinking
thē ſelues fit for that purpoſe came rūning
of their own accord crying Alarme which
Luther did not ſtick to boſt of ſaying as
Caluin reporteth *l. de reformat. p. 463. Behold
I call my ſelf Preacher and with this title haue I
adorned my ſelf*. And who readeth the liues
of our firſt Proteſtant preachers ether in
Bale or Fox, ſhall ſee that euerie one of
them fel to preach vnſent of anie. And the
forſaid Declaration of diſciplin *p. 145.* ſaith
plainly *that manie of their worthie mē for the loue they had to the Goſpel thaught it lawful for the
in theſe times to take vpō thē this Apoſtolical office.*

12. But this alone, that Luther Caluin &
ſuch like did preach and adminiſter ſacraments as Paſtors, being not ſent, nor hauing authoritie giuen them therto, wold
ſuffice to cōuince them to haue bene falſe
prophets, vſurpers, & theeues, though not
other exceptiō cold be takē againſt them.
For to preach, that is, as Paſtor to teach,
without lauful ſending or Commiſsion, is
flatly

See Bal.
Cent. 6 c. 85
Cent. 8.
cap. 100.
Manie
principal
Mini-
ſters
preached
vnſent.
The vvāt
of ſen-
ding in
Luther,
Caluin
and ſuch
like
vvold
alone
conuin-
ce them
to be
falſePro-
phets.

flatly againſt Scripture, againſt the example of Chriſt, his Apoſtles and all the Paſtors, of Gods Church, againſt reaſon, and
Finally againſt the doctrin and practiſe
now obſerved of Proteſtants. It is flat a-   1
gainſt Scripture. For *Rom.* 10. S. Paul asketh
how ſhall they preach vnles they be ſent? In ſo   Want
much as both the Prophets Chriſt and the   of ſen-
Apoſtles do bråd falſe Prophets with this   ding the
mark of coming vnſent. *I ſent not*, ſaith God   verie :
Hierem. 23. *Prophets & they ran. As manie* (ſaith   brand of
Chriſt *Ioan.* 10. *as came* (of them ſelues) *are*   falſe pro-
theeus & robers . Some going out of vs (ſaie the   phets.
Apoſtles *Actor.* 15.) *haue trobled you with words
whom we commanded not.* Loe how the holie
ghoſt hath branded falſe Prophets with
this note of coming vnſet. It is alſo againſt
the example of Chriſt & the Apoſtles. For   2
of Chriſt it is ſaid *Hebr.* 5. *Nether doth anie take
honor to him ſelf but who is called of God as Aaron.
So Chriſt did not clariſie him ſelf to be made a
Biſhop.* And *Ioan.* 17. and 20. Chriſt him ſelf
auoucheth his ſending by his Father. And
of the Apoſtles it is manifeſt that they   To preach
preached not before they were ſent of   vnſent is
Chriſt. Nether can Proteſtants produce   to imitate
anie Paſtor of Gods Church ſince the A-   Core
poſtles time, which preached before he   ande Abi-
was ſent. And to do the contrarie is not to   ron.
imitate Chriſt and his Apoſtles, but that
ſchiſmaticall crue of Core Dathã & Abirõ
                                    whome

See S. Cypr. lib. de sim- plic. Prelal. Tertul.de prascrip.

whome the earth therfore swallowed & hell deuoured. It is also against reason. For, as Pastor to preach and administer Gods Sacraments, is an act of spirituall and su- pernaturall authoritie , which none can haue vnles it be giuen vnto him, and lear- ning vertue or other talents what soeuer wherwith a man is fit to execute such au- thoritie are things far different from it, as is both euident by it self, and appeareth in woemen who may haue as much learning vertue and other habilities as some men, & yet none of them can as Pastors preach or administer the Sacraments , because they are incapable of Pastorall authoritie. Moreouer to be a Preacher and Pastor is to be Gods Embassador and steward or dispenser of his spirituall goods and miste- ries. And if none can be Embassador of an earthly Prince vnles he be sent, none ste- ward of his house vnles he be apointed, none officer ouer his people vnles he be constituted. How can any be Embassador to God without sending, steward of his goods without apointing gouernor of his people without his authoritie ? And I maruel how Protestants can call Luther, Latimer and such like their Apostles , and ether confesse that they were not sent at all but came of their owne good wills, or can not shew of whome they were sent,

feing

feing that the verie name of an Apoltle fignifieth one fent.

13. Finally Proteftants them felues condemne fuch preachers as come vnfent. Bilfon him felf *l.cit.we deteſt* (faith he) *theſe that inuade the paſtorall function without lavvfull vocation and election.* It *is not lavvfull* (faith the Englifh Clergie in the 23. Article of their faith) *for any man to take vpon him the office of publik preaching or adminiſtring the Sacraments. No man* (faith their Synod in Hagâ *Art.3.*) *ought to take vpon him to preach or adminiſter the Sacraments vvithout a lavvfull calling although he be a Doctor or a Deacon or an Elder.* And their Synod at Rochel 1607. *Art. 32. none muſt intrude him ſelf into the gouernment of the Church.* Thus teach all Heretiks after they haue gotten poffeſſion. But before their owne aptnes and talents, the glorie of God, and the faluation of foules, and truth of their doctrine was warrant and authoritie ynough for them to preach, as appeareth by what hath bene cited out of Bilfon, Caluin and others. But to conclude this matter with Luthers words. He 1. *Galat. fol. 11.* faith. *Let the Preacher of the Goſpel be ſure that his calling is from God,* and he calleth *phantaſticall ſpirits,* who intrude them felues. And *fol. 12. It is not* (faith he) *ynough to haue the word and pure doctrine, but alſo he muſt be aſſured of his calling,* and he that entreth without

Luther:

He that preacheth vnſent cometh to kil.

4

this assurance entreth t̃ano other end but to kill and destroie. Ibid. *the people haue great need to be assured of our calling that they maie know our word to be the word of God .* And in the same chapter. *Ther are manie* (saith Luther) *who complaine that they haue the talent of the Lord and therfore are vrged by commandment of the Gospel to teach, otherwise with a most foolish con-science they beleue that they hide the Lords money and are guiltie of damnation. The diuel* saith he *doth thu that he may make them instable in their vocation!* O good brother let Chr̃st quiit the of this *The Gospel* (saith he) *gaue his goods to seruants called. Expect his calling, in the mẽa time be secure yea if thou wert wiser than Salomon or Daniel yet if thou beest not called flie more th̃a hell to preach. If God need the he will call the.* And againe. *The diuel vseth to stir vp his Ministers that they run vncalled and pretend this most burning zeal that they are sorie that men are so miserably seduced that they wold teach the truth and de'iuer the se-duced from the snares of the diuel.* Thus Luther. and likwise Beza *epist* 5. and others, which I wold they had followed in their first preaching Protestancie.

14. As for Ca̍uins reason before cited , I saie that abilitie to preach cometh far more short of that spirituall and superna-turall power to preach and administer sa-craments which Gods Pastor hath , than abilitie to gouerne mens bodies & goods

in a

in a kingdom cometh thort of temporall power to gouerne such matters. And therfore if none(how able soeuer he be or think him self) may take vpon him to be an officer in the common wealth , vnles he be apointed, much les may one take vpō him to be a Pastor in the Church and gouerne soules vnies he haue authoritie therto giuen which the Declarer of the disciplin noted p. 32. When he said. *How fit soeuer a mā semeth to be for anie charge , yet nothing is to be taken in hand without the authoritie of God, who will vse in his affaires whom him pleaseth.* As for the example of the Iews brought by Bilson , I graunt they did ill in asking Christ and S. Ihon for their commission, because their preaching was both plainly fortold before by God, and then confirmed by the daily miracles of Christ, & others wrought for authorizing of Saint Ihon both in his conception and Natiuitie. If Luther were Christ, or Caluin S. Ihon , and their preaching as plainly fortold by God , and confirmed by present miracles, we shold do like to Iews in asking them for their Commission; But seing they produce nether extraordinarie holines, nor miracles, nor prophetie, not anie thing els to testifie their seding. we shold shew great lightnes of hart yea madnes to beleue them to be Gods messengers without all Commissiō.

VVhy the Ieues did ill to ask Christ for his commission.

VVhy vve do vvell to aske Luther for his.

The similitudes which Bilson bringeth
make nothing against as & may be returned against him self. For vs any man (or
woman too) when the house is on fire or
the cittie in danger, may crie fire & alarme if officers do not perceaue the danger.
So we saie that when a man (or womã also) perceaueth heresie to be taught which
the Pastor doth not, he (or she ether) may
giue notice or warning therof. But yet, as
not withstanding this none can, in what
danger soeuer, take vpon him to be Cap-
taine and command others of authoritie,
but he onely who hath such authoritie
giuen him. So none in what danger of heresie soeuer can take vpon him to be a Pastor and guider of soules preaching *tanquam
authoritatem habens* , but onely he who is
lawfully called therto . But Bilsons error
is, in that he distinguisheth not betwene
the aduertising or teaching of priuat mé,
and the preaching of Pastors, which is an
act of spirituall function and authoritie,
and therfore must suppose that authoritie.
From the same procedeth his bringing of
the example of Frumentius and Ædesius
who (as priuat men yea as woemen maie
in case of necessitie when no others is to
be had) being captiues amongst infideles
taught them the Christian faith . But nether of them tooke vpon him to be Pastor
to the

Great
differren-
ce betuen-
teahhing
of priuat
men and
preaching
as Pastors.

*Socrat.
lib. 1.c. 19.
Raffin.lib.1.
cap 9.
Theodoret.
lib. 1.c. 23.*

to the Infidels or as such to administer to
them the word and Sacraments, before
Frumentius came to S. Athanasius & was
by him made Bishop and lawfully sent.
And by as good example might Bilson
haue proued that women may preach
euen without sending, because a woman
being in like sorte captiue among infidels
taught them the Christian faith, and was
cause of their conuersion.

15. And thus thou seest (Gentle Reader)
euidently proued both by manifest proofs
and open confession of Protestants, that
Luther preached Protestancie without
sending and so without all authoritie, and
consequently that the Protestants Church,
is a companie without a Pastor, their
doctrine a message without an Embassador, and their Bishops and Ministers without prelacie or pastorall authoritie, but
such as S. Cipriã describeth *l. de vnit. Eccles.*
vvho amongst stragling companions of them selues
take authoritie vvithout Gods giuing, make them
selues prelats vvithout anie orderlie course, and no
bodie giuing them a Bishoprick chaleng the name
of Bishops. And not Catholiks onely thus
think but euen the purer sorte of our English Clergie. For the daugerous Positioner *lib. 3. cap.* 6. telleth how it was concluded by them in a Synod at Couentrie *An.*
1588. That the calling of Bishops is vnlavvfull.

Theodoret.
lib. 1. c. 24.

VVhat the
Protestãte
and their
doctrin
be, if Lu-
ther vvere
not sent
to preach.

English
Ministers
condemne
the calling
of the
English
Clergie.

Mm 3   *That*

That it is not *lawfull by them to be ordeined into* the Ministerie . That *Bishops are not to be acknowledged for Doctors, Elders, or Deacons, as haning no ordinarie calling* . And *cap.* 14. he recounteth how some Ministers renounce the calling which they had of Bishops and account ther orders *onely a ciuil thing necessarie for them to keep the ministerie*. And *c.16.* that, *the English Prelats haue no authoritie to make Ministers*. And thus much of Luchets want of Mission. Now let vs see his orders.

CHAP. XI.

That Luther was neuer ordered to preach the Protestants word , or administer their sacraments.

1. AS in the former chapter I did not denie that Luther was once sent to preach the Catholik word or doctrin. So Nether in this do I denie that he was rightly ordered to preach the same word, to saie Masse and to administer the Catholik sacraments. But as he brought a new word, so he brought also a new sacrament, consisting both of Chrifts bodie & bread also ; for preaching and administration of which new word and sacrament I saie he was neuer ordered. And that his Catholik prieft-

preisthood could be no sufficient Ministerie of the Protestant word and sacraments
is manifest manie waies. First, by reasō. For
preisthood cheefly cōsisteth in authoritie
to offer sacrifice for the quick and the dead,
as is euident by these words wherwith
men are made Priests . *Take power to offer sa-*
crifice to God , and to saie Masse for the quick and
the dead. And Caluin *4.instit.c 5. para 5* saith
we order *none but to sacrifice.* D. Suthf in his
Chaleng *pap.* 34. and in his answer to the
Cath. Supplicat. *sec.* 19. writeth that our
priesthood *is apointed onely to offer sacrifice for*
the quick & the dead. The like saith the *Declar.*
of *disciplin p* 20. and it is manifest. But the
Protestāt Ministerie detesteth all authoritie of saying Masse, of offering sacrifice, &
praying for the dead. *order to sacrifice* (saith
the said Declarer *l.cit. is to abolish the sacrifice*
of Christ ib. *hāds are laid vpō preists to an end most*
contrarie to the Gospel. How then can preisthood become protestātish Ministerie, vnles
one contrarie become the other ? or as the
said declarer saith well, *how cā one & the same*
ordering serue to giue one man at the same time of-
fices so diuers and contrarie one to the other ?

2. Secondly I proue it by the iudgment
of Protestants For D. Reinolds in his
epist. befor his *Confer.* calleth our priesthood
impious. D. Whitaker cont. Dur. *p.* 821. biddeth vs keep our orders to our selues. And

Mm 4   *p.*653.

Luthers
preishood
coula be
no Prote-
stant
order.

1

2

Reinolds

VVhita-
ker.

pag. 653. *vve iudge* (faith he) *no othervvife of your prieſts than of Chriſts aduerſaries, and enemies of his prieſthood* . And *pag.* 662. *you haue nether lavvfull Biſhops, nor prieſts nor Deacons.* Povvel in his Conſiderations vpon Catholiks reaſons. *The popiſh ordination* (faith he) *is nothing els but a mere prophanation.* D. Fulk Anſw. to a Counterf. Catholik *pag.* 50. *you are highly deceaued if you think we eſteme your offices of Biſhops, Prieſts or Deacons anie better than laie men, and you preſume too much to think that we receaue your ordering to be lawfull* . Penrie againſt Some p. 8. *Of this I am aſſured that Popiſh Prieſts are no Miniſters.* The forſaid Declarer p. 20. faith . *Prieſts oile and power of ſacrificing is no ſufficient warrant for them to be Miniſters it is a prophane oile, and can giue no men authoritie to diſpoſe of the Miſteries of God.* which he proueth their at longe, and calleth *it a ſhameles boldnes of Popiſh Prieſts to take in hand to be Miniſters of the Goſpel without anie new calling or apointing thervnto, and termeth their orders horrible orders.* D. Some alſo as Penrie faith *p.* 20. calleth Popiſh preiſthood *ſacriledg.* D. Sutlif Anſw. to Exceptions p. 82. *The Pope is nether true Biſhop nor prieſt, for he was ordeined preiſt but to offer ſacrifice and to ſaie Maſſe for the quick and the dead. But this ordination doth not* (faith he) *make a Prieſt, nor had true prieſts and elders euer any ſuch ordination.* And p. 87. *The Romiſh Church is not the true Church, hauing no Biſhops*

Povvel.

Fulke.

Penrie.

Declarer.

Shameles boldnes for Luther to plaie the Miniſter vvithout nevv orders. Some. Sutlif,

Bishop nor Priests at all, but onely in name. The like he hath in his Chaleng *p.* 33. *& seq.* Finally the Diuines of Geueua in the Proposions *pag.* 245. conclude that in the Romish Church *there is no holy order or Ministrie indeed no lawfull calling but a mere vsurpation.* Thus thou seest by the iudgment of learned Protestants, that Luthers priesthood was so far from right orders and lawfull Ministerie, as it was impious, opposit to Christ priesthood, a mere prophanation nothing better than lay men haue, maketh no Minister, horrible, secrilegi ous, and what not, And he hauing no other orders (as is certaine) what an impious, enemy to Christ, prophane, lay, horrible and sacrilegious Minister must he haue bene if he were any.

3. Thirdly I proue it by practise of Protestants that Popish preisthood is no Ministrie. For at Geneua when two Bishops, of Niuiers, and Troie, fled thither, and tooke vpon them the Ministry without all more ordering, the Consistory vpon mature deliberation therupon, concluded that they could not do so. And in England euerie one knoweth that it is made treasō to receaue popish preisthood and aboue one hundred haue bene executed therfor which they wold neuer do, if they thought it to be Protestātish Ministery.

rie, what a diforderly religion then muft
that be, which was begun by a man who
was neuer ordered to preach it or admini-
nifter the facraméts or feruice therof. But

*Lib. de
missa
angulari.*

what he did therin did only by vertue of
impious prophane, horrible, facrilegious
and treafonable orders, with which before
he had faid (as himfelfe confeffeth(Maffe
15. years togeather, And what orders hath

Note.

our Proteftant Englifh Clergie, wherof
the greater number (as euery one knoweth and both the Anfwere to an Examination printed at Geneua *pag.* 33. and o-
thers in Dange : Pofit *lib.* 2. *cap.* 13. confeffe)
in the beginning of Queene Elizab. time
were Popifh Priefts, neuer ordered to faie
the Comunion, but the Maffe quite oppofit therto? And albeit fome of the were ordered to fay Proteft. feruice, yet they were
made of fuch Bifhops, as etherwere Popifh
Priefts themfelues, as Couendale and Skorey were, or had byn made of fuch Bifhops

*See Suruey.
cap. 16.*

And fo all their orders were ether Popifh
or come originally from Popifh Priefts,
who not being able to giue other orders
than they receaued them felues, did ether
giue Popifh orders, or none at all, And our
Englifh ether haue them or none. Wherfore fith Englifh Minifters orders, came
from Parker who was firft Archb. of Canterbury vnder Queene Elizabeth, and that
he

he was made Bishop·(as Sutlif faith Answ.
to *Except. pag.* 88.) of Couendall & Skorey
who receaued their orders of Cranmer , &
he his of P. Clement, 7. I wold know what
orders, and what authority to giue orders,
the Pope gaue to Cramer? Surely no othere
did the Pope giue or meane to giue then
Popish, and if Cranmer receaued no other;
he could giue no other to Couendall ,and
Skorey, nor they any other to Parker, nor
he other to Ministers . Iudg then good
Reader what kind of orders they haue (if
they haue any) by their owne verdit , to
wit impious prophane, horrible. and sacrilegious. Iudg also what is to be thought
of them and their religion , who hitherto
haue , and yet doe permit Popish Priests
that is as they accout slaues and shauelings
of Antichrist, and enemies to Christ, prophane, and mere laie men, yea impious &
sacrilegious, no way degraded or new ordered of them, but but by vertue only (as
they speak) of their greasing of the Romish Antichrist, the mortal enemy of Protestancy, by power of their prophane , impious, & sacrilegious orders to be suffi-
ciet Ministers of their word and sacram. O
impious & Antich. word which can be
sufficietly ministred by vertue of impious
& Antichristiá orders. Can Antich. order
Chrifts lawful Ministers ? Shal his orders
                                    become

become Chrifts orders? fhall Antichrifts fhaueling flaues be fufficient Paftors for Chrift? Shall Chrift be ferued by no other officers thē fuch as ether mediatly or imme-diatly were made by Antichrift? Is Chrift comen to beg orders at Antichrifts hāds, to receaue paftors of his making? Can Anti-chrift giue fpiritual & fupernatural autho-ritie? And haue Chrifts paftors no other then what came from Antichrift. o fhame-ful Chriftian religion if this be chriftian religion which hath no bible or word of God but what came from Antichrift, no facrament but from Antichrift, no prea-cher but from Antichrift, no orders but from Antichrift, no fpiritual authoritie or iurifdiction but from Antichrift! what then maie we conclude but the religion is Antichriftian. And why fhold Proteftāts maruail to heare their owne brethren call their Bifhops and Minifters, *Bifhops and Mi-nifters of the diuel, enemies of God pettie Anti-chrifts.* and fuch like, fith all the orders they pretend they muft deriue from the pope whom they all account the true An-tichrift. God open the eyes of my deere Countrymen that as they partly fee that their Minifters haue nether right calling nor lawfull orders, fo they maie alfo fee that they haue no true religion, which wi-thout paftors both rightly called & law-fully

See Doue of Recu-fancie Luth. cont Anabapt.

See Survey cap. 8 3.18. Danger. Poft. lib. 2. cap. 13.

No true religion vvithout true cal-ling and right orders.

fully ordered can not ftand . And thus
hauing fhewed how vnfit Luther was to
be Preacher both for his life learning, calling and orders : now let vs come to his
doctrine to fee whether that be any whit
better.

CHAP. XII.

That Luthers doctrine was contra-
rie to the vniuerfall faith of
Chriftendom in his time.

1. THat Luthers doctrine was contrarie to the vniuerfall faith of Chriftendom at that time, I proue by many
waies. Firft. by the condemnation therof
by the cheefe heades fpirituall & téporall
of the Chriftiá people of that time. For, as   Luthers
Proteftants confeffe, Leo 10. than Pope, &   doctrin
fpirituall head of Chriftian people con-   condem-
demned it *An.* 1520. whofe Bull therof is   ned by P.
extant in Fox *p.*1166. And not longe after   Leo.10.
Hieremie Patriarch of Conftantinople, &
head (as he accounteth him felf) of the   By Here-
Greeke or Eaft Church condemned their   mie Patri-
doctrin in a booke which is called *Cenfura*   arch of
Orientalis, wherin he faith ther doctrine   Conftantinople.

                                     was

By char-
les.5
Emper.
Sleid.
also lib.1
fol.3.set-
teth
doune
Emper,
Maxmil.
letters
against
Luther.
Sleid.lib. 3.
fol. 30. 33.
50. 51.;
By K.
Henrie 8
Sla:d.lib3.
fol.34.

was *altogeather new and directly both against the Gospell of Christ, and right reason*, and calleth them *Heretiks.* And in the yeare 1521. Charles 5. then Emperor of Germany, King of Spain, Naples, Sicilie, and Sardinia, and Lord of all the low Countryes, first writ a letter to the States of Germany which is set downe in Fox *pag.* 778. in which he professed *to pursue Luther and all his adherents by all meanes that can be deuised for to extinguish his doctrine.* And sone after directed a solemne writ of outlawrie against Luther, and all them that tooke his parte, commanding the said Luther to be apprehended and his bookes burnt: Likewise the same yeare 1521. King Henrie 8. of England wrote a booke against Luther, in which (saith Fox *pag.* 780.) *First he reproueth Luthers opinion about pardons.* 2. *He defendeth the supremacy of the Bishop of Rome.* 3. *L boreth to refel Luthers doctrine of the sacraments.* And

By the
French
King
Sleidan
lib. 6.
fol. 68.
lib. 8.
fol.120:

againe in the yeare 1523. writ (saith Cooper in Chron.) *to the Princes of Germany against Luther.* And in the yeare 1525. (as the same Cooper writeth he *entred league with the French King to suppresse the sect of the Lutherans vvhich they thought to be no lesse dangerous than the Turkes power.* And *Anno* 1535. he writeth that six were burnt in Paris for Lutherans

before

before the French King his fight And
Anno 1543. that the French King made
ftrait proclamation againft the Lutherans , And as for Iames 5 . King of
Scotland and Grand-father to his Maiefty , a Scottifh writer teftifieth that
when King Henry 8. hauing fallen into
one point of Lutheranifme promifed to
make K. Iam s his heire if he would do
the like , he rather refufed fo great a pro-
fer than confent to his defire. And behold
the different rewardfrom God of the two
Kings King Henrie 8 iffue is quite extinguifhed , and Iames his royall pro-
genie wee behould not only flori-
fhing , but poffeffing King Henries
crowme and Kingdome. So hath God e-
uen in this life recompenfed,the religious
zeale of that moft Catholick King. And
as for Swizerland Fox p. 792. writeh that
Anno 1524. the States of that countrie in
their affembly Decreed *that no opinion of Lu-*
thers should be tought priuatly nor openly and
wrote to the men of Zurich , and do much la-
ment (faith Fox *) and complaine of this new*
broached doctrine which hath fet all men to-
geather by the eares through the occafion of
certaine rash and nevv fangled heades, and
vvill bring destruction both to body aud foule.
And as for the learned men of that age in
all Chriftian Countries their deteftation

of

By Ia-
mes.5.
King of
Scotlád.

Hamilton
Confut.
Caius.

Note:

By the
States of
Suizer-
land.
Sleidan.
ib. 3 *fol.* 54.
55.
By the
learned
men of
all partes
of Chri-
ften-
dome.

of Luthers doctrin is euident. For firſt the Vniuerſities of Louain, and Côlen, condemned Luthers bookes as hereticall in the year 1520. And in the next yeare the Vniuerſitie of Paris did the like. And in all Chriſtian Contries almoſt the cheefeſt learned men wrote againſt him, as Eckius Cocleus, Gropperus in Germanie; Silue-ueſter, Caietan, Catherin in Italy. Petrus a Soto, Alfonſus a Caſtro, Canus, Turria-nus in Spaine. Clictoneus and others in France. Biſhop Fiſherand, Syr Thomas More in England. Driedo, Tapper, Eraſ-mus, in Fianders. Hoſius in Polonie, and others otherwhere. And after in the Cou-cell of Trent (where the flower of all Chriſtêdom was gathered to gether from all parts of the Chriſtiâ world) his doctrin was côdemned by the ſubſcription of 255. Prelats. Wherby yow may ſee the vniuer-ſall hatred of Chriſtendome both in the Clergie & laytie, learned and vnlearned, both in the Eaſt & Weſt, Latin & Grecke Church againſt Luthers doctrin. Herevpô Eraſmus ſaith Luther was condemned with, *ſo many iudgments, confuted with ſo many bookes, ſtrooken with ſo many thanderboalts.*

2. Secondly I proue it by the teſtimony of diuers Proteſt. For, Fox*pag.* 789. accoun-teth it a miracle, that Luther (ſaith he) *one man, ſhould ſuſtain* (for his doctrin) *the hatred almoſt*

By vni-uerſiues.

Sleid. Engl. lib.1.fol.14. lib.3.fol.32.

By a gene-ral Coun-cel.

Of the Prelats. legats.4. Cardinals. 2 Patriar-chs.3. Aechb.25. Bishops. 168. Ab-bots.7. Procura-tors.39. Generals. 7.beſids a great number of famous diuines. Luthers doctrin condem-ned by all maner of vvaies.

whole world being set against him, and stand openly against the Pope Cardinals and Prelats of the Church, hauing the Emperors and all the Kings (saith he) of the earth against him. Iuel in his Apologie p. 13. speaking of the Protestants matters, saith, they *increased inuitis prope omnibus*, almost against all mens wills. And *pag.* 201. *The Gospel* (of Luther) *was at this time spread into the world inuitis prope omnibus against almost all mens wills.* Luther him self *L. de Captiu. cap.* de Eucharistia speaking of his enterprise, saith *I begin a hard matter as which being confirmed by the vse of so many ages, and approued by all mens consents, is so setled as it is necessarie to change and alter all the face of Churches.* And 4. Galat. fol. 187. *The world iudgeth vs to be most pernitious Hereticks destroyers of religion &c. fol.* 210. *This day the name of Luther is most odious to the world.* 6. Galat fol. 291. *The whole world most cruelly persecuteth and condemneth vs.* But because this matter is euident ynough out of that which hath bene saide in the first Chapter of this booke, I omit further proofe, and will add a word or twoe to shew what kinde of fellowes they were who began first to fauor Protestancie.

What Kinde of fellowes those Germans were who first fauored Protestants somewhat hath bene said before. As for the French men Caluin *Prefat. in Iustit.* saith

N n   they

Marginal notes: Luther had the Prelats and all Kings of the earth against him. Iuel. Luthers Gospel almost against all men. Luthers Gospel against consent of all men. *Sleidan Histor. praefat.* The beginning (of Protestancie) was full small and one man alone susteined the malice of all the world.

VVhat
kind of
men they
vverevvho
againſt
the
vvorlds
content
fauored
Luther.
VVhat
Dutrh.
VVhat
french.
VVhat
kind of
fellous
our firſt
Engl.
prea-
chers of
Proteſta-
cie vvere
Bilney.
Hovv per-
uerted.

they *were beggerly and abiect, wretches, miſerable
ſinners before God and in ſight of all men, moſt contemptuous the excrements & outcaſts of the world,
and if any thing can be named more vilde.* Yea of
their holy Cittie of Geneua he ſaith as the
Surueyer *cap.2.* writeth his words. That
the people were, *a diſordered Dunghil of rif-
raffe.* That the Senat of 200. were *a tumul-
tuous faction of rakhells and caſt awayes:* & that
the cheefeſt Magiſtrats of the Cittie yea
euen the Syndiks were *ringleaders of factions
and diſſentions.* And wil Engliſh men forſake
their worthy vertuous & renowned Anceſtors, and follow this ſcumme of the
world? And as for England, what kinde
of followers they were that firſt embraced
Proteſtancie, hath bene in parte touched
before. Wherfore I will here, add onely a
word of the firſt Preachers therof in this
Kingdome.

3. Bilney (whome Fox *pag.* 922. calleth *the
firſt framer of the Vniuerſitie of Cambridg in the
knowlegd of Chriſt,* and was burnt *An.* 1531. as
he ſaith *pag* 920.) This man (I ſay) was as
him ſelfe teſtifieth in Fox *pag.* 915. conuerted by priuie inſpiration of the ſpirit, in
reading Eraſmus Teſtament, and was ſo
ignorant as being apprehended *An.* 1527.
he writeth of him ſelf in Fox p. 918. thus,
*VVhither Chriſt haue bene a long time heard I
know not, for that I haue not heard all the Preachers*

chers of England. *And if I heard them, yet till it was within this yeare or two I could not sufficiently iudg of them.* Lo this fellow but a year be-before he was apprehended, could not iudg of Preachers whither they taught Chrift or not. So vnconstant alfo he was in his religion, as firft he tooke his oath that he fhould not teach, preache, nor defend any of Luthers opinions, but fhould impugn the fame euery where Fox *pag.* 910. And being again apprehended and condemned for Proftancie abiured it, fubfcribed to his abiuration, went before the procefsion in Paules bare headed with a fagot on his fhoulder, and ftood before the Preachers at Paules Croffe all the fermon time *An.* 1529. *ex* Fox *pag.* 919. And yet not withftanding *Anno* 1531. again fell to preach herefie, though at his death he recanted all, & dyed a good Catholick, as Syr Thomas More, then Chancellet of England, teftifieth and Tindal plainly infinuateth in Fox *pag.* 986. though Fox deny it.

4. Latimer the Apoftle (as Fox and Bale terme him) of England, was peruerted by this ignorant and inconftant Bilney, and before (as him felf faith in Fox *pag.* 919.) *VVas as obftinat a Papift as any in England.* VVhofe learning yow may gather by his Maifter, and his inconftancie by his owne

Hovv ignorant
Hovv often times he abiured Proteftancie.

1

2

3

Latimer.
Hovv peruerted.
Hovv ignorant
Hovv often times recanted

deedes. For he twife recanted Proteſtacie, once before Cardinall Wolſey , as yow may ſee in Fox *p.* 1575. and an other time before diuers Biſhops as yow may read in Fox. *p.* 1577. which Fox there ſaith *was no great matter nor maruel.* So little matter he maketh of his religion or his Apoſtles denying it. After this he was vnbiſhoped by King Henrie. 8. and by him caſt into the Tower where he lay all his time after, and at his own death vſed gunpowder to ſhorten his life *p.* 1606. Of Tindal an other Apoſtle, Fox telleth *pag.* 981. how he was a ſchol Maiſter, but mentioneth not how he came to Proteſtancie. And after this, wearie (as it ſeemeth) of this new doctrin, would haue bene as yow may ſee. *p.* 982. Chaplin to Biſhop Tunſtal a Notorious Papiſt *p.* 987. He would haue the real preſence accounted an indifferent thing. And *p.* 985. he telleth that he was ſtrangled before he was burnt, which manifeſtly ſheweth that he recanted at his death, which alſo I haue read other where. Thus yow may ſee what dubble and triple turncotes, what periured and abiured perſons were the Apoſtles and firſt preachers of Proteſtancie in England. The Foundations and cheefe Pillers (as Fox termeth them) of their Church. O what compariſon can thet be, betwene ſuch , and Saint

Auſtin

1
2

No maruel or matter for the Apoſtles of Proteſtants, to abiure their faith. Tindal. Hovv often times repenteth.
1
2

Auftin, S. Laurence, Saint Paulin? What madnes were it to leaue thefe to follow thofe?

CHAP. XIII.

That Luthers doctrine was neuer confeſſed by Catholicks to be ſufficient to ſaluation.

1. YOw heard before that the aduerſaries of S. Auftins doctrine, as wel the Britons then as the Proteſtants now, confeſſed that he brought the true way to ſaluation, and that many & great learned men haue followed him, and come to heauē by the way which he taught; which teſtimonie proceeding from aduerſaries mouthes muſt needes ſeeme to be the cōfeſsion of moſt euident & manifeſt truth. Here now it cometh in place to ſhew, that no one Catholick euer acknowledged that Luthers doctrine was the way to ſaluation or that any haue commen to heauen by following him which I ſhew. Firſt, becauſe not onely Pope Leo, but alſo the generall Councell of Trent confirmed by the Pope (which no Catholick thinketh

That no Cath. allovved Luthers doctrin as Proteſt. do S. Auſtins,

1

Nn 3   can

can erre) hath condemned and accurſed his doctrin. And his bookes are forbidden to be read vnder paine of excommunicatiō Secondly, becauſe euery Catholick beleeueth & profeſſeth that who keepeth not the Catholick faith wholly & vnuiolated ſhall without all doute periſh euerlaſtingly. Thirdly, becauſe no Catholicks words can be produced wherin hope of ſaluation is afforded to Luther & his followers. But on the contrarie as many Catholicks as write or preach condemne his doctrin for flat hereſie, and him ſelf & all his obſtinat followers for hereticks, out of Noes Arke, out of Chriſts ſould, out of Gods Church, out of al hope of ſaluation ſo long as they follow Luther.

Luthers doctrin condemned by all Kind of Chriſtians. By Greciās. By Anabaptiſts. By Caluiniſts. By Engl. Proteſtāts. By hovv manie: our Engl. Proteſt. religion is condemned. Sea Ihonſon againſt Iacob.

2. Nay, not onely Catholicks alow not Luthers doctrine but euen all other Chriſtians beſides condemne it. The Grecians, as is ſayd, condemn Proteſtants for Hereticks. The Anabaptiſts, as Luther ſaith, account them worſe than Catholicks: him ſelf affirmeth his followers to be ſeuen times worſe than Papiſts Caluin iudgeth Luthers opinion of the Euchariſt leſſe tolle rable than the Papiſts. Sutclif addeth that it is hereticall, by inference of ſuch concluſions as may be gathered therof. The Browniſts eſteeme our Proteſtant religion a medle or motle religiō. A thouſand

sand Ministers in their petition exhibited to his Maiestie 1603. affirm that it containeth abuses & enormities which they can shew not to be agreable to Gods word. Others propose some hundred of doubts against it as yow may see in the booke of Quæres and the late silenced Ministers in their solemne printed Challeng made to the Bish. protestãts saie that if that be truth which the Bishops maintain against them that then that is false which they both maintain against Catholicks, and that, *their departure from the Pope can not be iustified, but that he, yea Christ Iesus and his hauenly truth in him, haue had great wronge.* Finally his Maiestie with the tacit consent of the Bishops condemned all the Englishe Bibles (the very foundation of our Protestants faith) as ill tranflated, and gaue order to tranflate the Bible a new.

The silenced preachers prefer the Cath. faith befor the Protestant. The foundation of Engl Protest. faith condemned, by Protestãts. Confer. at Hampton. Court. p. 6.

CHAP. XIIII.

That Luther neuer confirmed his doctrine by miracles.

1. SOme Protestants say that Luther needed no miracles for confirmation

Nn 4 of

of his Doctrine, becaufe (faith Feild *lib. 3.* of the Church *c. 48. we teach nothing contrary to the confirmed & receaued doctrine of the Church of God then in the world when thefe differences betwene vs and our aduerfaries began.* This impudent faying of his may be ioyned to an other which he hath *L. cit. cap. 42. That ther is no materiall difference amongft the Proteftants, no not betwene Luther and Zuinglius in matter of the Sacrament, nor betwene Illyricus and others about originall finne, nor betwene Ofiander and others about Iuftification as fhalbe iuftified* (faith he) *againft the prowdeft Papift of them all.* But as for the ftrangnes of Luthers doctrine to all the Church of his time that hath appeared fufficiently here to fore , and fhall yet more hereafter. Wherfore Proteftants afcribe two kind of miracles to Luther, the one inuifible, which Luther him felf challengeth *to. 4. in Ifaiam c. 35.* where hauing tould that Catholicks obiect vnto him that he could not cure a lame horfe, but was altogether deftitute of miracles, replieth that by his preaching the fpirituall blinde began to fee the truth , the deaf heard the Gofpel The lame that fate in fuperftition and Idolatrie walk . But great fondnes it is to alleadg fuch miracles for confirmation of his doctrine. Firft, becaufe we demand vifible miracles. Secondly, Becaufe **Luther**

See Sleid. lib. 5. fol. 65 .

VVhat miracles Luther chalenged. Luthers allegation of his miracles difproued.

Luther(saith he)wrought those supernaturall effects, but no man seeth them.
Thirdly, Because euery Sectmaister can
say so. Fourthly, Because the question is
whether his doctrine be such as it can
work these spirituall effects. Therfore
fond it were to prooue his doctrine to be
such by these effects, vnles the effects were seene, or more manifest than the truth
of his doctrine. This is to prooue, *idem per
idem*, or, *ignotum per ignotius*. For it is all one
to say Luthers doctrine worketh those
spirituall effects, and to say that it is true,
or at least it is as doubtfull. Fox *Acts* p. 789.
and others aleadg this for a notable miracle, that *one man and a pore Frier creeping out of
a blind Cloister should be set vp against the Pope
and almost the whole world, and work that which
all the learned men before him could neuer com-
passe.* Mark good Reader how he confesseth his religion to haue begun of one mā,
and of one Frier creeping out of a blinde
Cloister, against almost the whole world,
and not compassed before of all the learned men that were.

2. But as I said before this is as great a miracle as to see stones roule from a hil: such
a one as that notable strumpet bragged of
to Socrates saying that her doctrine and
perswasion was more potent than his, because she with a few words could drawe

One
poore
frier
creeping
out of a
blind
cloister
began
Prote-
stancie.
See Bré-
tius an-
swering
the like
miracle
wrought
by zuin-
glius in
recog-
nit.cont.
Bullen-
ger.

his

cause she with a few wordes could draw
his scollers to follow her. But Socrates
rightly answered that it was no maruel,
because he lead them vp the hil to vertue
she drew them downe the hill to pleasure
Pleasure of marrying, hauing mony, and
liuing at commaund drew so many Friers
and Nonnes after Luther. Pleasure of eating flesh at all times, neuer fasting, neuer
confessing' neuer satisfying drew so ma-
ny lay people|after him Pleasure of liuing
out'of all spituall subiection, and getting
of Church goods and liuings, drew so
many Princes after him. And; great mar-
uell it is that more did|not run togeather
(as S. Peter speaketh *Epist.* 1. *cap.* 4.) *into*
the same confusion of leacherie. And that we
may speak to Luther as S. Hierom *lib.* 2.
did to Iouinian, *Glorie not that thou hast ma-*
ny disciples, that many fanour they opinion, that
is a signe of pleasure. For they fauour not so much
thy speach as their owne'vice. For alwayes false
Prophets promis pleasing things, and sooth much :
vertue is bitter and who preach it are reple-
nished with bitternes. And that I may not speake
of others Did not Arrius draw the whole world ?
Thus Saint Hierome . And what Iouinian, what Epicur what Libertin, hath
taught more licentious and voluptuous
doctrine thā Luther? Of which I wil giue
the Reader a taste by some points which I
                    haue

haue gathered out of of two litle bookes which he wrote in the beginning of his Proteſtancy. By which the reader may imagin what ſtore he vttered after, when he had more abandoned ſhame . *It will profit the ſoul (ſaith he l. de Libert Chriſtiana) nothing if the body pray and do what work ſoeuer can be done, in and by the body. Yea meditations & whatſoeuer can be done by the mind profit nothing . It will* ~~not~~ *hurt the ſoule if the body eate, drink commonly, pray not & emit all things which may be doneby hypocrits. No works whatſoeuer belong to the inward man. By only impiety & incredulity of the hart is he made guilty & ſlaue of ſinne to be damned & not by any external ſinne or work. All the cōmandements are equally impoſsible. Good works make not a good man, nor ill works an ill man. No ill work maketh man ill & damned, but incredulity* And *l. de captiu.* ⁵*There is no hope of remedy vnles recalling the Goſpel of liberty & all lawes of all men extinguished at once, we iudg & gouern all things according to it If we haue Gods law and natural wiſdome it is ſuperfluous yea hurtfull to haue writen lawes no law can be put vpon Chriſtians ether by men or Angels , but as much as they will them ſelues. By only faith although there vvant other works thou shalt be ſaued. A Chriſtian is ſo rich that though he would he can not leeſe ſaluation with what ſinnes ſo euer , vnles he will not beleeue . For no ſinnes can damne - but incredulitie*

A taſte of Luthers licentions doctrin,

Epiſt. ad Albert. Mogunt. Horribile eſt ſi vir ſine vxore in morte inueniatur

This

Thus Luther, & much more in two little bookes . By which thou maift fee good caufe whie diuers did follow him . And how temporall intereft maketh now diuers to follow the Puritan Minifters in England, the Surueier telleth *p.* 246. And *cap.* 2. how the like bayte drew the Geneuians to harken to Caluin and his mates. And the Dangerous Pofitioner telleth the like motiue in Scotland to follow Knox and his companions. Thus carnall pleafure, libertie, and profit were the miracles wherwith Luther periwaded his doctrin. 3. Wherfore Feild *lib.* 3. of the Church *p.* 48. infinuateth other kind of miracles of Luther, but referreth vs for them to Illyricus and Fox. And in Fox *pag.* 789. I finde thefe . Firft that Luther hauing had warning before, and the pictur of a Iew who meant to poyfon him fent vnto him, miraculoufly fkaped poifoning. That a ftone fell not from the top of a vaute before Luther rofe from vnder it. 3. That they who ftood vnder Luthers window where he ftoode praying , might fee him fhed reares. Fourthly, That by prayers he had obtained that fo long as he liued , the Bifhop of Rome fhould not preuaile in his Contrie . The Fift was that Luther compelled by prayer the Diuel to throw into the Church an obligation wherwith a

man

Luthers miracles out of Fox.

man had bound him felfe body and foule
to the Diuel. Sixtly, That when he preached they that heard him thought euery
one their own tentations to be touched.
Thefe are the miracles which Fox attributeth to Luther. Againft which I might
except (as they do againft miracles done
thefe dayes by Catholicks) that they are
auouched onely by Proteftants . I might
alfo obiect that Fox nameth no eye witneffe of any of thefe miracles. But I neede This
not. For befides the fift (which Fox him alfo the
felfe dare not auouch but referreth it to diuel
report faying, *if it be true as it is certainly re-* could do
ported.) What is there in any of the reft by col-
which might not be done naturally? Was to grace
it a miracle to efcape poyfoning by a man his fcho-
of whome he was warned before,& who ler.
was pictured ynto him . Might not the
ftone naturally haue ftood till that time
when Luther rofe?May not an Hypocrit
ftanding praying in a Window to be feene fhed teares ? May not Luther fain that
he obtained that of God which he faw
was not lykly to be otherwife. And fin al-
ly might not he who knew the difpofition of his fcollers and audients ; hit on
that wherwith they were tempted. Surely
thefe miracles we liken to thofe ridiculous miracles which the Fathers report
of the Montanifts.

4. But

4. But againſt theſe or whatſoeuer miracles are aſcribed to Luther, I oppoſe, firſt that himſelfe *lib. cit. in Eſai*; when it was obieſted him that he wrought no miracles, neuer mentioned any viſible miracles, yea he addeth that *miracula noſtro tempore corporaliter amplius non fiunt Quia Chriſtus* (ſaith he) *ad finem m undi infirmus eſt*: That himſelfe ſaith *Loc. Com. Claſ. 4. pag. 39. Nullas apparitiones Angelorum habeo.* And *pag. 40. pactum feci cum Domino meo ne vel viſiones vel ſomnia vel etiam Angelos mihi mittat* 3. That Fox himſelf ſaith *p. 1040. The time of miracles is expired, we hauing the ſcriptures to guide vs.* And Caluin *4. Inſtit. pag. 9. Temporale fuit donum miraculorum, & aliqua ex parte hominum ingratitudine, intercidit.* 4. Doctor Fulke. *Anot in Ioan. 15. Luther and Caluin work no miracles.* And *in Apoc. 13. yow know* (ſaith he) *that Caluin and the reſt whom yovv call Archereticks work no miracles.* Eraſmus alſo ſaid that Luther could not cure a Lame horſe.

Proteſtāts
denie that
Luther
euer
vvrought
miracle.

CHAP.

CHAP. XV.

*That Luther hath had no succession
and continuance of his doctrine
here in England.*

THe laft point wherin S. **Auftin** and
Luther are to be compared, is fucceffion & continuance of doctrine In which
leaft of all is to be faid. For albeit **Cramer**
were for a while and that fecretly in King
Henrie 8. time a Lutheran, as Fox tearmeth him *pag.* 1115. 1 yet fhortly after King
Edwards entrance, he reuolted from
that and fell to Zuinglius, denying with
him the reall prefence in the Euchariſt,
and for that cheefly was burnt, as yow
may fee in Fox. After whome nether
Archbifhop nor Bifhop was a Lutheran
in all England, but followed rather
Zuinglius or Caluin, albeit alfo they differ from them in diuers points of doctrin
as well appeareth by the Puritans who
profeffe to be the pure Caluiniſts. And for
continuance of Luthers doctrine himfelf
had fo fmall hope therof, as he could
not forbeare words of defpaire. For *in 3.
Galat. fol. 154. I feare* (faith he) *the*
proper

proper & true vse of the law wilbe after our time troden vnder foote. & vtterly abolished by the enemies of the truth. For euen now whiles we are yet liuing and employ all diligence to set forth the office and vse both of the law and the Gospel, ther be very few, yea euen among those that wilbe accounted Christians & make a profession of the Gospel with vs, that vnderstād these things rightly. VVhat think yee then shall come to passe when vve are dead & gon. And *fol.* 201. *VVhich thing* (that Protestants should not acknowledg Luther for ther Pastor) *shall one day come to passe, if not vvhilst vve liue, yet yvhen vve are dead and gon.* Sectaries vvhen vve be dead shall possesse those Churches which we haue won and planted by our Ministerie. And the like small hope our English Ministers haue of the continuance of their religiō, as appeareth by the Declarat. of Disciplin printed at Geneua 1580. *I am afrayd* (saith that Author) *lest God be come into England as into some Castle, in the way of his progresse for a small time.* Caluin in his preface before his Cathechisme did so despaire of posteritie of successiō in his religiō as saith he, *I dare scarce think therof.* Their cōsciences telling them all that their doctrin is not built vpō that rock on which Christ built his Church and Doctrine, but vpon the sandes of their human inuentions.

Luther forseeth that he shalbe forsaken

So Engl. Minister.

And Caluin.

Libri Secundi Finis.

THE

THE THIRD
BOOKE, IN. VVHICH

S. Auſtin and Luther, and their
doctrins are weighed together ac-
cording to their qualities.

Set dovvne and proued in the
tvvo former bookes.

PREFACE.

Itherto (Gentle reader haue
we ſhewed out of authenticall
and ſufficient witneſſes that S
Auſtin and Mar. Luther were
the firſt Founders of the Romã
Catholick and Proteſtant religion in our Engliſh Nation;
and we haue put each of them with his qualities in
his ſeuerall ſcale: Novv it remaineth that vvith an
euen hand vve lift vp the Ballance, and vveighing
them together, iudg according to thoſe qualities and
enduements vvhich naturall reaſon and true prudence teach vs, ought to be in a firſt Preacher and
founder of Gods religion in a Nation, whither it
more likly to come from God & bring his religion,
vvhither the contrarie?

Oo　　CHAP.

CHAP. I.

S. Auſtin and Luther weighed accor-ding to their learning.

How great a help learning is to diſcouer errors, and to finde out truth, and con-trarie wiſe how great a hinderance igno-rance is to attaine to truth, and an ayde to lyes; as a thing euident by it ſelfe neede no proofe. Herevpõ it hath bene vſual to the Sectmaiſters of all times , as they are the beginners of new doctrins vnknowne to their Anceſtors, ſo to impute to them igno-noráce, and to arrogat to them ſelues eſpe-ciall knowledg and learning , by help wherof (forſooth) they could diſcouer that truth which for ignoráce their Forfathers could not finde out. *It was* (ſaith S. Bernard ſerm. 65. in Cant.) *alwaies the trick of Hereticks to boaſt of ſingularitie of knowledg.* Thus the Donatiſts accuſed the reſt of the world of ignorance. At whome S. Auſtin *lib. 1. cont. Gaudent. cap. 19.* ieſteth thus. *O dolor fraudata ſunt tali magiſterio tempora antiqua ! O ſorrow that the ancient times wanted ſuch Maiſters.* And when the Pelagians in like ſort condem-ned the ancient Fathers of ignorance , he exclamed *lib. 2. cont. Iulian. cap. 10.* in theſe **words.**

words. *And darest thou call those blind? And hath long days so confounded the highest with the lowest, and shall darknes be so accounted light and light darknes, that Iulian Pelagius Celestius shall see and Hilarie Ambr. Greg. be blind.*

Yea in the time of Tertullian in the primitiue Church, ther were hereticks, who doubted not to impute ignorance to the Apostles them selues, whome Tertul. *l. de prascript.* refuteth thus, *what man well in his witts can thinck that they were ignorant of any thing whome our Lord gaue for teachers, had alwaies in his company, to whome he expounded aparte all obscure matters?* And when they bragged of their new light he merilie iesteth at them thus: *To these alone, & to these first was the truth reuealed,* Forsoth they obtained *greater fauor and fuller grace of the Diuel.* And how vsuall it is with Luther and Protestants to boast of their especiall knowledg, & new light, & to impute blindnes ignorance and errors to the former ages and ancient Fathers, no má that either conuerseth with them or readeth their bookes can be ignorát. *Audemus* &c. (saith Luther) *wee dare glorie that Christ was first published of vs* V Vigand *l. de Bonis & Malis Germ.* ascribeth to Luther *such a lightening of the Articles of faith as was not known in the world since the Apostles ty me.* Others cal him *the mouth of Christ, Chariot of Israel.* Finally some prefer him before all

Neandet. lib. 8 expli- cat. orbis terra. Fox p 416. edit. 1563. Iuel Apolog.

the Apostles but Paul, as Cyriacus Spangenbergius who wil iustifie thefe verfes.

Chriſtus habet primas habeas tibi Paule ſecundas
At loca poſt illos proxima Luther habet.

Let Chriſt be firſt and after him S. Paul be beſt
But next to the Luth. deſerus to go befor the reſt.

And as Luther challengeth more light & learning than the ancient, Fathers, ſo Zuinglius challengeth more light than he, and Caluin than they both. And in England the Proteſtats of King Edwards time challenged more light than thofe of King Henries, & thofe of Queene Elizabeth more than they both, and the Puritans challeng more light than the Proteſtant, the Brownifts than the Puritan *till at laſt* (as his maiefty fayde of the Scottifh Miniſters) *they run madd with their light*, or rather turn all into darknes of infidelitie & Atheifme, as dayly, experiéce theweth. Wherfore to fee whither indeede Luther were like to be better learned thã S Auſtin Let vs compare them together according to that which hath bene tould of them.

S. Auſtin was an Italian, Luther a Duch man: S. Auſtin ſtudied in Rome when ther was there a famous Vniuerſitie, Luther in Witteberg & places of no fame. S. Auſtins Maifter was S. Gregorie one of the fower Doctors of the Church, Luthers Maifter was a namèles fellow, and for Proteſtancy he

Confer. at
Hampt.
Court.

See all
thefe
points
proued
befor. l. 1.
c. 4. l, 2. c. 7.

he had no Maifter at all , vnles yow will
reckon his black Maifter S. Auftin is not
known to haue had any corporall impediment of ftudie , Luther is known to haue
had fo great a one as he could fcarce read
three leaues together. S. Auftin had teftimonie of S. Gregory that he was *repletus*
fcientia fcriptuarum: full of the knowledg of fcrip-
ture , Luther had teftimonie of his brother
Zuinglius that he was *imperitus vel nimis*
rudis Theologus an vnskilfull or too too rude a Di-
uine. S. Auftin reiected no part of Gods
word, Luther reiected diuers , S. Auftin
taught no abfurd doctrins, Luther by the
iudgment of Proteftants taught many. S.
Auftin ouercame the Britons amongft
whome were *plures viri doctiſsimi*, Luther (as
Catholiks write) was ouercome in publick
difputatiõs of one Eckius. S. Auftin taught
no herefies, Luther as Proteftants confeffe
taught diuers. Finally S. Auftin reuoked
none of the doctrin which he once taught
Luther reuoked & cõfeffed his ignorance
in many and weightie points. Befides all
this S. Auftin was nearer to Chrifts time
by 900. yeares and more, than Lu her, and
therfor more likly to learn what Chrift
taught thã Luther who was fo long after.
Now therfor (gentle reader) lift vp the
Ballance of thy iudgment with an euen
hand, & confidering that vpon this choice

goeth thie eternall saluation or damnatiō:
weigh these two men equally, and iudg
whether is more full, not of words, or
braggs, but of learning. Whether is liklier
to know what Christ taught, or to haue
erred of ignoráce. VVhether were likly to
haue bene blind, whether to haue seene.

CHAP. II.

S. Auſtin and Luther weighed accor-
ding to their vertue or vice.

1.　THe due consideration of the vertuous life of the first Preacher or
founder of Religion in any Country, may
giue to prudent men great light to descern
whether his Religiō be good or bad, come
from God or from the Diuel. For albeit
vicious men do often times preach and
continew the religion which vertuous
men first founded, as we see that the Scribes and Pharisies in Christs time taught
the Doctrin of Moyses; Wherupōhe bad
the people to do what they taught, and in
the day of iudgment there wilbe repro-
bats who haue prophesied in Christs name; yet notwithstanding if we looke into
the scriptures or Ecclesiastical Histories
we shall not finde but that those whome
God sent to be first founders of his religion

gion in any Nation or Contrie, were
when he sent them, vertuous and godly
men. Such a one was Moyses by whome
he founded his religion amongst the Ie -
es: *Mitissimus hominum qui sunt super terram.*
The most mildest man that was on earth. Such a
one was S. Iohn Baptist whome he chose
to first sound out the happy tidings of
Christian religion to the world. Such
were his Apostles who forsooke all and
followed him, euen Iudas when he cho-
se him for an Apostle, as S. Cyril in 6. *Ioan.*
Hierom *l.* 3. cont. Pelag. and others teach. S. Hierom proueth it inuincibly out
of these words *Ioan.* 17. *Father whome thou*
hast giuen to me I haue kept and none hath peris-
bed but the sonne of perdition. For if God the
Father gaue Iudas to Christ, surely he
was then good. And it may be prooued
out of the 54. Psalme, where he is pro-
phetically called *a man of one mind,* & said to
haue walked in Gods house with conset.
And before Christ would licence the A-
postles to preach to Nations, he bid
them abide in Ierusalem til they were indued with vertue from aboue, and made
them as S. Paul speaketh *Idoneos Ministros*
Noui Testamenti. Fit Ministers of the new Testa-
ment. Such also were those whome we call
the Apostles of certain Nations, as to omitt
others S. Patrick of Ireland. S. Ninian of

Pictland, S. Palladius the first Bishop of
Scotland. And the cause of this proceeding
of God in chusing vertuous men to be the
first promulgators of his lawe in any Contrie is manifould. First because it is more
honorable for him to chuse for instrumēts
of so notable a work of his, as is the conuersion of a Nation from infidelitie to
faith, and from seruice of the Diuel to his
seruice, men that are like to him selfe rather than men that are like to the Diuel,
his owne children rather than the Diuels
children, his owne seruants rather than
the Diuels slaues. Secondlie it is more effectual for the end which God intendeth.
For albeit God could couert a Nation to
his faith without vertue or miracles of
the Preacher or any other external help;
Yet because he *disponit omnia suauiter dispo-*
seth al things sweetly. he vseth these outward
helps wherwith he knoweth men to be
most draune to embrace his religion,
which are vertue and miracles. Of which
twoe though miracles be verie potent, yet
vertue is more poureful, as S. Chrisostom
sheweth by the comparison of S. Iohn
Baptist and Appollonius Tyaneus. Of
whome the one wrought no miracles as
the scriptur saith, & yet by his vertue stro-
ke the Iewes into such admiration of him,
as they doubted whether he were not the
Mesias

Messias of the world. And the other though
he wrought many wonders, yet had fewe
or no followers. And S. Chrisost. douteth
not to say, that if the Apostles had not
liued vertuosly, notwitstanding their
great miracles, the world would haue
counted them but seducers. And in the
conuersion of our English Nation, albeit
the miracles of S. Anstin and his fellowes
did cooperat therto, yet S. Beda *l.1.cap.26.*
attributeth it cheefly & almost wholly to
the vertue & holines of their life. Thirdly
this course is most proportionable & agrea
ble to the end for which God sendeth
Preachers to any Contry. For as the end of
his seding is vertue to be engrafted in that
Nation, so the meane most agreable and
sutable therto is vertue in the first preacher. Wherfore howsoeuer the Successors
or as S. Paule termeth them the Pedagogs
in Christ be yet the first Preachers or Fathers of a Nation who (according to Saint
Pauls phrase) *had begotte them in Christ,* ought
tobe very holy and vertuous men.

2. And the contrary course of sending
wicked & vicious men for first preachers
of doctrine is vsuall to the Diuell, and
wel be seeming him. For albeit vertuous
men may vpon ignorance fall into some
one or more errors, yet can they not, (so
longe as they keepe their xertue (be enti-
ced

ced by the Diuel to forsake their true faith
and worship of God, vpon which all vertue is grounded. But those who (as Saint
Paul speaketh of the Hereticks Hyme-
neus and Philetus) haue already made
shipwrack of a good conscience, and aba-
doned vertue, those the Diuell puffeth vp
with a proude conceit of their owne learning, and picketh out for Sectmaisters, &
for teachers of new doctrines. And therfore howsoeuer Archereticks may for a
time dissemble vertue, as S. Austin writeth of Pelagius, yet *mendacia* (as S. Cyprian writeth) *non diu fallunt.* Their Hy-
pocrisy will not *diu proficere, sed insipientia
eorum manifesta fiet.* Simon Magus before he
became an Archereticke would haue
bought Gods grace for mony. Arius before he became an Archeretick was noted
to be ambitious. Berengarius before he
broched his heresie was noted of enuie at
other mens glorie. Wicklef, before he began his doctrine was noted of anger, as
writeth Godwin in the life of Archb.
Simon Langhorn, & is euident in Stow
Chron. *Anno* 1376. Finally Luther before
he published his new doctrine was noted
of enuie againft the dominicâ Friers (as is
before shewed) & singularity. In so much
as Fox *pag.* 770. writeth that his freinds
did thinck euen before he fell from the
　　　　　　　　　　　　　　　Church.

Church, *that he would alter and abolish that
manner of teaching which then was vsed.* Thus
all Archereticks are branded with some
notorious vice or other. And perhaps
these Archereticks are the false Prophets
whome our Sauiour gaue a marke to
know by their life. For which cause also
both the scriptures and Fathers haue recorded the notorious vices of diuers Archereticks as a sure token that such men
were not they whome God first sendeth
as preachers of a new doctrine, or Apostles to couuert a Nation to him. Wherfor
let vs compare the qualities of S. Austin
& Luth. that therby we may see whether
was the more likly mā to be chosē of God
to be he that was first sent by him to conuert our Country to his faith & religion.

All this
vvas pro-
ued befor
l.1.c.5.
l.2.c.8.

3. S. Austin forsooke the world from his
youth and entred into religious life, Luther, not before he was 20. yeares ould &
then vpon feare that his companion with
whome he walked, was slayne with a
thunderboult. S. Austin was brought vp
vnder S. Gregorie, who as S. Beda saith
lib.1.cap.23. was *a man of greatest vertue and
learning of his time*, Luther vnder no man
of fame. S. austin profited so in vertue as
he was made by S. Gregory *Præpositus Mo-
nasterij:* of Luthers like profit no such proof.
S. Augustin kept his religious life, Luther
soone

soone shooke it of. S. Austin came a thousand miles to preach to Barbarous people Luther neuer went out of his Contrie for such purpose, and liued alwaies vnder sure protection of the Prince Eelector of Saxony. S. Austin liued *in continuall praier* (saith Beda *lib.* 1. *cap.* 26. *VVatching, fasting, preaching, despising the commodities of the world,* and single life, Luther after he became a Protestant, Wiued, feasted, tooke his ease and enioyed the pleasures of the world. S. Austin went commonly barefoot about England preaching, and had hard knees like a Camell by frequent kneeling in prayer. No such matter of Luther. S. Austin made Englilh men incoparable more vertuous than they were before, Luther made them much worse. S. Austin God approued by many miracles both aliue & dead. no such newes of Luther S. Austin is highly commended for his vertue by S. Greg. Beda & other writers to our age, Contrariewise Luther greatly discomměded eue of his owne brethren. Finally no great vice can be proued against S. Austin, Many and heinous vice are proued against Luth. Iudg therfore gentle Readee, God being determined to reduce our Natiǒ to Christs faith, whether of these two mě it is most likely he would make choise of, for to effect so notable and so pious a worke.

CHAP.

CHAP. III.

S. Auftin & Luther weighed accor-
ding to their motiues of preaching.

1.   MVch it auaileth to trie the sincerity of any mans counfel or actió
to examine whether the Counfeller or
Actor be like to reape any pleafure or có-
modity therby. For if he can not, moft
likly it is that he giueth fuch aduice vpon
fincerity & indgmét & otherwife the contrary may be fufpected, if it be not euidér.
Wherupon Cafsius gaue that prudér note,
which al wife mé in that cafe do obferue,
that we fhall mark *Cui bonum,* To whome
was the aduife good? To whom was ther
any commodity pleafure or preferment
like to redound. And if this courfe he obferued in trial of S. Auftin &, Luthers reli
gió, we fhal clearly perceaue that S. Auftin
is to be prefered befor Luthers. For S. Auftin left his Cótry, forfooke his freinds &
acquaintance, left his headfhip of a Monafterie, left his quiet aboad at home for to
come to preach his religion to our Natió
Luther left none of all thefe to preach his
S. Auguftin came a thoufand miles, and
aduentured his life her amongft a people
of a different religion, Luther neuer went
out of his Contrie to preach his doctrine,
                                        nor

These
points
proued
befor.*l* 1.
*c.*7.*l.*2.*c.*9.

nor euer came amongſt his owne Contry
men of contrary religion, without a ſafe
conduſt S. Auguſt got nothing but the
title of an Archbiſhop wherof he had
little or no hope at all when he came hither. Luth. got liberty, wife, riches & preferment of the world. Whetfore euident
it is that S. Auſtin was more likly to preach
his doſtrine vpon ſincerity & iudgment,
and for the good of them to whome he
preached, becauſe he loſt much, got litle,
& hoped for leſſe than Luther, who by his
preaching loſt nothing, and got much.

CHAP. IIII.

S. Auſtin and Luther weighed ac-
cording to their miſſion or ſen-
ding to preach.

SO ſure a mark it is of falſe Prophets to
preach without ſending as God almightie gaue it as a certain note of them
in the ould lawe Hierem. 23. *I ſent them not
and they did runne*. And our Sauiour in the
new law *Ioan*. 10. *VVho entreth not by the dore
into the ſheepfould, but climbeth vp otherwaies,
he is a theefe and a robber* ib. *All who ſo euer haue
comē* (without ſending) *are theeues & robbers.*
And the Apoſtles likwiſe *Aſt.* 15. *Some going
out of vs haue trobled yow with words, whome we
commāded not.* And ſo abſurd withal, as nothing

thing can be more. For if none dare take
vp̄o him to be the messēger or Ambassador
of a Prince, vnles he be sent, nor to gouern
his people vnles he be apointed, how absurd is it for any to take vpon him to be
Ambassador & Messenger of the Prince of
Princes, & be disposer of his misteries and
Stuard of his houshould, and guider of his
flock, vnles he be lawfully sent? Wherfor
let vs compare the missions of S. Austin
& Luther together, that therby we may
see whether was the true, whether the
false Prophet.

S. Austin was sent to preach of S. Greg.
successor to S. Peter, and first Patriarch of
Christendome, Luther when he first preached Protestancie, was sent nether of Patriarch nor Bishop nor any man els. S. Austin was sent by the sayd authoritie by the
which the first preachers of the most part
in Christendome were sent, Luther by no
authoritie at all. S. Austin came to preach
vp̄o obedience, Luther vpon disobedience.
S. Austin came of purpose to preach that
faith which he did preach, Luther at first
mēt onely to spite others for a time, & not
to found any newe faith. S. Austin neuer
ment to suppresse the faith which he begā
to preach, Luther oftētimes offered to suppresse his, if he had not bene bound to recant it. S. Austins sending was cōtested by
S. Pe-

All these differen-ces proued befor *l.*1. *c* 8 9 *l.*2. *c.*10.

S.Peters miraculous teſtimonie from heauen, Luther had no ſuch. Finally S. Auſtins
ſending was by God côfirmed in the ſame
ſorte that the ſending of the Apoſtles was,
that is. _God conteſting with ſignes & wôders_, Luthers wanted all ſuch côrmatiô. Iudg the
indifferent Reader whether of theſe two
mens ſending was more likly to be good.

CAAP. V.

S. Auſtin and Luther weighed accor-
ding to their orders of preaching &
adminiſtring the Sacraments.

CErtain it is that none câ lawfully adminiſter the Sacraments of God but
he that hath power & order therto from
God. For ar S. Paul ſaith hebr. 5. _Nec quiſ-_
quam ſibi facit honorem ſed qui vocatur a Deo tan-
quam Aaron Sic nec Chriſtus ſemetipſum clariſi-
cauit vt Pontifex fieret ſed qni locutus eſt ad eum,
tu es ſacerdos in æternum ſecundum ordinem Mel-
chiſedech. And if Chriſt could not offer ſacrifice before he was made Prieſt , how
ſhall man take vpon him to adminiſter
Gods ſacraments, Wherfore according to
that which hath bene ſaid, let vs weigh
both their orders. Saint Auſtins orders
were ſuch as S. Gregoryes were, and cô-
ſequently ſuch as all as Chriſtendome at
that

that time both approued & vſed Luthers
Miniſtrie (for of his Roman Prieſthood
we ſpeake not) was ſuch as the Chriſtian world neuer heard of before. S. Auſtin was made Prieſt at Rome by S. Gregory or his predeceſſors authority, and
Biſhop in France by his appointement
Luther was made a Miniſter of no man
at all. And ſuch orders as he had(he ſaith)
he receaued from Antichriſt, and in the
Sinagog of Satha. S. Auſtins adminiſtring
the word and Sacraments was confirmed
of God by miracles, of Luthers doings
no ſuch mention . S. Auſtins orders are
diſliked by none of his fellowes Luthers
orders are reiected euen by many great
Proteſtants, Iudg then good Reader whether thou thinkeſt beſt.

CHAP. VI.

*S. Auſtin and Luther weighed ac-
cording to the vniuerſalitie or
ſingularitie of their doctrine.*

THe word *Heretick* is originally a Greek
word ſignifying as much in Engliſh as
a *chooſer.* And an heretick is nothing els but
he who houldeth not the vniuerſall and
generall faith of Chriſtians, but maketh
choiſe of ſome points therof that he will
beleeue

beleeue, and denieth the reſt. And *Catho-licke* likewiſe is originally a Greeke word ſignifying as much as vniuerſal or Gene-ral. So that a Catholick Chriſtiã is he who profeſſeth the vniuerſall faith of all Chri-ſtendom. VVherfore if we weigh S. Au-ſtin and Luther according to this balance we ſhal ſoone ſee which of them was the Catholik, which the heretick. For S. Auſt. (as is before ſhewed) preached the vni-uerſall faith of Chriſtendome, making no ſinguler choiſe of his owne of any points of faith. But Luther as is before declared ſwarued frõ the vniuerſall faith of Chri-ſtendome and followed that which ether none or inuiſible perſons held, whom he neuer knew where or how many they were or rather none indeed knew it no not himſelfe before he inuented it.

Sup. *l. 1.*
a. 11. l. 2.
cap. 12.

CHAP. VII.

S. *Auſtin and Luther. weighed ac-cording to their aduerſaries alowance of their Doctrine*

ITmuſt needs be euident truth which the Aduerſaries confeſſe. For if it might iuſtly be doubted of ſurely ,they would neuer admit it. VVherfore this kind of weapon haue all men much eſteemed, & vſed

vſed as the ſword of Golias t ocut of his
owne head. This argument Moiſes vſed
Deut. 32 when he ſaid *For our God is not as
their Gods are and let our enemies be iudges.* This
argument vſed our Sauiour when being
accuſed of the Iewes for caſting out Diuels in Belſioub, he appealed to the verdict of their children. The ſame vſed S.
Paule whē againſt the Gentils he brought
the teſtimonie of their poets. The ſame
vſed the holy Fathers whē out of the hereticks owne Principles they ouerthrew
their Religion. The ſame now vſe Catholiks againſt Proteſtants, & Proteſtants
likwiſe indeuor to vſe the ſame againſt
vs, as you may ſee in Morton in his Treatiſe of equiuocation, Bel in his downfall
and others. And Atchb. Bancroft in his
Suruey *cap.* 8. arguing againſt the Puritás
out of their owne confeſſion ſaith *yow may
be hould to build vpon it for a truth that they are
ſo conſtrained to yeld vnto.* Wherfore by the
light of reaſon and example of all, that
Religion muſt needes be thought to haue
a great aduantage of the other, which is
by the Aduerſaries therof accounted good
and the other is not. But in this there is
no compariſon betwixt S. Auſtins and
Luthers religion. For wheras not only
the Britons then, confeſſed S. Auſtins doctrine to be *the true way of righteouſnes,* but

See *l.* 1.
c. 12 *l.* 2.
cap. 3.

alfo diuers Proteſtãts now, haue acknowledged it to be the *right beleefe, the perfect
faith of Chriſt, the true religion of Chriſt, pure
& incorrupte Chriſtianity*, as hath bene declared before, No one Roman Catholick
can be named that euer ſince Lurher began, afforded euer any hope of ſaluation
to thoſe that wittingly and willingly follow his doctrine.

CHAP. VIII.

S. *Auſtin and Luther weighed ac-
cording to their Miracles.*

VVHat a certain and infallible way of
truth Gods miracles are, hath bene
ſhewed before . And what can be ſaid for
S. Auſtins or Luthers miracles is already ſet
downe. Here it remaineth that according
to the rules of wiſdome we weigh & giue
iudgment whether of their miracles were
more likly to be true miracles, wrought
by God as ſet by him as it were his ſeales
to ether of their doctrin. By S. Auſt. meanes yow haue diuers things done which
could not be done naturaly . As the curing
of a blind man, and the healing of all lame,
diſeaſed, and deformed perſons, which
were cured by baptiſme at his apointmēt.
Of

See theſe
proued
befor *l.*1.
*c.*13 *l.*2.
*cap.*14.

Of Luther yow haue not heard one thing
which could not haue bene done naturally. As the bewraying of a Iewe of whome
he was admoniſhed to take heede. Of riſing before a ſtone fel. Of ſhedding teares
at his prayers, Of touching the tentations
of his hearers. Yea the caſting in of the o-
bligation by the Diuel (which yet Fox dare not auouch) might wel haue bene done
of the Diuels own accord. Of S. Auſt. miracles there were many eye witneſſes &
diuers of theſe enemies. Of Luthers wonderments not ſo much as friends alleadged for the witneſſes. S. Auſtins miracles
are teſtified by great Doctors and famous
Saints, as S. Gregorie, S. Beda and others,
who by their learning could know the
miracles, & for their holines would relate
no vncertain fables for certain miracles.
Luthers wonderments haue no ſuch teſtimonie S. Auſtins miracles were then confeſſed by his enemies the Britons, & now
by diuers his aduerſaries the Proteſtants.
No one paſt or preſent aduerſarie euer cōfeſſed Luther to haue wrought a miracle.
Finally no Catholik euer denied S. Auſtin
to haue wrought miracles, Diuers Proteſtants haue denied Luther euer to haue
wrought any. What man then is there that
iudging things according to rules of wiſdome, will not thinck S. Auſtins miracles

to haue bene true miracles. For(besides the testimony of the word of God which testified the miracles which we reade in scripture) what w̄ āt they to be accounted true miracles that any other miracles had? The Deedes were supernaturall, The effect of them was supernaturall & diuine vz:the conuersion of Infidells, The meanes of doing them holy,to wit prayer to God, The doers of them were Saints, The testimonie of these Deedes are of many, eye witnesses,freinds,and foes,learned, & vnlearned,holy, and Wicked,forrein and domesticall, and cōfessed of diuers which refuse S.Austins religion, Than the which greater testimonie for miracles can not be required, vnles we would haue God to speake from heauen . And on the other side,what prudent man is he that wil not iudg Luthers wonderments to be friuolous. The things reported o him were naturall, The testimonies for them are nether of eye witnesses;nor of enemies,nor of Saints,nor of great learned men, nor are they confessed of any who refuse Luthers doctrine. Yea they are denied by such as were both freinds and great scollers of Luthers. Whie then should we beleeue them ? Nay whie should we not deny them?

CHAP.

CHAP. IX.

S. Auſtin and Luther weighed accor-
ding to the Succeſsion or conti-
nuance of their doctrine.

TRuly ſaid Gamaliel *Acts.* 5. of the Chriſtian religion then preached by the A-
poſtles, *Si ex hominibus eſt conſilium hoc aut opus*
diſſoluetur, Si vero ex Deo eſt nõ poteritis d ſſoluere.
And in like ſorte of hereticks ſaid S. Paul 2.
Timoth 3. *Vltro non proficient .* And S. Auſtin
in *pſ.* 57. compareth the Catholik faith to a
Riuer, which hauing a continuall ſpring
euer floweth & neuer waxeth drie, & hereſie to a brooke riſing vpon raine, which
while the raine falleth, runneth boiſterouſ-
ly, and they who know not that it wáteth
a ſpringe would iudg that it would laſt See this
lõger than the quiet riuer, but as ſoone as it proued.
leaueth raining they ſee the water gon & *l. 1 .c. 14.*
the brooke dryed. Wherfor let vs ſeé whi- & ſeq.ad
ther S. Auſt. or Luthers doctrin hath cõ- fin.*l.2.c 15*
tinewed longer in Engl. in their followers
or rather we haue ſeene it alredy. For. S.
Auſt. hath had 69. ſucceſſors in his Arch-
biſhoprick ſucceſſiuly all of the 'ſame religion with him. 53. kings of Englãd beſides
diuers others as is before declared, & that
when the Crown & kingdome was twiſe

Pp 4   violent-

violently taken from the Englifhe men by
Danes & Normans , yet his raith was not
taken from his fucceffors Nor by fo many
fo long defolations of the Danes & many
feuere lawes, tirft by King Henrie 8. and
then by Queene Elizabeth, and fo manie
bitter torments hard banifhmets, ftreight
confinments, deep Dongeons could Iorns
great fines, Taxes,and paymets,& bluddy
deaths, could it be rooted thefe thoufand
yeares oute of this land , but that this day
God be thancked & S. Auft.)there are both
noble & ignoble clerks feculer & religious,
men,weemé,& Children, who not withftanding all lawes,threats,& dangers,will
profeffe to hould the faith of their Apoftle
S. Auft.to agree with him in all points of
religió to honor that See from whence he
came,& to refufe(as he did)to ioine in religió with them who obferue not the ma-
ner(as he faid to the Britós)*of the holy Romã,*
*& Apoftolik Church.*In fo much,as not with-
ftáding all the lawes,terrors,Proclamatiós
fearches,or paymets, Torturs,Banifhmets,
& executions which haue bene made thefe 50.yeares,yet Minifters in their printed
bookes dayly complaine of increafe of
Priefts and Catholicks And one lately in
his fermon at Pauls Croffe dedicated to
the preténted Archb. of Canterbury and
lyked of kim faith *pag.* 79. that *no bondage or*
                                            ard

Much
more
vvold S.
Auftin
haue for-
borne the
Proteft.
Church.

I B. in his
Taile of
Tvvoleg.
Foxes.*c.* 11

Som.
Collins.

hard measure can euer be thought able to suppresse or reclame vs. This, this, sheweth S. Austins worke to haue bene of God & the water wherwith he watred the plants of his religion to haue an euerlasting flowing fountain from Heauen, and the Church which he founded to be built vpon such a Rock as the gates of hel shall not preuail against it. And that they which spurne against it do (as S. Paule once did) spurne against the pricke. And on the other side Cranmer, if he were (as Fox saith) a Lutheran in King Henries time, it was but secretly; And if he professed it in King Edwards time, it was but for a verie short space, And long since was there not one true Lutheran Protestant to be found in all England. So soone was Luthers work dissolued, so soone was his brooke growne drie. And in steede of it runneth now Zuinglius or Caluins brooke, which though it seeme for the present to be ful, and runne strongly, yet if the Prince (whose harte is in Gods hands) would but ether disfancy it, or at least withould his seuere hád from Catholicks. yow should quickly see this ful brooke brought to a lowe ebbe, and quickly dreaned, and wax as dry as ether the brooke of Luther, or the brookes of 300. Archereticks more, wherof diuers haue runne far fuller and longer than ether

Luthers

Luthers or Caluins hath, and now no figne of them is left, yea scarce their names
are knowne. This Luther him selfe both
forsawe and fourtould, as is before declared. *l. 2. c. vlt.* And Caluin also in his Preface before his Cathechisme in these
wordes *of Posteritie I am so doutful as I dare
scarce thinck therof. For vnles God miraculously
help from heauen me thinks I see extreme barba-
rousnes hang ouer the world And I pray God that
a while hence our children feele not this to haue
bene rather a true prophecie than a coniecture.*
And if we mark we shall see, that as Vi-
pers broode killeth their Mother of whome they came. So new hæresies destroy
the ould from whence they sprange. Thus
the Puritan impugneth the Proteftant,
and the Brownist vndermineth the Puritan. Wherfor let all men that be careful of
their faluation harken to S. Hieroms aduise saying to a Luciferian Hæretick , *I
will tel thee my mind breefly and plainly. That
we should abide in that Church , which founded
of the Apostles, contineweth to this daye. For shall
we doute* (faith S. Austin *l. de vtil. Cred.*) *to
put oure selues in the lap of the Church wich from
the See Apoostolick by succefsion of Bishops in vaine Hæreticks barking about yt*) *hath gotten the
hight of authoritie.*

Epilog

Luther
epist. ad
Albert,
Mogunt.
An 1525.
forte
doctrina
mea ite-
rum sup-
primetur.

Epilog.

1. THus we see most deerly belóued Countri-men, that if we compare according to the true rules of prudence and wisdome, the Roman Catholike & Protest.religion in their first founders here in our English Nation, ether for learning or vertue, for mißiō or orders for moti-ues to preache, for vniuersalitie of religiō or con-feßion of Aduersaries, for miracles or succeßion and continuance, the Catholik religion is incom-parably to be preferred & chosen before the Pro-testāt. For if learning do help to espie truth S. Au-stin was liklier to find it than Luther, If vertue deserue to haue truth reuealed, S. Austin was more likely to haue deserued it thā Luther; If holy mo-tiues entice men to deliuer sincerly what they knowe to be truth, S. Austin was liklier to deale so than Luther. If laufull Mißion and true orders testifie a true preacher, S. Austin was more likly to be such than Luther. Or if consent of Christia-nitie, Confeßion of Aduersaries. Miracles & Con-tinuance make any thing for proofe of true reli-gion, S. Austins religion is incomparably before Luthers. And what I say of S. Austin in respect of Luther, may also be said (as appeareth by what hath bene writtē) of S. Austins followers in our English Natiō in respect of Luthers followers in the same Nation. And contrariewise if ignorance leade to lies, if vice hinder the reuelation of Gods truth, or cause the taking of it away, Luther is more lyke to erre than S. Austin. If worldly & naughtie mo-tiues drawe men to deceaue others, Luther was more like to deceaue thā S. Austin. If want of law-full mißion & right orders discrie a false Prophet, Luther is more like to be such than S. Austin. And finally

finally if want of confent of Chriftianitie, want of
acknovvledgmēt of Aduerfaries, want of miracles
and continuance, fhew any thing the vntruth of
of religicn, Luthers religion is more lyke to be
vntrue than S. Auftins. And ifany fhall fay that
albeit Luther and the Proteft.religion be inferior
to S. Auftin & the Romā religiō in all thefe points
aboue mētioned, yet are they fuperior in the word
of God, which is to be preferred before all other
confiderations whatfoeuer. If(I fay)any fhall thus
obiect. I requeft him to confider that one truth is
not cōtrarie to an other, nor Gods word to right
reafon nor his fpirituall light to the light of nature, nor faith oppofit to true prudence. And if
therfor right reafon light of nature, true prudence
ftand for S. Auftin & his religion, & giue fentence
againft Luther and his Proteftancie ; furely Gods
word(how foeuer it may feeme to fome in fhewe
of words) yet indeede & in fenfē ftandeth likwife
on S. Auftins fide, and condemneth Luther & the
Proteftant faith. For it can not but feeme ftrange
that any wife man fhould imagin that Gods word
fhould ftād on the one fide pofte alone, or accom-
pained onely with ignorāce. vice naughtie motiues want of lawfull Mifsion, & right orders, want
of approbation of Chriftianitie, of confefsion of
enemies, of continuance.and of miracles, And on
the otherfide with the Diuels word fhould ftand
learning, vertue, lawfully mifsion, right orders,
confent of Chriftianitie, cōfefsion of Aduerfaries,
cōtinuance & Miracles. VVould God difcredit his
word with fuch difgracefull mates, & countenāce
the diuels word with fo many & fo importāt titles
of commendation? Or can it finke into any mans
head that a man fhould be lawfully fent, haue the
approbatiō of Chriftianitie, the confefsion of Aduerfaries and Gods teftimonie by affured miracles
(as S.

(as S. Auſtin is plainly ſhewed to haue had) to
preach lyes? Or if I cā not obtaine ſo much of ſuch
a man, I requeſt him yet this, that he will pleaſe to
ſuſpend his iudgment till he ſee the ſecond parte of
this treatice, VVherin (Godwilling) he ſhall ſe eth:
Catholick religion to goe ſo far beyond the Proteſtant for right claime of ſcripture and true ſenſe
therof and other true grounds of religion, as he
ſeeth it exceed proteſtācy touching the firſt founder therof in England in all the points aboue mentioned. God for his mercies ſake open the eyes of
my deere Contrymē, that they may ſee that which
is truth. & mooue their harts to embrace & follow
that which they ſee to be his euerlaſting truth, &
their own æternall happines.

2. Here I wold haue made an end, but that I feared
that ſome though perſwaded by what hath bene
ſhewed in this booke, that the Catholick religion
is in all reaſon & wiſdome to be preferred & followed befor the Proteſtant, may notwithſtanding
perſwade them ſelues, that the Proteſtant religion
is good ynough & ſufficient to ſaluation, whom I
beſeech for God & their owne ſoules ſake to conſider theſe points following. Firſt, that howſoeuer
the Proteſtāt religion were a liklie waie to heaue,
yet ſith the Catholik faith is incomparably far
more liklie, it is no wiſdō in ſo weightie a matter
as is eternall ſaluation or damnation to leaue the
more ſecure (if not altogether certaine) waie, and
to take the more dangerous. What wiſe man that
feareth murthering wil trauel that waie wher he
hath iuſt cauſe to think that his enemies lie in
waie to kill him, when he maie goe an other waie
far more void of fear or danger? what prudent mā
being to paſſe a dangerous riuer will not chuſe to
paſſe rather that waie which manie expert paſſen-
gers haue vſed theſe thouſand yeares and more, &

by

An admo-
nition to
thoſe that
think men
maie be
ſaued in
both reli-
gions.

1

by which we are sure that diuers are safely arriue
on the other side; rather than a new waie which o
late some vnexpert & iangling fellows haue ima
gined them selues to haue found out, but we ar
not sure that anie one that hath gone that wais
hath escaped drowning and is landed in safetie
on the other side? And loue we our soules, desire
we heauen, fear we hell, & will we make the contrarie choise in religion.

3. Secondly I wold haue them to consider, that it is
2   euident by what hath bene declared that not onely
the Cathol. religion is in all reason to be preferred
See *l* 2.*c*.1. before the Protestãt, but that Protestãcie is indeed
7 8.9.10. no religiõ, but a humane deuise lately inuented of
& seq. one man, and him meanly learned, vicious, and for
naughtie motiues, disliked of him self, & at the first
condemned of all Christendom, and wanting all
See *l.*2 *c*.1 authoritie of lawfull Mission, of right orders, and
Miracles to approue it. Which kind of superstitiõ
rather than religion no man of wisdom can think
sufficient & able to saue him. For nether can Gods
religion be an inuention of mã, but an institution
of God him self, nether if it could, were it reasõ to
think that to be a good religion which a naughtie
& vnlearned man, vpon naughtie motiues had deuised, & wanted all authoritie of lawfull mission,
and right orders to vse it, yea which not onely all
Christendom at the first condemned. but euen the
inuentor him self for manie yeares disliked and
offered to suppresse.

3   4. Thirdly I would haue them to consider that the
Catholik & Protestant religion are not one & the
same religion in substãce, differing onely in some
small points, but are indeed two religions in substance, quite opposit in many most substãtiall partes of reliigon, namely; In the verie worship of
God: For Gatholiks beleue that they ought to
worship

worſhip God with externall ſacrifice which Proteſtants account ſacriledg: In the verie word of God. For Catholicks beleeue manie books to be diuine as Tobie Eccleſiaſticus Machabees &c. which Proteſtants reiect as fabulous. They are alſo oppoſit in the expoſition of Gods word; almoſt in euerie chapter and verſe. They are oppoſit in Gods Sacraments, the catholiks beleeuing ſeué wherof the Proteſtant reiecteth fiue: Finally to omit manie more great oppoſitions they are oppoſit in the foundation it ſelf. *For the foundation head and ſoul.* of Proteſtant religion as them ſelues account, is iuſtification by onely faith, which foundation Catholiks vtterly condemne. How then can anie reaſon which iudgeth the Catholick religion to be good and to come from God, think that a religion ſo oppoſit to it as the Proteſtant is can alſo be good and come from the ſame God? What argreement can ther be betwene Chriſt and Beliall, betwene light and darknes, betwene faith and hereſie. truth and lies.

See l c. 21.

5. Finally I wold haue them to conſider that not onely infidelitie in vtterly reiecting Chriſt and his doctrin, but alſo obſtinat denial of anie one point of his ſacred truth maketh a man an Heretik and ſubiect to damnation. And as S. Iames ſpeaketh of Gods Commandements, ſo we maie ſaie of Beleef, who offendeth in one point is guiltie of all. *If anie* (ſaith Chriſt Apoc. 22.) *ſhall diminiſh of the words of the book of this prophetie God will take his parte out of the booke of life. Vnles a man* (ſaith the Creed of S. Athanaſius) *keep the Catholik faith entire and inuiolate vvithout doubt he ſhall periſh euerlaſtingly.* F or as it litle helpeth a man to be found in all other members if he be deadly wounded in one. So it litle auaileth one to be found in all other points of faith if he be heretically

4

S. Athanaſius.

cally infected in one. And S.Auftin alfo *l.de heref*
pronounceth them to be Heretiks *qui fingulis aut*
non multo amplius dogmatibus oppugnant regulam
veritatis, who by one or not manie more opinions im-
pugne the rule of truth. To which doctrin alfo Proteftants agree as you maie fee in D. Sutlif againft
Exceptions *p,55.* and others. And the reafon is
manifeft becaufe the definition of Herefie is *per-*
tinatious error in faith, to which it is indifferent
whither the error be but in one or in manie points
of faith'And can anie Chriftian think that Herefie cã be a waie to heauen, that an Heretik (whom
Tertullian. S. Ciprian and all the ancient Eathers
account no Chriftian) fhall be coheir with Chrift,
That hærefie, which as oppofit to faith a theolo-
gical vertue, is one of the greateft finnes that is,
fhall enter into heauen when no fin fhall enter.
That he who deferueth to be excluded out of the
militant Church fhalbe admitted into the triumphant, who is condemned (as S. Paul fpeaketh) by
his owne indgment fhall not be condemned by
God, finally who giueth God the lie in one or manie points of his facred truth can be in Gods fauor and come to his kingdom, No furely, wherfor
affuring our felues that as their is but one God
and one faith, fo if the Cath. faith be Chrifts faith
Proteftancie is herefie if that be the waie to heaune, this is to hel if that be the path to faluatior
this is to damnation, let vs reiecting Proteftancie
embrace the Catholik faith. Amen.

F I N I S.